ILLINOIS CENTRAL COLLEGE
PN4121.E47 1966
STACKS
The art of speakin
A12900 282210

W9-BPO-782

THE ART OF SPEAKING

Second Revised Edition

E. F. Elson

Alberta Peck

with

George Willey

Samuel Hirsch

Theodore Moore

Earl Wynn

GINN AND COMPANY

Home Office, Boston, Massachusetts 02117
Library of Congress Catalog Card Number: 66-11099

Acknowledgments

Grateful acknowledgment is due to the following publishers, authors, and other holders of copyright material for permission to use selections from their publications.

DODD, MEAD & COMPANY, INC.: From "Lepanto," by G. K. Chesterton. Reprinted by permission of Dodd, Mead & Company from *The Collected Poems of G. K. Chesterton.* Copyright, 1932, by Dodd, Mead & Company, Inc.

DOUBLEDAY & COMPANY, INC.: "Experience" by Aline Kilmer, copyright 1919 by George H. Doran Company. From the book, *Candles That Burn* by Aline Kilmer. Reprinted by permission of Doubleday & Company, Inc.

E. P. DUTTON & CO., INC.: "Journey's End," from the book *Now We Are Six* by A. A. Milne. Copyright, 1927, by E. P. Dutton & Co., Inc. Renewal, ©, 1955, by A. A. Milne. Reprinted by permission of the publishers.

NORMA MILLAY ELLIS: From "God's World," by Edna St. Vincent Millay. Reprinted from *Renascence and Other Poems,* published by Harper & Brothers. Copyright 1913, 1941, by Edna St. Vincent Millay. By permission of Norma Millay Ellis.

GLADYS FICKE: "The Oracle," reprinted from *Selected Poems,* by Arthur Davison Ficke, by permission of Gladys Ficke. Copyright, 1926, by Arthur Davison Ficke.

HARPER'S MAGAZINE: From "Is the Welfare State Obsolete?" by Irving Kristol. Reprinted from *Harper's Magazine* (June, 1963) by permission.

HOLT, RINEHART AND WINSTON, INC.: "Stopping by Woods on a Snowy Evening," by Robert Frost. Reprinted from *You Come Too* by Robert Frost. Copyright 1923 by Holt, Rinehart and Winston, Inc. Copyright renewed 1951 by Robert Frost. Reprinted by permission of Holt, Rinehart and Winston, Inc.; "When I Was One-and-Twenty" and "Loveliest of Trees," from "A Shropshire Lad"—Authorised Edition—from *The Collected Poems of A. E. Housman.* Copyright 1940 by Holt, Rinehart and Winston, Inc. Reprinted by permission of Holt, Rinehart and Winston, Inc.

HOUGHTON MIFFLIN COMPANY: "The Plaint of the Camel," reprinted from *Davy and the Goblin* by Charles E. Carryl by permission of Houghton Mifflin Company; from "Patterns," reprinted from *Men, Women, and Ghosts* by Amy Lowell by permission of Houghton Mifflin Company.

ALFRED A. KNOPF, INC.: "The Warning," reprinted from *Verse,* by Adelaide Crapsey by permission of Alfred A. Knopf, Inc. Copyright, 1915, by Algernon S. Crapsey; 1934, by Adelaide T. Crapsey.

LEEDS MUSIC CORPORATION: "The Fox," arranged by Burl Ives is used by permission of Leeds Music Corporation. © Copyright MCMXLV by Leeds Music Corporation, 322 W. 48th Street, New York, N. Y. All Rights Reserved.

DAVID MCKAY COMPANY, INC.: From *The Status Seekers*, by Vance Packard (1962). Reprinted by permission of the publishers.

THE MACMILLAN COMPANY: From "The Congo," reprinted with permission of The Macmillan Company from *The Congo and Other Poems* by Vachel Lindsay. Copyright 1914 by The Macmillan Company, renewed 1942 by Elizabeth C. Lindsay; from "The Ghosts of the Buffaloes," reprinted from *Chinese Nightingale and Other Poems* by Vachel Lindsay. Copyright 1917 by The Macmillan Company, renewed 1945 by Elizabeth C. Lindsay; "Cargoes," reprinted with permission of The Macmillan Company from *Story of a Roundhouse* by John Masefield. Copyright 1912 by The Macmillan Company; renewed 1940 by John Masefield.

METHUEN & CO. LTD.: "Journey's End," from *Now We Are Six*, by A. A. Milne.

LAURENCE POLLINGER LIMITED: "Stopping by Woods on a Snowy Evening," from *The Complete Poems of Robert Frost*, published in England by Jonathan Cape Limited.

RANDOM HOUSE, INC.: From *The Iliad of Homer*, translated by Andrew Lang, Walter Leaf, and Ernest Van Ness Myers.

ST. MARTIN'S PRESS, INC.: From *The Iliad of Homer*, translated by Andrew Lang, Walter Leaf, and Ernest Van Ness Myers. Reprinted by permission of Macmillan & Company Ltd. and St. Martin's Press, Inc.

SOCIETY OF AUTHORS: "Loveliest of Trees" and "When I Was One-and-Twenty," by A. E. Housman have been granted by The Society of Authors as the literary representative of the Estate of the late A. E. Housman, and Housman's *Collected Poems;* "Cargoes," by John Masefield has been granted by The Society of Authors and Dr. John Masefield.

STANFORD UNIVERSITY PRESS: "Man and the Sea," by Tu Hsün Hao, reprinted from *A Garden of Peonies* by Henry H. Hart with the permission of the publishers, Stanford University Press. Copyright 1938 by the Board of Trustees of the Leland Stanford Junior University.

THE VIKING PRESS, INC.: From "Ornithology for Beginners," by Dorothy Parker. From *The Portable Dorothy Parker*. Copyright 1931 by Dorothy Parker. Reprinted by permission of The Viking Press, Inc.

A. P. WATT & SON: From "Lepanto," by G. K. Chesterton, reprinted from *Collected Poems of G. K. Chesterton* by permission of Miss D. E. Collins.

ANN WOLFE: "Thrushes," from *Kensington Gardens*, by Humbert Wolfe. Reprinted by permission.

The Authors

E. F. ELSON is assistant superintendent for instruction in the Sequoia Union High School District in California. He was chairman of the English department and a teacher of English and Speech at Sequoia High School, Redwood City. Prior to assuming his present position, Mr. Elson was director of curriculum for the Sequoia Union High School District. He holds two degrees from the University of California and has engaged in advanced studies at Stanford University.

ALBERTA PECK taught English and speech for ten years at Sequoia High School, following a period of teaching courses in public speaking for University of California Extension Division. She received her degrees from the University of California and the University of the Pacific.

George Willey is television producer and chairman of the Division of Mass Communications, Foothill College, California. He formerly managed WBNB-FM in Beloit, Wisconsin, and for ten years in various capacities directed the Radio-Television-Film Institute at Stanford University. Dr. Willey has revised the unit on radio.

Samuel Hirsch was formerly chairman of the Department of Acting and Directing, Division of Theater Arts, School of Fine and Applied Arts, Boston University. Professor Hirsch, who is also a contributor to professional organs, has revised for this text the unit on drama.

Theodore Moore is a teacher of English and public speaking and director of forensics at Abraham Lincoln High School, San Francisco. His contributions to the revision of this text are in prose reading, contest speaking, and debating.

Earl Wynn is Professor of Dramatic Art, chairman of the Department of Radio, Television, and Motion Pictures, and director of the Communication Center at the University of North Carolina. His degrees are from Augustana College and Northwestern University. He has prepared the television unit.

CONTENTS

A Note to the Teacher

The Art of Speaking is addressed to the student in language he can understand and in a manner which he should find inviting. For you, it is organized and treated in a way which we hope will make easier your traditional role as guide, director, and even participant in a pleasant community effort.

The purpose of this book is to help you to develop in our young citizens a liking for and a skill in oral expression, an awareness of its increasing importance, and a feeling of responsibility in its use. It is toward these ends that we have directed our efforts, emphasizing aims related to our philosophy, suggesting topics for thoughtful discussion, providing for careful planning of speech activities, encouraging the building of vocabulary, stressing the function of communication in human endeavor, and supplying more activities than you can use, activities which are varied enough to fit a range of student interest and ability.

The first of the book's three parts deals with principles and understandings that are basic to effective speaking; the second suggests ways and means of putting one's thoughts and words together in speech form; and the third extends instruction to a variety of speaking situations common in American culture. You will find that the twelve units comprising the first two parts can effectively be taught in chronological order, and the units in the third part may be taught in any number and in any order.

The Art of Speaking will give you all of the material you need for a full year's course, and you may, by judicious selection of material, make it fit comfortably into a semester course. If you are a teacher in the regular English program, you will find it convenient to use single units for your specific purposes. It is our hope that both you and your students will like the material, as well as the organization and presentation.

The Authors

THE ART OF SPEAKING

PUTTING SPEECH WORK INTO FOCUS

In this first section of the text you will consider human relationships, learn new terms and principles involved in speech work, increase your knowledge of the production of speech sounds, and delve into the problems of listening to others speak and of helping them to improve their speaking through helpful criticism. Perhaps most important of all is the attempt to put you into proper perspective with yourself as a speaker and as a listener.

WHAT YOU WILL FIND:

WHY STUDY SPEECH?

Being able to speak well is one of the greatest assets you can have; it will pay you dividends.

Right Now

1. **You can bring about personal improvement**
   Your voice, self-expression, and thinking will be improved.
2. **You can do school work better**
   Recitation, listening habits, and group work will be better.
3. **You can be a leader**
   Others will be influenced by your assured manner.
4. **You can excel in activities**
   Debate, Radio and TV, Speech contests, Politics, Dramatics
5. **You can prepare for life situations**
   Learning to communicate with others is valuable preparation.

Later

1. **You can succeed economically**
   Top-notch success is closely related to skill in speaking.
2. **You can be of service to your community**
   Clubs, church, and political organizations will welcome you.
3. **You can be at ease in social situations**
   Everyone likes a good mixer who uses language engagingly.
4. **You can increase your knowledge**
   Many skills are related to the study of speech.
5. **You can make everyday life more rewarding**
   Speaking, like other subjects, can be made an art.

Unit One

TAKING STOCK: Your Goals and Aims

What is the art of speaking?
How are speech and civilization related?
How important is speech training in today's world?
What are your goals and responsibilities?

Before you undertake a study of the art of speaking, it might be well for you to give some serious thought to the nature of speech and to some up-to-date concepts of its place in your life. Many of you may think of a speech course as one in which you learn to "make speeches," pronounce words correctly, train your voice, use gestures, and, in general, improve your "speaking" ability. These accomplishments are, in truth, a part of your training, but by no means does your study end there.

Speech is an act of communication which has assumed great importance today. The world is going through one of its great periods of change, causing many conflicts and complications and raising many problems. One of the most vital of today's needs is better communication between nations and peoples.

On a technical level, modern communication needs are well served by the scientific achievements in electronics affecting the telephone, radio, television, satellites (like Tiros, Nimbus, Relay, and Telstar), business data machines, tape recorders, programed learning, and synthesized speech produced by computers or "talking machines" which can construct speech artificially. But what about the human element? Most of the talking, convincing, and persuading that goes on every day is on a personal, man-to-man level. No matter how sophisticated the technical devices of communication become, there is no mechanical substitute for the creative and critical interaction that takes place when two people speak to each other. This is the grass-roots level of human communication. Let's investigate it in some depth in this unit before learning how to "make speeches."

What Is the Art of Speaking?

What do you do when you speak? You might dismiss the question by saying, "I make sounds. I utter words. I just talk." Actually, speaking is not that simple. It is a complicated process, rooted in thinking, that involves some rather complex mental and physical action on your part. If you tried to diagram the process as it applies especially to making speeches, you might come up with something like this:

THE SPEAKING PROCESS

Creating	**Delivering**	**Reacting**
(1) Generating ideas	**(1)** Using language to translate ideas into words	**(1)** Recognizing the effect of speaking upon the listeners
(2) Establishing a purpose	**(2)** Using voice for expressiveness	**(2)** Assessing the fulfillment of purpose
(3) Doing research	**(3)** Using body for added effectiveness	**(3)** Continuing the interchange of ideas with listeners
(4) Selecting material		
(5) Organizing thoughts		
(6) Adapting to listeners		

Sometimes this process is instantaneous and seemingly superficial, as when you are just chatting with friends. Sometimes the process is obviously lengthy and complicated, as when you are delivering a formal speech. In any case, speaking is concerned particularly with ideas, with their creation in your mind, their delivery by means of your voice, and the reaction to them by both you and your listener.

In its simplest terms, speaking is just person-to-person talk. However, at its highest level, speaking is an art because it requires expertness and proficiency in using the medium of the voice to create a pleasing form or effect from the raw material of language—ideas, words, sounds, and sentences. Thus, speaking is a *language art,* like reading, writing, and listening. It is one of the basic skills you need in order to function well in society. It is an instrument of social coordination.

In the process of developing your speaking skill, you will also be exposed to other learning disciplines, many of which will have a continuing effect on your ability to meet the demands of life. Here are some of those intellectual disciplines:

establishing values	discovering significant issues
developing ideas	making decisions
recognizing problems	listening critically
assembling facts	relating to people

grasping interrelationships of ideas

Speaking is an instrument of social coordination, a way by which you communicate ideas to people and through which you are able to meet and solve many of the problems of living in society.

Speech and Civilization

People have been speaking since the first primitive human being discovered he could communicate ideas by making sounds as well as gestures. Early man spoke before he wrote, even as you, when a child, learned to talk before you learned to read or write. This primacy of speech in man's long climb upward in the history of civilization assumes new significance in today's world. Recent research in anthropology by Dr. Ernst Mayr of Harvard University indicates that the size of man's brain, which is the most important characteristic that sets him apart from other animals, has remained more or less constant for the past hundred thousand years. As far back as twenty-two million years ago, according to Dr. Mayr, man's brain growth was stimulated by his need to communicate —to speak. The hazards and dangers he faced sharpened his mind and increased his need to communicate with others of his kind. In other words, among our earliest ancestors, those who could think best and communicate best were the ones who survived and passed on their intelligence to their children. Dr. Mayr thus suggests a strong relationship between communicative ability and civilization.

Throughout the course of history, men who could think clearly and communicate effectively influenced the destinies of nations, governments, and individuals. The idea of democracy that was born in the Greek city-states of the 5th century B.C. was strengthened by the exchange of ideas that took place in the agora, or marketplace. Orators like Demosthenes and Pericles, teachers like Socrates and Plato, and even the humblest Athenian freeman discussed great ideas of justice, truth, and freedom in open speech. Buddha, at an earlier time, and Mohammed, later, were religious leaders whose ideas were first communicated orally to their disciples. For Christians one of the greatest speeches of all time is the Sermon on the Mount. During Roman times it was Cicero who stirred men's minds and consciences. In the Renaissance it was Savonarola who spoke out insistently and powerfully. One can think of many others: Martin Luther, Edmund Burke, Patrick Henry, Abraham Lincoln, Woodrow Wilson, Franklin Roosevelt, Winston Churchill, John F. Kennedy. All were influencers of thought because they were masters of communication.

Thinkers and speakers continue to play their role of opinion-makers. Under our democratic system here in America, where we believe in free and open discussion, our need for leaders who are thoughtful, intelligent, accomplished speakers is especially great. In the halls of Congress, in the United Nations, in business corporations, in state legislatures, in schools and colleges, in fact, in all areas of human activity where ideas are discussed and decisions are made, we need *leader-speakers*, experts in thought and communication. They are the ones who help us make up our minds on issues which affect our welfare. We cannot all be experts on matters of public policy, but we can be well briefed by responsible, articulate leaders; and we do hold in our power the right to make the final decisions. It is part of our democratic ideal that when the public is well informed by intelligent and responsible leader-speakers, the people can properly judge what is good policy for themselves and their country. Thomas Jefferson said that "men are inherently capable of making proper judgments when they are properly informed."

In American life freedom of speech is a precious privilege granted by the Constitution. Amendment 1 of the Bill of Rights, adopted in 1791, states that "Congress shall make no law . . . abridging the freedom of speech," a guarantee which many foreign countries today deny their people. Furthermore, in Amendment 14, adopted in 1868, which states, "nor shall any State deprive any person of life, liberty, or property without due process of law," the Constitution protects freedom of speech from interference by the states. A double safeguard is thus written into the law of the land. Why? Because our founding fathers recognized that freedom of speech goes hand in hand with freedom of life. An informed citizenry, at liberty to speak its mind, is the best insurance for continuing freedom.

In the ceaseless struggle between East and West, the idea of freedom is one of our greatest strengths. Our tradition of freedom, our efforts to expand it, our pattern of independent thinking, and our values of life are extensively respected in many parts of the world. New nations and old are seeking ways to advance in civilization, to establish values of dignity and self-respect, and to reach for freedom. The battle for the minds of men goes on everywhere. The great issue is freedom. And if men are free to speak, they will speak for freedom.

> The best weapon in the arsenal of freedom is not bombs but ideas and the most effective delivery vehicle is not missiles, but the English language. . . . .
>
> —*from a speech delivered to members of the English Speaking Union, San Francisco, 1963*

How Important Is Speech Training?

In School. Evidence of the importance of improving yourself in the art of oral communication, both listening and speaking, is all around you. Consider, first, your life in school. It is obvious that you would do better work, get better grades, and enrich your school experience if you listened more carefully to class discussions, lectures, and assignments, if you contributed more constructively to class work, if you improved the quality of your recitations, homework, and oral reports, and if you took a more active role in school activities. The real purpose of being in school is to grow through learning. No matter what subjects you are taking, your growth can be greatly stimulated by your oral participation in classroom work. If you are one of those students who withholds himself from the free exchange of ideas in class or one who assumes an attitude of indifference, self-consciousness, rejection, cockiness, or conformity to what the "group" expects, you are hindering your growth as an individual and cheating yourself of a good education.

Your serious commitment to improving your ability of communicating with people, that is, "speaking your mind" effectively and responsibly and listening open-mindedly and objectively, can be very rewarding. As you improve, you'll do better in class work. You'll be more effective as a leader. You'll become a valued member of whatever group you become a part. Meet the challenge now by saying, "I *want* to improve my speaking," and let your class, whether it's English, history, mathematics, science, language, business education, or speech, be your laboratory.

In the Workaday World. Consider, second, your life in the practical workaday world when your schooldays are over. You may be a businessman, a career woman, a worker at one of the many trades, a housewife, or a professional man. Why is the ability to communicate important in this world? You'll be looking for jobs and trying to improve your living conditions. You'll be raising families, entertaining people, joining clubs,

Here, in the Security Council of the United Nations, communication affects the lives of billions of people.

doing committee work, taking part in community affairs. You'll be a leader in some cases and a follower in others. You'll talk, and talk, and talk. If you have any doubt as to the importance of being able to talk *well* in the working world, ask some adults the question, "What good will it do me to learn how to speak well?" The answer will be varied and positive and very likely will center upon the financial, social, psychological, and humanistic rewards that come to one who is adept at speaking. Whether you're applying for a job, conversing with friends, discussing business problems, running a happy home, talking on the telephone, or taking part in community life, you'll act more confidently if you've had some training in how to use your voice, how to speak with ease, how to listen intelligently, how to influence people.

In Your Relationship to the Larger World around You. Third, consider the nature of tomorrow's world, the world of space, science, and politics in which you'll be living for the rest of the 20th century. Barriers of space, time, mass, and energy, which once kept people isolated from each other, have been removed by science and technology. In 1963 a plane flew from London to Tokyo in five hours. How long will it take in 1980? Astronauts orbit the earth in less time than it takes you to drive a car a hundred miles.

High school students observing United Nations Week use the same principles of speech as are used in the Security Council.

Telstar makes it possible for you to see instantaneously what is happening halfway around the world. On your home telephone you will soon be able to dial directly almost any city in the United States. Computers reduce painstaking and lengthy work into instant action. The "hot line" puts leaders of the world in communication with each other within five minutes. In many ways the globe seems to have shrunk in size.

Yet the world is larger, too, in a sense. Our earthbound environment is being extended into outer space. Earth-orbiting is only a first step to exploration of other planets. Space stations will be no novelty. Communication with other planets may be possible. The ocean, too, is an unexplored frontier which the marine biologist will make a part of man's environment. The biochemist is penetrating the mystery of life with his discovery of DNA, the nucleic acids which determine our cellular being.

The scientist seems to dominate tomorrow's world, yet problems involving nuclear testing, space exploration, national defense, weather control, overpopulation, radioactivity, cell mutation, and the like are not only problems of science; they are problems of conscience, too. They require moral evaluations and political decisions affecting the welfare of everyone, decisions which must be made not by scientists alone, but also by government experts, politicians, churchmen, teachers, lawyers, doctors, businessmen, laboring men, housewives, secretaries—in fact, by all of you wherever you find yourselves in the adult world you'll soon enter.

The political nature of the world concerns you, too. Differences of opinion about the nature of government and the goals of society are national as well as international. A basic conflict is between East and West, the Iron Curtain versus the "open" society, the rule of force versus the rule of consent. It is a cold war but a continuing one, accounting for much tension and emotion in the world. Other conflicts, too, that are related to man's endless struggle for freedom have aroused strong feelings and led to violent actions both at home and abroad. Yet, as history gives abundant evidence, conflicts are rarely solved by violence. So what do we do?

We *talk*. We try to substitute cool logic for hot passion. We try to adjust our differences by discussing, debating, arguing, persuading, convincing, and reasoning with each other. Talking, of course, takes time. Delays, evasions, and postponements often tend to slow progress. Unreasonable attitudes and strong emotions often interfere with finding solutions. Consequently, people may become frustrated and impatient, sometimes concluding that it is better to "quit the talk and take action." All too often "reason goes out the window when emotion walks in the door." However, thoughtful people know that words are better than guns for solving differences. Communication lines accomplish more than battle lines.

Here is the crux of the matter: Common sense tells us that it is better to talk things out than to fight them out. Responsible leaders guide us in this direction and by their example give proof that problems can be settled reasonably with goodwill and good talk. If you feel the need of a general guide to a constructive communicative relationship with people throughout your life, then this simple Biblical quotation may well be your text: "Come now, and let us reason together."

Your Goals and Responsibilities

Up to this point you have given some serious thought to the broad aspects of the meaning and importance of speaking. Now is the time to look at some of the personal reasons you may have for being interested in speech training.

Why are you in a speech course? What are your personal goals, your objectives? To put it another way, what do you expect to learn in the months ahead? For a number of years members of public-speaking classes were asked to state why they wanted speech training. Samples of their answers are shown here. How many of them represent *your* reasons for being in this course?

1. I am very nervous when I get up to speak in front of people.
2. I don't speak distinctly.
3. There will be a need for speaking in the work I plan to do.
4. I want to learn how to interpret the prose and poetry of good authors.
5. I want to learn how to be logical in my speaking.
6. I expect to have a great deal of fun speaking.
7. I don't know anything about the use of gestures.
8. I want to be able to command respect when I speak.
9. My voice needs improvement.
10. The things I plan to say just never come out right.
11. I am majoring in English, and speech work is an important part of my intended work.
12. My speaking vocabulary is too small.
13. I have never known how to prepare a speech, especially how to organize one.
14. I am interested in being able to interpret the ideas of others and present them to a critical audience.
15. I hope to be a more interesting conversationalist because of my knowledge of speaking.
16. I need speech training because I am a leader in student activities.
17. I am very shy with people, and I can't bring myself to speak up when I'm in a group.
18. I want to learn how to become a good group-discussion leader.
19. My regular English classes don't give me enough experience in speaking.
20. My parents and my counselor believe that speech training will help me to develop self-confidence.

No one knows at this point what work you will cover or what your accomplishments will be. You, your teacher, and your speech texts will all define general goals. Among these you are sure to find more effective use of the voice, better listening habits and techniques, vocabulary building, acquisition of self-confidence and self-control, freedom in self-expression, techniques in specific speech activities, and skill in organization. At the top of this list might stand the general aim of your becoming a *happier person* through your learning to communicate more effectively. You'll have some specific and personal goals, too, like those in the chart below:

I Want to Learn How to

Use a microphone	Engage in debate
Read stories	Take part in a play
Give oral reports	Use a telephone
Select a speech topic	Be a better listener
Present demonstrations	Recite in class effectively
Organize a panel	Use parliamentary law
Give a sales talk	Plan a program
Work with groups	Give and take criticism
Give speeches for special occasions	Participate on a TV program
Use sources of information	Gain poise
Discover my prejudices	Evaluate an audience
Tell stories and jokes well	Influence others through speech

Achieve a feeling of personal accomplishment

Facing Responsibilities

A large measure of responsibility goes along with the satisfaction of acquiring the ability to speak well and the thrill that comes from having people listen attentively to what you say. A boy who learns to shoot a rifle must immediately assume the responsibility of seeing that he doesn't employ his newfound power dangerously. Anyone who drives an automobile upon our highways must be sure that his driving does not endanger others. A world that is willing to use atomic power must also be willing to face the extremely difficult task of choosing the only ways in which a civilized and conscience-directed society might use that power. In like manner, a person who learns to speak effectively will be able to influence those who hear him talk, so he must be sure that his influence is good. Do you begin to see your responsibility? Do you see why it is important to examine and reexamine your attitudes, convictions, opinions, and facts before passing them on to others?

The effective speaker is one whose words carry weight with people. The qualities that make him effective are many and varied. He may have a pleasing voice, a cultured manner, a smooth delivery, a sophisticated use of language. Or, at the opposite extreme, he may be rough-spoken, untutored in the niceties of delivery, weak in sentence structure, and awkward in manner. His effectiveness often depends not so much on his mastery of the techniques of speech (although the skilled use of such techniques adds much to a speaker's performance) as it does upon certain qualities within himself. What he is or stands for, how deeply com-

Winston Churchill, one of the greatest orators of the 20th century, addressing the United States Congress.

mitted he is to what he says, how dedicated and zealous, how "on fire" he is with ideas—these inner qualities may give him a kind of personal magnetism which audiences cannot resist. Listeners respond almost intuitively to inner dedication and intensity of thought and feeling. Many speakers in the past have given evidence of how significant this factor of personal magnetism is in effective communication. Consider these, for instance:

Patrick Henry • the firebrand of the Revolutionary provincial convention of Virginia in 1775.

Abraham Lincoln • said to have an unpleasant speaking voice and an awkward delivery, yet who can forget the Gettysburg Address or the compassionate words of his Second Inaugural Address?

Henry Ward Beecher • an orator of the old school, who attracted and held huge audiences with his brilliant speeches on controversial subjects.

Franklin Roosevelt • whose personal magnetism was felt by many Americans in his fireside chats and formal speeches.

Winston Churchill • though handicapped by a tendency to stammer, he became the man of the hour to whom millions of people rallied during the struggles of World War II.

John F. Kennedy • whose vigorous voice stirred Americans deeply.

You can think of others, too, like Richard Nixon, Everett Dirksen, Barry Goldwater, Nelson Rockefeller, Frank Church, Billy Graham, Bishop Fulton Sheen, Martin Luther King, and Norman Vincent Peale, to name just a few.

The great majority of school, community, national, and international leaders are people who can speak effectively. Having this power they can spread good or evil, depending upon their attitudes, their personal values, and the integrity with which they discharge their responsibility.

You, too, as you become more skilled in speaking, will have responsibilities, and one of the most important of them is to examine your prejudices. Reevaluate your convictions to see how many of them are little more than prejudice. Develop the habit of making sharp distinctions between fact and opinion. Make a practice of weighing your speeches in terms of their constructive contribution to your listeners' information, welfare, and happiness. Continue to look at new ideas and philosophies without fear or bias, assimilating and passing on those you approve. People will look to you for leadership. What kind of leadership will you give them?

How Curious Are You?

Do you remember the Greek myth about Pandora, the first mortal woman created by the gods? She was induced by curiosity to open a certain box, thus letting out into the world all ills and diseases. What a shock for Pandora, and how she must have regretted her action! Curiosity doesn't always get us into such predicaments, however; in fact, we are often rewarded handsomely for well-directed curiosity.

It is good to be curious about the nature of your course in speech, your new friends, your teacher, and your own reactions to this new situation.

It is even better to be *intellectually curious.* While it is important to take stock of your surroundings, asking yourself why you're studying speech, learning the names of your new classmates, and settling down for a year's work, it is even more important to develop a strong attitude of curiosity toward learning. Accumulating knowledge of new facts is intriguing, and exploring new ideas is like dealing with magic. Nothing in your life will be so baffling as coming to grips with a novel idea, one which is foreign to your way of acting or thinking, and nothing is more satisfying than producing an idea that is original and fresh.

There was a man who had an idea, and the wheel was born. There was a man who had an idea, and the steamboat was soon chugging on our rivers. There was a man who had an idea, and we have been able to talk great distances over wires. And countless other men and women have, through their curiosity, produced works of inestimable value to mankind.

Don't ever stop wondering about the new things you meet in life, and don't stop trying to find answers to your questions. Curiosity is a valuable attitude. Let it lead you into a rich and exciting life.

ACTIVITIES

1. Satisfy some of your curiosity this very moment. Take stock of your classmates by this simple and pleasant device. Let a volunteer stand up and tell his name, his year in school, and the district, or part of town, in which he lives. When he sits down, let another classmate introduce himself. Continue in this manner until all members of the class have had a turn—including your teacher.
2. Take stock of your school and city library to find out what research materials are available and where they are located. Pay particular attention to magazines, newspapers, pamphlets, dictionaries, encyclopedias, the card catalog, the *Readers' Guide to Periodical Literature*, and the nonfiction section of the library. Divide the work among volunteers and have them report to the class in a day or two what they find.
3. Make initial plans to start a speech notebook, one which will contain notes, speech topics, outlines and speeches, book reports, written evaluations of your speeches, special instructions and assignments, speech drills, vocabulary work, and any other related material. Begin the notebook by stating your personal goals with regard to speech training.
4. Test your intellectual curiosity. Listen carefully to all that goes on in class today and tomorrow and make a short list of words you don't know, statements you want to examine, and ideas you wish to explore. Keep this list in your notebook, and at the end of a week check to see where your curiosity has led you in providing answers and reactions.
5. Determine, from class discussion, what the members of the class consider to be important general goals for this course in speech. Write in your notebook a list of your personal aims, ones which you will bring up later when more definite steps are taken in organization of the year's work. Add to this list and delete from it as time goes on, but keep it—and keep it active! It will give you a good basis for checking on your achievement.
6. Look up the words *prejudice* and *conviction* in the dictionary. Discuss briefly the meaning of each word, and then listen as each member of the class states to the group what he thinks may be a prejudice of his, such as, "I don't like classical music," or "Poetry isn't worth reading," or "Boys are not so bright as girls." As each person expresses his prejudice, ask yourself, "Have I that prejudice, too? Why do I have it? What can I do to get rid of it?" Now, let each person in class state a conviction, a belief based on reason, such as, "Everyone can profit from training in speech," or "Unrestricted installment buying is not beneficial to the national economy." Are any of the convictions prejudices? What general conclusions can you reach about the difference between prejudices and convictions?

7. State the difference between *facts* and *opinions*. What is a speaker's responsibility in regard to both?

8. Give some thought to the following questions in class discussion. Try to explore your reactions rather than reach conclusions.

   a. Have I other responsibilities not mentioned in the text?
   b. What is the relationship between maturing and assuming responsibility?
   c. Why isn't my learning to speak well sufficient responsibility in itself?
   d. Since everyone has prejudices, what is the danger in my having a few of my own?
   e. Adults run the world, so why should I worry about my convictions until I go out to make my own living?

9. Discuss in class the following questions:

   a. In what ways is speaking a more important form of communication than writing?
   b. Does the right of freedom of speech impose any ethical or moral responsibilities on you? Explain.
   c. What reasons can you give for your personal interest in improving your speaking ability?

10. Test for yourself the importance of speech. Just for fun, using grunts, sign language, or gestures (but no words), communicate to your classmates these ideas:

I'm hot.	I'm thirsty.	Look!
I'm tired.	I'm sleepy.	Come here.

11. Now, to understand how vital speech and language are to us, try to communicate these more complex ideas without using words:

   a. We are living in a scientific world.
   b. The man in the third row seems unhappy.
   c. Charlie is shy and feels inferior to his classmates.
   d. I am delighted with figures of speech in literature.
   e. Long division is harder than addition for fourth graders.

12. Discuss the following terms as to their meaning and their relationship to communication and freedom of speech:

   a. filibuster
   b. academic freedom
   c. the Iron Curtain
   d. "taking the Fifth Amendment"
   e. Voice of America
   f. the "hot line"
   g. Radio Free Europe
   h. Telstar

13. Explain, in not more than three sentences apiece, how each of the following is important in the history of speaking.

   a. the Greek agora
   b. Pericles
   c. Socrates
   d. Demosthenes
   e. the Roman forum
   f. Cicero
   g. Quintilian

14. Find what specific evidence you can to support the statement that the following men were considered to be great "influencers of thought" through speech:

- **a.** Buddha
- **b.** Mohammed
- **c.** Pope Urban II
- **d.** Peter Abelard
- **e.** Saint Thomas Aquinas
- **f.** Savonarola
- **g.** Martin Luther

15. Discuss in class the ways in which the following terms are or may be examples of irresponsible speaking:

- **a.** rumor
- **b.** propaganda
- **c.** vituperation
- **d.** harangue
- **e.** slanting
- **f.** "loaded" words

What other examples of irresponsible speaking can you add to this list?

References:

Basic Public Speaking, by P. L. Soper. Oxford University Press.
Basic Training in Speech, by L. Thonssen and H. Gilkinson. Heath.
Effective Speech for Democratic Living, by R. T. Oliver. Prentice-Hall.
Oral Communication, by D. C. Bryant and K. Wallace. Appleton-Century-Crofts.
Speech: Dynamic Communication, by M. Dickens. Harcourt, Brace.
Speech: Its Techniques and Disciplines in a Free Society, by W. N. Brigance. Appleton-Century-Crofts.
The Communication of Ideas, by C. Bradford and H. Moritz. Heath.

Films:

Communication in the Modern World (Coronet). 11 min color or b&w.
Communication: Story of Its Development (Coronet). 11 min color or b&w.
Propaganda Techniques (Coronet). 11 min color or b&w.
Public Opinion in Our Democracy (Coronet). 11 min color or b&w.
Discussion in Democracy (Coronet). 11 min color or b&w.
Why Study Speech? (MH). 11 min b&w.

CHOCOLATE FUDGE
CHOCOLATE FUDGE

Unit Two

FRIENDLINESS: A Force in Oral Communication

There are men in every land who believe in measuring success only in terms of "getting to the top," regardless of how they get there. But many more believe that the "top" isn't a goal which must be achieved at any price, especially when that price is a rupture in human relations or a trampling on human beings. They are people who have a deep feeling for an important morality of mankind: no moral man should be deprived of the basic rights and essential privileges which other moral men in his society enjoy.

What is implied in this morality is a basic sense of justice, a feeling of the worthwhileness of the individual, and the conviction that in a civilized world no man can endure if all men can't.

There is the further implication that at the *heart* level, as well as at the *head* level, the world gradually is becoming—even if slowly, and sometimes discouragingly—a better place in which to live. To all corners of the world spread doctrines which embody the spirit of "Love thy neighbor." Around the world reaches the sturdy arm of the Red Cross. Genuine friendship lies in the "Hands Across the Sea" program. To countless desperate people the Salvation Army brings help and hope. Church missions and governmental agencies provide aid to the needy, the homeless, and the deprived. Private foundations and nonprofit organizations bring comfort and support to the crippled, the maimed, and the helpless. And in communities all over the world neighbors and strangers alike come bearing gifts to those who are the victims of calamity and dire need.

Friendship *is* an important aspect of the lives of men and of the destinies of nations, and its importance is increasing as the world shrinks and its population swells. Unless all of us find a way to live, to let others live, and to help each other in the process, our civilization may destroy itself.

"So what?" you may ask. "What have these observations to do with my speech work?"

Friendship and You

A speech course is, or should be, more than a succession of laboratory experiences in which you acquire technical skills used in oral communication. Hopefully, you should gain, too, new attitudes, new intuitions, new judgments, and new perceptions, some of which pertain solely to oral communication and many that will be related to the totality of living. One important quality or characteristic of human relations is friendship, *a force in oral communication,* as well as an influence in the affairs of nations and individuals. Your attitudes toward and perceptions of friendship, in its range from simple friendliness to moral obligation, are, therefore, a matter of concern and a subject for consideration.

The material in this unit is designed to help you to consider friendship from such viewpoints as your attitude toward yourself and others, your opportunities to develop habits of friendliness, your responsibilities as a friend, and your rewards for acquiring "the friendly touch."

As you read each of the sections that follow, measure yourself mentally, note the key words, phrases, or sentences on the side of the discussion material, and try to anticipate how you will answer the questions which appear as your first activity at the end of this unit.

You are important to yourself.

Putting Yourself into Focus. You are very important to yourself, and there's nothing wrong with this personal regard so long as it doesn't get out of hand. You *need* to have self-confidence and self- respect. At this time in your life *your* friends, *your* courses, *your* clothes, *your* grades, *your* parties, *your* car, and *your* opinions are of greatest importance to you. You tend to be self-centered about such matters; it's a natural part of the growth of your personality.

But if your self-concern leads you to become small-minded, conceited, egotistical, selfish, and unfriendly, so that you disregard the interests and problems of others, you haven't even started to grow up. You need other people unless you are a true hermit who wants only some berries, his cave, and splendid isolation. You need them for the things they can give you, and high on that list of gifts is acceptance of you and *your* gifts.

Others are important to you, too.

One step you can take toward growing out of your self-centeredness and into acceptance of and concern about others is to begin waging war on your snobbery, your feeling that you are better than other people. It's just possible, you know, that you, your group, your club, or your family may *not* be better than others; you may be only *different.* Besides, if you could in some reliable way prove that you are "better," what would you gain? Would *you* accept and feel warm toward someone who could prove himself superior to you in every conceivable measurement of a person?

Snobbery doesn't pay.

Finally, to put yourself into focus, take a good look at how you think others feel about *you.* If you think that everyone feels you are about the greatest thing to hit town, you should buy a new mirror; if you believe that nobody likes you, you need help. People who are talented, generous, friendly, and personable are popular, and those who have the opposite characteristics are not. Those who are in-between—and that's most of us—generally like and are liked by others. Don't be conceited, and don't feel sorry for yourself.

People generally like each other.

Keeping Your Emotions In Check. An ideal in emotional control is something like what a columnist has described as "class." "Class," he said, "is being or doing something so well that no one is aware of the tremendous skill that lies behind the unostentatious execution of the act." If your emotions are so controlled that others know your feelings but are not aware of the means by which you display them, or are not aware of those that you wish to conceal, you belong to an elite group. What is more possible, and certainly very desirable, is that you may exhibit a normal control of your feelings, neither winning laurels for perfection nor losing points for misbehavior.

Ideal control of emotions

Most distressing and embarrassing to others and most unbecoming to you are outbursts of temper. Be angry if you must, but recognize that making a spectacle of your-

Temper! Temper!

self or, worse, injuring human relations doesn't justify a flagrant advertising of your anger. In speech work, particularly, a show of temper will often ruin a group discussion.

Nobody loves a pouter.

At the other end of the scale of emotional expression, pouting and sulking are equally undesirable. Though they do not usually cause violent reactions in others, they do cause tension, anxiety, rejection, or active dislike. The pouter, trapped by his self-inflicted silence, must pout harder and harder to be able to endure his prison—and longer and longer to "save face." You can see that this kind of behavior is both painful and stupid, doubly stupid when you stop to think that the source of trouble can be examined and evaluated through the use of language and friendliness.

Control your likes and dislikes.

Another product of uncontrolled emotion is the extreme liking or disliking of someone. Schoolgirl or schoolboy "hates" and "crushes" are usually evidence of immaturity, but in many instances they reveal a more basic weakness in self-control. If you invest your energy in making *many* friends, you have less of it to give to clinging to one person or to hating him.

Don't be too sensitive.

Don't be too thin-skinned! Some people can't find time to be concerned about others or to be friendly to them because they are in a continual state of being injured. The least slight, real or imagined—and usually the latter—becomes a deep hurt, and the poison of the feeling of injury paralyzes their ability to be objective. Are *you* one of these people?

Remember the underdog.

Making Gestures of Friendship. One of the nicest, most significant, and most rewarding gestures of friendship that you can make is to go out of your way to be friendly and helpful to those who are apparently unloved, unpopular, or in trouble. They need you, and you need them. They are the ones who can best help you to learn the meaning of friendship as it applies both to personal relations and to human dignity. The gesture may not be easy. You must have the fortitude to withstand the possible disapproval of your friends, whose love you also need.

You can also explore "the friendly touch" by taking special steps to make strangers and shy associates feel comfortable and included in any group situation in which you are all involved. It is easy just to join your friends and let others fend for themselves; it is brave and thoughtful to bring the "outsiders" in.

Come, join us!

Who doesn't like a word of appreciation for his efforts? Or doesn't respond with warmth to a sincere compliment? And who doesn't radiate when you imply a compliment by showing an honest interest in his family, his fortunes, his problems, his plans, or his hopes? Who isn't almost fumblingly silent when he has been in deep trouble and has been helped to safety, having been paid the supreme compliment of his worthwhileness? And who doesn't turn away in disgust from ill-concealed flattery?

The warm touch of praise

At a lower, but no less real, level you can promote feelings of friendliness by your general attitude and demeanor. You can *think* a smile, and you can *wear* one. You can exhibit the physical manifestations of friendliness—and mean them—even in instances when you may feel disagreement with a point of view or disapproval of an act or an attitude of the other person.

Friendship wears a smile.

Behaving Well When Trouble Brews. When personal relations are poor, about to become poor, or are in the process of fast deterioration, you can make a real contribution by denying yourself the satisfaction of a sharp retort or a *coup de grâce.* Though every corpuscle in your body separately demands revenge or clamors for preserving the image of you as a formidable competitor, you will usually do better to seek your satisfaction through trying to solve the problem in human relations that confronts you. Neither by word nor by deed should you make a game, a contest, of trouble in personal relations.

Don't feed a grudge.

An important step in trying to solve the problem that confronts you is the deciding that you *want* to solve it, of resolving to take action toward that end. If you don't want to find a solution, if you prefer the struggle, forget the next two steps.

You must want to improve relations.

Identifying with others, engaging in varied activities, mingling with new people, asking questions, and listening attentively to the answers are steps to social maturity.

What is the other person's position?

For those of you who like solutions better than war-at-any-price, the next step is to reconnoiter the "enemy's" camp. What is he really like? What is *his* position in the quarrel? What do others know about him? Who holds him in esteem, and why? Does he want an improvement in relations? If he does, what is *his* proposal for a solution?

End a grudge by a definite act.

And last, if you are convinced that there is any chance at all to end misunderstanding or hostility, try to terminate the grudge match by a definite, friendly act. Don't hold out the olive branch at the sacrifice of honor or principle; rather, make an honest proposal, swallow a little false pride (you'll always have some left!), or simply make a generous overture which you hope will be matched by a similar conciliatory gesture. Since the original problem was most likely one of bad feeling, not of sharp issues, your act may be all that is needed to prompt a joint acceptance of a new, friendly feeling.

Learning to Know and to Understand Others. Some people—the introverts—are like icebergs, with only one-tenth of their personality showing above the surface. Other people—the extroverts—are like corks, exposing most of their thoughts and feelings to the world as they bob merrily in full view. Of course, no one reveals everything about himself, nor should he, for everyone needs a small private world into which he can retreat for relaxation, reflection, or some other kind of self-satisfaction. But, between everyone's private world and the submerged worlds of the icebergs lies a range of hiddenness in personalities that is fertile territory for friendly exploration. Your job, then, as one who wishes to develop a sincere friendliness toward people, both to help you in human relations and to improve your effectiveness as a speaker, is to learn to uncover personalities, to understand people's interests and problems, and to let others know you.

From iceberg to cork

You can start by knowing better all of the students who are in your various classes. Make a point of talking at least once to everyone in your classes during the school year—before, during, or after class, or at any time at any spot that you may meet them on or off the campus.

Know your classmates.

Don't get into the routine of running around with a clique all of the time. Certainly your group of friends is important, but it represents an extremely small segment of humanity. Try to identify with others in a variety of ways: special activities, clubs, teams, meetings, private chats, lunch, and dances.

Mingle!

And, if you want to add to your understanding of others, ask questions—not probing or impertinent ones, but friendly questions—and then *listen.* Stay off the air. Dispense with your favorite broadcast, the one in which you reveal modestly what a wonderful gal or guy you are. You'll have your opportunity later when the other person asks *you* questions.

Ask friendly questions.

Standing Up for What Is Right. It must seem strange to you that in a unit which is devoted to the importance of friendliness there should be an appeal to you to stand up for principle, especially since you know that such shows of

Friendship and principle

integrity always alienate someone and often many. How, you ask, can one be both friendly and understanding and at the same time take a stand which is surely to be regarded as hostile by some of his friends? There is no one answer to your question. Everyone, and that includes you, will have his own answer, one which will depend upon his personal values.

If you believe that a friend is a friend and that there isn't *anything* you wouldn't do for him, you have made a choice. If you feel that what others do is their own business and that keeping friendly relations is of highest priority, you have given your answer. Whatever your answer, in whatever situation, it will reflect your sense of values.

One point of view

It seems to the authors of this text that friendship must be viewed, as often as humanly possible, in the sense in which it was discussed in the introduction to this unit, as a genuine concern for all of mankind, as an essential ingredient in the maturing of a civilized society, and as a force for bringing to all of its citizens the basic rights and privileges of that society. Beneath this layer of somewhat impersonal friendship lie many layers of personal friendships that extend from the pleasantly casual to the warmly intense, and it is of these that we are most aware in our daily lives. It is the personal friendship to which most but not *all* of the material in this unit applies. There are times when you must rise above the comfort of having people like you, when you must *stand up for what is right.* In the long run you will have better personal friends and probably more of them than if you sit by and condone words and deeds that violate your sense of ethics. Equally important, you will grow in stature.

The chips are down!

So, speak out frankly to your friends when you know they are being snobbish, unfair, or selfish. At least try. You can be frank without being nasty. Further, refuse to support a cause, a statement, or an activity which is "out of bounds." Refrain from passing along injurious gossip. Forbear defending your ego and admit when you are wrong or your argument is faulty. Decline invitations to join others in an effort to discredit someone about whom you know little and against whom there is no substantial charge. Abstain from petty persecutions of unfortunates, "new kids," and unpopular ones. In brief, resign from the Club of the Go-Alongs and stand up for what is right—as you begin your development of *the friendly touch.*

ACTIVITIES

1. Reproduce the following personal checklist, answer the questions to which you feel you know answers at this time, and file the list in your speech notebook. Complete the checklist as the year progresses, making changes in previous answers as your understandings grow and your attitudes change. Your honest answers will be a mirror of your strengths and weaknesses in the area of friendly and thoughtful relations with others. Just for fun, ask a friend to weigh your answers against his own impressions of your behavior and attitudes.

Yes	No	Sometimes	
			1. Am I unduly concerned with my own interests, problems, and opinions?
			2. Am I free from petty snobbishness and social prejudices that make me feel I am better than others?
			3. Do I feel that other people like me and regard me as a friendly person, neither too shy nor too aggressive?
			4. Do I have "class" in emotional self-control?
			5. Am I able to avoid childish outburts of temper and name-calling?
			6. Do I pout and sulk when things don't go my way?
			7. Do I go overboard in my likes and dislikes, loving too hard and hating too much?
			8. Am I so sensitive, so thin-skinned that I am in a constant state of being hurt?
			9. Do I go out of my way to help the underdog, the unloved, the unpopular, the troubled?
			10. Do I make special effort to include strangers in my group? to make them feel comfortable?
			11. Am I the kind of person who takes the time and the trouble to praise others for their accomplishments?
			12. Do I make others feel at ease because I smile, shake hands, or make other gestures of goodwill?
			13. Do I nurture a grudge because I enjoy the conflict?
			14. Do I sincerely want to terminate conflicts?
			15. Do I ever take the trouble to find out the facts and feelings that underlie the other person's position in a conflict?

Yes	No	Sometimes	
			16. Do I try to end a grudge by taking a positive step, by a definite, friendly act?
			17. Do I take steps to uncover other people's personalities, to learn their problems and interests?
			18. Have I made efforts to know my classmates?
			19. Do I mingle with people, spending only a reasonable amount of time with my group of friends?
			20. Do I ask friendly questions and listen to the answers?
			21. Do I stand up for what I think is right, no matter who may be displeased?
			22. Am I a gossip?
			23. Do I admit my errors and turn to support those who have opposed me?
			24. Do I refuse to join in "witch hunts"?
			25. Am I willing to go along with the gang just to be "in"?
			26. Do I give the "new kid" a bad time?

2. Discuss in class the implications of friendship, trying to bring out both the distinctions between its simplest and its most complex forms and the honest differences of opinion which may exist with regard to its function, its application, and its value. Take notes on the discussion, and add them to your personal checklist (Activity 1) for future consideration.

3. Start developing the friendly approach in your speech work by giving a one- or two-minute chat about yourself. The following points will reveal the essential information about you that your classmates should find interesting:

a. Your name
b. Where you were born
c. Some entertaining facts about your home town
d. Where you live now
e. An incident of your childhood
f. Nicknames you've had and how they started
g. Your hobby and some interesting things about it
h. The things that interest you most in school, such as sports, other activities, or special classes
i. What you're planning to do when you finish school
j. Your greatest ambition

Here's a sample chat. Let it be a guide for you, but don't be a "copycat."

I live in Menlo Park. My family moved here about three years ago from a ranch in Arizona, where I was born. Our place was sixteen miles from Phoenix, and the thing I remember most about it was the fun our crowd used to have swimming in the irrigation ditches on hot summer days. The whole Salt River Valley, where our place was located, was crisscrossed with ditches that brought water down from the Roosevelt Dam to irrigate the farmland. We kids just about lived in that cool water when the red line of our thermometer hit over 100.

The most exciting thing that happened to me there was helping to train a palomino colt that Dad gave me. It took me a long time to teach Silver Mane her manners, but it was worth all the patience and work after she was broken, and the two of us could ride away for an afternoon in the desert like good pals.

Yes, someday I'd like to go back. But I have other plans for the future, first. Going to college to learn to be a construction engineer is one of them. I'm taking algebra and geometry now and maybe trigonometry later. But life isn't all work and no play by any means. I'm out for basketball and track, and I'd walk a mile to see a good baseball game. A dime in the juke box and a thick chocolate shake after class are my idea of relaxing after a hard school day. Maybe that accounts for my present nickname of Juke. My name is really Jack—Jack Edson.

While preparing your presentation, keep these suggestions in mind:

a. Stick to trivial, human-interest comments about yourself, not pretentious ones.
b. Write out your facts in the sequence in which you would like to give them.
c. If you practice your presentation aloud at home, try standing up and talking to an imaginary listener. Use your mirror for an audience, if you like.
d. Try not to memorize your material. Think of the *facts*, not the exact words.
e. Say to yourself, "They're my friends. I want them to know me and like me."

4. Consider an alternate to the previous activity. Exchange biographical information with a classmate. Then you can tell the class about him, and he in turn can tell about you.

5. Try another way of getting acquainted. Let pairs of students interview each other before class, or during class if it's the teacher's wish. The interview can be conducted like an ordinary conversation or like a man-in-the-street radio or television interview. If your classroom has facilities for radio or television broadcasts of the closed-circuit variety, you may wish to use this electronic medium.

6. Have a "guess who" program. Each student gives a brief biography of one of his classmates. The class may guess who the person is.

Films:

Are You Popular? (Coronet). 11 min color or b&w.
Developing Friendships (Coronet). 11 min color or b&w.
Feeling Left Out? (Coronet). 13 min color or b&w.
How Friendly Are You? (Coronet). 11 min color or b&w.
Improve Your Personality (Coronet). 11 min color or b&w.
Shy Guy (Coronet). 13 min color or b&w.
Friendship Begins at Home (Coronet). 16 min color or b&w.
Making Friends (EBF). 11 min color or b&w.

Unit Three

YOU AND YOUR LISTENERS: Audience Evaluation

To the inexperienced speaker an audience often seems like an ogre, an imagined monster lying in wait to swallow him. He holds the audience responsible for the long days of preparation, hard work, anxiety, and nervousness that precede his appearance before it; and he frequently blames it for the dry mouth, moist hands, and "butterflies-in-the-stomach" feeling he has when he finally faces it.

Fortunately, audiences don't devour speakers, a fact that you soon learn. Along with this knowledge come poise, skill, and maturity as experience increases, and soon you look forward to the stimulation that accompanies contact with an audience.

Part of the problem of fear, nervousness, or anxiety stems from the concept you may have of what constitutes an audience. If you think of it as a solid mass of people, a giantlike entity with a single mind but with dozens of eyes staring at you determined to make you ill at ease, you're on the wrong tack.

Think of an audience as a collection of *individuals* rather than as a monstrous unity. Even though the members of the audience sit close together, they are really far apart, for they don't have a way of reading each other's minds as the speech is given. Nor do *you* know what the audience is thinking unless there is a buzz of disapproval or applause, and then you know only that what you have said is liked or disliked. Since it is impossible for the audience to have a union of minds, you are, in a sense, never addressing more than one person.

Eliminating the fear of an audience is a part of the problem of understanding it. Realizing that you are talking to individuals who *want* you to succeed, who are uncomfortable if you are uncomfortable, and who are usually sympathetic to your problems as a speaker will be a big step toward that elimination. Then you are free to concentrate on the important task of establishing contact with the group to which you are talking.

Know Your Audience

Creating good contact depends upon understanding your audience, having something to say, and delivering your talk well. Other sections in this book will help you in your choice of subject matter and in your delivery; this one is concerned with your need to *know your audience.*

Your first question should not be, *What shall I talk about?* but *To whom am I speaking?* Any speaker who travels around a great deal, talking in many different sections of the country, must ask and answer this question. He must know what political and religious views his listeners hold, what their economic status is, how much formal education they have had, and whether they are friendly, indifferent, or hostile toward him. Unless he is speaking solely to adult groups, he must take into account the average age of those whom he is addressing. While your problems may not be those of the traveling speaker, they are like his in nature if not in extent. Let's look at some of them.

You Are Speaking at Assembly. Is it a general assembly of all classes or just of upperclassmen? of freshmen only? of English classes only? Are you speaking to your fellow students immediately *before* lunch when they are hungry or just *after* lunch when they tend to be sleepy? If your topic has been assigned, is it something new to the audience or have they heard it before? Are you trying to sell an unpopular idea?

You Are Speaking to a School Club. What are the special interests of the club? Are the members of uniform age? Are there both boys and girls in the group? Are you speaking as a member or as an outsider? Does the club meet for a *serious* or for a *social* purpose? Are you known to and respected by this group, or are you a stranger?

You Are Speaking at a Rally. Are your listeners all boys, all girls, or both? What do they want to hear? What is their mood? Will you need a lot of humorous material to fit the high spirits of the students, or must you give them some straight-from-the-shoulder talk about supporting a team that deserves their confidence?

You Are Speaking to an Adult Group in the Community. Is it a club or organization, or is it a random gathering of citizens? What is its purpose? Were you invited to speak, or did you secure permission because you have an idea to sell? Do you know these people? Are you speaking to members of one sex, or is it a mixed group? What do you judge to be the educational background and interests of your audience? What attitude do you think this group holds toward a high school speaker? Sympathetic? Indifferent? Bored? Hostile? Resigned? Did this group meet to hear you talk or to eat, your talk being the program that apologetically follows the main event, eating?

No matter what your speech assignment may be, make sure you have evaluated your audience. What you say and how you say it are always determined by the nature of your listeners. The degree to which you understand your audience is, therefore, an important factor in your selection of material and in your manner of delivery, which is just another way of saying that your giving a successful speech depends largely upon *knowing your audience.* Look beyond the frightening aspects of an audience and discover its heart. Earn the friendship of your listeners by treating them with consideration and respect. Think in terms of what you can do *for* your audience rather than of what it does *to* you. And when you are satisfied that you have established a good relationship with what is a Prince Charming rather than an ogre, then

1. Don't let that audience get away from you!
2. Look at the *people*, not out the window.
3. Make yourself heard.
4. Arouse the interest and curiosity of your listeners.
5. Invite them to follow your thinking, and then lead them.
6. Challenge them.
7. Make them think.
8. Make them laugh.
9. But don't *lose* them!

CHECKLIST FOR EVALUATING AUDIENCES

1. **Nature and size of audience:** Service club _____ School _____ Church _____ Fraternal _____ Political _____ Literary _____ Social _____ Random mixture _____ Known to me _____ Strangers _____ Other _____ Large group _____ Small group _____
2. **Age and sex:** Young _____ Old _____ Middle-aged _____ Mixed _____ Male _____ Female _____ Mixed _____
3. **Level of education:** Grade school _____ High school _____ College _____ A mixture of _______________________________
4. **Probable attitude:** Sympathetic _____ Indifferent _____ Resigned _____ Bored _____ Friendly _____ Hostile _____ Other ____

5. Time of speech: Before lunch _____ After dinner _____
When?____

6. Nature of meeting: Serious _____ Social _____ Mixed _____
Special occasion _____

7. Special information: (Audience mood, interests, motivation, and areas of conflict; approach to the speaking situation; speaker is or is not a guest; etc.)

____

____

____

____

The Value of Fear

The person who says he *never* feels keyed-up, anxious, disquieted, nervously concerned, or worried when he gets up to talk to an audience is either a liar or a nerveless automaton. To be afraid is a natural human reaction to most situations in which you must speak. You'll learn to control that fear, although you may never be entirely free from it. In fact, you should be glad that you're scared. Fear has a value that is often overlooked by beginning speakers.

A person who completely lacks fear of an audience often lacks sensitiveness and imagination also. He may have no feeling of responsibility toward his listeners and, therefore, may be too easily satisfied by an inadequate performance on his part. Your fear in speaking is usually rooted in your eager desire to do well before your audience. You want so desperately to do a good job that your nervous energy goes on a rampage, the result being what is called stage fright.

Psychiatrists assure us, too, that the emotion of concern is necessary to motivate accomplishment. When we are ambitious, we have considerable anxiety. We have feelings of insecurity and lack of self-assurance and confidence until we reach our goals. Worry and anxiety are normal, useful emotions when we can control them.

How to Control Your Fear

Much of your fear will be eliminated as time goes on and as you learn how to control your excessive nervous energy. Properly directed, that energy can lend force, vitality, and enthusiasm to your speaking. When the wild energy of the Colorado River was harnessed by the engineers who built Hoover Dam, the result was an enormous increase of electric power and controlled irrigation for Arizona and Southern California. So

As you speak, make individual friends out of what seems to be a mass of strangers. Address one person at a time.

it can be for you. Harness your nervous energy; turn it into an asset rather than a liability. Here are some practical suggestions for doing just that:

1. *Bypass your fears* by keeping your mind where it belongs—on your speech rather than on yourself and your worries. Much stage fright is caused by thoughts of inferiority and weakness and by fear of failure. Avoid a negative "I can't" attitude and think only good, strong, optimistic thoughts about your speech.

2. *Be thoroughly prepared.* The best insurance against fear is complete preparation. You can't be at your best if you start preparing your talk the night before you are to deliver it. Give yourself plenty of time to get ready, and use that time to good advantage.

3. *Make the most of any opportunity to inject humor into your speech.* Many speakers find that if they can get the audience to laugh a bit, there will be a greater feeling of ease and relaxation for everyone. The speaker feels less tension because he considers the audience to be more agreeable and sympathetic; the audience feels less tension because laughter and geniality are always relaxing. But beware of humor! It's tricky to handle. Jokes, stories, and anecdotes that are used where they don't belong show

poor taste and judgment. Any humorous references must be simple and appropriate, or they'll do more harm than good.

4. *Approach your audience with confidence.* Walk to the speaker's stand or table in a quiet and businesslike manner. Stand straight, throw your shoulders back, look proud. Acknowledge the introduction of your chairman and face your listeners with easy dignity. *Act* confident, even though your knees may be trembling.

5. *Begin speaking slowly, with short sentences.* If you rush the tempo of your speech at first or use long, involved sentences, you'll soon be breathless and uncomfortable.

6. *Look at individuals in your audience while you are speaking.* That may seem difficult to you at first because of your shyness or nervousness. But if you force yourself to do it, you'll find that it helps to make individual friends out of what seems to be a mass of strange faces. You'll soon *feel* more friendly and at ease with your audience, and you'll *look* more poised and relaxed.

7. *Make liberal use of pauses during your talk.* Beginners are often afraid of pauses while speaking. They feel that they must rush along with their words for fear they'll forget what they're saying. But purposeful silences have both a dramatic and a practical value. They command respect and attention from the audience, and they give the speaker time to take a deep breath and control his nervous energy. Deep breathing helps to relax tense muscles and to reduce nervousness.

8. *Conclude in a dignified and confident manner.* Let your listeners know that you have finished by stating your concluding words firmly and deliberately. Turn and leave the platform easily. Don't dash to your seat as if you were sliding to home plate. An appearance of poise hides many a quaking heart. Always put on a good front for your listeners.

Don't be misled by the simplicity of all these preceding suggestions. They are basic for good speech delivery. Courage, confidence, and self-reliance can't be acquired overnight, but a conscientious effort on your part to follow such suggestions will help you to control that cotton-mouthed, clammy-handed, scared-to-death feeling that all beginning speakers share.

Experience is a great teacher. The best way to conquer your fear of speaking is to speak. It's like learning to swim. You can read all about how to do it in books, you can listen to all the advice that your instructor and friends may give you, but in the final analysis it's what you do that counts. So take your first icy plunge with a positive mental attitude.

Learn to say, "I *can* do it and I *will* do it," rather than, "I'm scared!" And remember this: *Always give your talk.* No matter how frightened you are, and even if you are poorly prepared, *Don't be the first to fail!*

ACTIVITIES

1. Gain confidence before an audience by reading something to them. Select a short passage from a magazine or a short poem, not more than about two hundred words, and prepare to read it to your class. You might follow these steps in preparation:

   a. Understand thoroughly what you're going to read.
   b. Check the pronunciation of any words about which you may be doubtful.
   c. Practice aloud at home three or four times.
   d. Hold your book or magazine high enough so that your head is up, your eyes are free to look at your audience from time to time, and your voice is directed toward your audience rather than the floor.
   e. Force yourself to look confident. In Shakespeare's words, "Assume a virtue, if you have it not."
   f. Preface your reading with a brief account of where you got your material and why you think it worthwhile.

2. Help to lose your fear of an audience and learn to distribute your attention by trying this exercise. It rarely fails to give a speaker a degree of self-confidence. Choose a simple topic on which to speak, one that concerns an experience you have had recently, an article you have read, a TV program that has impressed you, a movie you have seen, or some activity in which you have been engaged. Plan a one- or two-minute talk and deliver it to the class.

   Don't worry much about the *content* of your talk. Your chief aim is to make friends with your audience. When you start speaking, have each of your classmates raise his hand to a comfortable halfway-up position. As you speak, look at each classmate for approximately a two-second count, at the end of which time he will lower his hand. Start by singling out a friend in class and feel that he is the only one in the room to whom you're talking. Is he looking at you? Does he seem friendly? Does his friendliness reassure you? Now talk to someone else. When all the hands are down, you will know that you have spoken to everyone personally. Shift your attention to different quadrants of the room; don't "mow down" your classmates by rows. When you have finished, you will realize that your audience is made up of friendly individuals and that it is not an ugly monster.

   Be sure to keep in mind the following suggestions for a successful delivery:

   Be prepared.
   Keep your mind on what you're saying.
   Try to *look* confident even though you *feel* nervous.
   Look at your listeners.
   Use a smile and friendly humor whenever possible.

3. Prepare a brief talk on some unusual current event or recent happening. After you have completed your talk, each of your classmates should help you to find

out how well you followed the suggestions in this unit by evaluating your effort. A checklist like the following is a convenient means of their evaluating your work and of your summarizing their criticism.

Name of speaker ______________________________

Comments	**YES**	**NO**
1. Speaker seemed well prepared	________	________
2. Positive, confident manner	________	________
3. Well-paced beginning	________	________
4. Eye-contact with audience	________	________
5. Evidence of humor	________	________
6. Sufficent pauses	________	________
7. Controlled breathing	________	________
8. Satisfactory conclusion	________	________

4. Diagnose the imaginary speaking situations listed below and decide in class discussion how sound your evaluations have been.

Here is a sample of what you'll do:

You are speaking to a high school assembly on the subject of pride in keeping the campus, or school grounds, clean.

Evaluation

a. This group is of my own age; I must not speak down to them.
b. The topic is "old stuff." What new approach can I make so that there will be interest in what I have to say?
c. I can't set myself apart and *accuse* my schoolmates of failure. I want cooperation, not resentment.
d. It is better for me to appeal to the natural pride in my friends than to threaten them with what school authorities will do if the grounds are not kept clean.
e. I know that a few good laughs will do much to get this crowd on my side. But I must not make a farce of my talk or the whole point will be lost.
f. If I can sell my idea to the assembly, I'll be able to gain more action by suggesting a few *definite* steps to be taken than by merely saying that we should keep the grounds clean.

Try these next items yourself. Let your evaluation be guided by consideration of age, special interests, educational background, size of group, aims of group, prejudices, mood, length of time the audience has been sitting, and any other conditions pertinent to your analysis. As an aid, use the checklist for evaluating audiences that appears in this unit.

a. *Parent-Teachers' Association.* You want help in building a student recreation building on the campus.

b. *All-boys assembly.* There has been a great deal of stealing from lockers in the boys' gym. As student-body president you are appealing to all the boys for fair play in recognition of property rights.

c. *All-girls assembly.* The dean of girls has called all the girls together to discuss appropriate dress for school wear, games, and dances. Because there has been a tendency toward carelessness in dress, the dean is eager to raise the standards. You are president of the Girls' Society, and your talk will be in line with the dean's concern.

d. *Speech club.* You are a member of the Speech Club, which is made up of about thirty students. You are presenting an informative talk on a present-day topic of national interest.

e. *Veterans Day program.* You are speaking to an all-school assembly on a topic related to world peace. Your talk is to be inspirational.

f. *Freshman classes.* As Commissioner of Cultural Activities in your school you are interested in getting freshmen out for the cultural activities offered by the school.

g. *A businessmen's service club.* This club meets for dinner and has its program afterward. You have been invited to speak from a student's point of view about the school's athletic program.

h. *Convention.* Representatives from a number of high schools in a section of your state have convened to discuss problems related to student government. You are speaking on the strengths and weaknesses of student courts.

5. Test student ability to adapt to audiences by this method. Have volunteers prepare brief talks for an imaginary but specific and realistic audience like one of those mentioned in Activity 4. Each volunteer should analyze his imaginary listeners carefully and adapt his material and delivery to the pretended situation. Then after the talks have been given, let the class evaluate the skill of the speaker in adjusting his speech and his manner of delivery to his specific audience.

Films:

Fundamentals of Public Speaking (Coronet). 11 min color or b&w.
Public Speaking: Movement and Gesture (Coronet). 11 min color or b&w.
Is There Communication When You Speak? (MH). 17 min b&w.
Your First Speech (Bailey). 11 min b&w.

Edison

Unit Four

SHOP TALK: The Mechanics of Speech

You are an exceedingly well-informed person if you can correctly identify all these terms: caliper, tandem disc, pulmonary edema, cultural lag, conduit. You are exceptional if you can define two of them. Yet any boy with a little shop experience knows caliper; any farm youngster can tell you what a tandem disc is; any girl in training to be a nurse can define pulmonary edema; any student majoring in education can give you his interpretation of cultural lag; and any plumber or electrician knows what a conduit is.

"So what?" you may ask. Just this. Every business, every trade, every profession, every special group of people has a vocabulary of terms not generally known. Even well-educated people may not recognize some of these terms. But if you belong to a particular trade, profession, or group, you soon learn the terminology peculiar to it, for such knowledge is your bread and butter. Every good workman knows the names of his tools, materials, and techniques.

Speaking, too, has a terminology of its own. In this unit you will find the particular terms, definitions, and explanations which are necessary for you to know if you would be a good workman in the field of speech. You'll find the answers to questions like these:

> What should you know about your voice?
> What part does your body play in speaking?
> How important are articulation and vocabulary?
> What standards of pronunciation should you follow?

The terms and processes that relate to the mechanics of voice production are the first ones which you should learn. Your voice is your most important tool of communication. Without it you can't speak; with it you can express your thoughts, feelings, desires, and problems in hundreds of different ways. Furthermore, your voice often reveals much about the inner "you," what kind of person you are, how you feel, what mood you're in, what sort of personality you have. The "image" you present to the world, whether shy, confident, serious, insincere, careless, indifferent, self-centered, aggressive, insecure, cultured, sophisticated, or boorish, is closely related to the way you use your voice. Since others judge you by how you sound, as well as by how you look and act, it is important that you should understand the voice production process and some of the techniques by which you can attain vocal competence. Let's begin with breathing.

How You Breathe

Your breath is the source of the energy which produces sound. You would have no voice at all without that essential stream of air that is expelled from your lungs as you exhale. We all take the simple act of breathing so much for granted that most of us don't give it a second thought. But since the correct use of your voice depends first upon correct breathing, you should learn what that process is. Here is a diagram of the breathing structure and an explanation of how it works:

The Breathing Structure

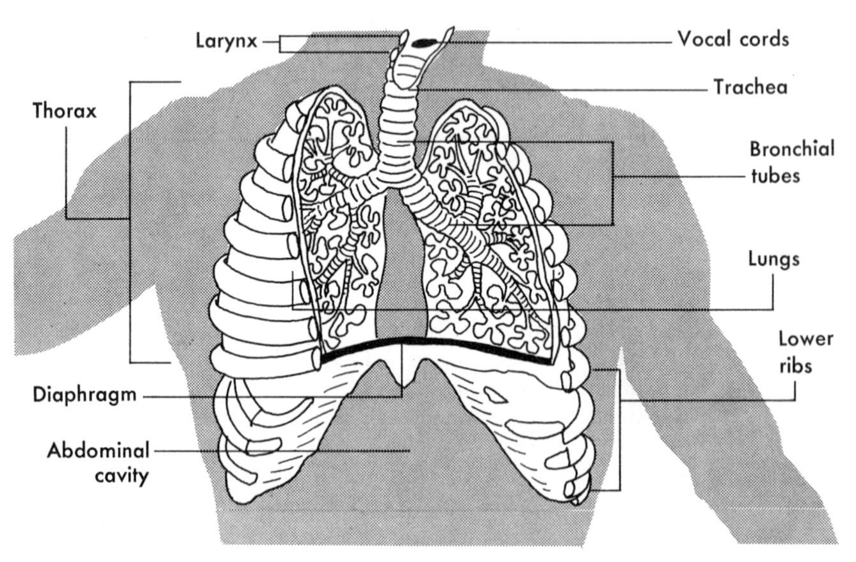

The *thorax* is the chest cavity from the neck to the abdomen.

The *ribs* are bandlike bones which encircle the chest cavity. The space between them is filled by two distinct layers of tissue consisting of the external intercostal and the internal intercostal muscles.

The *diaphragm* is a powerful, dome-shaped muscular wall between the chest and the abdomen. It performs a major function in the breathing process.

The *lungs* are saclike organs that fill with air when expanded and expel air when compressed.

The *bronchial tubes* are the two air passages leading from the lungs to the trachea.

The *trachea* is the windpipe, the main tube by which air passes to and from the lungs.

The *larynx* is the boxlike part of the trachea which contains the vocal cords.

This is what happens when you take a breath and prepare to speak:

Inhalation. The diaphragm contracts and flattens. At the same time the external intercostal muscles contract, forcing the ribs up and out. This process enlarges the size of the chest cavity, creating a partial vacuum. Air rushes in to fill this vacuum, entering through the mouth and nose, going down the air tubes into the lung cells and expanding the lungs.

A reverse action takes place when you exhale.

Exhalation. The abdominal muscles contract, pushing the diaphragm upward. At the same time the internal intercostal muscles contract, pulling the ribs in. This process reduces the size of the chest cavity and compresses the lungs, thus driving the air out of the lungs, through the air tubes, past the larynx (where sound is produced), and out of the body through the nose and mouth.

To be a good "breather," you must learn to use correctly the muscles of the middle part of your body—the abdominal and rib muscles—so that you can inhale quickly and deeply to give yourself a full supply of air for speaking. Breathing for speaking involves much more conscious control of your muscles than does just breathing for staying alive. One is a natural, unconscious act; the other is a planned, directed effort for a specific purpose, the creation and maintenance of sound.

As a speaker your prime interest in breathing should be centered on three things: *how to breathe correctly,* so that you will have a full supply of air to use while speaking; *how to control the output of that air,* so that you won't run out of breath at awkward moments; and *how to build up*

Inhalation and Exhalation

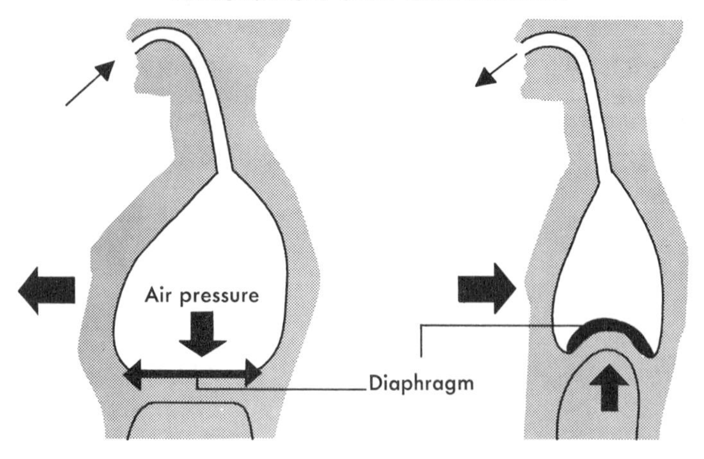

breathing power, so that correct and controlled breathing for speech will be easy and natural for you. You will find exercises later in this section to help you improve your breathing.

How You Make Speech Sounds

Breath is the first essential in the production of voice, as you've just learned. It supplies the motor power for speech. In addition, the *vibrators,* the *resonators,* and the *articulators* must be brought into action. Study the diagram on page 47 to become familiar with the terms you must know in order to understand the explanation of how speech sounds are made.

Vibrators. The vibrators are the vocal cords, located in the larynx or voice box. They are bandlike lips or folds of membrane, about one-half to three-fourths of an inch long, which have the ability to tighten or relax, much as your lips do. When you breathe normally, the vocal cords are wide open and relaxed, and no voice sound is produced as the air passes through the voice box during exhalation. When you whisper, the space between the vocal cords is slightly narrowed, causing a soft, breathy, yet voiceless rustling sound as the air passes through the cords and is manipulated into whispered words by the lips and tongue. When you speak, the cords tighten and move closer together, beginning to vibrate as the air stream strikes them and passes through. The vibration of the cords, an action called *phonation,* creates an audible sound wave. The thin bit of cartilage which folds back over the opening of the vocal cords to prevent food or

The Vibrators, Resonators, and Articulators

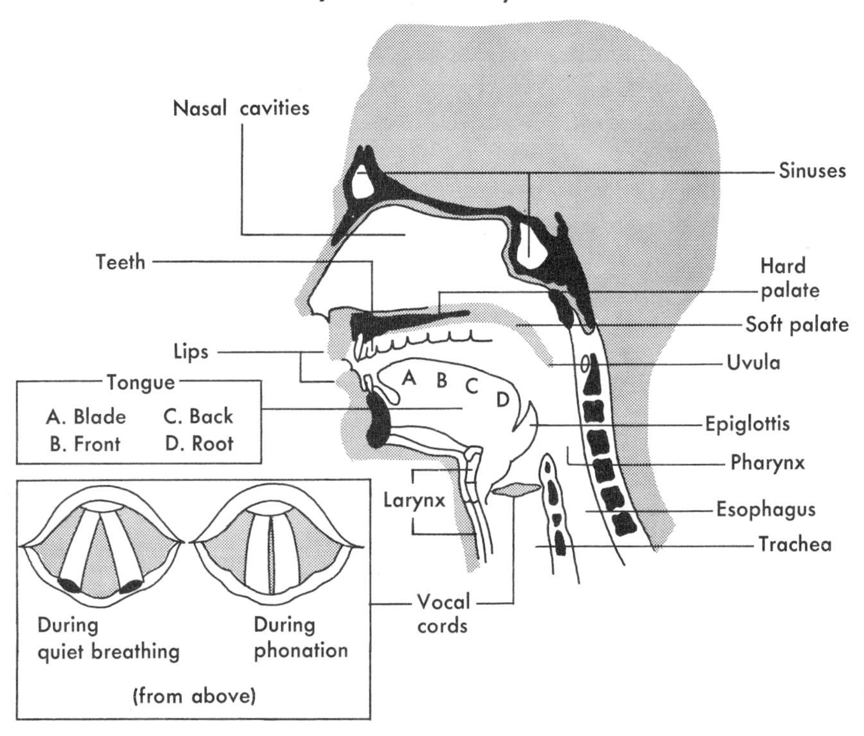

saliva from sliding down the trachea, or windpipe, when you swallow is called the *epiglottis.* The diagram above shows the position of the chords during breathing and phonation.

Resonators. The resonators are the mouth, the pharynx (the back of the throat, between the mouth and the esophagus), the nasal cavities, possibly the sinuses, and some of the bones of the skull. Their purpose in voice production is to furnish resonance, or amplification of sound. These cavities act like sounding chambers, magnifying the initial sound created by the vocal cords and lending depth of tone to your voice. Without resonators, your voice would be thin, faint, and squeaky.

Articulators. The articulators are the tongue, jaw, lips, and soft palate—the movable organs of speech. After voice has been produced in the larynx, the sound is carried by the airstream into the pharynx, mouth, and nose. There it is shaped and molded into consonant and vowel sounds by changes in the position of the lower jaw, tongue, lips, and soft palate. The tongue does most of the work in sounds like *t, d, s, z, l, n,* and *th*; the lips in sounds like *p*, *b*, *f*, *v*, *m*, *w*, and *wh*; the tongue and soft palate in sounds like *k*, hard *g*, and *ng*. It is the skillful use of the articulators which changes sound into words and completes the process of voice production.

As you can see, this process is a complicated and interrelated one. It starts with breathing, with the stream of air that is expelled by your lungs in exhalation. The airstream passes through the muscular folds in your voice box, setting the vocal cords into vibration and creating sound. That sound is then amplified by the resonators, molded and modified by the articulators, and finally released as intelligible speech. And it all happens almost instantaneously!

Preparing for Vocal Control

Obviously, your voice is a magnificent tool of communication. You may be wondering how people are able to communicate at all with so many involved processes going on at one time to produce a single effect—speech. Yet, in spite of what seems to happen "all by itself," there is much that you can do to *improve* the use of your voice. Most of it depends upon your ability to relax, control your breathing, and make use of the vocal techniques that help you develop variety and expressiveness.

Relaxation. The first key to achieving a well-coordinated voice is relaxation. Muscular tightness in areas affecting the vocal mechanism—your abdomen, chest, shoulders, neck, throat, jaw, tongue—will make you a muscle-bound speaker. Just as tight muscles in an athlete produce jerky motions, so will tight body, neck, and throat muscles produce erratic vocal and physical responses when you speak. Your aim, then, is to lessen tension by learning how to relax *before* you speak as well as *during* speech. You can't learn just by reading about it; you must *experience* relaxation by doing warm-up exercises, just as an athlete does before a sports event.

Control of breathing. Relaxation will clear the track for easy vocalization and muscle control, but only a steady, strong flow of air will produce a good voice tone. Two things you will want to learn about breathing, then, are how to use the abdominal and rib muscles properly to inhale deeply and rapidly and how to control the output of air during exhalation so that your words can ride on the crest of a strong air wave.

Your average rate of respiration (inhaling-exhaling) is about seventeen times per minute. During normal, speechless breathing you inhale only a fraction of the total capacity of air your lungs can hold. But during speech you speed up respiration and take in three or four times as much air to supply the necessary force to keep the vocal cords vibrating. You need to control that air as it passes out of your mouth and nose because such control helps you to avoid sounding weak and breathy and insures you against running out of air as you talk. You should spend some time on breathing exercises to establish the "feel" of controlled breathing.

Activities for Relaxation

1. Massage gently in downward strokes the muscles of your face and throat. Close your eyes; let your face feel limp, your jaw hang slack, and your tongue protrude slightly as if you were unconscious.
2. Drop your head forward, chin on chest. Raise it slowly, letting your mouth fall open. When your head is as far back as it will go, your mouth should be wide open and your lower jaw slack.
3. Let your head hang limp for a six-count, first on your chest, next on your left shoulder, finally on your right shoulder. Reverse the direction.
4. Open your mouth wide and yawn deeply while moving your head from side to side.
5. Rotate the head and neck in a clockwise fashion. Reverse the direction.
6. Relax the swallowing muscles by massaging gently with your fingers the soft part of your throat between the chin and Adam's apple. Then, with your fingers holding the muscles under your chin, swallow and feel the downward pressure in your throat.
7. Gently hold your Adam's apple between thumb and forefinger, moving it very lightly from side to side to feel its "floating" action.
8. Hunch your shoulders tightly and then let them fall suddenly. Repeat several times.
9. Bend forward slowly from your hips, with your knees straight and your arms hanging down loosely. Swing your torso and arms from side to side. Then slowly return to an erect position.
10. Place your hands on your hips, elbows out to the sides and feet slightly spread. Swing your trunk as far as possible to the right; return to starting position; then swing to the extreme left. Repeat, while inhaling through your nose and exhaling through your mouth.
11. Place hands on hips and rotate your trunk clockwise several times. Reverse the direction.
12. Yawn as you inhale; stop in the middle of the yawn and release your breath quickly. Repeat, but exhale slowly this time in a long, drawn-out whispered *hah-h-h-h-h* sound.

Making the test, described in Activity 2 below, as to whether or not breathing is being used to full capacity.

Activities for Control of Breathing

1. Sit in a relaxed position and place your hands on the "soft spot" of your abdomen, between and below your lower ribs, where the diaphragmatic muscle is located. Inhale slowly and deeply, feeling how the upper abdomen tends to push out against your hands. Exhale suddenly and notice how the abdomen sinks in. Inhale and exhale with force several times until you become fully aware of the in-and-out movement of the abdominal muscles. Try the same exercise lying down. You will then have little difficulty in noticing the correct action of the abdomen as it rises and falls. Your goal is to breathe in an erect position as easily and correctly as you do in a reclining position, with the effort centered at your diaphragm.
2. Stand up and place your hands on each side of your body just above your waistline. Inhale and exhale deeply and slowly, feeling your ribs move in and out as you breathe. Now, place your hands on your upper chest and feel the rise and fall there as you breathe in and out. If the

chest action exceeds the in-and-out movement of your ribs and abdomen, you're not breathing to full capacity. Don't let your chest and shoulders heave up and down as you breathe. The effort should be centered in the abdominal region.

3. Strengthen your abdominal muscles by lying down, placing several heavy books on your upper abdomen, and breathing in and out slowly and fully, causing the books to rise and fall in turn. *Feel* the pressure of your muscles against the books.
4. Inhale deeply and slowly, hold your breath for a ten-count, then exhale with force through your nose. Repeat, exhaling with a whispered *hah-h-h* sound.
5. Inhale deeply, then exhale (whispered *hah-h-h*) slowly to the count of ten, emptying your lungs when the final number has been reached. Repeat, raising the count to fifteen, twenty, twenty-five, then as far as you can go. Stop just before the air supply is exhausted. You're learning to control your outgoing breath.
6. Inhale, hold the air for a three-count, then exhale through pursed lips as *slowly* as you can. The object is to see how long it takes to exhale. Repeat, exhaling with mouth open in the continuous vowel sound of *ah-h-h-h.* Repeat, exhaling with a closed mouth in a long, continuous hum (*m-m-m-m-m*).
7. Inhale, then exhale in a prolonged whistle or an *s-s-s-s-* sound. See who can hold on the longest. Try other sounds like *z, sh, f, th.*
8. Inhale; exhale by counting 1,2,3 (hold), 4,5,6 (hold), 7,8,9 (hold), 10,11,12, etc. Try for smooth, prolonged control.
9. Inhale; exhale forcefully with puffs of air. Repeat, exhaling *Hip! Hip! Hip!* until breath is gone. Repeat, saying *Bay, Bee, Bye, Boh, Boo* in short, forceful releases of breath.
10. Practice swift, light inhalation and steady controlled exhalation while reading one of the following selections. At every place where the meaning of the selection might require a significant pause, take a quick breath to replenish your air supply. Then dole out your breath carefully during exhalation so that the last syllable is as audible as the first.

a. A thing of beauty is a joy forever:
Its loveliness increases; it will never
Pass into nothingness; but still will keep
A bower quiet for us, and a sleep
Full of sweet dreams, and health, and quiet breathing.

—John Keats

b. The great sea
And its waves
Are shallow
Compared to the heart
Of man.

When the waters fail
Or the flood dries up,
We can see
What was hidden beneath.
But to the day
Of his death
Who can really know
The depths of the heart
Of a man?

—Tu Hsün Hao

c. The world is too much with us; late and soon,
Getting and spending, we lay waste our powers:
Little we see in Nature that is ours;
We have given our hearts away, a sordid boon!

—William Wordsworth

d. We look before and after,
And pine for what is not:
Our sincerest laughter
With some pain is fraught;
Our sweetest songs are those that tell of saddest thought.

—Percy Bysshe Shelley

Voice Quality: Resonance and Timbre

What kind of voice do you have? If it is full, free, richly toned, and well modulated, you are fortunate. If it is tense, harsh, weak, thin, husky, nasalized, breathy, or restricted in some way, it will sound unpleasant. To improve it, you should learn to recognize and analyze your own special vocal quality, especially the two following elements.

Resonance. This term applies to the amplification of voice in the hollow chambers and bony structure of the head and upper body. When sound waves created by your vocal cords strike the resonators—pharynx, nasal cavities, mouth, skull bones—they set up additional vibrations that reinforce and intensify the original sound, giving it a full, rich quality. Vocal resonance may be compared with musical resonance. A vibrating tuning fork gives a thin, weak sound until you touch its base to a wooden table top. Then the vibrations are amplified, and the sound mellows and deepens. Pluck the strings of a ukulele or guitar when the sound-box opening is plugged with paper or cloth, and you'll hear a thin, weak tone. Remove the obstruction, and the tone becomes full and clear. So it is with your voice. The pleasing overtones that lend richness and fullness to your voice are created by resonance.

Vocal resonance is of two types: cavity and sympathetic. Cavity resonance occurs in the sounding chambers of your head where the major amplification of your voice takes place. Sympathetic resonance occurs in some of the bones of the head, neck, and chest, which reflect and pick up some of the vibration initiated by the vocal cords. Although you may be able to sense sympathetic resonance (hum forcefully and feel the vibrations in your head), most of the resonant quality of your voice is produced in the pharynx, mouth, and nasal cavities.

Timbre, or Tone Quality. These words are used synonymously to refer to the characteristic quality of a voice that identifies it as being different from other voices. If you were blindfolded in a crowd, you could still identify a friend by hearing his voice. You recognize people over the phone by the sound of their voices. It is the individual timbre, or tone, that aids your recognition.

Tone quality is affected by four elements: (1) depth and control of breathing; (2) the fundamental tone created by the vibrations of the vocal cords; (3) the overtones created by resonance, both cavity and sympathetic; and (4) the use of the articulators as they modify and manipulate the sound waves. How you control these elements and make use of the physical equipment nature gave you determines the inherent quality of your voice. Is it dull? Is it nasal? Is it harsh? Is it weak? Is it whining? Is it breathy? Is it booming? Is it full, rich, and resonant? You should know. Record your voice, to hear yourself as others hear you, so that you can analyze its quality and make plans for improvement.

Activities for Resonance and Timbre

1. Hum *m-m-m-m-m* in a steady prolonged monotone. Feel the vibration in your teeth, lips, nose, cheekbones, and forehead. Repeat with the sound of *n*, then *ng*.

2. Open your mouth as if to yawn; then intone deeply the sound *oh-h-h-h,* gliding into an *m* (*oh-h-h-m-m-m*). Feel the openness of your throat on the *oh* and feel the vibrations on the *m.*

3. Start to yawn, then exhale with the sounds *oh-no, go-slow, howl-owl, fowl-towel.* Do the same with this well-known practice sentence: "How now, brown cow?"

4. Yawn deeply, then say the following, prolonging the sounds:

   m-m-m-m-m-ay-ay-ay-ay
   m-m-m-m-m-ee-ee-ee-ee
   m-m-m-m-m-oh-oh-oh-oh
   m-m-m-m-m-ooh-ooh-ooh-ooh

Repeat with the *n* sound.

5. Say "hung," then glide into *ah-h-h-h.* Feel the change in position of the soft palate. Repeat *hung-ah, hung-ah, hung-ah.*

6. Say the following words, prolonging the *ng* sound: *ming, wing, sing, thing; hung, gung, sung, among.*

7. Repeat the following, intoning and lingering over the *m's, n's, and ng's*:

   Many men make a million.
   Nine mighty mice nibbled on my mailbox.
   Moaning in the gloaming

8. Practice saying the following with a relaxed open throat and full resonance:

   Home, home, sweet, sweet home!
   Be it ever so humble, there's no place like home!

   Roll on, thou deep and dark blue Ocean, roll!
   Ten thousand fleets sweep over thee in vain.

   For him who walks with eager, swinging stride across the boundless green of prairies lush with grain, there is no Night; there's only pulsing life that's born of Day and fertile plains and dreams of men.

9. For additional practice in quality and richness of tone, try reading aloud some of these poems:

   "Recessional," by Rudyard Kipling
   "Song of the Lotus-Eaters," by Alfred, Lord Tennyson
   "A Musical Instrument," by Elizabeth Barrett Browning
   "The Raven," by Edgar Allan Poe
   "Columbus," by Joaquin Miller

Some Technical Terms: Pitch, Range, Inflection, Pause

The voice that wins friends and pleases listeners makes use of a variety of techniques. Here are four of them.

Pitch. This word refers to the tone, note, or key on the musical scale which the voice assumes during vocalization. Everyone has his own natural pitch level, the limited area on the scale in which his voice performs most comfortably. Nature determines the pitch of your voice, such as bass or tenor, contralto or soprano. You cannot change overnight from high to low, but you can control and vary your pitch within the limits nature has set. Change of pitch is determined by the condition of your vocal cords and the speed with which they vibrate. Tense cords vibrating rapidly produce a high pitch; relaxed cords vibrating slowly produce a low pitch. Different pitch levels are used to suggest different emotions. Generally a high pitch indicates excitement, enthusiasm, alarm, fright, or annoyance. A low pitch may reflect seriousness, sadness, awe, or perhaps dramatic tension. Varying your pitch to match your meaning adds variety and flexibility to your speaking.

Range. The distance measured in musical notes between the highest and lowest pitches a speaker can comfortably use is called the range of his voice. The full extent of the human voice is at least three octaves (twenty-four full notes), but probably your range is limited to considerably less than one octave. If you happen to be a "Johnny-three-note," with a speaking range of only three tones, you are as hindered as a piano player who attempts to play a sonata on a three-keyed instrument. Limited pitch range results in monotony and lifelessness.

Inflection. Another manifestation of change of pitch is inflection, the rise and fall of the voice as it slides from one pitch to another during the utterance of a syllable, word, or group of words. Abrupt pitch changes are called *steps*; gradual pitch changes are called *glides*. Suppose someone makes a statement with which you disagree. You might say,

all
"You're w
r
o
n
g!"

Note that there is a definite stop in pitch between the first and second words. This change is called the step. Note also that the third word drops in pitch from high to low. This internal, gliding pitch change is the glide. Both steps and glides may go up or down. Sometimes the glides are double, the pitch level going up and down or vice versa. An example of such a change would be a person's saying *Oh!* as he suddenly understands a math problem being explained:

```
     o o
"O       o
           h!"
```

Generally, the upward, or rising, inflection suggests doubt, question, uncertainty, incompleteness, surprise, or possibly suspense. The downward, or falling, inflection shows completeness, positiveness, determination, authority, earnestness, or conviction. The double inflection often indicates irony, sarcasm, frustration, or doubt. Inflections enable you to add shades of meaning to what you say, to emphasize ideas, and to reveal inner feelings. They fulfill more functions than almost any other kind of voice modulation, occurring naturally and spontaneously as you talk, and adding subtlety, implications, overtones, and connotations to your words.

Pause. The pause, a brief suspension or hesitation of the voice, serves several purposes in speaking. In general it is an attention-getter, a device by which you may separate ideas, emphasize points, help listeners to focus on a thought, whet curiosity, arouse suspense, or create a dramatic effect. Pauses add clarity, emphasis, and expressiveness to your speech by directing attention to what you've already said, what you're going to say, or both. Also, they give your listeners a feeling that you're "thinking on your feet," that you are mentally and emotionally involved in what you're saying.

When you converse with people, you use pauses frequently and naturally as your mind actively plays with many ideas and shades of meaning, and you are spontaneously expressing your thoughts. When you give a speech, you must pause more consciously to get increased attention and to give increased emphasis, because your situation is more formal. Don't be afraid of the conscious pause; it will seem longer to you than it will to the audience. The audience needs time to absorb your thoughts and will listen more sharply because of the momentary silence.

Pauses might be said to "punctuate" spoken words, much as periods, commas, and semicolons punctuate written sentences; yet the grammatical construction of your speech is not a sure guide to pausing. You *may* use pauses whenever punctuation appears, but a better guide might be the intensity of your feeling, the significance of your thought, or the vividness of your ideas. Make your pauses meaningful.

Activities for Pitch, Range, and Inflection

1. Test the range and pitch of your voice with the aid of a piano. Say *ah* in what seems like a natural, comfortable pitch to you and match the sound with a note on the piano. Starting at that point, go up the scale as far as you can, then down as low as you can *without strain.* Your best speaking pitch will be in the lowest octave of that range, probably about one-quarter of the way up from the lowest note you struck.

2. Count slowly from one to eight, beginning on the lowest note you can comfortably produce. Reverse the direction, starting on your top note. Vocalize up and down the scale using the alphabet in the same manner. Jump from high to medium to low pitch and back again, saying the word *one.*

3. Say the sentence "This is my normal pitch" in your natural tone of voice, until your ear becomes accustomed to the sound. Then deliberately lower your voice at least three notes and say, "This is a low pitch." Finally, raise your voice to at least three notes above its normal pitch and say, "This is a high pitch." Practice doing this until your ear recognizes the changes in pitch and you thus become aware of your vocal range.

4. Speak the first words of the following passage in a low voice. Gradually raise the pitch of your voice as your excitement increases.

   There is no way. I couldn't face myself if I did what you suggest. It's impossible, utterly impossible. You can't expect it of me—you can't. I won't do it. I'll never do it. Never! Never! Never!

5. Practice the following sentences according to the instructions indicated:

   a. Keep to a medium pitch to indicate normal poise and ordinary conversational tone:

      I think I shall never forget the beauty of that October morning. From our vantage point we could see the lake below us, peaceful and unmoving. To our right lay the woods, spotted with bright autumn colors. And far above them both rose the massive dignity of Mount Lincoln.

b. Rise to high pitch to show excitement and tension:

There he is, over there! He's circling lower. He must be in difficulty! Look, look! The engine's on fire!

c. Drop to low pitch to indicate dramatic intensity:

There was always something sinister about this shaded path, even in daytime. Now in the darkness and the rain it seemed hostile and menacing. The trees were denser, the shadows blacker, the silence ominous.

6. Try saying the following words first with an upward inflection, as if asking a question; then with a downward inflection, as if expressing determination or firmness.

Oh? Yes? Well? No? So?
Oh! Yes! Well! No! So!

7. Tell a brief story to the class, either serious, funny, or mysterious, using *no* words, just letters of the alphabet or numbers. See if you can get the mood across by means of change of rate, pitch, and inflection.

8. Read names from a telephone book as if you were describing either an exciting or an ominous event. Cover a wide range of tones and use inflection to create your effect.

9. Read one of the following selections, using whatever pitch, range, and inflection techniques you feel are best suited to the meaning and mood:

a. They tell us, sir, that we are weak. . . . Sir, we are not weak. . . . The war is inevitable—and let it come! I repeat it, sir, let it come! . . . It is in vain, sir, to extenuate the matter. Gentlemen may cry, peace, peace—but there is no peace. . . . I know not what course others may take; but as for me, give me liberty or give me death!

—PATRICK HENRY

b. Bury the Great Duke
With an empire's lamentation;
Let us bury the Great Duke
To the noise of the mourning of a mighty nation;
Mourning when their leaders fall,
Warriors carry the warrior's pall,
And sorrow darkens hamlet and hall.

—ALFRED, LORD TENNYSON

c. I sprang to the stirrup, and Joris, and he;
I galloped, Dirck galloped, we galloped all three;

"Good speed!" cried the watch as the gate-bolts undrew,
"Speed!" echoed the wall to us galloping through;
Behind shut the postern, the lights sank to rest,
And into the night we galloped abreast.

—ROBERT BROWNING

d. When we two parted
In silence and tears,
Half broken-hearted
To sever for years,
Pale grew thy cheek and cold,
Colder thy kiss;
Truly that hour foretold
Sorrow to this!

—LORD BYRON

e. . . . David hasted, and ran toward the army to meet the Philistine.

And David put his hand in his bag, and took thence a stone, and slang it, and smote the Philistine in his forehead, that the stone sunk into his forehead; and he fell upon his face to the earth.

—1 SAMUEL 17: 48–49

Activities for Pause

1. Train yourself soon to become the master of pause, a kind of eloquent silence; it has a powerful effect in speaking. Notice how important pausing is when you read sentences like the following:
   a. Suppose that you were wealthy, that you could buy anything you wanted without thinking about its price. Would this be all you would need for happiness? I doubt it.
   b. Crouched in a corner of the dismal room, like a terrified animal that has been beaten unmercifully, was a little boy, Thad by name.
   c. It is a very odd thing, as odd as can be, that once we get what we set our hearts upon, we begin to have new desires.
2. Read with meaningful dramatic pauses and feeling: "Wait! Did you hear that? Listen. What was it? It sounded like—there, I hear it. I think it must be—yes, it's coming closer. What? *Sh-h-h,* it's stopped. No. I can't hear it now. What do you suppose it was?"

3. Here are some selections written without punctuation, capitalization, or regard to their original form. Read them aloud, making sense by using pauses to "punctuate" the idea-clusters. Disregard the way the lines appear; group the words yourself according to their meaning.

a. over
hill over
dale through brush through
brier over park
over pale through
flood through
fire I do
wander everywhere

b. I slip I
slide I gloom I
glance among my
skimming
swallows I
make the netted
sunbeams dance against
my sandy shallows

c. And out
again I
curve and flow to
join the brimming
river for
men may
come and men
may go but I
go
on for ever

4. Make full use of pauses in reading the following lines from Shakespeare:

a. Naught's had, all's spent,
Where our desire is got without content.

b. When our actions do not,
Our fears do make us traitors.

c. To die—to sleep.
To sleep—perchance to dream: ay, there's the rub!
For in that sleep of death what dreams may come
When we have shuffled off this mortal coil,
Must give us pause.

d. Tomorrow, and tomorrow, and tomorrow
Creeps in this petty pace from day to day
To the last syllable of recorded time;
And all our yesterdays have lighted fools
The way to dusty death. Out, out, brief candle!
Life's but a walking shadow, a poor player,
That struts and frets his hour upon the stage
And then is heard no more. It is a tale
Told by an idiot, full of sound and fury,
Signifying nothing.

e. Cowards die many times before their deaths;
The valiant never taste of death but once.
Of all the wonders that I yet have heard,
It seems to me most strange that men should fear,
Seeing that death, a necessary end,
Will come when it will come.

More Terms: Volume and Force, Intensity, Rate, Emphasis, Flexibility

Understanding and experimenting with additional vocal techniques like the ones discussed below is a necessity if you want to develop a voice that is responsive, expressive, and effective.

Volume and Force. These words are closely related in meaning, sometimes being used interchangeably. The dictionary indicates this relationship:

Volume: quantity, strength, or loudness of sound
Force: strength, energy, vigor, intensity of power

In general, volume refers to the amount or degree of sound produced, whereas force implies the energy or vigor with which you project that sound. You need both in speaking, as a means of reaching an audience in a large or acoustically poor room and as a device for communicating emotion. When you raise your voice in anger, defiance, or excitement, you not only change pitch but also add force and volume. When you lower your voice to express feelings of sorrow, sympathy, compassion, restraint, or solemnity, you decrease volume and force.

Your management of your outgoing breath is the factor that controls volume and force. When you speak loudly and forcefully, you need more breath than you normally use, you need to push it out harder to make the vocal cords vibrate more, and you need to direct its full strength into the resonating chambers without obstructions like a tight throat.

Intensity. Intensity is a quality in speaking that arises from strong feeling—a controlled vocal energy which reflects the emotions of the speaker as he reacts to what he is saying. It is not to be confused with volume and force, although both may be used in expressing intensity of feeling. Whenever you talk with great energy or emotion or thought, you are speaking with intensity.

Rate. Rate, or tempo, is the speed of speaking. Generally the term refers to how fast or how slowly you speak, the rate being determined by the duration of your pauses between individual words and sentences. When you say something weighty, serious, or complex, you tend to talk slowly as you choose the words and phrases your audience needs time to grasp. When you deal with trivial, light, or exciting matters, you tend to speed up, running words and sentences together. Rate varies from the slow, solemn eighty words per minute you might use for reading the Gettysburg Address, to the nearly two hundred words per minute you might hear an announcer using to describe an exciting hockey game. A variety in rate is what you should aim for in most of your speaking, and it can be powerful in producing a dramatic effect.

Rate may also refer to the *time* element or *duration* of sound used within syllables or words. For instance, the words "It's hot!" when shouted as a warning to a small child last only a fraction of a second. The same words used by a weary, perspiring, overheated traveler to describe stifling humidity might be prolonged—"It's hah-ah-ah-aht!"—to last as long as two or three seconds. Such time values or rate differences have an influence on speech because they reflect meaning and add variety and expressiveness to what you say.

Emphasis. Emphasis is any special attention that is given to something so as to make it stand out. In speech, emphasis may be the vocal stress given to a syllable, word, or phrase to give it prominence; or it may be contrasts and changes in volume, pitch, inflection, rate, pause, or tonal quality to make conspicuous a thought, significant feeling, concept, or a particular portion of a speech. Any method you use to enable main points to stand out or contrast with subordinate ones is helpful in showing a listener the relative importance of your ideas and in making the vital ones stick in his mind. Without emphasis they may be hidden by subordinate details.

Flexibility. Vocal flexibility is the ability of a voice to modulate or vary within a pleasant range of tone. The word *flexibility* suggests suppleness, adaptability, pliancy, freedom from restraint. A flexible voice is adaptable to the demands made upon it: it is responsive, easily manipulated, and well coordinated. Your ability to control and use many of the qualities already discussed in this section—those that lend warmth, color, and expressiveness to the voice—will determine whether you have flexibility.

Activities for Volume, Force, and Intensity

1. Stand erect. Place one hand on the abdomen. Inhale, then exhale, forcing the air out. As the last air leaves, shout *Hey!* and notice how the abdominal wall jerks. Try the following words in the same manner, using strong abdominal muscle power and explosive voice force:

   Hut! Two! Three! Four!

   Left! Right! Left! Right!

   Yo! Ho! Heave! Ho!

   Fee! Fye! Foh! Fum!

2. Read each of the following sentences three times, increasing force from soft to medium to loud. Don't substitute high pitch for force and intensity.

   The Campbells are coming!

   It must not happen again.

   Let him try his worst. I fear him not.

3. Prepare one of the following selections to read to the class. Let the volume, force, and intensity of your voice be adjusted to one of these conditions: (1) quiet reading directed at front row only; (2) enough volume to reach everyone in the classroom; (3) strong enough force and volume to reach the class across the hall (but don't *shout!*).

   a. We hold these truths to be self evident: that all men are created equal; that they are endowed by their Creator with certain inalienable rights; that among these are life, liberty, and the pursuit of happiness.

   —Declaration of Independence

   b. We are not enemies, but friends. We must not be enemies. Though passion may have strained, it must not break our bonds of affection. The mystic chords of memory, stretching from every battlefield, and patriot grave, to every living heart and hearthstone, all over this broad land, will yet swell the chorus of the Union, when again touched, as surely as they will be, by the better angels of our nature.

   —Abraham Lincoln

   c. The quality of mercy is not strained;
   It droppeth as the gentle rain from heaven
   Upon the place beneath. It is twice blest—
   It blesseth him that gives, and him that takes.

'Tis mightiest in the mightiest. It becomes
The thronèd monarch better than his crown.

—WILLIAM SHAKESPEARE

4. Study the feeling of the following three selections. One expresses pure joy and rapture; another is an angry challenge to man's conscience; the last has a tense, dramatic restraint. Practice reading them aloud, putting into your reading all the expressive intensity of feeling which each selection demands.

How good to be back! Every sound and smell and sight shouted its welcome to the eagerness that was in us. We had come home. There on the front porch stood Mother and Dad, arms outstretched, and halfway down the path lay ancient Wog, faithful, weary symbol of unquestioning devotion, wagging his matted tail in recognition of the prodigal children. Old hemlock tree, we're back! Old gabled roof, we're home again! How right the poet was when once she said, "World, I cannot hold thee close enough!" and how strange that such a fire should start these tears.

Gentlemen, you ask if your decision is not the only solution, and I say, "No!" For, if man can feed his stomach only by selling his soul, he solves no problems; he merely loses sight of them in a Darkness. You ask if your decision is not just, and I say, "No!" When is it just, when has it ever been, to make men crawl for the bread that they have earned? You ask if your decision is not a wise one, and I say, "No!" When is it wisdom's course to shred human dignity with a loathsome choice dictated by fear of hunger? Wisdom and justice are strangers to this room, and by your act you have covered not only this community, but all decent men, with the deepest shame.

Dark Corner

Long hours ago, a hidden mine
Upon a far Pacific beach
Reached up for you and drew you down,
And left me blind in scalding tears.
The searing of the shock has gone,
Yet every fiber of me yearns
To gorge myself on dark despair,
To come to you by my own hand.
Tonight my fingers gently touched
The soft wool sox you left behind,

The warm wool sox that I have kept,
And pain rushed back, no stranger now.
How wrong that Time will make amends!
The wound must bleed until the scar
Has hid from view the outward sign
Of loss, and then the heart will keep
A lonely vigil by that wound
In corner dark, for grief is there.

Activities for Rate

1. Watch the duration of sound *within* the syllables and words in the following sentences. Prolong the vowel sounds if the mood is slow, serious, or solemn; hasten them if the mood is swift, joyous, or excited.

a. The woodpecker's head jabbed frantically at the pole.
b. He inched his painful way over the rocky ledge.
c. This is the last time we shall be together, friends.
d. Two skiers were racing madly down the twisting course.
e. The long lines moved slowly up the path toward the flower-covered grave.
f. Very tenderly he leaned down to comfort the crying child.
g. If you take my picture, I'll smash your camera!
h. Very suddenly the feelings of the crowd changed, and a hush fell over the gathered mob.

2. Try reading these lines aloud, adjusting your rate of speaking to the mood of the selection.

a. Half a league, half a league,
Half a league onward,
All in the valley of Death
  Rode the six hundred.
"Forward the Light Brigade!
Charge for the guns!" he said.
Into the valley of Death
  Rode the six hundred.

—Alfred, Lord Tennyson

b. Now fades the glimmering landscape on the sight,
  And all the air a solemn stillness holds,
Save where the beetle wheels his droning flight,
  And drowsy tinklings lull the distant folds.

—Thomas Gray

c. The Cataract strong
Then plunges along,
Striking and raging
As if a war waging
Its caverns and rocks among.

—ROBERT SOUTHEY

d. And the night shall be filled with music,
And the cares, that infest the day,
Shall fold their tents, like the Arabs,
And as silently steal away.

—HENRY WADSWORTH LONGFELLOW

e. Haste thee, Nymph, and bring with thee
Jest, and youthful Jollity,
Quips and Cranks and wanton Wiles,
Nods, and Becks, and wreathèd Smiles . . .
Sport that wrinkled Care derides,
And Laughter holding both his sides. . . .

—JOHN MILTON

f. . . . hail! thou Goddess sage and holy!
Hail, divinest Melancholy! . . .
Come, pensive Nun, devout and pure,
Sober, steadfast, and demure, . . .
Come; but keep thy wonted state,
With even step, and musing gait. . . .

—JOHN MILTON

Activities for Emphasis and Flexibility

1. Read the following sentence aloud, bringing out different meanings by emphasizing the italicized words. What does each sentence imply?
   a. Did Nancy get an A grade in chemistry?
   b. Did *Nancy* get an A grade in chemistry?
   c. Did Nancy get an *A* grade in chemistry?
   d. Did Nancy get an A grade in *chemistry*?
2. Bring out by variations of emphasis and inflection as many meanings as you can in the following sentences:
   a. Is Betty going to fly to New York next summer?

b. Did Bill promise to meet Tom here at three o'clock?
c. Are you going to read that book for pleasure?
d. Why are you going to that movie?
e. That was a nice thing to do.
f. Sure, I had a fine time. I'll bet you did, too.
g. Are you going out that door?

3. Say, "Mr. Adams is going to talk to Dad about it," in the following ways:

casually	joyously	threateningly
indignantly	incredulously	soothingly

4. Speak the following lines with force and emphasis, using gestures, if you wish, to support the emphatic quality:

a. In the words of Franklin Roosevelt, "I hate war!"
b. Do you know how far the *Kon-Tiki* drifted? Forty-three hundred miles!
c. I know I am right. The facts I have here prove it.
d. Do you know what Mr. Poole did? He assigned fifty pages of reading over the Christmas holidays!

5. Practice reading some of the following selections for vocal flexibility. Use any techniques which help you to communicate the meaning or mood of the lines, including gestures.

a. This was the noblest Roman of them all.
All the conspirators save only he
Did that they did in envy of great Caesar;
He, only in a general honest thought
And common good to all, made one of them.
His life was gentle, and the elements
So mixed in him that Nature might stand up
And say to all the world "This was a man!"

—William Shakespeare

b. As Caesar loved me, I weep for him; as he was fortunate, I rejoice at it; as he was valiant, I honor him; but—as he was ambitious, I slew him. . . . Who is here so base that would be a bondman? If any, speak; for him have I offended. Who is here so rude that would not be a Roman? If any, speak; for him have I offended. Who is here so vile that will not love his country? If any, speak; for him have I offended. I pause for a reply.

—William Shakespeare

c. At these words the traveler, who was bent over, poking some embers in the fire with the iron-shod end of his stick, turned suddenly around, and opened his mouth, as if to reply, when the host steadily looking at him, added in the same low tone: "Stop, no more of that . . ."

—VICTOR HUGO, *Les Misérables*

d. In your hands, my dissatisfied fellow Countrymen, and not in mine, is the momentous issue of civil war. The government will not assail you. You can have no conflict, without being yourselves the aggressors. You have no oath registered in Heaven to destroy the government, while I shall have the most solemn one to "preserve, protect, and defend" it.

—ABRAHAM LINCOLN

e. If we could first know where we are and whither we are tending, we could then better judge what to do and how to do it.

—ABRAHAM LINCOLN

f. Though I speak with the tongues of men and of angels, and have not charity, I am become as sounding brass, or a tinkling cymbal.

And though I have the gift of prophecy, and understand all mysteries, and all knowledge; and though I have all faith, so that I could remove mountains, and have not charity, I am nothing.

—1 CORINTHIANS 13:1–2

g. When I was a child, I spake as a child, I understood as a child, I thought as a child: but when I became a man, I put away childish things.

For now we see through a glass darkly; but then face to face: now I know in part; but then shall I know even as also I am known.

And now abideth faith, hope, charity, these three; but the greatest of these is charity.

—1 CORINTHIANS 13:11–13

Films:

Mechanisms of Breathing (EBF). 11 min b&w.
Your Voice (EBF). 11 min b&w.

Your Body

Your body "talks" for you almost as much as your voice. Your listeners *hear* your words, but they *see* you, and are strongly impressed by your appearance, manner, and way of handling yourself. If your "actions speak louder than words," in a manner of speaking, what must you know in order to establish control of yourself and to make your speaking physically effective? Here are some fundamentals to learn and some more terms to meet:

Poise. Poise is a state of mind; it's balance and stability; it's assured self-control. Being poised means that you can keep your head in an emergency and that you will maintain an ease and dignity of manner no matter how nervous or upset you may be. It means, further, that you are showing maturity.

Evidence of poise, especially in your speaking, is usually revealed through body actions; and, though you may *feel* unsure, you can hide that fact if you can make your body behave. Gaining that ease of body and mind which indicates that you are poised is a slow and continuing process, but you can start now trying to *think* in terms of self-control.

If you feel panicky, stop and take a deep breath. Deliberately try to force relaxation by raising and lowering your shoulders, or by simply allowing your upper torso to droop, exhaling at the same time. Slow your rate of speaking briefly, or, if you feel the need, stop for a long pause and get hold of yourself. The main idea is to break the pattern of what you're doing for long enough to permit you to take some *other* action which will lessen your tension.

There are no special exercises that will teach you poise. You must learn it, as suggested above, over a long period of time and with conscious effort. Coming to speaking situations well prepared will nearly always help you to feel confident, and this feeling will be manifest in your relaxed and controlled body movements. Repeated success will gradually lead you to your goal: ease, dignity, and self-control—all of which spell *poise.*

Posture. Posture is carriage and bearing, the manner in which you handle your body when you walk, stand, or sit. "Stand tall and walk proud" is the advice given by many speech instructors. There are no rigid rules for good posture, since, as your speaking varies, so does the way you stand or sit. The Army, however, teaches its young men how to stand with the least fatigue. Essentially, the proper position is such that the body is in a straight line. For the average person this means that the head must be pulled back, the chin in, the chest thrown out, the stomach sucked in, and the hips rolled under the weight of the upper body. The sitting position is much the same. In neither position should there be tenseness or rigidity of the body, for such strain is tiring.

The speaker's standing position is much like that of the soldier at attention except that it is not so stiff, and the weight of the body, instead of being balanced on both feet, is rested mainly on the ball of one foot, which is slightly in advance of the other. A slight shift of position will enable you to change your weight to the other foot and at the same time to direct your attention to another part of your audience. The knees are not locked but are slightly loose to give a springy feeling. Arms hang naturally at your sides with the hands relaxed. Your neck muscles are stretched and your head held erect, as if a string attached to the top of your head were pulling it upright toward the ceiling. A feeling of lift and buoyancy should be your aim.

Sitting position should be comfortable and easy, but never slouchy or sprawling. Sit back in a chair with the base of your spine pressed against the lower part for support. In general, cross your feet rather than your knees, and don't move them restlessly or ungracefully.

Walking posture should be brisk, easy, and erect, reflecting alertness, dignity, and directness as you approach the audience. Avoid protruding your head, being round-shouldered, shuffling your feet, or acting disinterested, reluctant, or careless. You're "on camera" as soon as you get up to talk. Make that visual impression a good one.

Movement and Gestures. In a broad sense any bodily movement that expresses or emphasizes an idea may be called a gesture. It is a common but erroneous notion that gestures are made solely with the hands; facial expression and movement of the head, feet, shoulders, arms, or entire body are also classed as gestures. They are actions which should not be imposed artificially on your speaking but should spring from your inner desire to communicate.

Sign language came long before spoken language, you know, and continues to remain as a very significant carrier of meaning. If you travel in a foreign country without speaking the language, you can still make known many of your desires and thoughts by gestures being added to your words. Almost everyone recognizes a nod of the head for "Yes," a hand held up for "Stop," a frown and shaken head for disapproval, a smile and open hand for welcome and friendliness.

Normally, in everyday talk you don't think much about movement and gestures. As you feel, you act. In more formal speaking situations, how-

This Peace Corps teacher in British Honduras knows the value of a pantomime game as an icebreaker in her class.

ever, you might tend to be restrained and inhibited. Yet body action in your speaking is necessary if communication is to be complete. Stepping forward, backward, or sideways; turning your body from side to side; leaning forward; nodding, shaking, or tilting your head; using hand gestures; smiling, frowning, or looking serious; lifting an eyebrow; directing meaningful glances at the audience—all are ways of showing thought and feeling, of adding expressiveness and a personal quality to speaking.

You may find it easier to move about before an audience than to use hand gestures, yet hand movements can speak eloquently for you. Such gestures are used to fulfill many purposes: to emphasize a point, to describe an object, to locate an idea, to separate ideas, to register approval, to indicate rejection, to stimulate excitement or emotion, and to show your personal identification with your subject. There are only two warnings for you to heed about hand gestures: don't use them artificially and "do not saw the air too much . . . but use all gently," as Hamlet said.

Pantomime. The expression of meaning and feeling through body action—posture, movement, gestures, and facial expression—without the use of language is called pantomime. It is like acting without words. Practice in pantomime is of great help to you in learning how to free your body, how to identify with thoughts and attitudes, and how to acquire poise and grace in the use of movement and gestures. In practicing pantomimes for their greatest benefit to you, follow these five suggestions:

1. *Select an action* which has good possibilities for detailed movement and gestures.

2. *Identify emotionally* with the character or situation you're portraying.

3. *Feel the meaning* of what you want to communicate.

4. *Exaggerate slightly* the gestures, movements, and facial expressions in order to compensate for the lack of words. The *meaning* must come across clearly.

5. *Present the action in logical sequence,* as an organized unit with a beginning, middle, and end. In other words, plan your time so that you make an entrance, do the pantomime, and then exit.

In acting pantomimes, use your whole body—face, hands, arms, feet, eyes, everything—to show the action or portray the character or tell the story. Get into the mood of the situation or the character and forget yourself for the moment. You are learning the meaning of empathy, which is of value to you as a student of speech and human nature.

Audience Contact. This term means the establishment of a speaking situation in which the speaker sends out a message (communicates) and the audience receives that message (listens). The word *listens* is not a very good one to describe what the audience does, but we have no word that will tell the whole story. Actually, the audience hears, looks, thinks, evaluates, and undergoes emotional change if real communication takes place. A good speaker will bring himself closer to his audience by being aware of its reaction. He will watch like a hawk to see if everyone seems to be following him, using all the tricks and devices of his trade to keep the audience in a receptive frame of mind. A pause, a change of pitch, a story, a show of strong feeling, a confident manner of speaking, or some other device for establishing and keeping audience contact may be his tool. Of one thing the speaker may be sure: poor audience contact can reduce the best speech ever created to little more than a jumble of words and phrases without meaningful communication.

Delivery. Delivery is a word that means the "giving" of a speech, its utterance before a group of listeners. It relates not so much to *what* you say as to *how* you say it, although the content of a speech does have a relationship to the way in which you talk. Delivery is a combination of all such factors as gestures, posture, rate, volume, inflection, pitch, pause, emphasis, and poise. A more complete discussion of delivery will be found in Unit 12.

ACTIVITIES

1. Stand up, and assume good posture. Throw your shoulders back, pull your abdomen in, raise your head, and roll your hips under your weight until you feel comfortable. Extend one foot, and put the greater part of your weight on it. Shift your weight to the other foot.
2. Demonstrate good poise, posture, and movement in this brief assignment: Memorize a one- or two-line epigram or favorite saying and present it to the class. Rise, walk to the speaker's stand, take a breath, introduce your selection and deliver it, move back, turn away, and return to your seat.
3. Discuss with the class what natural gestures might help to intensify the meaning of the following sentences:
   a. I appeal to your sense of justice, now. How can we allow such an unfair situation to exist?
   b. How many of you are going to the game tomorrow? Let's see your hands. Come on; everybody who's going, hold up his hand! Up with your hands!
   c. It is difficult to refuse a request such as that, but our answer must be an unconditional "No!"
   d. All of us will be affected by the experiments now going on—everyone, including you and me.
   e. Here is the one idea which I want to put across, the most important idea of all.
4. Try this for a little fun and relaxation. Stand up and express some mood, idea, or state of mind by facial expression and bodily movement alone—no words. If you do well, your classmates should guess immediately what you are demonstrating. This exercise will help you to learn how gestures convey meaning.
5. Pantomime the following actions:

   direct traffic at a busy corner
   lead some school yells
   try to pick up and control a squirming puppy
   quiet a crying baby
   remove ice cubes stuck in a freezer tray
   remove a hot pan from the stove to the sink
   hang a picture on the wall
   put books on a high shelf while standing on a wobbly chair
   handle a freshly caught fish
   shoot off some firecrackers

6. Demonstrate without using words or objects how to do one of the following:

   tee off in golf
   kick a punt
   untangle a fishing line
   put up your hair in curlers
   get into a tight girdle
   change a flat tire
   hit a two-bagger
   iron a blouse
   serve a tennis ball
   thread a needle

7. Plan, rehearse, and present a group pantomime (two, three, or four students) like one of the following suggestions:
   a. Several students say farewell to a friend leaving on a train or bus.
   b. A girl teaches two of her friends a special dance step.
   c. A stranger asks directions of three people before he gets a satisfactory answer.
   d. A patient with a bad toothache disrupts the calm of a dentist's office.
   e. A boy has difficulty teaching a friend how to rig a fishing line.
   f. Two people build a campfire on a windy day.
   g. Two boys wash a small sports car.
   h. Three students share a bag of popcorn during an exciting movie sequence.
   i. A girl helps a friend shorten a skirt.
   j. Three people in a canoe find themselves in very choppy water.
8. Try these pantomimes without any properties whatever. They will give you practice in using your body to tell a story.
   a. Walk across your classroom "stage" in deep thought. Pick up a magazine and thumb through it until you discover something that startles you. Put the magazine down quickly, and go to your telephone with a worried but purposeful manner.
   b. You are having six guests in for dinner. You have social ambitions and are eager to impress them. Set the table carefully.
   c. Arrange a bouquet of flowers in a vase. You love the sight and the fragrance of the flowers, and you stop once in a while to smell a particularly lovely bloom.
   d. You are alone after having had a fight with a good friend of yours. You're still angry, and you pace about the room talking to yourself and to the imaginary friend as you relive parts of the quarrel. Your mood finally changes, and remorse sets in.
   e. Build a fire in the fireplace, and then turn your back to it, hands behind you, and enjoy it.
   f. You are being given a well-deserved lecture by your father. Show a variety of reactions to what he is saying. Try to break in once in a while.
   g. You are tired and have dropped into a chair. It's hot, and you show it. The desire to drowse is not quite so strong as your desire to read the paper. Your interest increases as you read until finally you are still and tense—and then you smile. The smile becomes a chuckle, the chuckle becomes a laugh, and the laugh turns into uncontrollable mirth.

Your Diction

The word *diction* has two meanings, both of which are important in speaking. First, it means *choice of words*: the way you choose and use words to express yourself; your vocabulary. Second, it means *articulation*: the way you speak words; the clearness and distinctness of your utterance; your enunciation. An examination of these two terms is necessary for your understanding of the part they play in speaking.

Choice of Words. Words are a speaker's stock-in-trade. You can't express ideas without them. The more extensive your vocabulary is, the better able you'll be to choose the right words for the right place.

You use words for accuracy, for enlightenment, for stimulation, and for beauty. Well chosen, they help you to speak with accuracy and precision of meaning as well as with warmth and richness of feeling. You should always use words that your audience can understand, of course, words whose sounds and meaning are within the range of your listeners' knowledge, emotional level, and experience. Audiences feel comfortable in familiar surroundings and are likely to respond to familiar words with the feeling "Now, you're talking my language!" Words commonly understood are essential for basic communication.

But words serve more than a utilitarian purpose. They are also conveyors of emotion and can stimulate and inspire your listeners. The Roman orator Cicero said, "The speaker must set forth with power and attractiveness the very same topics which others discuss in such tame and bloodless phraseology." A creative phraseology and an imaginative use of words can often drive home a point and stimulate the mind better than workaday words. So the use of figurative language—like similes, metaphors, and extended analogies—or of devices like rhetorical questions, repeated phraseology, comparisons and contrasts, restatement, and visualization contributes toward "dressing up" your speech.

Your diction, so far as choice of words is concerned, will be only as good as your perseverance in building your vocabulary. You need more than a handful of verbs, a few connectives to hold them together, an assortment of nouns, and some poor, tired, worn-out adjectives in your reservoir of words. You'll have to work at words, a little bit every day, in order to increase your supply. This book is filled with opportunities for you to improve this kind of diction. The booklet "Tests and Special Activities," which accompanies this book, is designed to help you. In Unit 5, "Listening: Developing Aural Skill," the part entitled "The Speaker's Responsibilities" will be of help, too.

Articulation. Of all the fundamentals you need to master for good speech, articulation is, perhaps, the most obvious. You may have good breath control, a responsive, well-modulated voice, poise, good posture, body flexibility, and a satisfactory supply of words to draw upon; but if you don't utter your words in a clear, distinct manner, your listeners will have difficulty in getting your message. They'll very likely be critical of your mumbling, slurring, and indistinct speech, and your communication with them will be thwarted.

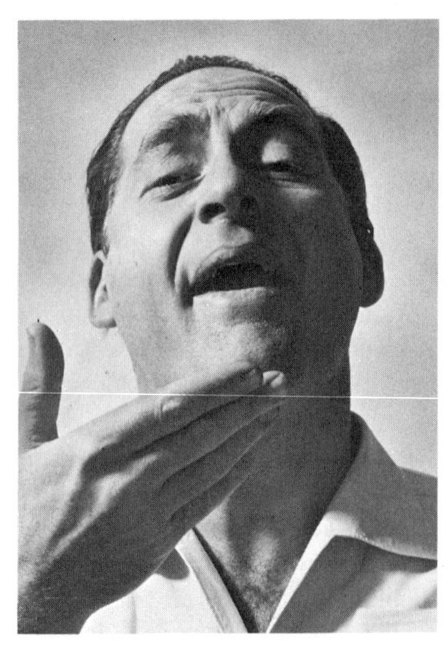

Determined not to have poor articulation, Sid Caesar begins his exercises with the lower jaw and the tongue.

Poor articulation is, unfortunately, quite common, especially among high school students, although they are not the sole offenders, by any means. In the normal process of speaking you tend to run or blend sounds together so that whole units of thought are said as if they were a single lengthy word. If you blend the sounds too rapidly or use your articulators too sluggishly, you end up with mushy, slovenly, or unintelligible speech, which might be adequate for very informal situations but which is out of place in more formal occasions when you want to make a good impression. Your diction, then, must be crisp and distinct; you must enunciate carefully.

Consonants cause the most trouble in articulation. Vowel sounds are comparatively easy to say because they are generally open sounds, flowing out of your mouth unobstructed by anything except the shape of the oral cavity, the possible tenseness of the jaws and throat muscles, and the action of the soft palate. Inadequate breath power or poor resonance can impair the sounds, making them weak or thin, and improper direction of the sounds through the nose can nasalize them; but, basically, vowels are produced more easily than consonants. Consonant sounds are formed by the action of the articulators—the lower jaw, tongue, lips, soft palate, and teeth, which obstruct the free flow of the sound waves. Good articu-

Photographs by Hans Namuth. Reprinted from *Holiday*. Copyright 1964, the Curtis Publishing Co.

He continues, now with the lips and the throat muscles. Not all speech exercises need to be quite this strenuous!

lation requires energetic and deft muscle action of the articulators, something which is either ignored or unrealized by many students whose habitual speech may often sound something like this:

"Hiya. Zenny buddy rown? Kinya kumovatuh myyows? Mebbe. Jeet jet? Nope, jew? Yawanna goadthanex show? Yeah. Howcumya gotta geddome serly?"

There are many reasons for poor articulation. You may be nervous or impatient when you speak and thus run your words together too rapidly. You may be lazy or find it difficult to use your articulators precisely, slurring words because you don't force your tongue, lips, or jaw to function quickly and energetically. You may be careless or unaware of the way the teeth and soft palate aid in making sounds distinct. You may be indifferent to the importance of speaking clearly. Or you may be so confined to the habitual speech patterns of your family or group or general background that you are unaware of how you sound to others or unwilling to improve your standard. Whatever may be the causes of your articulation weaknesses, remember that *good* articulation—free also from the other extreme of distortion or exaggeration—is a valuable technique for you to learn if you want to improve your speaking delivery and to be clearly understood by your audience.

ACTIVITIES

For choice of words:

1. Make a habit of doing crossword puzzles. They offer you a rewarding use of your leisure time.
2. Look for exercises, drills, questions, or games that will help your mind keep limber with words. You'll find such material in newspapers, magazines, and various kinds of books. Ask your librarian for materials dealing with vocabulary.
3. Choose the word that is nearest in meaning to the italicized one:

deft	quiet, skillful, foolish
suave	tricky, lovely, persuasive
pompous	fearful, fat, vain
erudite	scholarly, fictitious, comical
puerile	boyish, ridiculous, trivial
gullible	seagoing, naïve, self-seeking

4. Find the source of the following words, if you can, and make up a little story about them to tell the class. Most of them have colorful and interesting backgrounds, like the word *book.* It comes from an Anglo-Saxon word, *bōc,* which had the same base as the English word *beech.* Probably a long time ago the Anglo-Saxons scratched words on the beech trees in their forests and on pieces of beech wood, which were like books to them.

panic	sandwich
tantalize	colossal
lunatic	boycott
pecuniary	cereal
mercurial	salary
grocer	pajamas
tulip	alphabet
sugar	rabbi
deluxe	kimono

For articulation:

1. Say the following sounds, exaggerating your jaw and lip action:

a. *ah-oo*	*ee-oo*	*ee-oo-ah*
b. *mah-moo*	*mee-moo*	*mee-moo-mah*
c. *wah-woo*	*wee-woo*	*wee-woo-wah*

2. Practice saying *bay-bee-bye-boh-boo.* Repeat the vowel sounds, using other consonants: *p, d, t, v, f, l, s.*
3. Feel the action of the soft palate and back of the tongue as you say

a. *ung-ah*	*ung-ah*	*ung-ah*
b. *ing-ick*	*ing-ick*	*ing-ick*

4. Try some tongue twisters to develop agility with the articulators.
   - **a.** Amos Ames was an amiable astronaut.
   - **b.** A big black bug hit a big black bear.
   - **c.** Laugh and look pleasant while you lift your lid politely.
   - **d.** Robert gave Richard a rap on the rear because Richard roasted the rabbit too rare.

e. Peter Piper picked a peck of pickled peppers.
f. "That's that!" said the thirty thirsty thieves.
g. She sells seashells by the seashore.

5. Read these selections for practice in articulation:

When you're lying awake with a dismal headache, and repose
is taboo'd by anxiety,
I conceive you may use any language you choose to indulge
in, without impropriety...

—W. S. Gilbert

Advancing and prancing and glancing and dancing,
Recoiling, turmoiling and toiling and boiling...
And thumping and plumping and bumping and jumping,
And dashing and flashing and splashing and clashing...
All at once, and all o'er with a mighty uproar,
And in this way the Water comes down at Lodore.

—Robert Southey

And the muttering grew to a grumbling;
And the grumbling grew to a mighty rumbling;
And out of the houses, the rats came tumbling.
Great rats, small rats, lean rats, brawny rats,
Brown rats, black rats, gray rats, tawny rats....

—Robert Browning

This is the farmer sowing his corn
That kept the cock that crowed in the morn
That waked the priest all shaven and shorn
That married the man all tattered and torn
That kissed the maiden all forlorn
That milked the cow with the crumpled horn
That tossed the dog
That worried the cat
That killed the rat
That ate the malt
That lay in the house that Jack built.

—Unknown

Your Pronunciation

Pronunciation refers to the way you sound words, that is, what sound values you give to the vowels and consonants, how you break words into syllables as you say them, and what syllables you accent. What you do with these three—the vowel and consonant sounds, the syllables, and the accents—is largely influenced by your environment, your geographical location, your education, and your social group. Although no two people

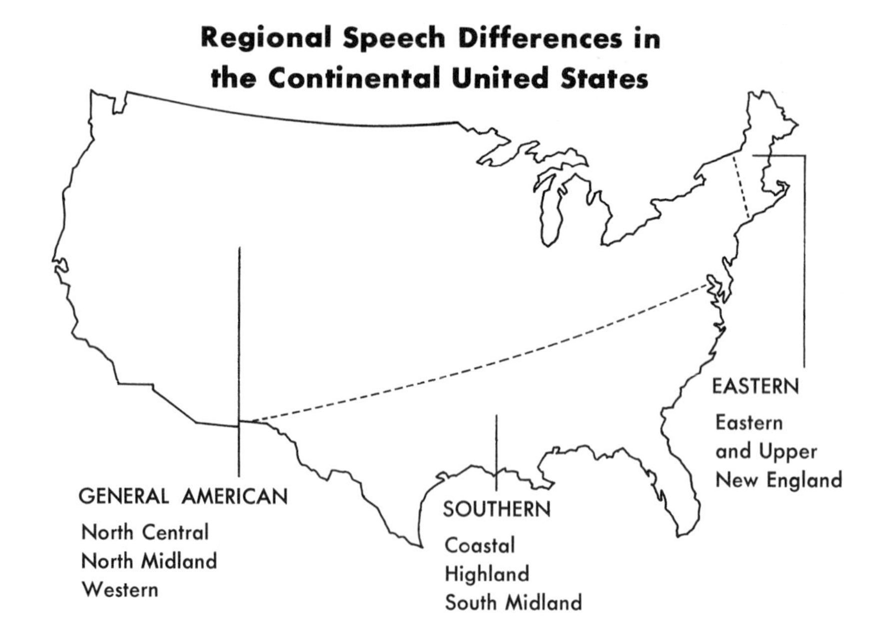

pronounce words exactly alike, most people do follow the general speech patterns of the group to which they are most closely related. The result is that in the United States there are many differences in pronunciation, not only between various regions of the country but also between individuals, a fact which often gives rise to confusion over how to pronounce a word and which stimulates all too often a "You're wrong! I'm right!" argument.

Standards of Pronunciation. There is no single, firm, "correct" American standard of pronunciation, no rigid rule that applies to everyone all over the country. There is no body of scholars or constituted authority in our country that undertakes to tell speakers what is "right" or "wrong" practice as do some language academies in France, Italy, and Spain. There is no need for a standard "King's" (or "Queen's") English, as there is in Britain, where distinct differences in dialects can be a barrier to general communication. Our regional differences in speech in the United States do not interfere with our free exchange of opinions and ideas. American English, whether it is spoken by a New Englander, New Yorker, Georgian, Texan, Iowan, Minnesotan, or Californian, can be understood without great difficulty anywhere within our borders. The practical necessity for a special single standard simply does not exist.

"Does it matter, then, how I pronounce words?" you may ask. This question is one you must decide for yourself. Good dictionaries don't attempt to dictate to you how to pronounce words. They merely record what the majority of educated people say. This information is obtained from hundreds of sources: men in public office, leaders in the business community, teachers, lawyers, university personnel, ministers, doctors, well-known speakers, radio and TV personalities, and specialists in phonetics—all sorts of literate people from all parts of the country. The result is no set standard of what is right or wrong, but rather a guide for you as to how well-educated people speak. If you will accept this guide, you will avoid making embarrassing mistakes, you will gain added confidence in speaking, and you will be able to go anywhere and speak acceptably in any group.

Pronunciation, then, is a very personal matter. It involves your background and environment, your education, your future goals, your sense of values, and your individual judgment of what constitutes an acceptable standard for you alone. The most sensible course for you to follow, perhaps, is to avoid any regional extremes that might interfere with good communication and in general to be guided by the best practices of the educated speakers in your community. You alone are the one who makes the final decision in answering questions like this:

Shall I say

data	dā′tə	or	dä′tə?
rodeo	rō dā′ō	or	rō′dĭ ō′?
either	ē′ŧħər̦	or	ī′ŧħər?
laugh	lăf	or	läf?
abdomen	ăb′dō mən	or	ăb dō′mən?
cigarette	sĭg′ə rĕt′	or	sĭg′ə rĕt′?
adult	ăd′ŭlt	or	ə dŭlt′?

Look for It in the Dictionary. Just a word about your good friend the dictionary before you start looking up some pronunciations. General usage, plus the influence of tradition, is what guides men in making the sound combinations they call *words.* General acceptance of what these sounds symbolize limits their meaning. The standard "authority" for acceptable sounds and meanings is the dictionary, or some other book like it, such as a *thesaurus,* a *lexicon,* or an *encyclopedia.* New words are constantly being born, and old words are either becoming obsolete or changing in their meaning or pronunciation. It is the responsibility of men who write dictionaries to keep up with all these changes.

The dictionary performs many services. It gives you pronunciations, meanings and shades of meaning, derivations, synonyms, antonyms, syllabication, drawings, charts, maps, tables, signs, symbols, foreign words and phrases, names of important persons and places, forms of address, and other miscellany.

An important part of any dictionary is its *guide or key to pronunciation,* a service that is often misused or not used at all because of ignorance. There is not one among you who would venture upon the highway in an automobile whose controls you couldn't operate; yet, sadly enough, many of you turn to a dictionary for the pronunciation of a word without knowing how to use the guide to pronunciation.

There are two well-known guides to pronunciation of which you should be aware. The first one is a scholarly, precise method in which all the sounds of speech in all languages are accurately pinpointed and represented by a special set of symbols. This system is called the International Phonetic Alphabet (I.P.A.). If you intend to go deeply into pronunciation differences, the I.P.A., when learned under the direction of a trained phonetician, can be very valuable to you. Many dictionaries include the I.P.A. in their guide to pronunciation.

However, the second system, a diacritical key, though less accurate and consistent than the I.P.A., is the one you will find more practical, since it is commonly shared by many dictionaries you are likely to consult. In general, this is what you will find when you look up the pronunciation of a word:

- The word is respelled, if necessary, to simplify the indication of sounds. (The word *chauffeur* may be respelled *shofer.*)
- The word is divided into syllables. (*sho-fer*)
- An accent mark is placed after (or, in some dictionaries, before) the stressed syllable. (*sho′-fer*)
- A set of symbols or diacritical marks is used to indicate the vowel and consonant sounds. (*shō′fẽr* or *′shō-fər*)

Many of the diacritical markings found in dictionaries are traditional ones, such as the macron (¯), the breve (˘), the dieresis (¨), the circumflex (^), and the tilde, or wave (˜). A recent introduction in some dictionaries is the schwa (ə), a symbol taken from the I.P.A. and used to show the sound of all unstressed vowels.

In fact, these symbols and marks vary a great deal from book to book and, therefore, may be confusing to you. Notice these examples, for instance, of the different ways in which well-known dictionaries indicate the pronunciation of the word *blazer*:

blaz·er (blā′zər)
(*The American College Dictionary*)

blaz′er, 1 blēz′ər; 2 blāz′er
(*Funk and Wagnalls New Standard Dictionary*)

[2]**blazer** \"\ *n*-s [[2]*blaze*+-*er*]
(*Webster's Third New International Dictionary,* unabridged)

blaz·er \'blā-zər\
(*Webster's Seventh New Collegiate Dictionary*)

blaz·er (blāz′ẽr)
(*Webster's New World Dictionary of the American Language*)

To indicate further the differences in guides to pronunciation, this is what you might find if you looked up the word *further* in several dictionaries:

further
1. fûr′thər
2. *FUR*·THER (-*th*ur)
3. \'fər-thər\
4. fũr′*th*ẽr

Do you begin to see what problems the different symbols and diacritical markings create? No two dictionaries use exactly the same ones. Each publishing company has its own editorial policy concerning what is the best method of showing how a word is pronounced. Obviously, if you don't know the meaning of the symbols, you cannot interpret the pronunciation. As the saying goes, "You can't enjoy the show without a program, folks!" Therefore, your most important responsibility is to study the "program" of whatever dictionary you're using. You must become familiar with its specific guide or key to pronunciation.

You will find such keys in various places in the dictionaries: on the inside of the hard cover; in the introduction or preface, under the heading "Pronunciation" or "Guide to Pronunciation" or "How to Use the Dictionary," or something similar; or at the bottom or top of every page or every alternate page. Look for them and learn to use them.

If an informal poll of your class indicates that there is a general lack of knowledge in regard to using the dictionary, have your teacher organize a lesson or series of lessons designed to acquaint you with the mysteries of this valuable tool. A useful aid is a test called "Cooperative Dictionary Test," put out by Educational Testing Service, Los Angeles, California.

Words are your stock-in-trade, both in usage and in pronunciation. You cannot afford to batter and bruise your audience with mispronunciations or *malapropisms.* (There's a word to look up, right now!)

Some Well-Known Dictionaries

The American College Dictionary. Random House.
Funk and Wagnalls New College Standard Dictionary. Funk & Wagnalls.
A Pronouncing Dictionary of American English, by JOHN SAMUEL KENYON and THOMAS ALBERT KNOTT. Merriam. (In phonetics.)
Webster's New World Dictionary of the American Language. World Publishing.
Webster's Seventh New Collegiate Dictionary. Merriam.

ACTIVITIES

For pronunciation:

1. Look up in a good dictionary the meaning of the following words: *vowel, consonant, diphthong, accent, syllabication,* and *diacritical marks* (or *diacritics*). These are terms with which you will work while studying articulation and pronunciation.
2. Refresh your knowledge of some commonly used diacritics by turning to the most recent dictionary you can find, preferably one published after 1960. Study the guide or key to pronunciation. What symbols does the dictionary use to indicate the following?

   a. the long vowel sounds
   - **a** as in *bay*
   - **e** as in *beet*
   - **i** as in *bite*
   - **o** as in *boat*
   - **u** as in *bugle*
   - **oo** as in *boot*

   b. the short vowel sounds
   - **a** as in *bag*
   - **e** as in *beg*
   - **i** as in *big*
   - **o** as in *bog*
   - **u** as in *bug*
   - **oo** as in *book*

   c. the soft Italian sound of **a** as in *father*

   Compare your findings with those of your classmates.
3. Look up the meaning of the word *schwa.* What is it? What is its symbol? What sound does it represent? Does it appear in your dictionary's guide to pronunciation? If not, what is used as a substitute? List five words in which the *schwa* or a substitute sound might appear.
4. Look up the pronunciation of some of the following words in at least two different dictionaries. Which pronunciation do you prefer, if there is a choice? In which dictionary did you find the pronunciation system easiest to interpret?

forehead	usual
wasp	wash
quintuplet	oleomargarine
Louisiana	Arkansas

5. Use the word lists in the "Tests and Special Activities" booklet, which accompanies this book, to check your pronunciation. Be sure you know which are the acceptable pronunciations of these words. If you find you've been mispronouncing some of them, practice these aloud until you master them. Begin now by turning to the "Check Your Pronunciation" sections of the booklet.
6. Begin to keep your own lists of commonly mispronounced words. Write down in your notebook any of your own mispronunciations which have been called to your attention. Add to your list throughout the school year and practice saying all the words correctly until you have mastered them.

7. Consult the map of regional speech differences in the United States. How do *you* say the following words? Do you detect different pronunciations in class?

egg	leg	keg	out	cow	house
tune	news	due	ten	cent	pen
horror	sorry	orange	greasy	absorb	absurd
path	glass	dance	law	cloth	Cuba
form	force	course	what	which	why
Boston	hot	rock	coming	running	calling

8. Consider these opposing points of view about the dictionary's role. With which do you agree? Why? Do you have a point of view differing from either?

Statement A:

A dictionary's function is simply to record language usage, not to pass judgment upon it. Dictionaries should not set up standards of correct usage or cling to traditional forms which are no longer in current use. Language changes are inevitable and should be allowed to happen naturally. The dictionary's aim should be *permissive*, merely showing what people *actually say*, not indicating what someone thinks they *ought to say*.

Statement B:

A dictionary should not only record what people say, but should also set up standards of speech and pronunciation. Dictionaries should label and describe several levels of usage, such as formal, informal, colloquial, slang, vulgar, or the like, and distinguish between "poor" and "good" English. Although language changes are inevitable, authorities should see that the change is an orderly, disciplined one. The dictionary's aim should be *directive*, helping people to use words with discrimination and telling them what they *ought to say*.

References:

A Drill Manual for Improving Speech, by William N. Brigance and F. Henderson. Lippincott.

Basic Voice Training, by E. Hahn and others. McGraw-Hill.

Essentials of General Speech, by A. C. Baird and F. H. Knower. McGraw-Hill.

The Art of Good Speech, by J. H. McBurney and E. J. Wrage. Prentice-Hall.

Training the Speaking Voice, by Virgil Anderson. Oxford University Press.

Voice and Articulation, by C. Van Riper and J. Irwin. Prentice-Hall.

Voice and Diction, by J. F. Bender and V. A. Fields. Macmillan.

Films:

Improve Your Pronunciation (Coronet). 11 min color or b&w.

Look It Up (Coronet). 11 min color or b&w.

Better Choice of Words (Coronet). 11 min color or b&w.

Healthy Lungs (Coronet). 11 min color or b&w.

Using Your Voice (MH). 10 min b&w.

Record:

Speak Well (Educational). One 12″ record 33-⅓ rpm.

Unit Five

LISTENING: Developing Aural Skill

There are only minutes before the final gun, and the stands are tense with excitement. Henderson receives the ball from center and fades back to pass. Back to the thirty, the thirty-five, the forty. He's being rushed. He sidesteps one tackler, but two more break through. He's hemmed in. It's too late. But no! In that last split second his arm whips back, and he rifles the ball in a long, low arc. From the milling cluster in the end zone a figure leaps high. A beautiful pass! But Henderson didn't complete it alone. The receiver had to function too.

Communication, likewise, is never a solo performance. Whether a message is oral or written, in Morse or semaphore, smoke signals or braille, the sender is helpless without a receiver. This truth is so plain that it is commonly overlooked. For example, a writer arranges a set of marks on paper in various combinations; but no communication occurs until someone else sees those marks, gives them attention, recognizes them as words, interprets them into ideas, and evaluates those ideas—a process we call reading. In a similar manner a speaker makes a series of curious sounds, but no communication takes place until someone hears those sounds, gives them attention, recognizes them as words, interprets them into ideas, and then evaluates those ideas—a process which we generally call *listening*. No matter what form communication may take, it requires teamwork.

The Listening Process

There is no adequate word in English, or in any other language, for the total process of listening. It is not hard to understand why. In the first place the act of listening is very complicated, requiring several skills and disciplines. In the second place the word *listening* is quite comprehensive in meaning, involving one, several, or all parts of the total process. Let's consider each of these aspects of listening and then add to our understanding of the whole process by examining diagrams of its parts.

The Listening Process Is Complicated. The listener has an extremely important and difficult job to do, yet he gets scant recognition for a fine performance. It's different in sports. When the left fielder makes a desperate throw to cut off a runner at third base, and the third baseman dives into the dust to scoop up the ball, we credit him with a brilliant catch. We recognize that his gymnastics have compensated for the wildness of the throw. But who shows appreciation for the skill and alertness of an expert listener who captures the intended sense of a hasty, garbled, or complicated message? Very few do, even though the listener's mental gymnastics include paying vigilant attention, swiftly sorting, discarding, and rearranging ideas, translating figures of speech, supplying unintentional omissions, linking disconnected items, and correcting misstatements. To make matters worse, many time the listening conditions are very difficult, whether at the dinner table, in the classroom, in the barber shop, or by the radio or television set. Add to these gymnastics and conditions certain problems that the listener will have to face because of his own attitudes, emotional reactions, or lack of knowledge, and you can easily see why the process is complicated.

The Term *Listening* Is Comprehensive. Ordinarily when we ask someone to listen, we are merely directing his attention to sounds, not just language noises, but any sounds—the screech of brakes, the patter of rain on the roof, a cry in the night, a knock in the engine, or the ringing of a telephone. Sometimes we are asking him only to recognize speech sounds. At other times we say, "Listen carefully, now," and we may mean anything from giving strained attention to thoughtful interpretation. And frequently we mean going beyond interpretation to a part of the process which involves a remembering of the important parts of what was said in a speech, a relating of those parts to a central idea, and an evaluating of any or all of the presentation. One thing is clear: the admonition *to listen* means that the listener is supposed to do something; how much he is to do, however, must be revealed by some other clue.

The Parts of the Listening Process. In simple terms the process of reading language might be described as a translating of written symbols into ideas. Similarly, the process of listening to language could be regarded as a translating of speech sounds into ideas. A diagram of the listening process could look like this:

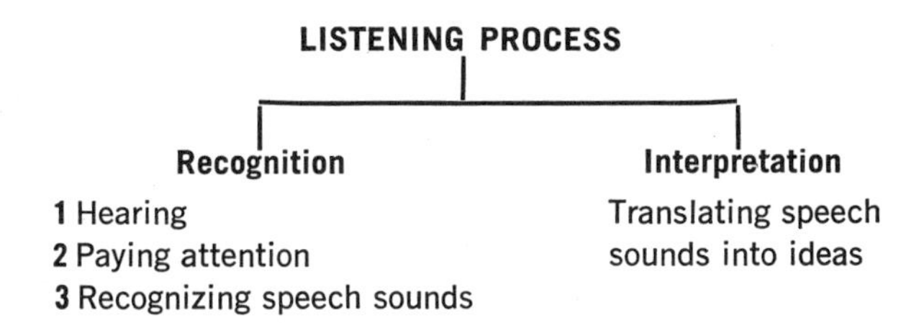

Strictly speaking, for both reading and listening, the process has technically ended when the steps of recognition and interpretation have been completed, when the *language function* has ended. What the reader or listener does with the material he has interpreted is regarded as a *post-language function.* In other words, once the machinery of your mind starts grinding on the ideas which enter it through the steps of recognition and interpretation, something new is happening, something different from the process of assimilation.

What is this "something different"? It is the *evaluation* of what you have assimilated, a third step which you may well add to the diagram above, because in actual practice your effectiveness as a listener does not stop with interpretation. You must also be able to recall the essence of an oral presentation and, often, many of its details. Further, if you are to become an intelligent consumer of oral propaganda, you must learn how to weigh it in terms of its basic worth and yourself in terms of your accuracy and fairness as an evaluator. For our purposes in this speech course, then, a diagram of the process of listening would have one more step:

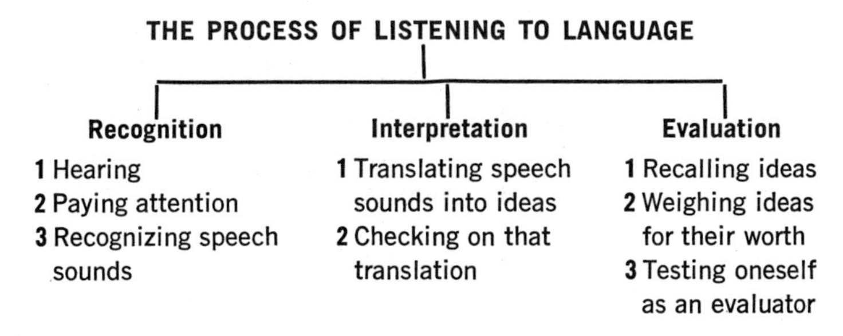

Problems in Oral Communication

There are many barriers to effective oral communication. Regardless of whether you are a passer or a receiver, some of these can be controlled or lessened, and others must be overcome or ignored. The problems in oral communication are related to the environment of the speaking situation, to the speaker, and to the listener. Many things can happen to the "ball" from the time it leaves the passer's hands until the time it meets the receiver's.

The Environment Fails. Environment, as used here, means circumstances that lie outside what the speaker creates or what the listener as an individual brings to bear on the receiving function. These circumstances are related to the room, the weather, the time of day, acts of an audience, conditions outside the room, and so on. For example:

Physical conditions of the room

- The room is too hot, too cold, too stuffy, too drafty, too musty, or too smoky.
- The room is too large, too small, too empty, or too crowded.
- The furniture is inappropriate or poorly arranged, the seats are too hard, or the lectern is inconvenient.
- The lighting is bad.

Audience reactions

- It whispers, talks, or shuffles its feet.
- It slumps, sleeps, or doodles.
- It makes restless sounds that come from hunger, fatigue, or expectation of imminent adjournment.

Outside noises

- Dishes rattle and voices carry from next door.
- A siren wails, a jet roars, a dog barks, or a storm breaks.
- The sharp sounds of construction or the popping of a lawn mower intrudes.

- The public-address system fails, or the microphone won't work.

Other barriers

- The lights go out—or won't come on.
- Members of the audience arrive late or leave early.
- An organization of hecklers is present.

The Passer Fails. You must take into account the inevitable poor passing, for there is almost no end to the number of ways in which a speaker may fail. Look at this partial list of possible failures, many of which are quite common.

- Articulation is so poor that words are indistinguishable.
- Volume is so low that only those near the speaker can hear, or it is so high that everyone is blasted.
- Rapid speaking runs his whole message into jargon.
- He directs his voice toward his notes on the table, toward the chart he is holding, or toward an illustration behind him—and nobody hears him.
- He mispronounces words or misuses them.
- He speaks with an accent that turns familiar words into strangers.
- He uses too many big words, too many technical terms.
- He produces bewilderment or disgust by expressing simple ideas in long, involved sentences.
- He alienates you by arousing your antagonisms or by offending your moral sense.
- He speaks with so little enthusiasm and in such a monotone that you have only two escapes: sleep or departure.
- He doesn't seem to have his purpose or central theme clearly in mind, and it isn't obvious what he wishes to communicate.

The Receiver Fails. The pass may be right between the goalposts and not a defender within yards, but "icy fingers"—and there are all kinds—will result in faulty reception. Can you identify yourself with the receiver in any of the following failures?

- He succumbs to personal discomfort—fatigue, hunger, illness, poorly regulated temperature, poor seating—and he either cannot or will not adjust to the conditions producing the discomfort.
- He has an exaggerated opinion of his knowledge, and, when he hears anything that sounds vaguely familiar, he partly or completely tunes out the speaker.

- He brings his "knitting" to the speech. In other words, he is always carrying on his interests and chores during a speaking situation, assuring himself that he can get all there is to get from the speech and still not "waste his time."
- He listens, as he often reads, to words, phrases, and sentences as separate pieces of a presentation. He is reluctant, or unable, to relate these pieces to each other or to a central idea of the speech.
- He can't adjust his listening rate to the speaking rate. Either he lags behind, wrestling mentally with what he has just heard and thus missing what the speaker says next, or he listens impatiently, thinking of other things while he waits to tune in again at what he believes will be the appropriate time.
- He is more interested in what he is *seeing* than what he is *hearing*—the splendor of the assembly room, the physical behavior of the audience, the dress or features of the speaker, or an activity (however small) that is taking place within the range of his vision.
- He is upset. Possibly he came to the listening situation with strong feelings of anger, resentment, hostility, frustration, or great joy. Maybe a strong emotion develops in him during the speech or discussion. Or, he may only be a victim of low-level anxiety that produces worry and fretfulness.
- He comes to a meeting with a closed mind and a dedication to uphold a point of view regardless of what may be said. Although you never hear the expression "Well, what I *meant to hear* is . . . ," the receiver might very accurately so describe his act of interpretation when he comes to a discussion or a meeting with a closed mind. He is guilty of hearing what he *wanted* to hear, *expected* to hear, or felt *obliged* to hear.
- He is not sure of himself, and he spends his listening energy in thinking of something to say which may enhance the opinion others hold of him.

Or the Passing Combination Fails. Usually failure in communication is something of a joint effort. An idea is intangible and often elusive, and the process of "capturing" it and turning it into words is seldom without error. If the speaker is beset by ignorance, haste, emotion, prejudice, or malice, the idea that he "captures" may be somewhat different from the one he started to pursue. The words he uses to describe his "captive" are now absorbed by the listener, who interprets them within the limits of his own intelligence, experience, emotional state, and attitudes, concluding that what he has heard is thus and so. In other words, the "captive" who was sent from the speaker's lips as a giant might easily come to rest in the listener's mind as a pygmy. If the listener can—and will—let the speaker know that he has just received a pygmy, there may be a fumbling toward understanding, with the speaker saying, "Well, what I meant to say is . . ." and the listener saying, "Oh, I thought you meant . . ." On the other hand, the speaker, never learning that the listener has a pygmy in mental tow, may not say anything further to change the image of the pygmy in the listener's mind; the listener will carry away with him a dwarf that never was.

In some instances faulty communication lies not in the kind of gross misunderstanding illustrated above but in the differences in mental images that words produce. For example, your friend Dick says "cat" and thinks of his blue-eyed Siamese; you hear "cat" and think of the green-eyed alley cat that hangs around your back door. Dick says "camping" and thinks of an overnight jaunt at the state beach park, but the word takes you quickly to memory of two wonderful weeks in Yellowstone Park. No serious miscomprehension has occurred between you and Dick at the level of "cat" and "camping," but think of what will happen both to feelings and to understanding when Dick discusses "capitalism" with you, and he has in mind an economic system that encourages free enterprise, while you picture an ugly, formless force which you blame for your family's poverty. Consider, too, what happens in communication when a speaker uses "good guy" words like *good, best, uplifting, honest, worthwhile, safe, economical, just, rewarding,* and *popular* to describe his plan or argument. He plants in the mind of the listener the idea that his plan or argument is full of merit because of the descriptive label, and only the very discerning listener will disregard the label in favor of convincing evidence.

Both the speaker and the listener have responsibilities in the improvement of communication—and in the specific task of improving listening skill. The more important of these responsibilities needs your attention.

The Speaker's Responsibilities

What are your responsibilities as a speaker in helping to overcome the problems of listening? How can you make language work for you, not against you?

Define Your Terms. Your chief aim is, of course, to use language that your listener understands, but this is not always possible. You may feel the need of using a familiar term in an unfamiliar way. For example, if you are going to use the handy word *gondola* to refer to a special type of freight car, you must be sure that the listener isn't thinking of a boat on a canal in Venice. Or you may simply want to use a term that you know is unfamiliar to most people. For example, if you were writing or speaking at length about language, you might find it convenient to use the word *semantics* to indicate that you were talking about the meaning of words rather than about their length or spelling or origin or pronunciation. But because the problem of semantics is not generally understood, the word *semantics* is a stranger. Whether it's the use of a term or the term itself that is unfamiliar, keep in mind the need of definition. Voltaire once said, "If you wish to converse with me, define your terms." Those words are worth remembering.

Chop Out the Deadwood. You will turn a sharp and eager listener into a bored one in a hurry if you make him search for meaning in phrases that don't contain any. When you say, "I just read a good book," he knows you liked the book; but the only other thing you have told him is that you have read it. If you add, "It was all about murder and things like that," he will say to himself, "What does he mean by 'all'? And what does he mean by 'and things like that'? There aren't many things quite like murder. Perhaps he means suicide. Maybe he means other crimes such as arson or robbery. He might mean that the story was just about murder. *Maybe he doesn't mean anything at all by those extra words.*" Such padding, or filler, will hardly conceal from the honest and intelligent listener the vacuum of your mind. He will mistrust you, and with reason. Chop out the deadwood.

Make Your Main Point Clear. Don't be satisfied with stating your central theme only once, and don't be misled into believing that your listeners will be offended if you repeat occasionally the main point of your speech. They need this kind of help because some didn't hear you the first time or two, and some didn't understand what they heard. If your logic, your supporting details, and your appeal to feelings are to be effective, they must relate to your big idea, your message, your main point. Your listeners will be drawn gradually to consideration of your central thought if you continue to focus their attention upon it, never letting them forget what it is and never giving them the opportunity to misunderstand it. You may be tempted many times, and with just cause, to feel that you have something to say and that your listeners can just jolly-well-listen-if-they-want-the-benefit-of-your-thoughts. Don't yield to this temptation if it means that you will stop emphasizing and repeating your central argument. Remember: a good passer looks good only when his receiver is catching the ball!

Shun Pretentious Terms. Avoid using big words with bulging muscles if their little brothers can carry the burden. Simple synonyms are always in good taste. An old saw, which goes something like this, "In promulgating your esoteric cogitations beware of platitudinous ponderosities," illustrates and pokes fun at pompous wording. The point here is not that all long words are pretentious; rather, it is that using longer and more unfamiliar terms in the place of their common synonyms is harmful to communication. Don't, in other words, say *appropriation* if *money* will serve. *Fire* is usually a better word than *conflagration* or *combustion*. Why use *therapeutic* when *healing* will make clear to more people what you mean? Or why substitute *eulogize* for *praise*? *purloin* for *steal*? *cogitate* for *think*? Shun pretentious terms.

Treat Feelings with Care. It is important not to use terms that arouse emotions so strong that they interfere with the reception of your message. Such terms will build up in your listeners a defense which reason cannot penetrate. You may, for instance, habitually shorten *Japanese* to *Jap* simply to save energy, unaware that you are causing hurt. You may be guilty of contempt for a people whom you don't know very intimately, and your friends of Japanese extraction will sensibly make allowance for this possibility. They will withhold judgment until they know whether you're being malicious or merely showing ignorance. But no thoughtful, healthy-minded person takes risks with words that may cause unnecessary pain. Those risks are greatest in the sensitive areas of nationality, race, religion, marriage, sex, politics, family and community customs, and personal reference. Don't take a chance. Treat feelings with care.

Welcome Questions. In spite of your best efforts to make your speaking simple, clear, and meaningful, the hazards of communicating anything more complicated than "Pass the salt" will almost guarantee that your listeners will have a few questions. Permit, and even encourage, those questions if you can. If possible, invite the interruptions of puzzled listeners, or even pause at intervals to ask if all is clear. Sometimes either the nature or the treatment of your subject will necessitate postponing questions until the end. In other instances, for whatever reason, you cannot accept questions, but on most occasions it is both courteous and intelligent to encourage sincere questions and to thank the listener for asking. Welcome questions.

Observe General Principles of Good Speaking

1. *Make your ideas personal, concrete, and interesting.* Aristotle said, "Generalities are the refuge of weak minds. Generalities are usually dull. Eschew them."

2. *Put sparkle into your talk.* Your audience will listen better if you are enthusiastic about what you say.
3. *Keep eye-contact with your listeners.* The Wedding Guest in *The Rime of the Ancient Mariner* was transfixed by the glittering eye of the sailor. Make your audience listen, too, but by keeping your gaze *comfortably* upon them.
4. *Let your gestures be spontaneous.* Bodily movements should spring from an urge to make language more expressive. Artificial gestures are not usually convincing.
5. *Check personal mannerisms.* Such distractions as smacking sounds made by the mouth, gasping for breath, fumbling with clothing, or involuntary twitching of the body must be eliminated.
6. *Have a neat personal appearance.* Extremes in dress, untidiness, and poor grooming attract unfavorable attention.
7. *Be sure your audience can hear you.* Inaudibility is highly annoying. What is the point in talking if no one can hear you? If you are speaking to an audience, adjust your volume to the people in the last few rows.
8. *Watch the beginning and ending of a talk.* In these two places you have nearly the complete attention of your listeners. Don't kill that attention by carelessness.
9. *Change your pace and pitch.* Monotonous speech is dull, tiresome, and sleep-producing.
10. *Stick to a plan.* Help your audience to listen by organizing your talk, making your plan clear, and by sticking to that plan. Someone put it this way: "First, tell 'em what you're going to tell 'em; then tell 'em; and, finally, tell 'em what you've told 'em."
11. *Set a time limit.* People generally know when a talk has reached its logical conclusion. If you're a smart speaker, you will make it your business to know, too. Don't talk yourself out of a victory.

The Listener's Responsibilities

Let's swing the spotlight from the speaker to the listener. Assume that you're the receiver now instead of the passer. If you are in a class of twenty-five students, you will listen twenty-four times more than you will speak. At home and out in the community it is much the same. Just as you read more than you write, you listen more than you speak. Yet there is amazingly little training offered in this activity. Probably it's because we tend to think of listening as a passive state rather than as a language activity that can be improved by training. We assume that oral communication is governed by the speaker's success or failure, when the fact is that the listener's success or failure is equally important. Very few even begin to develop their powers of reception. An examination of this problem will bring to light some exciting considerations for you as a listener, and it will contribute to your effectiveness as a speaker.

What are some of the specific things you can do to lighten the speaker's burden? Can listening skill be improved, as we know physical skills such as wrestling and boxing can be, through training? Will your listening power, like your reading power, grow through concentration and directed exercise?

Give the Speaker Your Attention. How gratifying it would be if the giving of attention were as simple as the suggestion! It *isn't* that simple, however. Haven't you been told to "pay attention" so many times that often the reminder is little more than an unpleasant noise? Isn't it true that sometimes with little effort you can direct your attention to what is being said, but at other times you can do little more than turn your eyes toward the speaker while you fight against sleep or the intrusion of your own thoughts and feelings? The fact is that there are times when conditions make paying attention improbable or impossible: illness, emotional upset, extreme personal discomfort, or faulty reception, to name the major ones.

You can, however, learn to pay attention to spoken language under reasonable conditions, just as you can acquire any other kind of desirable habit. A strong factor in this learning is self-discipline, and a key to self-discipline is *practicing total attention.* Such practice is important because it is the basis for building up both an attitude toward and a skill in "receiving." Begin your practice on short attention spans, allowing nothing to divert your attention. Force yourself to take notes on what is being said, brief notes that will help you identify thoughts, not long ones which will take your attention away from the speaker. Just as soon as you find you are not giving total attention, check your watch or the wall clock to see how long your span lasted. The next step, obviously, is to make the next span longer.

Just as self-discipline can be effective in helping you to eliminate pleasant daydreaming during an oral presentation, so can it help you to overcome inattention which springs from worries, a chief cause of inattention. People who carry their worries to bed will fret, toss, and turn, unable to sleep. They have to unlearn, and often with a doctor's help, the habit of worrying in bed and then to learn a new habit of thrusting worries away from conscious consideration. Habitual and even casual worriers need help. If you are one, go to someone in whom you have confidence

The rewards of total attention are many: listeners can follow a speech with interest, can ask intelligent questions, and can discuss the topic later.

–your favorite teacher, your counselor, your parents, your doctor–and talk about what is troubling you. Your emotional well-being is important not only to your effective listening but to the whole of your existence.

Listening to a broadcast in a foreign tongue will convince you that paying attention is not enough to guarantee understanding. Nor is it even an assurance of understanding your own language. But you recognize that comprehension can hardly happen *without* it. You know, too, that habits of inattention cannot be turned off like a faucet. There is no secret shortcut to control. You get it as a pitcher does, by being aware of your weakness, by throwing one ball at a time, and by practicing at every opportunity. You get it as the diver does when he practices holding his breath under water before being forced to the surface for air. You get it as the magician does, through willpower, infinite patience, and endless practice. And, your hardest and your *best* workouts will be those under the exasperating conditions of fatigue, boredom, irritation, and distraction.

Gain Word Power. A wide knowledge of words is a powerful weapon. A narrow vocabulary is a kind of blindness. If you are bored or baffled or embarrassed in the company of enlightened people, it is probably not so much that their ideas are beyond you as that the words they use to express those ideas are strangers. Your limited vocabulary puts you in the position of feeling stupid, inferior, and frustrated, and your personality is poisoned by this feeling. The trained speaker will try to adjust to what he judges your language capacity to be, but he shouldn't have to stoop to a childish level of vocabulary to be sure that you understand. How, then, can you make new word-friends that will give you added listening power?

You can do a great deal through reading if you will choose books and articles with a mature vocabulary. By keeping your dictionary handy and turning to it frequently you will make the happy discovery that the ideas are neither so dull nor so difficult as you supposed. As you meet a new word in your reading, remember that its sound as well as its meaning is important to you as a listener. Check its pronunciation; it may surprise you. In this respect English is trickier than any other language because the events that gave English the richest vocabulary on earth gave it also the queerest spelling system. Foreign scholars learning English discover this to their dismay. They are distressed to find, for example, that *-ough* is pronounced *awf* (cough), *ow* (bough), *uff* (rough), *oo* (through), *oh* (though), and *aw* (thought).

You didn't have much trouble with these common words because you had learned their sounds and meanings before you saw them in print. But without the help of a dictionary or a well-educated companion many other words you learn to recognize by appearance will remain strangers to your ear; words such as *ennui, err, rapine, hearth, crochet, gauge, indict, ague,* and *victuals*; and proper names such as *Thames, Freud, Bentham, Cowper,* and *van Loon.*

There are many radio and TV programs that can contribute to your fund of useful words; further, you will find these programs stimulating and satisfying once you begin to break down the barriers of vocabulary. Tune in on some of the round tables, debates, panels, lectures, and quiz programs that radio and TV have made accessible to you. Do this in the company of a friend or member of the family who can help you with some of the more troublesome terms. But don't overlook your friend the dictionary.

It is stupid to guess what words mean when you can be sure. It is often simpler to learn meaning from the person who uses an unfamiliar word than to hunt for it in the dictionary. There is a wealth of words in the course of daily discussion that is yours for the asking. Because of the importance of the habit of inquiry it is given separate emphasis under the next heading.

Ask the Right Questions. In spite of the efforts of the speaker to make his message clear, and no matter how well informed and attentive a listener you may be, some of the speaker's points will remain obscure. It is your responsibility to assist him, as well as yourself, by asking courteous and intelligent questions if there is opportunity. During formal addresses, radio speeches, and the angry outbursts of superiors it will be either unwise or impossible to interrupt, but on most occasions the speaker will welcome the aid of a sincere question if you frame it courteously and clearly. You should not, however, abuse a speaker's invitation to ask questions, nor should you mistake it as a challenge to debate. On the other hand, it is a clear case of cowardice, dishonesty, or misguided courtesy for you to pretend by your silence that you understand when you don't. The habit of courteous, intelligent, and courageous inquiry is one of the greatest assets of an expert listener. Cultivate it.

Be Courteous. Courtesy is always a mark of mental health and human decency. In a listener it is more than that. It is an attitude and a practice that can be neglected only at the expense of communication. Your discourtesies will be interpreted by the speaker as signs of indifference and hostility. His assurance, his poise, and his enthusiasm will be affected. If, on the other hand, he is stimulated by your interested attention, his task is lightened and his performance improved. Treat him as you would like to be treated if you were in his place, and he will do a better job, just as you would. Your attitude of interest and consideration will, moreover, sharpen your reception and interpretation of what he has to say. The very act of aligning yourself with him, of identifying yourself with his point of view, and of wanting him to succeed gives you a position of advantage that you cannot have if you're indifferent, apathetic, or unsympathetic. Thus your courtesy to the speaker becomes a service to both of you.

Give thoughtful consideration to these suggestions for courteous behavior:

1. Let the speaker know he has your full attention.
2. If it is necessary to take notes, do so unobtrusively.
3. Look and act interested in what is being said.
4. Ask questions only if they are in order, phrasing them in friendly terms; don't heckle.
5. Avoid the kind of behavior that offends *you* when you are speaking.
6. And by all means:

   Don't whisper to your neighbor.

   Don't shuffle your feet, rustle paper, jingle coins, or play with objects.

   Don't chew gum or eat candy.

Don't engage in such activities as reading, writing, knitting, or drawing.
Don't make preparations to leave before the speaker has finished.
Don't perform acts of personal grooming.

Be Open-minded. The best program on the air cannot reach you if your radio or TV is turned off. Closed minds are like dead sets. When you are determined to resist the plea of the speaker and when you already know what you are going to think regardless of what he says, your mind is closed. Neither accurate interpretation nor sound evaluation is possible. There are several questions you should ask yourself in your search for open-mindedness:

1. Do I immediately reject what has been said merely because it is *different* from what I believe?
2. Am I accepting or rejecting the idea on the basis of my reaction to the speaker? or because of his reputation?
3. Am I casting aside this proposal which affects group welfare because of my self-interests?
4. What is my own attitude? Do I *want* to believe this statement is true, or do I *want* to believe it is false?
5. Do I welcome the speaker's ideas as warmly as if they were my own?
6. Does personal, family, or group loyalty blind me to the truth?
7. When I see the truth, do I cling to my loyalties?
8. Do I have such an exaggerated opinion of my own knowledge that I listen with half an ear, shutting my mind to the acceptance of what someone else says?

You are indeed a superman if your honest answers to these questions verify yours as an open mind. You are fortunate if they do no more than indicate much room for improvement. Look upon every listening experience as a kind of treasure hunt in which there are unlimited prizes if you'll just keep your mind open.

Evaluate What You Receive. Evaluating the ideas of a speaker is usually the most difficult phase of the listening and post-listening process. So far, we have been discussing the solution of problems related to hearing and interpreting what has been said, but now we must ask, "Of what *value* is this material?" To answer this question we shall go through three steps in evaluation: breaking through barriers of interference, checking on interpretation, and weighing ideas. Let's take them in order.

Breaking Through Barriers of Interference. Consider first that speaker you heard the other day at assembly. A hush settled over the audience as he walked to the stand, paused, looked out, and smiled. The first sounds of his resonant voice thrilled you pleasantly. His anecdotes made you chuckle. His easy, graceful manner was soothing and sympathetic. The flow of his faultless diction lulled you to sleep as if it were a magic sleeping potion. You had never, simply never, heard such a fascinating speaker. A vote for him and for his platform, you felt in a vague and blissful sort of way, would be a vote for Culture and for Truth.

Yesterday when you tried to recall for your father what that "wonderful" speaker had said, you remembered only the smile, the voice, the eloquence of gesture, the sheen of polished phrases—the *shower of charm.* Why could you recapture neither the gist nor the details of his speech? Why did you remember only pleasant sensations and emotions? The answer is that reception was made so easy, so delightful, and so entertaining that you discarded your responsibilities of evaluation. Maybe the speaker said something important, but you'll never know; you were either hypnotized or just having fun.

This illustration underlines a truth: it must be kept in mind that you are evaluating the speech and not the speaker; you are evaluating the depth of the speech rather than its glitter. The chrome on a car may increase its desirability but not its horsepower.

The type of interference illustrated by the story is only one of several. Another block to evaluation is your *personal friendship* with the speaker. Yours is an exceptionally well-trained mind if you can test the words of a friend with the same cold logic that you apply to those of a stranger. Likewise, it is hard to control the *antagonism* you often feel, whether it is created by personal mannerisms of the speaker or by his ideas. For example, his foreign accent may cause you to doubt his knowledge. His features may arouse your prejudice. His mannerisms may annoy you. Whatever it is that antagonizes you will interfere with evaluation. Still another obstacle in the way of critical appraisal is the *authority* of the speaker. His fame or his age or his position may lead you to accept what he says without question, or maybe you'll reject his statements because he isn't an acknowledged expert. Finally, you may be so *intimidated* by the subject or so *exhausted* by the difficulties of determining what the speaker meant that you simply swallow what you do understand without question.

Checking on Interpretation. You must remember that evaluation is important, that it is often the most critical phase of the listening process. You must be alert to the types of interference discussed above. But your responsibility doesn't end there. The next step is a check on your interpretation. Ask yourself these questions:

1. Did the speaker say what he intended to say? Did I mistake poor statement for poor thought?

2. Could I have misunderstood him?

3. Is there another possible interpretation of his statement?

4. Could I have missed a key word that would explain an apparent inconsistency or contradiction?

5. Does the proper interpretation of what I have just heard depend upon something the speaker has already said?

Weighing Ideas. Having satisfied yourself that you have done your best to discover his meaning, it is time to consider its worth. This third step is one of weighing.

1. What is the speaker's *motive*? Has he an ax to grind?

2. Is his statement the result of *strong feeling* or of *solid reasoning*?

3. Have I, where possible, separated *opinion* from *fact*?

4. Is the statement *relevant* to the question being discussed?

5. Does it support the speaker's arguments?

6. Is there evidence of his dishonesty? Does he distort facts? Does he gloss over items to which honest answers would be damaging? Does he lay false claim to authority? Is he guilty of false reasoning?

7. What about me? Am *I* prejudiced? Does my desire to believe or disbelieve affect my judgment? Am I discrediting the idea because it is new or different?

If, to the best of your ability, you have tried to separate the good from the waste by following such a thoughtful procedure as the one just presented, you have discharged your final responsibility as a listener. Learning to listen and maintaining a high standard of listening once good habits have been formed are phases of a lifelong task. The degree to which you succeed will depend upon your interest, your thoughtfulness, and your perseverance.

ACTIVITIES

1. Identify for yourself some of the ways in which the passer, the environment, and the receiver may fail in communication. Put each as a heading at the top of a sheet of paper, and during your speech class—or all of your classes if you wish—list under each heading a sample of what you regard as a failure. At the end of a period of time to be designated by your teacher, bring your research to class for discussion. Answer these questions:

a. How do your findings compare with statements made in this text?

b. Which of the barriers to communication have you found to be of greatest importance?

c. Which barriers are hardest to eliminate or control?

2. Prove to yourself some of the hazards of oral communication by playing the game which is commonly known as "Gossip." One person writes on a piece of paper a brief message and puts it away for reference. He then whispers the message to his neighbor, who passes it on by whisper. When the last person in the room hears the message, he writes it on paper. The two written messages are compared. The game can illustrate a point and provide some amusement for extra measure.
3. Talk informally before your class on some phase of school work with which your classmates may not be familiar. Use and define some unfamiliar terms. When you have finished talking, ask several of your classmates some questions for the purpose of determining how well you explained your strange ideas and words.
4. Find some short, easily recognized synonyms for these words:

sagacious	esoteric	equestrian	somnambulist
discourse	horrendous	ebullition	grandiose
magnanimity	replete	itinerary	discommode

5. Rewrite the following short introduction. Chop out all of the "deadwood" that you can find. Make any changes you wish.

My throat is pretty sore today, but I'm going to give my talk anyway, of course. It's all about my experiences at the Indianapolis racetrack and some other things. Maybe you haven't been there and maybe some of you don't like this racing jazz, but you don't know what you have been missing, let me tell you. In case you didn't know it, race cars are my hobby in a way. Well, anyway, there are all kinds of things to see at the racetrack. Before the day is over you are sure to see lots of wrecks and such stuff. I'm sorry my voice is so raspy. Also I'd like to tell you about how I lost my ticket before I went in. I guess most of you girls don't like car racing, but that's your business. Everybody to his own taste.

6. Make a list of epithets (disparaging names we often give to people) which are used in casual conversation and sometimes even in talks. These nicknames, not always used in jest and with affection, may arouse negative feelings which lessen the effectiveness of communication and damage personal relationships. Here are a few easy ones to start your list:

Slim	Tubby	Chink	Baldy	Gringo	Fatso

7. Try deliberately to extend your span of attention to spoken language, whether in the classroom or outside. Carry with you a card or piece of paper on which to keep a running record of your efforts. In each instance jot down the time you begin paying attention and the time you find yourself tuning out. Try quickly to identify the reason why you tune out. Is it the speaker's fault or yours? Is it an aspect of environment which could be ignored with a little self-discipline? At the end of two weeks compare your beginning and ending spans of attention. What have you learned about attention—and about yourself?
8. Practice control of attention on a companion whose chatter always bores you. Don't try to escape from him; stay right with him and listen carefully as if you had to report his conversation to a superior officer handling espionage.

9. Time your attention spans in the reading you are doing for classwork. If you can make your attention behave here, you are gaining a discipline that will carry over into listening situations.
10. Turn on your radio or TV (in class or at home) to any discussion program. Deliberately choose something to which it seems difficult to listen. Put all your power of concentration into your listening activity and try to discover the answers to the following questions. Repeat the results to your teacher.
   a. When did your attention lag?
   b. What caused your listening difficulty?
   c. How long were you tuned out?
   d. What did you do to force yourself back to listening attentively?
   e. What were the main points the speaker made?
11. Interest a friend or member of your family in this experiment. Find in your radio or TV log a lecture, discussion, or word-game program to which all of you can listen. Provide everyone with pencil and paper; follow these instructions:
   a. Write down every word you can't define.
   b. Write down every word you think others may not know, whether you know it or not.

   When the program is over, or the allotted time has elapsed, compare notes to see who admitted to the most impoverished vocabulary. Next, let each person test the rest of the group on the words listed under *b*, orally if he wishes, though written work will be fairer and more accurate. Count up your scores!
12. Observe and list for just tomorrow all of the discourtesies that come to your attention during any kind of oral communication. Try to determine how much of your accumulated evidence applies to your own listening behavior when you're not on guard.
13. Test your attention span and your ability to interpret material which is read to you by your teacher or a classmate. A good editorial, a short essay, an article from a newspaper or magazine, or a portion of a speech from a book of speeches or a speech magazine, such as *Vital Speeches*, is good material for your purpose.

References:

Language in Action, by S. I. Hayakawa. Harcourt, Brace.
Language in Thought and Action, by S. I. Hayakawa. Harcourt, Brace.
The Tyranny of Words, by Stuart Chase. Harcourt, Brace.

Films:

How to Concentrate (Coronet). 11 min color or b&w.
Effective Listening (MH). 15 min b&w.

Filmstrips:

How to Listen (SVE). 4 fs b&w. (1) Tell the Difference between Essentials, Details—43 fr (2) Discover the Purpose of a Speaker—48 fr (3) Tell the Difference between Facts, Opinions—42 fr (4) Information; Persuasion; Propaganda—40 fr.

Record:

A Word in Your Ear (ERC). One 12″ record 33⅓ rpm.

Unit Six

GIVE AND TAKE: The Value of Criticism

The boy who wants to be first-string guard on the football team expects the coach to tell him when his blocking is good or his tackling is bad. The girl who is cutting out a dress pattern for the first time expects to be corrected if she mistakes the front for the back. Your English teacher suggests improvements for your themes. Your history teacher evaluates your reports. Your science teacher checks your experiments. And in this speech class it will be your listeners, teachers and classmates together, who will comment on your efforts and judge your work.

In a class like this, more than in others, you'll find it necessary to take personal suggestions. How can you know whether you are speaking distinctly if someone doesn't tell you? Are you sure you have good posture and poise? Have your thoughts been presented clearly and logically? Did you talk too rapidly? Was your subject interesting and well chosen? Did you make any mistakes in pronunciation or grammar? These are some of the things you must know in order to improve your speaking. Learning how to take criticism graciously when you're a speaker and how to give it generously when you're a listener is part of your responsibility from now on. Let's help each other.

Some Basic Understandings

Since learning to give and take critical comments is a necessary part of your speech work, you ought to know what good criticism is, and you should set up some general rules to follow. Here are a few suggestions. Can you think of others?

Understand the Purpose of Criticism. Criticism is an act of evaluation and analysis based on knowledge and conducted with good manners. It is not "faultfinding." In the giving, it demands a sensitive consideration of others' feelings; in the receiving, it requires an open-minded, objective desire to improve. Because speaking is a highly personal activity, evaluation of it must deal with highly personal matters, such as your posture, appearance, mannerisms, voice, language, and ideas. It is important to your maturity as a speaker that you learn to see yourself as others see you. That's why you need the help of your teacher and classmates.

Be Willing to Accept Help. You're in a speech class to learn, to improve, or to master a skill. Whatever may be your specific personal reasons for studying speech (have you read Unit 1?), your goals may be unattainable without a strong desire to succeed and a willingness to accept help and to profit by it.

Contribute to a Friendly Classroom. Get acquainted with your classmates. Trust the sincerity and guidance of your teacher. Everyone's in the same boat, so pull together and develop a kind of morale which is based on your friendly concern for the other fellow's problems and a strong pride in your own achievements as you improve. A vital speech class can be a creative workshop for you.

Keep Your Standards High. Expect the best of yourself and look for the best in others. Careless or purposeless effort deserves disapproval, yet criticism must be sympathetic and constructive. Poking fun, being sarcastic, being "picky," dwelling on nervous personal mannerisms or speech defects, overdoing negative comments ("don't do this" or "don't do that")—all these should be avoided. Stress the constructive, important values and deal lightly with trivialities. Treat feelings with care in public and reserve strong adverse criticism for private sessions.

Ask Yourself Some Basic Questions.

- Do you want to be praised or appraised?
- Do you have a hard or a soft shell?
- Will you go on the defensive under criticism, or are you mature enough to face yourself honestly?
- What can you learn from being a critic as well as from being criticized?

How to Give Criticism

Your eager question "How'd I do? How'd I do?" should be answered as promptly as possible after you've given a class talk and while your speech and its delivery are still fresh in your listeners' minds. Oral comments made by your teacher and classmates just after you've spoken are necessarily brief and limited, but they offer you an immediate evaluation of your performance. Written criticisms, on the other hand, can be more detailed, even though there may be some delay in your receiving them. Both play an important part in giving you an appraisal of your work, and both follow these general rules:

1. *Be tactful.* Most people's feelings are easily hurt. It is always wise, therefore, to *think* before you speak critically of someone. To be rude, cruel, unkind, bitter, or sarcastic in what you say about another person's efforts is not being *critical*; it's simply being small and petty. There's an old saying, "You can catch more flies with honey than with vinegar." Remember to be thoughtful, courteous, and tactful in your criticisms.

2. *Be constructive.* Criticism is not mere faultfinding. It has a constructive meaning, too. The best criticism is that which builds up as well as tears down. You may pick out specific faults in a student's speech, but you should also make definite constructive suggestions for overcoming those faults. Your aim is to *help,* not *hurt.*

3. *Be definite.* Vague, general comments too often are meaningless. To be helpful to a student, you should make your criticism definite, accurate, and specific. Hurried and abrupt statements, such as "I didn't like the way he spoke," are too general. Instead say, "His volume was well regulated, but he spoke too rapidly and his enunciation was not clear."

4. *Be thorough.* Criticism that is complete and thorough is more helpful than that which is sketchy and hurried. There are more things to criticize in speaking than you may realize. It isn't possible to comment on *everything* a speaker says or does; nevertheless, it is wise to try to make as thorough an analysis as possible. The charts for criticism you'll find later in this unit are intended to show you how thorough you can be.

Oral Criticism. In giving oral criticism you must be sure to follow the general rules already established. Your attitude should be sincere and helpful, your manner straightforward and honest, and your comments tactful, constructive, direct, and as thorough as you can make them. Look at the following criticisms which were made by members of one speech class after several students had finished their talks. Do you agree that they are fair, honest, and direct?

Jim had well-chosen, interesting material, but he fidgeted too much and mispronounced two words which he should have known.

His opening sentences were real attention-getters; yet he spoiled the effect by racing on too fast. His rapid rate of speaking also made it hard for me to concentrate on his ideas. They came too fast.

Why didn't she prepare more thoroughly, so that her delivery would have been smoother? She had a good topic and some clever expressions, but her delivery was awkward and halting.

After a nervous start, Betty got hold of herself and really put her ideas across. I liked her seriousness and her general attitude, but she ought to look at us more often and try to put on a more confident manner.

Ted seemed to be bluffing his way through this one. He had too good a subject to let it down like that. His speaking voice is one of the best in class, but his manner didn't seem sincere. I'll bet he didn't put enough time on this speech.

Nancy always gives a good talk. Her subject was interesting, her organization was good, and her delivery was effective. What about those slurred words, though, and her habit of using slang so much?

This talk was delivered well, but it wasn't original. I read it in *The Reader's Digest* last month.

Although her delivery was mechanical and her voice was monotonous, Eunice showed she'd spent a lot of time in preparing this talk. The subject was a little deep, though, for this kind of audience.

These comments were far more helpful to the speakers than the hurried and abrupt statements that are sometimes made by thoughtless or untrained students. Look at these, for instance:

He spoke too fast.
I didn't like the subject.
She mispronounced a word.
I didn't get the point.
She fiddled with her notes.
He didn't pause enough.
Her voice was bad.
It wasn't interesting.
He made a mistake in grammar.
He said *er* too much.

Good oral criticisms, like the first ones, can be given in your class, too. Notice that the students looked for specific strengths *and* weaknesses in the talks to which they listened and that they mentioned *both.* Of course, it takes time and effort for a critic to analyze someone else's efforts fairly so that the resulting comment will be helpful to the speaker. But if you try to do your best in giving oral comments, your classmates will find them very valuable as a quick check of their efforts.

Written Criticism. Oral criticism isn't enough in a speech class. You may forget what your teacher or classmates said unless it's written down. If you want to see yourself as others see you and if you want to check on your improvement in speaking, you should plan to have some visual record of the criticism that is offered you.

One of the commonest methods of recording criticism is for either the teacher or the students or both to write a short comment on each speech. These written comments are then given to the speaker for him to read and keep. Obviously, this is a time-consuming task for everyone, with the critical appraisal being necessarily brief.

A better way of giving written criticisms which may be kept as a record of improvement is to prepare an outline or chart on which specific points to be checked are indicated and on which space is left for a short written comment, if the critic desires to add one. With the help of your teacher you and your classmates can make a chart of this kind, one that is general enough to cover all the major phases of speaking and yet specific and detailed enough to include an evaluation of the individual characteristics of the speaker.

The guide which is included in this section is a sample of the kind of standard form you can use for each speech assignment throughout the year. It covers the necessary general speech areas; it suggests definite critical terms after each general topic; it leaves room for additional written comment by the critic; it is flexible enough to cover critical comment for almost any kind of speaking you may do; it can be reproduced on standard notebook-size paper so that it will fit easily into your binder. The simplest way to use the chart is to have one before you as you listen to a speaker. Check or circle the appropriate words which apply to the speaker's efforts, and then, if you have time, add a brief written comment on the reverse side.

The chart could be used exclusively by your teacher, or a different student-critic could be selected for each speech assignment or for each individual speaker. The important thing is that every speech or oral reading you give in class should be criticized, and a record of that criticism should be kept by the speaker.

Remember: much of your improvement in the art of speaking depends upon the regularity of helpful critical evaluation and upon your active effort to profit from it. Written summaries, critical guides, and check-charts, whether detailed or limited in coverage, give you a permanent record of each speaking performance. By keeping your charts in consecutive order in a folder or binder, you may easily use them for quick reference or for more extended analysis.

SPEECH-EVALUATION GUIDE

SPEAKER ______________________________

TOPIC ______________________________

CONTENT:

TOPIC	ORGANIZATION	ORIGINALITY	RESEARCH
challenging important acceptable pointless	strong plan satisfactory not clear no plan	imaginative ordinary doubtful dull	outstanding adequate unnecessary neglected
errors of fact:			

DELIVERY:

AUDIENCE CONTACT	PREPARATION	POISE	POSTURE
compelling aware indifferent no attempt	complete satisfactory memorized inadequate	assured evident uncontrolled lacking	striking effective awkward slovenly
VOICE	ARTICULATION	VOLUME	RATE
pleasing flat flexible weak resonant booming "colorful" harsh persuasive strident monotonous	precise clear careless cluttered	regulated satisfactory erratic too high-low	flexible satisfactory monotonous too fast-slow

LANGUAGE:

COMMUNICATION	VOCABULARY
achieves purpose fully gets most ideas over occasionally makes point fails in purpose	rich adequate slangy impoverished
GRAMMAR	
errors:	
PRONUNCIATION	
words mispronounced: provincialisms:	

SPECIAL PROBLEMS:

breathlessness nasality "uh" and "ah" stuttering lisping hissing *L* sounds *R* sounds foreign accent

COMMENTS (use reverse side of sheet if necessary):

CRITIC ______________

As you become familiar with such a guide and as you progress through your speech course, you can condense the chart, if you wish, to fit a small card, like this:

SPEAKER ________		TOPIC ________
CONTENT	Organization ________	
	Originality ________	
DELIVERY	Audience contact ________	
	Poise ________	
	Posture ________	
	Articulation ________	
	Volume ________	
	Rate ________	
	Voice ________	
	General effect ________	
LANGUAGE	Vocabulary ________	
	Grammar ________	
	Pronunciation ________	
SPECIAL COMMENT	________	
	________	

You can prepare a separate chart for a particular speech assignment, too, if by common class consent you want to limit criticism to one or two special points instead of covering the whole field. For instance, when you are learning how to organize talks, class criticisms may be centered on that topic alone. Your condensed chart may look like this:

SPEAKER ________		TOPIC ________
INTRODUCTION	Method used ________	
	Effect on audience ________	
DISCUSSION	Order of points ________	
	Effectiveness ________	
CONCLUSION	Method used ________	
	Effect on audience ________	
SPECIAL COMMENTS	________	
	________	
	________	
	________	
	________	
	________	

A GRADING CHART FOR SPEECH EVALUATION

SPEAKER ____________________

TOPIC ____________________

General Evaluation **Specific Evaluation**

GRADE			A	B	C	D	F
	CONTENT	Well-Chosen, Interesting Material					
		Clear, Definite Purpose					
		Well-Unified Theme					
		Careful Selection of Detail					
		Interesting Illustrations					
	ORGANIZATION	Attention-Getting Introduction					
		Logical Arrangement of Ideas					
		Easy Transitions					
		Effective Conclusion					
	DELIVERY	Mental, Physical, Social Poise					
		Natural, Sincere Manner					
		Pleasing Vocal Qualities					
		Clear, Distinct Speech					
		Effective Audience Contact					
		Meaningful Gestures					
	LANGUAGE	Good Choice of Words					
		Correct Pronunciation					
		Well-Composed Sentences					
		Acceptable Grammar					
		Originality of Style					
	AUDIENCE APPEAL	Ability to Hold Interest					
		Consideration for Audience					
		Projection of Personality					

The possibilities for creating useful guides for written criticism are endless. Whatever method or form you decide to use in class, keep in mind that you're aiming at a practical and efficient way of getting a visual record of your good and bad points. That record should be thorough in coverage, detailed enough to be helpful, and easy to use.

How to Take Criticism

There are two sides to criticism: the giving of it and the taking of it. The taking may be hard for you, so let's establish a sound basis for learning to accept what others say.

1. *Take it gracefully.* It isn't always easy to take criticism. Even the average person, who is not usually shy or sensitive, may find it difficult to listen to personal comments about his appearance, voice, or delivery. Human nature being what it is, we're not too happy about being criticized. However, criticism is a necessary part of speech work; it is designed to help you to improve. If you understand its purpose and the spirit in which it is given, you can learn to accept it gracefully, even thankfully.

2. *Be objective.* Again you must remember that comments on your speech work are aimed at helping you to improve. Being objective means being detached, impersonal, unprejudiced, unemotional. Never view a fair criticism as if it were a personal attack on you. Avoid being too self-conscious about suggestions that are given you. Think of the purpose behind criticism in a class like this and don't ever allow yourself to feel resentment, anger, or displeasure. Ask questions about points which you don't understand, but don't do it with a chip-on-shoulder attitude.

3. *Keep a record.* As was said earlier in this unit, it is wise to keep some kind of accounting of your strengths and weaknessess as a speaker if you want to watch your development. Oral comment is not enough. The charts suggested in this unit could be used and filed in your binder as a visual record of your continuing improvement. Decide in class what form would be efficient, and be persistent about keeping your record up to date.

4. *Make use of criticism.* Criticism is of little value to you if you don't use it. The time and effort that a critic takes in making comments on your performance should be balanced by the time and effort you put into eliminating your weaknesses and improving your strengths. A good plan to follow is to make a point of correcting at least *one* of your weaknesses as soon as you can after it has been called to your attention. Observe other people to see how they may handle the same problem. Another thing you might do is to make a composite list each month of all the points on which you have received adverse criticism. Errors which persist on that

list are the ones which you should concentrate on eliminating in the future. In any case, *DO* something about the criticisms given you.

Without the helpful personal suggestions and comments you can get from others, you'll not know how well you're progressing as a speaker or what improvements you still need to make. Be grateful for all evaluations, and help each other.

Review of Criticism

If you are the critic:

1. Judge others as you would be judged.
2. Be fair, honest, and tactful.
3. Have a friendly, helpful feeling.
4. Say something good along with the bad.
5. Whenever possible give definite suggestions about how to improve, not vague, general comments that are meaningless.
6. Be objective in your criticism, not personal and negative.
7. Emphasize major criticisms first; the more unimportant, last.

If you are being criticized:

1. Read carefully or listen attentively to whatever criticism is offered
2. Accept all comments graciously at face value.
3. Ask questions about points which you don't understand.
4. Keep a record of all criticisms, including your self-criticism.
5. Make a point of correcting at least one weakness at the first opportunity after it has been called to your attention. You can't do *everything* at once, but you can start with small points and then work up to the large.
6. Observe others to see how they may handle the same problems you have and how they improve.

Criticizing Written Speeches

Your thoughtful study of well-known speeches in their written form can teach you much about how speakers of experience organize and express their ideas. Saint Augustine said, "If a man desire to speak not only with wisdom but with eloquence . . . I would rather send him to read . . . eloquent men than advise him to spend time with the teachers of rhetoric."

Because a written speech may be pondered over and examined minutely, you have an opportunity to analyze in detail the soundness of the speaker's ideas, his organization, and the devices used to impress listeners and clarify points. The following form may be helpful in such analysis.

READING REPORT FORM

(for evaluating written speeches)

NAME: **DATE:**

Source of speech (where found): ____________________

Speaker: ____________________

Title or subject: ____________________

Occasion: ____________________

____

Central thought: ____________________

____

____

Memorable details, phrases, sentences, or ideas: ____________________

____

____

____

Strengths	Weaknesses
____________________	____________________
____________________	____________________
____________________	____________________

Was the speech worthwhile reading? Why? ____________________

____

____

As you gain experience in reading and listening to speeches, you will become more sophisticated in your critical evaluations. The Advanced Guide for Criticism of Speeches, which is included in this section, may then be helpful to you. It is intended to focus your attention not on the delivery of a speaker but on the principles and devices he uses to add clarity and interest to the content of his speech. Consider this guide as a supplement to others included in this unit. It may be used for evaluating both written and oral speeches.

Advanced Guide for Criticism of Speeches

Background:

- What was the occasion of the speech?
- What do you know about the speaker?
- Is there any special historical, political, literary, or social significance to the speech?

I. Introduction to the speech

A. How did he get attention in the opening sentence?
B. How did he relate his subject to the interests of his audience?
C. Did he establish a central thought, a main thesis, early in the speech?

II. Body of the speech

A. What were the main points?

1. In what order were they presented?
2. How was each point supported and developed?

B. What devices were used to make ideas clear?

1. Logical plan?
2. Concrete details?
3. Definitions?
4. Comparison and contrast?
5. Repetition and restatement?
6. Transitional signposts and cue phrases?

C. What devices were used to make ideas interesting?

1. Vivid examples and illustrations?
2. Personal reference? Reference to audience?
3. Humor?
4. Special word usage and sentence style?
5. Appeal to emotions? self-interests? common experiences?

III. Conclusion of the speech

A. Where did the conclusion begin? Was it long? short?
B. What method was used to "wrap up" the speech?
C. Was the conclusion effective?

Summary:

- As you think over the speech, what do you feel was the speaker's ultimate, as well as immediate, purpose? his motive?
- Can you summarize the theme, or central idea, in a single sentence?
- What parts do you think were most effective?
- What did you like best—or least—about the speech? Why?
- How honest and valid was the speech? How worthwhile?

ACTIVITIES

1. Arrange a panel discussion, to be followed by audience participation, on the subject "Criticism." Consider these questions as possible topics to discuss.
   - **a.** Are young people quick to take offense under criticism? Why?
   - **b.** Can boys take criticism better than girls can?
   - **c.** Are girls more tactful than boys in making suggestions?
   - **d.** Specifically, what can be done in your speech class to help create a good atmosphere for criticism of your speech work?
   - **e.** What kinds of comments are likely to be hurtful rather than helpful?
   - **f.** How should you tell a boy that his personal appearance is not neat?
   - **g.** How should you tell a girl to improve her posture?
   - **h.** What method of critical evaluation would you like to see used in this class?
2. Let everyone in class prepare a one-minute current-event report. An individual student-critic should then be assigned to each speaker. The critic's duty is to give oral comments on the speaker's efforts as well as a brief written evaluation at the conclusion of the talk. Here is a suggested chart to use:

NAME:	**TOPIC:**
Easy approach to audience? ____________________	
Interesting beginning? ____________________	
Good poise and posture? ____________________	
Easily heard and understood? ____________________	
Good contact with audience? ____________________	
Satisfactory ending? ____________________	
Was the delivery effective? ____________________	
Was the subject worthwhile? ____________________	
Would you grade it good, average, or fair? ____________________	

3. Ask the teacher of some class other than your speech course for personal criticism of your efforts when you give your next talk in that class. Give the teacher a copy of the Grading Chart for Speech Evaluation included in this unit for checking specific items. File the completed evaluation in your speech notebook

as evidence of how someone outside the speech field has judged one of your oral presentations.

4. Listen to a well-known speaker or news commentator on radio or TV and give a brief critical evaluation in class of his voice, delivery, projection of personality, and general effectiveness. Some possibilities are Chet Huntley, David Brinkley, Frank McGee, Eric Sevareid, Walter Cronkite, Harry Reasoner, David Susskind. You can think of others well known in your locality or in the nation.
5. Read or listen to (on TV, tapes, or records) a speech by one of the following men. Each one has appeared frequently before the general public and is known for his own special style, manner, or ability in speaking. Either write a theme or report to the class on what you heard or read, evaluating the general effectiveness of the content and style of the speech.

Frank C. Baxter	Robert McNamara
Ralph Bunche	James P. Mitchell
Erwin D. Canham	Richard Nixon
Frank Church	Norman Vincent Peale
Everett Dirksen	James A. Pike
Dwight D. Eisenhower	Walter Reuther
Barry Goldwater	Nelson Rockefeller
Billy Graham	William Scranton
Hubert Humphrey	Fulton J. Sheen
Robert M. Hutchins	Rabbi Abba Hillel Silver
Lyndon B. Johnson	Adlai Stevenson

6. Read a famous speech and write a brief criticism of it, using the Reading Report Form included in this unit.
7. Submit a written speech of your own for evaluation by the teacher or one of your classmates. Have your critic refer to the Advanced Guide for Criticism of Speeches for suggestions.
8. Take notes the next time you hear a visiting speaker at school or fill out an evaluation guide as you listen to him. Then have a discussion during the next meeting of your speech class and compare your evaluation with those of your classmates. Be sure to cover the following questions:
   - a. What was the central idea of the speech?
   - b. How did the speaker try to make it clear and interesting?
   - c. What were the strong and weak points of delivery?
   - d. How effective was the language style?
   - e. Were there any special listening problems which distracted you?

Speeches to Read for Criticism

"Address to Congress," by Douglas MacArthur, *Congressional Record* (April, 1951), pp. 4123-4125.

*"Aloha Ke Akua," by Abraham K. Akaka.

*"Anti-Westernism: Cause and Cure," by Vera M. Dean.

"Blood, Toil, Tears, and Sweat," by Winston S. Churchill, in *Blood, Sweat, and Tears*. Putnam.

*"Eulogy on Eleanor Roosevelt," by Adlai Stevenson.

*"How Would You Have Us?" by RUFUS E. CLEMENT.
"Inaugural Address as Governor of Pennsylvania," by WILLIAM W. SCRANTON, January 15, 1963.
"In Memoriam," by FRANK CHURCH, November 24, 1963. (See Appendix B.)
*"The Prospect for Civilization," by FRANCIS H. HORN.

*These speeches may be found in *Representative American Speeches,* by A. C. BAIRD or L. THONSSEN. Wilson.

Sources to Consult for Written Speeches

American Speeches, by W. M. PARRISH and M. HOCHMUTH. McKay.
A Treasury of the World's Great Speeches, by H. PETERSON. Simon and Schuster.
The Age of Danger: Major Speeches on American Problems, by H. F. HARDING. Random House.
Congressional Record.
The New York Times.
Vital Speeches of the Day.

Films:

Effective Criticism (Coronet). 11 min color or b&w.
Making Yourself Understood (EBF). 14 min b&w.

PUTTING A SPEECH TOGETHER

In this portion of the text you will come to grips with the problem of organizing formal and informal oral presentations. You will be starting with ideas and raw material from which you will fashion those presentations, asking yourself in the process such questions as these: What shall I talk about? How is purpose related to my topic and its development? How and where do I find speech material? What is an effective plan for a speech? How do I develop such a plan? Is there more than one kind of effective plan? What is a good way to begin my presentation? What makes a conclusion more than a mere stopping point? How can I develop a desirable delivery? Many answers to your questions may be found in the material of this section.

WHAT YOU WILL FIND:

SOME KEYS TO SUCCESSFUL SPEAKING

Before You Speak

- Have a *purpose,* or goal, in mind.
- Choose a *subject* that's interesting, challenging, entertaining, and timely.
- Have a *plan,* and set a time limit.
- Understand your *audience* and adjust your material to it.
- Use plenty of illustrations, stories, quotations, and similar *interest-arousing* devices.
- Pay careful attention to your *beginning* and your *ending.*
- Use *repetition* and *restatement* to emphasize main points and important ideas.
- Find room for a bit of *humor.*

When You Speak

- Be *poised,* neatly dressed, and confident.
- Speak with *vigor* and *enthusiasm.*
- Keep *eye-contact* with your listeners.
- Let your *posture* and *movement* be dignified and easy, your *gestures* spontaneous.
- Use *language* that is simple, colorful, and correct.
- *Enunciate* clearly and *pronounce* correctly.
- Vary your rate, pitch, volume, inflection, and pauses to *avoid monotony.*
- Cultivate a warm, friendly, sincere *manner.*
- Keep *notes* on small cards or not at all.
- Observe the *time limits* you have set.

HEARING
SPEAKING
All
creatures
communicate
many creatures
HEAR
things unheard
by man

Unit Seven

HAVE SOMETHING TO SAY: Topics and Purposes

Language in oral form has brought to human beings one of their greatest pleasures, the exchanging of information on personal desires, plans, ideas, anxieties, accomplishments, sorrows, satisfactions, or any other topic which suits them. Possibly most people would rather talk than listen, for talking satisfies a strong urge for self-expression; but the listening part of the communication is important, too, because it is an avenue of pleasure and because it is a necessary factor in giving meaning to the talking. Language is more than a vehicle of pleasure, however, for it permits us to carry on the process of civilization, and use of oral language in situations more formal than conversation often carries with it a responsibility and accompanying pressure that give the speaker a case of "butterflies."

You're comfortable in most conversational groups of your friends because you are talking about matters of common interest. In fact, it's hard to get a word into the conversation when the surge of communication is high. But have you ever tried seriously to analyze what you talked about? Have you ever tried to examine your discomfort when you felt that the conversation excluded you? In other terms, have you ever wondered about the sources from which most communication springs?

Communication Comes from What You Know—Feel—Do

You talk best when you're talking about something with which you are familiar, about which you have special knowledge, and for which you feel enthusiasm. When you have something to say, the words come. You converse. You communicate. You impress. Your listeners may be quiet in the sense of not making human sounds, but they are responding to your communication because there is vitality in your contribution.

Though you may want to reject the idea at first, will you consider the position that all of your oral self-expression has its sources in what you *know*, what you *feel*, and what you *do*? The *know* represents your knowledge, training, understanding, and general mental sophistication. It also represents what you may suddenly be obliged to learn, if you are in a formal speaking situation, to discharge your responsibilities as a speaker. The *feel* portion of you is that segment which encompasses your emotional reactions to environment, your honest opinions as they are related to feeling, your interpretation of yourself. The *do* about which you can talk is what you have done, what you are in the process of doing, or what you are planning or hoping to do. The three areas may be designated by these terms: knowledge, feeling, and experience.

". . . Thought on Fire"

Though "giving a talk" and "just talking" have much in common, since communication is their common denominator, they differ in that a speech requires planning, no small part of which is soul-searching effort.

To answer the question "What shall I talk about?" you first must say to yourself, "No matter what the subject is, I must have something to say. I must make some kind of point. I must accomplish a purpose. I must bring to this presentation a quality that only I can create." Maybe your talk won't have the quality of a *message*, but you can help yourself by thinking of it as being *important*. When you *want* to say something, the quality of sincerity affects in a positive manner both your thinking and your speaking. In other words your speech gains effectiveness from your attitude. William Jennings Bryan said, "Eloquence may be defined as the speech of one who knows what he is talking about and means what he says—*it is thought on fire*." Though you may modestly, and justifiably, deny your readiness to sway audiences with your oratory, you will do well in your speech training to search for the quality of speaking that is described in Bryan's statement.

Choosing and Limiting a Speech Topic

In addition to your topic's being important to you, it must be appropriate in other ways. Is it in good taste? Is it within the limits of your ability to present and of your listeners' to understand? Will it be interesting to others? Will it fit into the time at your disposal?

It would be wise to discuss your proposed topic with someone else—your teacher, for instance. He probably will be able to suggest ways to make your presentation most effective, such as selection of a purpose that best fits your material and the manner in which you may limit content. Or, if you simply have no topic in mind, he may suggest one which will fall comfortably into your know-feel-do area. Before you turn to him, though, see what you can do on your own by studying the suggestions that follow.

First, consider these **DO's** and **DON'Ts:**

DO choose your subject with thought and care.

DO select a subject early and let it grow in your thinking.

DO consider how appropriate the subject is in relation to the audience and the occasion.

DO dig into your own head and heart and examine *your* thoughts, *your* feelings, and *your* accomplishments in regard to the subject.

DO choose subjects from a variety of fields. Let your interest guide you where your knowledge is limited.

DO have a clearly identifiable purpose in mind as you choose your subject.

DO choose a subject which is fresh and about which you probably know more than your listeners do.

DO have confidence in your own unique qualities. There is no one like you, and what you can tell has a special worth, flavor, or importance.

DON'T pick a subject at random and hope to find something to say about it later.

DON'T procrastinate and then try to do a week's work in thirty minutes.

DON'T choose a subject blindly, without concern for your listeners' needs and desires.

DON'T "lift" thought from publications without putting them through the mill of your own mind. Be original!

DON'T be afraid of a subject about which you know little. If you're interested, you can find facts.

DON'T decide to select a subject and just talk about it as you go along.

DON'T let your interest and energy wane to the extent that you merely try to warm up some old hash.

DON'T fall into the trap of thinking that everyone else knows what you know or thinks as you think.

Next, consider some of the general fields from which a topic may be chosen, trying to find an area of interest if your topic is still elusive.

Travel	Transportation	Exploration and Discovery
Hobbies	Journalism	Vacation Experiences

Movies	Medicine	Strange Experiences
Sports	Photography	Legitimate Theater
Music	Literature	Student Government
Art	Science	Fraternities and Sororities
Business	Forestry	Forms of Government
Crime	Atomic Power	Traffic Problems
Housing	Racial Segregation	Retirement Security
Aviation	Famous People	Labor Unions
Education	Odd Sights	The World of Tomorrow
Television	Radio	Unemployment
Physical Fitness	Space Travel	International Relations
Religions	Mathematics	Extrasensory Perception

Do you notice that all of the suggested fields don't have the same degree of generality? For example, music is a much more general topic than student government; science encompasses a greater range than radio; medicine is larger than extrasensory perception; and the world of tomorrow includes more considerations than space travel. It is practically impossible to equate general topics and just as impossible for a speaker to relate all that is known about any fields. What must be done is to select for presentation a *facet* of the general topic, a segment that can be treated in a reasonable length of time after a reasonable amount of preparation.

For example, any of the following subtopics might come from the general topics, and, if you wished, you could reduce these subtopics to sub-subtopics. Where you stop in the reduction process depends upon the degree of refinement that is necessary to your purposes and upon the extent of your knowledge about the finer points. If you are like many speakers, you will, unfortunately, seek the comfort of making general statements that are hard to disprove rather than to aim for specifics that can be closely examined; but the strength of a speech, like the strength of a piece of writing, lies to a great extent in those specifics.

Suppose you are interested in the general field of *Medicine.* The following subtopics limit the general topic to *some* extent:

Socialized Medicine
Hypnotism Has a Place in Medicine
The Fight against Polio
How Medical Research Is Carried On
The Miracles of Plastic Surgery

Now, let's look at that first subtopic with a view toward reducing it into sub-subtopics. Here are some possibilities:

Socialized Medicine

England's Experiment in Socialized Medicine
Medical Service behind the Iron Curtain

Strength and Weaknesses of Socialized Medicine
Blue Cross: Modified Socialized Medicine
Why Most U. S. Doctors Oppose Socialized Medicine

To illustrate that the process of reduction can easily go further, let's break the first sub-subtopic above into several parts:

England's Experiment in Socialized Medicine

How the English People Like Their Medical Service
England's Private Practitioners Speak Out
The Cost of Medical Service in England
Have English Health Standards Improved?
A Foreigner Looks at English Medical Service

Now, take one of the parts above and see how far you can carry it into smaller and smaller segments. This process, incidentally, is practically identical to the process of selecting and developing main points for a speech, which will be discussed in Unit 10. For the moment, however, let's turn back for ideas from some of the general areas which have been listed. Perhaps you would be interested in *Strange Experiences*:

My Trip to the Petrified Forest
Two Hours in the City's Sewer System
We Didn't Know We Were Being Hypnotized
Riding Out a Storm in a Jet Liner
A Visit to an Indian Burial Ground

If your present interest lies in the general field of *Aviation*, one of these topics may suit you:

The Thrill of Being in the Air
New Safety Devices for Our Planes
Air Cargo Is Big Business
Atomic Power for Planes of Tomorrow
Air Traffic Regulations Must Be Tightened

These are possibilities from the field of *Sports*:

Mortality Rates of Professional Athletes in Popular Sports
Are Gamblers Controlling Collegiate Sports?
Rigged Wrestling Is Wrong
What Is Woman's Place in Athletics?
Are Foreign Athletes Superior to American Athletes?

Use your imagination to develop ideas from *The World of Tomorrow*:

My Home Is Forty Feet Underground
Three Meals in Three Pills

Deepfreezing the Human Body for Interstellar Travel
Have Your Own Telephone . . . Wear It on Your Wrist
No More Front-Seat Driving . . . Cars of the Future

The field of *Traffic Problems* has an abundance of topics. Here are a few:

We Must Establish National Traffic Regulations
The Highway Building Program Is Consistently Too Little and Too Late
State Highway and Main Street Should Not Mix
What Would You Do If You Were a Traffic Officer?
Bottlenecks That Cause Traffic Snarls

Maybe you are a "whodunit" fan or are seriously interested in *Crime*:

Has Centuries-Old Capital Punishment Served a Useful Purpose?
The Modern Sherlock Holmes
Who Is a Criminal, and How Did He Become One?
High-Priority Target: The Narcotics "Pusher"
Is a Robbery-Proof Bank Possible—and Practical?

Your Topic and Your Purpose

Related to the process of reducing a general field to a topic of speaking size is the *purpose* you wish to accomplish, and both the way you state your topic and the material you select to present it should reflect that purpose. If, for example, you have chosen from the field of aviation the topic "The Thrill of Being in the Air," it seems apparent that you are going to talk about something which you have *done* and that you have as your general *purpose* the sharing of your feelings about this experience. If most of your listeners have also been up in an airplane, your purpose is not to tell about feelings in an informational sense but to share your *particular* feelings, to bring to some of your listeners a new dimension about their own feelings of flying, and to present yourself in a new light.

If, however, you choose from traffic problems the topic "We Must Establish National Traffic Regulations," your purpose would seem to be to convince your audience that you have a reasonable solution for a recognizable problem. The title of your speech is no guarantee of your purpose, though; only *you* can know what influence you want your speech to have. You could, for instance, make a serious speech on "The Modern Sherlock Holmes," pointing out significant changes in detective work. But, using the same topic, you might just as easily present an entertaining speech, one in which you poke fun at today's detectives as you compare them with the infallible Holmes, a character who is as invincible as Paul Bunyan.

One classification of speeches according to purpose is that of putting them into these five categories:

The solar system is as vast a topic as anyone could be assigned. How would you reduce it to a sub-subtopic?

To inform—Tell the listeners something which they don't know.
To convince—Gain the listeners' acceptance of a statement of truth or of a point of view.
To persuade—Rouse the listeners to take action on a proposal.
To entertain—Provide the listeners with material which will bring them enjoyment.
To impress or inspire—Create in the listeners strong emotional reactions.

Although speeches may be classified according to purpose, it is well for you to keep this distinction in mind: only *speakers* have purposes; the speeches have *characteristics* which should reflect the speaker's purposes. The material in the speech should enable each speaker to achieve his purpose; the speech itself is just a vehicle to serve that purpose.

Consider for a moment some of the difficulties in the establishment and identification of purpose. First, there is the problem of classification, or identification, of what you as a speaker have as your purpose. Suppose, for example, that you want to tell your audience about a strange experience, and you desire to *impress* them with its weird qualities, to make them *feel* the eeriness. You decide that your purpose is *to impress.* Later, your listeners tell you that yours is one of the most *entertaining* talks they have ever heard. Were you wrong in your identification of purpose?

Look at another situation. You have just given a speech on the need for a new traffic signal at an intersection in your neighborhood. Your purpose was *to convince* your listeners of the need; you were not asking for action. After your speech, however, several members approach you, shake your hand, and tell you that you have really *persuaded* them to go after that signal and they start to discuss enthusiastically plans for getting one. Were you wrong in your identification of purpose?

In neither instance were you "wrong" and neither were your listeners. If there is error anywhere, it is in the oversimplified classification of speeches according to purposes, or it is in the assumption that either the speaker's purpose or the effect of his speech upon the listeners can be pigeonholed strictly into one category.

A second difficulty, one which is closely related to the first, is that of overlap in the establishment of purpose. Let's go back to your speech on the traffic signal, the one in which your purpose was *to convince* but which had the effect of being *persuasive.* Suppose your intention had been only to bring *information* to the group about the hazards at the corner because of no signal; but suppose, further, your information was so complete and given with such *feeling* that your listeners responded as if you had tried *to persuade* them. What can we conclude? You may have believed your purpose was only *to inform,* but apparently you had hidden purposes which were stronger; what happened was that unconsciously you brought into your presentation those qualities of appeal which both *convinced* and *persuaded* the group. Thus, you had an overlapping of purposes even though you had thought you had only one.

On the other hand, you can be quite aware of having more than one purpose and can still have difficulty in identifying the main one. For instance, you intend to give a talk on your trip to Mexico, and your material will include the usual what-I-saw, what-I-did, where-I-went, and what-I-felt. Is your purpose *to inform* or is it *to entertain?* As far as you're concerned, it is both, and neither is uppermost in your mind. Your position is a most defensible one. If your teacher, though, insists that you choose one of the two as your major purpose, how can you both be right?

You are right because there is no speech material so pure that it supports only one of the purposes which a speaker may have, and many times several purposes are in evidence. It isn't hard to see, is it, how a talk designed only for entertainment might rely on *information* and *emotional appeal* and would be effective only if it persuaded the listeners to feel what you set out to have them feel?

But your teacher is right, too, for he knows that it is possible for you to designate a major purpose; and, once the designation has been made, it is also possible for you to treat your material in such a way that the major purpose will be emphasized, even if only subtly. The emphasis, which is a focusing of your presentation, sharpens your communication so that you and your audience keep your message in perspective.

ACTIVITIES

1. Start several lists of topics from which you may give future talks. Let one of them be a classified list of Know-Feel-Do areas. For example:

Something I Have Done

a. My Trip to Hawaii
b. Model Ships as a Hobby
c. I'm a Salesman on Saturdays
d. Extra Pennies for Hostessing

Something I Want to Do

a. I Want to Be an Engineer
b. Russia Is My Next Stop
c. How to Train to Be a Diver
d. Harvard for Me!

Something I Know About

a. Important Women in History
b. Secrets of Electricity
c. Famous Dishes from Foreign Lands
d. Chess Champions

Something I Want to Know About

a. Deep-sea Denizens
b. Qualifications for Being an Astronaut
c. What Are the Causes of War?
d. Life on The Galapagos Islands

Something I Feel

a. All Men Must Have Equal Rights
b. Purposeful Work Is a Good Tonic
c. Life in the City Is Exciting
d. Firearms Should Be Purchased through Permits

2. Let the second of your lists be general fields that have been broken down into more specific topics, like the ones discussed and illustrated in the first part of this unit. Try to have several topics listed under each of your general fields.
3. Make up a third list of topics chosen at random from the stimulus of reading, conversing, going to a play or movie, attending a meeting, hearing a lecture, conducting an interview, seeing an event or incident that moves you, or becoming aware of a change in your own feeling and thinking. This list is your source list for the year; it will change and grow as you change and grow. From it you can get material to refine, classify, and add to the other two lists.
4. Make an early determination of your major purpose, as you would see it now, for each of the speech topics that you have listed in the activities above. Whenever you add a topic, also jot down what you *think* your major purpose would be if and when you talk on that topic. You will thus build an attitude of thinking of purposeful speaking, and you will have at hand not only a list of topics but also a record of how you originally thought you might best present them.

Films:

Ways to Better Conversation (Coronet). 11 min color or b&w.
Say What You Mean (MH). 20 min b&w.

Unit Eight

BE A GOOD ORGANIZER: Planning and Outlining

Practically all of man's activities are planned to some degree. Even nature, which appears wild and lawless, is guided by a plan that man is always trying to discover.

Take yourself, for example. You plan parties, excursions, meetings, vacations, your year's courses in school, your wardrobe, the way you will spend the evening, and many, many other aspects of your life. It seems as if you do nothing but plan, although you know this is not true, for both in your own life and in that of your community you may recognize innumerable instances of unplanned or poorly planned activity. Mainly, however, your most successful ventures have been preceded by careful planning.

Speeches Must Be Planned, Too

A good speech plan is a way of directing and focusing your speaking energies. Rain can fall gently over great areas and the water will hardly be noticed, but let rivulets and streams grow into surging rivers, and water becomes a rushing force. When energy is focused and directed, it is powerful. It is your goal as a potential speaker to learn how to focus your speaking energy, and it is your obligation as a citizen to direct this force into desirable ends.

The purpose of this unit is to help you understand the meaning of planning and the relationship between planning and outlining, to identify the major divisions of a speech, and to learn some forms of outlining.

The Meaning of Planning. Perhaps you noticed that *plan* was used above both as a noun and as a verb. As a noun, *plan* means a method of procedure or an arrangement of parts. Often it bears no other name than plan; but sometimes it has, for purposes of particular reference, a more descriptive and limiting name, such as *design, diagram, drawing, scheme, blueprint, sketch, prospectus,* or *outline.* It would seem obvious, then, that *plan* used as a verb would mean *to do* or *to make* any of the objects described by the noun form, which is true, but the truth is somewhat oversimplified. Lying behind that "doing" or "making" is a great amount of complex mental activity.

When an architect sits down at his drawing board and creates a plan for a building, he is creative, logical, critical. His hands do the bidding of his mind, and a plan emerges on the drawing board, one which helps him to visualize the final product—the building. Thus, though his process of planning is primarily a thought process, it is also the recording of those thoughts on paper so that they may be remembered and may be communicated to others. Like the architect, you will find that your planning activity in speech work is a blending of thinking and the recording of your thinking, a process that is more or less continuous during the preparation of a speech, even if it occurs in "fits and starts." Like the architect, too, you will be guided by a "master plan," or major purpose, which you must have clearly in mind.

Some Characteristics of a Good Planner

1. His planning is flexible in that initially he creates many choices.
2. He weighs choices carefully, discarding the weak ones.
3. He makes new choices as new ideas and new information come to him.
4. He places his final choices in effective relationship to each other.
5. He is willing to revise or abandon a plan that turns out poorly.
6. His planning is always controlled by a major purpose.

The Relationship Between Planning and Outlining a Speech. Even though planning a speech is a somewhat continuous process, occurring at various stages of a speech and in various ways and degrees according to the needs of the planner, the establishment of a tentative master plan must occur early in the total development of that speech. This tentative plan may exist only as a mental picture in the mind of the planner, or it may be recorded in some form on paper, usually as a short outline.

Referring to what was said above, you can see that your planning is chiefly mental effort, and your outline is a recording of that effort, a visualization of the thoughts you have chosen to start your speech plan. As your outline develops, it becomes a record of choices that you have examined and kept, a record that you probably would have difficulty in retaining as a mental image. You can now with much greater ease examine the record for its effectiveness as a total effort and for the soundness of its parts. Thus, the outline emerges as a valuable part of planning and as a servant to the planner.

Some Other Values of an Outline

1. It provides for you as a speaker, in its final form, a visual convenience for recall of material to be presented.
2. It provides for both you and your teacher an aid to evaluation of a proposed speech.
3. It becomes a permanent record for you to use in recalling the speech at a later date, for the teacher to use when you present your speech, and, if printed in quantity, for the members of any audience to use to recall the contents of a speech at a later date.

Major Divisions of a Speech. The most basic fact to keep in mind about the composition of a speech is that a speech has a beginning, a middle, and an end. What goes into each of the three parts depends upon a number of factors, but for your immediate purpose some working generalizations will serve.

The beginning, or *introduction,* usually has four parts; or, to put it another way, the speaker has four tasks to perform in the introduction: to catch the attention of the audience, to reveal his purpose in speaking, to show how the topic concerns the audience, and to give some indication of what will be discussed. These ingredients, as separate parts, as combinations, or as implications, are generally regarded as essential in serious, formal speeches; but the speaker must always remain the judge of what material he considers necessary to launch his speech successfully.

The middle, or *body,* of a speech, carries the burden of the speaker's message. It consists of the main points, subdivisions, and supporting detail.

The end, or *conclusion,* will usually include a brief summary of main points, a return to the speaker's purpose, and appropriate closing comments, particularly in a formal speech. Like the introduction, however, it must include only what the speaker believes to be important and effective.

A deviation from the speech composition described above is the organization that is called the "Bull's-Eye" plan in this textbook, a plan which

Senator Everett Dirksen of Illinois, a noted orator, is also adept at presenting his ideas in informal talks.

has five steps. The first two steps might be considered as an introduction, the next two as the body, and the last one as a conclusion, though such an attempt to classify these parts has little to do with the use of the plan. It is a simple but effective plan for short talks, sales talks, informal chats, impromptu talks, or any talk that is not too long and detailed. Its name suggests its nature; it gets directly to the heart of the topic that is being presented.

The five steps of the plan are these:

Step 1. *Wake Up!* This is the opening, the attention-getting device. Arouse interest quickly. Get everyone looking at you and listening to you.

Step 2. *This Concerns You.* In this step you tell your audience why you woke them up. How does the subject fit them? Why are you talking?

Step 3. *Generally Speaking.* State clearly the point you want to make. This general statement is what you hope to prove by *examples*; it is the substance of your message.

Step 4. *For Example.* Give your audience some specific illustrations of your generalization. This step is the heart of your talk, and your examples must be interesting and convincing.

Step 5. *What to Do.* It's time now for the clincher. You should have your audience saying, in effect, "Your idea sounds fine. We agree with you.

So what?" Step 5 should answer that question. You must establish clearly and definitely at this point the line of thinking or the course of action you desire to be taken.

Further reference to the "Bull's-Eye" plan will be made in Unit 10, where development of main points is treated.

The "Bull's-Eye" plan represents a variation in speech planning. There are even variations of the "Bull's-Eye" plan itself. Also, the many logical arrangements of the body of a speech, several of which are presented and discussed in the next unit, may themselves be adapted as overall speech plans. A fact that you must never forget is that there are no rigid rules governing the creation of speeches; there are only general truths that guide you in preparing material for presentation, with a variety of specific ways to observe those truths.

Sometimes successful communication can take place under odd circumstances, when seemingly most principles of good speaking are violated; but in such a case the speaker is probably not an amateur. The suggestions for speaking that are being offered to you, the plans that are illustrated, and the specifics that are found in the pages of speech texts all represent a body of general knowledge that has come to us through centuries of man's experience. You must study this text with that thought in mind, just as you must keep it in mind when you read this statement: *Regardless of the plan used, all good speeches have in common a beginning, a middle, and an end.* Let's turn now to forms of outlining.

Outline Forms. A good speech, like a good piece of expository writing, has a skeletal structure which is related to the whole speech just as the trunk and limbs of a tree are related to the whole tree. This is the skeleton that you create during your planning of a speech; this is the skeleton that has as its parts the major divisions of a speech and the main points and subdivisions of each; this is the skeleton that is your speech outline. But how much of the skeleton should you include in an outline, and how should you label its parts?

As you would expect, there is no certain answer to either question. Need is a determining factor in the decision on what to include, and personal choice, or teacher preference, will dictate your system of labeling.

You may, if you wish, use phrases and single words for the parts of your outline; you may use sentences, following the style generally employed in debate briefs; or you may use a combination of these practices. For example, suppose you were planning a talk on the topic "The Case for the Compact Car" and your first main point concerned economy. With sentence style, your outline might look like this:

A. The chief reason for owning a compact car is economy.
  1. Initial cost is less than for standard-sized cars.
  2. Gasoline consumption is lower, as evidenced in the latest Mobil Economy Run.
  3. Repairs and replacements are cheaper.
  4. Insurance rates are lower.
  5. General upkeep involves less energy and expense because of smaller size.

The same point, with the use of phrases, could be:

A. Economy
  1. Low initial cost
  2. High gas mileage
  3. Inexpensive repairs and replacements
  4. Low insurance rates
  5. Minimum general upkeep

Which of the two styles is better? Only you can answer—in terms of your needs and responsibilities. The first might help you to clarify your thinking and might suit your teacher better as evidence of your planning. The second, however, could serve you well as a reminder during the delivery of your speech, or it could even be the style you like for your initial planning as you explore for possible ideas.

Now, what about the system of labeling? Shall you use the familiar system of Roman and Arabic numbers in combination with capital and small letters? For example:

II. Body
  A. Economy
  B. Maneuverability
    1. Turning radius
    2. Fast steering response
    3. Light weight
      a. Less sway on curves
      b. Advantages in snow, sand, mud, etc.

Or shall you use the newer decimal system, the one in which Arabic numbers serve for all divisions? Each new subdivision is set off by the addition of a decimal point, and the number of items in that subdivision can be as large as you wish. For example:

2. Body

2.1 Economy
2.2 Maneuverability
2.3 Style
  2.3.1 Sports car appeal
  2.3.2 Clean lines
    2.3.2.1. Simple design
    2.3.2.2. Less "brightwork"
  2.3.3 Miniature scale attractiveness

Again you have choice. Neither style has superiority, and you may even combine them, using Roman numerals for major speech divisions and the decimal system for all other divisions. There is an easy-to-use, mathematical precision about the decimal system; but as the subdivisions become smaller, the labeling becomes a little cumbersome. The other system runs out of "pure" labels after the fourth category, and you have to repeat the labels, adding such distinguishing marks as parentheses or single quotation designations. Further, the alphabet contains only twenty-six labels, and such a device as double letters, *aa.*, *bb.*, *cc.*, etc., would have to be employed next. Since your speech outlines may not extend either system to its undesirable features, why not experiment with both?

Another choice concerns the format. Shall you include, and how, the words *introduction, body,* and *conclusion* in your outline?

FORMAT A

Introduction

I.
II.
III.
etc.
} Essentials of introduction

Body

I. First main point
  a. First supporting detail
  b. Second supporting detail, etc.
II. Second main point, etc.
III. etc.

Conclusion

I.
II.
etc.
} Essentials of conclusion

FORMAT B

I. Introduction
  A.
  B.
  C.
  etc.
  } Essentials of introduction
II. Body
  A. First main point
    1. First supporting detail
    2. etc.
  B. Second main point
  etc.
III. Conclusion
  A.
  B.
  etc.
  } Essentials of conclusion

Or shall you omit reference to the major divisions of the outline and treat all of your material as a series of main points? For example, using "The Case for the Compact Car":

FORMAT C

I. The compact car is worth considering.
  A. Everyone is interested in a good buy.
  B. Proper information helps influence people.
  C. Compact cars are economical, maneuverable, stylish, and dependable.
II. Compact cars are economical.
  A. The initial cost is low.
  B. Gas mileage is high.
  C. etc.
III. Compact cars are maneuverable.
IV. Stylish, etc.
V. Dependable, etc.
VI. The compact car seems to be a good buy.
  A. You are invited to check the evidence presented.
  B. Remember that compacts are economical, maneuverable, stylish, and dependable.
  C. Make a compact car your next purchase.

Because even authors must make choices, the form for speech outlines that follows Format B has been chosen arbitrarily as the one which will be used as a teaching device. Future reference to speech organization, in whole or in part, will be in terms of the organization that this outline exemplifies. Note that the Roman numeral-capital letter-Arabic number-small letter system of labeling has also been an arbitrary choice not only in the suggested outline form but also in the examples under FORMAT A, FORMAT B, and FORMAT C.

Suggested Form for Speech Outlines

I. Introduction
  A. Opening: pertinent questions, story, quotation, or other
  B. Revelation of the purpose of the speech
  C. Indication of how the subject will concern the audience
  D. Statement of the main points to be made

II. Body
  A. First main point
    1. First item supporting this point

a. Elaboration of above item
b. Further elaboration

2. Second item
(Repeat as above, where necessary.)

3. Third item
(etc. . . .)

B. Second main point
(Repeat form shown under A.)

C. Third main point
(Repeat form shown above and continue with as many main points as are needed.)

III. Conclusion

A. Summary of main points
B. Return to purpose to remind listeners of central idea or message
C. Closing: impressive statement, question, quotation, story, or some similar device which rounds off the speech effectively

Whether you use the suggested form or one of your own, you may find these comments to have some practical value:

- Any outline form is a guide for general use and will not fit *every* speech situation. Unless you have been instructed to adhere closely to a specific outline form, always feel free to adapt any outline form to *your* needs.
- Be consistent in your use of letters and numbers in your outlining system so that each part of your outline, each division, or each level of subordination is identified always with the same kind of letter or number.
- Be consistent in your use of words, phrases, and sentences to build your outline. If it is an all-sentence outline, use only sentences; if it is an all-phrase outline, use only phrases for the parts; if the main points are all sentences, but the subdivisions are phrases, maintain their use consistently. Even when you are using only single words for parts of your outline, either main points or subdivisions, keep parallel structure by using the same parts of speech for the same kind of points in the outline. For example, if you start with nouns as main points, use nouns for *all* main points, and if your subdivisions can be expressed as adjectives, make all of them adjectives.
- Whether you use words, phrases, or sentences, the first word of each new point and subdivision should be capitalized and each main point and subdivision indented in a consistent manner.
- Frequently evaluate your subdivision material, as you build your outline, to be sure that each item properly supports the larger division of which it is a part.

- No proper outline shows a *single* subdivision under the point which is being supported. If there isn't a minimum of two subdivisions, the one subdivision which you have created is actually a part of the point it is pretending to support.
- Unless you are participating in a speech contest, preparing script for a radio or TV show, or writing a speech that is supposed to be read, *don't* write your speeches out! Use your outline, instead. Writing speeches in final form leads to memory work, a crutch that speakers must throw away as soon as possible. It is, however, not only permissible but also desirable to write out and memorize the opening and closing parts of your speech. This much memory work will assure you of a smooth beginning and effective ending. Include the portions to be memorized in your outline.
- You will find that a short form of the suggested outline can be a very useful part of your preliminary planning for a talk and helpful as a reminder of your main points when you are making a presentation. Here is an example of how it might appear:

The Game of Chess

I. Introduction (a statement which will capture the idea you wish to open with, or, if you prefer, a writing out of your opening remarks)

II. Body

A. Origin of the game
B. How it is played
C. Its value or importance

III. Conclusion (a statement which indicates the thought which you want to use in closing, or, as in the introduction, a writing out of all of the closing remarks)

ACTIVITIES

1. Organize the following scattered points into the short outline form suggested above. Use whatever labeling system you choose.

   a. *Last Saturday's Football Game*

   (1) The game itself
   (2) The crowd
   (3) Preparing to go to the game
   (4) Celebrating later
   (5) Outstanding players

   b. *Nuclear Bombs*

   (1) How they explode
   (2) The need to understand nuclear bombs
   (3) How they are made
   (4) Their power of destruction
   (5) Present types
   (6) A look into the future

c. *Rocketry*

(1) The importance of discussing rockets
(2) Summary of important points
(3) The latest experiments
(4) Notable types in our present arsenal
(5) Its origin

2. Rearrange the following points into a Format B outline. The introduction and conclusion will have three points each and the body four.

a. There is an abundance of social life at the beach.
b. A vacation at the beach need not involve major expenditures.
c. III. Conclusion.
d. To convince audience that a beach is the best place for a summer vacation.
e. Summary of the main points of the body.
f. Open with a beachcomber story.
g. II. Body
h. Remind listeners that your purpose is to get them to a beach when summer comes.
i. I. Introduction.
j. End with some device. For example, "Where else can you get so much for so little? Come join me at the beach!"
k. There are personal satisfactions in terms of feeling healthy, vital, and suntanned.
l. The beach offers a variety of recreational activities.
m. Indicate main points: variety of recreational activities, good social life, rewards in terms of health and appearance, moderate expense.

3. Go back to one of the short outlines which you organized in Activity 1 and develop it to the same extent that the outline in Activity 2 has been developed.

4. Select a speech from a collection of famous speeches, study it carefully, and outline it, using the suggested outline in this unit. Some sources are:

American Public Addresses, by A. C. BAIRD. McGraw-Hill.
Representative American Speeches, by A. C. BAIRD. Wilson.
Representative American Speeches, by L. THONSSEN. Wilson.
Selected American Speeches on Basic Issues, by C. G. BRANDT and E. M. SHAFTER, JR. Houghton Mifflin.
Treasury of the World's Great Speeches, by H. PETERSON. Simon and Schuster.
World's Great Speeches, by L. COPELAND. Dover Publications.

5. Think of a general truth you would like to observe in relation to one of the following personalities, and make an outline of a "Bull's-Eye" plan for a talk.

Madame Marie Curie
George Washington Carver
Dwight D. Eisenhower
Winston Churchill
Eleanor Roosevelt
Lyndon B. Johnson
Martin Luther King
George Bernard Shaw
Michelangelo

Films:

Building an Outline (Coronet). 11 min color or b&w.
Planning Your Talk (MH). 13 min b&w.

Filmstrip:

How to Prepare a Speech (SVE). 40 fr b&w.

Unit Nine

GATHER MATERIAL: Research and Selection

Your most perplexing problem, after you've decided what to talk about, will be, "Where, oh, where, can I find any material on this subject?" The most obvious source is books. Your first impulse, after you've been assigned a subject or have chosen one independently, will be to dash to the library and hunt frantically for a book or magazine that will give you "ammunition." But wait a minute. Take it easy. Think! Ask yourself a question first.

What Am I Looking For?

The kind of material that makes speeches interesting, lively, challenging, and convincing is that which is concrete and which comes within the experience of your listeners. Another unit has already pointed out to you how many things can distract a listener's attention. Armed with this knowledge, you should plan to look for the kind of speech material which can help to overcome such distractions. That material must be concrete, vivid, familiar, alive, and challenging. Build up a reserve supply of details, examples, facts, stories, incidents, descriptions, comparisons, quotations, pictures, charts, drawings, and samples which you can use to support abstract ideas or general statements. Every talk should be packed with these items, some of which will be explained here.

Looking for Facts. A fact is anything which is true or which has existence. Facts form the foundation of every speech. If they are new and unusual, they are particularly fascinating to people. They arouse immediate curiosity and stimulate interest. Here are some samples of facts which can be found in newspapers, dictionaries, almanacs, encyclopedias, pamphlets, magazines, books, newsreels, radio and TV talks, and conversation. They can be used as the basis of a talk, or they can serve as illustrations for a talk.

Four popular kinds of cameras are the box, the folding pocket type, the twin-lens, and the 35mm. miniature.

The *Nautilus* was the world's first atomic-powered submarine.

John F. Kennedy, the thirty-fifth President of the United States, was assassinated on November 22, 1963.

The deepest place yet found in the ocean is off the island of Mindanao in the Philippines group, where the recorded depth is 35,400 feet.

Salvador Dali, a Spanish artist, is noted for his surrealistic painting.

The average sixteen-year-old girl needs 2250 to 2800 calories per day in a properly balanced diet.

Herman Melville's most famous book is *Moby Dick*, a novel which relates the conflict between the master of a whaling ship and a great white whale.

The Surgeon General's Advisory Committee on Smoking and Health reported that cigarettes are a major cause of lung cancer and chronic bronchitis.

It has been said that an educated man is one who knows where to find what he does not know. How well educated are you? Suppose you are preparing a talk on the steel industry and you need some facts about the amount of iron ore mined in the United States. Where will you look? The most logical place is the *World Almanac,* since it is the best book on specific facts in its field. If you want facts about the policies of our present Secretary of State, try the *Statesman's Yearbook* or the *International Yearbook.* How many people live in your own community? Why not ask your Chamber of Commerce? Are you having a hot argument over the latest political fight in Congress? Newspapers, magazines, the *Congressional Record,* the *Congressional Digest,* or the *United States Daily* ought to give you some ammunition. Do parents think this generation is spoiled and undisciplined? Ask your mother and father. Yes, possible sources of material are almost endless. It's up to you to be a good ferret and dig out useful material.

Looking for Illustrations or Examples. Any details, instances, stories, descriptions, quotations, comparisons, or samples which throw light on a statement, helping to make it clearer and more easily understood, are called illustrations. There is no more important kind of speech material than this. As soon as you say, "For instance . . ." or "Here's an example of what I mean . . ." or "Let me illustrate . . .," people prick up their ears and give better attention. Illustrations are pictures in words. An idea that may seem vague, abstract, or too general to a listener can be translated into familiar terms which he can immediately understand and appreciate, merely by the the use of specific details and concrete examples. In the following samples notice how a single general statement is made vivid and meaningful by illustrations:

The old adage "Haste makes waste" was proved to be true in our family last Monday. We all got up late that morning, thus throwing the whole household into an uproar. Mother tried to hurry breakfast and overcooked three eggs and burned four pieces of toast. Dad tried to hurry while shaving and cut a neat nick in his chin. I tried to hurry downstairs, slipped on the bottom step, and crashed into the hall table. It now has a beauty of a scratch. I drove the car out of the garage for Dad in a hurry and scraped the right front fender. Dad called up later that morning to tell Mother that in his hurry to get to the office he had forgotten his briefcase. The whole morning was upset for everyone, all because we tried to hurry.

Men of strong will and personality dominated the scene during the second World War. There was Winston Churchill, the indomitable and highly articulate Prime Minister of England. There was Benito Mussolini, dissolute, iron-jawed braggart. There was Joseph Stalin, enigmatic master of 190,000,000 Russians. There was Adolf Hitler, half mad with dreams of power. There was the remote Chiang Kai-shek, revolutionary leader of China's millions. And there was our own preeminent chief, Franklin Roosevelt.

Gypsum is one of the world's most versatile materials. It was first used by the Egyptians over four thousand years ago as a wall plaster, and it is still used in more than 90 percent of all present-day plastering. In addition, it can be used for fertilizer, for fireproof building board, for casts to correct broken bones, for cement, crayons, matches, paper, and glass, and for casting metal parts for precision instruments. It has literally hundreds of uses.

Looking for Quotations. Statements or testimony from authoritative and reliable sources can also be forceful in a speech. Many times a quotation from someone important or well known can serve the purpose of adding weight to what you say. The theme of a paragraph or of an entire speech can often be summed up in the expressive words of someone else. For instance, suppose you want to establish the point that careful attention to small details may often make the difference between the success or failure of a project. You could use the following quotation to give strength to your statement. It is well known, authoritative, and interesting. Benjamin Franklin wrote it in *Poor Richard's Almanac.*

> A little neglect may breed mischief:
> for want of a nail the shoe was lost;
> for want of a shoe the horse was lost;
> for want of a horse the rider was lost.

Make a practice of collecting apt quotations; you will find them very useful in speaking.

Looking for Statistics. Facts which have been classified and compiled into significant figures are known as statistics. They often prove a point better than other material will, but you must be sure that they are accurate, easily understood, appropriate, and interesting. Don't bore people with a long string of figures. Whenever possible, translate statistics into comparative terms which your listeners can understand and remember. For instance, in describing Hoover Dam, you might say something like the following:

Hoover Dam, formerly known as Boulder Dam, is the tallest concrete dam in the world. It is 726 feet high, or as tall as a 55-story office building. It contains over three million cubic yards of concrete, enough to build foundations for 100,000 average-sized houses. Its reservoir, Lake Mead, the largest artificial lake in the world, is over 115 miles long, a distance greater than that between New York City and Philadelphia.

Looking for Anecdotes. A little story always attracts a listener's attention. People especially like to hear stories that have a human-interest appeal. Stories need not always be humorous, although a joke which has a good point, which fits into what you're saying, and which is well told helps to lighten a speech. Nothing is worse, however, than a badly told anecdote that has, at best, a poor relationship to the speech. Unless you are a good storyteller, handle anecdotes cautiously and stick to those stories that appeal to people's interests. Here is an ancedote that could be used to make a light reference to what has happened to many people when they have spoken before an audience.

A little girl in grammar school got up to deliver her first speech. The occasion was Washington's birthday. "Washington is dead–," she began, and then paused nervously. "Washington is dead–," she said again, and faltered once more. There was a painful silence while she tried to remember what came next. Then gathering herself for a final effort, she said doggedly, "Washington is dead–and I don't feel very well myself!"

Looking for Incidents. The description of an event, occurrence, or experience involving other people always interests an audience. Reference to your own experiences is also good if not too lengthy. Again it's human-interest material that catches attention and keeps a listener interested. Look for incidents that are dramatic and unusual, yet related to people's experiences. The following incident could be used to point out the dangers that lurk in what seem to be harmless war souvenirs.

When Bill Jackson returned from overseas service, he brought home two war trophies that he prized highly. One was a fountain pen that had been given him by a German soldier, and the other was the warhead of a sixty-millimeter shell that Bill thought would make an excellent paperweight for his brother's desk. Bill's buddies had said that both were safe, that the warhead had been deactivated, and that a fountain pen was bound to be harmless. But when Bill tried to take his pen apart one afternoon to clean it, it exploded in his hands; and Bill, who had escaped injury all through the war, lost three fingers. Bill's family then became suspicious of the warhead paperweight and sent it, wisely, to an Army ordnance expert for examination. The expert's report revealed that the "harmless" paperweight had an explosive charge in it sufficient to kill several people.

Looking for Analogies. Comparisons, or analogies, add color to what you say at the same time that they make meaning clearer. Often you can create lasting impressions by means of vivid comparisons, showing the similarities between two objects or ideas. Some of the simplest analogies that we use almost unconsciously in everyday talk are the figures of speech called *metaphors* and *similes*.

A metaphor is an implied comparison, like the following:

The audience suffered under his barrage of words.
He snaked his way through the tall grass.
She pecked aimlessly at her food.

Your talk on Yosemite might begin with an overview and then close up on a wonder such as Bridalveil Falls.

A simile is a directly expressed comparison. Here are some examples:

Her voice was smooth and like honey.
A speech is like a bridge between the mind of the speaker and his audience.
His smile was like a benediction.
The old lady was as fretful as a sick child.

Analogies also can be more extended than the simple figures of speech mentioned above. Pointing out similarities at greater length helps listeners to see the main idea of the comparison more clearly. For instance, notice the following effective comparisons:

I'm going to plan my next speech the way Dad planned our summer trip to Yosemite Valley. We drove in by the way of Oak Flat Road. When we passed El Capitan Ranger Station, Dad stopped the car and said, "See, there's the valley below us. There's the Merced River; we can have a picnic there later. Over there is Bridalveil Falls; we'll take a close look at it tomorrow. And around the bend of those cliffs is Camp Curry; we'll watch the fire-fall from there tonight." That was our introduction to the valley and that's going to be the way I shall begin my speech. I'll mention what I'm going to talk about, list the main points, and indicate what they will include. Then in the body of my talk I can develop those points, giving the audience a close look at them, the way we saw the river, the falls, and the camp at close range after we dropped down into the valley. For a conclusion, I'll review my main points for my listeners from a different angle, the way Dad did when we left Yosemite by the Wawona road. He stopped at Inspiration Point on the way out to give us a last look. "There she is, boys," he said, "one of the great scenic wonders of the world. There aren't many places where you can see such lofty cliffs, so many high waterfalls, or such picturesque views as right here. Take a good look; we probably won't be back for a long time."

Looking for Epigrams. Bright or witty sayings can summarize a general idea so that its point is brought home effectively to the audience. Adages, proverbs, maxims, and popular sayings are all more or less the same as epigrams. They are usually skillfully and tersely expressed so that a whole thought is condensed into a few words, and they usually depend on clever wording for their full effect. Here are some typical examples. You can collect even better ones.

If you have too many irons in the fire, some of them will cool.
Everything happens to everybody sooner or later, if there is time enough.
Birds of a feather flock together.
In this world nothing is certain but death and taxes.
A friend is one who knows all about you and loves you just the same.
Every man is as Heaven made him, and sometimes a great deal worse.
A closed mouth catches no flies.
You're leaping over the hedge before you come to the stile.
You cannot put the same shoe on every foot.
In the night all cats are gray.

Looking for Visual Material. Charts, drawings, photographs, samples, or demonstrations always help an audience to *see* what you mean. This kind of material speaks a language all its own, the language of the eye, and it appeals to almost everyone, since most people agree with the adage "Seeing is believing." Be sure that your visual material is large enough to be seen by everyone, that it is appropriate, that it is simple enough to be easily understood, and that it is handled skillfully And take care that the attention of your listeners does not shift *permanently* to the chart, drawing, or object you are displaying. The audience should listen as well as look. Suggestions for using visual items may be found in Appendix A of this book.

Gathering material like what has been discussed here is one of the most important tasks you'll have to perform. Facts, examples, quotations, statistics, stories, incidents, analogies, epigrams, and visual items constitute what are called specific details. They help you to clarify, support, and illuminate your general ideas, and they help the audience to understand, believe, and remember what you say. Keep looking for them.

Where Can I Find It?

"But where can I find all this material?" you may ask. "In books? In magazines?" Yes, but wait again. Start with yourself first. Take time to analyze what you already know, and plan ways of expanding that knowledge. This takes patience, but it will repay you. Here are five answers to the question raised by this paragraph:

1. *Think.* The first step is to ask yourself what you have experienced and what ideas you have on the subject you're going to talk about. You may be surprised at the amount of random information you have. It may be unreliable and may need confirmation, but at least it is *your own* and will have the personal touch that comes from you alone. *Jot it down!*
2. *Observe.* Most people learn by watching. Incidents are always happening which, if you note them carefully, can be used in a speech. You can store up facts, impressions, attitudes, feelings, and reactions by watching closely the world about you. Speech material will not come to you; it must be hunted. Look, watch, observe. And when you see something that has a connection with your speech subject, *jot it down!*
3. *Talk.* Good conversation is a gold mine of speech material. One of the most interesting and profitable adventures you can have is to explore the thoughts of other people. Learn to talk to other people and to ask intelligent questions. You will gather information and material which will help you in many ways. *Jot it down!*

Among the many offerings of a library is a pleasant invitation to browse.

4. *Experience.* Actual experiences are always fresh and interesting. People like to talk about their own experiences and to hear about those of others. Your own interests, hobbies, and adventures make good speech material; use them. If you have a subject with which you have had no firsthand experience, think about it, read about it, talk about it all the more. And *jot it down!*
5. *Read.* At last you come to reading material. After you have thought, observed, talked, and experienced what you can about your subject, you'll be ready to read. And whatever you read in relation to your subject, *jot it down!*

"Reading Maketh a Full Man"

Reading is the last answer to the question "Where can I find it?" and offers you perhaps the fullest source of speech "ammunition." Because our knowledge and experience are limited, we all probably turn more readily to reading as a means of getting information than to any other method. We can get not only facts, but also opinions, arguments, and inspiration from our reading. As a potential speaker you should recognize the value of reading, you should develop the habit of browsing in the library, and, above all, you should become familiar with some of the standard reference sources which will be useful to you. Here are some of them:

Newspapers. Get the newspaper-reading habit and keep up with what's happening in the world. Some of the most reliable sources of news are *The New York Times, The Atlanta Constitution, The Washington Post,* the *St. Louis Post-Dispatch, The Christian Science Monitor,* and *The Observer* and *The Manchester Guardian,* English papers. Your local papers that have good coverage of news, reputable correspondents, and an intelligent editorial policy are the ones which can help you a great deal, too. Don't judge a newspaper by its comic section and sports coverage alone. Become acquainted with the editorial page; that's where you'll find the most valuable ideas and opinions.

Magazines. You can't be expected to read all the magazines that are published, but you should be familiar with at least one good weekly and perhaps two or three monthly ones. Investigate what your library has and make a regular habit of reading some of them. Here are a few:

The Atlantic Monthly
Aviation
Business Week
Catholic World
Changing Times
The Christian Century
The Commonweal
Current History
Fortune
Harper's Magazine
Holiday
Life
Look
The Nation
Nation's Business
The National Geographic Magazine
Natural History
The New Republic
The New Yorker
Newsweek
Poetry
Popular Science Monthly
The Reader's Digest
The Saturday Review
Scholastic
Scientific American
Sports Illustrated
Theatre Arts
Time
Today's Health
Travel
U. S. News & World Report
Vital Speeches

If you're looking for articles on some particular subject see the *Readers' Guide to Periodical Literature.* It offers you a classified list of subjects under which are listed all the articles on that topic that can be found in standard magazines. It gives you the title and author of the article, the name of the magazine, the number and the date of the issue, and the page on which the article may be found. For instance, if you look up the topic *Atomic Power* in the *Readers' Guide,* you'll find references like this:

Atom blasts for research. Sci N L 79:374 Je 17 '61

The above reference means that an article entitled "Atom Blasts for Research" will be found in *Science News Letter,* Volume 79, page 374, issued June 17, 1961. Other references concerning atomic power might look like this:

Atom power two decades old. A. Ewing il Sci N L 82:322–3 N 17 '62
Atom runs a chemical plant. il Bsns W p 144+ N 17 '62
Atomic anniversary. Commonweal 77:305–6 D 14 '62
Atomic energy: new peaceful uses. P. Fozzy il Bul Atomic Sci 18:42–4 Ja '62
Atomic power: the long view. Sci Am 204:82+ Mr '61

It will be to your advantage to learn to use the *Readers' Guide* efficiently. Consult copies from past years, not just the current ones; learn what the abbreviations and symbols mean; find out what periodicals your library has so that you won't waste time looking for magazines that are not available; always list more articles than you intend to consult, since very often you'll find that some articles whose titles sound interesting are actually of little use to you. You may sometimes be impatient in searching for suitable material, but in the long run you'll find the *Readers' Guide* to be a helpful timesaver.

Pamphlets and Bulletins. Much interesting material on a variety of subjects may be found in the bound pamphlets put out by corporations, large business organizations, and city, state, or national departments. All libraries have some material of this sort. If your city or country library doesn't have exactly what you want, look for a catalogue or index of bulletins or pamphlets and send directly for what you need. The cost is usually trivial. Here are a few sources:

1. Government bulletins cover a very wide range of topics, including such subjects as forestry, taxation, infant care, soil culture, nutrition, control of insects, and raising crops. They can be obtained from Washington, D. C., by writing to such departments as the United States Department of Agriculture, Office of Education, Bureau of Labor Statistics, Department of the Interior, and others.
2. For material on topics of state interest, write to the Departments of Education, Agriculture, Motor Vehicles, Health, or similar ones at your state capital. Your local or state Chamber of Commerce also offers pamphlets that may be useful.
3. Among miscellaneous bulletins that discuss social, economic, and political problems, the following are well known:

Public Affairs Pamphlets. Public Affairs Committee, Inc., New York, N. Y.
Foreign Policy Reports and Foreign Policy Bulletins. Information Department, Foreign Policy Association, New York, N. Y.
Congressional Quarterly Reports, Congressional Quarterly, Inc., Washington, D. C.
Freedom Agenda, Carrie Chapman Catt Memorial Fund, Inc., New York, N. Y.

4. Pamphlets that give special information in limited fields can be obtained from numerous other sources, such as automobile manufacturers, steel companies, glass manufacturers, utility companies, national foundations, life insurance companies, farm implement manufacturers, bus, railway, airline, and steamship companies, and many others. If you need special pamphlets that your library does not have, write for them.

Books. Books are generally the best source of information to which you can go. When you're looking for material for a speech, a panel discussion, a term paper, or a debate, you'll invariably want to rush to the library for a book that deals with your subject. It would take too much space here to list all the good reference books that are available in most libraries. You'll have to find out for yourself what your school, city, or county library offers. However, a few suggestions may be helpful to you. Consider those that are made here under the following questions:

1. Are you looking for general facts and statistics? Try the *Encyclopaedia Britannica, Encyclopedia Americana, Lincoln Library of Essential Information, Collier's Encyclopedia, Columbia Encyclopedia,* or *The World Book Encyclopedia.* Books that are published annually, such as the *Britannica Book of the Year, The World Almanac and Book of Facts, Statesman's Yearbook, Statistical Abstract of the United States,* and *Information Please, Almanac,* will give you current facts and figures.

2. Are you looking for biographical sketches? Consider books like the *Dictionary of American Biography, Dictionary of National Biography, Who's Who* (British), *Who's Who in America,* and *The New International Yearbook.* Consult the card catalog in your library for complete biographies of important people.

3. Are you looking for controversial material on social, economic, or political topics? The pros and cons of many arguments can be found in books like the *Debate and Discussion Handbooks,* published by the National University Extension Association, *Reference Shelf, University Debaters' Annual,* and *Intercollegiate Debates,* as well as in periodicals like *Congressional Digest, Annals of the American Academy of Political and Social Science, Daedalus: Journal of the American Academy of Arts and Sciences,* and *Current History.*

4. Are you looking for an elusive quotation or an appropriate anecdote? Look in books like these:

Familiar Quotations, by John Bartlett. Little, Brown.
The Home Book of Quotations, by Burton E. Stevenson. Dodd, Mead.

The Home Book of Proverbs, Maxims, and Familiar Phrases, by BURTON E. STEVENSON. Macmillan.

Hoyt's New Cyclopedia of Practical Quotations, by KATE L. ROBERTS. Funk & Wagnalls.

Dictionary of Thoughts (Revised), by TRYON EDWARDS. Classic.

The Public Speaker's Treasure Chest, by HERBERT PROCHNOW. Harper.

When It's Laughter You're After, by STEWART HARRAL. University of Oklahoma Press.

The books which have been mentioned above are, of course, only reference books. You will use them when you are looking for specific information. But the world of books is large, indeed, and your exploration in it should bring you more than just information. Make it a habit to read many books of all kinds: novels, short stories, poems, biographies, histories, plays, travel books, essays, speeches, and books about religion, philosophy, science, politics, economics, and social problems. They will help your mind to grow, will widen your knowledge and your interests, and will help you to build up a stockpile of ideas that will serve you well throughout your life.

A student who takes notes preserves the best of his reading. In the process he becomes a more careful, critical reader.

Where Can I Keep It?

Have you ever misplaced anything? Have you ever searched frantically for a lost book or telephone number or letter or something you read last week that you really wanted to keep but didn't take time to put away properly? Remember the old saying, "A place for everything and everything in its place"? It all applies here. After you have searched for and found suitable material for your speeches, you should stow it away carefully so that you'll be able to find it when you want it again.

Keeping a notebook or file of speech material is almost a *must,* for it is essential that you keep a record or classification of good items for use in the future. Your storehouse will then always be filled, and you will have insurance against failure of memory. Our memories simply aren't reliable. The facts of today will slip the mind tomorrow. About one-half of what your mind takes in is forgotten within a half-hour; three-fourths is forgotten within a week; four-fifths within a month. As you progress in speech training, your experience will prove that a notebook or file of some sort is indispensable.

Most students prefer keeping a notebook, one that is small, loose-leaf, and easily carried. You can divide it into sections where you can stow away facts, arguments, reasoning, unusual thoughts, statistics, quotations, clever sayings, jokes, anecdotes, illustrations, figures of speech—anything which may be of use to you in later speech work.

Some students prefer a card index, or file. Its advantage over a notebook is that classification is simpler and finding material is quicker. A few people use Manila folders or large envelopes for keeping newspaper clippings, diagrams, pictures, drawings, charts, or other visual material not easily kept on cards or in a notebook. Still another method is the use of a scrapbook. It doesn't matter very much which method you use so long as you find some helpful way to keep speech material. Abraham Lincoln used to jot down facts, stories, and sentences on scraps of paper and stow them away in his tall black hat. The whole point is simply this: when you find something worth remembering: *Jot it down* and *stow it away.*

Taking Notes. Keeping material is one thing; taking notes from material is another. An orderly system of note-taking will help you to recall what you've read and to organize your material. These notes are not to be confused with the hand notes you may want to use as you're delivering a speech. Those hand notes represent a brief outline of your talk; these are summaries of what you've read and are to be used in the building of your speech. Write your notes on stiff 3″ × 5″ or 4″ × 6″ cards. A good system to follow is described here:

1. At the top of the card write the identifying phrase, topic, question, problem, or issue.
2. Center your notation, which should consist of a quotation, a summary in your own words, or a brief statement of fact relating to the topic.
3. Write direct quotations accurately, using the exact words and proper punctuation.
4. In making formal reference notes that will later be sorted, organized, and worked into formal speeches or term papers, take full notes and identify complete sources.
5. In making informal reference notes for simple talks, use abbreviations, shorthand, or any useful but readable shortcuts.
6. At the bottom of the card, place the reference: the author's name, specific source (book or magazine), publisher, date, and page. Include brief facts about the author if needed for authoritative proof.

Sample Quotation Card

Status symbols: color

"The Color Research Institute of Chicago has found . . . that people in the higher classes (higher income and higher education) favor muted and delicate colors, whereas the lower classes like their colors in brilliant hues and large doses. They particularly like the warm, bold reds and orange reds."

Vance Packard,
The Status Seekers, p. 72
David McKay Co., N.Y., 1959
(A.B.; M.A.; Associate Member of American Sociological Society)

Sample Note Card

Peaceful use of atomic energy

Project Plowshare: an account of the success of the AEC experimental program to determine feasibility of digging canals by nuclear explosion. Experiments listed; conclusions given.

Time, Jan. 31, 1964, p. 36

Deciding what material to put on your note cards depends, of course, on the aim of your speech. As you read and think about your subject, the controlling purpose guiding you in selecting material should be based on the answers to questions like these: What am I trying to accomplish? How does this material serve my purpose? Does this item fit into my plan? Answering such questions involves your logical sense and requires some mental discipline. If you're persistent and patient in "keeping your eye on the ball," you'll learn to eliminate irrelevant items and take notes only on such material as furthers and strengthens your purpose. Remember these additional suggestions:

1. Read your material critically, taking time to think about it before putting it into note form.
2. Don't take notes sentence by sentence. You'll bog down in too much useless detail.
3. Look for the large unit of thought, the "big" idea or the central point of a paragraph, chapter, or article. Condense it in your own words.
4. Look, too, for factual supporting material, like dates, names, statistics, examples, and illustrations that strengthen the main points.
5. Limit each card to a single item. You'll avoid clutter and confusion of ideas and make it easier to sort and arrange your note cards when organizing your material later.

The importance of building a reservoir of material will become evident to you every time you give a talk, write a paper, or make a report. You already know from experience that when assignments are made, your first concerns are, What shall I write or talk about? and Where can I find some material? You'll find that a private storehouse of interesting ideas and unusual items is a great help. It's never too late to start a collection for yourself. You might begin now to browse around in your school or town library or among the books and magazines that you have at home to look for ideas, facts, quotations, stories, diagrams, jokes, verses, pictures, examples, figures of speech, analogies, well-worded phrases, or exceptional thoughts. You'll soon have a sizeable collection, and your mind will be enriched in the process. So begin now. Don't wait.

ACTIVITIES

1. Test your own ability in finding material by answering the following questions, giving the facts and the sources:
   - **a.** What is the present United States government debt?
   - **b.** How do you pronounce the name of the man who founded our public library system—Andrew Carnegie?
   - **c.** About how many thunderstorms occur daily on the earth?

d. How many people were killed or injured in automobile accidents in the United States last year?
e. What is the March of Dimes, and how did it start?
f. What is the average seasonal rainfall in your community?
g. Who was James Audubon, and for what is he best known?
h. What is the fastest speed that man has traveled in the air?
i. What was Pickett's Charge at the Battle of Gettysburg?
j. How many high schools are there in your state?

2. Choose one of the following general statements and support it with as many specific illustrations, examples, and facts as you can find:

    Abraham Lincoln had a great fund of humorous stories.
    There have been several changes in car models this year.
    There have been great achievements in space exploration since 1960.
    I had a wonderful vacation last summer.
    Smog is caused by many factors.
    Skin diving requires special equipment.
    There were many outstanding performances at the 1964 Olympic Games.
    Oceanography is an increasingly important science.

3. Explain how the following quotations might be used as the theme of a speech or as the illustration of a point:

    "The best way to have a friend is to be one."
    "No man is an island, entire of itself."
    "The family is the best place to learn human relations."
    "Any man's death diminishes me because I am involved in mankind."
    "A house divided against itself cannot stand."
    "Man does not live by bread alone."
    "Generalities are the refuge of weak minds."

4. Start a classified list of quotations for your notebook or for a filing box if you keep one. These should be related to several general topics in which you're interested or on which you might be giving talks during the term.
5. Make the following statistics more vivid by adding additional explanations which will help to translate the cold facts and figures into terms that are closely allied to the experiences and interests of the average person.
    a. The New York World's Fair of 1964 housed more than 175 pavilions on 646 acres. A million cubic yards of dirt were moved, and 50 miles of pipe plus 500 miles of cable were laid underground for utilities.
    b. There were 40.2 million pupils enrolled in the U. S. public elementary and secondary schools in 1963.
    c. During the seventeen-day period the Berlin Wall was opened for holiday visitors in December, 1963, a total of 1,240,000 people passed through to East Berlin.
    d. The Golden Gate Bridge in San Francisco has a span of 4200 feet.
    e. Within two months after John F. Kennedy's death, his widow had received 700,000 messages of sympathy. The peak volume of mail was 50,000 pieces in one day.
    f. About 5 per cent of the labor force in the U. S. is unemployed.

6. Turn to some recent newspapers or magazines and read through several stories in which there is an abundance of factual material. Newsmen are conscious of the need for translating statistical data into round figures. Find examples of clever use of statistics and bring them to class for examination.
7. Support the following statements with specific facts, examples, or explanations:
   a. These, I feel, were the outstanding features of the New York World's Fair.
   b. Of all our national parks, these two seem to me to be outstanding.
   c. The warning signals in the event of an enemy attack should be understood by all of us.
   d. The Federal government's debt in 1964 totaled about 309 billion dollars. Do you realize what this means?
   e. San Francisco offers the visitor several unusual attractions.
8. Find a clever anecdote and tell it to the class, explaining how it might be used in a speech. *The Reader's Digest* is a good source.
9. Start a class collection of stories that may be useful throughout the term. Contribute to the class file by bringing at least three anecdotes. Classify them under such general headings as Public Speaking, Sports, Movies, Newspapers, Shyness, Nervousness, Doctors, School, and Teachers.
10. Answer these questions:
    a. What books containing anecdotes and jokes are available in your school library for ready reference?
    b. What magazines have you found to be good sources for anecdotes?
    c. From what other sources besides books and magazines might you be able to get some anecdotes?
11. Recollect a number of dramatic incidents that have happened to you. Choose one of these and relate it to your class. The incident should have a dramatic value, human-interest appeal, and a significant point or moral.
12. Relate to the class some experience of a friend of yours that fulfills the same requirements mentioned in the above activity.
13. Look through magazines like *Time* or *The Reader's Digest* and find some unusual incidents involving personalities in the news which you can relate to the class.
14. Find an interesting simile, metaphor, or extended analogy to read and explain to the class. Your best sources may be famous speeches of the past, literary selections, poems, editorials, or even advertisements.
15. Using one of the following as an opening sentence, write a short paragraph which is an expansion of the idea contained in it.
    a. The weather was as changeable as the whims of a small child.
    b. Overconfidence is a trap for the unwary.
    c. Men who think in advance of their times are like shepherds who lead the flock: they must fight the wolf.
    d. Planning a speech is like building a house from foundation to roof.
    e. To some people life is a perilous journey; to others it is a gay adventure.
16. Select an epigram from this unit and develop the idea it contains in a short paragraph of your own. Then read it to the class for criticism.
17. Choose one of the following five sayings and use it as the theme or central idea of a one-minute talk. Develop your theme carefully and shrewdly without

mentioning the particular saying you're illustrating. When you've finished, let the class guess the one on which your talk was based.

a. Hitch your wagon to a star.
b. First things should come first.
c. What's sauce for the goose is sauce for the gander.
d. He was between the frying pan and the fire.
e. A bird in the hand is worth two in the bush.

18. Turn to Bartlett's *Familiar Quotations* or some similar reference book and thumb through it casually, selecting what you consider to be five good epigrams. Read them to the class, and show how you think they might be useful in some future talk.

19. Bring a chart, a drawing, a photograph, a cartoon, or a simple article to class and explain it briefly to your classmates. Later, hold a class discussion on how well the visual material was handled.

20. Prepare and deliver a two-minute talk in which you demonstrate how to *make* something or how to *do* something. Use at least one kind of visual material in your brief talk—for instance, a diagram on the chalkboard, a picture from a magazine, or an object you can display. If, for example, your talk is on the topic "I'm Making a Coffee Table," you could show a picture of the table, a diagram showing a detailed section of the table, or a piece of the wood you are using. Here are some suitable topics:

Playing Golf	Making Costume Jewelry
Leathercraft	Cutting Dress Patterns
Baking Cookies	The Game of Badminton
Woodcarving	Making Christmas Cards
Football Plays	Repairing a Broken Lock

21. Explain fully the meaning of every item in the following references taken from the *Readers' Guide.*

a. Building a new boat. W. T. Snaith il Yachting 114:42–5+ Ag '63 (to be cont)
b. Secret weapons save the Yanks. R. Creamer. il Sports Illus 19:12–15 Ag 5 '63
c. How to choose the right diet. W. Bar-Illan bibliog il Sci Digest 54:32–8 Ag '63
d. Spending into trouble; with editorial comment. D. D. Eisenhower Sat Eve Post 236:15–19, 82 My 18 '63; Same abr. with title We are spending ourselves into trouble; without editorial comment. Read Digest 83:60–8 Jl '63
e. NATO's nuclear dilemma. H. A. Kissinger il Reporter 28:22–33+ Mr 28 '63; Discussion. 28:6+ Ap 25; 8+ My 9 '63

22. Using any book, magazine, or pamphlet for your source, find some material to put on two note cards: (1) a direct quotation; (2) a brief summary in your own words of an interesting topic or item. Follow the sample forms given in this unit.

23. Bring to class an example of what you think is an unusually striking bit of illustrative speech material. It may be a fact, an illustration, a quotation, an anecdote, an incident, an analogy, or an epigram. Read it to the class and explain how you think it could be used in a speech. You'll find good "ammunition" in books like the following:

A Subtreasury of American Humor, by E. B. and K. S. WHITE. Coward–McCann.
Try and Stop Me, by BENNETT CERF. Simon and Schuster.

The Lincoln Reader, by CARL SANDBURG. Rutgers University Press.
Here Is Your War, by ERNIE PYLE. Holt.
Myths after Lincoln, by LLOYD LEWIS. Harcourt, Brace.
Toaster's Handbook, by PEGGY EDMUND and HAROLD WORKMAN WILLIAMS. Wilson.
Thesaurus of Epigrams, by EDMUND FULLER. Crown.

24. Look over the magazines in your school or town library and select just *one* magazine that you think will be a useful source of speech material for the future. Bring the magazine to class and explain your choice to your classmates. When everyone has been heard, select the three most popular magazines by class vote.

25. Start a class file of illustrative stories, anecdotes, and jokes. Everyone in class can bring in from day to day material that he has come across in his reading. Since there will be repetitious items as well as undesirable ones, you will need to control the material that goes into the file. One way to accomplish this control is to direct all items through a committee, selected on the basis of interest and ability, which will weed out unwanted items and then classify and file those that remain. Probably you will want items classified as to the subject covered; the divisions of classification may be as elaborate as you choose, but this is a matter for you to decide. If your storehouse is an ordinary filing box, you will find that your material is more usable and more durable if it is fastened to filing cards by glue or transparent tape. Start this class file *right now* so that it can serve you throughout the term.

Films:

How to Observe (Coronet). 11 min color or b&w.
How to Judge Facts (Coronet). 11 min color or b&w.
Importance of Making Notes (Coronet). 11 min color or b&w.
Getting the Facts (EBF). 12 min b&w.
What's in a Story? (FAC). 14 min color or b&w.

Unit Ten

SUPPORT THE CENTRAL IDEA: Selecting and Developing Main Points

Just as a composition has a central idea which is presented through the use of several main points that explain and support that idea, so is a speech built of divisions of material that enable the speaker to present a message, or central idea. In both the composition and the speech, the major organizational divisions are the introduction, the body, and the conclusion; and these divisions, in turn, have subdivisions, each of which may be further subdivided for the purpose of preserving subordinate details in a desirable relationship to each other and to the idea of which they are a part. The bodies of both the speech and the composition contain the chief thoughts that support and clarify a central idea, and these thoughts are called the *main points.*

You should understand that a main point in any oral or written presentation is *main* only in a relative sense. In other words, a point is a main point whenever it is a major division of thought supporting a central idea, and the size of that idea is immaterial. Do you recall the process of reducing a general topic to a more specific one in Unit 7? You could stop at any stage of that reduction process and choose your topic, and the thoughts you would use to support the central idea of your topic would be your main points. Let's consider your speech book as an illustration.

The title, *The Art of Speaking,* may be regarded as the central idea and the three main sections as the main points. In outline form the relationship would look like this:

Central idea: There is an art to speaking.

Supporting main points: First, you must understand yourself and others in the speaking situation.
Second, you must learn how to put a speech together.
Third, you must learn how to employ speaking in a variety of ways.

Suppose, however, that we are not looking at the book as a whole, that we are considering only the second section, *Putting a Speech Together.* In the outline below you can see that the points which would have been subdivisions in the outline above are now main points:

Central idea: You must learn how to put a speech together.

Supporting main points: First, you must learn how to select a topic and a purpose.
Second, you must learn how to organize a talk.
Third, you must learn how and where to find material—and the kinds that will help you.
Fourth, you must learn how to select and develop the main points of your talk.
Fifth, you must learn how best to begin and to end a talk.
Sixth, you must learn how to present the material which you have developed so that it indeed becomes a speech.

Let's go one step further. You are now taking Unit 9, "Gather Material: Research and Selection," as your starting place.

Central idea: You must learn what kinds of material can help you and how and where to find it.

Supporting main points: First, you must learn to know what you're looking for.
Second, you must learn where and how you can find it generally.
Third, you must learn the importance of reading as a source of material and how to use special sources.
Fourth, you must learn how to record and preserve the results of your research.

If you turn to Unit 9, you can see at a glance how the first part, "What Am I Looking For?" could easily be treated as a central idea and each of the headings under it as the main points; and, if you worked at it, you could use the headings as central ideas and develop main points from the material under each. Do you feel that you have clearly in mind now what a main point is?

What IS a Main Point in a Speech?

1. It is a division of the central idea of your speech, one which should support, describe, clarify, or expand that idea.
2. It is a segment of speech organization which helps to bring order into the presentation of material.
3. It is a classification of a body of related details.
4. It is an identifiable unit of thinking, one which helps the speaker to prepare his speech and to communicate the thoughts in it to the listener.
5. It is a unit, the magnitude of which is determined by the scope of the speech topic.

Main Points May Have Different Forms

The main points in the outline of the body of your speech will appear in various forms, ranging from a word to a phrase to a sentence. The words and phrases can be used for main points that are simple divisions such as those of time, space, matter, or function; sentences will serve you better when your main points are questions, generalizations, or specific statements. The examples that follow should illustrate the various forms that main points may take.

As Words and Phrases

Space

Speech topic: Exploring the United States

II. Body
- A. The Eastern Seaboard
- B. The Deep South
- C. The Southwest

Function

Speech topic: Catching a Big Trout

II. Body
- A. Selecting bait, or lure
- B. Casting
- C. Setting hook and "playing" fish
- D. Netting and landing

Matter

Speech topic: My Favorite Rock Garden

II. Body
- A. Trees
- B. Ornaments
- C. Plants
- D. Rocks

Time

Speech topic: My Summer in Japan

II. Body
- A. A week of introductions
- B. An evening on the town
- C. A month of traveling

As Sentences

The main points in any of the examples above *could* have appeared as sentences, as you can see in this illustration:

Speech topic: My Summer in Japan
II. Body
- A. My first week was one of amazing and amusing introductions to Japanese life.
- B. I had an evening on the town which was unforgettable.
- C. My final month was one of exciting tours.

Or sentence form may be used to present generalizations as main points:

Speech topic: Night Football Games Should Be Restored
II. Body
- A. The reasons for restrictions are not valid.
- B. The restrictions impose a hardship on the students and on the community.
- C. The restrictions impose a hardship on other schools in the league.
- D. The restrictions don't solve the problem of bad behavior.

Speech topic: The City Council Should Be Recalled
II. Body
- A. Major civic enterprises under this administration have failed.
- B. New proposals for solving civic problems are unimaginative and unsound.
- C. People in this community are in a rebellious mood.
- D. Continuation of the present situation will result in losses both to individuals and to the community.

In the following examples the speech topic and the main points are the same, but the main points appear first as *statements* and then as *questions*.

Statements	*Questions*
Speech topic: Laguna Seca Racetrack	Speech topic: Laguna Seca Racetrack
II. Body	II. Body
A. The setting is unique and beautiful.	A. What kind of setting greets the visitor to the racetrack?
B. The circular course provides spectators an excellent view.	B. Why is the course ideal for the spectators?
C. The tricky turns challenge drivers.	C. Why do drivers find the course interesting and challenging?
D. Many cars can be parked both inside and outside the course.	D. How adequate are the facilities for parking?

Main Points May Have Different Arrangements

To be sure you haven't forgotten, let's note again this important fact: Your decisions concerning the form and arrangement of main points in your speech, the introduction and conclusion that you choose, and the kind of supporting material you select will depend upon your *purpose.* You *must* have in mind clearly what you intend to achieve, the message you wish to convey, the thesis you desire to project, the argument you want to present, the effect you are seeking to build. Such clarity of direction will make your task easier and your product more effective.

One consideration in the achievement of your purpose is the arrangement of your main points, and three general arrangements will be illustrated for you in the material that follows. They are known by the names of *chronological, climactic,* and *logical.* All three, in a general sense, are logical arrangements if logical means sensible, reasonable, orderly, and planned with a goal in mind. In a more restricted sense the first two kinds of arrangements have an easily identifiable main characteristic, while the third has a number of characteristics. Let's consider each.

Chronological Arrangement of Main Points. When you use a chronological arrangement, or time order, you start at the beginning and tell

Telling about the first morning at Sun Valley—breakfast at Challenger Inn and the sleigh ride—would be a correct beginning for a chronological description.

how something happened—or how something happens—which means that you are describing a step-by-step process. Necessarily, then, only matters which are related to the passage of time can be treated chronologically. You would not, for example, in a speech designed to persuade a customer to buy a product, arrange your arguments in chronological order.

On the other hand, as stated in an earlier unit, you must never feel obliged to tell of an experience in time order just because it happened that way. Many times it is to your advantage to explain what followed, or follows. More often, however, people will be interested in the highlights of an experience and won't enjoy your step-by-step recountal—unless, like the Ancient Mariner, you are able to hold them spellbound. Since no rule can be employed, you will have to use your judgment in the use of time order. In planning your presentation, try to think of yourself as a *listener,* not as a speaker, and choose the arrangement that you would like to hear.

Regardless of the words you use for your main points—whether they're names of time units, names of steps in a process, or names of major events in the chronology—you are still following time order in this arrangement.

To illustrate a chronological arrangement in greater detail and to provide a vehicle which can be used to compare and contrast logical and climactic arrangements, let's suppose you are planning a talk on your trip to Sun Valley, Idaho, during Christmas vacation. You had four glorious days there. You saw your first snow, stayed at the Lodge, swam in the glassed-in pool, went skiing on Dollar Mountain, saw many celebrities, and met Audrey Hepburn—the experience that impressed you most. Though you can't help giving *information* in this talk, your primary purpose is *to entertain* your audience, to share with them vicariously the joys of your trip. You have decided to group your experiences under four main headings: First day at Sun Valley, Second day, Third day, and Fourth day. Here is how the body of your outline, with subdivisions included, might look:

II. Body

A. First day at Sun Valley
  1. Eating pheasant breakfast at Challenger Inn
  2. Sleigh riding
  3. Visiting with a friend in a nearby town
  4. Dining and dancing at the Lodge

B. Second day
  1. Skiing on Dollar Mountain

2. Lunching at the Lodge
   a. Meeting Audrey Hepburn
   b. Not having money to pay for my lunch
3. Swimming in glassed-in pool
4. Seeing celebrities at dinner

C. Third day
1. Discovering light snow in the morning
2. Exploring the shops and grounds
3. Skiing in the afternoon
4. Going to the Opera House
   a. Frank Sinatra, guest star
   b. Midnight supper party after the play

D. Fourth day
1. Sleeping late and reading in bed
2. Eating big lunch at the Lodge
3. More snow—skiing behind a station wagon
4. Attending farewell dinner

Climactic Arrangement of Main Points. The climactic arrangement is one in which the most important or most dramatic point is saved until last. Neither you nor members of your audience could mistake an obviously dramatic or important point, and you could not go wrong in choosing a climactic arrangement to include such a point.

If your talk has a climactic arrangement, the highlight of your Sun Valley trip—meeting Audrey Hepburn—would be saved until last.

There is the chance that you may have less than spectacular success if you choose and give weight in a climactic arrangement to a point in which there is not general interest. For example, you may be a chess fan, and you have saved for your climax what you regard as an absolutely stunning play that ended in a checkmate. The winning player cleverly used only two bishops and a knight to trap his adversary, who still had a castle and queen and bishop in play. If you are not a chess player, the sentence you have just finished reading should begin to give you an idea of what your classmates, who are not likely to be a group of chess players, would feel if they were to be subjected to your "climax." If you were presenting this talk to a *chess club,* though, then you might indeed have an excellent final point. The success of this arrangement, therefore, will depend, first, upon whether your final point is in fact important or dramatic and, second, upon whether the members of the audience are sufficiently informed to recognize this quality.

In Sun Valley the most dramatic event for you was your talking with Audrey Hepburn. Will this also be the highlight for your classmates? Your outline for the body of your speech might look like this:

II. Body

- A. Satisfying experiences
  1. Riding by sleigh from the station to the Lodge
  2. Exploring Sun Valley shops and grounds
  3. Sleeping late and reading in bed
  4. Dancing at the Lodge
  5. Having a midnight supper party after the play
- B. Highlights
  1. Seeing first snowfall
  2. Skiing on Dollar Mountain
  3. Eating pheasant for breakfast
  4. Seeing the celebrities
  5. Going to the play at the Opera House—Frank Sinatra's appearance
  6. Swimming in the glassed-in pool
  7. Attending the farewell dinner
- C. Meeting Audrey Hepburn
  1. Recognizing her and speaking
  2. Eating lunch together
  3. Making a "date" to meet next Christmas at Sun Valley
  4. Having no money with me to pay for my lunch
     - *a.* My discovery
     - *b.* My panic and embarrassment
     - *c.* Audrey Hepburn's amusement and paying the check
  5. Discovering that Hepburn is great—and a "regular gal."

In a logically arranged speech, skiing would be one detail of a main point—fun.

Logical Arrangements of Main Points. As pointed out earlier, logical means sensible or reasonable in a general sense, but in a more restricted sense it pertains to a form of logic. In formal speaking, particularly in debate, forms of logic are frequently employed to strengthen argument. For example, the main points of a speech might be the three steps in a syllogism—the major premise, the minor premise, and the conclusion, or the main points might be those that you would use in trying to establish causal relationship. In other words, you are starting with a known cause and arguing that a certain effect will result, or you are starting with a known effect and trying to present evidence which will prove that a particular cause is responsible for it. Another approach to setting up the main points would be reasoning from analogy—comparing two ideas, problems, or situations, one of which is familiar to the audience. In this type of argument you try to show that the unfamiliar idea, problem, or situation is like the familiar one, and then you make whatever point you wish to make because of the similarity. These forms of logic, incidentally, are discussed at greater length in the unit on debate.

Formal, logical arrangements will not be explored and exemplified in this unit; rather, attention will be given to three kinds of arrangements which are in common use and which are logical in a more general sense. The first of these is logical because it is a selected, orderly, and sometimes sequential arrangement of main points, all of which are chosen by the speaker because he thinks they will help him to carry out a particular purpose. You will find an example of this sort of grouping of related ideas in the Sun Valley outline that follows, an arrangement which illustrates a selection of most impressive features of an experience.

After the Sun Valley example you will find three more illustrations of how, within the limits of a single subject, you can make various arrangements of main points, all different, yet logical, orderly, and systematic in their own way.

The other two arrangements, which are also logical in a general sense, but which have more specifically sequential structures, are the problem-solution order and the "Bull's-Eye" plan. Further comments on them and examples of each will conclude this section on the selection of main points.

General Logical Arrangements. So, it's off to Sun Valley! You have decided to focus attention on experiences, and you have selected scenery, people, food, and recreation as main areas of experience.

II. Body

A. The beauty of Sun Valley
   1. Smooth, snow-covered hills
   2. High mountains in the distance
   3. The valley when snow is falling
   4. View from Dollar Mountain

B. Interesting people
   1. Quick friendships made while skiing
   2. Celebrities on vacation at Sun Valley
   3. Charming guides and instructors
   4. Frank Sinatra, guest star at the Opera House
   5. Introduction to Audrey Hepburn

C. Wonderful food
   1. Pheasant for breakfast
   2. Venison from frozen-food locker
   3. First taste of mountain sheep
   4. The farewell dinner

D. Fun—indoors and out
   1. The midnight supper party after the play
   2. A dance at the Lodge
   3. Sleeping late and reading in bed
   4. The sleigh rides
   5. A swim in the glassed-in pool
   6. Skiing

The examples that follow also illustrate the general logical arrangement used in the Sun Valley outline. The subject and the speaker's purpose are the same for all examples, but there is a different emphasis in each. Let's assume that you are the speaker and that you are going to describe a scene or painting. Here are three different arrangements; would you like to work out a fourth?

Example 1: An orderly classification by type, with the common denominator's being color

II. Body

A. The predominant green colors
B. The outstanding brown colors
C. Other interesting colors and shades

Example 2: An orderly classification by type, but with the added dimension of most-to-least sequence and with the common denominator's being points of interest

II. Body

A. The center of interest
B. Secondary, or supporting, points of interest
C. Special points of interest

Example 3: A selected group of maximum features that will strengthen a general description

II. Body

A. Unusual autumn colors
B. Points of interest
C. Line and texture
D. Sun and shadow

Problem-Solution Arrangement. Now, let's consider the problem-solution arrangement, a type which is in fairly common use and with which you may have had some previous contact. It is a balanced, step-by-step, orderly, methodical, *progressive* arrangement of main points which will aid you in any serious speaking situation when you are trying to help your listeners solve a problem. It is different from the first kind of general logical arrangement in two chief respects: it has an established pattern of questions, and this pattern represents a progression of thought from one arbitrary point to another arbitrary point. The material that follows identifies the four questions that make up this arrangement and exemplifies them with a familiar topic:

	Your Main Points
	II. Body (on topic of socialized medicine)
1. Is there a problem?	A. Adequate medical care remains a problem in the United States.

2. What is the proposed solution to the problem, and is it *possible*?	B. Socialized medicine provides a solution to the problem, and the experience of others shows it to be a realistic solution.
3. Is the solution desirable?	C. This solution is desirable because it is *financially* possible and *acceptable* to our society.
4. Is there a *better* solution?	D. No existing plan, such as the many health insurance plans in existence or help from the county, reaches all of the people who need medical care.

"Bull's-Eye" Arrangement. The last example of general logical arrangements is the "Bull's-Eye" plan, which was presented to you in outline form in Unit 8. It is a five-step, progressive arrangement that strongly suggests the feeling of movement and climax. Its orderly sequence includes identifying the listener with the topic, giving him one main thought to consider, reinforcing that thought with numerous examples, and ending with a plea for action. Because you already know what the outline for this arrangement is like, the example that follows will illustrate its full development:

Main Points (developed)

Step 1 WAKE UP!

Today's assembly is in honor of one of our students who went beyond the call of duty. He wasn't afraid *to go that last mile*!

Step 2 THIS CONCERNS YOU

He lived a long time ago, but his name, his achievements, and the legends about him live on. He made possible the Teen-Age Center. The city's recreation park bears his name. Stories about his heroism during the earthquake that leveled this town are told and retold. Why is Brick Thompson remembered? What made the man great? What quality should we try to develop to be like him?

Step 3 GENERALLY SPEAKING

It's not always easy to say why one man achieves fame while another remains in obscurity, but it is reasonable to believe that *going the last mile* is a good explanation. It's doing that extra chore when others have quit for the day. It's trying to gain one more foot after you have been tackled and stopped in your tracks. It's having courage to struggle on when others have dropped by the wayside. It's helping others when personal cost is high.

Some years ago magazines, films, and radio made popular the story of an American country doctor who, with little tangible reward, served his community beyond professional obligation. Somehow, the community woke up to the fact of his greatness as a fellowman. They showered tardy love and gifts upon him in a public demonstration. They recognized, I'm sure, that he had never been afraid, never reluctant *to go that last mile.*

Step 4

FOR EXAMPLE

Who is unaware of the blessings of radium to mankind? And who has not read the story of the gallant Frenchman and his lovely, courageous Polish wife in their long, heartbreaking fight to take radium from pitchblende? The Curies won because they would not acknowledge fatigue and disappointment and didn't know the meaning of defeat.

The list stretches on and on. The Wright brothers and their improbable contraption—everybody laughed at them; Louis Pasteur—thought to be a fool; Sister Kenny—her name was associated with quackery; Albert Schweitzer—achievement was painfully slow and the hazards were great in African jungles; James McDivitt and Edward White—the success or failure of our space pioneering depended on their own faith and courage; Jacqueline Kennedy—who, in her most tragic and trying hour, demonstrated endurance and bravery beyond comprehension.

Step 5

WHAT TO DO

To me, the answer to our question is obvious. The quality that made Brick Thompson what he has been to this community also made the Curies, the Wrights, and the others great men and women. If you want to join their ranks, you may—if you're *not afraid to go the last mile*!

Selection of Main Points

Comments and Cautions

1. Main points, as used in this text, are the major divisions of the body of the speech.
2. Main points, as they appear in a speech outline, may take the form of words, phrases, or sentences.
3. Main points may be arranged in several different ways: logical order, chronological order, or climactic order.
4. Don't choose too many main points. Usually, three or four will be enough for any speech you wish to give. Two could easily be enough for some speeches.
5. Try to select and develop your main points so that they have about the same weight, or value. You have reasonable leeway here, but you quite obviously would not want some main points that are two or three times more prominent than others.
6. Never select main points that are closely alike or that contradict each other. This caution on contradiction does not apply to a speech in which, for example, you are giving the pros and cons on an issue and have developed information on each as a main point.
7. Never select as a main point any information or idea which is clearly a subdivision of another of your main points.

Developing Main Points

So far in the unit, you have seen a number of examples of main points in a variety of speech situations; and, in the Sun Valley examples of main points in several arrangements, you have been shown some supporting details. Let's think a little about the problems and processes involved in developing the main points in the three examples and then turn to an imaginary situation in which we try together to develop some main points for another kind of speech.

First, you should recognize that in the Sun Valley examples you were dealing with one of the easiest kinds of speeches—an entertaining, informational talk on *an experience*. YOU WERE THERE! Everything you did, felt, saw, and heard became your larder of materials, your barrel of content for the speech. Your chief task was that of selecting the materials you wished to share and organizing them in the most effective way for final presentation. Your research had been done, and there were no issues to be resolved by critical thinking. In the final analysis it would be your enthusiasm, your sense of humor, your feeling for drama, your personality, your ability to share feelings that would make your speech a success—not its unique content. Precise words, "color" words, and perky details would also help. But not a single member of your audience would be sitting in judgment on your logic; no one would be testing the clarity of your thinking.

Even if you tried to add life to your Sun Valley talk by using some color slides, excerpts from tape recordings, and realia from the Sun Valley area—which wouldn't be a bad idea—you still would not have an especially difficult time in preparing your speech.

But what if you want to do something more serious and more difficult, and choose as that something the preparing of a speech to convince (persuade?) your classmates that cigarette smoking is most undesirable in terms of health? You know that smoking is an individual matter, that people smoke or don't smoke for many reasons, and that sheer exhortation won't change people's habits. What you have to do is to convince them that there is danger in the smoking habit, and then you have to leave to them the choice of whether they wish to risk the danger. Now plan the campaign.

Get Some Reference Material. If you're going to draw support from the movement that started a number of years ago, gathered force in 1963, and culminated in early 1964 with the report on cigarette smoking from the Surgeon General of the United States Public Health Service, you must find some material. The high school library will provide much, and the public libraries in the vicinity will have much more; so much, in fact that you won't be able to search it all out or to use it all. Suppose you come up with an armful, such as the following:

BRECHER, RUTH, and others. *The Consumers Union Report on Smoking and the Public Interest.* The Consumers Union, 1963. Mount Vernon, New York.

Cigarette Smoking and Cancer: The Evidence Upon Which the American Cancer Society's Position and Programs Are Based. The American Cancer Society, 1963. New York, N. Y.

HAMMOND, E. CUYLER. "The Effects of Smoking," *Scientific American*, Vol. 207, No. 1 (July, 1962).

SALBER, EVA J., M.D., and others. "Reasons for Smoking Given by Secondary School Children," *Journal of Health and Human Behavior*, Vol. 4, No. 2 (Summer, 1963).

"Teen-agers and Cigarets," *Changing Times* (March, 1962).

Many states—California, for example—have similar publications and you might find references such as these to add to your collection:

"Cigarette Smoking and Health, Part I: A Review of Studies in California; Part II: Expressions of Authoritative Opinion," *California's Health*, Vol. 21, No. 5 (September 1, 1963) and Vol. 21, No. 6 (September 15, 1963).

"Smoking and Sports." Comment by the National Federation of State High School Athletic Associations and the Committee on the Medical Aspects of Sports of the American Medical Association. Distributed in California by the California Interscholastic Federation. (Mimeographed)

Further, let's assume that the librarian gave you a folder of information and brochures put out by the American Cancer Society. You selected, at random, *To Smoke or Not to Smoke?, 1960 Cancer Facts and Figures, Teaching About Cancer,* and *Free Education Films.* In the latter you noted that two appropriate filmed productions are available:

To Smoke or Not to Smoke? filmstrip, 84 fr, accompanying record, 1962.
Is Smoking Worth It? 16 mm film, 16 min, color, sd, 1962.

Make Some Decisions. Before you select your main points, make a few other decisions. Perhaps after spending about thirty minutes skimming through your references, you are a little confused and somewhat overwhelmed by the mass of it, yet you know it's only a small part of all the writing available on the topic. You're going to be faced with limiting the search, which means some kind of delimiting of your topic. It will be well, too, to think about the introduction and conclusion. These decisions, then, will help:

1. Your purpose will be *to convince* your listeners, through information, of the seriousness of the effects of smoking cigarettes, and you can take an extra step by trying *to persuade* them to read at least one article from a list you will provide.

2. You can point up the problem by opening with a strong quotation, one of the many in Volume 21, Number 6, of *California's Health.*

3. You can show why the topic is of particular concern to everyone by listing numerous agencies and persons who have expressed alarm about the serious effects of cigarette smoking upon health.

4. Your conclusion can end with a strong quotation much like the one in the introduction and taken from the same source. You can start looking for the several articles which you will mention in the conclusion as your appeal for action, your attempt *to persuade* the listeners to take a step by reading just one of them. Do you think you should have the list duplicated for distribution?

5. You have discovered that the two volumes of *California's Health* are résumés of fact and opinion which can serve you rather well, making possible your having a wealth of usable material without having to extract it from all the other documents, though you will be able to use some of them, too.

Select Your Main Points. Your decision, then, is to use these volumes extensively. *Select your main points.* Knowing that preaching about the evils of smoking is a waste of time, choose several areas of *information* as main points, information with status. One way to develop a clear, specific plan is to ask yourself questions and then to develop answers.

Question	*Answer*
Shall I make expense a main point? I could talk about the increase in cigarette smoking, the burns in clothing, damage to furniture, loss of homes, loss of lives, and other losses.	No, I don't think so. The actual expense of cigarettes every day is small, and the expenses involved in the other matters is part of calculated risk. I don't think that people are frightened by such possible expenses.
Well, then, what about damage to heart, damage to lungs, and other damages? *There* are three good points for the talk. . . .	Not bad. . . . Ordinarily, the idea might appeal to me, but I want a better coverage this time. I'm thinking about beginning with causes. . . .

Good idea! What about having as the first main point, *Why students say they smoke*? The Newton study will help us here.

This was my first idea and I still like it. Such information is certainly related to why they may quit or not start.

Could I use Volume 21, Number 5, of *California's Health* as the basis for the second point? I could call the point *What studies show about cigarette smoking*.

It appeals to me because it helps to carry out my purpose and because it seems to have a comparable importance or comparable weight. Actually, there's more material than I can use, however.

Should I also make use of Volume 21, Number 6, for material to support *What authorities say about cigarette smoking*? It would fit the pattern of information-giving we set out to accomplish.

I like that, too, but it seems to me that the dramatic facts in Number 5 are more important than the opinions in Number 6. I'd like to switch the two points around and aim for a *climactic* arrangement.

Why not have a fourth point and let it be the showing of the film "Is Smoking Worth It?" If I want a climax, that film will give one. . . . It could be followed by a brief conclusion and appeal.

How much time am I allowed for this talk? It would be a wonderful fourth point, but. . . . I'll talk with my teacher and find out if I can give a special talk and use the film. If I can't have the time, I'll just stick with the three points I've chosen.

Develop Your Main Points. Forgetting for the moment the use of the film as a fourth point, deciding to switch the second and third points, you can set up the main points in the body like this:

II. Body

A. Why students say they smoke
B. What authorities say about smoking
C. What studies show about cigarette smoking

First Main Point. As you pointed out, there is a limit to the time at your disposal, so you can't tell *all* that students say, that authorities say, or that studies show. You must make some abitrary choices of supporting details. With regard to the first main point, you have read Dr. Salber's "Reasons for Smoking Given by Secondary School Children" and have made some random notes which look like this:

Study of 7000 teen-agers, grades 7-12, Newton, Mass. Over 50 percent of smokers gave "conformity" as reason for their smoking and for why they thought other teen-agers smoked. Smokers rated "enjoyment and tensions release" as second in explaining their own smoking, but ranked "to impress others" as second in explaining why others smoked. Teen-agers who had smoked and discontinued the practice listed "impressing others" and "conformity" as being nearly equal reasons for other teen-agers' smoking. Teen-agers who had not smoked judged that others smoked, first to "impress others" and, second, to "conform." Reasons for smoking that had lower ratings: "adult emulation," "curiosity," "rebellion," and "enjoyment and tension release." Reasons for discontinuing smoking in order of importance: boys—"no enjoyment," "health," "athletics"; girls—"no enjoyment," "influence of parents," "aesthetic or moral." Reasons given by nonsmokers for not smoking: boys—"health," "aesthetic or moral," "no enjoyment"; girls—"aesthetic or moral," "health," "no enjoyment."

From these notes you might select as your first rank of supporting details these subdivisions: identification of study, smokers' reasons for their smoking, smokers' reasons for others' smoking, discontinued smokers' reasons for others' smoking, nonsmokers' reasons why others smoked, low-rated reasons for smoking, reasons for discontinuing smoking, and nonsmokers' reasons for not smoking. Your first main point, with supporting detail, might look like this:

A. Why students say they smoke (or don't)
  1. Identification of study
    a. Newton, Massachusetts
    b. 7000 teen-agers
    c. Grades 7-12
  2. Smokers' reasons for their smoking
    a. Conformity—first choice by over 50 percent of smokers
    b. Enjoyment and tension release—second choice
  3. Smokers' reasons for others' smoking
    a. Conformity—first
    b. To impress others—second
  4. Discontinued smokers' reasons for others' smoking
    a. Impressing others } nearly equal
    b. Conformity }
  5. Low-rated reasons why others smoked
    a. Adult emulation
    b. Curiosity
    c. Rebellion
  6. Nonsmokers' reasons why others smoked
    a. Impress others—first
    b. To conform—second
  7. Reasons for discontinuing smoking (in order)
    a. Boys
      (1) No enjoyment

(2) Health
(3) Aesthetics
b. Girls
(1) No enjoyment
(2) Influence of parents
(3) Aesthetic or moral
8. Nonsmokers' reasons for not smoking
a. Boys
(1) Health
(2) Aesthetic or moral
(3) No enjoyment
b. Girls
(1) Aesthetic or moral
(2) Health
(3) No enjoyment

You now will note that the sequence of eight subdivisions is different in the outline from the listing in the paragraph that preceded it. There is *some* sequential nature in the material, but not too much, and you have choice here. What choice should you make?

It is obvious to you that the choice of first-rank subdivisions was somewhat arbitrary. For example, the outline might just as easily have turned out like this:

A. Why students say they smoke (or don't)
1. Identification of study
a. Newton, Massachusetts
b. 7000 teen-agers
c. Grades 7-12
2. Smokers' reasons for smoking
a. For their own smoking
(1) Conformity—first choice by over 50 percent
(2) Enjoyment and tension release—second
b. For others' smoking
(1) Conformity—first
(2) To impress—second
3. Others' reasons for the practice of smoking
a. Discontinued smokers' reasons why others smoke
(1) Impress others } nearly equal
(2) Conformity }
b. Nonsmokers' reasons why others smoke
(1) Impress others—first
(2) To conform—second
4. Low-rated reasons why others smoke
5. Reasons for discontinuing smoking (in order)
6. Nonsmokers' reasons for not smoking

It must also be obvious to you by this time that still other choices remain to you in putting the outline together, not only in arrangement of ideas but in delimiting them too. Further, you can dress up the material in that outline, if you wish to do some additional work, by looking for other statistics, for visual material to exhibit, for an illustrative anecdote, and so on. But let's turn to your second main point, *What authorities say about smoking.*

Second Main Point. Fortunately, you have a relatively easy task in supporting this main point, the hardest part being that of delimiting the material. Volume 21, Number 6, of *California's Health* has twenty-eight separate expressions of authoritative opinion; and, in addition to those from the United States, there are others from the United Nations World Health Organization, International Union Against Cancer, Great Britain, Sweden, Holland, Iceland, and Norway. The material is all good, and your choices are almost as easy as flipping a coin, but you *do* have to choose. You can be guided in your choices by two factors: (1) geographical distribution of opinion and (2) the appealing quality of content.

The outline for the second main point could look like this:

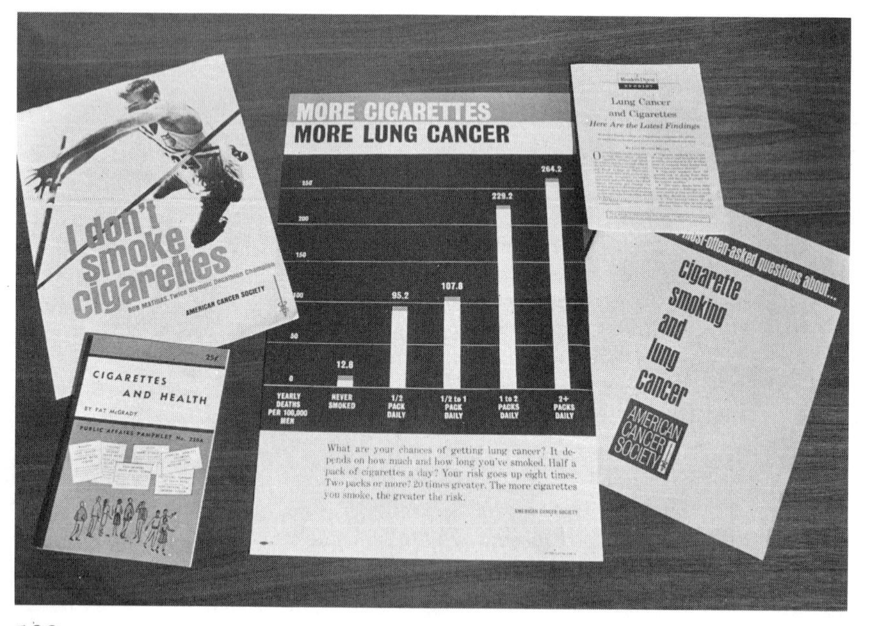

The official materials here would fit "what authorities say about smoking." The athlete's testimonial, a supporting detail, adds a human touch.

B. What authorities say about smoking
   1. March 6, 1957, Joint Report of the Seven-Man Study Group (of the U.N. World Health Organization) on smoking and health
   2. March 9, 1957, Holland, Health Council
   3. September, 1957, Surgeon General of the United States Public Health Service
   4. June 30, 1958, International Union Against Cancer
   5. October 21, 1959, American Public Health Association
   6. June 22, 1962, Norway
   7. March, 1963, Resolution of House of Delegates, California Medical Association.

You have arranged the subdivisions in chronological order. The arrangement may not be of as much value in your speech as you think, but it is a kind of climactic order of subdivisions in the sense that the final item is the most recent of the seven which were selected; and it has the strength of a steady and continuing expression of concern.

You may want to use more than seven subdivisions, but that number is convenient because the content of the quotations represented by that number takes approximately the reading and speaking time that you want to devote to the second main point. Further, the seventh, the shortest of the group, happens to be more than expression of opinion; it has the element of action in it and makes a good ending point. This is what it says:

> *Resolved:* That the California Medical Association take steps on a statewide basis to publicize, particularly in schools and homes, the harmful effects of cigarette smoking.

Third Main Point. Now for the third and last main point, last that is, if you decide not to use the film "Is Smoking Worth It?". *California's Health,* Volume 21, Number 5, contains a review of studies which, not counting introductory and concluding material, is covered under three main headings: Cigarette smoking and mortality, Cigarette smoking and morbidity, and Cigarette smoking and physiologic impairment. Also included are seven figures and one table. Six of the figures are bar graphs, and one is a line graph. Mortality, as used in this review, means *death rate*; morbidity means *disease rate,* or proportion of the persons in a community who are diseased or disabled.

Because you can enlarge and use any or all of the graphs shown in the review of studies, you need not include in your notes some of the details which those graphs show and which are also given in the written material of the reviews. Your notes, then, might be something like these:

Cigarette smoking increases many times the risk of lung cancer. The greater the amount of smoking, the greater the risk. Also increases substantially the risk of dying from coronary heart disease and other diseases, such as chronic bronchitis and emphysema. In a follow-up study of 68,154 middle-aged men, cigarette smoking (with all amounts combined) increased risk of lung-cancer death fourteen times. Two-pack-a-day smoking increased it twenty-six times. Risk of death from coronary heart disease about twice as high among smokers as among nonsmokers; risk from other diseases increased about one-third among smokers. Activity limitation and days of disability occasioned by chronic conditions substantially greater among men smokers aged 26–64. Frequency of conditions such as coughing much higher among smokers. Pulmonary function studies show physiologic impairment to be associated with cigarette smoking. Studies of airway conductance and measurement of carbon monoxide in expired air indicate that one-tenth of light smokers, one-fifth of moderate smokers, and one-third of heavy smokers *exceeded* the level of carbon monoxide which corresponds to 7 percent carboxyhemoglobin in the blood; when carboxyhemoglobin extends into the 5–10 percent range, physiological impairment apparently begins. Greater frequency of symptoms of respiratory disease (cough, sputum, shortness of breath, wheezing, etc.) among men who had smoked ten years or more than among those who had smoked less than ten years or not at all.

How will your notes look in outline form? After you have read the comments that follow, turn to the first activity to try the outline suggested.

Supporting Details. One way in which the developed form of three main points could be improved would be by the addition of some supporting details that will personalize or humanize your message. Consider these possibilities:

Personal reference

Have you given up smoking? Has a member of your family had to give up smoking for health reasons? Have you had any personal experience outside the family which you could use as testimony?

Results of a local study

Has any group in your community, church group, school group, club, etc., engaged in a study that you can use to illustrate a point?

Quote from local paper

Has your local paper carried a feature article, news story, or editorial which will provide you with a quotation that will bring one of your points closer to home?

Testimony from one known well to the group

Testimony from a national figure is useful here, but try to get testimony from a former school athlete, the mayor, a celebrity who lives in your town, or from anyone known and respected by your audience.

Anecdote or story

The material in your talk on smoking is pretty heavy, and you can use an occasional anecdote or story for relief. Do you remember the porter scene in *Macbeth* which Shakespeare used for this same purpose—relief? Turn to the magazines and joke books for help here, and keep your ears open for appropriate illustrative stories that may be making the rounds.

Or you may be able to dramatize some of your points by using photographs, pictures, or slides. Further, you may be able to extract from the many other sources of material assembled for this speech project additional testimony, quotations, or facts that will enrich your subdivisions. Such enriching material might be found, for example, in "Teen-agers and Cigarets" or in *The Consumers Union Report on Smoking and the Public Interest,* which would also be an excellent reference to put on your list of readings, if you were to follow the suggestion of passing out such a list to your listeners after you had made an appeal in your conclusion for them to read at least one of the items. Finally, after you have begun working on your speech for delivery, don't hesitate to eliminate material that doesn't sound effective, don't be afraid to rearrange subdivisions or even main points if they sound better another way, and don't be reluctant to look for new material to fill gaps that appear or to replace the material which you have eliminated.

ACTIVITIES

1. Study the random notes that were gathered during the imaginary joint session on the third main point of a proposed speech on the effects of cigarette smoking, and develop these notes into outline form. Following the process that was used for outlining the first main point, select your first-rank subdivisions first, and subordinate to them all the material which you wish to use, employing as many subdivisions as you need. If you wish to enrich your outline by including material which has come from your own research, feel free to do so.
2. Develop an outline of your own on the subject of effects of cigarette smoking, using as little or as much of the example as you wish. Secure some reference material to aid you in your development, either some of those listed in the sample development or others which may be either more easily procured or more recent. If your final product is better than the example, which is most probable, try to determine *why* it is better.
3. Write out several main points, according to *form,* for each of the following topics and suggested form:
   a. My Trip to Canada—simple divisions of *time*
   b. The Geography of Our Community—simple divisions of *space*
   c. The Materials in a House—simple divisions of *matter*

d. How to Ride a Surfboard—simple divisions of *function*

e. Everyone Should Have Health Insurance—main points as *generalizations*

f. Texas Is an Unusual State—main points as *statements* or *questions*

4. Decide which of the following arrangements of main points are *chronological,* which are *climactic,* and which are *logical.* If you think any one of them isn't clearly identifiable as one of the arrangements, discuss it in class.

II. Body
- **A.** First impressions of the fair
- **B.** Wonders of the science hall
- **C.** Winning a prize with a lucky number

II. Body
- **A.** The view from the cabin
- **B.** Wildlife in the area
- **C.** Magnificent trees
- **D.** Beauty of the lake

II. Body
- **A.** We are still having trouble with our service points.
- **B.** An interschool council is necessary to study the problem.
- **C.** Students are dissatisfied with the present regulations.
- **D.** Only joint action among the schools will get at the heart of the problem.

II. Body
- **A.** How the fight started
- **B.** The battle itself
- **C.** The police arrive
- **D.** The aftermath

II. Body
- **A.** The tension in the game
- **B.** Some beautiful plays
- **C.** The turning point
- **D.** Thrill of my home run

II. Body
- **A.** The first day of school
- **B.** Time for semester grades
- **C.** Importance of education
- **D.** Why colleges have to maintain admissions requirements

5. Choose a topic for a "Bull's-Eye" talk. On a sheet of paper write down the main steps of the plan, leaving plenty of space between them. Now work out a talk, referring as necessary to the requirements for each step. Would one of these topics interest you?

Don't Make Promises; Make Good
Death Rides with Drivers Who Drink
It Can't Go Off; It's Not Loaded
Our Deeds Are Our Epitaphs
Man's Best Friends Are His Books
Tomorrow May Be Too Late
An Ounce of Praise Is Not Enough

6. Let everyone in class write on a slip of paper (get your teacher in on it, too!) a topic for a short "Bull's-Eye" talk. Put the slips into a container and give them the usual shaking. Start the talks by having someone draw a topic. Allow him a minute for preparation and approximately a minute for speaking. Continue in the same manner with the rest of the class. You will be surprised to see how well these little impromptu talks turn out. If the time suggested doesn't suit you, vary it. *You* make the rules.

If you especially want to save time, assign a speaking order and then let everyone draw his slip at the beginning of the talks. No one may look at his topic until the speaker before him has started talking. Should anyone fail to speak for a full minute, the person who follows must be allowed additional time for preparation.

7. Search reading material for articles or stories which exemplify the three methods of organizing main points: chronological, climactic, logical. Newspapers, magazines, and short stories should all be good sources. Identify and list the major points. When you find an example of climactic order, decide whether you agree with the author in his choice of point saved for last. Some sources of such examples are occasional feature stories in *Time* magazine and some of the short stories written by Thomas Bailey Aldrich, Bret Harte, and O. Henry.

8. Bring out in class discussion why news stories always have the gist of their message in the lead, or first part, of the story. Why don't they use climactic order?

9. Find a topic that is acceptable to two members of your class and have one of them prepare a short speech, organizing it by topic outline. Let the other prepare his speech in the manner of the "Bull's-Eye" talk. Since the same topic will be treated by both speakers, you should find a comparison between the two presentations an interesting one.

Films:

Learn to Argue Effectively (Coronet). 11 min color or b&w.
Tobacco and the Human Body (EBF). 15 min b&w.
Building an Outline (Coronet). 11 min. color or b&w.

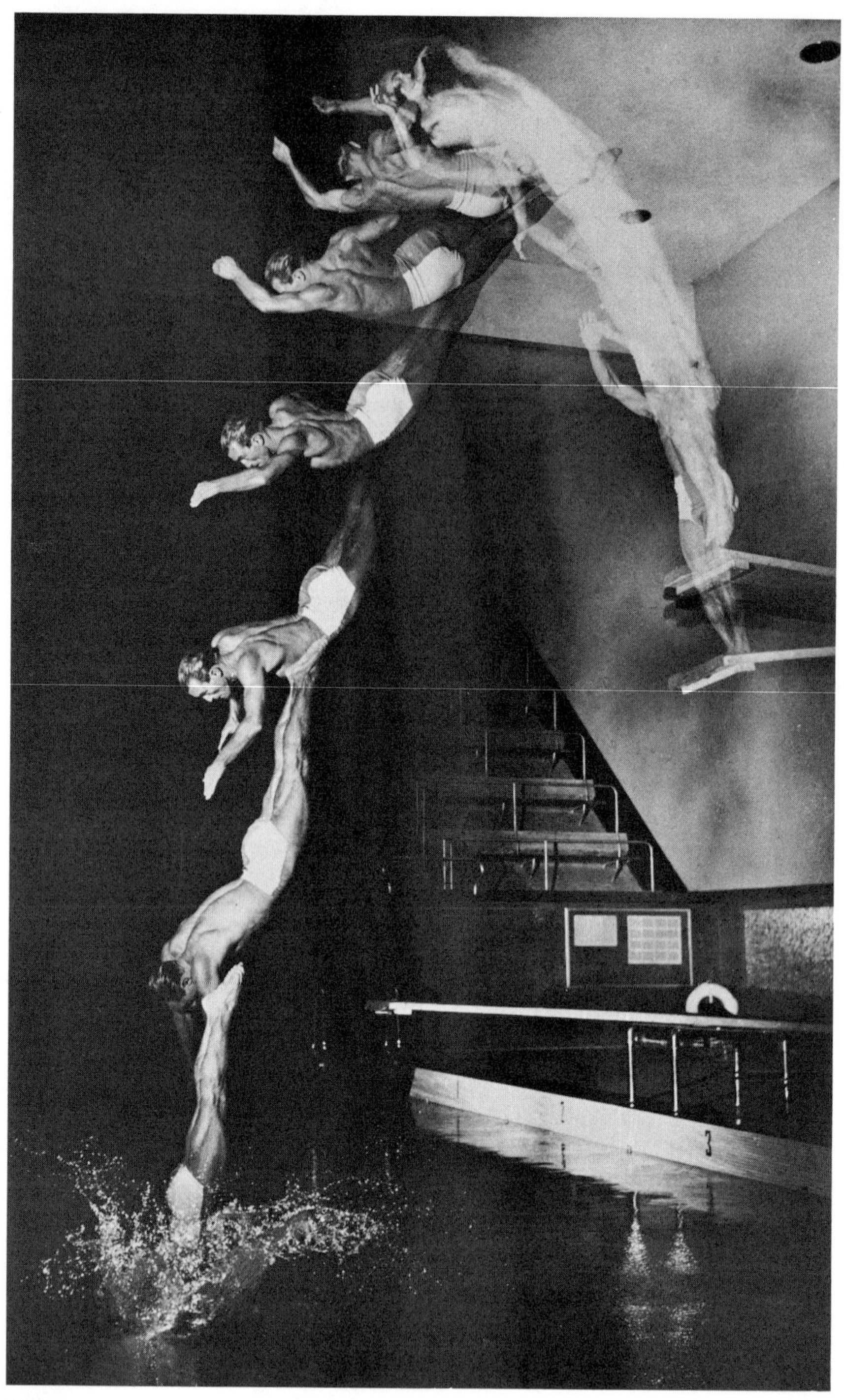

Unit Eleven

BEGIN AND END WELL: Your Introduction and Conclusion

A girl just out of college was applying for her first teaching job in a country school. She had interviewed three of the four members of the board of trustees and was now on her way to see the fourth. As she trudged up to the small farmhouse, she came upon a group of youngsters concentrating on a game of ticktacktoe in the dust of the road leading into the yard. Quietly she stepped around the absorbed children without disturbing their marked squares, offering a cheery "Hi!" as she continued on to the house for her interview.

It was several days later when she received the final decision of the board on her application. To her great delight she had been appointed, and to her greater surprise she received this compliment from the fourth board member:

"When you came down that dusty lane to my house, I was watching you from the window. Anyone who shows the consideration for others that you showed when you stepped around the children's game is someone I want my children to know. You made a good first impression on me. I thought then, as I did after talking with you, that you are the girl for the job."

Good first impressions *are* important, and the purpose of the instruction and the examples that come next is to help you make good first impressions in the speeches which you will be giving in the future. To be more specific, let's talk about the *introduction* to your speech.

Reference to the proposed outline form in Unit 9 indicates that the introduction should accomplish four objectives: a catching of interest, a revelation of purpose, a relating to the interest of the audience, and a preview of the main points which will be made. Must these objectives, clearly identified, always appear in the outline of an introduction and in the speech itself? No, they are general goals. When the speech is formal and the material is expository in nature, there is perhaps greater need for inclusion of all the elements of the suggested introduction. How do you know what to include and when to include it? You don't really ever *know*; you learn, both by instruction and by experience, to *judge*. In general, you try to get attention, to gain a favorable audience reaction, to arouse interest, to stimulate your listeners to hear you out, to let them know what you hope to accomplish, and to help them identify with your subject. Sometimes your purpose and what you expect of the audience are quite clearly implied; at other times you have to be quite explicit in these matters.

Your introduction, depending upon the nature and the scope of your speech, may vary in length from a few sentences to a few paragraphs. In days past, orators were quite leisurely about "getting down to brass tacks"; nowadays, most speakers fall into line with the spirit of the times and streamline their introductions.

The Roman orator Cicero said that the purpose of the introduction of a speech was "to render the hearers well-disposed toward the speaker, attentive to the speech, and open to conviction." In the two thousand years that have passed since his time, no one has put it much better than that; but knowing what should be done and knowing how to do it are hounds of different kennels. Your immediate task is to consider some of the many ways that speeches may be introduced.

The examples that accompany the suggested approaches are just one person's interpretation of what might be done, and, as such, should be regarded only as examples, not models. You will have to fashion your introductions to fit your personality, your particular problem, your audience, the occasion, and many other aspects of the speaking situation in which you will be placed.

Ways to Start Talks

The following kinds of openings will be presented in brief discussion and examples:

Immediate consideration of the subject
Immediate revelation of purpose
Use of a quotation
Reference to the occasion
Making a personal reference

An appeal to self-interest of the audience
Asking a pertinent question
Issuance of a challenge
Use of suspense
Use of an illustration
Use of anecdote or humorous reference
Use of an exhibit
Use of a startling statement

Immediate consideration of the subject

Without any fanfare you can let your listeners know immediately *what* you intend to talk about. The subject itself carries the burden of arousing interest. This method of opening a talk is popular, simple, and always in good taste.

Topic: "The Atom Bomb, Hiroshima, and You"

Purpose: *To convince* audience of the urgent need to control atomic energy

It's time to talk again about what the atom bomb did to Hiroshima. What happened there is still vital to all of us, because it is a constant reminder of what can happen to our cities, to our people, and to future generations in the event of of another war. Today's bombs have unbelievable destructive force, and more and more nations are capable of using them. Atomic energy must be controlled if civilization is to endure.

Immediate revelation of purpose

Similar to the method shown above, immediate revelation of purpose leaves no doubt about *why* you are talking. It is a very direct means of getting started and is frequently employed when it is important to get to the heart of a matter without wasting time. If your speech is to be short, the introduction can easily be telescoped without losing its force.

Topic: "Voorhies for President" (campaign speech at high school rally)

Purpose: *To convince* audience Voorhies is the best candidate and *to persuade* them to vote for him

I'm on this platform for just one thing—to convince you that Jerry Voorhies is the best candidate for student-body president and to ask you to vote for him in tomorrow's election. There are four other candidates running for this office, all of them with good records and fine qualifications. But I believe Jerry has that *extra* bit of ability and personality that makes him *the* man for the job. Let's review his scholastic record, his participation in activities, and his influence in school affairs.

An appeal to self-interest

If you appeal to the desires

Topic: "Selling Magazine Subscriptions"

Purpose: *To inform,* to tell about some-that move people, they will listen—and often act. Making money, self-preservation, dressing well, having a good time, being complimented, gaining an important position, and being popular are just a few of these desires. They reflect the ego that is in all of us; they are matters of self-interest.

thing, but a hidden or implied purpose may be *to persuade*

Everyone of us could use an extra dollar. No matter how much your allowance is, or how profitable your after-school job may be, or how generous your parents are with extras, there's always a place for another dollar. So, if you'd like to know how to make that extra dollar with a minimum of effort and on a flexible time schedule, I'll give you a recipe: Sell magazines!

Asking a pertinent question

Asking a pertinent question is a simple and sure way of getting your audience to think *with* you. You arouse interest and curiosity, while letting your listeners know the nature of your subject. Which *is* the pertinent question in the example? How is it helped by the other questions?

Topic: "How Long Will You Live?"

Purpose: *To inform* listeners of today's life expectancy

Do you know that a parrot may live to be two hundred years old? Are you aware that toads have been known to live forty years? Do you know that the giant tortoise has a life expectancy of at least one hundred years? And how about you? How long will *you* live? There are some interesting new statistics that may surprise you.

Issuance of a challenge

This method is closely related to an appeal to self-interest, because it strikes at a person's ego. If the challenge is reasonable, response is quick. In a speech, the challenge may carry the listeners along in active mental effort, even though by the end of the speech they may be largely convinced of the speaker's argument. What is *your* reaction to a challenge?

Topic: "Our Grading System"

Purpose: *To convince* this audience of the merits of the grading system.

Quarterly grades were handed out last Monday, and it seems to me I have heard nothing but grumbling about what a "lousy" system of grading we have in this school. I think it's about time for us to put up or shut up. I challenge anyone in the room to come up with a better system. Now, before you accept that challenge, I want you to listen to some facts about grading systems. I say it isn't likely that we will get a better system than ours—and I can prove it.

Use of suspense

Tease your audience, arouse

Topic: "Time"

Purpose: *To inform*; to bring interesting

its curiosity, whet its appetite, and then reveal the subject of your talk. Beware of trying to build a high pitch of curiosity about a topic in which your listeners will have a minimum of interest. What is your evaluation of the example in this respect?

and important facts about time to the audience

With the possible exception of the weather, it is the most talked-of topic in the country. Millions of TV fans may groan on a Saturday afternoon when the announcer mentions it. It was discussed at the dinner table last night; it was talked about before class today. Its passage is uncontrollable, and its effect on everyone is inevitable. What is it? It's *time*!

Use of a startling statement

The dramatic effect of the startling statement upon the listener is such that his attention is gained quickly. The caution here is to be sensible in the use of this device. If your effort sounds phony, unduly exaggerated, or bizarre, the attention you gain may be lost quickly in negative reactions that will be built up in the audience. The startling statement can be effective, but it can also backfire.

Topic: "The Influenza Epidemic"

Purpose: *To inform,* but mostly *to convince* the audience of the seriousness of the epidemic

Before this week ends, one person in this room will be dead! There is some comfort in that figure, though, because it may be only a statistical death. Records show that the influenza epidemic raging in this city is claiming every week one life in fifty. Hospitals are filled to overflowing, and rest homes and private homes are being pressed into service. Death is showing no favoritism to young or old, to male or female. *You* may be lucky, but the death rate is tragic.

Use of a quotation

What someone else says is nearly always of interest to people, particularly if the person quoted is well known and respected, and the quotation has either immediate importance or a universal truth. Quotations that are famous and easily recognized establish a feeling of familiarity with the subject and

Topic: "The Finer Things in Life"

Purpose: *To arouse emotion;* to inspire the listeners to new feelings and appreciations of certain values in life

"Man shall not live by bread alone." The truth of this Bible quotation has been recognized for thousands of years. It means that food and drink and sleep are not enough to sustain man, that practical things—either luxuries or necessities—are not sufficient to keep man content, create in the audience a mood of acceptance toward the idea you intend to present.

Reference to the occasion

This simple and obvious way to begin can sometimes be quite effective and may other times be very ordinary although appropriate. It is particularly appropriate when the occasion of the speech is of major importance.

Making a personal reference

People are interested in other

that man has a soul and yearns for the finer things in life. What *are* these finer things? How do we recognize them? How do we get them?

Occasion: Lincoln's birthday assembly

Purpose: *To arouse feeling*; to pay tribute

We have gathered here to pay tribute to the memory of an outstanding American, a President who served his country well and who gave his life in that service. Because it is his birthday, and because his greatness grows with the years, it is "altogether fitting and proper" that we take time today to remember what Abraham Lincoln was and what he did.

Topic: "Diving for Abalone"

Purpose: *To entertain* is the chief effort, although much information will also be given in the talk

If your topic is something like "Diving for Abalone," you might begin your talk by telling how your own experience with the sport came about.

people and what they do. Brief personal references usually arouse interest and sympathy, or empathy. Your audience will be pleased to hear something personal about you. Personal references must always be in good taste, reflecting discretion in content and the avoidance of boastfulness.

About three years ago my family and I went to Laguna Beach for our summer vacation. It's a wonderful spot for swimming and fishing, and in the month that I was there I had a liberal, demanding, and exciting education in both. A couple of new friends were especially good at diving for abalone, and when they found out I was interested, they took me along and taught me the tricks of this dangerous sport. If you have a few minutes, let me tell you about this exotic "shell" game.

Use of an illustration

We all have curiosity about most things in life—the things we can understand and those that mystify us. Especially are we curious about people, and an illustration that has human-interest value will capture attention and put your audience in a good listening mood. Do you believe this to be true?

Topic: "Home Accidents"

Purpose: *To convince*; to sharpen the awareness of your listeners of the dangers lurking in home situations where accidents can occur

Douglas Keller was a promising young instructor in journalism at Duke University. At 8:15 on the night of October 15, he decided to take a bath. Because he wanted to finish reading an article while he was soaking, and because he needed extra light in the bathroom, he brought in a standing lamp from his bedroom. Then he got into the tub, relaxed, and started to read. A glare from the lamp bothered him a bit, so he reached up to shift the lamp slightly, and his hand came into contact with the socket. You know what happened. The doctor, who arrived too late, shook his head and said, "Far too many people die from accidents like this."

Use of anecedote or humorous reference

Humor is difficult to handle. Be cautious in using it as the

Topic: "Thrift"

Purpose: The example that follows would permit a choice of purpose. What is *yours*?

It was a drowsy summer day in Salt

chief ingredient of your opening. Its effectiveness lies in your ability to put your point across and to tie it to what follows. If your effort fails, you're off to a bad start because your audience is no longer neutral; it is now a little bit against you. Generally, anecdotes are safer than attempts at pure humor.

Lake City. Few people were on the streets; traffic moved lazily. All of a sudden an automobile swung noisily around a corner and moved down the middle of State Street—backward! People couldn't believe their eyes. Two cars dashed for the curb, and a bored cop, no longer bored, sprang into action. The culprit, when apprehended, offered this explanation: He was renting the car on a mileage basis, and he was driving backward because the speedometer didn't register in reverse! How's that for thrift?

Use of an Exhibit

Though visual aids are more commonly used during the body of a speech than during the introduction, the device of starting a talk with an "eye-catcher" rarely fails. Visual aids help to focus attention, to enliven, to enhance, to clarify, to emphasize, and to reinforce. You must learn the knack of making an exhibit do those things *for* your speech, and you must learn to keep it from taking attention *away from* your speech.

- Know your exhibit well enough to be able to direct your speaking at least partly to your audience and not exclusively to the exhibit.
- Use only exhibits large enough to be seen by everyone.
- If the exhibit is used as a device for opening your speech, follow it quickly with speech material that is related to the exhibit and that is as interesting as you can make it.
- Hold such exhibits as photographs, maps, charts, and diagrams at an angle convenient for the viewers, and swing them *very slowly* in a flat arc as you show them.
- Beware of using exhibits that are so unmanageable that your performance becomes acrobatic and is itself the exhibit.
- Avoid displaying a mechanism whose appeal depends upon its *operation*, and, if you are planning to demonstrate a mechanism, be sure you can operate it.
- If you are using a projector—filmstrip, opaque, transparency, slide, or film—*know* how to use it, and have your materials carefully selected and in order, if sequence is important.
- In general, use exhibits that are closely related to your talk and which quickly add interest or make a point clear.

The example that follows illustrates the use of a simple exhibit to open a talk.

Topic: "How Matches Are Made"

Purpose: *To inform,* as the speech title clearly indicates

I want you, all of you, to look at this for a moment. (Holds up a match.) Here is a simple, useful article used by millions of people all around the world every day. (Strikes the match and holds it flaming before his audience.) Despite the fact that modern technology has provided us with many kinds of lighters, both manual and automatic, that use inflammable liquids, electricity, and even flint, we still burn billions of matches a year . . . and we still find something fascinating about striking a match. But I wonder how many of us know how matches are made.

Other Tips on Openings. There is always a gap between a speaker and his audience, particularly at the beginning of a speech, and more particularly when the speaker is facing a group which is tired, bored, or hostile. Your first step in an attempt to bridge that gap is to introduce yourself and your speech in a way that will put both in as favorable a light as possible, which means that your words, your manner, your sensitivity to the mood of the audience, and your ability to make a quick adjustment in your remarks are all important ingredients of an introduction. As stated before, the examples you have studied are examples, not models. They were made for imaginary audiences, but they are guides for introductions to speeches before real ones. If you should find yourself speaking to a hostile group, your opening should reflect awareness of that hostility and should be aimed at reducing it. You might appeal to self-interest of the audience or to their sense of fair play. You could, if it seemed appropriate and you feel capable of doing it, use humor to lessen tension and gain a degree of acceptance. Or, you might go immediately to the reason for the hostility and deal with it directly, reasonably, and firmly, but in a manner which does not make the audience feel that you yourself are hostile and argumentative. Whatever your approach, you won't reduce hostility if you are uncompromising, vindictive, insensitive, dishonest, inaccurate, or ambiguous in what you say and either fawning or frightened in the way you say it.

Laying aside the difficult task of gaining the favor of a hostile audience, let's turn to a few tips on openings for most circumstances:

Memorize your opening sentence. Starting off without faltering, stumbling, or repeating yourself will give *you* assurance and *your audience* a good impression.

Open with short, forceful sentences. Short sentences have a directness that lends them punch. Long sentences, because they are harder to say and harder to follow, create an obstacle for both the passer and the receiver.

Get to the point. Tie your introduction in with your subject and purpose as quickly and effectively as possible. Early ramblings may lose your listeners beyond recovery.

Make your opening inviting. Try to make every member of the audience feel that you are talking to him and that he'll enjoy going along with you. Make him feel included and wanted in the experience you are to share.

Have faith in yourself. Don't apologize for your preparation or for what you plan to say. Such explanations slow the beginning of a speech and may lose for you the respect and interest of the audience.

ACTIVITIES

1. Discuss in class the method which might be the suitable way of beginning a talk on each of the following topics:

Pets I Have Had
The Empire State Building
Save Our Forests
Seat Belts in Every Car
Why Read Shakespeare?
The Presidential Succession
A Trip to the Grand Canyon
Traffic Problems in the 1970's
How Old Is a Teen-ager?
Tolerance toward Others

2. Bring to class a sample of the introduction to some published speech famous or otherwise and be prepared to discuss it in terms of these questions:

a. What method, or approach, is used?
b. Does the introduction arouse interest?
c. Does it create a friendly relationship between speaker and audience, insofar as you can judge?
d. Does it lead smoothly and directly into the body of the talk?
e. Are the opening sentences clearly stated and brief enough to be immediately understandable?
f. What improvements do you suggest?

3. Make up an introduction for an imaginary speech on a topic from the list in the first activity above, and deliver it before the class. Let your classmates evaluate it on the basis of the questions in the second activity.

4. Imagine yourself to be the last speaker on a program. You expect to face an audience which is restless from listening to several speeches. Your topic is "The Red Cross Needs Your Help"; your purpose is to persuade your listeners to contribute money to a worthy cause. How can you begin? Write a sample introduction and compare it in class with those written by your classmates. Which introductions were most appealing, and what qualities made them so?

5. Review the various kinds of introductions, select one you feel would be suitable for an oral book report, and write out your introduction. Read it to your speech class and ask for criticisms and suggestions for improvement.

6. Change, rearrange, or add to the following statements so that they become an introduction built upon the technique of opening with a question or questions:

This high school is now the largest one in the state, both in its physical size and in enrollment. At the present time there is an average daily attendance of 3246 students. The gymnasium is capable of seating more than 4500 spectators. The school grounds cover an area equal to four of our city blocks. A fleet of twenty buses is required to bring in students from outlying sections of the district. Next year the enrollment will be larger. Some new buildings are needed. Bonds must be passed to insure adequate housing for future classes.

What have you discovered to be the main subject under consideration?

7. Develop an introduction that is opened by one of the following quotations:

a. "Now would I give a thousand furlongs of sea for an acre of barren ground."—WILLIAM SHAKESPEARE

b. "Let tomorrow take care of tomorrow . . ."—CHARLES SWAIN

c. "He too serves a certain purpose who only stands and cheers."—HENRY ADAMS

d. "Goodwill is the mightiest practical force in the universe."—CHARLES DOLE

e. "No man can be a patriot on an empty stomach."—WILLIAM COWPER BRANN

8. Rewrite the following introduction, in which sentences have been jumbled, so that the *purpose* of the talk appears quickly. Make any other changes you wish.

What we do is up to you to decide. As you know, our purchases are necessarily on a cash basis and must continue to be. If we can't raise extra funds, we have two alternatives. I'm here to ask for money, so don't let your moneybags leave the room. The float that our club is entering in the Mardi Gras is nearly completed, and it's beautiful, but there are expenses we didn't anticipate. If present plans are to be fulfilled, we must spend a little more money.

9. List as many self-interests as you can think of, and then in class discussion try to relate these interests to various groups in your community. Which self-interests seem to be identified with every group? Which pertain only to special groups? Which seem to belong to individuals rather than to groups? How can an awareness of the powerful motives that impel people to act be of use to you in certain speaking situations or, for that matter, in many life situations?

10. When you plan for your next class talk, select *two* of the methods for opening that appeal to you and write an introduction for each. Compare them for effectiveness and appropriateness, choose the one you think is better, and write the reason for your choice. As a follow-up, ask your classmates to evaluate your introduction in terms of the questions listed under Activity 2.

11. Prepare several introductions to the same speech which is to be given to each of the following groups:

a. Boy Scouts
b. Parent-Teacher Association
c. Saturday Afternoon Garden Club
d. High School Age Church Group
e. Rotary Club
f. Retired Citizen's Community
g. Student Body of Neighboring School

Would you use the same introduction for each group? Is it important to consider the goals, interests, desires of your audience when planning an introduction?

The Function of a Conclusion

The conclusion consists of your closing sentences, beginning when the middle, or body, of the speech is completed. It is that part of your talk in which you highlight your central theme and leave your listeners with a clear, definite, and favorable impression. It may include a summary of main points, if you have that kind of speech, or it may have some other kind of ingredient which will serve your purpose. Perhaps you have heard the advice given to all would-be speakers: "Stand up, speak up, shut up!" The conclusion is the "shut up!" part of your speech and it must be done well.

The conclusion should be a natural outgrowth of your subject, not just something tacked on the end because everyone expects a conclusion. Those closing sentences are strategic and, because they are the last words your audience will hear, they may be remembered longer than other parts of your speech. The end of a speech is just as important as the beginning and must be accorded its proper allotment of preparation. No matter what specific method you use to conclude your speech, you must be sure that your conclusion does two things: it gives your audience a feeling of completeness or satisfaction in terms of your having done what you set out to do, and it centers attention on the whole idea of your speech rather than on any part of it. In short, it must drive home the central idea.

Ways to End Talks. There are many ways to end speeches, just as there are many ways to begin them. If you want to leave the effect of logic with your listeners, you may simply summarize what you have said, or you may prefer to put into a capsule the extended syllogism of the body of your speech; if you want to touch their feelings, you may make an emotional appeal or project them into the future; if you want to get them to *do* something, you make a definite appeal for action; or, if you want to highlight your main idea, you may use a clever story or quotation as a clincher.

It is impossible to set specific rules for concluding all speeches, since there are too many variable factors to consider. As with your introduction, you must create a conclusion that fits the speech situation. Consider the type of speech you are giving, the purpose behind it, the mood of your audience, the nature of the occasion, the materials at your disposal, and your own talent and then put together the best ending your time and skill will permit. And remember: don't make it too long!

Until you feel comfortable in not doing so, make a regular practice of writing out your conclusions as well as your introductions in full sentence form. It may be well for you to memorize the introductions and conclusions of your first few talks. Such memorization can often give you a feeling of greater confidence when you begin and can serve as a form of insurance for your ending.

The following methods for concluding a speech will be discussed and exemplified:

Return to method used in the introduction
Summary of main points
General summary of your theme
Visualization of the future
Suggesting definite action
An appeal to emotion
Appropriate quotation
Illustration, story, anecdote, or personal reference
Decision-provoking question

Return to Method Used in Introduction

This method of conclusion gets its strength from the elements of emphasis and drama. An audience can have a feeling of pleasure and satisfaction from the reinforcement that unexpected repetition brings, and the repetition won't be resented. You may repeat the exact words of your opening sentence or sentences if they are memorable, you may paraphrase those words, or you may refer to them in such a way as to evoke their impact. Several of the methods of introduction could be utilized in this manner, but only one will be exemplified here. For example, do you recall the introduction on "The Influenza Epidemic"?

Topic: "The Influenza Epidemic"

Purpose: *To inform,* but mostly *to convince,* audience of seriousness of the epidemic

There is no doubt about the tragic possibilities that face us. As I said in the beginning, one person in this room will be dead, statistically, before the week ends. One life in fifty will be claimed by death in our present epidemic. The shortage of space to take care of the ill and dying is acute. Whether I'm to be the next statistic—or you are—is no longer important. What *is* important is that we recognize the epidemic's force, give up being complacent, and join in an effort to halt it.

Summary of main points

Restate essential facts or major points of your talk. If your

Topic: "The Miracle of Nylon"

Purpose: *To inform* audience of nylon

Truly, nylon is a word to conjure with.

speech has been long or technical, this method helps to refresh the memory of your listeners. Overuse of this approach could bring monotony to speech endings, but for certain kinds of material it is almost necessary.

As we have seen, first, it is a product of the magic of chemistry; second, its manufacture seems like sleight of hand; third, its present uses are artful and ingenious; fourth, its future possibilities are as startling as the sight of a white rabbit pulled out of a magician's hat. Another miracle of the modern world of science—that's nylon!

General summary of your theme

Your closing sentences should be centered upon the main idea of your talk, removing any possible doubt about what you've been saying. This commonly used method fixes attention on the theme of the speech rather than on any individual part, and it reinforces a general truth rather than supports a particular act.

Topic: "The Red Cross and Mankind"

Purpose: *To impress* the audience of the worthiness of Red Cross

The Red Cross, certainly, is a most worthy organization. People everywhere respect its symbol because it stands for help and compassion, regardless of religious conviction, race, ideology, or geographical location. Its concern is always for the welfare of mankind, and our present concern should be the support of its worthwhile activities.

Visualization of the future

Project your audience into what may lie ahead, trying to make a responsible generalization about the future. We are both frightened and intrigued by the unknown, and its being anticipated in a realistic manner can greatly influence our present behavior. This method makes a good conclusion for talks to convince or impress.

Topic: "Soil Conservation"

Purpose: *To convince* listeners of our wastefulness in certain agricultural practices

Without additional soil-saving efforts on the part of farmers and the government, we face a threatening future. Rolling fields now rich and fertile with topsoil will be eroded and cut by gullies. Good grazing land will be covered with thin, weedy growth. Once virgin soil of the Texas black lands is already worn down to the white limestone which will grow nothing. Today's productive prairies will tomorrow fill the rivers of the flat Middle West with life-giving silt washed away by rain. We will all pay for this shameless waste, but especially our children and their children will pay. We must not let this happen.

Suggesting definite action

If you want people to do something, you must ask and ask. In a persuasive talk you must not fail to conclude with a request for action, no matter how or where you made your previous requests. Sales talks and pep talks always end with such requests. You will find more detailed discussion of appeals for action in Unit 13.

An appeal to emotion

However logical we like to think ourselves, we most often are moved by an appeal to our feelings when an appeal to our cold logic will not sway us. An appeal to the heart may be long remembered, while an appeal to the head may be soon forgotten. Among the best appeals to human feelings that have been made in public addresses are those by Lincoln in his Second

Topic: "Improve Your Vocabulary"

Purpose: *To persuade* listeners to take an actual step in learning new words

A good vocabulary, then, can give you a real sense of power and a feeling of pleasure. If you learn a new word every day, in a year's time you will have three hundred and sixty-five new sources of power and pleasure. Why not start *now*? Try this. Look up the word *genial* in a dictionary before you leave school this afternoon. Use it correctly in conversation three times before tomorrow's meeting of this class, and the word will be yours to keep unless, of course, you already own it. You'll be on your way to possessing an excellent vocabulary if you'll just start now!

Lincoln's Second Inaugural Address

Fondly do we hope—fervently do we pray—that this mighty scourge of war may speedily pass away. Yet, if God wills that it continue until all the wealth piled by the bondman's two hundred and fifty years of unrequited toil shall be sunk, and until every drop of blood drawn with the lash shall be paid by another drawn with the sword, as was said three thousand years ago, so still it must be said, "The judgments of the Lord are true and righteous altogether."

With malice toward none; with charity for all; with firmness in the right, as God gives us to see the right, let us strive on to finish the work we are in; to bind up the nation's wounds; to care for him who shall have borne the battle, and for his widow, and his orphan—to do all which may achieve and cherish a just and lasting peace among ourselves, and with all nations.

Inaugural Address and by Patrick Henry in his famous and now-familiar speech before the Virginia House of Burgesses in 1775. Here are the closing sentences of each:

Patrick Henry's "Liberty or Death" Speech

It is in vain, sir, to extenuate the matter. Gentlemen may cry peace, peace—but there is no peace. The war is actually begun! The next gale that sweeps from the north will bring to our ears the clash of resounding arms! Our brethren are already in the field! Why stand we here idle? What is it that gentlemen wish? What would they have? Is life so dear, or peace so sweet, as to be purchased at the price of chains and slavery? Forbid it, Almighty God! I know not what course others may take; but as for me, give me liberty or give me death!

An appropriate quotation

Your quotation may be the stirring words of some great man, a bit of poetry, or merely some doggerel. If it is unusual, to the point, and appropriate, it can add immeasurably to the effectiveness of your ending.

Excellence in a quotation is not enough; it must also be appropriate!

Does the example meet this standard?

Topic: "World Peace"

Purpose: *To impress* the audience with the thought that world peace is not futile, not unrealistic

World peace is not hopeless, not impossible. Compassionate and understanding men yearn for it today as they have for thousands of years. If we work constructively toward that goal, and if we are steadfastly resolute, the prophecy of the Bible may yet be fulfilled. "They shall beat their swords into plowshares, and their spears into pruning hooks; nation shall not lift sword against nation, neither shall they learn war any more."

Illustration, story, anecdote . . .

Any one of these devices can make your main idea more vivid and can reinforce your logical appeal by capturing it in a funny or interesting nutshell. Just be sure that your illustration doesn't overshadow the point you wish to make. In other words, don't

Topic: "The Responsibility of Voting"

Purpose: *To persuade* listeners to vote

So, when the polls open tomorrow and you ponder your choices, remember that the candidates are all worthy of your *consideration*, but what they need are your *votes*. Don't be like the kindly old lady who knew all of the candidates in a small-town election and thought them all to be such nice people that she couldn't choose let your audience lose sight of the forest because one of the trees is so interesting.

Decision-provoking question

Such a question, though it may reveal the speaker's bias, is not so intended. Rather, it should focus the issue and put it squarely before the listener, leaving him with a choice of decision but *not* with the choice of procrastinating or doing nothing. The talk itself is primarily informative, but the conclusion ends on the note of pushing the listener to act, to make a decision.

among them; so she simply wrote on the bottom of her ballot, "God bless you all!" Our candidates tomorrow don't want your blessing; they want your votes.

Topic: "Our Traffic-Bound Community"

Purpose: *To inform* and *to persuade* the audience to face a problem and to make a thoughtful decision

The decision is up to you. If a freeway is built, the community loses taxable property and some of you will have to sell your homes. If nothing is done, you must live with the traffic snarls that are making community life miserable. The issue must be faced; a stand must be taken. I suggest that you ask yourselves: Which can my children and I better afford—the tax burden and personal losses we may sustain or the increasingly frustrating traffic delays that are paralyzing our community?

Know how and when to conclude—don't bore your audience!

Other Tips on Conclusions. The length of your own conclusions will depend upon the overall length of your speech, as well as upon the type of ending you choose. You have noted, for instance, that the examples have varied in length, with types such as visualization of the future and an appeal to emotion requiring more thorough treatment than those which concluded with a summary, a story, or a quotation.

Don't bore your audience by being long-winded and rambling in your closing remarks. Be brief, and your audience will be grateful.

Don't stop too abruptly, or you may fail to emphasize your main point and will leave your listeners with a feeling of incompletion.

Don't introduce new material which should have been in the body of your talk. If you have not already presented your basic arguments, provided essential information, or moved your audience to desired feelings, you can only hurt your effort by trying to go back to recoup. Even if you have forgotten an important point, don't cram it into the conclusion.

Don't use long, involved sentences. Shorter sentences in the conclusion, like shorter conclusions themselves, tend to carry listeners quickly and comfortably to the end of a speech, an end that good listeners expect.

Don't fail to work out the details of your conclusion. Plan every ingredient essential to the type of conclusion you have chosen. Write out as much as necessary. Memorize at least the last sentence. Practice saying your conclusion until you feel it will produce the impact you desire.

ACTIVITIES

1. Consider the following points to have been made in a speech you gave in support of a candidate. Summarize them in a short conclusion.

   a. The candidate has a good general education.
   b. He is well trained in his particular field.
   c. He is capable.
   d. He has shown much interest in public affairs.
   e. He gets along well with people.

2. Turn back to the two examples given under an *appeal to emotion* and analyze them for the kinds of appeal that were made. Why was an appeal to feelings important in both of these conclusions?

3. Listen carefully to any talks you may hear in the next few weeks around school, on radio or TV, or at a public meeting and concentrate on the conclusions. What type of conclusion is used in each case? Does it leave a lasting impression? Did it seem effective at the moment? If it failed to "reach" you, why did it?

4. Study the following sample conclusions and write your reactions to each. Do they omit essential material? contain items which should not be included? violate concepts of acceptable construction? or fail in *any* way, in your judgment? How do your evaluations compare with those of your classmates?

a. **Topic:** "New Uniforms for the Band"

Purpose: *To arouse* audience to raise funds for these uniforms

As William Cowper Brann said, "No man can be a patriot on an empty stomach." Our band has been dressed in the same old uniforms for years, and they're a pretty ratty-looking outfit. They may not have empty stomachs, but who can put his heart into playing good music when he is shabby? I'm not musical myself, but I *am* interested in science, and I know that you can't very well conduct experiments if you don't have a laboratory. So I think we must do something to help the band get new uniforms. I'm sure everyone in this room joins me in wanting the band members to look like first-rate patriots!

b. **Topic:** "Your University"

Purpose: *To convince* students that they should enroll at their own state university

Why should you go to your own state university? That's the question which I hope I have answered. One reason, that I didn't mention, is the fact that the registration fee and the dormitory rates are among the lowest in the nation. You can get board and room for seventy-five dollars a month, and the semester registration will cost you only fifty dollars. Because the university is centrally located in the state, you can also save money on transportation. So, if you are really interested in saving some money, don't forget the state university.

c. **Topic:** "Polishing Rocks"

Purpose: *To inform* listeners how rocks are polished

Well, I guess that's about all there is to be said. I certainly like to polish rocks, and I want to thank you for letting me tell you how to do it. My favorite rocks are those in the chalcedony family, such as an onyx or an agate.

d. **Topic:** "Daily Exercise Plan"

Purpose: *To arouse* the listeners to start a plan of daily exercises

As I said at the very beginning, everyone wants to have good health, no matter who he is, but not many people are willing to work hard to get it, which is one of the reasons I am proposing the simple, short exercises that I have described, assuming, of course, that you regard eleven minutes a day as a short time and that you think the exercises themselves are really simple, which I do. I'm really very serious about getting you to start these exercises. Actually, I forgot to bring the exact title of the exercise book or the name of the publisher with me today, but I promise I'll bring it to class in the *very near future.* Now, that's a promise! Meanwhile, keep this thought in mind: a stitch in time saves nine!

5. Using the topics and purposes in the examples in the fourth activity, write your own conclusions. Lift from the examples any ideas that will serve you, and use any method of conclusion that is attractive to you.

Film:

Writing a Good Paragraph (Coronet). 11 min color or b&w.

DENT OF THE U

Unit Twelve

ON THE PLATFORM: Delivery Technique

So far in this central section of the book you have learned about selecting a topic, identifying a purpose, planning the general content, gathering material, outlining an orderly arrangement of ideas, developing the main points, and preparing a beginning and an ending. In effect, you have explored how to develop a solid, organized, well-motivated body of material for the content of a speech. You are now ready for the final step: preparing for its delivery. How can you best present what you have written on paper or stored in your mind—the thoughts and feelings that have been generated through the long process of building your talk? What methods, mechanics, techniques, devices, or simple practicalities may help you to "deliver the goods" effectively? How can you make a good impression on your listeners, strengthen your relationship with them, and gain for yourself a feeling of satisfaction and well-being through your delivery? Let's find some of the answers now. The problems which you will have to solve and which are discussed in this unit are suggested by the four general instructions below:

- Use the *method* which seems best suited for the occasion, purpose, and audience.
- Plan to coordinate *delivery* and *content.*
- Anticipate and meet *special problems*: mannerisms, handling notes, using a speaker's stand, using a microphone, adjusting to different groups, meeting the unexpected.
- Follow a definite plan for *practice and rehearsal.*

Methods of Delivery

Extemporaneous Speaking. Of all methods of delivery, extemporaneous speaking is probably the best for you to learn. Although it may seem difficult for some of you to master at first, it will in the end prove to be the most realistic, practical, and useful.

An extemporaneous speech is one that is thoroughly planned ahead of time as to thought and arrangement of ideas but in which the wording is left to the moment of speaking. It demands that you know more than you say. It requires you to have complete understanding of the idea-content of your speech, a full supply of material to draw upon for elaborating your main points, a good, clear, logical plan, and a desire to communicate in the best sense of the word on a person-to-person basis with all members of your audience.

This method best meets the demands of modern life. The standards and tempo of living today require people to be well informed, efficient, adaptable, and able to communicate freely. The person who trains himself to speak well extemporaneously is helping himself to meet such requirements. He learns how to assemble ideas and facts, to organize them in his mind, and to deliver them in a direct, conversational manner.

The challenges and values of extemporaneous speaking are exemplified in this study of the late Dag Hammarskjöld, who was Secretary-General of the United Nations.

The challenges and values of extemporaneous speaking lie in its freedom. When you discipline your thinking in order to be free in expression, the advantages to you and your listeners are many:

- *You can adapt your speaking* to whatever the time, place, or occasion demands—the mood of the audience, the significance of the place or the occasion, recent or immediate happenings, the chairman's introduction of you, an interruption, a shortened time limit.
- *You can express yourself with freshness* and spontaneity because you are not tied to a manuscript nor bound to a succession of memorized words which you might have difficulty in recalling.
- *You are free to establish a warm, personal relationship* with your listeners through an informal, straightforward conversational manner of speaking.
- *You have an opportunity to develop sensitivity* to the way your listeners react to ideas, thus increasing the communicativeness between you.
- *You will find yourself talking with people instead of at them* as you become deeply involved in the ideas you are expressing and more committed to putting them across with vigor, animation, and earnestness.
- *You will become more fluent in the use of language* because you are not reading or speaking words from memory, but are creating as you talk, uninhibited by set word-patterns.

Because of your past speaking experiences, especially in grade school, you may hesitate to leave the security of a written manuscript or memorized material. A greater security, however, awaits you when you conquer the extemporaneous method. It is the most mature, acceptable, practical, effective way of speaking today. Once mastered, it will serve you well in meeting almost any speaking situation that you will face.

Tips on Extemporaneous Speaking

- *Speak from a Full Mind.* The more you know about your subject, the better you'll talk. If you have a wealth of material and specific details in your mind, you'll speak with greater sureness and confidence.
- *Study Your Outline.* Knowing the chief ideas and following their logical progression keeps you on the right track.
- *Practice Orally from Your Outline.* Once started, keep going without backtracking or repeating. As you practice, take mental note of spots which give you trouble and concentrate on those later.

- *Don't Memorize Words!* Too much oral practice may lead you into repeating the same word-patterns and cause you to lose the extemporaneous quality of speaking. Think in blocks of ideas rather than words. Change your wording each time you practice, but cling to the orderly plan of your outline.
- *Let Vigor and Animation Characterize Your Delivery.* Your deep involvement with the ideas you're presenting and your sensitive awareness of the interaction between your listeners and yourself helps stimulate enthusiasm and earnestness.

Memorized Speaking. Delivering a speech from memory is generally not recommended as an effective method of presentation. The results are too often mechanical and artificial. It is a popular method, however, for some young or inexperienced speakers who feel unable to verbalize under pressure or who are reluctant to try extemporaneous speaking. You may be one of these. From your early days in school you have probably leaned on memorizing whenever you've had to "give a speech," and you may find it difficult to change your habit now. Yet the more sophisticated you become as a speaker (and as a listener, too), the less you will be attracted by this method. Because memorized speech is rigid in form, its delivery *sounds* memorized, lacking the life, warmth, earnestness, and freedom of the extemporaneous method. It seems more like a production than like communication. Except for times when orations, declamations, formal tributes, eulogies, or rituals in fraternal organizations are to be given, you will do well to stress extemporaneous rather than memorized delivery.

If you *must* memorize a speech (or poem or literary selection), remember to be letter-perfect and well rehearsed. It takes skillful artistry and acting ability to bring life and freshness to memorized words. You must become more an actor than a speaker.

Tips on Memorized Speaking

- *Rehearse, Rehearse, Rehearse!* An early start with plenty of time for frequent repetition and recall will make delivery easier.
- *Memorize the Whole, Rather Than the Parts.* Keeping your mind on the main blocks of thought and the forward movement of your script helps you to avoid memorizing single sentences parrotlike. Don't backtrack. If some sections are difficult, repeat the entire block of thought where those sections appear.
- *Establish Sympathy with the Material.* This means putting yourself

into the mood and feeling of the script. Make the words your own by pretending they are fresh and new each time you speak them.

- *Employ Good Delivery Techniques.* Don't race; don't mumble. Proceed deliberately, suiting your pace, pause, emphasis, and action to the meaning of the words.

Impromptu Speaking. The word *impromptu* is defined as "in readiness; without preparation or advanced thought; offhand." In speaking, it generally applies to a talk that is given on the spur of the moment to meet a special occasion (see Unit 14); but, as a method of delivering a talk, impromptu speaking is unreliable and hazardous. It is almost synonymous with "unprepared."

There are times, however, when you will speak in impromptu fashion during the course of a prepared speech. Under such circumstances impromptu speaking involves a quality of spontaneity and informality that is associated with conversational repartee or the give-and-take of a lively discussion. If an unexpected or interruptive situation occurs which requires your immediate response, such as answering a question, responding to an unexpected introduction, or coping with other unforeseen circumstances, you will be speaking impromptu. You will be on your own, indulging in "instant" speech.

President Johnson has marked the words he wishes to emphasize in his address.

There is always room in speaking for ad-libs and bon mots, for the inspired improvisations, apt witticisms, and well-tempered humorous comments that may be said impetuously because the moment or situation demands creativeness and invention. Good taste, good humor, good intentions, and good sense will have to be your guides when such times arise. Ordinarily, however, impromptu delivery cannot take the place of the extemporaneous method.

There is frequent confusion over the meaning of impromptu and extemporaneous, some people believing they are essentially the same. They are not! Without belaboring the difference, just remember that impromptu delivery occurs on the spur of the moment and involves *no* previous preparation or advance thought. It is neither a synonym nor a substitute for extemporaneous delivery.

Reading a Speech. This method of delivery is generally a poor one. In special cases, when exactness and precision are necessary, such as in radio speaking, where the limitations of time and programing may require your reading from script, or perhaps in a committee meeting or a convention, where formality and accuracy demand the reading of a special study or report, this method is acceptable. But under ordinary conditions reading is a poor substitute for speaking. Most people read aloud very badly, either racing meaninglessly through the script or droning along in a listless, impersonal, halting fashion that almost kills communication. If you must read a speech aloud to an audience, try the READ-SPEAK plan that is discussed under Composite Methods in the following section. Putting feeling and animation into lifeless words is your greatest problem in reading a speech skillfully. Unit 21, "Reading Aloud: Prose and Poetry," will help you gain such skill.

Tips on Reading a Speech

- *Glance Ahead at Thought Units.* Your eyes should be one jump ahead of your voice. After you glance at a group of words, raise your eyes and look at the audience while uttering them; then glance quickly down again to take in the next thought-group.
- *Blend Sounds Together.* Speak whole groups of words together as if they were one unit of thought, as you do in normal speaking. Reading words instead of groups of words leads to artificial, stilted, unrhythmical delivery.
- *Watch Your Rate and Articulation.* A deliberate pace and distinct enunciation will help you to avoid racing over the words or mumbling them.
- *Make Full Use of Pause and Emphasis.* Mark your script, if you wish,

by heavily underlining the words or phrases you intend to stress vocally and by using dashes (—), diagonal lines (/), or lettering (P) to indicate places for pausing.

- *Thorough Familiarity Breeds Confidence.* As with memorizing, oral practice and strong identification with the thought-content will aid delivery.

Composite Methods. Sometimes delivering a speech involves a little of everything: memorizing, extemporizing, making impromptu comments, and reading from manuscript. For instance, you may memorize your outline and also go one step further by memorizing the key sentences which introduce each new block of thought. Such memorizing may help you to recall the structure and the key sentences of your speech and to keep you on the track.

Some speakers use a straddle device with great success. They memorize the introduction and the conclusion word-for-word in order to insure a smooth beginning and ending, but they deliver the body extemporaneously. You might find this compromise to your liking, since it combines security with freedom. Just remember, however, that to bridge the gap between what is memorized and what is extemporized, your manner of delivery must artfully conceal the difference as you slip from the memorized introduction into the extemporaneous body and then into the set words of the conclusion.

Impromptu remarks, as we have seen, may also be part of a composite method. You may wish to begin a talk with a few personal observations that are unprepared. You thus allow yourself some freedom in responding to the chairman's introduction or to the occasion or to some happening relating to your topic or your audience, before getting into your planned speech.

Another combination involves what you may call the READ-SPEAK method. Here you come to a speaking situation with a fully developed outline or manuscript of your speech from which you both read and talk. You consult your material from time to time, read from it, if necessary, to stress a point or refresh your memory, and extemporize from it when you have good command of the main points and plenty of specific details in your mind. You combine reading and speaking, alternating from one to the other as your talk progresses. The method is a practical and realistic one, enabling you to put your entire attention on the ideas you are presenting without worrying whether you'll forget something and thus assuring your listeners that they'll hear everything you planned to say.

This method is commonly used in the business, scientific, and social world at meetings, conferences, panel discussions, lectures, and similar sessions where it is important to give a report, state a problem, explain a position, or give information accurately, quickly, and efficiently. If it seems not to fit into the traditional forms of speaking, being half of one and half of another, remember that customs and standards change with the times. By today's practical communication standards, READ-SPEAK is a very acceptable method for meeting real-life situations. Whereas an extemporaneous speech in its purest form may be more highly artistic, effective, and suitable for most occasions, its successful presentation requires much time, broad knowledge, careful preparation, great fluency with words, and a considerable amount of oral experience. Under the pressures and tempos of modern life the average person may not be able to give the time and effort required for the perfectly delivered extemporaneous speech. So he takes the shortcut, freely using his manuscript, outline, notes, or other material as he puts across his message. He gets the job of communication done informally and efficiently by combining the best of two methods.

Tips on Read-Speak

- *Don't Neglect Preparation.* Just because you're using notes or script freely for frequent reference, don't skimp on planning and practicing your talk.
- *Maintain an Extemporaneous Quality.* An informal, conversational manner with a close communicative feeling toward your audience is important. Don't let your reference to notes interfere with your audience contact.
- *Handle Your Material with Skill.* Because you are committed to reading your material, you must rely on it primarily during your speech. What you *can* do, however, is to leave your script frequently and complete, extemporaneously, the thought of a sentence you have started to read. Such action will give something of the feeling of extemporaneous speaking. Further, you can improvise a new idea which may occur to you, make an aside, remember an illustration, or adjust to your audience's reception in a manner which you think will help communication. Free yourself from the security of your written-out speech from time to time to bring life and sparkle to your talk. Your problem in skill is to jump from printed material to free thought frequently and easily.
- *Use the Best of Both Methods.* Apply the suggestions given in this unit under *Tips* for both extemporaneous speaking and reading.

As you gain experience in speaking, you will use some or all of the methods discussed in this unit, discovering for yourself which one is best suited for different audiences and occasions and which one gives you the greatest sense of accomplishment. As a goal in terms of training yourself in speaking skill, the extemporaneous method is an excellent one. The READ-SPEAK method, on the other hand, is a practical, realistic way of meeting most real-life situations.

Coordinate Delivery and Content

Delivery is the total of *how* a speech is given. It involves such factors as poise, posture, breath control, movement, gestures, and the vocal techniques of pause, emphasis, rate, volume, pitch, inflection, and the like. All of these were discussed in Unit 4 and should be familiar to you by now. Your use of these factors affects the general visual and aural (look for this word in the dictionary) impression you make on your listeners, an impression which often determines how well the audience receives what you say and is affected by it. In preparing to deliver a speech, then, you should consider the many ways you can impress your audience favorably and coordinate your delivery with the content.

Beginning the Speech. Your first impression will be made as you approach your audience and make your opening remarks. People will look at you curiously, noting your bearing, poise, voice, and general appearance. What should you do?

- Act calm and confident, hiding your inner tension.
- Look directly at your audience, glancing over the entire group.
- A friendly smile works wonders, too.
- If you feel very nervous before you rise to speak, take a few quiet deep breaths, swallow several times, slightly tense and relax your hands, arms, or leg muscles in an unobtrusive manner.
- If you tend to be dry-mouthed, keep a lozenge in your mouth until just before your turn to speak.
- Address the chairman and the audience. The words are not so important as a friendly manner, a direct glance, a clear voice, and some judicious pauses:
  "Madam Chairman (pause) and members of the audience . . ." (pause)
  "Thank you, Mr. Chairman (pause). Good evening, ladies and gentlemen . . ." (pause)
  "Mr. Williams (pause) and fellow students . . ." (pause)

During the Body of the Speech. The good impression you make during the middle part of your speech is closely related to how interesting, challenging, persuasive, or inspiring your material is and how closely identified you are with it. If your speech is well organized, with easy transitions from point to point, and with supporting material that has much interest value and impact, your delivery problems are simplified. With good material upon which to lean and with which to associate yourself, you are likely to reflect your pride and confidence through an animated, vigorous presentation. If, in addition, you make use of a few cue phrases, introductory words, or other transitional devices as you talk, you can help your listeners to follow your thinking by preparing them for shifts of thought and leading them from point to point. Such devices give you natural opportunities to pause, to emphasize a word or phrase, to shift your weight, to gesture, or to otherwise indicate visually and vocally the significant ideas and the forward movement of your talk.

- To indicate main points, include cue phrases like the following:

  "My first point is . . ."
  "In the second place . . ."
  "Third, we have . . ."
  "The next major issue is . . ."
  "Finally . . ."

- To indicate transitions or to introduce illustrative material, include devices like these:

  "To illustrate this point . . ."
  "For example . . ."
  "In other words . . ."
  "Furthermore . . ."
  "Let's look at it this way . . ."
  "A continuation of this idea is . . ."
  "On the other hand . . ."
  "Consequently . . ."
  "Therefore . . ."

- Place such cue words or phrases at the beginning of your paragraph or block of thought.
- Repeat key words occasionally to keep the thought flowing from sentence to sentence.

  "The members of the committee were shocked by the *findings. These findings* were . . ."
  "Because of a lack of recreation facilities, children must play in the *streets.* Let me describe *those streets* to you . . ."
  "At the end of 1963 *there was some doubt* that Congress would pass a tax-cut bill. Not only *was there some doubt,* but also . . ."

- Watch your audience for evidences of uncertainty, puzzlement, or inattention, and make a special effort to reach them by restating, reemphasizing, or reviewing a point you feel they're not getting.
- Match your delivery with the mood of your speech, whether serious, humorous, emotional, rational, concerned, angry, or sad.

Concluding the Speech. Your final impression should be a strong and effective one, for audiences are likely to remember best the last points a speaker makes. Whether your conclusion is a summary, a quotation, a question, an appeal, a projection into the future, or any other type, treat it as a natural outgrowth of your subject, not something tacked on, and give it a full measure of attention.

- Indicate your approach to the conclusion by any of various means: a more deliberate pace, a change of position, measured words, a dramatic pause, a more intense manner, a lowered pitch, some cue phrases, or whatever suits the mood of your words.
- Keep your voice strong and clear until the last words are said. Don't race, if time presses you, or mumble hurriedly. Maintain your poise to the end.
- Pause momentarily for a final effect. As your concluding words are said, look at the audience and, perhaps, give a barely perceptible nod of farewell.

Meeting Special Problems

The ease with which you handle yourself under varying conditions has a definite bearing on the impression you make on an audience. Here are some problems and situations to consider, inasmuch as they do have an effect on your delivery.

Mannerisms. You will need to eliminate aimless actions or mannerisms that detract attention from your speech. Are you guilty of any of these? Ask someone to help you recognize and correct your personal weaknesses.

Don't:

- twist fingers, hands, or notes
- sway restlessly back and forth
- touch face, hair, or clothing
- clear throat, smack lips, click tongue
- stare at floor, wall, ceiling, window

- make wry faces, frown, twist mouth
- use *er, ah, uh, and-a* between words and sentences
- move feet or hands nervously
- repeat fixed gestures

Handling Notes. Notes are a useful device that help beginning speakers to build confidence, recall the succession of ideas, insure against "blackout," and prevent unnecessary digressions, Don't be ashamed to use them; just use them well.

- Copy the large divisions of your outline on 3″ × 5″ cards, inked or typewritten on one side only.
- Hold notes in one hand, both hands, or place them on speaker's stand, whatever is most comfortable for you.
- Glance briefly and easily at your notes when necessary, without hovering over them or depending on them too much; then return your glance to your audience.
- Shift notes from hand to hand if desired, but never call unnecessary attention to them by shuffling or "fiddling" with them.

The Microphone and the Speaker's Stand. Both these aids are in common use whenever acoustical problems or the demands of the occasion

Senator Mark Hatfield of Oregon, a dynamic speaker, gestures while maintaining proper microphone stance.

dictate their need. Learn to regard them as aids to communication, not as hindrances to delivery.

- A speaker's stand or a table serves as a convenient place for your notes, script, or reference material such as that used for debates, lectures, and some formal talks.
- Stand behind the stand or sit at the table without slouching, leaning over it, hiding behind it, or holding it with both hands.
- Feel free to move or gesture if you wish, but in general maintain your position behind the stand or table.
- The microphone may be free-standing, placed on the speaker's stand or table, suspended over you like a "boom mike," or hung around your neck. Whatever the case may be, do not let it attract your attention or the audience's attention away from what you're saying into it.
- Pretest the microphone, if possible, to determine the best speaking distance from it. In general, 10–15 inches away is satisfactory for speaking into a table or stand microphone.
- Keep your eyes on your audience, not on the microphone.
- Microphones limit your body movement somewhat, but not your gestures, although their full sweep must be restrained.
- Be careful of the sounds you make and the things you do that might be magnified unpleasantly by the microphone: 1, "blasting," or the distortion caused by sudden change in volume, energy, or sudden explosion of breath, as in sounds like *p*, *b*, *t*, *d*, *k*, *g*, *s*, *sh*, *z*, *zh*; 2, "fading," or loss of sound caused by weaving back and forth, dropping your head too low when referring to notes, or turning too far away from the microphone while speaking; 3, microphone noise or unpleasant sounds caused by coughing, clearing throat, breathing heavily, rustling script, striking, or nervously adjusting and handling the microphone; speaking too close to it; harsh or raspy voice quality; strained or high pitch.

Facing the Unexpected

There's an almost endless list of unexpected things that may happen to you when you deliver a speech, and no one can tell you with any certainty the best way to meet a crisis. In general you will have to assess an unusual situation rapidly, maintain your poise, and decide on the spot what action to take. Common sense will generally come to your rescue, the key to your decision-making being questions like these:

1. Is the occurrence a minor, temporary distraction which will not lose me my audience? If so, can I ignore it or make a slight adjustment to it?

2. Is the occurrence a major disturbance which seriously affects my relationship with my audience? If so, what definite action should I take?

Minor distractions, such as coughing, whispering, light traffic sounds, noisy passersby, latecomers, books falling, chair scraping, feet shuffling, dropping your notes, stumbling, hitting the microphone, bumping a chair or table—these are all either ignored or lightly passed off because they are temporary interruptions which do not seriously alter your speaking situation.

Major disturbances, however, require definite adjustment because they break into the communication bond between you and your listeners and may destroy the rapport or sympathetic harmony you build up in speaking. Here are some of the problems you might face and a few suggestions for action:

The problem	A suggestion
• A noisy group arrives late.	• Pause and wait for them to get settled, pointing out empty seats, if you wish. Make a friendly comment or jest, if the occasion is informal; then promptly return everyone's attention to your speech.
• Someone interrupts you with questions.	• Answer as best you can or politely tell the questioner to wait until later.
• The microphone works improperly or not at all.	• Don't fuss with it. Point out its inefficiency; then "go it alone." Increase vocal volume to insure everyone's hearing you.
• You forget part of your speech.	• Don't just *stand* there; *do* something! Acknowledge your error, refer to your notes or script, and pick up the thread of your speech without losing poise.
• You omit part of your speech.	• If the omission is minor, don't backtrack. If the omission seriously weakens your speech and you have not yet reached your conclusion, ease into the omitted part with a covering transition, like "One more point we must not forget is. . . ." If you've already gone into your conclusion, don't introduce the omitted part. The best speeches are made on the way home; that's when you remember all the things you should have said.
• You overrun your time limit.	• If you've almost finished, maintain your rate and poise to the end. If you've badly misjudged the time, conclude as gracefully and quickly as you can.
• You forget to address the chairman or the audience.	• Forget it! Once you've started speaking, keep going. Your lapse of good manners will be less noticeable than an abrupt interruption of your speech.

There are many other situations that you might face, too. What would *you* do, for instance, if

- the chairman introduced your name or subject incorrectly?
- you were faced with an annoying heckler?
- the lights went out?
- you had to quiet a noisy audience?
- the introduction you'd planned was inappropriate?
- a panel member hogged the discussion when you had something important to say?
- your audience was very small and the room quite large?
- a very disturbing noise occurred outside?
- the room was extremely hot or cold?

In most cases your main concern should be for the audience, its comfort and welfare. Just as you thought of it in choosing your subject and planning your talk, selecting material with your listeners' interests in mind, so should you now do what is best for your listeners. As for yourself, dignity, an appearance of ease and coolness, and a good-humored manner are important at the moment that you face the unexpected. You can fall apart later.

Adjusting Delivery to Different Groups

Even as the content of your speech is adapted to different audiences, your delivery, too, is adjusted to your listeners and to the conditions under which you speak. Consider, for instance, what your outward manner should be in these various situations:

In the Classroom. Here you are in a learning situation, engaging in recitations, discussions, reports, and speech assignments. The room is likely to be small, the atmosphere informal, the group-feeling casual and intimate, conditions which should not tempt you to lower your behavior standards. Your good speaking manners can contribute to the classroom situation, so speak courteously, clearly, distinctly, and loud enough to be heard by all. Don't clown or show off or lower your dignity to get cheap attention. Your classmates are likely to lose respect for you, just as they are quick to notice an untidy appearance, a slovenly manner, an indifferent attitude, or annoying mannerisms.

Before Student Groups. Speaking in committees and clubs, at rallies and banquets, in class and student-body election campaigns, or at rallies and assemblies involves larger audiences and often larger rooms. Except on occasions of pure fun, you will find conditions to be slightly more formal than in the classroom. Project a responsible, likeable, dignified image with a friendly, enthusiastic, earnest manner, and make an extra effort to capture your audience. Dress neatly and appropriately, and speak as you would like to be spoken to, observing the accepted standards of good speaking.

Before Adult Groups. Sometimes you might talk at P.T.A. meetings, luncheon groups, women's clubs, service organizations, speech contests, or even graduation night, when adults make up the majority of your listeners. Now's the time to put on your "party" manners. Match the formality of the situation with your best skills of language, mature poise, good posture, well-dressed appearance, clear voice, and distinct articulation. Take extra pains to be courteous, friendly, and self-controlled. It's the grownups you want to impress this time, so project an image of maturity and responsibility through your manners and bearing.

An aid to many speech skills is practice before a mirror—here, turning to include each section of the audience.

Practice and Rehearsal

> "Practice yourself, for heaven's sake, in
> little things; and thence proceed to greater."
> —EPICTETUS

You learn to speak by speaking. Speaking becomes an art when you commit yourself, like an artist, to the many painstaking disciplines which help you to create form, beauty, and style out of a hodgepodge of shapeless material. Up to this point in preparing a speech you have learned how to give order and shape to what was originally a jumbled mass of ideas, and you have considered many techniques of presenting those ideas to a body of listeners. Now is the time for the final discipline: the polishing and refining of your speech through practice and rehearsal.

It is through intensive oral rehearsal that you become keenly and personally aware of what you *can* do and what you *must* do to deliver a speech well. Oral practice is a sort of self-confrontation, a time when you test yourself, face up to some of your weaknesses and strengths, and learn how your mental and physical equipment functions under the stress of speaking. Although you may be practicing for a specific performance, you are laying the groundwork for a greater goal, your future confidence and skill in meeting further speaking situations. So look upon practice and rehearsals as a time for refining habits, developing skills, and establishing the individual style that will be your personal art of speaking.

The success of your final effort depends largely upon how thoroughly you have prepared prior to rehearsal time and how intensively you work during practice. There's no strict rule about how to proceed, but you may find the following suggestions useful. They apply particularly to the rehearsal procedure for rather formal speeches—those given on special occasions at club meetings, assemblies, adult organizations, speech competitions, banquets, commencement time—or for special oral assignments like formal talks, book reviews, projects, or term papers. Any planned talk, however, whether formal or not, would be improved by the practice that could make it perfect.

Practice and Rehearsal Do's

Generally	*Specifically*
Begin early and allow plenty of time.	• Begin rehearsing formal speeches, contests, debates: ten days ahead, minimum. • Practice informal speeches: five days ahead.

- Plan five to ten *complete* practice periods.
- Allow a half hour to an hour for each practice.

Practice alone at first.

- Find a quiet place; a full-sized room.
- Stand erect. Pace back and forth to release tension.
- Pretend audience is present.
- Visualize the occasion.
- Concentrate! Eliminate distractions like radio, friends, family.

Be sure that your outline or manuscript is fully completed.

- Write out your planned introduction and conclusion.
- Know the order of your main points.
- Be sure that all supporting details are in place.

Study outline or manuscript to fix in mind its progression of thought.

- Read silently to see the sequence of ideas.
- Read orally to hear the sequence.
- Memorize the orderly succession of the ideas.
- Be able to duplicate the outline from memory—what follows, what next, etc.

Practice orally with the outline as a guide, noting places which cause difficulty.

- Concentrate on the whole speech, not individual parts.
- Once started, keep going. Don't backtrack or repeat.
- Revise, add, discard, or rearrange material that may "write" well but not "talk" well.
- Pinpoint lapses of memory, omitted details, wrong sequences.
- Prepare hand notes of the main points of the outline.
- Practice three or four times, gradually decreasing dependence on outline or note cards.

Practice orally without the aid of outline, manuscript, or notes.

- Know your introduction and conclusion.
- Maintain the forward movement of the thought pattern. If you forget, continue to the next part.
- Feel the stimulation of the ideas you're presenting.
- Strive for earnestness, sincerity, and power.

- Concentrate on the thought, not the words.
- Be thoroughly familiar with your hand notes, but try not to use them.
- Repeat and repeat until you feel confident.

Coordinate your delivery with the content of the speech.

- Note mentally or mark on manuscript all important climaxes, transitions, and similar places which inspire special emphasis, pauses, phrasing, change of rate, pitch, or body movement.
- Watch, as you practice aloud, for overly long sentences, pronunciation difficulties, and articulation traps. Avoid unpleasing sound combinations.
- Don't mumble, race, run out of breath, slur your words, drop the ends of sentences, or fall into monotonous sound patterns.
- Use your mirror for checking poise, posture, movement, and gestures, unless such use disturbs you.

Taper off.

- Avoid last-minute changes and a feeling of rushing.
- Review mentally the key points of the sequence of ideas plus the introduction and conclusion.
- Plan your last practice for the day before presentation.
- Remember: thorough preparation is a great fear-remover. If you've been conscientious in preparation and practice, you're well insured for success.

ACTIVITIES

1. Arrange a panel discussion on *Methods of Delivery*, using a plan similar to what is suggested here:

   Purpose: To discuss and evaluate methods of delivery
   Chairman: Opening remarks
   Panel member 1: Report on the various methods presented in Unit 12
   Panel member 2: The chief advantages of each method for both speaker and audience
   Panel member 3: The main disadvantages of each method for both speaker and audience
   Panel member 4: Report on what method most students actually use, based on personal experience, interviews with students, observation, and hearsay

Audience participation: Asking questions, volunteering personal experiences, making suggestions, or challenging statements made by panel

Chairman: Summary of discussion and closing remarks

2. Use your classroom as a workshop to practice an oral assignment you've been given in some other class, like the explanation of a mathematics problem, lab experiment, shop project, home economics report, history reading, or translation into English of a foreign-language assignment. Ask for a class evaluation of your efforts so that you can make improvements in your delivery.

3. Practice good delivery manners in rising, approaching the audience, addressing the chairman, reading from manuscript, and leaving the audience. Prepare one of the following for presentation, marking your script for emphasis and pauses:

I expect to pass through this life but once. If there is any kindness or any good thing I can do to my fellow beings, let me do it now. I shall pass this way but once.

—WILLIAM PENN

A thoughtful mind, when it sees a Nation's flag, sees not the flag only, but the Nation itself; and whatever may be its symbols, its insignia, he reads chiefly in the flag the Government, the principles, the truths, and the history which belong to the Nation that sets it forth.

—HENRY WARD BEECHER

Humanity can be welded together only by love, by sympathy, by justice, not by jealousy and hatred. . . . It was but an historical accident, no doubt, that this great country was called the "United States"; yet I am very thankful that it has that word "united" in its title. . . . The man who seeks to divide man from man, group from group, interest from interest in this great Union is striking at its very heart.

—WOODROW WILSON

4. Bring to class a two-hundred-word paragraph copied from a historical or modern speech. Mark your script for pauses and emphasis and read it to the class as you think it should be delivered. Some speech sources are the following:

American Observer
Congressional Record
Senior Scholastic
Vital Speeches of the Day
American Speeches, by W. M. PARRISH and MARIE HOCHMUTH. McKay.
Representative American Speeches, by A. C. BAIRD. Wilson.

5. Set up a microphone in class and have each student in turn approach it, adjust it to proper height, speak three or four sentences into it, and return to his seat. Check for the following:

- Easy, poised approach
- Proper distance from microphone
- Deft handling of microphone
- Posture of body and head
- Eye-contact with audience
- Fading, blasting, volume, sibilance, breathiness, harshness
- Dignified retreat from the microphone

6. Hold a "buzz" session having the class discuss ways in which a speaker might meet embarrassing or unexpected situations that are his own fault, like forgetting part of his speech, scattering his papers, dropping notes, striking the microphone noisily, running over time limit, and similar blunders. Follow the discussion with pantomime or words to illustrate what might be done to retrieve one's poise.

7. Test your ability to meet the unexpected by facing an actual situation. Let a student committee, with the help of the teacher, plan secretly for some interruptions to occur during the next few class-speaking activities. Your performance "under fire" should be evaluated by the teacher and the class.

References:

A Guide to Effective Public Speaking, by L. H. Mouat. Heath.

Fundamentals of Public Speaking, by D. C. Bryant and K. R. Wallace. Appleton-Century-Crofts.

Practical Public Speaking, by E. E. White and C. R. Henderlider. Macmillan.

Principles and Types of Speech, by A. H. Monroe. Scott, Foresman.

Public Speaking: Principles and Practice, by G. W. Gray and W. Braden. Harper.

Speech: Idea and Delivery, by C. W. Lomas and R. Richardson. Houghton Mifflin.

Films:

Public Speaking: Movement and Gesture (Coronet). 11 min color or b&w.
Function of Gestures (MH). 10 min b&w.
Platform Posture and Appearance (MH). 9 min b&w.
Stage Fright and What to Do about It (MH). 10 min b&w.

Filmstrips:

How to Deliver a Speech (SVE). 39 fr b&w.
Relation of a Personality to Communication (SVE). 41 fr b&w.

Record:

And the World Listened (ERC). One 12″ record 33⅓ rpm.

PUTTING PRINCIPLES INTO ACTION

By this time you have come a long way in your understanding of communication through oral media. You have completed a great deal of basic work, and you're ready to put principles into action. You will test theory, add some necessary new principles to your stock, and experiment with a variety of speaking situations. Perhaps most important of all, you will begin to discover your own talents. What do you like? Radio and TV? Parliamentary procedure? Panel discussion? Debating? Choral reading? Sales talks? Choose your areas of interest from the abundant experiences described in this section, and lay your plans for the remainder of the course.

WHAT YOU WILL FIND:

Unit Thirteen

TYPES OF SPEECHES: How Purpose Affects Their Development

In learning how to put the principles of good speaking into action, you will experiment with a variety of speech activities; however, most of your basic work in class may very well center upon the preparing and delivering of all kinds of talks, both formal and informal. This unit will classify such presentations by their purpose into five major types and will provide guidelines for you in preparing and delivering each type.

If you have already studied Unit 7, you will remember that speeches must be purposeful. Or, to be more accurate, *you, the speaker,* must be purposeful; you must have a definite aim in mind if you wish to be effective in communication. If you don't know what your goal is in a speech, if you have no particular objective, you'll find yourself on an aimless and uncertain journey without a destination, like the wanderer who said, "I'm on my way, folks, but I don't know where I'm going."

It is your *purpose* in speaking that strongly affects the characteristics of the different speeches you'll give. Purpose is responsible for the kind of material you'll use, the plan you'll follow, the presentation you'll make, and the response you'll try to get from your audience. It is generally recognized as the determining factor in the classification of all sorts of speaking, regardless of whether it's a debate, a panel discussion, an after-dinner speech, an interview, an everyday conversation, a play, a sales talk, a book report, or a speech contest.

As you learned in Unit 7, most speakers put speeches of purpose into these five categories:

Your Purpose	What You Do	The Listener's Response
To inform	Tell the listeners something that they don't know.	"Thanks for the facts and information. I understand what you are talking about."
To convince	Gain the listeners' acceptance of a statement of truth or of a point of view.	"You've convinced me. I agree with you."
To persuade	Rouse the listeners to take action on a proposal.	"I'll do it!"
To entertain	Provide the listeners with material which brings pleasure and enjoyment.	"I enjoyed your talk."
To impress or inspire	Create in the listeners strong emotional reactions.	"What you said has touched me deeply."

You may also remember that you can't always pigeonhole a speech into just one category, that there may be an overlapping of purposes within a single speech. What you plan as a purely informative talk may also be entertaining to your audience, or an inspiring speech may also be convincing. Regardless of such overlapping, however, you should recognize that it is not only possible but also wise to designate a *major* purpose for your speaking and to focus your presentation upon that single purpose in order to keep your message in perspective.

Before you set yourself the task of studying these types in detail, you must not lose sight of some of the general principles of speaking which have been presented to you up to this point in the book. Let's look at them again to reemphasize this general truth: *speaking is communication*, and communication becomes more effective when

- your ideas are fresh, worthwhile, and relevant.
- your material is interesting and accurate, where accuracy is essential.
- your speech organization is strong and appropriate.
- your general statements are supported by valid and varied details.
- your use of language shows maturity and facility.
- your delivery reflects your poise, sincerity, understanding, and skill.
- your presentation gives evidence in its entirety not only of your continuing awareness of your own aims but also of how the audience is reacting to them.

Let's turn now to a specific consideration of each of the five types of speaking you are likely to use most. The suggestions will fall under the following general headings: *Your Goal, Plan to Follow, Material to Use, Things to Avoid,* and *Topics for Talks.*

The visual device, the map, adds clarity and interest to this speech to inform.

Speeches Which Inform:

Communication That Adds to Knowledge and Understanding

An important purpose in communication is to state facts and to give information. Actually, most speaking, regardless of its specific purpose, is largely informational; however, when the giving of information becomes the *chief* aim and purpose of a speaker, the resulting speech may be classed as informative. Such a speech may range from giving simple directions (Where's the library?) to explaining a complicated theory or process (What is photosynthesis?). It may encompass a mere announcement of facts (the plans for the next school dance) or a formal project report based on reading and research (some of the causes of the Civil War). In each case the emphasis is primarily on statements of fact; the appeal is chiefly to the understanding of the listener.

People like to know things. They're curious. It makes no difference whether they're finding satisfaction in poking around in their own little private investigations or getting it from being handed information on a silver platter; they still like to know something new. It's this curiosity that makes informative speeches favorites with audiences, and it is the fun of telling people something they don't know that makes such talks popular with speakers. A dash of suspense in an informative talk may lead you to discover new depths of curiosity in people.

You will find yourself dealing with factual material a great deal during the course of your life—in classroom recitations, in school projects, in club activities, at home, in social situations, and on your job. Part of your responsibility in developing your communicative skill depends upon your ability to avoid vague, ambiguous, misleading, or unproved statements and to recognize and to use facts, examples, statistics, illustrations, and quotations as concrete evidence to support whatever you say. Learning how to select and present relevant information is a valuable skill for you to acquire.

Your Goal

Your aim is to add to the knowledge of your listeners, to give them information. You shed light on a subject by sharing facts which you have learned through experience, observation, talking with people, and reading. You explain, describe, report, clarify, exemplify, or otherwise supply material that is vital to understanding. You introduce facts that are new, observe old facts in a new light, clear up misinformation and misunderstanding, or point out relationships between facts which your audience knows and those which it is just learning. Your main responsibility is to be accurate, objective, and clear. The response you want from your listeners is simply, "I understand what you said."

In order to achieve your goal, consider the following general suggestions:

1. *Aim for clearness.* It is extremely important that your audience understands you, that it is not left uncertain or puzzled about what you have explained.

2. *Be a slave to accuracy.* Check your facts. Are they authoritative? Can you verify them? Is the source reliable? Don't make a statement unless you are sure of its truth.

3. *Be wary of broad generalizations.* To be accurate, a general statement needs the support of many specific facts.

4. *Control your feelings and prejudices.* Strong opinions or feelings may lead you astray from your original purpose. To *inform* does not mean to convince or to persuade. Be objective.

In learning how to master the informative speech, start with simple talks, ones which deal with facts that you know well, or have experienced or observed. Then proceed to speeches which require reading and research, like the reports you give in many of your classes.

Plan to Follow

1. Arrange your major points in whatever order will best fit the material you have to present. Tell first those things which are necessary to the understanding of what follows. Review Unit 10 for help in understanding some of the plans you might use.

2. Use the chronological, or time, order for relating biographical or historical events, describing travels, explaining a step-by-step process, or telling personal experiences in which the exact time sequence seems important to follow.

3. Climactic order is effective for an account or a narrative in which the facts logically build up to a dramatic ending or a strong climax.

4. Arrange the main points in a space pattern, jumping from one location to another, for describing a building or a scene, giving directions for finding a location, explaining a plan or design, describing a geographical place, or talking about a trip, if moving from place to place seems a logical plan to follow.

5. Arrange the main points in order of size, importance, difficulty, or interest (as from least difficult to most difficult or from most important to least important) depending upon your judgment of where the emphasis should be placed. This small-to-large or large-to-small order is a generally logical one for explaining or describing almost anything.

6. If you have a difficult topic which involves terms, definitions, or concepts which are new or unfamiliar to your listeners, arrange your points in a generally logical simple-to-complicated form which starts on familiar ground and moves gradually into unfamiliar territory. Establish a common understanding and then proceed step by step from what they know to what they don't know. This plan is important to follow in explaining scientific, political, philosophical, or technical ideas not easy to understand.

Material to Use

1. Use an abundance of illustrative material—facts, statistics, examples, comparisons, incidents, stories, quotations—anything which helps to catch the audience's interest and to clarify a point.

2. If appropriate, use visual devices as an aid to clearness and interest, such as maps, pictures, drawings, charts, diagrams, exhibits, demonstrations.

3. Whenever possible, relate your points to the special interests of your audience by referring to things they know, feel, or have done.

4. Use definitions, examples, descriptions, comparisons, and restatements to explain difficult terms, words, or ideas.

5. Repeat and restate the key facts and essential relationships of your subject in as many ways as you can, especially in your conclusion.

6. Use transitional devices between main points, and employ cue phrases from time to time to help listeners to follow the progression of your material.

Things to Avoid

1. Too many small details that may bore or confuse your listeners.

2. Insufficient facts to support your main points or the omission of necessary details for clear understanding.

3. Expression of opinion about facts. Don't attempt to convince, persuade, or impress your audience if your *main* purpose is information.

4. Technical subjects that are too difficult or too remote from your audience's interests.

5. Poor organization, rambling, inaccuracy, uncertainty, vagueness, incompleteness, dull or lackluster presentation.

Topics for Talks

Our Present Space Program
What to Do for a Third-Degree Burn
The World's Largest Telescope
Some Causes of Juvenile Delinquency
What Is Communism?
Some Recent Fads
How the United Nations Works
The 24th Amendment to the Constitution
The Formation of the Grand Canyon
Our Exploration of the Moon
Conversion of Salt Water into Fresh Water
What Is a Laser Beam?
A Balanced Aquarium
The Causes of Smog
Weather Forecasting
Our Newest Satellites
Jazz–America's Music
A Great American Architect
Atomic Submarines
What Is a Good Driver?
Some Outstanding Accomplishments of the F.B.I.
America's Peace Corps
Some New Wonder Drugs
What Is Abstract Painting?
Measuring Rainfall
How to Catch Abalone
The Control of Polio
Training a Porpoise

ACTIVITIES

1. Be accurate, brief, and clear in explaining to the class one of the following directions:

HOW TO GET TO—

- the post office
- the nearest gas station
- the police station
- any church in town
- the hospital
- the state Capitol
- a drugstore
- the airport
- a nearby city
- where you live

HOW TO—

- change a tire
- build a barbecue fire
- write a thank-you note
- make artificial flowers
- start a coin collection
- give artificial respiration
- use a microscope
- rig a fishing pole
- learn the keyboard in typing
- select a pair of skis

2. Listen to one of your classmates give a brief biographical sketch of some famous person. Evaluate his performance on the basis of the following questions:

CRITICISM GUIDE

1. *Did he give you basic information?*
2. *Did he have too little, too much, or just enough detail?*
3. *Was his explanation clear?*
4. *Did he follow a recognizable plan?*
5. *Did he stick to purely informative material?*
6. *Was he interesting?*

3. Give a brief informative announcement of some school-related event or happening. Be sure to include *what* it is, *when* and *where* it will be, *how* to get there or *how* much it costs, and *why* it is worthwhile or important. One of these might be a suitable subject:

- class party
- school dance
- special assembly
- school election
- yearbook sale
- appointments for class pictures
- rally
- football game
- club meeting
- concert or play
- special TV program
- basketball tournament

4. Inform yourself and the class in a one- to two-minute talk of the main reasons why any one of the following men is remembered as an orator, political speaker, or opinion-maker:

- Edmund Burke
- Patrick Henry
- Henry Clay
- Abraham Lincoln
- Edward Everett
- Frederick Douglass
- Theodore Roosevelt
- Woodrow Wilson
- Winston Churchill
- William Pitt
- John Randolph
- Daniel Webster
- Stephen A. Douglas
- Wendell Phillips
- Henry Ward Beecher
- William Jennings Bryan
- Booker T. Washington
- Franklin D. Roosevelt

5. Plan a three- to five-minute talk of information in which you use some visual devices like charts, drawings, pictures, maps, and objects. Consider topics listed earlier in this unit or some like these.

    The Climbing of Mount Everest
    Rare Coins
    Newest Fashion Ideas for American Women
    Our State's Driving Laws
    Smog Control Devices on Cars
    The Latest Space Exploit
    What Happens in a Nuclear Reactor?
    The Newest Automotive Ideas from Detroit
    Learning How to Surf
    Bats
    Scuba Diving

6. Find enough information on a topic like one of the following to write a one-page outline for an informative talk. In what order will you arrange your points?

    A Famous American Woman
    The College of My Choice
    An Outstanding Athlete
    A Trip to Hawaii
    A National Park
    The Newest Jet
    The World's Fair
    The Game of Chess
    A Visit to a TV Studio
    The Alaska Earthquake
    A Famous Bridge
    A Book I Read

Speeches Which Convince:

Communication That Brings About Belief and Conviction

Scarcely a day passes when you don't argue about something, assert a belief, defend a position, or take a stand for or against some idea. The need to speak convincingly is an almost continuous challenge in your life, whether you are arguing about the best baseball player, trying to convince your parents that you want more freedom, taking sides in an election, engaging in a heated classroom discussion, debating with yourself about some course of action, or presenting your convictions in a formal speech. Whenever you attempt to settle a problem, instill belief in a listener, change his mind, get him to agree with you, or otherwise influence his thinking so that he is "with you" instead of "against you," you are giving a convincing speech.

Your Goal

In content the speech that convinces is somewhat linked with the speech that informs; both require factual material for their base. But, in a sense, the convincing speech "takes off" where the informative one ends. The method of handling the material is different because the speaker's purpose is not merely to present facts but also to use those facts as evidence to support a contention or belief, to reason and argue *from* the facts.

Your goal in the convincing talk is to create a favorable impression, plant your belief, remove doubts, and get your audience to agree with you. You do this by appealing both to the mind and to the feelings. You present facts, reasons, and arguments to satisfy the rational needs of the audience, and then you invite, urge, lead, or "pull" your listeners into accepting your point of view by the weight and skill of your argument. If you're successful, you'll have your audience saying at the conclusion of your talk, "You've convinced me. I agree with what you said."

Plan to Follow

1. A logical plan is essential since your main approach is to reason, although you may also use a psychological or emotional appeal to accomplish your purpose.

2. The problem-solution plan is very effective: (*a*) state the facts of the problem; (*b*) suggest a solution; (*c*) prove that your solution is practical and workable; (*d*) argue that your solution is the best one to solve the problem.

3. The climactic order is also useful. You arrange your thoughts in a step-by-step pattern establishing a chain of reasoning that leaves your strongest argument for the last.

4. The "Bull's-Eye" plan (see Units 8 and 10) is useful because it immediately identifies the listener with the topic, gives him one central thought to consider, reinforces that thought with numerous examples, and ends with a personal appeal, which in this case is for conviction.

5. A causal relationship plan may be used, such as the following:

a. Here's the situation
b. This is its cause.
c. The effect is this.
d. Here's what should be done about it.

Material to Use

1. Use plenty of acceptable evidence—facts, statistics, examples, incidents, and the testimony of reliable authority.

2. Tie your evidence together in a chain of reasoning so that every general statement is supported by proof of some kind and every argument is plausible.

3. Analogies, or comparisons, are useful, but be sure that they are valid, truly comparable, and acceptable to your listeners.

4. Be sure that your material and your arguments appeal to the *common* desires, beliefs, interests, and goals of your audience. Stress the points with which they can agree.

5. Appeal to the emotions by means of human-interest material—stories, anecdotes, personal references—material that illustrates your points and serves to make your audience feel that your argument concerns them personally.

6. Bring variety into the body of evidence so that your appeal will keep people listening.

7. If appropriate, enliven your talk with such visual evidence as photographs, pictures, slides, charts, diagrams, and sample exhibits. Sometimes "seeing is believing."

Things to Avoid

1. Ignoring the interests and feelings of your listeners or forgetting to identify with them.

2. Statements of strong opinion unsupported by facts or based on weak reasoning.

3. Anything that might antagonize your listeners, like tactlessness, abruptness, cockiness, aggressiveness, a show of temper, impatience, or pressing too hard.

4. "Lecturing" your listeners or becoming too argumentative or accusative.

5. A wordy, heavy, humorless, plodding, pedantic, or overrighteous presentation.

6. Leaving an impression of insincerity or of not really caring about or believing in what you're saying.

7. Stubbornness about recognizing weakness in or objections to your own point of view and an unwillingness to meet honestly the other points of view.

8. Presenting your arguments in an overdramatic or overemotional manner.

Topics for Talks

These topics have two sides; take either one.

The Voting Age Should Be Lowered to Eighteen
Everyone Needs to Diet
Our School Curriculum Should Have Some New Subjects
I Like Modern Art
The Honor System Will Work
Our High School Should Have a Pep Band
A Hobby Is Good for You

Liability Insurance Should Be Required of Every Automobile Driver

Physical Education Should Be Optional in the Last Two Years of High School

Culture Is for Everyone

Young People Should Work Part of Their Way through College

Freedom Is Everybody's Job

Four Years of English Should Be Required in High School

Jazz Is an Important Part of American Culture

Don't Be a Litterbug

Schools Should Be in Session Eleven Months of the Year

Capital Punishment Should Be Abolished

You Shouldn't Believe in Superstitions

We Need a New Kind of School Spirit

The Federal Government Should Arbitrate All Labor Disputes

There Should Be a United States of Europe

Land and Water Travel Surpass Air Travel

The Case for the Compact Car

Foreign Aid Should Be Continued

Everyone Should Be Required to Have an Annual Chest X-Ray

TV Is Desirable Entertainment

Science and Religion Are Antagonistic to Each Other

The Military Draft Should Be Abolished

Success Means More than Just Gaining Economic Security

The Oscar Awards Should Be Discontinued

Our Government Is Too Paternalistic

We Need National Speed Laws

There Should Be No Limit Placed on the Number of Times a President May Be Elected

Nuclear Testing Should Be Controlled by an International Commission

ACTIVITIES

1. Find a short editorial or a brief article which attempts to convince the reader of some truth or belief. Read and explain it to the class and analyze its effectiveness, using the following questions as guides:
   - a. What was the main idea?
   - b. What facts were used to support the point of view? What reasons?
   - c. What was the tone of the argument? reasonable? aggressive? emotional? humorous?
   - d. How effective was the argument? Did it *convince* you?
2. Listen to a discussion, a political talk, or some other kind of program on TV that attempts to convince the viewer of some belief or point of view. Report briefly to the class some of the methods used by the performers to accomplish their purpose. Did the use of facts play an important part in influencing the audience? What sorts of arguments and appeals were effective? How did the personality and delivery of the speaker affect your acceptance of his point of view?

3. Have someone read a challenging or controversial statement to the class. Each student can give an impromptu reaction to the statement, agreeing or disagreeing with it. Follow an orderly progression of thought in speaking, like:
   a. "This statement means . . ."
   b. "I agree (or disagree) with it because . . ."
   c. "One reason I think so is . . ."
   d. "Another reason is . . ."
   e. "To summarize my belief . . ."

4. Don't pass up the opportunity to try your argumentative skill in an informal debate. Challenge one of your classmates to argue against you on a debatable subject, like those suggested under "Topics for Talks." Build your case on two or three "reasons why," support those reasons with strong evidence, and argue with vigor and force for your contentions. Also, try to anticipate what your opponent will say, and have arguments and facts ready to refute him. Your "debate" can be evaluated on the basis of the following questions:
   a. Were the main arguments clearly stated?
   b. Was the proof sufficient and convincing?
   c. Were there any weaknesses in reasoning?
   d. Did the speakers sound convincing?

5. Choose one of the following broad generalizations and make it meaningful, specific, and convincing by qualifying it and supporting it with some facts, examples, comparisons, or arguments so that your listeners can believe its truth.
   a. Great crises produce great leaders.
   b. Whosoever would be a man must be a nonconformist.
   c. The family is the best place to learn human relations.
   d. Men who think in advance of their time are persecuted.
      (They who lead the flock must fight the wolf.)
   e. The frontier lies wherever man confronts a new fact.

6. Contribute your convictions to a classroom discussion of one of the following questions. Use facts and examples to strengthen your arguments, appeal to both reason and feeling, and speak in a vigorous, compelling manner.
   a. Are TV programs too juvenile?
   b. Is it necessary to go to college to be successful in life?
   c. Should people stop smoking?
   d. Should people be forced to retire from work at sixty-five?
   e. Should a woman work after she marries?
   f. Should the legal voting age be reduced from twenty-one to eighteen?
   g. Is our culture becoming too materialistic?

7. Plan and present a formal convincing talk using any topic on which you have some earnest convictions. Try to follow these suggestions:
   a. Gain the goodwill of your listeners.
   b. Identify your arguments with their interests and knowledge.
   c. Present strong and abundant evidence.
   d. Avoid antagonism.
   e. Use a logical plan that leads to the conclusion you want to reach.

Confidence, vigor, and sincerity are essential when you are making a speech to persuade. The use of gestures helps to emphasize your call for action.

Speeches Which Persuade:

Communication That Rouses People to Action

The purpose of the persuasive speaker goes beyond that of the informative or convincing one. Although he seeks understanding and presents facts and information, and although he uses argument and reasoning to implant belief and get agreement, the speaker who wants to persuade has a final difficult task to perform: he must transform understanding, belief, and agreement into definite *action;* he must get his listeners to *do* something.

Human nature being what it is, that final step is not easy to accomplish. The old adage "You can lead a horse to water, but you can't make him drink" applies here. Getting people to *do* what you want requires patience, understanding of the psychological appeals to which people respond, and considerable skill and effort in applying the techniques which can result in action. **The most important factors for you to understand, if you want to become a good persuader, are these two:**

1. *The fundamental drives or impelling motives that cause people to act,* such as patriotism; feeling of brotherhood, self-preservation; sense

of duty; curiosity; generosity; love; pride; loyalty; desire for approval, for affection, for power, for status, for recognition, for ownership of property, or for satisfying personal tastes.

2. *The mental and emotional factors that hinder the acceptance of reason and argument and cause resistance to action,* such as prejudice, bias, stubbornness, fear, doubt, indifference, selfishness, "crooked" thinking, resistance to change, a closed mind, laziness, resentment, hostility.

These drives, motives, and resistances are shared by all of us and exist in each one of us in varying degrees. Sometimes the desire or needs are strong and easily stimulated, like coming to the defense of a friend, going along with the crowd, buying new clothes, or learning to drive. Frequently our needs are hidden or inactive so that we are unaware that a certain action might fulfill a desire; or we may even be unconscious of *having* a desire, like going to college, deciding what to be in life, finding a way to earn money, or being proud of a member of the family. In many cases our drives are in conflict, our resistance is strong, and our failure to act desirably may be due to our being guided by selfish rather than unselfish motives, such as being rude to strangers, uncooperative with adults, procrastinating with our homework, or being unwilling to take responsibility for our actions. This is the way we are—all of us—and it becomes the task of the persuasive speaker to understand these various drives and motives if he wants to influence people's thinking and action.

The point for you to remember is that people *can* be induced to act, to do something new or to change their old course of action, if you touch them deeply enough in the areas of their greatest human needs or concerns. The basis of persuasion is this: Show your listener that something he needs or wants is either available to him or is threatened. Then show him how he can get what he needs or wants or, if it is threatened, how he can protect it against loss or change. You awaken desire, if there is none; you propose action which will satisfy that desire, and you show that the action you propose is possible. And you do all this in the most appealing way you can.

In school or community life you hear and probably take part in many variations of persuasive talks. There are pep talks, sales talks, election talks, campaign talks, and contribution talks—those that are appeals for worthy causes, such as the Cancer Fund, the Red Cross, civic improvements, the needy at home, the needy abroad, victims of disaster, memorials to the dead, and so on. Someone is always going to be asking you to *do* something; and you will find yourself, in turn, asking action of your schoolmates, family, and community. Furthermore, as you mature and take your place in the adult world, you may find yourself in many leadership situations where the ability to be persuasive can pay you extra dividends. Executives, managers, lawyers, ministers, committee chairmen, politicians, coaches, salesmen, clubwomen—all, and more, find that getting things done requires the persuasive touch. In discussions, conferences, staff meetings, and other groups where courses of action must be formulated and policies adopted, the persuader is needed. Why not begin to be knowledgeable and adept in this type of speaking now?

Your Goal

Your goal is action, either immediate or delayed. You lead, urge, and induce people to *do* something. You overcome normal human resistance to action. You appeal strongly to the motives which stimulate action. You arouse interest, get the listener personally involved in the subject, sharpen his desire to act, and make what you're asking reasonable enough so that action is almost inevitable.

Your personality—that is, the total manifestation of your character—is an important factor in persuasion. People are not always rational. They are often influenced by personalities more than by logic or evidence, frequently making decisions on the basis of their personal reactions to someone. You should try, therefore, to establish a constructive personal relationship with your listeners, seeking common ground, identifying with their interests, being candid and sincere, and presenting yourself and your appeals in such a pleasing manner that you will win their respect and confidence as a human being. If your listeners like you, trust you, and believe you, they're more likely to do what you ask.

Don't be misled into thinking that you can fool an audience by "putting on a front" or persuade them by the clothes you wear, the dazzling smile you give them, or the line you hand them. Most people are quick to spot a phony, and the persuader's cause is lost when doubt and distrust are raised.

Persuasive speaking, because of its effect on people's thoughts and actions, demands of you a sense of responsibility. If you can arouse others to action, be certain that it is constructive action, both socially and morally desirable. The world has had plenty of Hitlers and Mussolinis, and more than enough of rabble-rousers, "pitch" men, high-pressure salesmen, and fast-talking "con" men. Just examine your own motives when you start looking for action. Keep your goal high by being concerned about *how* you persuade people and by being morally senstitive about *what* you're persuading them to do. Then you can take pride in getting the response you want from your listeners: "I'll *do* it!"

Plan to Follow

1. The "Bull's-Eye" plan suggested in Units 8 and 10 is a good one to follow because of its direct attack and progressive movement. Its five steps and their purposes as adjusted to persuasion are summarized here:

Step 1. WAKE UP!	Arouse attention and stimulate interest dramatically.
Step 2. THIS CONCERNS YOU	Get audience personally involved and establish motivation.
Step 3. GENERALLY SPEAKING	Explain what action you want and why it is desirable.
Step 4. FOR EXAMPLE	Give facts, reasons, arguments, and appeals to support your request and win agreement.
Step 5. WHAT TO DO	Be specific about what you want and "wrap it up" with so strong an appeal your listeners won't forget or evade your suggestion for action.

2. The climactic order of points is useful for a longer, more leisurely speech in which you take time to orient the listener's full attention to the subject by piling up facts, evidence, reason, and arguments, and building your appeals to a strong, dramatic conclusion.

3. Any other generally logical plan is usable provided that you stimulate interest early in your talk, sustain attention, and keep the audience personally involved by emotional appeals as well as logical ones. The essentials are to establish good rapport with your audience, present plenty of evidence and arguments, and end your talk with a strong conclusive appeal.

4. Be definite, clear, and direct in what you're asking your listeners to do. Understanding is fundamental to persuasion. Your audience must know the full extent of your request and not misunderstand you. Particularly, they must not be confused about what specific action you want.

5. Whatever plan you use, build your talk on *facts* plus *reasoning* plus *appeal* plus the strength of your *personality*.

Material to Use

1. In general, use the same materials as those listed under "Speeches Which Convince" (p. 245) because of the similarity between these two types of speeches. However, emphasize material which has a human, emotional, activating appeal, since your final goal is belief *plus* action.

2. Use *facts* to bring knowledge to your audience; use *arguments* to bring about belief; use *suggestion and appeal* to bring action.

3. Let the audience help convince itself by showing it the *desirability and the possibility* of action. Then get it personally involved by urging it to think for itself and to apply its own insights to the problem.

4. Use attention-getting devices in the beginning, state points clearly, make use of frequent restatement of your strongest points, employ clear transition words to help your listeners follow you, use plenty of "since . . . then" construction ("Since all of us could use a little extra money from time to time, *then* let's see what we can do about getting some"), and use strong imperative sentences in the concluding portion of your talk (they help to stimulate action).

5. Conclude your appeal with a definite suggestion for immediate action. Your listeners have been prepared psychologically to act, and with every passing moment their resolve weakens. Listeners cool off after the stimulus of speaking; be sure to make your appeal for action so effective that they will want to carry on *after* the speech is over.

6. Use visual aids—charts, diagrams, slides, motion pictures, and drawings—to help "sell" your suggested action. Substantiate your claims wherever feasible by using testimony, affidavits, expert opinion, and demonstrations.

7. Delivery techniques: an air of poise and confidence; movement, gestures, eye-contact for emphasis; a vigorous, compelling manner combined with a sincere, constructive, believing attitude.

8. The use of friendly, well-chosen humor always helps to win friends and influence people.

Things to Avoid

1. A mere recitation of points and arguments without any personal commitment, conviction, sincerity, or interest on your part.

2. The extremes of too much dependence on logic alone or too much emphasis on an unreasoning, overemotional appeal. Balance the rational *with* the emotional.

3. Rousing antagonism or resentment by your manner, argument, or voice, such as threatening, dictating, begging, bullying, being sarcastic,

pushing too hard, playing on prejudices, being cynical, or exhibiting a selfish motive.

4. Talking so far past the point of "closing the deal" that your audience becomes bored, wearied, or impatient.

5. Overconfidence, lack of thorough research, too many uninteresting details, too many statistics, artificial devices or tricks to capture attention, inadequate understanding of your specific audience.

6. Rabble-rousing; overplaying upon feelings of anger, fear, or prejudice to get action.

Topics for Talks

Keep the School Grounds Clean
Let's Redecorate Our Clubroom
Go to See the ________ Movie
Read This Book
Start a Savings Account
Plan a Program of Daily Exercise
Be Punctual for Appointments
Join the ________ Club
Learn How to Give Artificial Respiration
Vote For ________
Help the Red Cross
Listen to the ________ TV Program
Join the Republican (or Democratic) Party
Get Some Seat Belts
Make Friends with Your Counselor
Make Worthwhile Use of Your Summer Vacation
Come to the Prom
Subscribe to ________ Magazine
Give Some of Your Spare Time to a Worthwhile Activity
Eat at the School Cafeteria at Least Once a Week
Visit an Art Gallery
Let's Elect Dick Richards Class President
Buy a Student-Body Ticket
Begin Now to Build Your Own Library
Learn to Swim
Begin Your Advanced Education at a Small College
Support Proposition ________
Get a Weekend Job for Extra Spending Money
Attend an Opera
Aid the ________ Drive
Don't Be an "Ugly" American
You *Can* Improve Your Grades
Go on a Diet
Stop Smoking Today

General topics which can be made to apply to specific local or national current problems:

Let's Get This Job Done
We *Can* Solve This Problem
We Need Your Help
It's Time to Change Our Course of Action
This Must Not Happen
Let's Stop the Proposed Action

ACTIVITIES

1. Here is a list of a few manifestations of the fundamental drives or impelling motives that cause people to act. Discuss in class any people or incidents that you've read about, observed, or experienced which might be specific examples of these, or similar, manifestations. For instance, what probably motivates a boy who wants to own a car when he's sixteen? a girl whose hair style is like that of her closest friend? a student who won't report the cheating of others in an exam? a volunteer in the Peace Corps? a man like Martin Luther King? Fidel Castro?

   a. Giving devotion and protection to the family.
   b. Exhibiting pride in family, community, state, and nation.
   c. Feeling loyalty to the "gang."
   d. Trying to improve health standards.
   e. Buying insurance; accumulating savings.
   f. Defending freedoms that have been gained; struggling for those that haven't.
   g. Finding satisfaction in being noble or generous.
   h. Trying to outshine the neighbors.
   i. Reacting to a sense of justice.
   j. Organizing unions, cooperatives, brotherhoods, and clubs.
   k. Buying or making things that satisfy aesthetic tastes.
   l. Voting bonds for civic improvement.
   m. Undergoing long periods of education or training.
   n. Making great personal sacrifices.
   o. Subordinating personal desires to those of the group.
   p. Creating and maintaining government.
   q. Adhering to customs, styles, etiquette, decorum, fashions, and taboos.
   r. Guarding property by patents, copyrights, and other laws.
   s. Inventing and using machines that save time and labor.
   t. Combatting pestilence and disease that bring man pain and premature death.

2. Bring to class something you own but would like to "sell." Deliver a sales talk to the group. Set about gaining attention and interest, as you try to do in all your talks, and then work hard to bring about the desire for ownership. If you can create the desire, all you have left to do is show how it is possible to "buy."

3. Has your school suffered from lack of school spirit? Is your favorite club in a slump? Does your class need some pep? Give a short pep talk to your class, for whatever purpose you desire, and see if you can raise some enthusiasm.

4. Unless you are different from the average high school boy or girl, there is something you'd like to do, something you'd like to have, or somewhere you'd like to go, and so far your parents haven't been sold on the idea when you've asked their permission. Now is the time to try again, since you are armed with new ammunition. Ask a favor of your parents. Prepare your appeal carefully in advance, and then present it as skillfully as you can. Make a report on the results.

5. Read a number of advertisements in magazines having national circulation. What impelling motives have been recognized by the advertisers?

6. Listen to some TV or radio commercials and evaluate their appeal and direct suggestions for action. What do you notice about the vocabulary used?

7. Choose for the subject of a class talk something you think your classmates should be doing but are not. If you wish, speak to them as citizens of the community rather than as school citizens. Prepare a three-minute "Bull's-Eye" talk on your topic, keeping in mind the points that follow:
   a. Your classmates must believe in your plan.
   b. They should benefit by your request for action.
   c. The plan should be simple and definite.
   d. You must appeal to the fundamental drives.
   e. Your conclusion should carry power and punch.
8. Prepare a persuasive talk approximately three to five minutes long, using climactic order, saving your best argument for the last.

Speeches Which Entertain:

Communication That Brings Pleasure and Enjoyment

To most people the word *entertainment* implies fun and amusement, something that people do or observe in their spare time for pleasure and enjoyment. Trips, plays, movies, sports, games, dancing, parties, delicious food, books—all these things and many more offer entertainment because they tend to free a person from his worries and daily routine, giving him stimulation, relaxation, or a feeling of well-being.

Among the forms of entertainment that cost little or nothing is everyday communication between people. Exchanging ideas in conversation is a pleasant activity. Most people enjoy chatting; they like exchanging jokes, stories, and anecdotes, or just "passing the time of day."

Another kind of speaking that gives pleasure to both speaker and listener is more formal than just plain talk. It is the sort of entertainment that is found in humorous or dramatic readings, monologues, skits for club meetings and programs, after-dinner speeches, or simply speeches whose primary purpose is to entertain. It is with this latter type of speech that this section deals.

An important ingredient in the entertaining speech is humor, a quality that causes us to smile, chuckle, laugh uproariously, or even laugh silently. People like to have their "funny bones" tickled. The humor may be lightweight and superficial, a simple expression of fun and hilarity; or it may be deep-centered and highly perceptive, reflecting a high degree of compassion, tolerance, and sympathetic understanding of the frailties of human nature and the ludicrous, absurd, and comical things that people do. The humor may be preplanned, or it may be spontaneous, growing out of the occasion, the content, or the audience reaction. It may lie in *what* you say or in *how* you say it.

Victor Borge makes an art of the speech to entertain.

It is true that there are few speeches, however serious, that won't be more effective if dashes of humor are added, a fact that too few speakers remember. Yet you will find yourself enjoying many speeches that are very entertaining without being funny or humorous. Any good informative talk which deals with unusual, odd, novel, and interesting facts or experiences can be entertaining, such as a travelogue, a hobby talk, an adventure, or an explanation of some fascinating device or process. Speeches whose chief purpose is to convince may also be entertaining, like a vigorous debate or a timely political speech. Impressive or inspiring speeches, too, entertain in the best sense of the word by holding attention, stirring emotions, or having a stimulating intellectual appeal. But when your *primary* purpose is to entertain, then you make use of all that you can muster—humor included—to please your listeners.

Your Goal

Your specific aim is to hold the attention of the audience, to interest it, divert it, and perhaps amuse it. You want to give pleasure and enjoyment. You should strive for originality of thought or approach, presenting either new ideas or old ideas with freshness. You may develop humor in your talk along the lines that best fit your ability and personality. You should maintain a relaxed, light, easy manner of delivery that puts no strain on your listeners. Your personal appeal to the audience is important, since people respond with pleasure to a personality that is genial, friendly, and good-humored. If, in addition to lightness of touch, you can give your listeners something solid with intellectual or emotional appeal, you'll give satisfaction as well as pleasure and can look forward to the response you want: "I enjoyed your talk."

Plan to Follow

1. The order of major points is not a particular problem in this type of talk. Any simple logical plan is possible to use. Even a hodgepodge of points might be successful if the material is interesting.
2. The climactic order is a good one if your material is dramatic and filled with suspense or if you want to adhere to the principle that your talk should become stronger as you go along.
3. The chronological order is usable for a travel talk, an exposition, or a narrative.
4. Get favorable attention quickly, sustain it by carefully chosen interesting material, and then make your conclusion short and "snappy."

Material to Use

1. Capitalize on material that is unusual, novel, queer, funny, unbelievable, mysterious, ludicrous, exciting, or otherwise highly interesting.
2. Use material you can identify with your audience. Both group and personal references, if relevant and kindly, make people feel pleased.
3. Look for humor among human weaknesses. Procrastination, forgetfulness, making excuses, exaggerating our troubles, repeating ourselves, being defensive, rationalizing, and always putting ourselves in the best light are grist for the humor mill. Don't forget to laugh at yourself, too.
4. Try to inject humor of a personal sort *throughout* your talk rather than by just pulling in some jokes. Use cleverly worded sentences and phrases or try your natural wit instead of telling stock stories, if you can.
5. Recall events; tell stories; describe incongruous situations; make exaggerated comparisons; relate whimsical incidents or bits of conversation; or reveal absurdity as a way of introducing a humorous element.
6. Exploit your personality; bring out vigor, zest, drollness, mannerisms, or quirks—whatever makes you pleasingly different from other people.
7. If you have any tricks, "gags," or devices that have proved effective in catching attention, making people feel relaxed, or getting a friendly response, use them; but be sure they are suitable to the occasion.

Things to Avoid

1. Choosing a dull, heavy topic that shouldn't be treated lightly.
2. Being long-winded or slow in putting your points across.
3. Overuse of stories and anecdotes. They are good for highlighting a talk but lose strength if used too freely or tritely.
4. Trying too hard to be funny.
5. Being insensitive to your audience's response. Emphasize the material that receives favorable response and cut out what doesn't.
6. Unwise choice of material that you *think* is humorous. Use this guide: *If you're in doubt, don't say it!*

Topics for Talks

A Case of Mistaken Identity
Styles That Bring Smiles
Only Ants Enjoy Picnics
I Met a Ghost
Skiing Looked So Easy
My Dentist Scares Me
Caught in the Act
The Oddest Person I Know
If I Were a Millionaire
My First Slumber Party
A Traveler's Tale
Hairdos
I Saw Stars
Oh, Women!
Some Amusing Superstitions
I Was Embarrassed to Death
The Things My Mother Tells about Me!
Have You Heard about My Operation?
Men Are Worse Gossips than Women
A Small Brother Can Be a Pest
A Practical Joke That Backfired
It Wasn't Funny at the Time, But–
The Travels of a Secret
A Look at Some Amusing Speakers
My First Day behind the Wheel
I Am a Teen-Age Monster!
If Politicians Kept Their Promises
My First Flight

ACTIVITIES

1. Listen critically to a number of TV programs headed by big-name stars in the field of comedy. What characteristics do the programs have in common? How do they differ? What special ability does each star have? Notice especially how these professionals make use of suspense, pause, timing, inflection, and pace.

2. Stand by your seat and tell in one minute, or less, of some incident that you thought rather amusing. Go back in your memory to the part of the incident that caused you to laugh. What were the details that lent humor to the situation?

3. Tell the class a short story or joke that you especially like. The reaction of the class will give you some notion of how popular your sense of humor is and how well you have told the story.

4. Ask your teacher to bring to class a number of stories that he likes. Let him read one; then several of you try to retell it. Repeat the activity until everyone has repeated a story. Let the class decide who are the best storytellers.

5. Try telling a story in dialect. Very few people can tell such stories well. Those who can will always have an eager audience. Maybe *you* have some talent.

6. Choose a topic for a short humorous talk and prepare it in this manner:
   a. Make a short outline of the main points.
   b. Plan an introduction to get attention and put your audience in a good mood.
   c. Select details that add to interest and humor, distribute them throughout your talk, and inject your personality into the selection of the details.
   d. Build a conclusion that carries a punch and leaves your listeners smiling.
   e. Present your talk to your family or a friend for reaction to the humor and suggestions for improvement.
   f. Forget your talk for a day or two; then go back over it alone to polish it.

Speeches Which Inspire or Impress: Communication That Stirs the Emotions

The inspirational or impressive speech is one that appeals primarily to the emotions. Its purpose is to impress the listener by creating an effect which stirs him deeply, leaving a memorable imprint upon his mind and feelings. It may even stimulate and impel him to some creative or effective effort, a kind of inner action which is similar to the objective action that a persuasive talk attempts to accomplish. Aggressive action, however, is not the aim of the inspirational speech. Rather, its purpose is to arouse depth of feeling, strong sentiment, or quiet reflection about the general truths and human values that add enrichment to life.

Inspirational talks are frequently idealistic in nature, dealing with abstract qualities like beauty, faith, love, nobility of character, generosity, brotherhood and self-sacrifice—any of the great words that are the symbols of man's best ideals. No doubt you have heard talks of this type a number of times, as in church, at impressive club meetings, at memorial services, when special honor is given to a public figure, on a commemorative holiday, at large gatherings like Billy Graham's spiritual crusades, or similar special occasions. You may also have heard impressive talks that were chiefly descriptive ones, as on the beauties of nature, a man's courage, a woman's love, a dog's devotion, or some heartwarming experience.

Any talk that causes people to feel deeply and respond emotionally may be called impressive, regardless of what emotions are aroused. But the truly inspirational speech is on the highest level of feeling. It touches the good in people; it appeals to their unselfish drives and desires; it affects their conscience. Learning how to deliver a sincere message, which reflects your own feelings about something good, true, and beautiful and which touches the hearts of your listeners, is a satisfying experience.

Billy Graham is one of the most famous inspirational speakers in America. Here he opens a spiritual crusade in Washington.

Your Goal

You want to stir the emotions of your listeners, making them *feel* deeply about something, and inspiring them to rise above their ordinary thoughts and feelings. Ideally you want to lift them out of themselves and direct their thoughts to stimulating ideals and spiritual values. You want them to be cheered, heartened, encouraged, and perhaps even exhilarated by what you say. You offer them universally accepted and approved general truths, giving them courage to accept new ideas, goals, and ideals and renewing their faith in old, established ones. You appeal to sentiment, you touch their hearts, you affect their conscience. You impress and inspire them. And if you speak with sincerity and earnestness of belief, you'll get the response: "What you said touched me deeply."

Plan to Follow

1. Decide what impression you want to make. What mood do you want to create? What emotions do you want to stir? To what fundamental drives do you want to appeal? What "good" do you want to stress?

2. Give your listeners time to get into the proper mood and then build up slowly to the desired emotional response.

3. Unify your audience by stressing common hopes and desires, and relate your subject to the present audience and the present times.

4. Any progressive plan that moves toward a strong conclusion is suitable: climactic order, the "Bull's-Eye" plan, or any general-logical step-by-step order.

5. Watch that conclusion! Make it sustain the emotion you set out to achieve, but don't drag it out.

Material to Use

1. Present universally accepted and approved general truths or abstract ideas, but support your generalizations with well-chosen details. Employ proverbs, adages, fables, quotations from Scripture and from philosophy, and warmly human stories for illustration and example.

2. Strive for *reasonable* idealism; talk in terms of basic human values.

3. Use psychological suggestion. People like to imitate the actions of people of prestige and to identify with good causes and right-doing.

4. Be saturated with personal conviction about your subject and phrase your statements so that they have dignity and sincerity.

5. Use frequent and varied restatement of your main thesis.

6. Use vivid words, descriptive words, "feeling" words. Add charm by using figures of speech: metaphors, similes, and personification.

7. Use striking comparisons and contrasts to reinforce your thought and create a vivid impression.

Things to Avoid

1. Glittering generalities that may sound impressive but are empty of meaning to your audience.

2. Subjects too broad, too complex, too intellectual, too trite, too threadbare, or too matter-of-fact.

3. An oratorical manner; attacking your subject with "sound and fury"; flag-waving; emotionalism. Also beware of overrighteousness.

4. Insincerity; artificiality; triteness; clichés—anything which detracts from honest emotion.

Topics for Talks

What It Means to Give
Nature Paints a Wonderland
The Valiant Die But Once
Frowns Lose Friends
A Test of Courage
The Grand Canyon Is Awe-Inspiring
Is Honesty an Outmoded Virtue?
Music Waves a Magic Wand
Integrity Has Its Rewards
Blunt Statements Have Sharp Edges

What Price Democracy?	Are You a Quitter When the Going Is Tough?
I'm Proud to Be an American	Everyone Must Have Faith in Something
The Unknown Soldiers	Youth Has Not Failed Its Obligations
America the Beautiful	Don't Sign Your Name to Unworthy Deeds
Our Parents, the Forgotten People	
Words Are Windows to Our Souls	

ACTIVITIES

1. Find and study a eulogy (a speech or piece of writing in praise of a person) of a famous person. Read to the class parts which you find especially impressive or inspiring, explaining why you chose them. The speech *In Memoriam,* by Frank Church, which you will find in Appendix B, may be used for class study.

2. Describe a place, a work of art, or a natural wonder as impressively as you can in a two-hundred-word paragraph. Read it to the class for evaluation of the devices you used to make your description impressive. Here are some suggestions:

The Lincoln Memorial	John Kennedy's Grave	A Lonely Mansion
Mount Rushmore	Yosemite Valley	Michelangelo's *Pietà*
The *Mona Lisa*	A Tropical Sunset	A Gothic Cathedral

3. Plan a short inspirational talk on a person who has gained fame through an impressive record of deeds. Point to the ideals for which this person was well known, like courage, devotion to duty, love of his fellowman, or faith; and build your talk upon the things he did which prove his idealistic qualifications.

4. List some of the outstanding national and international problems of our time. Choose one of them and write a paragraph in which you make an emotional appeal concerning the need or way to solve the problem. Deliver it to the class.

5. Find some speeches by well-known speakers of the present or past, and bring to class examples of inspirational passages from them for reading and discussion.

6. Choose a topic for a talk to impress or inspire. Remember these points:

a. The choice of impression you want to make is essential.
b. Dignity and sincerity are chief factors.
c. People understand and respond to statements of simple, human truth.
d. "Feeling" words, figures of speech, and comparison and contrast help to establish mood.
e. A short, forceful conclusion is best.

Films:

Give Me Liberty (TFC). 24 min color.
Planning Your Talk (MH). 13 min b&w.

Filmstrips:

Relation of Ideals to Communication (SVE). 37 fr b&w.

Record:

Great American Speeches (Caedmon). Two 12″ records 33⅓ rpm.

Unit Fourteen

SPECIAL SPEAKING: Talking That Fits the Occasion

There will be a number of times in your school life, as well as in the adult world, when a knowledge of what to say on certain special occasions will be of great help to you. For instance, what should you do when you are suddenly asked to give an impromptu talk? Are you able to talk interestingly about books you've read? When you are a committee chairman, can you give an efficient report of what your committee has done? Are your telephone conversations all that they should be? Could you introduce a speaker to an audience? Are you at ease in introducing people to each other? Can you make an interesting announcement? What should you say when presenting or accepting a gift? If you found yourself in the position of having to deliver a welcome talk, could you do it? Do you know how to make a nomination or campaign speech? Do you want to enter a speech contest? This unit will help you to answer these questions.

Impromptu Speaking

Being called upon unexpectedly to give an impromptu speech can be a harrowing experience. It's like having a jack-in-the-box suddenly pop up in your face when you least expect it. You feel a sudden shock of surprise, followed by a mental numbness that can cause you to lose poise, unless you know just what to do.

An impromptu talk is one which is given on the spur of the moment. You have no opportunity for deliberate preparation; you simply gather your thoughts together quickly and do the best you can with what comes to mind. Your success depends upon how large a supply of material you generally carry around in your mind, upon how rapidly and effectively you can organize some of that material so that it will fit the occasion, and upon how well you maintain your poise in the face of an emergency. If your mental storehouse is full, your mind quick and alert, and your personality pleasing, you will be able to meet your impromptu situation with some degree of success. The ability to speak well on short notice can be a valuable asset to you. Some practice in this type of speaking will help you to collect your wits, think fast, organize quickly, speak simply, and drive home a point.

A Plan to Follow. When necessity demands that you get up to "say a few words" or "make a few remarks" in an impromptu situation, there's no better plan to follow than the one with which you are already familiar. Reread the part of Unit 8 which tells you about the "Bull's-Eye" plan, and pay special attention to the sample "Bull's-Eye" talk included in Unit 10. That's the way an impromptu talk could be given. There are no strict rules, of course; but if you could make that plan a part of your thinking, you would find yourself able to meet an unexpected situation with greater confidence. Let's review that plan as it applies to impromptu speaking.

YOUR AUDIENCE	YOU
STEP 1. *Wake Up!*	Start with a good attention-getting opening sentence.
STEP 2. *This Concerns You*	Explain why your subject is important or worthwhile.
STEP 3. *Generally Speaking*	Follow with a general statement of what you're talking about.
STEP 4. *For Example*	Back up that general statement with two or three examples and illustrations.
STEP 5. *What to Do (or Think)*	Conclude with striking sentences that quickly summarize your idea.

Here is a sample written speech based on that plan. You will recognize that it is somewhat more polished than most of the impromptu speeches you will give or hear, but don't let that discourage you. It represents a *goal* as well as an *example*.

Who's afraid of the big, bad wolf—besides the three little pigs? Almost everybody is! The big, bad wolf to most of us in this class is the thought of getting up and speaking in public. That gets us down. It scares us. It worries us. We begin to feel that no one else has ever suffered as we have.

But we are not alone. Almost everyone has met that frightening wolf. Even some of the most famous people in the world have had the same feeling that we have. Let's look at some of them.

Mark Twain said that the first time he gave a lecture he felt that his mouth was filled with cotton and his heart was hammering its way out of his chest.

There are few more famous speakers in the world than Winston Churchill; yet he overcame severe nervous stuttering to become a powerful voice against Fascism.

The first time Charlie Chaplin spoke over the air the "butterflies" in his stomach kept interfering with his voice, and he felt as if he were riding out a February storm on the Atlantic.

Lincoln's voice was shrill, high, and unpleasant. His manner was painfully shy, his face wrinkled and sallow, and his posture awkward. He frequently confessed to feeling nervous and ill at ease. Yet who can forget the Gettysburg Address?

These examples could be multiplied a hundred times to prove that all speakers have been afraid at some time in their careers. So take heart, fellow sufferers. If others have faced the wolf and mastered him, so can we. With patience and persistence we can tie him up in knots and put him where he belongs.

Word of Warning. Understand that impromptu talks are not good substitutes for carefully prepared talks. *There is no substitute for preparation.* You may speak fluently and therefore feel that you don't have to prepare your work carefully. But if you do feel that way, you're on dangerous ground. Hasty preparation leads to hasty and ill-considered thinking, to loose generalizations, to rambling sentences, to slovenly language. *Don't be guilty!*

ACTIVITIES

1. Practice impromptu speaking on one of these topics. Pick one at random, give yourself about five minutes to think about it, then stand up and talk for sixty seconds—if you can!

a. A Person I'll Always Remember
b. The Value of a College Education
c. Everyone Should Learn to Swim
d. Drive Well and Survive
e. It Pays to Increase Your Vocabulary
f. The Dog Is Man's Best Friend
g. Everyone Should Have a Hobby
h. Follow the Golden Rule
i. We Need Friends
j. We Can't Do without TV

2. Write each of the following topics on a separate slip of paper. Shake the slips up in a container and have each member of the class draw one. Then without *any* time for preparation, give an impromptu talk on the subject you have drawn.

Dreams	Men	Apologies	Relatives	Hairpins
Flowers	Junk	Gossip	Christmas Cards	Cold Feet
Spring	Pets	Storms	Maple Syrup	Clouds
Vacation	Fashions	Rubber	Dates	Smiles
Rain	White Lies	Diets	Prunes	Fire

3. Write on the board five or six sentences, each of which could be the opening sentence of a brief talk, like "People do the craziest things!" or "Let's talk about the weather." Give a one-minute talk on whatever sentence your teacher or class chairman picks for you as a surprise topic.
4. Try some "chain-talks" for impromptu practice. One student starts a talk on any topic of his own choice. After several sentences, he stops, points to another student, and sits down. The other student picks up the topic, continues the talk for a short while, and then tosses it to someone else. This chainlike procedure continues until five or six students have spoken. The last one to speak must wrap up the topic with an appropriate conclusion.

Book Talk

Talking about books you have read is one of your responsibilities in many classes in high school and college. In your history, science, English, and social science classes you have opportunities to report on books you read outside of class. The suggestions included here are intended to help you to prepare such reports or reviews.

Let's establish a difference between a book report and a book review. When you give an account of the contents of a book, stating the facts, items, details contained in it, you are giving a *report*. You relate facts, give information, itemize details. But when you exercise your critical judgment and deliberately survey, examine, and appraise the contents of a book with the intention of setting a value on them, you are giving a *review*. You are not merely telling *what* the book contains; you are passing judgment on it. You assess its worth and values, and you express an opinion about its importance and significance. A report is objective and informative; a review is subjective and convincing. It is like the difference between a newspaper reporter's account of the weekend traffic accidents in your town and the editor's comments on their tragic consequences and the need for more careful driving. In one case the emphasis is on *facts*; in the other, on *opinion*.

Book Reports. *Be a good reporter.* In giving a factual *report* on books you have read, you will have to learn to be a *good* reporter and have a "nose for news." You must decide, first of all, what is important to talk about and what is trivial or ordinary. You can't tell *everything* that a book contains; you must select those details which will give your listeners the clearest picture of the book and which will also give them the most pleasure as they listen to your report. The same general principles apply here as in speeches to inform. You might look over the first part of Unit 13 again to be sure you have in mind the goals of informative talks.

Specifically, there are certain points that are customarily included in book *reports.* Here they are. You may use some or all, in any order you wish, depending on what you decide is important.

1. The name of the book.
2. Something about the author.
3. A statement of the general purpose of the author or the main idea of the book. Every book has a theme, a reason for being. Find out what it is and let your listeners know.
4. A *brief* summary of the content. Be very careful here not to become boring or dull to your listeners. Too much rambling and overemphasis on minor details will spoil your report. Limit your account to what will interest your audience or add to suspense.
5. Discussion of the most interesting *characters, incidents, details, facts,* or *chapters.* Select details carefully. If you come across something especially worthwhile, you may read a sample to your listeners; but be brief.

Book Reviews. *Be a good reviewer.* The editor of a newspaper or a magazine directs the policies of his publication, passes judgment on principles, sets a value on what is worth printing, appraises facts, and leads in forming public opinion. His editorials reflect his critical opinions. So it is with a book *review.* It should reflect your critical opinion. The emphasis should be on your reaction to the book and on your evaluation of it.

Good judgment grows out of experience. As you grow older your sense of values will become deeper, broader, more reliable. You are not too sure yet about artistic and literary values. But you're learning! If you have an adventurous mind and are willing to meet challenges, you can say much more about a book than just "I liked it" or "I disliked it." The next time you read a book, give a *review* of it instead of a *report,* trying out these suggestions:

1. Deal *very* briefly with the content. A few sentences are sufficient.
2. Stress the theme, the purpose, the problem, the *idea* behind the book. What does the author want to say? Can you state in a few significant sentences the motive behind his book? Is it worthwhile?

3. If your book is a novel, who are the most interesting people in it? Why? If it is a biography, what are the outstanding characteristics of the main figure? What constructive things can you learn from his life? If it is a travel book, what are the best incidents? If it is a technical book, what is the best feature of it?

4. Discuss the style of the book, its personality, its use of language. Is there any dramatic description or colorful detail? Does it touch your heart? Does it appeal to your mind? How does the author handle humor? Does the personality of the author show? If so, how? Can you quote or read any illustrative passages? Can you tell what view of life the author has?

5. Make a general statement as to the values contained in the book. Does it reveal any weaknesses in our society? Does it examine a problem? Does it offer a solution? Does it attempt to examine the character of a man's life? Does it add to your historical or literary background? Is the book primarily useful, entertaining, instructive, inspiring, exciting, or what? Will you remember it for a long time? Should you like other people to read it? Why? What did you like *best* about it?

6. Take time to have a critical reaction to what you read and express an honest, sincere, fair, thoughtful opinion. Don't be content to say "I liked it" or "It was amusing" or "The characters didn't appeal to me" or "It was pretty long" or "I recommend it" without further explanation. *Support your reactions with evidence.*

7. Always look for significant relationships, subsurface meanings, symbolism, and philosophy when you review literary books. Don't limit your review to what is obvious and superficial. Dig deep for meanings and values that are related to human needs, desires, and problems.

These suggestions are all leading ones; they should open new doors for some of you, and they may guide you further in learning what lies behind words on a page. Your teacher will have many more suggestions for you. It is enough now to point out to you that a thoughtful, well-prepared book *review* covers more ground than a factual, cut-and-dried book *report*.

ACTIVITIES

1. Choose one of the books on your required reading list and give a *report* on it. Remember that you are primarily interested in reporting upon the *facts*, as you find them. Follow the steps outlined above.
2. Turn to your Sunday paper or to some national magazine in which there is a section devoted to new books. Examine the comments carefully to determine which of them are factual reporting and which are opinion.
3. Find newspapers, magazines, or other publications that contain book reviews. Select a review which appeals to you, bring it to school, and read it to your class,

Cartoon by Franklin Folger

"The treasurer wishes me to announce that if certain members don't soon pay their back dues, she will simply scream."

pointing out the method the writer has used in appraising the book. The Sunday literary supplement of *The New York Times, The Saturday Review,* the *Book Review Digest, The Reader's Digest,* the American Library Association *Booklist,* the London *Times,* and perhaps the Saturday or Sunday issues of your own local newspapers are some of the sources to which you may go.

4. Give a five-minute review of a book you have recently read. Follow the seven suggestions listed in this section and let your classmates evaluate your review.

Giving Reports

Almost everybody gives reports. In your English classes you may give book reports (reviews might be better, remember?). In your history or science classes you may work on a project for several weeks and then give a report on your work. If you are a member of the student-body council or some similar group, you will bring back a report of its activities to members of your homeroom or activity room or basic-course class. If you are the treasurer of some school organization, reports of financial conditions are a part of your responsibility. Perhaps you will be sent to some convention as a representative of the student body, the scholarship society, the debating club, the athletic organization, or the school paper. A report on what happened will be expected of you by the stay-at-homes.

No student completes a school year without becoming familiar with the word *report* in some form or other.

Project Reports. Most reports are simple informative speeches. The best thing for you to do in planning project reports is to read carefully the part of Unit 13 entitled "Speeches Which Inform" and follow the suggestions given there. Simplicity and clarity are essential, since you are dealing primarily with facts and details rather than with opinions and impressions. Therefore, avoid too much detail unless it is specifically required in your report, and be sure to select the details carefully for their novelty, significance, or interest.

Committee Reports. All organizations depend on committee reports when group ignorance, lack of complete information, or lack of time make it impractical to take immediate action. A committee can speed up the business of a club by making investigations and recommendations on its own time. Its importance is recognized by parliamentary law in placing committee reports immediately after the reading of the minutes and requiring them to be heard before any other business is considered. The basic essentials to be included in a committee report are the following:

1. The purpose of the committee
2. What it found, and the sources of its information
3. Conclusions and recommendations

If the committee report contains no recommendations for action, it may be accepted by the group without vote. But if recommendations are included, the report must be accepted or rejected by a group vote.

Convention Reports. Too many convention reports are boring because they are too detailed. The goal of a successful convention report should be simplicity and clearness. The organization which you represented at the convention is interested only partially in where the convention was held, how you got there, what you did, and how you felt. Its real interest lies in the new ideas you picked up there, the impressive message which you may have received from one of the speakers, the interesting facts or suggestions that it can make use of. If you need any further suggestions as to what to include in a convention report, look at the following questions:

1. *What* was the convention about?
2. *When* was it held?
3. *Where* was it held?
4. *Who* was there?
   a. Organizations represented
   b. Outstanding speakers

} light emphasis

5. *Why* was it held?
6. *How* does it affect your organization?
   a. Benefits to be derived
   b. Inspiration for future activity

(items 5–6: strong emphasis)

As with all speeches, reports should be well planned in advance. Thoughtful preparation is the best guarantee against long-windedness and overindulgence in uninteresting details. Make your reports as brief as you can, as interesting as your subject allows, and as helpful to your listeners as possible.

ACTIVITIES

1. Present a three- to five-minute report on a project that you are preparing for some other class or on a school project being sponsored by a group in which you are active. Remember, your report will be like a simple informative talk and should be prepared as carefully as any other speech you give.
2. Imagine that you are the chairman of a committee for some organization, and that you are expected to report on your activities at the next regular meeting of the group. Plan a suitable report for any one of these situations:
   a. Treasurer's report on the financial status of your class.
   b. Finance-committee report on expenses incurred for some class activity.
   c. Program-committee report on class plans for a special program during Book Week.
   d. Activity-committee report on plans for a homeroom project of giving a Christmas box to a needy family.
   e. Block-letter organization report on the cost of sweaters to new members.
   f. Reading-committee report to an English class on new books available in the school library.
   g. Special-committee report on plans for the school Red Cross drive.
   h. Student-representative report on what took place in the last student-council meeting.
3. Give a convention report on one of the following situations. Follow the procedure suggested by the questions listed above.
   a. A report from a representative of the debating club on a recent Debate League meeting.
   b. A report on the results of the journalism convention attended by members of the staff of the school paper.
   c. Results of any special convention, such as are attended by members of the Scholarship Society, a church group, a school group interested in youth problems, journalism students, student-body officers, or athletic representatives.

Telephone Talk

Talking over the telephone has become an accepted part of our daily speaking activities. Scarcely a day goes by without our resorting to this convenient method of talking with people; yet most of us give no thought to how we sound over the telephone. The average person has never been taught how to develop a telephone technique that is efficient, courteous, and pleasing. We take our telephone manners as much for granted as we do our conversation manners, and often the results are feeble, if not painful. For instance, read the following telephone conversation:

Hello?

Hello.

Is this Steve?

No.

Is this Steve Lapham's house?

Yes.

Well, is Steve there?

No, he isn't.

Do you know where he is?

No, I don't.

Will he be back soon?

I don't think so.

Well, this is Bill Ott.

Who?

Bill Ott.

Oh, yes.

I'd like to get in touch with Steve.

Well, he–uh–I don't know just when he'll be back.

I guess I'd better call later.

All right. Or I can take a message for him.

Well–er–O.K.

What do you want me to tell him?

Tell him I called and to call me back before one o'clock, if he can.

All right.

And tell him I called because Dad lent me the car today and we can go to Searsville for a swim if he gets in before one o'clock.

All right; I'll tell him.

O.K. G'bye.

G'bye.

With a little friendly, helpful, courteous coöperation that conversation could have sounded something like this:

Hello, Steve?

No, Steve isn't here. This is his mother speaking. May I take a message for him?

Please. This is Bill Ott, Mrs. Lapham. If Steve comes home before one o'clock, would you have him call me? Dad has lent me the car today, and I thought Steve might like to come out to Searsville Lake with me for a swim this afternoon.

That sounds like fun. I'll tell him, Bill.
Thank you, Mrs. Lapham. I'll be waiting to hear from him. Good-bye.
Good-bye, Bill.

The first conversation uses 145 words. It sounds awkward and unfriendly; it wastes time and words. The second conversation requires only eighty-seven words to accomplish a more efficient and a more pleasing result. The point of this comparison is that a little cooperation, common sense, and good manners can go a long way toward changing an ineffective telephone conversation into a helpful and courteous one.

We use the telephone to make business, social, and pleasure calls. Developing a technique which will be satisfactory for all three is not too difficult. When you analyze *why* you are talking, when you know *what* you are going to say, and when you consider *how* to say it most effectively, your ability to communicate via the telephone will change for the better. A little practice will help you to improve your technique.

Business Calls. In business calls you want to accomplish something as quickly and as effectively as possible. Efficiency is desirable whether it is in placing a grocery order, making a complaint, asking for information, answering an advertisement, making an appointment, or concluding some other business arrangement. Consider the following suggestions:

1. Be sure you have the correct number.
2. Identify yourself as soon as you get your party.
3. Know exactly what you intend to say and state your business directly. Jot down notes before you call so that you won't forget anything important.
4. Have necessary materials ready at hand in case you need them as you talk: pencil, note pad, grocery list, newspaper advertisement, order blank, or a letter to which you may need to refer.
5. Don't "hem and haw." Time is valuable in the business world.
6. Speak clearly and in a businesslike manner, and remember the courteous "thank you" that should always bring a conversation to a close.
7. Don't ever be rude, discourteous, irritable, or just plain "ornery" during a business call.

Social Calls. The telephone is especially useful in meeting informal social responsibilities. When you extend an invitation or accept one, when you make a "bread-and-butter" or "thank-you" call, you are either meeting a social obligation or attending to social affairs in which etiquette plays an important part. In addition to this more formal area of social relations, there is the one in which you sometimes find it necessary to

Representative Patsy Mink of Hawaii uses the telephone as an aid to efficiency.

straighten out misunderstandings, smooth ruffled feelings, or simply maintain a contact that busy daily routine tends to destroy. Read the following suggestions for good social manners over the phone:

1. Avoid making a social call at an inconvenient time, such as early in the morning, during the dinner hour, or late at night.
2. When you get your number, ask immediately for the person to whom you wish to speak, identifying yourself at the same time.
3. Indicate your purpose in calling, and deliver your message directly without vagueness or generalities.
4. In extending an invitation be sure to make important details clear, such as date, time, place, occasion, or special arrangements. In accepting an invitation give your acceptance or rejection without dillydallying.
5. After accomplishing your purpose, converse briefly and courteously about topics of common interest. Don't hang up too abruptly.
6. Conclude with the familiar courteous remarks that usually end all telephone conversations. The person who places the call is responsible for bringing it to a conclusion.

Pleasure Calls. Your purpose in this kind of telephone call is just plain fun. All of us enjoy talking with our friends, passing the time of day with them, engaging in casual chatter and bits of news. Perhaps some of you indulge in too much of it, to the annoyance of other people on your line and to the chagrin of your parents. In any case, watch the following suggestions:

1. Don't play childish tricks, such as saying "Guess who this is" or calling strangers just for the fun of it.

2. Find out if your friend is busy; if so, call back later.

3. Be informal and friendly in your manner and let the conversation develop naturally.

4. Avoid too lengthy or too frequent visiting over the telephone. Someone else may want the line, or perhaps the person to whom you're speaking has more important things to do.

5. Avoid using the telephone for pleasure during the rush hours. You can find out from your telephone company what those hours of peak load are if you don't already know.

Your Telephone Voice. Your voice is the only means you have of making an impression on people to whom you speak over the telephone. Your listener cannot see your face, your eyes, your hands, or your body, all of which usually add expressiveness to speech by means of gestures and facial expression. Your voice and the language you use are what people judge you by. Look over the following suggestions:

1. Keep your voice pitched low and well modulated. The telephone picks up and distorts unpleasant sounds, particularly shrill, rasping ones.

2. Speak slowly enough to be heard easily.

3. Articulate clearly, watching *s* sounds especially. Don't hold the mouthpiece too close when you speak into it.

4. Avoid shouting or raising your voice. Loudness is not a proper substitute for clearness.

5. Your voice will reflect your moods and attitudes. Try to keep your telephone personality cheerful, friendly, alert, and interested.

ACTIVITIES

1. Discuss in class items you think are essential to efficiency in business calls. Demonstrate them in some imaginary business calls before the class.

2. Pair with a classmate and make up a telephone conversation based on one of the following:

   a. Call a friend and ask him about some homework assignments.

   b. Make an appointment with a doctor, dentist, or beauty-shop operator.

   c. Call for some information from the bus or railroad depot, the library, or the post office.

d. Call a theater and inquire about the program for the night, when the feature begins, and when the show is over.
e. Place a call to your family doctor late at night on behalf of your mother, who has suddenly become ill.
f. Place a call in answer to a newspaper advertisement concerning the sale of some article in which you're interested.
g. Call your newspaper agent and make a complaint about nondelivery of your Sunday paper.
h. Send a fifty-word night telegram to a relative.
i. Place an emergency call for an ambulance.
j. Report an automobile accident to the police.

3. Pair with a classmate and make up a telephone conversation based on one of the following:

a. Refuse or accept an invitation to a party, a picnic, or a show.
b. Call two of your friends and invite them to go with you and your family to a beach party next Sunday.
c. Thank your best friend's mother for the birthday dinner to which you were invited last night.
d. Call a friend of yours, a girl or boy back from his first semester at college, and bring him up to date on hometown news.
e. Make an excuse or an apology for some misunderstanding that has arisen between you and your best friend.

4. Keeping in mind the suggestions for social and pleasure calls, talk with a friend of yours tonight about some school event, some bit of news you'd like to pass on, or about anything that is fun. After you have finished your telephone conversation, evaluate it on the basis of the following questions and write a brief theme on telephoning:

- When did you place your call?
- How long did you talk?
- Did you inconvenience anyone?
- Did you have privacy when you telephoned? Were there any disturbing factors?
- What is your parents' attitude toward your use of the phone?
- What is your opinion about why teen-agers spend so much time on the phone?
- How do you assess your own telephone technique? In what areas can you improve?

5. Write and present a short skit in which you show, first, some common faults in telephoning and, second, the proper ways to place various kinds of calls.

6. Compile a list of the qualities that constitute a good telephone voice. When your list is complete, make a telephone date with a classmate for tonight. Talk about whatever you wish, but be sure to keep in front of you the checklist so that you may evaluate each other's telephone voice. Don't report to each other what your evaluation is until class time tomorrow.

7. Prepare a group of talks or a panel discussion on one of the topics listed here. Consult with your local telephone company or write to the American Telephone and Telegraph Company in New York for material.

a. The Historical Development of the Telephone
b. Correct Telephone Habits
c. How to Place a Long-Distance Call
d. The Correct Use of the Telephone Directory
e. Technical Aspects of the Telephone
f. How Telephone Operators Are Trained
g. The Telephone of the Future

8. Make up your own chart of "telephone hints" and post it near your telephone at home. You'll be surprised at the number of times it will be a helpful reminder to you of ways in which you can improve your telephone talk.

Introducing the Speaker: A Chairman's Duties

Getting off to a good start is important in almost everything. It is especially important to a speaker, particularly when he is facing an unfamiliar sea of faces and feeling the nervous tension that always precedes talking to an audience. Courtesy demands that we give every speaker the most favorable send-off we can, that we place him in harmonious relationship with his audience, that we make the audience want to listen to what he will say. The guest speaker, especially, who has put effort into preparing his speech, who has traveled some distance, perhaps, to come to your school, and who has taken time to bring you a message which he considers worthwhile, deserves every courtesy that can be given him. A good speech of introduction is one way of extending him courtesy, of helping him to feel at ease, of bridging the gap between him and his audience.

Remember Who's Speaking. Introducing speakers to audiences in a pleasing, effective manner should be one of your many accomplishments by the time you have finished your speech course. As chairman of a program you should try to get the occasion, the speaker, the subject, and the audience together as quickly, as interestingly, and as gracefully as possible. You should be brief because the speaker is more important than you are, and what he has to say is of greater interest to the audience than what you may say. Your position is subordinate to his. A chairman once forgot this. He was introducing a former pole-vaulting champion, who was also a famous lawyer and speaker, to a group of sportswriters at a banquet. The program was long and the time was growing short, but the chairman was ambitious. He first talked at length about the accomplishments of the vaulter and then became absorbed in the subject that was to be discussed by the speaker. He was probably fascinated by the sound of his own voice, for he went on and on in spite of anxious glances from the speaker-to-be. At last he finished, after fulsome oratory, and said, "Mr. Eastman will now give us his address." And Mr. Eastman did just that. He said, "My address is 365 Mills Building, Kansas City," and sat down. The audience rocked with laughter, at the expense of the chairman. You can do better than this chairman if you keep in mind your purpose: to get the speaker and audience together quickly, simply, and courteously.

Plan Introductions Wisely. The plan of your speech of introduction will depend upon which is the more important, the speaker or his subject. If the speaker is well known, interest will be centered in his personality, his achievements, his fame. For instance, if Richard Nixon or Robert Kennedy were to be the speaker in the auditorium at your next school assembly, attention would naturally be focused upon him at first, rather than upon his subject. On the other hand, if a stranger addressed a high school audience on a challenging subject like *Whom Do You Hate?* or *How to Make a Million,* attention would probably be centered in the topic rather than in the speaker. It is the responsibility of the chairman to decide what the audience is most interested in and to balance that interest with other facts that should be mentioned. Here are the main points to be covered in an introductory speech. Make use of as many of them as you need to.

1. Reference to the occasion.
2. Who the speaker is.
3. Why he is important.
4. Human-interest material about him.
5. His subject.
6. Its importance or significance.
7. Anticipation of pleasure in listening to him.
8. Presenting the speaker to the audience.

When you have introduced the speaker, it is customary for you to remain standing until the speaker has come forward and has acknowledged the introduction. It is also well to plan to thank the speaker briefly when he has finished, making some simple complimentary reference to his speech and expressing sincere gratitude for his speaking. Friendliness and sincerity are always in good taste.

This sample, which includes both fact and fiction, will help you to see what a speech of introduction may contain:

All people make mistakes, but not many people like to talk about them. Our guest today, Dr. Ogden Ramsey, is an exception. He enjoys talking about his mistakes, and he says he has made plenty of them. In fact, he believes that his many past mistakes are the direct cause of his present success.

In 1962, when Dr. Ramsey first became a member of the staff at Charter Hospital, he won public acclaim by restoring life to a sixteen-year-old boy. The boy, victim of a traffic accident, was pronounced dead upon arrival at the hospital. But Dr. Ramsey, after making a quick examination, injected a powerful stimulant directly into the boy's heart and brought him back to life. It was a scientific miracle.

Much painstaking laboratory work and many heartbreaking mistakes lay back of that miraculous result. It is of his work and his mistakes that Dr. Ramsey will speak today.

With pleasure, then, I present to you our distinguished visitor, Dr. Ogden Ramsey, whose subject is "Today's Mistake Can Be Tomorrow's Success." Dr. Ramsey.

Introductions may be very informal and friendly, or they may be formal and dignified, depending upon the occasion, the speaker, and the type of audience. In any event, your duty as chairman is to see that the speaker and his listeners meet on the best terms possible. These final suggestions may help you to accomplish your purpose:

1. Arouse interest and curiosity in the speaker and his subject.
2. If the speaker is important, give sincere compliments; avoid flattery.
3. If the occasion is important, make specific reference to it.
4. If the topic is unusual, draw attention to it.
5. Get the facts straight about the speaker and the subject.
6. Pronounce his name correctly.
7. Don't discuss the speaker's subject at length.
8. Be friendly.

ACTIVITIES

1. Write out a brief presentation in which you introduce an imaginary speaker to an audience. Exchange your paper with that of your neighbor, and let him criticize yours while you do the same with his. Here are some possible subjects:

- **a.** The Next War May Be the Last
- **b.** A Summer in Mexico City
- **c.** Glassblowing
- **d.** The European Situation
- **e.** Is a College Education Necessary?

2. Plan and deliver an introduction suitable for one of these situations:

- **a.** A well-known writer speaking to your English classes about new books.
- **b.** The town chief of police speaking to the entire school on traffic violations.
- **c.** A former Air Force pilot speaking about radar to the Physics Club.
- **d.** A former student speaking about the importance of college training.
- **e.** A famous football player talking about sportsmanship to an assembly of boys.

In this situation, as the young woman introduces her friend to her mother, what would be appropriate remarks for each of the three to make?

3. Notice particularly the introductory remarks of the chairman the next time you have a guest speaker at school. Write answers to the following questions and bring them to class the next day for group discussion:
   a. How did the chairman establish a friendly feeling between the speaker and the audience?
   b. What did the chairman emphasize? The speaker? The topic? The occasion? Or what?
   c. Was the length of the introduction satisfactory?
   d. What suggestions have you for improving the introduction?

Introducing People

Some of the most awkward and embarrassing moments you've suffered have probably come from situations in which you have been making introductions or in which you were being introduced. It's an experience everyone shares. A girl introducing her new boyfriend to her family feels the same nervousness that a boy does when he goes to a party and is introduced to the hostess's parents. They are both worried about what to do and what to say. Such situations occur frequently; the only way to meet them is to acquire the poise and confidence that come from knowing what is the right thing to do and from practicing correct procedure.

Making Introductions. The rules of etiquette which govern the proper methods of making introductions are based on three items: age, sex, and rank. We have all been trained to defer to age. Even among primitive tribes older people have always been shown respect and thoughtful consideration. The same courteous respect is paid in civilized society to girls and women. Since before the days of chivalry in the Middle Ages woman has been granted a position of special privilege. And rank has always been regarded as indicating a degree of success or distinction, a fact which accounts for our extending special courtesies to VIP's, that is, Very Important Persons. *Age, sex,* and *rank,* then, are the basic guides in introducing people to each other. A friendly and sincere manner is oftentimes more important to remember than the formal laws of etiquette; however, you'll find that a knowledge of the following simple rules of courtesy will add much to your social poise. Here they are:

1. *Mention the name of an older person first.* Courtesy demands that young people should be presented to older people. The usual practice is to mention first the name of the person to whom the courtesy is being extended, then follow with the conventional words of introduction, and finally mention the younger person's name.

Dr. Whitcomb, this is my friend, Bob Daley. Dr. Whitcomb has been our family physician for longer than I can remember, Bob.

Mrs. Mills, may I introduce Miss Griffin, my gym instructor?

Dad, I'd like you to meet my teammate, Tod Morgan.

Miss Taylor, my sister Eileen.

Mr. Watson, this is Ann Whiting.

2. *Mention the name of a girl or woman first, if you are presenting a member of the opposite sex.* Follow the same general procedure mentioned in the preceding paragraph.

Jean, I'd like to have you meet my cousin, Tom Blake. Tom, this is Jean Wells.

Miss King, may I introduce my father? Miss King is my English teacher, Dad.

Aunt Alice, this is my friend Bob Phillips.

3. *Mention the name of a person of rank or high position first.*

Miss Palmer, I think you may remember my sister Jean. She was in school three years ago, when you first became our dean of girls.

Professor Stewart, may I present Mr. Prentis? He has just returned from the University of Iowa, where you formerly taught.
Colonel Parker, this is Mr. Henry Lewis of *The Denver Post.*

4. *Usually mention the name of your mother first,* unless you feel the position of the other person outranks that of your mother.

Mother, I want you to meet Mrs. Firbanks, our school librarian. Mrs. Firbanks, my mother, Mrs. White.
Mrs. Knowland, may I present my mother, Mrs. Holt? Mother, this is Mrs. Knowland, the governor's wife.
Mom, I'd like you to meet Sally Patten, our new neighbor.

5. *Usually mention the name of a stranger or slight acquaintance first,* when the age, sex, and rank are the same. Extending slight courtesies to strangers is one way of making them feel welcome and at ease.

Miss Nichols, this is my neighbor, Janet Grant. Janet, Sue Nichols.
Mr. Tucker, my uncle, Mr. Baker.
Mildred, I'd like to have you meet my sister Grace and my brother Bob.

6. *If there is a situation involving conflict of the preceding rules, use your own judgment.* For example, if you are acquainting a woman with a man of rank or position, follow your better judgment in proceeding by either rule 2 or 3.

When you are introducing people, it is your task to follow up your introduction with a few casual comments, a bit of interesting information, or some personal details about the people involved. Without this help, those you have introduced may feel awkward and ill at ease, wondering what to talk about. Getting a conversation started is not a simple matter.

Sometimes you may have to introduce *yourself* to a stranger or a group of people. If you're friendly and willing to take the initiative, you can get over the hump something like this:

Hello! I'm sorry I don't know your name yet, but I'm June Allen. Did you just arrive, too?
May I join you? My name is Ed Whiting. Mary Lou seems to be busy just now, so I thought I'd introduce myself.
I'm sorry I arrived late and missed being introduced to you. I'm Mary Moore. I'm sure I've seen you around school, but I don't think I know your name.

Responding to Introductions. Knowing how to respond to an introduction is just as important as knowing how to introduce people. Here are the conventional statements that are used in response to an introduction:

How do you do.
How do you do, Mrs. Mills.
How are you, Bob?

Often in informal situations you may add or substitute a courteous comment like one of the following:

I'm glad to meet you.
I'm very happy to meet you.

Don't say "Hello" unless the occasion is a very informal one; avoid saying, "I've heard a lot about you"; and be careful not to slur your responses so that you say "Howjado" or "Haryuh."

It is not necessary to shake hands upon being introduced to a person. However, if the person to whom you're being introduced offers his hand, shake it firmly and quickly as a matter of courtesy. When people of opposite sex are being introduced to each other, the boy or the man should take his cue from the girl or the woman; deciding whether or not to shake hands is a feminine prerogative.

When you are being introduced, it is your task to respond quickly to any lead you may be given and to keep the conversational ball rolling. You may ask the person you've met to repeat his name if you've forgotten it, and then try to find an area of common taste, interest, experience, or knowledge for starting the conversation.

You'll probably have some bad moments in your experiences of introducing people, but remember that there's no substitute for genuine friendliness and thoughtfulness for others. A friendly smile and a courteous manner go a long way in helping you to meet people. As a final hint, keep in mind these suggestions:

1. Show the best side of your personality.
2. Take the initiative in starting introductions and conversations.
3. Get names straight and pronounce them clearly.
4. Follow up an introduction with helpful information that will aid conversation.
5. Be quick to meet awkward silences.
6. It's usually courteous to stand while introducing people or while being introduced.

ACTIVITIES

1. Practice the rules presented in this section by making the following introductions:

a. A noted scientist and your father
b. A newcomer to class and a friend of yours
c. Your girl friend and your mother
d. Your father and your principal
e. A woman teacher and your mother
f. A man teacher and your mother
g. A friend of your mother's and a neighbor who has just dropped in
h. Two of your school acquaintances who are strangers to each other

i. Your entire family (consisting of your mother, father, and small sister) and your teacher
j. Your minister and your boyfriend
k. Two girls and two boys
l. An out-of-town friend and five of your classmates
m. A late arrival at a party and your mother and father
n. A person whose name you don't know and your best friend

2. Make the proper responses after you have been introduced, in imaginary situations, to:
   a. A student new to your school.
   b. An out-of-town friend of your parents.
   c. A member of the city council, who has come to speak to your class.
   d. A member of the opposite sex whom for some time you have been eager to meet.
   e. A club-member acquaintance of your mother.

3. With two classmates put on an imaginary drama involving introductions. Let one member, acting as host, introduce the remaining two to each other and then walk away, leaving the newly introduced "strangers" to continue a brief conversation. After a few minutes of practice, switch places, giving each member a chance to play a new role.

Announcements

Announcements are short informative speeches which tell of some coming event. You've heard many of them. If you participate in any school activities, you may be called upon sometime to make an announcement concerning one of them. There are no rules to follow, but the suggestions included here will help you to plan this simple type of speech.

Rudyard Kipling's advice to young news reporters is worth mentioning here because it applies to announcements as well as to news stories. He maintained that a reporter, in order to cover all the essential material that belongs to a good news story, should be sure to tell the *what, where, when, how, why,* and *who* of an event. If you keep that advice in mind, perhaps omitting the *how,* you'll include everything of importance that belongs in an announcement.

What to Say

What? The *event* you're announcing, its *purpose,* and the *price* of the tickets.

Who? The *people* concerned and perhaps something interesting about them.

When? The *date* and *time* of the event.

Where? The *place* where the event will be held and the *place* to get tickets.

Why? The significant details which may explain the importance of the event.

How to Say It. Arrange your material in whatever order you wish, but be sure your coverage is complete. Plan exactly what you want to say, giving careful thought to ways in which you can dress up the facts with some of your own originality. In general, follow these hints:

Be brief. Remember—announcements should be short.

Be clear. Use repetition and restatement of your essential facts at the end of your talk, so that those who didn't hear you the first time will be sure to get the necessary details.

Be interesting. Originality of style and cleverness in arranging the facts which you are announcing will help to arouse interest.

Be objective. Your main purpose is to give information, to put across facts; therefore, keep *yourself* out of your talk, and avoid overdramatizing or overselling those facts.

Here are two examples of announcements:

1. If you're able-bodied and like a good time, you shouldn't miss the opening of our new recreation center this Saturday night. There are four ping-pong tables, a badminton court, a jukebox, five sets of checkers and chess (if you can concentrate!), a dance floor, and a coke and sandwich bar. Every student in this high school and his date are welcome. Admission is 75¢ a couple, 50¢ for stags. The time, 8.00 P.M. The place, the old library building at 10th and Main Streets. It's the grand opening! Come and have the time of your life this Saturday night.

2. It isn't often that a small city like ours has the privilege of playing host to a musician like Yehudi Menuhin. He has been a master of the violin since the age of seven and now ranks as one of the greatest violinists in the world. It is our good fortune to have him appear here in concert at the Muncipal Auditorium one week from tonight at eight o'clock. While they last, tickets for this one-night performance may be bought at Dillon's Drugstore or at the Bazaar. Main floor seats are $3.50, balcony seats, $2.75. We are indebted to the Ladies' Guild for arranging with Mr. Menuhin to appear. Remember, eight o'clock April 19, one week from tonight. That date brings us an opportunity we have not had before in our town, one we shouldn't miss.

ACTIVITY

Give an announcement of a real or an imaginary event. Be brief, but cover all the essential points, and try for originality. Here are some possibilities:

At some time in your life you may be receiving an award. Will you react like Hayley Mills or like Don Knotts?

1. A football game with a rival school
2. The drama group's production of a new play
3. A school rally
4. A school dance
5. A band or orchestra concert
6. An interschool debate
7. A school radio program
8. A meeting of the scholarship society or any other club group
9. A hayride or picnic
10. A lecture by a well-known speaker
11. A song recital or glee-club concert
12. The purchase of the school annual
13. The sale of class rings or sweaters

Presentation and Acceptance Talks

Sometime you may be called upon to present or to accept a prize, award, honor, gift, medal, certificate, or scholarship. Even if the occasion is informal, you will be expected to make a few appreciative remarks as a matter of courtesy. These talks are brief, usually spontaneous, often loosely organized, and invariably simple and sincere. There should be no pretense, exaggeration, or flowery words. Your own naturalness of manner and possibly your originality in rising to an occasion will determine what you say. Sincere compliments and expressions of genuine appreciation are always a part of these talks.

If You Present. The aim of a presentation talk is the bestowal of an award in a complimentary manner. Here is an effective plan with a typical development:

1. Refer to the occasion.
2. Explain the award.
   - *a.* Its purpose
   - *b.* Who's giving it
   - *c.* The requirements
3. Compliment the receiver.
   - *a.* His accomplishments
   - *b.* The reason why he is deserving
4. Present the gift.

In the past three years Lincoln High has celebrated Saint Patrick's Day with an annual Gingerbread Fair and Rummage Sale, the proceeds of which are given to our recreation center. Each year a special pennant is offered to the class which contributes the most to its success. This year the award goes to the hard-working class of 19__ for its effort, its enthusiasm, and the nickels and dimes, amounting to $392.50, which it collected from its sales.

This sum is the largest ever received from any class. It means more records, more games, more furnishings for our recreation center, and therefore more fun for all of us. The student-body officers, on behalf of the whole school, are proud, therefore, to present to Mal Whitcomb, president of the class of 19__, this fifteen-foot pennant, which may be flown from the main flagstaff for the rest of the year in honor of Lincoln's class of 19__. Congratulations, Mal.

If You Accept. When you are on the receiving end, you face a slightly different problem. Let us hope you have had some warning about the presentation to be made. You will then have some time to plan what your response will be. But if the whole situation is entirely unexpected, you will find yourself giving an impromptu speech. Your quick wit, your sense of good manners, and your past training in speech will have to come to your aid. In either case, prepared or unprepared, you may find the following suggestions of value in learning how to accept gifts or honors graciously:

1. Pick up the mood or the remarks of the presentation speech and carry on in the same vein.
2. Give a simple expression of thanks.
3. Introduce a personal touch.
   a. Meaning of gift to you
   b. Work involved in winning it
   c. Personal or humorous reference to yourself or organization you represent
4. Express your appreciation to the donor.

This is the way it might be done:

Thank you, Steve Gordon. Lincoln's class of 19__ is more than happy to accept the honor of flying this flag for the rest of the year. It's been a matter of class pride with us for the past two years to try to beat the class of 19__ and win this award. And now, at last, we've done it. We're also proud of the fact that our contributions mean more pleasure for more students at our school recreation center. We've had fun working for the success of the fair, and we intend to keep up the good work next year. Thank you again for the flag, and long may it wave for Lincoln's class of 19__.

If you have been elected to some student-body, class, or club office, courtesy usually demands a simple acceptance talk. It is only natural that your organization should expect an expression of appreciation from you and perhaps a preview of what it can expect of you as one of its leaders. This talk, then, should be carefully organized and prepared by you, particularly if you are a newly elected president and thus are responsible for the future accomplishments of your office. Again, your naturalness of manner, your sincerity, your enthusiasm, and your dignity are highly important in winning the goodwill of your listeners. As far as planning what to include in your talk is concerned, try these suggestions:

1. Express appreciation for support in the election.
2. Recognize the success of the retiring officer.
3. Explain what you hope to accomplish.
4. End on a note of friendliness.

This is a sample:

While the votes were being counted yesterday afternoon and evening, I kept wondering how I'd feel if I won the election. Then when the final tally was made and Jack Carlson turned to me and said, "Bob, you're it!", I found out. My knees felt weak, my mouth felt dry, and my heart beat a tattoo against my ribs. Seriously, being elected to the office of commissioner of student welfare gives me a feeling of much pride, sincere appreciation, and real responsibility. There is pride because of the honor which this office holds, there is appreciation for your support in the election, and there is a keen sense of responsibility for the continuing welfare of the student body.

Jack's accomplishments this year as our leader have established a high record for the school, a record which will be difficult to match. We owe him our best thanks and appreciation for a job well done. This coming year should see a continuation of Jack's policies and the setting up of new goals under new leadership. With the help and cooperation of all of you, we should be able to expand our club program and include more students, we should add more activities to our recreation center, we should pep up our student-council meetings, and we should increase our support of our football and basketball teams. I'd like to see all students out for at least one activity this year. It will add greatly to school spirit We can do all this and more, too, if we can keep our interest in student affairs at the same high pitch that it was during the election. With your help in the year ahead, I'll do the best I can to match Jack's record. With your *active* support we might even better that record! Let's try!

ACTIVITIES

1. Prepare presentation and acceptance talks for the following imaginary situations. Pair with a classmate if you wish, one of you presenting the gift or award, the other accepting it. Notice that the situations emphasize *you,* whether you are the one who presents or the one who accepts.

- **a.** The principal awards you a hundred-dollar scholarship on graduation night.
- **b.** The community director of the Red Cross gives your homeroom class a token of appreciation for its efforts in the recent Red Cross drive.
- **c.** You present a class gift to a popular teacher at the end of the school year.
- **d.** As football captain you are called upon to accept the championship cup for the season.
- **e.** You are the editor of your school paper, which is being given an all-American award for the second time in its history.
- **f.** On behalf of your classmates you present a gift to a well-liked classmate who is recovering from a serious illness.
- **g.** You are an officer in a young people's church group. Present one of the members with a "best attendance" award.
- **h.** You are being presented with the winner's award in a public-speaking contest.
- **i.** A well-to-do man presents a television set to the Radio-Physics club. You are the club president.

2. Prepare a talk of acceptance which would be suitable for one of these situations:

- **a.** You've been elected president of your club and you are expected to make a few remarks as you take over the gavel from the outgoing president.
- **b.** The election returns are in, and you're the new class president. Accept your new position from the outgoing president.
- **c.** You have been installed as leader of your fraternal organization for young people. Accept the honor that has been given you.

Welcome and Response Talks

Welcome and response talks are much like presentation and acceptance talks. Basically they are speeches of courtesy which depend upon sincere compliments and gracious acceptance of those compliments for their success. Of necessity they are simple in construction and brief in delivery. Situations in which they may be appropriate are many: a debating team from another school may be visiting your school; an honored guest may be present at a banquet; the national president of a club may meet with your social club; an out-of-town visitor may be a special guest at an assembly; a benefactor of the school may be present at graduation; the donor of a scholarship award may come to a scholarship-society meeting; a student committee from a neighboring school may sit in on a student-body meeting; a former well-known member of the student body may be present at a special assembly.

The Welcome. The purpose of the welcome speech is to make the person concerned feel at home. It is simply a cordial greeting to a guest or newcomer which should make him feel that he is gladly received and honestly appreciated. You might include the following:

1. Pleasant reference to yourself or to the occasion
2. Mention of the guest
   a. Who he is
   b. Where he's from
   c. Why he's here
3. Friendly appreciation of his presence

This is a sample:

When I was twelve years old and a student at Lytton Grammar School, I entered my homemade racer in the May Day hobby show. I remember with much gratitude the compliments I got from the man who directed that show when my proudly decorated "buggy" almost won first prize. Now I have a chance to return those compliments. Mr. Charles Stewart, who did so much to encourage me and many other boys in finding worthwhile hobbies, is our honored guest today. He came to see our Hobby Club off to a good start this year. I want to assure him that his presence is most welcome to us. You're a real friend, Mr. Stewart, and we're very glad you're here today.

The Response. The speech of response which follows this is a simple expression of thanks with complimentary reference to the person or group that is responsible for the welcome. Perhaps something like this would be useful:

1. Express thanks for the welcome.
2. Remark on pleasure in being present.
3. Compliment hosts.
4. Anticipate friendly future relationship.

Here is a sample response:

Thank you, Dick; you're very generous. I thought at first that you fellows might not exactly like to have an old duffer like me around when you held the first meeting of your Hobby Club, but your invitation to come and watch you get started was so sincere that I couldn't resist it. You're off to some wonderful adventures when you find and follow an absorbing hobby, and I envy you all your enthusiasm and your abilities. If there is anything I can ever do for you in any way, let me know. It's *my* hobby to see that *your* hobbies keep going. Good luck to you.

ACTIVITIES

Prepare both a welcome and a response for these situations:

1. A former student returns to visit your club. He is welcomed by the president.
2. A former coach attends a school rally and is welcomed by one of the members of the football team.
3. A speech student from a neighboring school pays a visit to your public-speaking class to find out about its organization and activities. He is welcomed by a member of the class.
4. It's Youth Day in your town. You've been elected mayor for a day. The real mayor welcomes you to your office.
5. You're a guest at a service club downtown. You've been invited by an adult friend because you have expressed interest in the activities of the club. Your friend introduces you to the club, and the president, on behalf of the members, welcomes you.

Nomination and Campaign Talks

Under ordinary circumstances the nomination of a candidate for an office is a simple matter. When nominations are in order, according to the rules of parliamentary law, you merely stand up, receive recognition from the chair, and say, "Mr. Chairman, I nominate Bob Whitney." The president then says, "Bob Whitney is nominated," the secretary writes down the nomination—and that's that. But sometimes, especially in large and active organizations, you may be given an opportunity to speak of the requirements of office and the qualifications of your candidate as you present his name. In short, you *inform* people about your candidate.

There are still other occasions, such as the annual student-body elections, when you may be expected to go even further. Your purpose then

An effective nomination or campaign speech is brief and factual, but full of enthusiasm.

is to do more than *inform;* your aim is to *convince* your listeners that your candidate is the one who most deserves their support.

These talks, whether nominating or campaign, are always brief. Their success depends largely on the personality of the speaker, his originality of expression, his enthusiasm for his candidate, and his sincerity of manner. Since *what* you say is rather limited by the occasion, *how* you say it becomes very important. Remember, enthusiasm can be contagious. As far as the content of your talk is concerned, the most you can do is to state who the candidate is, why he is well qualified, what his platform is, and why he should be supported. This is the customary form of a talk in behalf of someone running for office:

1. What is the office?
2. What are its requirements?
3. How does the candidate fill these requirements?
   a. His experience
   b. His abilities
   c. His character
4. What is the candidate's platform?
5. Appeal for support

It isn't necessary to include all the above suggestions, nor is it always wise to follow the numbered order of topics. Use your own judgment in deciding how much to include when you face an actual occasion, and let your originality of expression add interest. Here is an example of a campaign speech:

Fran Nelson for Commissioner of Cultural Activities! That's what the campaign banner hanging over the library entrance has been proclaiming for two weeks. That's what I want to put across now. Fran Nelson for Cultural Activities! She's the girl for the job—and here's why.

This office requires plenty of experience in cultural activities. Fran has it. She's played two leads in the past two years for our Dramatic Workshop productions. She sings in the Treble Clef. She is a member of the debating club. She's on the planning board for this year's Varieties. She's contributing editor to the school paper.

This office requires good scholarship. Fran has it. She is a member of the Scholarship Society and has a B+ average this quarter.

This office requires personality. Fran has it. Those of you who saw her in last month's play will remember her charm and acting ability. And she ought to have an Academy Award for her smile alone!

But since we don't hand out Academy Awards here, let's give Fran something more practical than an Oscar. Let's give her our votes next Tuesday and elect her Commissioner of Cultural Activities. She'll play a leading part for our school. Vote for Fran and watch her lead!

The most important things to avoid in talks like these are triteness, overconfidence, lengthiness, and sermonizing. And don't forget that it is never good manners to belittle other candidates or to deal in personalities.

ACTIVITIES

1. Prepare a nomination or campaign talk for an imaginary situation, but use one of your classmates as candidate.
2. Give a campaign talk in the student-body elections this year and let your classmates grade it for you.
3. Give a campaign talk for one of the possible candidates for the next President of the United States.
4. Listen to campaign speeches that are delivered on TV and radio when election time comes around, and give a report on what you hear to your class.

Speech Contests

If you like competition, you can broaden your speech experience and test your speaking ability by entering a speech contest or tournament.

Such activities, generally sponsored by service organizations, colleges, and high school speech and debate leagues, are growing in number and popularity in recent years. Many of them are conducted on a local level, but state and even nationwide contests are increasingly common.

One purpose of a speech contest is to give you the chance to test your best speech against that of other students of similar background and experience from other schools or even regions. If, in such a contest, you learn what your speech abilities are or can be, you have won a great deal, whether or not you win the first prize. If you have spent much time and energy in careful preparation, you may be surprised to learn how well you can speak "when the chips are down" in a contest.

Original Oratory

Most service organization speech contests are oratory contests. An original oration is a speech written by you alone. Of course, some research on the topic is necessary, and the advice of your coach is desirable; but the basic ideas and wording must be your own. Usually the speech must be memorized and delivered without notes. Here are some hints in preparing for an oratory contest:

Start Early. You will need several weeks to select a topic, think, research, outline, write, rewrite, polish, memorize, and rehearse your speech. An oration is usually expected to be a formal speech, well written and well rehearsed.

Choose an Appropriate Subject. In many contests a general theme or topic area is demanded. You will then need to choose some specific aspect of the subject to narrow it to something you can handle. If no topic is required, then choose a subject that will be appropriate for the audience and judges, and one that interests you. Look at happenings, problems, and controversies in the world around you for a subject that stirs your blood, an idea that you feel strongly about, a message that you feel needs to be communicated. Don't be discouraged if you can't think of something that is completely unique. Nothing is new under the speech-contest sun, either. The skill is to communicate well an old, even familiar, message in *a new way*. Ask your teacher for help with approaches to the topic.

Decide Your Purpose and Message. After thinking, reading, and talking about your subject, construct a brief outline of what you want to say. Indicate clearly what message you are trying to communicate. The purpose of your communication in an oration should usually be to convince, to persuade, or to inspire, rarely just to inform. Review Unit 13 for suggestions about purpose.

Employ Effective Devices As You Write. As you develop your speech in your first draft, remember that you will be most effective if you *show* the audience the problem or situation instead of merely telling them about it. In addition to a careful analysis of a problem, present stories and incidents which are vivid examples of it. Use effective, polished, and imaginative vocabulary. Construct your sentences to achieve maximum effect, using contrasts, parallel structure, and repetition for strength.

Rewrite and Polish. As you rewrite your draft, say it aloud to yourself and consider these questions:

1. Does the wording sound effective like that in a good essay or a good speech?
2. Are the examples clear, forceful, and appropriate? enough? too many?
3. Have you made good use of the standard speech devices? an arresting introduction? a strong conclusion? vivid examples? appropriate quotations? important facts?
4. Have you avoided either becoming so lost in the details that your message is obscured or so vague, overgeneralized, and abstract that your ideas seem to have no connection with concrete reality?
5. Have you avoided being overly dramatic, maudlin, or tear-jerking?
6. Are you communicating what you wish to communicate?

Memorize and Rehearse. You will find memorizing your own words relatively easy, although you should allow yourself plenty of time. As you memorize, avoid mouthing the words mechanically without thinking about what they mean, lest you memorize a mechanical delivery pattern as well as the words. Make each memory session a rehearsal of the speech as well. Although it is usually convenient to memorize a few sentences or a paragraph at a time, be careful to keep reviewing the speech as a whole so that you are not weak on the transitions from one paragraph to another. Do not be concerned if you alter a few words or phrases. The important thing is the overall message and impact of the speech. On the other hand, solid memorization can give you great confidence. As you rehearse, speak slowly enough so that you can give emphasis to the important word or phrase in each sentence and so that you can give vocal color to contrasts, repetitions, unusual phrasings, and examples. Strive for naturalness, sincerity, and enthusiasm. If possible, rehearse with your teacher and follow his suggestions.

Oral Interpretation

Many speech tournaments include contests in interpretation, sometimes of several different types. The key distinction between original speaking and interpretation is that the material, the words and ideas, are *not* those of the contestant. Usually the contestant is expected to choose a selection of a particular kind from a published short story, play, dramatic poem, or speech. The selection is then cut to fit the time limit of the contest, rehearsed, perhaps memorized, and delivered in such a way that the message and mood of the author is communicated to the audience. Remember, an interpretation is not paraphrasing or putting into your own words the message of the author, but is the delivery of his actual words.

Cutting the Selection. Because the words are not the contestant's own, the problem in interpretation is to make the delivery seem natural yet effective. Meeting the problem starts with cutting or eliminating parts of the selection to bring it down to the required time limit. When cutting a full-length play or novel or lengthy speech, do not eliminate just the beginning, middle, or end at random, but rather cut the selection in such a way that a complete story is told or a complete message communicated. Keep material that will be most effective orally and eliminate passages difficult to put across. Do not add to the story or message, or introduce a subplot, character, or idea that you do not have time to develop fully.

Preparing for Delivery. Make yourself a copy of the selection exactly as you will deliver it. Do not try to use the complete version with some parts crossed out, as this method will only confuse you. If you will be allowed to hold the manuscript as you deliver the selection, familiarize yourself with it almost to the point of memorization so that you can have good eye-contact with the audience. If the contest requires that you must memorize the selection, follow the suggestions for memorization of an original oration. Remember to begin your memorization early so that during the contest you can concentrate on delivering the selection, not just remembering it. Plan an introduction to your selection which will give the audience whatever background is needed.

Dramatic Interpretation. Choose a literary selection from a play, novel, short story, or dramatic poem which enables you to suggest, through your delivery, the thoughts and emotions of the author. Selections which require you to suggest characterizations by means of your voice can be very effective. Be sure your selection tells a story that has a beginning, middle, and end, a story that presents some conflict or problem which is finally resolved. Since not every selection may be suited to your ability and voice quality, you will need the advice of your teacher as to the appropriateness of your choice. Analyze the thought, mood, and characters, and try different ways of achieving their communication. Your interpretation will be successful if the audience forgets the contest and becomes engrossed in your story. Avoid, therefore, a presentation which pulls attention away from the story you are telling and to the "technique."

Humorous Interpretation. Since it is difficult to compare a very amusing selection with a very serious dramatic selection, separate contests are sometimes held for humorous interpretation. Here the problem is to find a selection from published literature that is funny and in good taste. Avoid using material that is inappropriate, that is amusing when it is read silently but not aloud, or that depends entirely for its humor upon a long, slow build-up to one joke. Because the field of humor is limited, there tends to be much repetition of particular selections in humorous interpretation. Look for selections which contain amusing everyday situations, "punch" lines, and good-natured humor rather than biting sarcasm.

Oratorical Interpretation. In oratorical interpretation a speech previously given by some other speaker to a "live" audience and subsequently published is delivered from memory by the contestant, usually without notes. A good speech to select is one with a message still timely and important for the audience and judges who will hear it. Choose speeches which have a lively style, contain effective examples and phrasing, and use material that is not too technical, out of date, or vague.

Cut the speech to fit a ten-minute time limit, *leaving out* irrelevant or inappropriate material, but *not changing* or *adding* to the speech. You may wish to prepare a draft of the speech exactly as you will give it, including the underlining of the words and phrases to emphasize and the marks for pause or, perhaps, for rising or falling inflection. Although minor changes in wording, unplanned omissions of paragraphs, and similar errors of memory will probably go unnoticed by the audience (unless you call attention to your mistakes), complete memorization will assure you of the opportunity to deliver a good speech effectively.

The goal of your delivery is to present the speech in such a way that the audience forgets that you are interpreting someone else's words and feels that the speech is your own important message for them.

Extemporaneous Speaking

Extemporaneous speaking is another category in speech contests, one which is quite different from those already mentioned. It challenges the depth and extent of your practical speaking ability; and it tests your ability to think clearly, to construct an original speech under pressure, and to speak effectively without the benefit of any lengthy preparation or delivery rehearsal. Usually you will be informed in advance of the contest of the general area from which the speech topics will be drawn. Often the area centers upon some of the important current events of the previous three months. Upon arrival at the contest, you will draw three topics from a pile at random, choose one, and then have thirty to sixty minutes to prepare a speech on that topic. Usually you may consult any books or magazines you have with you during your preparation time, but you may not get help from any other person.

How to Prepare. Before the day of the contest you prepare yourself by reading as widely as possible in news magazines, such as *Time, Newsweek,* and *U. S. News and World Report.* However, preparation for the most successful extemporaneous speaking is broader than simply reading a few magazines. Knowledge gained from your social studies courses, such as United States history and civics, can be of much help. In any three months there will be some events and problems that are bound to be among the topics from which you will draw. Preparing a file of information on these topics, discussing and analyzing them in and out of class, getting background on the historical development of current problems, and finding and evaluating suggested solutions are all invaluable to the extemporaneous speaker. For example, if there have been important developments in Southeast Asia recently, you would want to find information covering questions like the following:

1. What has been the recent history of the area?
2. What is the nature of the problem?
3. What are the conflicts?
4. Who has what to gain?
5. Why is the area important to the United States?
6. What is the prospect for the future?
7. What solutions to the problems of the area have been suggested?
8. What are the prospects, consequences, and value of these solutions?

Although effective delivery is demanded as in any speech contest, the principal emphasis is upon mastery of the facts and ability to analyze, evaluate, and interpret a sometimes complex event. Seldom does a student begin with all these abilities. Fortunately, he often will develop them as he participates in many extemporaneous speaking contests.

Impromptu Speaking

As a contest, impromptu speaking is designed to test your ability to speak effectively and coherently on a general topic with a minimum of preparation. In a typical contest you will be given three general topics—they may be brief, thought-provoking quotations on a general subject, such as "Thrift," "Honor," or "Friendship," or they may be topics of current interest, such as "United Nations," "Integration," or "Divorce." You will have from two to five minutes to prepare before speaking, usually with a five-minute time limit for the speech. The most you can hope for in your preparation time is to decide upon a point to make, an interesting introduction, and perhaps a few examples and a conclusion. Obviously, you must then "think on your feet" as you deliver the speech.

The best preparation for impromptu speaking is to gather anecdotes, facts, quotations, and examples that may be applied to many different topics. Generally, delivering impromptu speeches on words and quotations taken at random from dictionaries and books of quotations is the best practical rehearsal. If you think clearly, speak fluently, and have an interesting store of material, you will be an ideal impromptu speaker.

Don't Forget the Judges

Regardless of the type of speech contest you may enter, you will generally find that your experiences have these common characteristics:

1. In a speech tournament you will probably be expected to deliver your type of speech, such as impromptu or extemporaneous, more than once and in competition with two or more sets of other speakers.

2. Ranking of speakers in each category is a procedure designed to match contestants of nearly equal ability and to hasten the process of elimination. Often, a panel of speakers, usually from two to eight, is heard by one or more judges and rated in order of excellence as a preliminary step to the final rounds of competition. Judges are guided by standards set up in the ballots, by their own experience and understanding of the principles of good speaking, or by other general personal standards.

3. Judges will tend to be influenced approximately equally by the content of the speech and by the skill of delivery.

4. In a contest where your abilities are very similar to those of other speakers, the judges' decisions may be made upon very fine points. Be sure you understand exactly what is expected and give your best effort.

And Don't Forget the Ground Rules

Keep in mind the following general rules in preparing for and participating in contest speaking:

1. *Read the Official Version of the Rules for This Contest.* Don't assume that the rules for *this* contest are the same as for some previous or similar contest. Many contests are lost by the student's not knowing or following the exact rules.

2. *Observe the Time Limits Carefully.* Many contests have only a maximum time limit, while others have a minimum time as well. In some contests time signals are given by a timekeeper, while in others no signals are permitted. If time signals are given, be sure that you know *beforehand* who will give the signals and what the signals mean. Overtime is often the best way to lose a contest.

3. *Prepare the Right Kind of Speech.* Be sure you understand what is expected. Don't be told, "Your speech was good but not the right kind" (or not on the topic required).

4. *Begin Your Preparation Early.* Most contest speeches are expected to be formal, well-rehearsed, and well-polished performances. Only thorough preparation can give you the confidence and polish that win speech contests.

5. *Follow the Advice of Your Coach.* What you or your classmates think will be effective may not be what the adult judges will approve. Football games and speech contests are won by capable competitors who follow the directions of the coach.

6. *Test Your Speech on Various Audiences.* In preparation for the contest, try to present your speech to several audiences. Note their reactions and discuss them with your coach, making adjustments in your content and delivery if necessary. Such "dress rehearsals" will give you confidence and smoothness in your contest performance, as well as an opportunity to view your speech objectively.

7. *Concentrate on the Message of Your Speech.* When you begin to speak, try to forget that this is a contest and concentrate on communicating the message of your presentation. If you are convinced that it is worth communicating, you will be able to carry on. Avoid dwelling on all the things that could go wrong.

8. *Be Physically and Mentally at Your Best for the Contest.* A good night's sleep, arriving in plenty of time for the contest, and trying to remain calm will help you to be at your best. Be well groomed, too. Boys should wear a suit and tie. Remember to avoid flashiness in dress which will call attention to itself and away from your speech.

9. *Be Confident But Not Cocky.*
Remember that the other competitors are students like yourself who are trying to do their best. In a good contest the abilities of the competitors will be similar. Do your best and accept the results with good grace. Cockiness or discourtesy is bad manners and hurtful to your efforts.

10. *Learn from the Decision in Each Contest.*
Remember that the decision was made by a reasonable sample of responsible people. They, or people like them, will be in audiences you will speak to for the rest of your life. If a decision goes against you, try to find out why—and turn this knowledge to your advantage.

ACTIVITIES

1. Organize a speech contest in your class. Each student should select one of the categories of contest speaking in which to compete and should prepare his speech according to the suggestions given in this unit. After eliminations the final contest may be presented before English classes in school.
2. Listen to some tapes or recordings of original oratory and of dramatic, humorous, or oratorical interpretations. Evaluate the speeches through class discussion.

Graduation Speeches

One approach to graduation speeches is the practice of presenting two speeches, a speech of welcome by the salutatorian and a speech of farewell by the valedictorian. This approach is one based on recognition of scholarship, the valedictorian's being the student with the highest academic standing and the salutatorian's being second highest. Some schools vary the practice by trying to recognize both leadership and scholarship, in which case the class president will give the speech normally accorded to the salutatorian.

Another approach to graduation speeches, one which reflects the quality of modern competition, is that of having open tryouts for the speaking assignments. Let's examine both approaches.

The Traditional Approach

The Salutatory Speech. The speech of welcome should be brief. Custom dictates the following coverage:

- Include an introduction to the ceremonies and a specific welcome addressed to the audience.

- Comment on the special nature of this graduation, or, if a theme for the ceremonies has been chosen, explain its significance.
- Offer genuine and restrained nostalgic comments relating to matters concerning the class, including a brief review of accomplishments but excluding overly sentimental references that are pointless.
- If sufficient time is allotted, or if school tradition dictates, an idea or message should be developed to supplement the specific welcome function of the salutatory speech.

The Valedictory Speech. The valedictorian—literally, "farewell sayer"—usually delivers the principal student address. In his preparation he should aim for a good speech that is suited to his audience of parents, friends, teachers, and fellow students and which is appropriate to this special occasion. Thus, this is not the time to prepare a State Department policy paper, an F.B.I. crime report, or a rally pep talk. A sincere message which assesses the future and refers to the graduating class's preparation for it is always acceptable. The effect of this speech should be reasonably formal, with accompanying positive feelings. It should be shown that though our problems and prospects may be discouraging at times they can and should be balanced by our progress and aspirations.

The Modern Approach

It is misleading to imply that the valedictorian-salutatorian type of presentation is not used today with great satisfaction to many speakers and to many audiences. But it *is* true, however, that many young speakers and many speech coaches have rebelled against the traditional approach and have gone to open tryouts for speakers who give evidence of ability to verbalize in a representative fashion the social attitude of their classmates and to present with skill their own articulate thinking. The top academic students in the class may, or may not, be among the winners.

Organize a Speech Team. In the modern approach the two or three best speakers in the tryouts are awarded assignments for the graduation speeches, and the next-best speaker becomes the chairman of the speech team, the person who issues a note of welcome and introduces the theme which ties the speeches together, who presents the speakers, and who makes concluding remarks. Tryouts should be held at *least* two months before graduation so that the speaking team has time for group discussion, decision on the theme and its individual topics, preparation, critiques with the speech coach, and polishing of content and delivery.

Your Goal. The modern approach, though like its traditional counterpart in many ways, is different in that it makes less of a bow to ritual and expected content and more of a nod to unexpected, independent thinking. The objective is for a team of speakers to present to the audience a fair sample of the basic feelings and thoughts, the ungarnished judgments, and the honest expectations of the Class of 19—. Further, a worthwhile objective is to deal with subject matter which is within the reach of the speakers, within the range of audience interest, and within the realm of reality. Far too often student speakers overreach themselves and deal with lofty generalities, full of hope, oblivious to reality, and determined to meet challenges which they don't even understand. Another practical goal, if not a final one, should be the achievement of these objectives by each speaker in a period of time which doesn't greatly exceed five minutes, because still another reality is that both the graduating class and the audience are waiting for just one thing—the handing out of diplomas.

Films:

Describing an Incident (Coronet). 11 min color or b&w.
Room for Discussion (EBF). 25 min b&w.
Getting Yourself Across (MH). 21 min b&w.

Filmstrip:

Relation of Interests to Communication (SVE). 41 fr b&w.

Records:

Consult sources like *Schwann Long Playing Record Catalog* or the original manufacturers like Caedmon, Spoken Arts, etc., for listing of recordings like these:

Edna St. Vincent Millay. Selections of her poetry, read by Judith Anderson (Caedmon). One 12″ record 33⅓ rpm.
Leaves of Grass by Walt Whitman. Selections read by American actors (Folkways). One 12″ record 33⅓ rpm.
Abraham Lincoln, selected readings by Carl Sandburg, Orson Welles, Walter Huston (Decca). One 12″ record 33⅓ rpm.
John Brown's Body by Stephen Vincent Benét, dramatization directed by Charles Laughton (Columbia). One 12″ record 33⅓ rpm.
Frank Lloyd Wright (Caedmon). One 12″ record 33⅓ rpm.

Tapes:

Visual Aids Service, University of Illinois, Urbana, Illinois, can supply tapes of readings on a variety of literary and historical subjects. You might also consult your own state tape-recording libraries for tapes of high school speech contests and tournaments; for example, the Oregon High School Speech League Championship Finals, Oregon School of the Air, Corvallis, Oregon.

Unit Fifteen

CONVERSATION: The Art of Good Talk

Conversation is vital to all of us. It is the friendly and informal oral exchange of sentiments, observations, opinions, and ideas. It isn't talking *at* or *to* people so much as it is talking *with* them. That's what the *con* in *conversation* means. **You** talk; someone listens. Then **he** talks, while you listen. And so the conversation continues, with ideas being tossed back and forth in an atmosphere of mutual interest, stimulation, and respect.

Some critics say that good conversation is a lost art, as extinct as the dodo. They feel that there are too many demands on people's time and too much preoccupation with spectator entertainment, like TV, radio, movies, and sports events. There is no longer the kind of leisurely, witty, far-ranging, sophisticated talk that in times past made conversation an art. However, as long as man desires the companionship of his fellows, he is going to talk. Companionship and conversation go hand in hand.

What Is *Good Conversation?*

Ordinary conversation is mostly small talk. "What's new? Where'd you go? What'd you do? What'd he say? Did you hear this?"—these questions are clues to what might be called the trifles of everyday talk. There is nothing profound, intellectual, or seriously stimulating in such talk, but it *is* communicative and it serves to help you establish common ground with people and open the door to further exploration of ideas and personalities.

Sophisticated conversation, on the other hand, deals with larger talk. Ideas are likely to be challenging, topics are likely to be both deeper and larger in scope, the language more carefully chosen, the repartee quick and stimulating, the humor witty and sophisticated, and the manners more polite and socially oriented.

Business conversation is chiefly practical talk. It fills the communicative demands of daily living in establishing and keeping contacts, arranging business affairs, discussing and solving business problems, exchanging ideas, or just engaging in "shop talk." Conversations at all levels—from the chitchat around the water cooler or the buzz-session after a meeting to the polished conversations at highly social affairs—all affect much of the world's business. Many a deal is concluded over a luncheon table or after a pleasant dinner conversation. Such talk is the kind that gets things done while mixing business with pleasure.

In any case, *good* conversation follows most of the general principles of good speaking with which you are already familiar. Here are some qualities which are characteristic of it:

WORTHWHILE. What you talk about need not be overserious, but it should have importance and substance. No aimless chatter; no pointless talk; no mean and hurtful gossip; no thoughtless personal comments; no persistent "wisecracking."

INFORMAL. A conversation may drift along without a definite goal, or it may develop a conscious direction and accomplish something worthwhile. No formal purpose or aim; no pretentious language; no special manners in delivery.

FLEXIBLE. Be prepared to adjust yourself to changing topics and to be responsive to others' opinions. A conversation is very pliable; it is not rigid in form or matter. There is almost complete freedom in expressing ideas. No planned introduction, discussion, conclusion; no definite time limit; no limitation of subject.

RELAXING. You should maintain a comfortable alertness but keep yourself free from tension. You have more time to be at ease and to make yourself clear by pausing frequently, repeating, restating, and asking questions. No nervous tension as when you are facing an audience; no vocal strain; no delivery problems.

INTERESTING. You should make much use of human-interest details and lively personal experiences. No boring repetitions or dull, endless observations; no ax-grinding; no narrow or self-centered hogging of the conversation.

A Good Conversationalist

And now consider what makes a good conversationalist. A person who has sparkle—one who talks vigorously, interestingly, and courteously—is always popular. Look around you. Can you pick out some member of your class who is well liked because of his conversational ability? You've gone to parties where much of the fun has centered around "gab fests" in the kitchen or in some corner. Everyone contributes to the stories or the witty remarks or the thoughtful comments, but usually one of the group stands out. What makes him good? How can you be like him?

Develop a Background. You can widen your horizons by reading more, by observing people and their traits, by acquiring more hobbies and interests. Remember what was said in Unit 7 about the "know–feel–do" area? You always talk best about things that you know well, feel strongly about, or have done. So, if you want to be a good conversationalist, enlarge your background of knowledge and develop your interests.

Have Something to Say. An empty mind and an indifferent manner will quickly mark you as a poor conversationalist. Conversation is built upon knowledge that leads to opinions and upon a desire to express those opinions. A worthwhile idea and a bubbling-over feeling about sharing it with others are important for the person who wants to talk well.

Speak with Vigor and Vitality. People like a person who has spirit, vitality, and alertness. Your voice is the flexible and expressive instrument that reveals your attitudes and feelings. If you have a lively interest in ideas and people, your voice should reflect your enthusiasm and energy in the give-and-take of conversation.

Stimulate Your Listeners. Conversation can be a lively, two-way, person-to-person adventure in communication when you give your listeners *ideas* that are stimulating, exciting, exhilarating, or challenging. Idle gossip and pointless chatter pass time, but they do not set people's thoughts on fire or add stature to the speaker or substance to a conversation.

Be Interesting. The kind of material that holds people's attention is either that which is so unusual as to challenge interest or that which is so familiar as to come within anyone's experience. Conversation picks up when people find that they share common acquaintances, tastes, judgments, or ideas. Instead of talking generalities, they talk particulars. Specific instances, illustrations, and details help keep a conversation from being dry.

Be a Good Listener. Remember you're talking *with* people, not *at* them. There is no surer way of killing conversation and winning the scorn of your friends than by "hogging" all the talk. Give the other fellow a chance to talk, and listen to what he has to say. A good conversationalist is interested in the experiences and opinions of his companions.

The best conversations are sparked with ideas and spoken with vitality.

Be Courteous. It simply isn't good manners to monopolize a conversation, to interrupt a speaker, to contradict rudely, to argue violently, or to be stubbornly opinionated. A conversation can be stimulating and even argumentative without being a verbal brawl.

Getting Started

Many good conversations grow out of the small talk that starts them. What begins with a bit of trifling chatter may lead to an invigorating exchange of opinions and ideas on a higher level. Anything goes as a starter, since the little pleasantries are only an opening wedge, serving to split the barrier of strangeness or self-consciousness. In general:

- Start with what interests you; lead to what interests others.
- Start with little things; lead to bigger ones.
- Make use of well-chosen questions that may start a chain reaction of talk.
- *Listen* to what others say, then link their comments with your own.

Remember that conversation is informal, that it flows from one topic to another, that it has no premeditated goal, that it is guided only by the interests of the people who are talking and by the responses they make to what is said. You may feel awkward or self-conscious when you first enter a conversation, but the chances are that once you're in it and forget about yourself, you'll talk without much difficulty. People never rehearse or practice conversations, and yet they somehow manage to express themselves clearly and possibly even cleverly when they really have something to say. Here are some summarizing Do's and DON'T's:

Do	**DON'T**
1. Listen courteously.	1. Interrupt rudely, monopolize the conversation, argue stubbornly, or belittle other people's ideas.
2. Take your fair share of the conversation.	2. Refuse to take part because you're bored, and don't contribute only abrupt monosyllables.
3. Talk about things that will interest other people and that will get them to respond.	3. Talk about yourself all the time or overuse the personal pronoun *I*.
4. Learn to talk about worthwhile things.	4. Gossip or make mean personal comments or spend all your time in idle chatter.
5. Look interested and attentive, building rapport with your eyes.	5. Let your eyes wander restlessly or give other evidence of being attentive.

ACTIVITIES

1. Find some quotations which define or describe conversation and read them to your classmates. Here is a sample:

> Conversation is but carving!
> Give no more to every guest
> Than he's able to digest.
> Give him always of the prime,
> And but little at a time.
> Carve to all but just enough,
> Let them neither starve nor stuff,
> And that you may have your due,
> Let your neighbor carve for you.
>
> —JONATHAN SWIFT

2. Consider the following topics for conversation and decide whether they are suitable for "small talk" or for "big talk." How may they help to start conversation?

Your Surroundings — The Occasion

Your Host and Hostess	The Weather
Vacations	Hobbies
Similar Interests	Books
People in the News	Music, New Records
Plays or Movies	School Events or Classes
Games and Sports	Pets
Social Problems	Magazine Articles
New Cars	Mutual Friends or Acquaintances
Food	Clothes and Fashions
The News Event of the Day	An Unusual Experience or Occurrence

3. Test your conversational ability by presenting a few "sociodramas" for your classmates. A sociodrama is an impromptu playlet in which a scene that involves the solution of a real-life social problem or situation is portrayed by various people who assume set roles. This technique of solving problems is popular in many schools and lends itself admirably to practice in conversation.

First step. A true-to-life problem is discussed by a group.

Second step. A probable solution is enacted conversationally by certain members of the group.

Third step. The acted solution is then analyzed and discussed by the entire group, actors and audience alike.

Here are some real-life problems which you can enact as sociodramas, making up suitable conversation to fit the situations as you meet them:

Problem 1. Tom is delivering an important message from his father to a man whom he has not met. When he arrives at the man's house, Tom is asked to come into the living room, where he finds four men who are total strangers to him engaged in conversation. Discuss in class the various ways in which Tom may introduce himself and deliver his message; decide which way would be the most satisfactory solution of Tom's problem; have five class members dramatize that solution; and, finally, discuss the results of the acted solution in class.

Problem 2. Three students are grouped around the main entrance of school at lunchtime waiting for the next period bell to ring. They're engaged in an urgent last-minute review of some questions they expect to have in a quiz in their next class; then one of the school "characters" breaks into the conversation. He always tries to monopolize attention. Employing the sociodrama technique, demonstrate how the others can continue their conversation without being rude.

Problem 3. A rather timid girl finds herself in the position of being a wallflower at an informal party. The hostess and a friend notice her predicament and, wanting to make her feel more at ease, they approach, start a conversation with her, and gradually lead her into another group having a good time talking about that day's football game. Show how the others include the timid girl in the group activity without pointedly recognizing her problem.

Problem 4. Two boys and two girls are trying to decide what movie to see Friday night. While they are discussing the possibilities, an acquaintance of one of them joins the group. He is the aggressive type who likes to "horn in" on other people's plans. How can the group carry on its conversation without being discourteous to the newcomer, yet without including him in their plans?

Problem 5. Bill, who owns a car, picks up Jack and Fred on his way to school in the morning. Fred, who is a recent transfer from another school, is not very well acquainted yet. Bill and Jack start a conversation which at first omits Fred. Then, remembering their companion and noting his silence, the two boys try to include him in their talk. How do they accomplish this?

Problem 6. Three girls who are in the same history class, but who are not very well acquainted with each other, are waiting for the bus after school. One of them starts a conversation in a friendly manner. Emphasize what the other two girls can do to keep up the conversation so graciously started by the first girl.

4. Arrange your class in groups of five or six. Let each group get together in a different corner of your classroom. Sit or stand around informally and start talking. The situation is artificial, of course, and things will go slowly at first; but, if everyone shows interest, you'll find the conversation rolling along in time. At the end of fifteen minutes call a halt and compare experiences with the other groups.

5. Write down as many appropriate opening sentences as you can think of that might help you to start a conversation with a new acquaintance. Use the following general topics as guides:

a. The Weather
b. Your Surroundings
c. The Occasion
d. Common Friends
e. Similar Interests, such as Sports, Reading, Hobbies, Pets, etc.
f. Your School
g. Yourself

6. Prepare a "talking" letter by having five or six students take part in an informative conversation about what they've learned or done so far in their speech course. Make a tape recording of the conversation and send the tape to a speech class in a neighboring school, asking them to reply by a similar tape.

References:

The Art of Conversation, by Milton Wright. McGraw-Hill.
The Seventeen Book of Etiquette and Entertaining, by Enid A. Haupt. McKay.
Everybody's Book of Better Speaking, by Dorothy Uris. McKay.

Films:

Ways to Better Conversation (Coronet). 11 min color or b&w.
Let's Discuss It (MH). 9 min b&w.
Conversation (MH). 12 min b&w.

Filmstrip:

How to Converse (SVE). 41 fr b&w.

INFORMATION

Unit Sixteen

BUSINESS TALK: Selling and Interviewing

There is scarcely a day in your life that you don't have business contacts with people. You're buying or selling, giving or receiving, interviewing or being interviewed, or engaging in an exchange of money, goods, ideas, plans, views, enthusiasms, and energies. Yes, business is a particularly vital force in America, and it is businesslike talk that settles most business transactions, for the tongue is mightier than the pen in these matters.

A knowledge of businesslike talk is useful. While you're in school, you may ask your counselor to change your program; you may request information from your librarian; you may interview your principal about a school problem; you may sell tickets to a school dance, play, benefit, or game; or you may apply for a vacation job.

When you're out of school, the possibilities increase. Someday all of you will have the experience of applying for a permanent job. Most of you will have the experience of interviewing people for various business reasons after you have a job. Many of you will be in positions where a knowledge of selling techniques will be valuable. And there will be numerous other occasions in life in which you will find businesslike talk necessary: making a complaint about telephone service, returning an unsatisfactory article to a store, ordering groceries, asking for a raise, buying from a door-to-door salesman, or consulting with your boss about your job. And notice this: they are all situations in which we meet people face to face for the purpose of doing business. To meet such situations successfully you should understand salesmanship—both as a seller and a buyer.

Five P's of Salesmanship

Salesmanship is the technique of getting people to do what you want them to do. Successful selling requires a knowledge of sales psychology, careful planning, effective presentation, perseverance, and a pleasing personality. Not all of you, of course, will become salesmen, but most of you will meet situations in which knowing how to persuade people will be helpful. A review of the suggestions given in Unit 13 under the headings "Speeches Which Convince: Communication That Brings About Belief and Conviction" and "Speeches Which Persuade: Communication That Rouses People to Action" will help you in your study of this unit.

Sales Psychology. Sales psychology is the special branch of psychology that considers what makes people buy. If you are to be a good sales psychologist, you'll have to understand the motives that lead people to action. Your problem will be to overcome natural inertia, strong prejudice, or active opposition, and you'll have to know what makes your prospective customer "tick." Ask yourself such questions as these: To what kind of person am I trying to sell? What are his likes and dislikes? Why have other salesmen failed with him? Does he like to bargain, or does he want a best offer immediately? Is he vain? Does he like to think he is besting the salesman?

Planning. Planning is essential to your sales campaign. There's nothing casual, hasty, or accidental in good selling. Put yourself in both the buyer's and the seller's position at the same time, and let your planning follow these lines:

THE BUYER'S FEELING	THE SELLER'S PLAN
1. I'm not interested.	1. Get attention.
2. Hm-m-m-m-m.	2. Create interest.
3. But–.	3. Meet objections.
4. Well, maybe you're right.	4. Make strongest appeal.
5. It sounds good.	5. Get action.

Presentation. Presentation is partly a matter of applying sound psychology and partly a matter of following the dictates of effective communication. Start by establishing good feeling between yourself and the customer. Continue to be friendly and courteous, but don't fawn. When logic is appropriate, use it; when an appeal to feelings is in order, don't ignore them. Make your customer feel that the course of action you are suggesting is desirable and possible, even easy. Keep avenues of suggestion open by such devices as association, repetition, and comparison. And by all means maintain your poise, regardless of how the buyer behaves. Try to give your presentation the quality of *leading* rather than *pushing*. It is perhaps unnecessary to say that irritability, flippancy, antagonism, familiarity, mispresentation, and criticizing competitors are absolutely taboo.

Perseverance. Perseverance is a salesman's talisman. You just can't give up easily. Thomas Edison said that his job was 1 percent inspiration and 99 percent perspiration. A well-known maxim states, "If at first you don't succeed, try, try again." A proverb points out, "Constant dripping weareth away stone." A scientist drew attention to the fact that a thousand-pound mass of steel suspended vertically by a chain next to a cork hanging on a string can be forced into pendulumlike motion if the cork is kept swinging regularly so that it strikes against the steel in exactly the same position. The lesson for you as a salesman is obvious.

Personality. Personality can be enhanced even if it cannot be shed. What you can do to develop your strong points and submerge your weak ones is suggested by the list of personality traits that follows:

Positive traits	*Negative traits*
Is a good conversationalist	Never says anything interesting
Seems interested in people	Is interested only in the sale
Has a happy expression	Is a sour-looking old bird
Has a sense of humor	Never makes or enjoys jokes
Apparently has worlds of time	Is always aware of the clock
Always lifts people's spirits	Depresses people
Gives others a chance to talk	Never stops talking
Wears clothes that reflect good taste	Wears clothes that draw unfavorable attention
Welcomes criticisms	Resents any kind of criticism
Is quick to admit error	Never is wrong
Is sensitive to people's feelings	Seems oblivious of another's mood
Recognizes a positive "no"	Can't recognize reasonable refusal
Is courteous	Is boorish
Is generous	Is stingy

The Sales Talk

A sales talk is a persuasive speech which presents organized information and then makes an appeal for action. A "pep" talk to get a better attendance at football games, an appeal for money for the

POGO
BY JING! I'M QUITTIN'... NOBODY IS EVER BEEN SO UNAPPRECIATED ANYWHERE.
THE HON. BREWSTER B.
I TRIES TO HELP EVER'BODY! SETS MYSELF UP AS A HIGH-CLASS INTERPRETER OF DREAMS AN' WHAT HAPPENS?

ALL I GET IS SCORN!
THE BIG BREWSTER

WHAT I GOT FOR THIS SWAMP IS NOTHIN' BUT SCORN!
HOO HOO! I'LL TAKE A DOZEN IF THEY'S NICE.
OL' BRUISE
8-17

SCORN SCORN SCORN!
SCORN!
HOO HOO

THEY'S ALL A BUNCH OF CHEAP TOMATOES--- CHEAP TOMATOES
HOO HOO! GIMME A COUPLE POUNDS OF THOSE TOO.

SCORN! YOU CHEAP TOMATOES!
THERE'S A REAL SALESMAN, SIS.
MY SAKES.

I SCREAM FOR YOUR HEADS!
ICE CREAM FOR OUR HEADS?
BOAT'S EMPTY

THE POOR MAN'S MAD. HE AIN'T GOT NOTHIN' FOR SALE.
SCOR-UGK!
A PITY.

DIN'T HAVE SO MUCH AS A STRING BEAN.
I KNOW! BUT COULD HE SELL CORN... LAND!
© 1958 WALT KELLY

Community Chest, selling tickets to the latest school play—these are all sales talks. The speaker gives his speech without interruption; the audience merely listens. The listener's doubts, objections, or questions must be anticipated by the speaker and the answers included within the body of his speech. There is no opportunity for give-and-take conversation between speaker and listener as there is in a sales interview. When you give a sales talk, you're making a speech, not engaging in conversation. Use a simple plan of organization like the following and present your case as reasonably and attractively as possible.

1. Get interested attention.
2. State your case logically and clearly.
3. Win confidence and interest by using illustrations, examples, authority, personal reference.
4. Appeal to human motives.
5. Make it easy for people to act.
6. Have a good conclusion that calls for the desired action.

Plan some practice sales talks now in which you apply the above suggestions.

ACTIVITIES

1. Have five students volunteer for a bit of selling competition. The volunteers will be magazine salesmen; the remainder of the class will be prospective buyers, well supplied with imitation "money" with which to buy the magazine of their choice. Each of the five salesmen should have a different magazine to sell and should present his sales talk in turn. When all talks have been completed, the salesmen should pass among the buyers and complete as many sales as they can in five to ten minutes. Buyers may purchase more than one magazine, but their subscriptions should be given to those salesmen who, they think, have demonstrated the best sales technique. When it's all over, discuss the results in class.
   - **a.** Which salesman got the most subscriptions? Why? Was it because of his clever use of psychology? appealing arguments? good planning? pleasing manner? or merely personal popularity?
   - **b.** How could the other talks have been improved?
   - **c.** What was the best opening, or sales approach? The best conclusion, or clincher?
2. Have a classmate join with you in some competitive selling. Let each of you choose a different brand of the same article and then prepare a three-minute sales talk on the brand of your choice. For instance, one of you may push the sale of a Neverfail pencil, while your competitor uses his sales technique on an Airlite pencil. Or one of you may sell an Enchanting lipstick while the other one plugs for another brand. Since the general type of article you are selling is the same kind as that of your competitor, you must know your article thoroughly

and marshall the best reasons for the superiority of your brand. Is it quality? use fulness? beauty? style? durability? price? popularity? Anticipate any superiorities which your competitor may show his brand to have and be ready to match his arguments with better ones of your own. But be sure *not* to belittle his product or to indulge in personal remarks concerning his salesmanship. Let the class decide who is the better salesman after each of you has talked for three minutes.

3. Prepare a one-minute radio or TV commercial which advertises some well-known product. Pack all the sales appeal you can into your sixty seconds without being artificial. Be sincere in trying to put across your product.

4. Prepare a three-minute sales talk on one of the following articles. Bring your article to class so that you can display it or even demonstrate it to your listeners.

fountain pen	camera	Thermos bottle	kitten
binder	lasso	lipstick	bracelet
goldfish	phonograph record	mousetrap	class ring
pair of socks	chocolate bar	typewriter	shaving soap
toothbrush	school annual	comb	nail polish
wallet	Christmas cards	harmonica	portable tape recorder

The Sales Interview

A sales interview is a businesslike conversation between two people, one or both of whom wish to sell something to the other. When somebody tries to sell you a ticket to the school play, a copy of the school annual, or a class ring, or when you try to persuade the boy down the street to trade his electric drill for your radio, you're taking part in a sales interview.

The sales interview differs from the sales talk in that it is a two-way conversation, a discussion that has no set speeches, even though the seller may have learned a patter which he often employs. In some highly structured presentations the seller will ask the potential buyer to permit a presenting of an entire idea or plan before the discussion stage begins. In the business world you'll find that the sales interview occurs far more frequently than the sales talk and that a knowledge of sales psychology is important to both the buyer and the seller. Consider these specific points:

The Seller Must–

- Establish a friendly, person-to-person basis.
- Quickly find common ground and begin to evoke "yes" responses.
- Arouse interest and plant the idea of action that the buyer will take if the sale is to be successful.
- Cultivate desire and a feeling of need for the product.
- Show how easily desire and need can be satisfied.

- Understand a great deal about human nature, knowing when to "push" and when to "coast."
- Encourage the customer to talk and to state his objections, meeting those objections tactfully and constructively.
- Distinguish between valid objections and those which are an excuse to get rid of him.
- Return frequently to the sales points which seem best to satisfy the customer.
- Make the buyer feel strongly that his satisfaction is more important than the sale.
- Allow the buyer to do some of the selling; let him express his desires and answer some of his own questions. Make him feel secure in his effort to weigh facts and make a wise decision.

The Buyer Must–

- Be willing to listen with an open mind.
- State his objections frankly but not belligerently.
- Try to ascertain the seller's honesty, accuracy, knowledge of his product, and determination to make a sale regardless of the circumstances.
- Be sure to understand the "fine print" of all conditions of payments, guarantees, dividends, replacements, repairs, etc.
- Distinguish between need and desire and look very frankly at the cost of satisfying desire.
- Avoid hasty decisions, especially when the commitment is sizeable.
- End the interview graciously when he has decided upon his action.

ACTIVITIES

Pair with a classmate and prepare a sales interview, one being the buyer, the other the seller. The interview should be treated as a real-life situation. It should be a business *conversation* with a give-and-take spirit, not a sales monologue. At first the buyer may be unwilling to consider the salesman's arguments. He may use some of the following objections, common answers of most buyers:

"I'm not interested."
"I already have one."
"I don't like it."
"It costs too much."
"I don't need it right now."

If the seller is able to meet those objections with appealing arguments of his own, so that the buyer is fully satisfied and can think of no other reasons for *not* buying, then a sale has been made. Try one of these sales situations:

a. Sell a subscription to a newspaper or magazine.

Listening and speaking alternate in a good interview.

b. Get a signature on a petition.
c. Solicit an advertisement for a newspaper.
d. Sell a ticket to a show or dance.
e. Get a contribution to the Junior Red Cross.
f. Try to get a friend to sell you his car.
g. Sell a pair of ice skates, a charm bracelet, a bow tie, a pair of jeans, a T-shirt, a fishing rod, a pair of earrings, a portable radio, a camera, a tennis racket, a compact, a binder, a coin purse, bobby socks, toilet water, or a bathing cap.
h. Try to borrow five dollars from an unwilling friend.

Applying for a Job

The person-to-person relationship that occurs in a conversation in which your purpose is not to sell an article, but rather your services, differs from that of an ordinary sales talk or interview. When you apply for a job, your purpose is to give your prospective employer all the information he needs about you and to make a good impression on him. You'll do most of the talking, but your leads *should* come from him. It will be your personality, ability, experience, and potentialities that are under examination. You're not selling a product; you're selling yourself.

A prospective employer is a businessman. His aim is to select the applicant best suited for the position. He will want information about you;

but he also will observe your appearance, your manners, your poise, your personality, your voice, and your language as you talk with him. During the interview he probably will discuss with you things like these:

Your general education
Your training for a job like this
Your previous experience
Your reasons for being interested in this particular job
Your ambitions
Your special interests and abilities
The duties and responsibilities of the position
The possibilities for advancement
Salary
Your references
Interesting facts about the company, the employees, or the position
Your health
How you get along with people

If you are wise, then, you will be prepared to have something to say on most of these points. In general it will be your businesslike manner and talk which will make the most immediate impression on your employer. He will study your other qualifications after you've left.

Remember these hints when you are applying for a job:

1. If possible, make an appointment for your interview.
2. Know in advance what you intend to ask or say regarding the position.
3. Plan some courteous remarks as an opening.

a. The weather
b. The latest news
c. The surroundings
d. Some interesting object in the room
e. A subject of local interest
f. Appreciation of interview

4. Take your cues from the employer. Let him take most of the initiative, but assume your fair share of the conversation, too.

5. Let your manner and appearance help to sell you. The way you look, the way you talk, and the way you act are important.

a. Be straightforward and candid.
b. Be respectful, but not afraid.
c. Be honest with your employer, yet fair to yourself.
d. Be cheerful, confident, and willing to cooperate.
e. Be neatly and conservatively dressed.
f. Use good English.

6. Don't overstay your welcome. When you sense that the important things have been said, be ready to leave courteously and graciously.

ACTIVITIES

1. Make a personal application for a job. Have your teacher or a classmate act as the employer, or have a local businessman who wants to employ a high school student come to your class and interview interested students. After the interview, discuss the applicant's performance on the basis of the following questions:

a. Was the applicant's appearance attractive?
b. Was his manner courteous and confident?
c. Did he answer questions clearly and concisely?
d. Did he act alert, enthusiastic, and eager?
e. Was there a good give-and-take between the interviewer and the applicant? Did the applicant take any initiative in meeting and answering questions? Or were his bearing and manner too retiring and timid, and his answers monosyllabic?
f. Was anything important omitted in the interview?

2. Plan the strategy which you would use in making a personal application for any of the following positions:

OFFICE ASSISTANT
Must have had some training in typing. Neat appearance, good judgment, patience with detailed work necessary. Salary to start, $60 a week. Apply in person, Room 302, Bank of America Bldg.

The Menlo Park Tribune
Wants a high school boy, interested in learning journalism from the bottom up, for part-time office work. Come in and talk it over with the City Editor.

CAR WAITRESS wanted. Apply in person. Tally-Ho Drive-In Restaurant. Corner of Sixth and Main.

NEWSPAPER route boy wanted for one-hour job every morning. Car or motor scooter necessary. Liberal commission and mileage. Phone 4404 for appointment.

STORE CLERKS
Wanted for Christmas holiday season. Must be polite, alert, and dependable. Salary, $70 a week. Character references required. Apply to Mr. Burns, Manager, Young's Dept. Store.

Part-time Filing Clerk
Twenty hours per week guaranteed. Experience unnecessary; will train on job. Salary to be discussed. Apply Paul Bunyan Lumber Co., Room 10, Nevada Bldg., 514 Bryant Street.

3. Pretend that you have written a letter of application for the position mentioned in the advertisement and that you have been asked to interview the employer. Make an outline of what you intend to state or ask during the interview.

WANTED

High school student, age 16 to 18, for position as a part-time clerk in Cowle's Five-and-Dime Store. Must be quick to make change, have neat appearance, and be courteous to the public. Salary open for discussion. Apply Box 181, *Times* Office.

Giving and Getting Information

The personal interview, in addition to being almost a requirement in applying for a job these days, is also a very practical means of communication when it is necessary to give or get information. Newspaper, radio, and TV interviews of personalities in the fields of sports, the theater, politics, literature, and music are popular and common. Local radio and TV stations often have man-in-the-street interviews on current topics and happenings. There are other occasions, closer to your current experiences, in which interviewing for the purpose of getting information is desirable. For instance, when you're preparing a social studies report, a debate, a platform speech, or a report to a club, you may find it helpful or necessary to ask questions of someone whose knowledge and experience you respect. Talking casually with people is an age-old way of gathering facts and opinions. The interview method is simply a more modern, purposeful way of accomplishing the same objective.

Because the technique of radio and TV interviewing is covered in the units that are devoted separately to these two media of communication, the material that follows, though necessarily general in its application, is directed toward the accomplishment of successful formal and informal interviews that occur between people in the daily business of living.

When Getting Information

- Be sharply aware of the particular purpose of the interview which you are conducting.
- Pay attention to the characteristics of the person you are interviewing.
- Prepare your questions in advance, but be ready to ignore them or change them as the interview develops.
- Conduct the interview in a businesslike manner, but lighten it by in-

formal chatting, personal references, and some conversational side-tracking.

- Phrase your questions so that they are easily understood and do not encompass an unduly large range of consideration.
- Ask provocative questions, as well as those to which concise answers may be given, so that discussion may develop and replace a laborious question-and-answer procedure.
- Try to bring about easy transitions from one topic to another. If you are successful in this effort, you ease the tensions of both participants and listeners—when there is an audience; you encourage sprightliness; and you help to give the interview a quality of unity.
- Listen carefully to the answers to your questions and be alert to the interviewee. Perceptiveness on your part will help you to discover "gold mines" and to avoid "tar pits."
- In general, try to create a climate of interchange which will permit you to get at fundamental—not superficial—information and reaction.

When Giving Information

- Cooperate with the interviewer in every reasonable way that you can.
- Aim for a type of response that is informal, conversational, and friendly.
- Answer questions fairly, honestly, and as fully as time and common sense allow.
- Refrain from monosyllabic replies which tell little about your reactions and which force the interviewer into greater effort to draw you out.
- Give supportive evidence for statements which you wish to be accepted as fact, and use examples and illustrations to clarify comments which are complex or difficult to understand.
- Be sensitive to the purpose of the interview and to the intent of the interviewer's questions, especially when those questions seem a little vague, so that you may help to carry the interview forward. You can do much by a friendly request for clarification to refocus the interview and to ease the tension that a poor question might produce.
- Keep in mind the fact that you are not in competition with the interviewer and that your utmost cooperation and creative effort are essential in the giving and getting of information.

ACTIVITIES

1. Interview someone you know who holds the kind of job in which you think you might be interested someday. He or she might be a mechanic, service-station operator, bookkeeper, waitress, doctor, businessman, teacher, plumber, interior

When interesting visitors come to school, you might arrange a special interview.

decorator, sales clerk, carpenter, lawyer, airline hostess, gardener, real-estate operator, beauty-shop operator, typist, nurse, dental assistant, librarian, cashier, theater usher, photographer, newspaper reporter, farmer, forest ranger, or actor.

Your aim is to collect as much reliable information as possible from the person you are interviewing and to report the results to your classmates. Be prepared with a list of questions like the following:

a. What do you like best about your work?
b. Is there anything you do not like?
c. What are your duties?
d. What is the beginning salary?
e. Are there opportunities for advancement?
f. How many hours a day do you work? Is there overtime? Are you paid extra for it?
g. Is the work relaxing or nerve-racking? Is there any danger involved?
h. Exactly what do you do in a typical day?
i. Are the people with whom you work pleasant and congenial?
j. How should you advise me to prepare myself for a job like this?

2. Pair with a classmate and prepare an imaginary interview to put on before the class in which you are a reporter getting information for the next edition of your paper. Your classmate may take the part of one of the following persons:

a. A traveler returned from an extended vacation to Mexico
b. A soldier back from overseas duty
c. A well-known graduate of your school who is back in his home town for a visit

d. A visiting student from an out-of-state school
e. A local celebrity
f. The school principal upon his return from a convention
g. An athletic coach upon the completion of a successful season

3. Plan with another student a radio interview (see Unit 23 for suggestions) in which your purpose is to bring out information concerning some particular school activity. If the interview is a previously planned one, the questions, answers, and dialogue must be prepared carefully beforehand and read from manuscript. If the interview is to be impromptu, like the man-in-the-street type, the interviewer should have the questions jotted down on cards and should keep the discussion alive and moving at all times. A three- to five-minute interview should be sufficient for either type. Here are some suggestions about whom to interview.
   a. A football player, on the school's football prospects for the year
   b. A member of the debating team, about debating activities for the year
   c. A student-body officer, on his plans and accomplishments during the year
   d. A United States history student, on what his class is now doing
   e. An art-club student, on the projects being completed in his class
   f. A member of the chess club, radio club, camera club, or any other club, on the activities of his group
   g. A staff member of the school newspaper, about some interesting stories that have been covered and the work he is doing
   h. A student of a science class, about some experiments and activities in which his class is interested
   i. A member of a school dance or picnic committee, on the plans it is formulating
   j. A member of the band or orchestra, about the activities of his group
   k. A typing or shorthand student, on what she is learning in her class
   l. A student in the machine shop, on the projects being worked out in class
   m. A drama student, on the plays that have been and will be produced this year

Discussing Personal Problems

There is still another kind of personal interview to consider, the one which involves the settling of personal problems. Remember what was said in Unit 2 about *you*? You are both a great problem and a great joy to yourself during your school years. Personal affairs loom large in your life, and you find numerous occasions when you want to ask advice, make protests, seek consolations, or share enthusiasms about many personal matters. You will probably do this by talking with your closest friends, with members of your family, and with other adults whose knowledge and wisdom you admire and respect. This kind of face-to-face talk is like any informal conversation except that it is usually more purposeful and businesslike. Your aim is specific: to settle a personal problem in a friendly manner without waste of time. Your success will depend both upon *what* you say and *how* you say it. These suggestions may prove helpful:

Some Do's

Be honest in your evaluation of the problem.
Be moderate in your demands.
Be fair in your criticism.
Be reasonable in your attitude.
Be tactful in your remarks.
Be courteous and pleasant in manner.
Be willing to make reasonable compromises.
Be persistent enough to explore satisfactorily the various aspects of the subject under consideration.

In the event that matters are not settled to your personal satisfaction in an interview of this type, by all means, remember these Don'ts:

Some Don't's

Don't sulk.
Don't lose your temper.
Don't feel sorry for yourself.
Don't be vindictive.
Don't refuse to see the other side of the problem.
Don't give up if you're still convinced you're right.

ACTIVITIES

Pair with some member of your class and dramatize a personal interview for the class. Follow the general procedure explained for the sociodramas in Unit 15:

1. Explain a low semester grade to your definitely disappointed mother.
2. Ask your English teacher for an extension of time for completing a theme which you *knew* was due today.
3. Ask your counselor's advice about a change in your program for next term.
4. Talk over with your coach your failure to make the first team.
5. Request the use of the family car from your unwilling father.
6. Defend yourself to a policeman against a traffic violation charge
7. You've had a serious misunderstanding with your best friend. Try to make it up.
8. Explain an unexcused absence to your teacher.
9. You've caused a disturbance in study hall and have been sent to the principal.
10. It's 2:30 A.M. You've just arrived home from a school dance to find your mother waiting up for you. She had instructed you to be home by 12:30. What happens?
11. You need an increased allowance, but your parents feel unable to grant it. Talk over your problem with your best friend and ask his advice about what to do.
12. A friend of yours has been accused of something he didn't do, and you want to intercede for him. State the problem to an older person and ask his advice.

Unit Seventeen

GROUP DISCUSSION: Talking Things Over

Discussion in groups has been a common experience for you during most of your school life. Most often your teacher has been the discussion leader; but, as you have progressed through the grades, there has been an increasing amount of student-leader discussion. Outside the classroom you have also taken part in many activities that have called for settling problems in the huddle, and for the rest of your life there will be opportunity for you to engage in group discussion: college activities, clubs, lodges, councils, boards, committees, church groups, community welfare groups, and many others.

All of these groups have in common their being an assemblage of people who want to accomplish one or more purposes by the exchange of ideas through oral language. Most, but not all, seek to take some kind of action, a step which should logically follow, but not precede, discussion. Some are not action groups but are seeking only to gain information, to increase understanding, to find personal satisfaction in the group experience. All, however, rely upon the exchange of ideas to achieve their many purposes.

What Are Groups Like?

They range in size from very small, as in a conference of a club's officers, to very large, as in a town-hall meeting. They come into existence by designation, by self-constitution, and even by accident. Sometimes they are a collection of friendly people with an easily recognizable common purpose, sometimes a hostile group with personal axes to grind and bitter challenges to hurl at each other, sometimes an angry group with a common enemy, or sometimes a neutral group without much certainty of why they have been called together.

Often a group, such as a standing committee, has a continuing responsibility, but a special group—an *ad hoc* committee, for example—may exist only for a brief time to accomplish a specific task. Some groups study and discuss at great length in private sessions; others discuss items briefly and take many formal actions, most of the time in public. Still another kind, the advisory group, digs hard into every aspect of a problem in an effort to help a leader make decisions that he alone can make.

Sometimes, as in the symposium and the panel, a small group has as its chief purpose the communicating of ideas or information to an audience, with expectation that large-group discussion will occur when the audience participates. On the other hand, audiences may be informed and influenced by listening to a small decision-making group in action; but this group does not have as its chief purpose the communicating of information to the audience and may, indeed, have strict rules of procedure that deny any kind of audience participation. Still another important kind of group discussion is that which goes on among a small number of people who are studying the phenomenon of the group itself, who are trying better to understand their own motivations as well as the many other factors that influence communication within a group. Such discussion is, of course, important to everyone, but it is especially valuable for those who have, or plan to have, leadership roles in discussion groups.

What Factors Influence Group Communication?

- *Physical environment.* How large is the meeting room? Is it too hot or too cold? In what arrangement are the participants? How comfortable are the seats? What other factors may have an influence on the group?
- *Time of day.* Is the meeting in the morning when energy is generally high? after lunch when some may be sleepy? late in the afternoon when fatigue has taken its toll, or frustrations have made members tense?
- *Feelings.* Who is angry? Who came to the meeting with feelings of hostility? Who is bored? Who feels so insecure that he is silent—or nervously defensive? Who is happy? confident? sullen? exhausted? frightened?
- *Actions of group members.* Has someone decided, for whatever reason, to play the role of the clown? Who is aggressive and domi-

nates the discussion? Who seals himself off from participation? Who leaves the room? taps his foot or his pencil? keeps looking at his watch? yawns? drops off to sleep? shuffles papers? asks irrelevant questions? gets away from the subject? makes tiresome speeches?

- *Size of the group.* Is the group a large one which can operate only under well-defined and enforced rules of behavior, such as the Congress, House of Representatives, United Nations, or a public forum? Is discussion limited? Is the group a small one in which everyone has opportunity for full expression? Is it a group that is neither small nor large, but one in which the chairman must exercise group control and the members must maintain self-control to insure successful exploration of all points of view?
- *Time limitations.* Is the length of a meeting so short or the number of meetings so few that discussion is limited and decisions are reached without desirable exploration of alternatives or of the possible effects of the decisions themselves?
- *Vested interests.* Does someone have such a large ax to grind that all of the group energy goes into resistance to or support of the grinder himself rather than into examination of the merits of the ax? Has selfishness caused an impossible tug-of-war?
- *Choice of language; manner of speaking.* Do you remember the part of the unit on listening that discusses the difference between the image created in the mind of the speaker when he used a word or phrase and the one created in the mind of the listener when he heard it? Do you recall from the same unit discussion on the impact of certain words on people? If you don't, review both; they apply significantly to group discussion. And are you aware of what you can do to another by a challenging question? the tone and pitch of your voice? the look on your face? your rate of speaking? your lack of volume? your mumbling speech?
- *Sensitivity; perception.* How sensitive are you to the feelings of others? How well do you perceive the causes and effects of what people say and do to each other? Do you know beforehand that what you say will silence another member, obscure an issue, create a personal schism, or kill further discussion? How much do you give vent to your own feelings, no matter what you believe to be your justification, without regard to what others may be thinking or feeling? To what extent do you willingly take advantage of your strengths in debate to vanquish another for personal reasons and with no concern for what this attack may do to the member or to the group function?

How May a Group Behave?

- It may be TENSE, INDIFFERENT, or EAGER when it is newly formed.
- Members tend to SIT IN THE SAME PLACE, either in the same chair or in the same location in the room.
- There are occasional SILENCES. Some members can't stand silences and become known in the group as silence-breakers. Long silences have a stronger effect on the group than short silences, with the not-unusual result of the group's having to stop and talk about the silence before any further group activity can occur.
- LONG, TIRESOME DISCUSSION of a major topic or issue often takes place for no other reason than that the group wishes to avoid coming to grips with an unpleasant problem.
- One or more members will often RALLY TO THE DEFENSE of another member when it is felt that he is being "picked on" by anyone present.
- Members will RESIST IDEAS AND SUGGESTIONS for action that come from outside the group and will support those which come from within, with special reference to "outside" as meaning higher authority or strangers and "inside" as meaning compatriots or friends.
- Members will exhibit FEELINGS OF SATISFACTION when "tasks" have been completed and interpersonal relations have been pleasant—and dissatisfaction when the reverse is true. Most groups are "task-oriented," which means only that they are more used to working on the solution of a problem than to being engaged in evaluation of themselves, Thus, when anything or anybody gets in the way of problem-solving (completing a task), negative feelings are aroused.
- GETTING OFF THE SUBJECT, despite the desire of all members to complete tasks (solve problems, reach decisions, soothe feelings, etc.), is a common experience. The reason for this kind of group behavior lies in the members' particular interests, feelings, inability to understand what is going on, compulsion to make a contribution to the group in the only way they know how, and in the "daisy-chain" effect of one conversation's following another without intervention and refocusing by the group leader.
- Often a group is WILLING TO MAKE ANY KIND OF DECISION on a problem in order to bring about adjournment or to avoid prolonging an unpleasant and difficult discussion, unless a member with sound judgment resists and forces the group to an acceptance of responsibility for more mature behavior.

If you were chairman of this group, what would you need to keep in mind about group communication and behavior?

- Related to the item above, and seemingly contradictory, is the disposition of a group TO PROLONG AN ARGUMENT, even though repetition has set in and a solution of the problem remains remote. The explanation for this kind of behavior lies in high feeling, frustration, the need for personal vindication, and the vain hope that group discord will disappear if enough discussion can occur. It is not impossible for a group to resolve a prolonged argument, but, usually, only strong group leadership will provide the setting for such a resolution.
- TERMINATION BEHAVIOR is another readily identifiable aspect of the functioning of any group. If the termination means only adjourning for the day, the symptoms appear as restlessness, stealing glances at a clock, folding papers, pushing back in a chair, looking expectantly alert, or turning from the main topic to get in a quick personal comment. If termination means a breaking up of the group for a long period of time or permanently, the symptoms are often more subtle, appearing as sudden evaluations of how important the group has been, invitations to the group to "let's get together for a party when this is over," withdrawal of members from active participation in group discussion, challenges to the leader, questions about future activity of the group, and similar expressions of insecurity and apprehension.

Making Group Effort More Effective

Molding any group into an efficient working unit, either as a task for the leader or for the group itself, is not a simple achievement. Many of the factors that interfere with effective group discussion, for example, are related to our weaknesses as humans, and we can't change human nature by exhortation. We *know* better than we *do.* So, you ask, what can I do to make group efforts more effective?

You can learn to recognize the factors of interference and to understand their influence; and, through understanding, you can gradually modify your behavior by yielding less and less to *feeling* and more and more to *reason.* You can learn when to drive and when to give, when to laugh and when to be serious, when to support discussion and when to be silent. In short, you can learn how to become more perceptive in human relationships, which is the formal way of saying that you can learn to "read" others.

Solutions to most problems of behavior in a group are suggested by the problems themselves, but rarely are there "pat" solutions.

- If you can't be heard in group discussion, even though your voice is quite normal, group members must make you aware of the fact, and all you have to do is increase your volume–and possibly improve your enunciation.
- If you speak softly because you are shy or because something is wrong with your normal voice production, the solution to your problem ranges from the difficult to the near-impossible, and you need expert help.
- If you are a person who tends to monopolize attention but who isn't aware of what he is doing to group discussion, you may be able to modify your actions by having them called to your attention. If, on the other hand, you are a monopolizer because you feel a strong need to be in the limelight, you cannot with ease turn to being a "mouse" in the group, for your need lies deep in your personality and you may or may not be able to change either the need or its many expressions.
- If you are using language that is inappropriate because it is imprecise, vulgar, too sophisticated, abstract, or charged with extravagant emotion, you can easily learn–and members of the group will help you–to turn to terminology that will be acceptable. If you use abstract terms such as *democracy, communism, cooperation, prejudice, loyalty,* and *equality,* be sure to define them in light of what you intend them to mean. In general, choose from your vocabulary good "working"

words that won't act as a block to the understanding of your ideas. Don't use epithets, profanity, words that arouse antagonism, or any words which in your judgment will shock some of your listeners to the point that they will begin to condemn your *message* because they have an unfavorable opinion of *you.*

The preceding comments on solving problems in group behavior are not intended to be more than a brief exploration into the nature of such problem-solving. *Awareness* of the factors that affect communication, an understanding of those factors as they are related to you as a member and to the group as a whole, your interest in improving your actions in group work, and, in particular, your opportunity to participate in group experience will eventually bring you a reasonable degree of sophistication in group behavior. If you like people and have a better-than-average understanding of what causes them to act and feel as they do, you will intuitively tend to behave in a manner which is acceptable to groups. You can improve your performance, however, by continuing to learn more about human behavior and about the technical aspects of group discussion.

A Capsule of Suggestions for Making Communication Within the Group More Effective

- Be a *catalyst:* help to resolve conflicts, suggest alternatives, bring others into the discussion, ask leading questions.
- Practice the kind of *courtesy* that will encourage positive feelings and harmonious reactions in others.
- Pay attention to oral communications, *listening* carefully when others speak and *limiting your own speaking,* both in frequency and in length of comments.
- Control your *feelings.*
- Examine your *motives.* Are you trying to block action? Are you trying to discredit a group member? Are you genuinely trying to solve a problem?
- Avoid being *stubborn,* but hold fast to your *convictions.*
- *Come to the group prepared,* if preparation is necessary to your group's discussion.
- *Stick to the topic* under discussion, unless deviation will further some purpose which is acceptable to the group.
- Speak *clearly* and with *sufficient volume* to be heard.
- Use language *appropriate to the occasion* and to the *sensibilities* of the rest of the group.
- *Be aware constantly* of the total process of group dynamics, and gauge your actions to be in tune with that process.

A thirteen-year-old girl, Ann Brooke, addresses the Massachusetts legislature.

Approaches to Group Discussion

As you have observed in your own experience, discussion groups have many sizes and purposes. *Small-group discussion* falls mostly into the category of what is called round-table discussion, and *large-group discussion* is generally identified with the forum, or open forum, though the term *forum* is often used to apply to the group itself and originally was used as the name for a public meeting place in ancient cities, with special reference to those in which law courts and public offices were located. Now we think of a forum as being a public meeting, such as a town hall meeting, or as the audience-participation period that follows a speaker's address, a panel presentation, or a symposium.

Large-Group Discussion. Large-group discussion has existed wherever and whenever democracy has flourished; it is freedom of speech in action. There a man has the *right* to speak his mind, the *privilege* of speaking it, and the *responsibility* for living with what he has said. Sometimes his utterances are very satisfying to him, in that his fellowmen show approval or he himself feels pride, even though such utterances may later prove unacceptable to both himself and his fellows. Sometimes his observations cause men to distort their faces in angry rejection, even though later he may be acclaimed as a man "too early for the times." But, for whatever he says, he must assume responsibility.

At its best, a large-group discussion truly is discussion by a group, where the important aspects of a problem are aired, though everyone doesn't speak; at its poorest, it may be a verbal brawl, a harangue before a group that can only listen, or stifling of group expression by an organized, articulate minority who have come to shape and use group power for selfish purposes.

Ideally, the *open forum* represents the most democratic kind of discussion because it provides all citizens an opportunity to state their views. Realistically, all the citizens cannot be housed at general meetings, and, if they could be, all would not be able to speak. Further, large-group discussion often suffers from lack of focus and lack of leadership as well as unpreparedness, timidity, or aggressiveness on the part of the members.

In general, it is true that large-group discussion will be successful if the chairman is a good leader, if the group wants to solve problems on a rational basis, and if an expression of representative points of view occurs. It is also generally true that a strong factor in the success of large-group discussion is the chairman; but no chairman, however talented, can bring about success if the group will not permit an operation of the ground rules and the persuasion of reason. There is one more observation to be made: what has been said under the heading of large-group discussion is not specifically true of the activity that occurs in such special large groups as official state, national, and international assemblies. Such groups function under strict rules of procedure, most members are sophisticated in the use of these rules for both their protection and their advantage in attack, and the chief purpose of most speakers is to win a point, not to promote discussion.

Perhaps it should be said that these special large groups are not different from others except in sophistication, status, and degree of responsibility, and that all of their members are not necessarily motivated by integrity, a sense of fair play, a desire to reveal truth, or a compulsion to serve mankind—regardless of state or national boundaries. It is obvious, however, that the structure of many of today's societies demands large-group discussion, and our own nation employs it freely and profitably. Your task is to help in its preservation and in its improvement. When you are the chairman of a large meeting, your goals are much the same as if you were chairing a small group, but the demands upon you are different:

- The size of the audience and the volume of sound that comes from it put greater pressure on you, and you must put additional energy into being alert.

- Because people often feel freer to express strong feeling in the anonymity of a large group, there is greater challenge to you to maintain poise if language and action become violent and abusive.
- If many audience members wish to speak, your plans for accommodating them must be well organized. Lack of such a plan may easily produce near-riot when feelings are high.
- You must be sure that ground rules for the discussion are set up and *understood,* and you must enforce them, being sensitive to the need for free expression, the wastefulness of repetitious speeches, and the importance of moving the audience toward a conclusion which will not violate good sense, decency, or principle.
- You are always dealing with your group at long range, often by microphone, and you never have the advantage of quick and easy interchange to clear up a point, close-range facial expression to help communication, or the thought-filled pauses that can help a small group to maintain perspective. Urge that comments be reasonably short; break in with a question, a suggestion, or a brief summation when comments become overly long; and try always to have your own statements show the sympathy, understanding, and tolerance that will dignify the speaker's efforts—no matter how you personally may evaluate them.

Although the panel and the symposium may be part and parcel of large-group discussions, they will be treated under the following section on small-group discussion. There is an intellectual problem in their classification, one which may intrigue you and lead to class discussion; but there is good reason to skip that problem in the interests of getting at the basic problem of how these and other forms of group discussion are carried on.

Small-Group Discussion. Small discussion groups, because of their size and their informal nature, are usually very satisfactory to the participants. They are easy for a chairman to run. Everyone may have an opportunity to talk a number of times. The manner of speaking is conversational. Ideas can be exchanged, explored, and evaluated. But the most important advantage of the small group is the possibility for *group thinking* to take place. Though much fun has been poked at committees and their inability to accomplish anything, they do have the ingredients for unusual accomplishment. When all members participate, when they put aside defending a pet point of view, and when they join in developing an idea, a unique kind of thinking can take place. Each member builds on the central idea, not only from his own reserves but also from the stimulation of others' thoughts; and the chain reaction that occurs has tremendous power.

A round-table situation stimulates the flow of ideas. Each member makes his contribution in an atmosphere that is conversational and relaxed.

The Round Table. Round-table groups that you know best are your own classes, whether discussion takes place casually as a lesson progresses or more formally when a topic has been assigned for class discussion. If your class has no more than twenty to twenty-five members, if your teacher is not addicted to lecturing, and if you are actually seated in a round-the-table arrangement, you have conditions that will enhance group discussion. You must recognize, however, that a school class has somewhat less freedom than smaller groups not only because of the size but also because the teacher is usually the chairman. It is his obligation, in the learning process, to take the floor more often than a chairman usually does, so that he may point out errors, direct the discussion along new lines, stimulate ideas, or improve participation.

The Committee. The term *committee* generally means a small working group which has been appointed or elected to complete a task, though some groups form and call themselves a committee so that they may be identified and have a degree of official recognition. Committees all have a chairman, nearly always keep minutes of proceedings, and follow parliamentary procedure in varying degrees. What may be called a committee in one organization or in one community may be called a board or a council in another, but, whatever the name, a committee is a group that sets out to solve a problem by study and discussion. Except for large committees established by state, national, and international agencies, most conduct their business as round-table discussion. You are probably not surprised to learn that, with the possible exception of "conferences," committees outnumber all other forms of organizational units for group discussion.

The Conference. What is a conference? Quotes were used above to indicate the wide range of this particular category, not its questionable existence. The conference extends all the way from an extremely informal meeting of two people to discuss a problem to a formal, highly structured gathering of hundreds of people, a gathering which may also be called an assembly or a convention. If you are wondering why the conference is treated under small-group discussion when it has such a range, the answer is that most conferences, by far, occur as small, informal or semi-formal meetings. In 20th-century man's daily existence, no matter what agencies, companies, organizations, or corporations are involved, there are countless conferences—and their effectiveness as group discussion is a strong factor in the determination of his welfare. Small conferences are usually round table in nature, may sometimes not have an appointed leader, may often not keep minutes of the meeting, and more often than not will be "one-shot" meetings.

The Panel and the Symposium. While it is true that both the panel and the symposium are small groups, neither, in the strict sense of the word, should be classified as small-group discussions. The symposium is not group discussion at all, if interchange of ideas is an acceptable criterion. Panel members, on the other hand, do have the opportunity to carry on small-group discussion; but, like the members of the symposium, they have as their chief purpose the bringing of information to an audience. With both the symposium and the panel, regardless of how each presents a discussion of a problem, group discussion must occur as a phenomenon of the total group, which means the inclusion of the audience. Both symposium members and panel members may answer questions, pose questions, and join in large-group discussion; but, until they do join in large-group discussion, they are serving the special purpose of presenting and presumably clarifying a problem of general interest.

The *symposium* is a presentation of a number of prepared speeches on a topic or particular problem. It is expected that each speaker represents a reasonable degree of expertness in his field, that the speakers as a group will present the important aspects of a problem or issue, and that the presentation will either be an end in itself—in that it brings important information to the audience—or will provide the particular background of information necessary to intelligent and effective large-group discussion. It is quite possible for the symposium to turn, after the formal speeches have been completed, into a panel discussion which will make for easy transition to large-group discussion; but whether or not this transformation takes place usually depends upon preplanning.

The *panel* must also bring out important aspects of a problem, but the members do not, or should not, have prepared speeches. Revelation of the many facts of the issue being discussed should come not only from planned statements made by the panel members but also from responses they make to questions and challenges arising from their group. Skillful and perceptive panel members will try to anticipate and to discuss questions which they believe to be in the minds of the audience.

Let's suppose that you are to be the chairman of a panel presentation. How should you go about your task?

The Chairman Conducts a Panel

In the unit on parliamentary law there are some tips for the chairman. Those suggestions apply to chairmen in most circumstances whether they are presiding at a round table, conducting a forum, heading a panel, or guiding a meeting by the use of formal procedure. Also generally applicable to the behavior of the chairman are the suggestions for the behavior of any group members in "A Capsule of Suggestions" earlier in this unit. A chairman must be tactful, able to separate sense from nonsense, sensitive to the mood of the group, capable of keeping discussion in progress, expert at keeping discussion on the topic, able to restrain himself from talking too much, and aware of the value that a touch of humor has in easing tension or dispelling apathy. Let's assume that you have these skills and many others. Your problem right now is to collect a panel, organize it, and conduct it in a manner that will insure profitable group discussion.

Preparing the Panel

1. *Evaluate the situation.* To whom will the panel be presented? How large is this group? Has the topic been assigned, or is its selection up to you? Will the topic be discussed by the panel members in round-table fashion, or will each member have specific responsibilities for presentation of material? Will there be a need for microphones? How long is the meeting to be? Will there be a need for a rehearsal with all members

Several meetings of the panel before presentation are necessary for organization, informal discussion of the topic, assignments, and progress reports.

before final presentation, or should it be a spontaneous presentation? Or should each member present at a rehearsal just a general résumé of material he intends to cover?

2. *Select the topic.* Follow the same principles of selection that you employ in selecting a speech topic. If your topic has been assigned, you must be sure you know exactly what is expected of your panel, and then you must decide upon the best approach to exploration of the topic.

3. *Choose your panel members.* Steps 2 and 3 may have to be reversed. For example, you may be instructed to choose a panel and to decide with the members what the topic is to be, or you may have difficulty in securing the members you particularly desire, in which case you probably will want to delay selection of the topic until the panel membership is established. Other reasons for reversal are: the panel may already be in existence, the choice of members may be somewhat automatic or restricted, or you may be the kind of chairman who believes that a choice of topic should never occur without the participation of all members. Regardless of how the topic is chosen, try always to select panel members who represent a *variety of interests,* if the presentation is informational, and *different points of view,* if the topic is debatable.

4. *Organize the panel.* Call your panel members together and discuss

the topic informally. Take the initative in making suggestions and asking questions. Panel members will soon follow your lead. Discuss sources of information: reading matter, authority, a survey, or a questionnaire. Tell the members what procedure they are to follow in the presentation and what time limits must be observed. Unless you have been otherwise instructed, or have a strong personal preference, find out whether your panel would prefer to have the audience participate during the presentation or to wait for an ensuing forum. Now, unless the presentation is to be an unstructured, round-table discussion, assign to each member the phase of the topic for which he is to prepare and *be sure he is agreeable to the assignment.*

5. *Meet with the panel.* Hold progress meetings with your group to determine the success of your planning to date. Have members been able to find resource information? Are your assignments still acceptable to both the members and you? Has a reasonable amount of work been completed? Are there problems that have arisen? Are there new ideas for improving the presentation? Use your judgment in deciding upon the number of progress meetings needed.

Too much emphasis cannot be placed upon the importance of informed discussion, and when you meet with your panel members you must stress the value of research, helping them to use such sources of information as the *Readers' Guide* and leading them to the practical realization that lack of adequate information produces hesitancy in contribution, dull generalities, and sense of inadequacy—all of which frustrate discussion. An audience can soon tell whether it is being subjected to a barrage of opinion or a body of facts. The quality of discussion that follows a panel presentation will reflect, accordingly, the quality of that presentation.

Seating Arrangements for a Panel

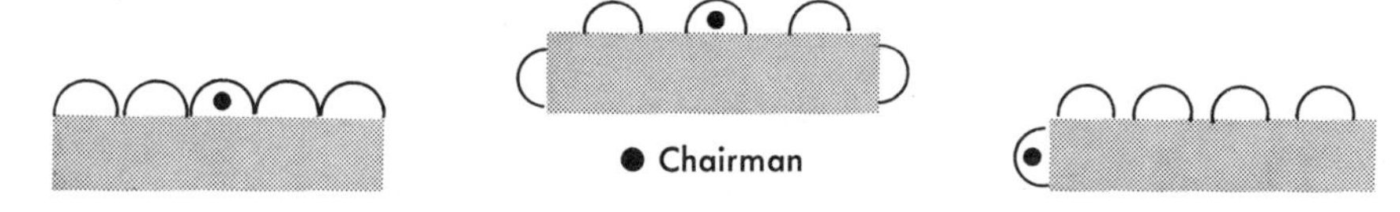

Conducting the Panel

6. *Seat your panel.* Physical limitations or a seating arrangement predetermined by someone else may dictate the manner in which your panel will be seated, but conventionally most panels are seated at a long table—

with the chairman in the center position—in front of an audience. Any arrangement that will allow the panel to be seen and heard is acceptable.

7. *Define procedure and rules for the discussion.*

8. *Introduce the members of the panel.*

9. *Announce the topic and introduce it so that discussion by the panel may follow easily and logically.*

There is no rule about the order of steps 7, 8, and 9, and a skillful chairman may either reverse their order in some fashion or combine them as a single operation. However *you* proceed, don't forget that discussion of the topic by the panel must be preceded by an introduction that makes discussion an obvious and easy next step.

10. *Run the show!* This step is a test of your true skill, for you are now on your own, and you must be alert. You are reminded to:

a. Keep the discussion lively.
b. See that all panel members make contributions.
c. Control members who want to "hog" the discussion.
d. Hold discussion to the topic.
e. Don't permit heated arguments based on personalities and prejudice.
f. Allot a reasonable amount of time to each phase of discussion.
g. Make brief summary statements, when necessary.
h. Limit your own talking.
i. Insure audience participation, because discussion by the *whole* group is your objective.

11. *Summarize briefly the main contributions brought out by the group discussion, and adjourn the meeting.*

Topics for Group Discussion

How Meaningful Is Student Government?
Grades Are Necessary
New Courses Our High School Should Offer
School Letters for All School Activities
An Evaluation of School Assemblies: Problems and Proposals
Strengths and Weaknesses of Student Court
Is the High School Diploma Outmoded?
Poor School Spirit at the Last Game
The School Needs Facilities for Noontime Recreation
The New Rules Concerning Tardiness Are Unfair
Student Ownership of an Automobile Should (Should Not) Be Discouraged
Who Needs Shakespeare?

What Parents Don't Understand
The Pros and Cons of Going Steady
"Going Along" with the Gang: When Yes? When No?
Whose Business Is Moral Behavior?
Who Is a Good Leader? A Good Follower?
Youth, Traffic, and Safety
A Critical Look at Compulsory Education
Medical Care for Everyone
Labor and Management Must Join Forces
Strikes: Their Cost, Their Effectiveness, and Their Future
International Control of Atomic Energy
Mid-Century Gains by Racial Minority Groups
The Place of Programed Instruction in Modern Education
America's Houses of Tomorrow
What Every American Must Know about Communism
The United Nations as a Step Toward World Government
Trends in Today's Travel
What Does "Progress" Mean, and How Do We Measure It?
After the Moon, What?
Security after Retirement
Can Science Outlaw War?
Who Should Pay for Education?
The New World of Food Preparation
Our Outmoded Transportation Facilities
The Psychological Effect on a Civilization of Building Underground
Automation Versus Manual Effort; Tomorrow's Jobs
The Tyranny of College Degrees in Education
The Present Jury System Versus a Panel of Professionally Trained Jurors

ACTIVITIES

1. Plan a survey of group activity for the next week to answer these questions:
   a. How many kinds of group discussions have come to your attention during the week, and how many times were you an observer or a participant in each?
   b. Which of the factors that influence group communication, as listed at the beginning of this unit, did you particularly note as being either helpful or detrimental to group effort?
   c. Which of the kinds of group behavior, as listed early in this unit, did you observe?
2. Discuss in class the results of your survey, bringing out in your discussion the answers to these questions.
   a. Did the survey make you more aware of group discussion in terms of its nature, its frequency of occurrence, and its problems?
   b. Which of the factors that adversely affect communication in a group did you note most often?
   c. From your observation what individual acts of behavior made discussion suffer in the group? Which ones helped?

3. Attend, if it is at all possible, a meeting in your community at which there is to be public discussion. Pay particular attention to and report to your class on the following items, as they seemed to affect group discussion: size of the meeting, physical environment, display of feelings, use of language, and appropriateness of remarks. Add to your report any comments you care to make on significant acts of group behavior.

4. Choose for discussion in class one of the topics from the list in this unit, preferably one which will bring out both difference of opinion and feeling. Prepare for discussion in the manner and to the extent that your teacher determines, assuming that he is to be chairman. Your chief responsibility, when the class discussion is held, is to help make communication within the group more effective by following the suggestions in this unit. Use the Capsule of Suggestions on page 337 or, if you prefer, make a list that has been developed in class. Be sure to leave a period of time after class discussion of the topic for evaluation of the discussion and the parts played by the discussants.

5. Try, before the school year ends, to allow everyone in class to be the chairman of a class discussion that resembles the one above, even if the discussions are not quite so long. Right now, in whatever time there is for such activity, you and one or two of your classmates should be able to take turns at being chairman. Select a topic which is acceptable to your classmates, give instructions on preparation, and assume your role as discussion leader. Your class group is larger than a panel and smaller than a forum, so you will have to turn to the suggestions for chairman of each to select those items which will be your guide during your chairmanship. There will be a class evaluation of your effort!

6. Set up, through any process of selection which is acceptable to your class, five or six conference groups, each of which will have a problem to discuss. Perhaps it would be best for your teacher to prepare the topics but not to reveal them until they are handed to each conference group for a proposed solution. It will be the group's responsibility to select a chairman, discuss the problem, and propose a solution—within a specified time limit. Your teacher will circulate, making notes on behavior in each group for later evaluation. When the time is up, the chairmen will take turns announcing their problems and their solutions and commenting on pertinent aspects of group communication.

7. Let four members of your class who are interested in science present a symposium on "Atomic Power and Man's Survival." They may select a fifth member to act as chairman, working with him in separating the main topic into four subtopics. After the symposium the chairman should open the class meeting to general discussion of (*a*) the topic itself, (*b*) how well the topic was covered, and (*c*) how successful the symposium and the discussion on the topic were as parts of a group-discussion technique.

8. Divide your class into convenient groups of five or six members. Let each group elect a chairman, choose a topic (see list in this unit), and organize a panel discussion to be presented to the class. Half of the groups should plan to follow the method of allowing class participation *after* the panel has finished, and the other half should allow participation by the audience *during* the presentation. Your teacher will be your chief consultant while you are working on the

five steps of preparation for the panel and your chief evaluator when you go through the six steps of conducting it.

9. Plan to take a well-prepared panel out into your community for adult review. Delay this activity only until you have finished class consideration of group discussion and feel confidence in your ability to act as a panel member. There are many adult groups—church, service clubs, parent-teacher organizations, and special-interest groups—that will welcome you; all you have to do is to make some contacts and let it be known you have a presentation to offer. To protect the name of your school, to bolster your own pride, and to insure your being invited back, choose an interesting topic, prepare it well, and *stimulate lively group discussion.*

10. Prepare a panel for broadcasting. An increasing number of radio and television stations are allowing school groups to air their views, particularly in educational matters, through a panel discussion. Call or write to the manager of a station that is near to you and has broadcasts in the public interest. *Don't miss this opportunity!* If you are accepted, put on your Sunday best; if you are rejected, don't give up until the last possible station has been questioned.

    If, because there is no station available, you cannot broadcast a panel discussion, turn to your own school's radio station or closed-circuit television services. If your school has neither of these, don't give up; you still have another avenue open. Surely your auditorium or multipurpose room has facilities for amplifying voices from the stage—or from a position in the front of the room. You can set your panel up and present your material just as if it were going over the air.

11. View a film which stimulates thought and encourages discussion. Some of those listed below may provide a take-off point for class discussion.

Films:

Learn to Argue Effectively (Coronet). 11 min color or b&w.
What about Drinking? (MH). 11 min b&w.
What about Prejudice? (MH). 12 min color or b&w.
Other People's Property (MH). 11 min b&w.
Organizing Discussion Groups (EBF). 21 min b&w.
Room for Discussion (EBF). 25 min b&w.
Group Discussion (MH). 12 min b&w.

Unit Eighteen

"Mr. Chairman . . .": Procedure in Meetings

No matter how hard you try, you can't name a game that doesn't have at least one rule or more. Think you can? Is it basketball? Tennis? Baseball? Hide-and-seek? Bridge? Authors? Twenty Questions? Cops and Robbers? Chess? Monopoly? No, it's none of these, nor is it one you're likely to recall. Even professional wrestling, in which nothing seems to be barred, has its rules. And it's the same in your school, in business, in your social life, in your home, in your community, and in the world. Everywhere there are rules.

In the most serious game of them all, living with one's fellowmen, there is a maze of rules, regulations, taboos, and customs. Civilized man has surrounded himself with more rules—laws—than he can remember or apply, but still he goes on and on making more. Why? If you can judge by his reaction when a highway patrolman stops him, or when income-tax time rolls around, or when the game warden catches him, you can't help reaching the conclusion that he hates rules. If you can judge by the number of times he pleads ignorance of the existence of certain laws, you can hardly see why he wants more rules. Why does he?

The best answer seems to be that man is trying to make the game of living with others a little cleaner, a little fairer, a little more fun. He often kicks like a bay steer when he has to conform to the rules he has helped to create, but this rather natural reaction doesn't mean he wants them abolished. His real resentment comes from unfair application of regulations or from being subject to laws enforced upon him by some outside agency that isn't particularly interested in his welfare. Because of this resentment there has been a centuries-old struggle of men *against* tyrants, despots, and dictators, and *for* freedom to be self-governing, for the right to make rules in which there will be more *justice*. It is this concern about fairness that has led to the development of rules to govern decision-making activity in groups.

Justice in Meetings

If you understand why games have rules that fit all players alike, then you understand a great deal about justice, democracy, and the business of living with other people. You will keep in mind, too, that since the rules are man-made, they are often unsatisfactory or inadequate and so must be enforced with wisdom. With this concept of fair play to guide your actions, you should have no difficulty in joining with other people in a formal meeting and applying the rules that help to guarantee democratic procedure, *parliamentary law*.

When you go into a business meeting, you expect at least that you will have the right to speak and that something will be accomplished. *Parliamentary law* is the set of rules that ordinarily will guarantee these expectations, for it brings justice and order to meetings. It is not, as many people think, a complicated procedure that only confuses members and delays action. Try always to run your meetings according to the best accepted rules, and discover that working with others can be both enjoyable and profitable.

Most organizations use as their guide for parliamentary law *Robert's Rules of Order*, Revised. Because it is rather formidable reading, you may find that one of the simpler texts listed at the end of this unit will best serve your purpose in solving problems not discussed here.

How to Learn Parliamentary Law

The use of parliamentary law, like any other skill, is not learned quickly, nor will it remain a skill unless it is employed with some degree of regularity. The material offered in this unit and in the one that preceded it is an *introduction* to a field of knowledge in which you may become as proficient as your time and your desires allow. The activities listed at the end of this unit present you with the opportunity to go beyond basic information.

For best results organize your class early in the school year and conduct your class work according to parliamentary law whenever possible and practicable. This long-term contact with proper procedure will fix practices in your mind much better than a single concentrated unit can do. Deliberately introduce new types of motions after you have become familiar with the old ones; observe, increasingly, the restrictions placed upon a group by formal procedure; give everyone a chance to be chairman; be careful and accurate in your interpretation and application of all rules.

Organizing a Club

"Let's start a club!" Those are the words that usually mark the beginning of an organization. As soon as people with common interests in some activity start talking about meeting together regularly to share those interests and to expand that activity, the idea of a club is born. The first step is taken when the interested persons talk over the possibility of organizing a club and decide to call a meeting of those who are in sympathy with the idea. Word is passed around or a notice is given as to the date, time, and place of the meeting. When that time arrives, all who are interested gather and follow the official procedure which will bring their club into being.

Procedure to Follow. Usually three meetings of a group are necessary before a club is legally organized. This is what generally happens at those meetings:

First Meeting

1. Explanation of purpose of meeting by interested parties
2. Election of a temporary chairman and secretary
3. Passing of motion to organize a club
4. Appointment of a committee to draw up a constitution for approval at the next meeting
5. Discussion by the group of what should be included in that constitution
6. Fixing of time and place of next meeting by temporary chairman
7. Adjournment

Second Meeting

1. Call to order by temporary chairman and reading of minutes of first meeting by temporary secretary
2. Report of committee appointed to write a constitution. The chairman of the committee reads the whole constitution to the group and then moves its adoption.
3. Acceptance of constitution. The temporary chairman of the group restates the motion for acceptance and asks for a rereading of the constitution, one paragraph at a time. Suggestions for changes in wording or

amendments to be added should be made and voted on at this time. When the rereading has been completed, a vote is taken on accepting the *entire* constitution as changed or amended. After the constitution has been accepted, all interested persons should sign it, thus becoming charter members of the club.

4. Appointment of a nominating committee to select a roster of permanent officers for approval at next meeting
5. Fixing of the time and place of next meeting for the election of permanent officers as provided by the constitution
6. Adjournment

Third Meeting

1. Call to order and reading of minutes of last meeting
2. Report of nominating committee
3. Election and installation of permanent officers
4. Appointment of standing committees by newly elected president
5. New business
6. Adjournment

You have noticed that this general procedure calls for *three* meetings to accomplish the full organization of a club. In some cases, when a group is small, when its members desire to proceed more swiftly and informally, and when the constitution does not provide for a report of the nominating committee, the nomination of permanent officers may be made from the floor during the second meeting, and their election may be held at the same time. In other cases there may be problems of conflict that will delay quick formation of a club, and more than three meetings will be necessary. More important than the exact number of meetings is the accomplishment of the items suggested under each of the three headings above.

Writing a Constitution

A constitution is the law of the club. It is more basic, essential, and permanent than bylaws. It can be changed usually by a two-thirds vote of the club, but only after careful deliberation and after previous notice of the proposed change has been given. Therefore, wisdom dictates that you should proceed slowly and carefully in forming the original draft. The committee appointed by the chairman at the first meeting has the responsibility of writing the constitution for the club and should be ready to present it at the second meeting.

Many large and active groups, such as your student-body organization, may have bylaws attached to the constitution. Their purpose is to state the minor regulations and details which enable the provisions of the constitution to work smoothly and efficiently. It is becoming a customary practice, especially in small clubs, to make no distinction between the terms *constitution* and *bylaws*. General Henry M. Robert, whose *Robert's Rules of Order* is the most acceptable final authority in such matters, has suggested that for practical reasons bylaws alone may be considered sufficient for a small group. They contain the same general headings, but they include more working details than the constitution does, thus making a more compact and often more usable body of regulations. Consider the following regulations, which are a combination of material usually found in constitutions and bylaws. They are designed for a small group interested in debating.

Sample Constitution or Bylaws

ARTICLE I. Name and Purpose

Section 1. The name of this organization shall be the Parkhurst Debating Club.

Section 2. The purpose of this organization shall be to encourage interest and participation in interscholastic and interclass debating and to provide members with an opportunity to learn and to practice techniques of debate and of parliamentary procedure.

ARTICLE II. Membership

Section 1. Any students of Parkhurst High School who are interested in debating shall be considered members after they have signed the constitution.

Section 2. Any member who is absent from regular meetings for three consecutive times shall be dropped from the roll.

Section 3. The annual dues of all members shall be fifty cents, payable at the third meeting after joining.

ARTICLE III. Officers

Section 1. The officers of this club shall be a president, a vice-president, a secretary, and a treasurer.

Section 2. All officers shall be nominated from the floor and elected by ballot at the first meeting of each semester, and shall continue in office until the end of the semester.

Section 3. A majority of all votes cast shall be necessary to constitute an election.

Section 4. The duties of the officers shall be such as their titles imply.

Section 5. Vacancies in office may be filled by special election called by the president.

ARTICLE IV. Meetings

Section 1. Regular meetings shall be held on Wednesday of each school week.

Section 2. Ten members shall constitute a quorum.

Section 3. The order of business shall be as follows:

a. Call to order
b. Reading of the minutes
c. Reports
d. Unfinished business
e. New business
f. Adjournment

ARTICLE V. Committees

Section 1. At the time of his election the president shall appoint a parliamentarian, who shall serve as a committee of one throughout the president's term of office.

Section 2. The duties of the parliamentarian shall be such as the title implies.

Section 3. There shall be a standing program committee consisting of three members.

Section 4. The program committee shall be responsible for planning a debate once a month and shall make arrangements for its presentation to the club.

ARTICLE VI. Parliamentary Authority

Section 1. *Robert's Rules of Order,* Revised Edition, shall be the parliamentary authority of this club, subject to special rules which have been or will be adopted.

Cartoon by Franklin Folger

"Before introducing our speaker I just want to say it's very important that you do not leave during his lecture as cake and ice cream will follow."

ARTICLES VII. Amendments

Section 1. This constitution may be amended at any regular meeting of the club by a two-thirds vote, the proposed amendment having been presented in writing and read to the club at the previous meeting.

Order of Business

In most clubs and organizations the order of business will vary little from this order:

1. Call to order
2. Reading of minutes for approval, with correction if necessary
3. Unfinished business
4. Reports (Steps 3 and 4 are often reversed.)
5. New business
6. Adjournment

In most meetings the reading of communications is not a very important item of business and is usually handled at the discretion of the chairman. He might, for example, make a point of reading a communication *before* new business is in order if he thinks the group will want to take some kind of action in regard to it.

Minutes of the Meeting

Organizations keep diaries because people have faulty memories and often have different interpretations of what they heard or thought they heard at a meeting. The diary of the organization, known as the *minutes,* is a factual record of group action during the time the meeting is in session. There is no place in such a record for the secretary's opinion; fact, insofar as the secretary is able to report it, is all that goes into the minutes. More specifically, the secretary should be *sure* to include in his minutes:

1. The name of the organization, date and time of meeting, whether the meeting is regular or special, and the name of the chairman if he has not regularly presided before.
2. A record of all action taken by the group. This includes motions that have been defeated as well as those that have been passed.
3. The names of those who made the motions.
4. Statements of whether or not motions passed. Usually clubs are not interested in how many voted "Aye" or "No"; but in organizations which are serving the public and whose records are open to scrutiny by all, it is the practice to record the exact vote. It is also common practice in any organization to record *unanimous* votes in order to show group accord.
5. A brief account of reports and communications.
6. The signature of the secretary at the conclusion of the minutes, preceded by the expression "Respectfully submitted."

The secretary *may* include:

1. The names of those people who seconded motions.
2. A record of discussions, if it is the desire of the group.
3. The place of meeting. If the nature of the organization is such that meetings are held in different towns, cities, or states, the place of meeting *must* be included.
4. The name of the chairman, even though he was elected for a long term and always presides. In his absence the special chairman *should* be named.
5. The date, time, and place of the next meeting. If the committee meets regularly, this item is a *should* include, not a *may* include.

Being a good secretary isn't easy, and very few people like the job, but it's an important one and must be done well. Unless you can take notes in shorthand, you will make no attempt to write your minutes in word-for-word manner. Nor will you try to write the minutes in final form during the meeting. Take down the essential information in shortened form, being sure to get *the exact wording of all motions,* and then write the minutes in their final form just as soon after the meeting as you can.

What about You, Mr. Chairman?

Yes, Mr. Chairman, you have a difficult job, too. You're running a six-ring circus, and the acts haven't been rehearsed. You're working with people, and that means you'll run into ignorance, prejudice, emotional outbreaks, conflicts between personalities, and violations of the rules. You're the moderator, the judge, the referee, the umpire, the one responsible for the well-being of the meeting, but you are *not a dictator.* You are here to see that people accomplish group action, but not at the expense of minority and individual rights. Do you still want the chairmanship? Good! Here are some tips to help you:

1. See that a motion has been introduced before a discussion starts, for such discussion is out of order otherwise.
2. Don't let unproductive lulls come into the meeting. Ask for whatever action is necessary to carry the business forward.
3. Make a special point of knowing parliamentary law so that your decisions will not embarrass you or your group, hinder action, deal out injustice, or create problems that need never have existed. If you haven't a parliamentarian in your group for final authority in problems that may arise, bring to meetings some parliamentary-law text to which you may refer.
4. Don't let anyone speak unless you have recognized him.
5. If two members stand and ask for the floor at the same time, you may recognize either one, unless (*a*) one of them has spoken before, in which case it is better to call upon the other, or (*b*) you know they represent opposite points of view, one of which hasn't yet been presented, in which instance you should allow the unstated point of view to be expressed.
6. Recognize and tactfully stop all discussion that is not related to the motion pending.

7. *Never* be guilty of allowing a faction in the group to "railroad" a motion, even if you're in extreme sympathy with it, by failure on your part to permit full discussion of the measure or by failure to call upon members who are opposed.

8. If a situation develops in which tempers have flared and discussion is being lost in heat, you will have to take positive action. You can first try recognizing members who do not seem to be angry. If this fails, you will have to warn the assembly that it is out of order and that, unless order can be restored, you will entertain a motion to postpone action, to lay on the table, or to adjourn.

9. To the limit of your ability plan the agenda for your meetings carefully, start promptly, and encourage adjournment at a reasonable time. Long meetings tend to discourage membership as well as to cut down efficiency. Don't bring too much business before the group. Arrange for more meetings if there is a great deal of work that the *entire group* must accomplish.

10. Watch *yourself*! Don't argue, harangue, nag, lose your temper, offer opinions, except in accordance with a chairman's parliamentary responsibility, or keep the floor for yourself because you like the sound of your own voice. *Be a good umpire.*

Some Working Definitions

Main Motion. A motion designed to bring before the group a subject for consideration. Any motion that brings up business when no other motion is pending is considered a main motion. It should be clear and not loaded with several separate proposals. Only one main motion may be pending at any time. A motion that *rescinds* or *ratifies* another motion is usually classified as an *incidental main motion.*

Incidental Motion. A motion arising during the course of business and having relationship to the question immediately pending. It takes precedence over the pending motion and must be decided first. Examples: *suspension of the rules, point of order, point of information, objection to consideration of a question.*

Subsidiary Motion. A motion that may modify, delay action upon, or dispose of main (and certain other) motions. Examples: *to amend, to postpone definitely, to lay on the table.*

Privileged Motion. A motion that is not related to the motion pending, but has such importance or urgency that it demands immediate consideration. Examples: *raising a question of privilege, to take a recess, to adjourn.*

Take Precedence. If a motion takes precedence, the meaning is that it is in order for that motion to be made and considered, even though another motion is pending.

Pending. A term referring to any uncompleted action before the group. As soon as the action is disposed of, either temporarily or permanently, it is no longer pending.

Discussion. Consideration of a motion by members of an organization. Discussion cannot *precede* a motion.

Debate. Another name for discussion. *Debatable* means that a motion *may* be discussed according to parliamentary rules.

Majority. Any number more than one half. In voting the term refers to more than half the number of votes cast.

Plurality. More votes than any other candidate receives, when there are more than two candidates.

Quorum. The smallest number of members that must be present before an organization can legally do business. Usually the constitution states the number required for a quorum. If it does not, the customary number is a majority of membership. If membership is for any reason hard to determine, those present in the meeting constitute a quorum.

Enough Law to Run a Meeting

This unit contains a table showing most of the motions used in formal parliamentary procedure, their classification into types of motions, and some of their limitations. You won't need all these motions to conduct business in most organizations. In fact, you'll need only a few. Your own personal interest can take you as far in the study of parliamentary law as you like to go, but the average person has no need for many refinements. Further, unless you are dealing with parliamentary law constantly, you will forget the intricacies you have learned. What are the basic motions you should know, then, to be able to take part in your high school or community club?

What You Want to Do	*Name of Motion*
Start action	Main motion
Change proposed action	Amend
Retract action	Withdrawal of a motion
Postpone action	Lay on the table or postpone definitely
Resume action that has been postponed	Take from the table

To function fairly and efficiently, a lawmaking body must make use of parliamentary procedure. Here the New York legislature assembles at Albany.

Question procedure	Point of order
Get information	Point of information
End the meeting	Adjourn

1. *Main Motion.* As pointed out before, a main motion brings before the group a subject for consideration. Remember to keep your motion clear and on one topic. Customary procedure dictates that you say "I move that . . ." rather than "I make a motion that. . . ." A main motion must be seconded, is debatable, may be amended, and may be passed by a simple majority. Don't forget that a motion must be made *before* discussion can start.

2. *Amend.* An amendment may add to, strike from, or substitute a phrase or clause in a motion. It *must* be *related* to but *may not* be *contrary* in intent to the motion it is changing. Many motions cannot be amended; and, if you become extensively engaged in parliamentary law, you must learn which these are. It is not in order to have more than two amendments pending at once, although it is possible for a motion to have a great many amendments. Motions and their amendments must be voted upon in precisely the reverse order of their making. An amendment must be seconded, is debatable, may be amended (unless it's the second

amendment pending), and may be passed by a simple majority. Don't forget that the first amendment pertains to the motion and the second amendment to the first amendment.

3. *Withdrawal of a Motion.* If you make a motion and then decide to withdraw it before the chairman has stated it, you may do so without anyone's consent. Once the motion has been stated, however, it belongs to your organization and cannot be withdrawn without consent. If there is not unanimous consent, the chairman may ask the group to vote, or someone from the floor may move that your request be granted. A simple majority vote will permit you to withdraw your motion. A request to withdraw a motion does not require a second and is not debatable.

4. *Lay on the Table* or *Postpone Definitely.* It is quite likely that many times in your meetings you will want to give up consideration of a question before it comes to a vote. You may wish more time for study of a motion; you may need more information than is available at this time; you may feel that another matter needs immediate attention. Whatever your reason may be, your proper course is to move that the question be laid on the table. If the majority of the group feel as you do, the motion can be tabled. It requires a second and only a majority vote. Here's a word of warning, though. This motion is *not* intended as a means of suppressing debate, even though it may have that effect. Once it becomes evident that it is being used generally to stop debate, a simple majority vote is no longer sufficient; a *two-thirds* majority is now necessary.

Be sure that you understand the spirit of this motion. It is to bring about desirable delay, not to stop discussion or kill final action. No discussion is in order except that which the maker of the motion may wish to offer if he has not had the opportunity of speaking on his motion.

The fact that a motion to *lay on the table* takes precedence over other subsidiary motions makes it a strong motion.

The purpose of the motion *postpone definitely* is to postpone action on the question that is pending for a definite length of time. Action must not be postponed longer than the next regular meeting. This motion takes precedence over the three subsidiary motions below it in rank, but yields to higher subsidiary motions. The *necessity* for this motion can be debated, and the length of the postponement may be changed by amendment. A simple majority vote will pass the motion.

5. *Take from the Table.* As soon as the reason for a motion's having been tabled no longer exists, the motion may again be brought up for discussion, in the same state as when tabled, by a motion to *take from the*

table. If, after the intervention of business or at the next regular session, a motion is made to take up again the tabled motion, the rules of parliamentary law apply. For example, if a speaker has already spoken twice on the question during the session, he may not speak again. Or, if the question has been called for, a vote must be taken without further debate. This motion requires a second and a simple majority vote and is not debatable. If defeated, it may be renewed (remade) again and again, but *only* after other business has been transacted before each renewal.

6. *Point of Order.* A point of order, or *question* of order, is not a motion in the strict sense that it is moved, seconded, and voted upon. But it is a motion in its intent to bring about necessary action. Whenever you think there is a violation of parliamentary law, rise—even interrupting a speaker—and without waiting for recognition say, "Mr. Chairman, I rise to a point (question) of order." The chairman will respond by saying, "State your point of order." If your objection is valid, the chairman will uphold you by saying that your point of order is well taken and by directing the proper procedure. Sometimes the chairman asks the group to help him to make his decision, or he may ask the parliamentarian. If at least two people, one to make an appeal and one to second it, disagree with the chair's decision, an appeal may be made, and the assembly will settle the issue by a simple majority vote.

7. *Point of Information.* The parliamentary inquiry and rising to a point of information resemble raising a point of order in their form and application. The difference between them is slight and in most meetings is not recognized. The parliamentary inquiry, strictly speaking, concerns questions on procedure; the question of information is more general. They may serve young clubs and organizations well, for their purpose is to bring out information pertinent to proper procedure and group welfare. Many times you may find that you want to do something in meetings or object to something's being done, and you have no knowledge of how to proceed toward action. All you have to do is rise and say, "Mr. Chairman, I rise to a point of information," or "Mr. Chairman, I rise to a parliamentary inquiry." The chair hears your inquiry and sees that you get the information, and you can then determine your next step. This motion needs no second, is not debatable, takes no vote, and does not lead to an appeal.

8. *Adjourn.* The motion to adjourn, as it is usually applied, takes precedence over all other motions. It requires a second, is not debat-

The information in this table comes primarily from *Robert's Rules of Order,* Revised, and covers most of the motions used in parliamentary law. The mark **x** in each column at the right indicates that the heading of that column applies to the motion. The numbers in the column are explained in the footnotes.

Class and Name of Motion	Out of Order if Someone Has the Floor	Requires a Second	Debatable	May Be Amended	Simple Majority	2/3 Majority Required
1. Main motion (original)	x	x	x	x	x	
2. Subsidiary motions						
a. Lay on the table	x	x			x	
b. Previous question	x	x				x
c. Limit debate	x	x		x		x
d. Postpone definitely	x	x	x	x	x	
e. Refer to committee	x	x	x	x	x	
f. Amend	x	x	x	1	x	
g. Postpone indefinitely	x	x	x		x	
3. Privileged motions						
a. Fix time to which to adjourn	x	x	2	x	x	
b. Adjourn (if unqualified)	x	x			x	
c. Recess (unprivileged)	x	x	2	x	x	
d. Question of privilege	x	x	x	x	x	
e. Call for orders of the day					x	
4. Incidental motions						
a. Questions of order					3	
b. Questions of appeal		x	x		x	
c. Suspension of rules	x	x			4	
d. Objection to consideration of a question						5
e. Division of assembly					x	
f. Parliamentary inquiry					6	
g. Request for information					6	
h. Withdrawal of a motion	x				x	
5. Main and unclassified motions						
a. Main (incidental)						
(1) Rescind	x	x	x	x	7	
(2) Ratify	x	x	x	x	x	
b. Unclassified						
(1) Take from the table	x	x			x	
(2) Reconsider		x	8		x	

1. The first amendment to a motion may be amended but not the second, since only two amendments may be pending at once.
2. This motion may not be debated if it is made when another question is pending.
3. Usually requires no vote unless the assembly is called upon to decide whether or not there has been a violation of parliamentary law.
4. If a "standing rule," it may be suspended by simple majority; in other cases a two-thirds majority is necessary.
5. The objection must be made after the question has been introduced and before debate has started.
6. No vote need be taken.
7. See *Robert's Rules of Order,* Revised, pages 9 and 10, for exceptions.
8. Undebatable when the motion to be amended or reconsidered is undebatable.

able, cannot be amended, and may pass with a simple majority vote. This kind of motion to adjourn is classed as *unqualified.* If it has a provision or qualification, or if it would dissolve the organization because no future meeting time is set, it is no longer a *privileged* motion and is open to debate and amendment just as is any main motion.

A motion to adjourn may be made at any time except when a member is speaking or a vote is being taken. If defeated, the motion cannot again be introduced until business has intervened.

From Idea to Action

Let's suppose your organization is meeting and you have an idea which you would like to transform into group action. What are the necessary steps? In the section below is a chronological order of the steps, followed by the dialogue that might bring about the action.

STEP 1. You rise and address chairman. "Mr. Chairman."

STEP 2. Chair recognizes you. "Bob Johnson."

STEP 3. You present your motion. "I move that this club sponsor a float in the parade."

STEP 4. If no one voluntarily seconds the motion, the chair asks if there is a second. "Is there a second to that motion?"

STEP 5. Some member offers a second. "I second the motion."

STEP 6. The Chairman states the motion and the fact that it has been seconded. "It has been moved and seconded that this club sponsor a float in the parade."

STEP 7. Chairman asks for discussion (if motion is debatable) and acts as referee while discussion is carried on. "Is there any discussion of this motion?"

STEP 8. When discussion dies down, the chairman may ask if the club is ready to vote. "Are you ready for the question?"

STEP 9. Members indicate they are ready. "Question," they reply.

STEP 10. The chairman restates the motion and asks for the Aye vote. "It has been moved and seconded that this club sponsor a float in the parade. All in favor say 'Aye.' "

STEP 11 Those in favor vote. "Aye!"

STEP 12. The chair asks for the No vote. "Those opposed," or "Contrary."

STEP 13 Those opposed vote No. "No!"

STEP 14. The chairman states the results of the voting. "The motion is carried."

To present a motion for group action, rise and address the chairman—in this case "Madam Chairman"—who will give you the floor by stating your name.

The chairman doesn't always ask if the members are ready for the question; usually some member, followed by other members, calls, "Question." If the chairman is sure discussion has been adequate, he may proceed to asking for the vote. If, however, he is not sure, or if some members indicate they are dissatisfied with an early end to discussion, he should call for a *vote* to determine whether or not the majority want further discussion. Any member may at any time during discussion force a vote on the question by getting recognition and saying, "I move the previous question." This motion cannot be debated, cannot be amended, and must be passed by a *two-thirds* majority.

If the outcome of an oral vote is doubtful, any member may ask for a more specific vote by calling for a "division of the house." This motion is in order unless a new motion has been introduced, needs no second, is not debatable, and may be passed by a simple majority.

A Sample Meeting

Although the following model loses some of its force because it is shortened to save space, it will serve its main purpose—to show you procedure under parliamentary law with reference to the more common motions.

Chairman. The meeting will please come to order. [*Waits for order to prevail.*] The secretary will read the minutes of the previous meeting.

Secretary. The regular meeting of the Junior Toastmasters was called to order by the chairman at 3:15 P.M. on September 18. The minutes of the previous meeting were read and approved.

Chairman Mike Durand called upon Tamalee King for a report of the program committee. Tamalee stated that the semester's plans were nearly completed and that all members would be given mimeographed copies of the plans at the next regular meeting.

Gene Kopecky, reporting for the finance committee, suggested that, since club funds were low, a special assessment might be considered by the club.

As there was no unfinished business, the chairman called for new business. Jack Mulcahy moved that each member be assessed fifty cents to increase the club funds. The motion was seconded by Rebecca Barlow. After discussion of whether or not this amount was enough, the motion carried.

Mike Rich moved that the club ask the Student Council for permission to meet in the Council Room. Seconded by Ralph Farquharson. Discussion.

Ed Cotton moved to amend the motion to include the Girls' Club Room. Seconded by Susan Bowen. After much discussion the amendment was defeated.

The chairman then called for a vote upon the main motion, which was passed unanimously.

Bob Bryan moved that the meeting be adjourned in order that the committees might get together and work on plans for the semester. Seconded and passed. The meeting was adjourned at 4:15 P.M.

Respectfully submitted,
Christina Angle, Secretary

Chairman. Are there any corrections or additions to the minutes? [*Pause.*] If not, the minutes stand approved as read. Is there any old business to come before this group?

Darrell Dorfmeier. Mr. Chairman.

Chairman. Darrell.

Darrell. Have we had any report of the action taken by the Student Council on our request to use the Council Room for our meetings?

Chairman. No, we haven't, Darrell. I understand, unofficially, that the Council had to wait until this week's meeting before a final decision could be made. I think I should hear by tomorrow. Is there any other old business? If not, are there any committee reports ready?

Tamalee King. Mr. Chairman.

Chairman. Tamalee.

Tamalee. I'd just like to remind everyone that the mimeographed copies of the semester's programs are ready and that I'll distribute them right after the meeting.

Chairman. Thank you, Tamalee. It looks as though our club is off to a good start this year. Are there other reports? [*Pause.*] This meeting is now open for new business.

Gordon Scott. Mr. Chairman.

Chairman. Gordon.

Gordon. I move that we enter the speech contests sponsored this fall by the Kiwanis Club and the PTA.

Robert Berg. I second the motion.

Chairman. It is moved and seconded that Junior Toastmasters enter the speech contests sponsored by the Kiwanis Club and the PTA. Is there discussion?

Bill LeBlanc. Mr. Chairman.

Chairman. Bill.

Bill. I don't think I understand that motion. Does it mean that this club enters a contestant, or that everyone in the club enters, or what?

Gordon Scott. Mr. Chairman.

Chairman. Gordon.

Gordon. I admit my motion is a little vague. I had in mind, however, that we'd enter one or two representatives, unless everyone wanted to enter.

Bill LeBlanc. Mr. Chairman.

Chairman. Bill.

Bill. I move to amend the motion to read that Junior Toastmasters enter two contestants in each of the contests sponsored by the Kiwanis Club and the PTA.

Don Bunce. I second the amendment.

Chairman. It is moved and seconded that the main motion be amended to read that Junior Toastmasters enter two contestants in each of the contests sponsored by the Kiwanis Club and the PTA. Is there discussion on the amendment?

A number of the group. Question! Question!

Chairman. The question has been called for. All those in favor of the amendment say "Aye." Those opposed say "No." The "ayes" have it, and the amendment is carried. Is there discussion on the main motion as amended?

Ginny Bliss. Mr. Chairman.

Chairman. Ginny.

Ginny. These contests seem like a good idea to me, but I'd like to know more about them, so I move that Gene Kopecky be appointed to get all the information he can and bring it back to the club.

Dan Gray. Mr. Chairman, I rise to a point of order.

Chairman. State your point of order.

Dan. Ginny's motion is out of order because there's a main motion already pending, and her motion is obviously not an amendment.

Chairman. Your point of order is well taken. Ginny's motion is out of order. Is there further discussion?

Ginny Bliss. Mr. Chairman.

Chairman. Ginny.

Ginny. I still want more time to think over the action we're about to take. I feel we're not ready to vote, so I move that the motion as amended be laid on the table.

Jim Forsberg. Second.

Chairman. It is moved and seconded that the motion as amended be laid on the table. All those in favor say "Aye." Those opposed, "No." The "ayes" have it, and the motion to lay on the table is passed.

Don Way. Mr. Chairman, I rise for information.

Chairman. State your question, Don.

Don. Why didn't we get a chance to discuss Ginny Bliss's motion? Did you forget?

Chairman. According to parliamentary law the motion to lay on the table is not debatable. Once it has been seconded, the vote must be taken.

Ginny Bliss. Mr. Chairman.

Chairman. Ginny.

Ginny. I move that Gene Kopecky be appointed to get all the information possible on the two contests and bring it back to the club.

Ernie LeBlanc. I second the motion.

Chairman. It has been moved and seconded that Gene be appointed to get all the information possible on contests and bring it back to the club. Is there discussion? [*Silence.*] Are you ready for the question?

Several. Question! Question!

Chairman. All those in favor of the motion as stated say "Aye." Those opposed, "No." The "ayes" have it, and the motion is passed.

Tom Carter. Mr. Chairman.

Chairman. Tom.

Tom. I move that we appoint Mr. Keller one of our contest judges for the semester.

Diane Harris. I second the motion.

Chairman. As stated, Tom, your motion is out of order, since we have no right to appoint a faculty member to any position. If you mean "appoint" in the sense of expressing our wishes, your motion is in order. However, because Mr. Keller may take over the Radio Speech Club soon, he is likely to have activities conflicting with our meetings. Perhaps you should withdraw your motion.

Tom. Mr. Chairman.

Chairman. Tom.

Tom. I wish to withdraw my motion.

Chairman. Tom asks leave to withdraw his motion. Is there any objection? [*Pause.*] Since there is none, the motion will be withdrawn. Is there further business?

Gail Duckworth. Mr. Chairman.

Chairman. Gail.

Gail. I move that we adjourn.

Wendell Ferguson. Second the motion.

Chairman. It is moved and seconded that we adjourn. Will those in favor say "Aye"? [*Response.*] Opposed, "No"? [*No response.*] The meeting stands adjourned.

ACTIVITIES

1. Prepare to take this True-False test. Write on a sheet of paper the letters **a** to **t**, inclusive. After each letter write *T* if you believe the corresponding statement in the test is true and *F* if you believe it is false. When you have finished, check your answers by referring to the text. Do *not* write in your book.

Parliamentary-Law Test

a. Parliamentary law helps to promote justice through democratic procedure.
b. The secretary's minutes must always include the number voting for and the number voting against a motion.
c. A chairman who is afraid to argue with the group may fail in his job.
d. The motion to adjourn is not debatable.
e. A subsidiary motion is intended to bring change to a main motion.
f. A member must always be recognized by the chair before he speaks.
g. A motion that takes precedence over the motion pending must be considered first.
h. There cannot be more than two amendments to a motion.
i. Rising to a point of order is out of order if someone has the floor.
j. The order of business is usually determined by the chairman.
k. Once a meeting is in session, discussion is in order whether a motion has been made or not.
l. To lay on the table is a motion designed to delay or kill action by a minority group.
m. The maker of a motion can withdraw his motion whenever he pleases.
n. Not more than two amendments may be pending at one time.
o. An amendment may not be offered if it is contrary to the intent of the main motion.
p. Most motions require a two-thirds majority vote to pass.
q. It is possible for a motion that has been tabled during a meeting to be taken from the table during the same meeting.
r. General Robert, author of *Robert's Rules of Order,* invented parliamentary procedure.
s. A main motion is in order at any time during a meeting.
t. A call for "division of the house" will settle the doubtful issue of an oral vote.

2. Organize your class as a club and plan to hold regular meetings for the rest of the school year. Use the *three-meeting* plan presented at the beginning of this unit.
3. Go to a club in your school or community and ask some of the members how it came to be organized. Make notes on the procedure which was followed to bring the club into being and report to the class the information you receive. Compare the plan of organization with the procedures that have been stated in this unit.
4. Write a model constitution or bylaws for a speech club, following the suggestions given in this unit.
5. Procure from any school clubs already in existence, or from organizations in your town like the Rotary Club, the Women's Club, and the Parent-Teacher Association, copies of their constitutions, if they are available. Study them and compare them for their completeness, correctness, and workability. Which one seems to be the best? Are there any ideas you would like to incorporate in your own club constitution?
6. Study the following account of a meeting and discover the errors in procedure. Discuss these errors with your classmates.

Chairman. The meeting will please come to order. Does anyone have any business to bring before this group?

Tom Johnson. Mr. Chairman.

Chairman. Tom.

Tom. I make a motion that we have a debate or something in this club.

Barbara Moffet. Mr. Chairman.

Chairman. Barbara.

Barbara. I think that's a good idea, too, but it's too indefinite. I move that the motion be amended to add "on January 18."

Shelley Bernardo. I second the motion.

Chairman. It has been moved and seconded that we have a debate on January 18. Personally, I don't think we're going to have time to work up a debate as soon as that, but it's up to you.

Ann Andrews. Mr. Chairman, I agree with you. Semester exams come at that time, and I think we'll be too busy. I move that we amend the motion to add "on February 15" instead of January 18.

Steve Christensen. I second the motion.

Chairman. It is moved and seconded that we have a debate on February 15. Are you ready to vote on it?

Don Way. Mr. Chairman, I think that . . .

Chairman. Yes, Don.

Don. . . . that debates are dry. Let's face the facts. We'll never get that debate completed. Last year we tried debate, and you remember what happened. A mock trial is much more fun. I make the amendment that we substitute "mock trial" for "debate."

Steve Christensen. Second the motion.

Chairman. It has been moved and seconded that we have a mock trial on February 15. Are there any objections?

Tom Johnson. Yes, Mr. Chairman, I object. I want a debate, and since my motion is being changed so much, I withdraw it.

Chairman. Well, I guess you have that right. If there's no other business, the meeting is adjourned.

7. Study the following script, assign parts to class members, and present the material to your class in play form. It will help you to fix in mind proper parliamentary procedure. This script primarily concerns the *point of order* and *whom the chair should recognize,* and illustrates incidentally several other aspects of parliamentary law.

Chairman. The meeting will please come to order. Will the secretary read the minutes of the previous meeting?

Secretary. [*Stands and reads minutes.*]

Chairman. Are there any corrections or additions to the minutes? If not, they stand approved as read. Is there any unfinished business to come before the house?

Lawrence Cox. [*Stands.*] Mr. Chairman.

Bill Foulas. [*Remaining seated.*] Mr. Chairman, I move that the class . . .

Chairman. Point of order, Bill. The chair recognizes Lawrence for two reasons:

first, he was first to speak after rising in an orderly way, and secondly, Bill, you did not wait for recognition from the chair. Lawrence, you have the floor.

Lawrence. Thank you, Mr. Chairman. I move that this class study and practice the procedure for conducting a meeting every Wednesday.

Jeann Hafkenscheid. I second the motion.

Chairman. It is moved and seconded that this class study and practice the procedure of conducting a meeting every Wednesday. Is there any discussion?

Adrianne Carveth. [*Stands.*] Mr. Chairman.

Bill Foulas. [*Standing.*] Mr. Chairman, I think it's a great . . .

Chairman. Point of order, Bill. You *must* be recognized by the chair before speaking. A violation of a rule of procedure disqualifies you in favor of another speaker. The chair recognizes Adrianne.

Bill. I stand corrected.

Adrianne. Mr. Chairman, I think the study of the procedure of conducting a meeting on Wednesdays is a good idea, for then we'll feel more comfortable when we attend meetings. We'll know how to act.

John Banich. [*Stands.*] Mr. Chairman.

Bill Foulas. [*Standing and speaking at the same time.*] Mr. Chairman.

Chairman. Bill.

Ilonk Hafkenscheid. Mr. Chairman, I rise to a point of order.

Chairman. State your point of order.

Ilonk. Mr. Chairman, I believe you should call on John, because he hasn't asked for the floor before.

Chairman. Your point is not well taken. In case two persons stand and address the chair at the same time, the chair should recognize the person who has tried to speak before but has not yet been given the opportunity. You may speak, Bill.

Bill. Mr. Chairman, I just want to say that I like the idea and think we should pass the motion.

Chairman. Is there further discussion? [*Silence.*] All of those in favor of the motion to have study and practice of the procedure of conducting a meeting every Wednesday say "Aye." [*Ayes vote.*] Those opposed say "No." [*Silence.*] The motion is carried.

8. Work out for your own use some scripts using any or all of the following sets of motions. Include other motions if you wish, but emphasize those suggested. Use a parliamentary-law text for reference.

Set 1
a. Rise to a point of information
b. Make amendments
c. Call for a division of the house

Set 2
a. Rise to a parliamentary inquiry
b. Withdraw a motion
c. Move the previous question

Set 3
a. Lay on the table
b. Question of privilege
c. Unqualified motion to adjourn

Set 4
a. Take from the table

b. Refer to committee
c. Appeal the decision of the chair

Set 5
a. Postpone definitely
b. Suspension of rules
c. Qualified motion to adjourn

Set 6
a. Object to consideration of a question
b. Postpone indefinitely
c. Reconsider

9. Start a class meeting with a temporary chairman, a secretary, and a parliamentarian. Let all the members of the class try to introduce new motions, putting the chairman "on the spot" if possible. After a short time, change officers, repeating this process throughout the class period. At the end of the period, cast votes to determine who did the best work in each office.

10. Prepare three- to five-minute talks on the following topics:

a. What the Secretary's Minutes Should Include
b. Parliamentary Law and Justice
c. The Ideal Chairman
d. Characteristics of a Good Meeting
e. Why Parliamentary Law Is Not Just Red Tape
f. Why Some Motions Should Have More than a Simple Majority for Passage
g. Parliamentary Law Insures Democratic Action
h. What a Group Can Do about a Member Who Tries Unreasonably to Delay Action
i. The Real Purpose of the Motion to Lay on the Table
j. Unfair Use of Lay on the Table
k. The Difference between Lay on the Table and Postpone Definitely (or Indefinitely)
l. Why Debate Must Sometimes Be Limited
m. The Reasons for Some Motions Being Undebatable
n. The Function of Amendments
o. The Importance of Committees
p. Rights and Privileges of Members
q. How Proper Procedure Is Safeguarded
r. Should the Filibuster Be Outlawed?
s. Appropriate Times for Suspension of the Rules

11. In the parliamentary problems that follow you are given six choices for solution. The sixth choice, the blank space, is a solution which you think is right but which is not included in the first five choices. On a piece of paper write numbers that correspond to the numbers of the "parliamenticklers." After each, write the letter of the solution you choose. If you choose 6, be sure to write out your own solution. Because all of these problems cannot be solved on the basis of information provided in this unit, you will probably have to turn to a book on parliamentary law for help.

a. A motion is before the house. It has been discussed and there is a silence. A member arises, gains recognition, and makes a new main motion because he believes the motion before the house is inadequate. You are a member of the general body. You feel that it is time to take proper action. You should

(1) remain silent.
(2) move the previous question.
(3) rise to a point of order.
(4) ask for withdrawal of the motion.
(5) call for a division of the house.
(6)

b. A member has moved that your club revise its constitution immediately. Another member has moved to amend the motion to provide for revision next semester rather than immediately. You realize that the club is too busy to do the task now, but that next semester is too much of a delay. Your action is to

(1) object to consideration of the question.
(2) move to postpone indefinitely.
(3) rise to parliamentary inquiry.
(4) move to lay the matter on the table because there is a difference of opinion.
(5) help to kill the amendment and offer a new amendment.
(6)

c. At the last meeting of your group a motion was tabled. Now that you're in session again, you feel that discussion of that motion should be continued. You should

(1) move to reconsider the tabled motion.
(2) rise to a question of information.
(3) move the previous question.
(4) make the motion over again, using the same wording.
(5) move to ratify.
(6)

d. There has been in your club much discussion of a motion to change the name of the organization. It seems that a majority of the members want a change, but you can't be sure. You belong to the apparent minority who don't want a change. You'd like to know how many favor the change without having the motion come to vote. Your action is to

(1) raise a question of privilege.
(2) rise to a parliamentary inquiry.
(3) move to lay on the table.
(4) move to postpone indefinitely.
(5) call for a division of the assembly.
(6)

e. The longer you think about it, the more dissatisfied you are with the motion you helped to pass earlier in this meeting. It becomes increasingly obvious to you that the minority were more level-headed than the majority. You feel that a mistake has been made, and you want to rectify it. Your action is to

(1) ask for a withdrawal of the motion.
(2) move to ratify the motion.
(3) move to reconsider.
(4) call for consideration of the previous question.
(5) move to rescind the motion.
(6)

f. Your club meets at 3:30 P.M. on every other Wednesday, as provided by your constitution. Two weeks from today, however, there's a football game in the afternoon that all of you want to see, especially *you.* Changing the time for your next meeting seems the best way out. Your action is to

(1) move suspension of the rules.
(2) move to postpone definitely.
(3) rescind the rule which states the time of meeting.
(4) go to the game and let the others carry on the meeting.
(5) move for a recess.
(6)

g. The motion before the house is one that you made. The first speaker has pointed out, to your embarrassment, that the motion is in bad taste, for a reason you had overlooked. He has asked for defeat of the motion and has expressed regret that it will be part of the club's minutes. You are eager to correct your error. The action you should take is to

(1) object to consideration of the question.
(2) offer an amendment that will make the original motion sound a little better.
(3) remain silent but vote *against* your motion.
(4) move that the motion be tabled.
(5) ask leave to withdraw the motion.
(6)

h. There is a motion before the house that has been discussed and is almost ready to be voted upon. You are sure that the group is not ready to cast a vote, that more time is needed for thinking the matter over. But you don't know what action to propose to delay voting. Your best course is to

(1) ask for suspension of the rules.
(2) suggest the maker withdraw his motion.
(3) rise to a parliamentary inquiry.
(4) remain silent and wait for developments.
(5) rise to a point of order.
(6)

References:

- **Senior Manual for Group Leadership,** by O. Garfield Jones. Appleton-Century-Crofts.
- **Come to Order!** by M. W. Card and E. M. Wines. Doubleday.
- **Robert's Rules of Order,** Revised, by H. M. Robert. Scott, Foresman.
- **Handbook of Parliamentary Procedure,** by H. A. Davidson. Ronald.
- **Parliamentary Law for the Layman,** by J. F. O'Brien. Harper.
- **Sturgis' Standard Code of Parliamentary Procedure,** by A. F. Sturgis, McGraw-Hill.

Films:

- **Parliamentary Procedure** (Coronet). 11 min color or b&w.
- **Parliamentary Procedures in Action** (Coronet). 13 min color or b&w.
- **Conducting a Meeting** (MH). 12 min b&w.
- **Mr. Chairman (The Fundamentals of Parliamentary Law)** (EBF). 13 min color or b&w.

Filmstrip:

- **How to Conduct a Meeting Using Parliamentary Procedures** (Basic). 59 fr color.

55

Unit Nineteen

PROGRAMS: Planning and Execution

Good programs don't just happen. They are the result of planning, teamwork, and a great deal of effort. A fifty-minute assembly program, for instance, might take ten, twenty, or even more hours of preparation and still might not be successful if it hadn't been created with imagination and ingenuity. Let's consider, then, some of the basic elements of successful programing.

What Makes a Good Program?

Definite Purpose. A good program should have a purpose, a goal, a reason for being put on. Is it to entertain? Is it to instruct? Is it to impress? Is it to convince? Is it to show student talent? There may be an intercrossing of purposes in a program, but one *main* goal should be clear to the program director, the participants, and the audience.

Worthwhile Theme. Most programs are built upon some central idea, theme, or motif. Sometimes the theme is determined by commemorative holidays, such as Veterans Day, Thanksgiving, Christmas, Lincoln's Birthday, Washington's Birthday, Easter, and Memorial Day, or other occasions of local or national significance. Sometimes the central theme is determined by the group before whom the program is to be presented. For instance, the Parent-Teacher Association may request a student program on "How Our High School Teaches Democracy"; the Rotary Club may want to hear a sports roundup entitled "This Year's Athletic Accomplishments"; a church group may be interested in "What Do Young People of Today Believe?" Sometimes a motif is selected to highlight the spirit of an occasion like a class reunion, a club luncheon, or an end-of-the-year banquet. The theme is like a thread on which the items of the program are strung; it has to have meaning and interest for the audience, it should be appropriate to the occasion, and it should be stimulating to the participants.

Audience Appeal. Audience response is the test of a program's success. If the audience understands the purpose of the program, is interested in the theme, appreciates the efforts of the performers, and is generally pleased with the results, it will express its good feeling in generous applause. Make it easy, then, for the audience to understand and follow the program. Try for a fresh, original, imaginative approach. Use material which is stimulating, informative, pleasing, and varied in interest. Employ a variety of talent and enliven the program, if it is appropriate to do so, with music, skits, films, tapes, or novelty numbers. Make use of a variety of such speaking activities as choral reading, recitations, dramatic sketches, informal debates, interviews, or discussions. If a program must be limited to speeches alone, encourage the speakers to make liberal use of illustrations, incidents, personal references, stories, and humor to enliven their talks. All these things tend to give variety and animation to a program and will help the audience to enjoy it.

Careful Planning. Good programs are the result of careful planning by cooperative committees under responsible leadership. If your class were asked to put on a program, how would you proceed? Here's a general plan:

1. Discuss the purpose, analyze the audience, select a theme, and decide on the overall plan, or format, of the program.

2. Discuss possible segments, such as speeches, skits, music, films, or novelty numbers and set a time limit on each segment.

3. Divide into groups, each group being responsible for working out the details for one segment of the program and for writing or selecting a suitable script.

4. Present the scripts of each segments of the program for class discussion and approval.

5. After revision and correction of scripts, select the performers, appoint necessary committees to work out production details, and set up a rehearsal schedule.

6. Rehearse individual segments of the program as much as necessary.

7. Keep a sharp eye on timing both during rehearsals and at final presentation.

You can modify this plan or adapt it to any kind of program you want to produce. Just remember that good planning and cooperative effort are important for success.

Good Leadership. The personality and ability of the master of ceremonies, the chairman, or the leader often determines the effectiveness of a program. He carries a great burden: he establishes the mood for the occasion, he makes appropriate opening remarks, he introduces the various participants, he draws the program to a successful close. He should be a good speaker, quick-witted, alert, and reliable. His duties will vary with different situations, but always he's the ringmaster, the man in charge.

Cooperative, Able Participants. When all is said and done, a program is only as good as the people who take part in it. You'll want to select the best talent you can, of course. But there should also be room in all programs for those people whose ability has not yet fully developed, but whose willingness to work and desire to participate should be encouraged. Since we all learn by doing, programs planned by high school students should provide an opportunity for as many students as possible to express themselves and develop confidence before groups. Whenever you're in a program, do your best willingly and cooperatively.

Assembly Programs

Assembly programs that entertain, inform, or inspire can be a vital part of the school curriculum. They are a real part of your school life and can offer you valuable opportunities for educational experiences that are not otherwise provided in the school program.

General Form for Assemblies

Formal Opening	• Sets tone of assembly, creates unity, and stresses fundamentals in the American way of life • May include flag salute, patriotic songs and music, school creed, inspirational reading • Often followed by school announcements
Introduction of MC	• Marks beginning of main body of program

Hobbies can provide the subject for a varied assembly program.

The Program	• Surveys reveal student preferences for programs to be entertainment, student talent, music, dramatics, and films. The program should be planned with this fact in mind.
Formal Closing	• Rounds off assembly and serves as ceremonious conclusion • May be handled by MC, student officers, or principal • May include music, songs, words of acknowledgment and thanks, announcements, and formal dismissal

Program Material for Assemblies Is Where You Find It. You can find material in all phases of student life both in class and out, among faculty members, in community groups and organizations, or even in "package deals" which can be bought from reputable sources. Keep your eyes open for talent, let your imagination take wing, and you'll be able to put together an assembly program with something of interest for everyone.

Some Ideas for Assembly Programs

Science in Action	an informative program of talks, interviews, skits, demonstrations, and films
Hobbies	a program which brings to light interesting, unusual, or profitable student and faculty hobbies

College Days	music, talks, skits, readings, debates, interviews, and films stressing the values of college education
Speech Festival	a sampling of the varied activities of the speech, drama, debate, interpretation, and radio-TV classes
Liars Unlimited	a storytelling contest varied with skits about famous characters and authors of tall tales
The World Today	a documentary of significant events affecting young people
Campus Capers	a variety program revealing hidden talent among students
What's My Secret?	a panel program similar to *What's My Line?* involving school personalities
Class-Day Revue	a year's-end review of the outstanding, interesting, or humorous happenings of the school year

Club Programs

Most clubs and organizations today set aside a specific time in the agenda of their meetings for a program of some kind. This program usually follows the regular business meeting, generally aims at informing, stimulating, or entertaining the members, and very often centers upon some sort of speech activity. The format varies from club to club, depending upon the aim of the organization and the interests and needs of the members. But the basic elements of good programs, suggested earlier in this unit, still apply.

Format. If you are on the program committee, try to avoid falling into the stereotyped pattern just of finding a speaker to fill the time. Speeches generally serve a good purpose because they are an obvious, simple means of bringing information, giving entertainment, injecting controversy, or stimulating the thinking of club members. However, unless their standards are very high and the personalities of the speakers are outstanding, a repetitious diet of nothing but talks, talks, talks can dull the interest of club members and may have unhappy effects on the attendance figures. Be inventive and creative, therefore, in planning a program. Add interest and variety by trying speaking activities other than the straight speech. Many such activities have been presented in this book, as the following example shows:

Speaking Activities Suitable for Club Programs

Purposeful talks (Unit 13)	After-dinner speaking (Unit 19)
Impromptu speaking (Unit 14)	Debating (Unit 20)

Book reviews (Unit 14)
Contest speaking (Unit 14)
Sociodramas (Unit 15)
Panel discussions (Unit 17)
Forums or symposiums (Unit 17)
Interpretative reading (Unit 21)
Choral speaking (Unit 21)
Plays, skits, pantomimes (Unit 22)
Radio interviews (Unit 23)
Documentaries (Unit 23)

Planning. You may find the following general suggestions useful when you are planning a club program:

- If a specific theme or definite subject matter has been requested by the officers or membership of the club, you should conform to their wishes and fill the request to the best of your ability.
- If the choice of theme, subject matter, or talent is left up to you, look for material which is fresh, varied, and different, yet close to the vital interests of the club. Something that offers both stimulation and relaxation is a happy combination for most groups.
- Lay your plans well in advance.
- Check all details relating to the physical set-up and the necessary props, such as tables, microphones, screens, projectors, and tape recorders.
- Insist on the performers' keeping within the time limit set for them.
- Have an ace-in-the-hole alternate plan or idea in mind in case your planned program is delayed, canceled, or changed.

Dinner Programs

In many schools a formal banquet or an informal dinner program is a traditional social event which highlights the year's activities of some groups of students. It may be a junior class get-together; the football team may have a dinner meeting at the end of its season; the Latin club may plan a Roman feast; the drama group may want a dinner party; the shop boys may give a supper for their fathers; the scholarship society may have an end-of-the-year banquet; there may be a reunion at commencement time. All these occasions require a program of after-dinner speeches and entertainment. Here is what you should consider:

The Occasion. A dinner, supper, or banquet is a *social* occasion. That means that there is more informality, friendliness, relaxation, entertainment, and fun than there is at the club meetings or school assemblies. It is an occasion for displaying good humor and enjoying good fellowship. It is a time for wit, banter, and repartee between toastmaster and speaker. It is a time for reminiscences, congratulations, complimentary references, personal anecdotes, and stories. It is also a time for good taste. The primary purpose of an after-dinner program is entertainment; there is no place for showing off, endless wisecracking, or indiscreet remarks.

The Program. A dinner program should reflect the friendly, familiar, lighthearted spirit of the occasion; yet it should have a serious note tucked in it somewhere. The program usually consists of speeches and toasts, perhaps interspersed with music, skits based on the evening's theme, novelty acts, or other brief forms of entertainment, and it may be presented during or after dinner.

The Toastmaster. The toastmaster is the chairman, or master of ceremonies. He must be "tops." His job is to foster the spirit of good fellowship, engage in skillful repartee, be alert to reactions from the audience, keep the tempo of the program active, introduce the participants with clever and appropriate remarks, and see that the whole affair runs smoothly. He should be quick-witted, tactful, humorous, and well poised. The toastmaster's task requires much personality and skill. Often the success of the entire program depends on him alone.

After-Dinner Speeches. These speeches are given for the main purpose of adding to the joviality and fun of the evening. They belong in a class by themselves and require more originality, versatility, good taste, and good humor than almost any other type of speech. The following generalizations apply:

1. May be informative, impressive, or inspiring, but should be primarily entertaining
2. Should have interesting material, well planned and prepared
3. Will be enlivened by stories, anecdotes, quotations, puns, witty remarks, and humorous local and personal references
4. Should fit the occasion
5. Should reflect a genial mood
6. Should emphasize good feeling, goodwill, and pleasant associations
7. May include spontaneous, impromptu thoughts
8. May seem rambling and undirected; yet should have a basic theme and should put across a definite point
9. Should be brief

The Toast. A toast is a very brief tribute to a person, a group of people, a cause, or a sentiment. The tradition of the toast is said to have been originated by ancient Celtic singers and storytellers at feasts, as they drank wine or ale in which floated pieces of toast. If the giving of a few toasts is to be included in your dinner program, be sure that the speakers proposing them do so briefly and in the correct manner.

A variation of the "after-dinner" program is the introduction of speakers and entertainment at the beginning of, and during, the dinner.

The Speakers. Most people want to be entertained during dinner programs; therefore, after-dinner speakers are usually expected to provide enjoyment for their listeners and to be amusing, charming, convivial, and clever. Unless a dinner program is specifically planned to be serious and thoughtful, the speakers who have the ability to entertain an audience in a lighthearted way will win the most favor. Remember, however, that humor should not be forced on an audience, that at its best it grows naturally out of a situation, and that when it is mixed with a touch of the serious, it can bring a program down to earth and can be an inspiring reminder of the good feeling and earnestness that lie behind the festive mood. The speaker who can combine successfully the humorous with the serious and who is able to entertain his listeners by his good-humored manner and his clever treatment of material is skillful indeed; he will be much in demand as an after-dinner speaker.

Radio and TV Programs

Radio and TV programs are different from the kinds you have been considering so far in this unit. They are more like productions than simple programs. They reach a larger audience in a less personal way. They function under a strict pressure of time, moving at a faster rate. They require direction and technical assistance. They are often dependent upon a script or restricted in the amount of the material that can be covered. In planning them you must take into consideration all these factors that set them apart from assembly, club, or dinner programs.

If you are able to produce a radio or TV program in either your school or your community, you should follow the *general* principles of planning and production that have been presented in this unit. The *particular* skills and practices which are associated with these media are presented in Units 23 and 24. Turn to the appropriate unit, if you are planning a broadcast, for suggestions and instruction that will help you in your task.

ACTIVITIES

1. Discuss in class suitable themes and possible programs for **(a)** a welcome assembly for freshmen at the beginning of the school year, **(b)** a school spirit or "pep" assembly, **(c)** an exchange assembly with a neighboring school, **(d)** a program publicizing the speech activities in your school.
2. Plan an hour's student-talent show following these suggestions: choose a theme, add an MC or two, get five or six main acts, work in four or five short between-act features, end with an entire cast finale, and tie the whole program together with good musical selections.
3. Discuss in class program ideas suitable to present to **(a)** a school hobby club, **(b)** a town service club on Washington's Birthday, **(c)** the monthly PTA meeting at your school, **(d)** a language club.
4. Plan a thirty-minute program with a patriotic or educational theme and present it to some adult organization in your community. Consider the following titles:

   America: A Land, a People, a Way of Life
   Our School: Its History and Achievements
   What Education Means to Us
   Democracy in Action in Our School
   Safety Is Everybody's Business
   Speech Is for Everyone

5. Prepare a program for Visitors' Day (or Open House) in which you explain and demonstrate the work being done in your speech class. Here is a sample which you might find helpful in working out the format of your own program:

MC:	Welcome remarks and introduction of the segments of the program
Speaker:	"Why We Study Speech"
Panel discussion:	"An Explanation and Evaluation of Our Speech Course"
Oral reading:	Suitable selection of poetry or prose
A ten-minute debate:	"The Most Important Issue of the Day"

Demonstration:	Recording the Voice
Skit:	A parody on speech—"Before and After Taking This Course"
MC:	Concluding remarks

6. Plan an informative program for a simulated broadcast in your classroom, using a documentary format similar to the example you'll find at the end of Unit 23. Plan to have an announcer, a narrator, and several participants, who dramatize the information you want to put across in a series of key scenes that are connected by the comments of the narrator. Here are some possible topics for you to explore:

Teen-Agers and Fads	What about Driving?
Choosing a Vocation	Grades: How Important Are They?
The Pressures We Face	Dating
Should Girls Pay Their Own Way?	Teen-Age Drinking
Early Marriage	What Do We Want from Our Parents?
Homework	Student Dropouts
What Is School Spirit?	Are Athletes Given Too Much Recognition?

You may prefer to present these topics by means of the interview or the panel discussion method.

7. Plan a dinner program for your class or club, using one of the following themes or motifs:

Song Titles	A Musical Show	Down on the Farm	TV Westerns
A Circus	Dogs	Transportation	A Carnival Sideshow
Book Titles	Newspapers	School Spirit	Jazz
Travels	Outer Space	Mardi Gras	The Zoo

8. Give a three-minute humorous talk on one of the following topics as if you were an after-dinner speaker at a banquet:

Horseshoes	Dieting	Baby-sitting
Twenty Years from Now	Stagestruck	Laughter
Cheerfulness	Lies	A Fish Story
The Next Step	Nicknames	The Weather
Talkers	Spotlights	Comedians
Bare Feet	Slang	Hometowns
Courage	Women's Hats	Examinations
Space Travel	Chatter	String

General Program Sources:

U. S. Office of Education, Washington, D.C.—lending service of scripts, plays, skits, and pageants for school programs.

National Education Association, 1201 Sixteenth St., N.W., Washington, D.C.—materials and suggestions for all types of educational programs.

Children's Book Council, 175 Fifth Ave., New York, N.Y.—suggestions and material useful for planning programs about books, reading, and libraries.

Pan American Union, Washington, D.C.—folders of materials for use on Pan American and Columbus Day.

National Conference of Christians and Jews, 43 West 57th St., New York, N.Y.—bibliography of material for junior and senior high school assemblies.

School Activities, School Activities Publishing Co., 1041 New Hampshire St., Lawrence, Kansas—a magazine of suggestions for all student activities including assemblies, $4.50 per year.

Plays, Inc., 8 Arlington St., Boston 16, Massachusetts—book collection of plays, skits, group readings, recitations, etc., suitable for classroom or assembly programs. Also publishers of *Plays, The Drama Magazine for Young People,* $6.00 per year.

National Recreation Association, 8 West 8th St., New York 11, N.Y.—suggestions for adult service organizations.

National Council of Teachers of English, 508 South 6 St., Champaign, Illinois.

Senior Scholastic Magazine, 50 West 44th St., New York 36, N.Y.

Wetmore Declamation Bureau, 1631 South Paxton St., Sioux City, Iowa.

Expression Publishing Co., Magnolia, Massachusetts—catalog of choral speaking material.

Film:

Developing Imagination (Coronet). 11 min color or b&w.

Unit Twenty

DEBATING: The Clash of Opinion

Americans like debating. Perhaps we like it because it appeals to our sense of fair play, for both sides have an opportunity to be heard. We tend to think that an idea is like a defendant in a jury trial. He may be guilty, but he has a right to a good defense and a thorough presentation of his case. Perhaps we like debating because we have confidence that a jury or an audience or the voters will make a good decision if both sides of the question are presented clearly. Perhaps it is that we are constantly discussing and arguing the merits of everything from foreign policy to baseball strategy, and a debate seems like a familiar experience. Whatever the reasons, we have based our elections, our legal machinery, and even our economic system on the belief that the people can be trusted to make the most important decisions after hearing both sides of an issue ably presented. In totalitarian countries debating is just an interesting intellectual exercise. For us, debating is a part of our heritage.

Historically, American interest in free debate stems from the days of the Revolution. Matters of public concern, then as now, were argued vigorously by people everywhere, in legislative bodies, town meetings, political rallies, private clubs, even in the taverns and around the cracker barrels of the country stores. Free speech is one of our incontestable rights, one of the cornerstones of democratic life. To encourage free discussion, to promote intelligent argument, to foster fair debate, therefore, is a responsibility every American should share. Any student of speech should have a particular awareness of the importance of sound argument and fair debate in these times, when the settlement of national and international differences of opinion is of such great consequence to all of us.

The word *debate* is often loosely used. Originally it meant "to engage in strife and combat." Now it may mean any oral controversy. It may be an informal dispute between individuals who examine some question and consider the arguments on both sides; it may be an open argument before the public between two opponents; it may be a formal, highly regulated discussion of a given proposition between two matched teams as a test of their forensic ability; or it may be simply an argument in your own mind over some decision you must make. Most of us debate about something almost every day. You're debating when you're deciding whether to wear your brown slacks and sport jacket or your blue suit to the school dance Saturday night. You're debating when you're trying to decide whether to go to a small college or to a large one. You're debating when you get into any argument that has opposing sides. For instance, look at the following questions. You could begin an argument on any one of them.

1. Should public speaking be a required course in high school?
2. Which is better for college-preparatory students, the study of Latin or of a modern language?
3. Should more students be encouraged to go to college?
4. Is war inevitable?
5. Should capital punishment be abolished?
6. Should all automobile owners be compelled to carry liability insurance?
7. Should all national resources except agriculture be owned by the government?
8. Is corporal punishment justifiable?
9. Have labor unions gained too much power in the United States?
10. Should we have a system of complete medical care provided by the Federal government?

Debate or Discuss?

You may notice that all these questions can be answered "Yes" or "No." But a problem which you cannot frame easily into a simple question is likely to be more suitable for discussion than for debate. Discussion seeks to explore a problem area and perhaps find one or more solutions. If your discussion comes down to one solution or two clearly defined alternatives, you are ready to debate the solution or alternatives. Sometimes, although you are not sure what the best solution is or whether there is more than one solution needed, it may be helpful to assume that there is only one solution and to debate it in the hope that the debate will help the audience to understand the problem better. So, when you discuss, you are usually looking for the right questions as well as for their answers. When you debate, you assume that you know the answer and try both to convince others of its validity and to improve your own understanding of the problem in the process.

When you can argue convincingly and forcefully on questions like those above, you will have grown up, mentally, more than you may realize. Debating disciplines the mind. It is a difficult speech activity to master, but once mastered it can serve you well. Under ideal conditions it develops qualities in you that make for good citizenship and good leadership, interest in public affairs and current problems, the ability to see questions from two sides, recognition of the importance of forceful statements backed by proof, thoroughness in analyzing problems, clear thinking, the ability to express opinions with confidence and force, and appreciation of the rights of others. Lawyers, judges, members of legislative bodies, members of policy-making committees, governmental officers, labor leaders, and industrial managers all find that a knowledge of debating technique is always useful. You may never engage in formal debates for a living, but you need to understand what makes an argument strong or weak. The skills you learn in this stimulating activity will be useful not only in a speech class but can be applied also to any situation in which choices must be made and alternatives argued.

General Principles of Debating

Whether you plan an informal debate in which two people present two sides of a question as effectively as they can and without set rules, or whether you wish to prepare for a formal team debate following the traditional rules that have been developed over the years, you need to understand the basic principles of all argumentation and debate. If you do not, your debate will be a haphazard and vague sort of activity which will leave you and your audience dissatisfied. Let us suppose that you are planning a debate as a classroom activity. Here is an outline of what you will find in this section—the general procedures, basic to all debating, with which you should become familiar:

I. Getting started.
  A. Choose a topic.
  B. Choose a side.
II. Preparing your case.

A. Decide the issues.
B. Understand the nature of proof.
C. Find the evidence.
D. Use sound reasoning.
E. Organize your case.

III. Debating effectively.
A. Use good delivery.
B. Refute opposing arguments.
C. Win listeners' favorable response.

Getting Started

Choose a Topic. Before you can begin your preparation of a debate, you must select a question which is debatable, and you must choose one side of the argument.

The most obvious requirement for a debate question is that it must be debatable, but the obvious is often overlooked. A debate needs a single, clear, and specific question on which there is a conflict or basic clash of opinion. Generally, the more specific and concrete the issue is, the better debate topic it is. For example, you can't easily debate automobiles in general, but you can argue with your father about the necessity of your using the family car tonight, a specific proposal. You can't very well debate about voting in general, but you can argue that the power of the veto as it now exists in the United Nations should be changed, a definite change from the present system. You can't debate the value of Latin in general, but you can argue that one year of Latin should be compulsory for college-preparatory students. As these examples show, a general topic must be narrowed to a question which clearly shows a conflict in opinion and which can be debated.

A good question for debating should have two equal sides so that each side has a fair chance to prove its arguments; it should be centered in only one main idea so that only one debate is possible, not two or three; it should be clearly and simply worded so that no confusion arises over terms; and it should be so stated that the affirmative advocates some change and assumes the burden of the proof, leaving the negative in a defensive position. The way a question should be worded for a formal debate will be discussed in more detail later. For an informal debate it may be stated either in a simple declarative sentence or in question form.

In addition to being debatable, a question should be interesting, timely, and important. We live in the present and look to the future. Questions which deal with current problems, affecting as they do both our immediate

The 1858 debates between Stephen A. Douglas and Abraham Lincoln, then candidates for the United States Senate from Illinois, made Lincoln a nationally known figure.

and future welfare, are best for debate. At the time of the Lincoln-Douglas debates, slavery was a hot issue. Today, subjects like arms control, automation, civil rights, foreign policy, and changes in the American educational system could be worded as topics which lend themselves to spirited debate. Questions for debate, in order to be acceptable, then, should have a basic clash of opinion on a definite proposal, two equal sides, clear and simple wording, and present-day interest. In addition, debaters should try to agree beforehand on the meaning of the words in the question. For example, does "college-preparatory students" mean those planning to attend junior college, too?

Choose a Side. Every debate question has two sides, pro and con, also called affirmative and negative. You should decide which you will defend. In other words, will you support the proposition or oppose it? Before you decide, consider:

- How much do you know about the subject? Do you need some preliminary thinking and reading before you take a stand?
- Might your convictions change with more information?
- Should your choice of a particular side be determined by the opportunity to express your personal convictions? to strengthen a personal bias? to broaden your understanding of the question? to give the audience a balanced view of the question?
- Should you defend what looks like an unpopular or difficult side to assure that it is given the best possible presentation, or should you choose the easier and more popular side?

Let your good sense and conscience be your guides in answering the questions above. Nothing is quite so effective as the enthusiasm of a speaker who is convinced that he has framed a strong argument with strong proof to support him. So do some preliminary research on the topic to see what arguments are available. Talking and reading about a topic will help you to make up your mind about taking sides in a debate.

Of course, every debater should recognize the wholeness of an argument and see the two sides of a question, both pro and con. If you are in contest debating, you may be obligated to present *both* sides of a question, alternating from one side to the other as you progress from round to round at a forensic meet. However, in informal classroom debating you will, for practical reasons, probably present only one side.

If your topic is merely a question of preference or opinion—such as "Are compact American or foreign cars the best buy?"—the debate will be a relatively simple matter of advancing as many reasons for your choice as possible and answering the reasons of the other side. But if your topic proposes a definite, concrete change from the present practice, then your audience will expect that each side meet certain responsibilities:

1. *The affirmative, or pro, should*

   a. State the topic and give the background of the problem.
   b. Clarify any words in the topic that might cause confusion.
   c. Prove that there is an unsolved problem to be dealt with.
   d. Explain the affirmative plan for coping with the problem.
   e. Show that the affirmative plan will be the most beneficial, practical, and desirable.

The affirmative has a difficult task, the assumption of what is usually called the *burden of proof*. This term means that the affirmative must show that a problem exists and that its solution is the best one. On the other hand, the negative has the responsibility of *clash,* which means that the negative must meet each of the affirmative arguments head on instead of simply speaking against the affirmative position in general. Usually several courses are open to the negative.

2. *The negative, or con, should*

   a. Prove that no serious problem really exists, or
   b. Prove that the problem has been exaggerated by the affirmative, and that the extreme solution of the affirmative is therefore unnecessary.
   c. Prove that the affirmative solution neglects, ignores, or mistakes the real cause of the problem.
   d. Admit that there is a real problem but show that the affirmative solution is unworkable, too costly, and would do more harm than good.
   e. Offer another solution, called a counterplan, and make the debate a choice between the two solutions to the problem.

The negative may rely on several of these attacks, since a combination is often the most effective.

No matter which side of the debate you take, you must be prepared to do two things: build up and tear down. You build up your own case and tear down that of the opposition.

Remember, getting started in a debate is a matter of careful choice of a debate question and of a side to support.

ACTIVITIES

1. Read the following topics for debate, decide which are debatable, and explain your answer in each case.
   a. Lincoln was a greater President than Washington.
   b. Interscholastic high school football should be abolished.
   c. A nuclear war is inevitable.
   d. All citizens should have full civil rights.
   e. Our Congress should restrict immigration.
   f. The planet Mars is not inhabited.
   g. The pen is mightier than the sword.
   h. Everyone benefits from athletics.
   i. There are too many commercials on television.
   j. Voting should be compulsory.

2. Bring to class three topics. The first should concern current events; the second, a school problem; the third, a topic of local interest. Discuss these in class and select one for a practice debate. Word it so that it has a good clash of opinion, is timely and interesting, has a clear definition of terms, but doesn't cover too much ground.

3. Examine the following topics for debate and choose two. Be prepared to tell what the affirmative would be expected to prove and what the negative would be expected to prove.

   a. Typing should be a required course in high school.
   b. The world is becoming more civilized.
   c. Television programing should be censored by the government.
   d. Peace Corps volunteers should be exempt from the draft.
   e. English should be an elective high school course.
   f. High schools should be small.
   g. All school dances should be free.
   h. Students on athletic teams should be excused from gym.
   i. Our plan of student-body government should be reorganized.
   j. The sales tax should be abolished.
   k. This school should have a detention room for disciplining students.

4. Which words in the above topics need clarification or definition to prevent confusion? Define the words in the two topics you selected.

5. After you have clarified any ambiguous terms for one of the above, have an informal class argument about it. Are you well informed? Does the class seem evenly divided?

6. After the informal argument in class, construct a chart showing the best arguments "pro" and the best "con."

Preparing Your Case

After you have begun by choosing a topic and the side you wish to support, you need to

A. DECIDE THE ISSUES
B. UNDERSTAND THE NATURE OF PROOF
C. FIND THE EVIDENCE
D. USE SOUND REASONING
E. ORGANIZE YOUR CASE

You may find yourself doing all of these tasks throughout your time of preparation, often several at the same time, and not necessarily in the order above. For example, you cannot really determine the issues until you have found some evidence and thought about the total organization of your case. But unless you make a tentative decision as to the issues now, your preparation will be haphazard and inefficient.

SAMPLE CHART #1

TOPIC: One year of public speaking should be required of every student in high school.	
AFFIRMATIVE ARGUMENT	**NEGATIVE ARGUMENT**
FIRST ISSUE: Do all students need more speech training than they are getting?	
1. Yes. a. There is an increased need in both the business and social world for oral skill in the use of language. b. Too few students take our present elective courses.	*1. No.* a. The demand is not for everyone to have these skills, just for more to have them. b. All students who want or need training in speech may elect to take it.
SECOND ISSUE: Would all students benefit from a required speech course?	
2. Yes. a. The speech of all students would be improved in high school. b. Students would benefit from speech training in later life.	*2. No.* a. Some might be harmed by a course to which they are unsuited. b. One year's study of speech would have little lasting effect.
THIRD ISSUE: Would a required course in speech be practical?	
3. Yes. a. The program could be taken in place of third-year English. b. Third-year English could become an elective for students who want or need it for college preparation.	*3. No.* a. The curriculum is already overcrowded with required courses. b. Third-year English and all presently required courses are needed by all students.
FOURTH ISSUE: Is a required course in speech the only way to meet the problem?	
4. Yes. a. Half measures have not worked in the past. b. Only in a required speech course can students all achieve a general improvement in speech.	*4. No.* a. The elective program has been successful. b. More speech training could be introduced in present English classes.

SAMPLE CHART #2

TOPIC: Should capital punishment be replaced by life imprisonment without parole?	
AFFIRMATIVE ARGUMENT	**NEGATIVE ARGUMENT**
FIRST ISSUE: Is capital punishment morally wrong?	
1. Yes. a. Killing should be permitted only as a means of self-defense. b. The value of life is cheapened by capital punishment.	*1. No.* a. The people inflict the death penalty in self-defense against the most desperate criminals. b. The criminal has forfeited his right to life, and taking his life protects the life of others.
SECOND ISSUE: Is capital punishment effective as a deterrent to crime?	
2. No. a. Only a small percentage of murderers are actually executed. b. Juries are often unwilling to convict if they know the required punishment is death. c. The poor, the undereducated, the underprivileged are more likely to be executed than those who can afford an expensive defense.	*2. Yes.* a. Capital punishment protects the innocent victims of would-be murderers since the murderer fears capital punishment. b. Courts and juries decide each case on its merits, but even one execution deters the would-be murderer. c. Adequate defense is guaranteed to all under the Constitution.
THIRD ISSUE: Will life imprisonment without parole be as effective as capital punishment in preventing future crimes?	
3. Yes. a. Most condemned criminals never imagined that the death penalty would be applied to them. b. States without the death penalty often report fewer murders than states using capital punishment.	*3. No.* a. Many criminals regard imprisonment as a light punishment compared to death. b. Some states have returned to capital punishment after a trial of other punishments; other states not using capital punishment are less populous and have lower crime rates generally.
FOURTH ISSUE: Is life imprisonment without parole a practical punishment?	
4. Yes. a. It is used by many states. b. Crimes committed in prison could be punished by hard labor or solitary confinement.	*4. No.* a. A change in the law or officials might result in the prisoner's release, perhaps to murder again. b. The only effective deterrent to killing a guard or other inmate is the threat of the death penalty.

Decide the Issues. The issues are the main points on which the whole debate hinges. They are the bones of the skeleton to which the flesh clings. You find them by listing the main beliefs of *both* sides, asking yourself, What are the strongest, most sensible points I can bring up to win my argument? What are the strongest points of my opponent? When you have them listed, check them against each other, keeping only those to which the affirmative can answer a positive "Yes" and the negative a definite "No." You should have two, three, or four big issues on which there seems to be no compromise. These are the points on which there is the most violent clash of opinion. The charts on the previous pages illustrate the clash of opinion and argument on issues.

Often the issues can be discovered by answering questions such as these:

1. What is the real problem the topic is concerned with? What caused it?

2. Is the problem being solved by present methods? If not, why not? Can the present methods be improved without a drastic change?

3. Will the proposed solution really solve the problem? Is the solution directed at the real cause of the problem or just at the symptoms?

4. Is the proposed solution beneficial? practical? expensive?

5. What harmful result might the solution cause? Will it do more harm than good?

6. Will the solution result in too much expense, government control, complicated enforcement, or restriction of individual freedom and initiative?

7. Are there other solutions which would be more effective and/or less harmful?

Finding the issues on which a debate depends is not easy. It takes much reading and thinking to pick out those major points upon which disagreement exists. You can't invent issues or arguments; they must grow out of the essential differences that exist between the two sides of the question.

Don't depend only on what you *think* or *feel* is right. You may be biased or may lack information about a topic. You cannot analyze a question or proposition without first gathering knowledge. Therefore, to understand the essential clash of the debate, do plenty of reading and research covering both sides of the question.

After you've read widely, covering both sides, the best thing to do is to look at the question from two points of view: yours and your opponent's. First, pick out those arguments or contentions which your reading and common sense tell you must be considered in order to convince a reasonable person that your side is right. Then, put yourself in your opponent's shoes, look at the question from his side, and pick out the points he must establish in order to convince a listener. Balance his points against yours. Those in direct conflict will be the main issues upon which the debate rests and which you must support or attack with plenty of proof.

Understand the Nature of Proof. When reading the issues and unsupported arguments on the sample charts, you will notice that each side is making statements which the other contradicts. You may want to ask of each side, "How do you know?" or to say, "Prove it." Like most people, you are not satisfied by personal opinions of the debaters, statements without proof, and clever phrases. You realize that no contention can stand up without some kind of proof; so you need to understand what proof is and where you can find it for your arguments.

PROOF = EVIDENCE + REASONING

Properly speaking, proof consists of evidence plus reasoning from that evidence. Proof is like a wagon wheel. There is a hub (the main point you want to make); there are spokes (the evidence you want to present); there is a rim (reasoning) which holds the spokes together. Without a hub (main point), the wheel has no central point to attach it to your whole case. Without spokes (evidence), the wheel has no strength and will collapse under a load. Without a rim (reasoning), the spokes are not connected and the wheel will not perform its function of rolling.

Let's assume that your analysis of the issues reveals a main point you should prove. Your next step is to find evidence.

Find the Evidence. Research is necessary for two reasons: first, to find the evidence, and second, to get a deeper understanding of the whole topic so that you know what additional evidence you need. As you learn more, you may find it necessary to change your ideas about the issues and even the meaning of the topic itself. Don't let this discourage you; you are growing in your understanding of the topic. But now you need to look more closely at the spokes of the wheel of argument—the evidence, the material you need to support your arguments.

1. *Where to Find Evidence*

   a. Read current newspapers, magazines, and books.

   b. Listen to television and radio programs, commentaries, discussions, documentaries, and news programs. Talk to adults and other students about the topic.

   c. Research the topic in your school or public library. This is a must!

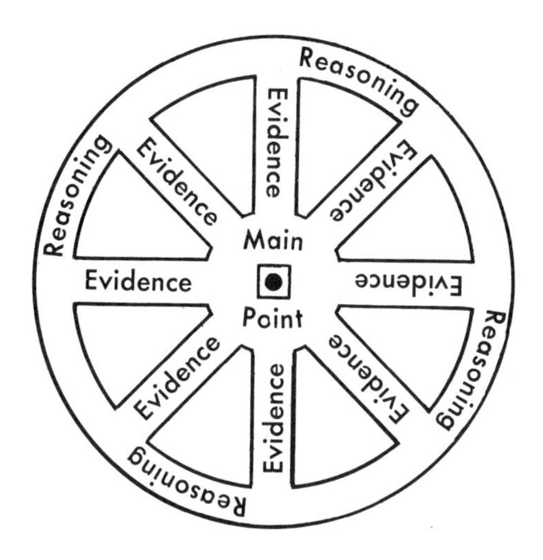

2. *How to Find Evidence*

   a. *Review* "Where Can I Find It?" in Unit 9.

   b. *Check the card catalog of books and the* Readers' Guide to Periodical Literature *for magazine articles.* Look up your subject under several headings. For example, material on "Medicare" might be found under "National Health Insurance," "Socialized Medicine," "Welfare," "Hospitals," "Insurance," "Social Security," "King-Anderson Bill."

   c. *Consult standard reference works* such as encyclopedias, yearbooks, almanacs, and textbooks on your topic.

   d. *Read pamphlets* distributed by government agencies, corporations, foundations, universities, and private associations.

3. *Kinds of Evidence*—Facts, Examples, Statistics, and Quotations

   a. *Facts* are actualities or statements of actuality. You cannot deny established historical facts, but you can offer opposing facts, and you can dispute the interpretation and meaning of the facts.

   b. *Examples* consist of particular instances, cases, illustrations, comparisons, situations, conditions, or occurrences which help the listener to understand and accept a statement. You must be sure to have typical examples and enough of them to demonstrate your point.

   c. *Statistics* are figures based on facts. They are powerful if they are extensive, up-to-date, and reliable. You must learn to use them effectively. These rules may help you:

(1) *Use round figures.* It's better to say "nearly six million" than to say "5,987,612."

(2) *Summarize the meaning.* Most people won't remember the numbers very long, but they will remember the point if you stress the meaning of the numbers.

(3) *Tie the meaning* of the statistics to your main point. Be sure that the relationship between the statistics and your main point is clear.

(4) *Be brief.* A few reliable and typical statistics well explained and presented are more effective than dozens that confuse and bore the audience.

(5) *Make it visual.* Use charts, diagrams, or effective gestures to assist the audience to see the relationship and meaning of the numbers.

d. Quotations are evidence if they are:

(1) *An authority's opinion.* An authority is one whose job is to know about your subject and who has a reputation for accuracy and sound judgment.

(2) *A complete and accurate quote.* Don't "short quote" by omitting a portion of the statement that does not support your stand. Your opponent might supply the missing portion.

(3) *An unprejudiced opinion.* Avoid authorities who have a personal stake in the problem.

(4) *A support for your argument,* not a substitute for your argument.

4. *Tests of Evidence.* Evidence can be challenged. While you are learning to convince others by means of facts, examples, statistics, and quotations, you should learn to test your evidence and the evidence of your opponent. The character and source of evidence can be tested by applying the following questions to a bit of evidence:

a. Character

Is the evidence honest? Is it a typical example?

Is it consistent with known facts and common experience?

Is it contradictory to what the speaker has already said?

Is it pertinent? Does it apply to this argument?

b. Source

Is the source of the evidence definitely stated?

Is it reliable? Are the authorities sincere, unprejudiced, and capable?

Is it recent?
Is it acceptable to the audience?

c. Timeliness

Is the evidence up-to-date and relevant to the present situation?
Is timeliness an important factor in the argument?

5. *Evidence Cards.* Since you cannot carry in your mind all the material you need to prepare a debate, keep your evidence on filing cards, a separate card for each item. Cards can be filed, rearranged, and found quickly. The usual way is to head each card with the major issue it applies to, list its source completely, and state the evidence fully. Use quotation marks if you quote directly because later it will be hard for you to remember whether you quoted or summarized the material. Here's an example on the subject of National Health Insurance;

> **NEED** met by private insurance.
>
> "We already have a nongovernmental pattern of medical insurance—two-thirds of the American population is now covered by surgical and hospital insurance issued by nonprofit organizations such as Blue Cross or Blue Shield or by private insurance companies."
>
> from "Is the Welfare State Obsolete?" by Irving Kristol in *Harper's Magazine,* June, 1963, p. 42

Now that you know where to find evidence, how to find it, the kinds of evidence, the tests for good evidence, and the use of evidence cards, don't forget that the more evidence you can find, the better. You need at least three times as much as you expect to use. You need it not only to construct your arguments but also to meet the arguments of the other side.

Use Sound Reasoning. The most crucial part of the wheel of proof is the rim—reasoning. Fundamentally, reasoning is the process of discovering and explaining relationships. In a debate, reasoning or logic is the interpreting of evidence (the relating of the evidence and its meaning), the relating of one piece of evidence to another, the systematic reaching of a conclusion from the evidence, or the relating of one conclusion to another conclusion. You have been reasoning since you first began to answer such questions as "Why?" and "How?" When you explain why something happened, you are reasoning because you are relating cause and effect. When you point out the similarity between two happenings, you are reasoning because you are explaining their relationship. When you write an outline of debates or a history chapter, you are reasoning because you are showing the relationships between facts, events, causes, and trends.

Since reasoning is such a useful and common activity, we might expect that there are rules to follow which will make our reasoning accurate and efficient. There are such rules, but few people consciously apply them. They are usually satisfied to say that a statement or an argument makes sense or that it doesn't. But for centuries philosophers and psychologists have studied reasoning, have classified its types, and have pointed out some obvious examples of crooked thinking. Studying these types and the fallacies or errors in reasoning will not guarantee you sound reasoning, but it will help you to recognize crooked thinking when you meet it (or use it) and to understand what went wrong in the reasoning process.

1. *Kinds of Reasoning*

a. Generalizations are conclusions drawn from similarities in a group of facts. For example, each automobile accident is a fact. If you examine the accident reports of several agencies such as the police department, National Safety Council, automobile clubs, and insurance companies and find that more serious injuries were suffered by persons not wearing seat belts than by persons wearing them and involved in similar accidents, you can generalize that the wearing of seat belts appears to reduce the chances of serious injury in an automobile accident. You have generalized from many facts to reach one conclusion.

Generalizations are only as valid as the facts they are based upon. To check your generalizations, ask:

Are there *enough* facts to justify the conclusion?
Are the facts *typical*?
Is the conclusion *contradicted* by other known facts?

b. Analogies are conclusions based on comparisons. When objects, facts, systems, or ideas are shown to be essentially similar, you may argue that they are alike in other ways, too. For instance, you can argue that since your neighboring high school has a successful and active debating club, your own high school, which is similar in size, student interests, teaching personnel, and community support, can succeed with a debating club, too. Test the strength of analogies by asking this question:

Are the two cases alike in essential points?

c. Cause-and-effect relationships are useful in a debate. Here are three kinds:

(1) Effect to cause. You observe a certain known event or effect and seek to determine its cause. For example, you note the increasing rate of unemployment among the unskilled (effect) and you attribute it to automation of industry (cause).

(2) Cause to effect. You begin by describing a known or proposed event and then show that it will produce a certain effect. For instance, you argue that a decrease in defense spending (cause) will result in a business slump (effect).

(3) Effect to effect. From one effect you predict another effect. When you say that a falling barometer means a storm tonight, what you really mean is that the falling barometer (one effect) is caused by a change in atmospheric pressure (a known but unexpressed cause) which will also produce a storm (another effect).

In all cause-and-effect relationships, errors can occur when you fail to link the correct cause with the correct effect or when you overlook the probability that most effects have several causes and that conditions surrounding one cause-and-effect sequence may change with the passing of time.

d. *Deductive* or syllogistic reasoning is reasoning from the general principle to the particular example. You start with a general law you know to be true or a generalization you have proved and draw a conclusion about a particular case. Thus, if you know that all grown rattlesnakes are rather thick-bodied and large-headed and have rattles at the end of their tails, you can conclude that the snake you saw in the woods last summer, which conformed to this description, was a rattler.

The basis of this type of reasoning is the syllogism, a form of argument consisting of a general law, a particular truth related to the general law, and a useful conclusion that results. For instance:

General law (major premise): All citizens of the United States are guaranteed equal protection of the laws under the Constitution.
Particular truth (minor premise): I am a citizen of the United States.
Conclusion: Therefore, I am guaranteed equal protection of the laws under the Constitution.

You will notice that the first term in the major premise is a general class (citizens) under which the second term of the minor premise (a citizen) belongs. This gives the two premises a common meeting point and leads to a conclusion. It's like saying in a mathematical proof,

$$\begin{aligned} \text{If } & A = B \\ \text{and } & C = A \\ \text{then } & C = B \end{aligned}$$

A syllogism is valid only when both major and minor premises are proved true, when the minor premise contains a specific example of the general law of the major premise, when there is no basic change in the meaning of the common term from one premise to the other, and when the conclusion is justified by the premises given.

2. *Fallacies in Reasoning.* Fallacies are errors in reasoning. If you imagine logical reasoning to be like a straight road, leading from what the audience accepts to what you wish to prove, a fallacy is like a wrong turn in the road. Fallacies are usually caused by stating a relationship that doesn't exist. Here are some typical kinds of fallacies:

a. *Hasty generalizations* are fallacies based on too few or too limited examples. Consider this generalization: "I went fishing three times in the Rogue River and didn't have any luck. It's not a good river to fish in." The error of this conclusion lies in the fact that the fisherman has not considered weather, season, types of fishlines, or even his own skill in fishing as factors in his failure. The most that he can conclude from his examples is that *his* luck at fishing in the Rogue River has not been good. He does not have sufficient information to prove a more general conclusion about fishing at the Rogue River in general.

b. *False analogies* result from overlooking essential differences in the two things being compared. Examine this analogy: "Williamson Trade School and Thomas Proctor College Preparatory School are both educational institutions. They both have the same size faculties; both offer English and history; both engage in sports; both have good reputations. Therefore, a student would receive the same education at either school." The analogy is false because one essential difference has been ignored: their curriculum. One is a trade school, the other a college-preparatory school.

c. *Ignoring the question* is the fallacy of sidestepping the basic argument or real issues. It may be easier to attack the character, motives, or ability of your opponent, but it is poor debating. For instance, Stephen Douglas tried to cloud the issue in his debates with Lincoln by belittling Lincoln's political motives, by sarcastically attacking his early background, and by hinting that Lincoln's opposition to the Mexican War was unpatriotic. Lincoln disposed of these "little follies" of Douglas by refuting them effectively and bringing the argument back to the main issue, slavery.

d. *Irrelevant conclusions* result when you violate the rules of logic and common sense and arrive at a conclusion that does not necessarily follow the evidence or premises of your argument. What is wrong with this syllogism? "Citizens are guaranteed equal protection of the law by the Constitution. I am a citizen. Therefore I always receive equal protection." The fallacy is that being guaranteed equal protection by the Constitution does not necessarily mean I *will* always receive it. It merely means I *ought* to receive it.

e. *Begging the question* is assuming the truth or falsity of what you are proving before or while you are proving it. Sometimes the simple choice of words can beg the question. For instance, the statement "The present dominance of athletics is bad for our school" begs the question. The word *dominance* assumes both that athletics do dominate, which is unproved, and that this is bad, since *dominance* has a harmful ring to it.

Organize Your Case. After you have discovered your main points or arguments by deciding the issues, have gathered your evidence, and have checked your reasoning which ties them together, it is time to look at your whole case. Whether or not you plan to use notes while delivering your debate, you should get your case organized on paper in some way. Use the method that suits your topic, your teacher's instructions, or your personal preference.

1. *Evidence cards* can be shuffled into the proper order in which you plan to to use them. Numbering them in this order will prevent a mix-up.
2. *An outline* of your case will give you an overall view if it includes:

   a. Topic wording.
   b. Meaning of confusing terms.
   c. Issues and your stand on each.
   d. Proof for each stand.
   e. Evidence cards attached or indicated by number where they fit in the case.

3. *A brief*, as used in a formal debate, reveals the full case. It is a complete and extensive outline, written in sentence form, in which every bit of argument and evidence on either side of a given question is compiled in a tightly arranged, step-by-step, logical order.

If you have decided to have a team debate with at least two on a side, you must arrange with your partner how you will divide the case. Indicate this in your plan. As a final check, look at your plan as objectively as possible and, posing as a listener, ask yourself:

a. Would I understand this case?
b. Would I judge that the real issues are met?
c. Would I think that the evidence was sufficient?
d. Would I be convinced by this case?

ACTIVITIES

1. Find the main issues in any two of the following debatable propositions:

a. Young people under eighteen should be forbidden to drive cars.
b. Our school should plan immediate purchase of closed-circuit television.
c. Our town should establish and support a community theater.
d. Every member of this school should be required to pay annual dues of five dollars.
e. This school should establish a form of student government.

2. Choose for debate any topic already listed in this unit and write down answers to the following questions:

a. With what problem is the topic concerned?

b. Is the present way of meeting the problem satisfactory? Why?

c. If not, what seems to be the best solution?

d. Is that solution necessary? desirable? workable? better than any other?

3. Bring to class some evidence—facts, examples, statistics, and questions—to support one of the following statements. Test the strength of the evidence by answering the questions under the heading "Tests of Evidence."

a. The American Indian has been unjustly treated.

b. Automation has thoroughly changed the nature of labor and management problems.

c. American missiles are the best insurance against another war.

d. Excessive buying on credit is dangerous to our national economy.

e. Because capital punishment does not deter crime, it should be abolished.

f. Unemployment is related to lack of education.

4. Look in some newspapers for an argumentative editorial or in a magazine for an article which uses evidence to prove the point. Bring it to class and read it to the class. Test the character and source of the evidence used.

5. Complete the following syllogisms:

A

Lawbreakers should be punished.

Jim Davis in violating the state speed limit of 50 miles per hour became a lawbreaker.

Therefore, . . .

B

To be a good fisherman requires skill and patience.

Sid Graves is a good fisherman.

Therefore, . . .

6. Bring to class three syllogisms of your own and test their validity in class.

7. Discover the error in each of these syllogisms:

A

All soldiers are brave.
Ted Beckett is a soldier.
Therefore, Ted Beckett is brave.

B

Cleveland High defeated Jefferson High 14—7.
Lincoln High defeated Cleveland 6—0.
Therefore, Lincoln will defeat Jefferson in next Saturday's game.

C

All sports are beneficial to health.
Tom Gaines is out for football, a major sport.
Therefore, Tom's health will be benefited by his playing football.

D

All the students in our school take gym.
Bonnie takes gym.
Therefore, Bonnie goes to our school.

E

All the tomatoes raised in Magic Valley were blighted this year.
The Johnsons raised tomatoes in Magic Valley this year.
Therefore, people will stop raising tomatoes in Magic Valley.

8. Bring to class a series of related facts. What generalizations can be drawn from them? What hasty generalizations should be avoided?

9. Find the generalizations that can be derived from this statement of fact:

"The building of a community recreation center in our town is supported by . . ."

The Parent-Teacher Association	The school trustees
The City Council	The churches
The Mayor	The parochial schools
The Civic League	The Y.M.C.A.
The Chamber of Commerce	The Boy Scouts
The Rotary Club	The Women's City Club

10. Bring to class an example of each of the three types of causal relationship, **(a)** cause to effect, **(b)** effect to cause, **(c)** effect to effect, and show how each is a sound argument.

11. Detect the fallacies in the following arguments:

a. Military training should be compulsory for young men because they need the discipline which it imposes.

b. Juvenile delinquency has increased because our national divorce rate has increased.

c. Anyone who is able to speak can succeed in debating.

d. Final examinations are fair tests of student knowledge.

e. Wars have never settled anything in the past, so they cannot be expected to settle anything in the future.

f. We can't grow tomatoes on our farm because our crop has been destroyed by blight for three years in succession.

g. All men are created equal; therefore, women cannot be considered the equal of men.

h. Those houses certainly look alike on the outside. They must have the same inside floor plans, too.

i. All poorly organized programs that are detrimental to the welfare of the people should be abolished.

j. Yesterday when I was walking in the woods I saw four quail. The woods must be full of them.

k. A big dog bit a girl over on the other side of town yesterday. Today a child down our block was bitten, too. It was probably the same dog.

Debating Effectively

With a well-prepared debate case you are ready to engage in the debate. But, before you begin, remember that your audience is composed of people, not computers, to analyze the logic of your arguments. The purpose of your debate is both to convince your listeners and to demonstrate your skill in the presentation of arguments. Your presentation must be far more effective than a simple reading of your notes, outline, or brief. How?

A. USE GOOD DELIVERY.
B. REFUTE OPPOSING ARGUMENTS.
C. WIN LISTENERS' FAVORABLE RESPONSE.

Use Good Delivery. All the principles of good speaking apply to a debate. Poise, posture, and freedom of movement will add greatly to your appearance before the audience. A pleasing, vigorous voice and clear, distinct enunciation will ensure audibility. Good English usage, adequate vocabulary, and correct pronunciation will make your language more effective. More specifically,

1. *Open your speech* by addressing your audience in some way. The method depends upon custom, ranging from simply "Hello" to "Mr. Chairman and Ladies and Gentlemen." Your teacher can tell you what is customary in your area.
2. *Speak extemporaneously* if you can. A memorized speech lacks flexibility and probably will not clash directly with your opponent's arguments. Memorized delivery makes you sound like a walking tape recorder. Argue from your readings. Don't read your arguments.
3. *Speak forcefully* but not belligerently.
4. *Be courteous* to your opponent. Sarcasm, personal remarks, and debating your opponent instead of the arguments are bad debating and bad manners.
5. *Watch your time limit* and don't overstep it.

Refute Opposing Arguments. The two words that are used to define the process of answering an opposing argument are *refutation* and *rebuttal.* They both mean essentially the same thing, the contradicting by evidence and argument of an opponent's main points. Logical contradiction of what someone says, whatever form the argument may take, is *refutation.* The term *rebuttal* appears most often in formal debate as a name for the two- to five-minute period each debater has following the presentation of all the formal arguments. Certainly you will make no mistake in using the terms interchangeably.

A good way to prepare a refutation is to anticipate and list all opposing arguments that occur to you. By reading, talking, and thinking you try to determine the best proof your opponent can advance, and then on the

basis of apparent or possible weakness in his proof you build your defensive case, your counterattack. This defense should be included in your own case.

An effective way to include refutation in the body of your argument is as follows:

1. State clearly and fairly the argument you anticipate or are meeting.
2. Show why it seems important to the case of your opponent.
3. Contradict it, using facts, examples, statistics, quotations, *and* argument.
4. Summarize the contradiction, pointing out that your argument is stronger than that of your opponent.
5. Indicate how you have undermined not only your opponent's argument but his whole case as well.

Of course you must be sure that you are dealing with *major* points, not minor ones, and that your reasoning doesn't leave you open to attack in return. Thoughtless preparation on your part can lead to embarrassing situations. It is very uncomfortable to be pinned down by your opponent with an argument that you haven't thought of at all, one which you can't answer, or one that you can answer only feebly.

Finally, here are some direct and effective expressions to use in exposing weakness in the other person's argument, *if* you can follow your statements with reliable evidence and reasoning.

1. The proof is insufficient.
2. The argument is inconsistent.
3. The statements are false and misleading.
4. The authority is unreliable and prejudiced.
5. The reasoning is not sound.
6. The statement is contradicted by other acknowledged authorities.
7. The argument sidesteps the main issue.

Win Listeners' Favorable Response. Before you are ready to present your ideas in a debate, you must put your speech to one final test. What appeal will win a favorable response from your listeners? Often logic and reasoning are not sufficient to win your cause for you. Woodrow Wilson said, "We talk a great deal about being governed by mind, by intellect, by intelligence in this boastful day of ours, but as a matter of fact, I don't believe one man in a thousand is governed by his mind."

Facts and sound reasoning will get a sympathetic reception when they are supported by constructive emotional appeal. It will pay you well to analyze in advance the feelings of the audience or the person whom you are anxious to convince. For example, an appeal to our love of justice and fair play is especially strong in an argument. During the violence of the Civil War when Henry Ward Beecher went to England to win support for the cause of the North, he was faced at Liverpool with a howling, threatening audience in an ugly mood. This is how he began:

> It is a matter of very little consequence to me, personally, whether I speak here tonight or not. But one thing is very certain; if you do permit me to speak here tonight, you will hear very plain talking. You will not find me to be a man that dared speak about Great Britain three thousand miles off, and then is afraid to speak to Great Britain when he stands on her shores. And if I do not mistake the tone and temper of Englishmen, they would rather have a man who opposes them in a manly way than a sneak that agrees with them in an unmanly way. Now, if I can carry you with me by sound convictions, I shall be immensely glad; but if I cannot carry you with me by facts and sound arguments, I do not wish you to go with me at all; and all that I ask is simply fair play.

Notice how Beecher stated that he wanted to carry his audience with him by facts and sound arguments alone. Yet he appealed to his listeners' sense of fair play and justice to win their favorable response. This is an excellent example of a speaker's understanding of the motives which influence human actions.

There are many other fundamental urges or drives. It is enough that you recognize their existence and realize that they have much to do with people's beliefs and actions. What you do with that knowledge depends upon your own ability to analyze your listeners and to weave into the fabric of your speech such appealing arguments as will touch the character of your particular audience.

A few important *Don't's* are in order here:

Don't appeal to passions, prejudices, intolerances, or base emotions.

Don't attach a mere appeal to the conclusion of your talk and think you are being convincing. It must be part of the whole talk.

Don't be too dramatic, too oratorical in delivering an argument. Simplicity, sincerity, and honesty are more appealing.

Don't antagonize your audience by confusing them. Tell what you are trying to prove. Use examples to clarify as well as prove your point. Summarize often, emphasizing the relation of one point to another.

REVIEW OF GENERAL PRINCIPLES OF DEBATE

1. Be sure the question is debatable.
2. Know the meaning of the question and understand the problem involved.
3. See that the issues are clear and important.
4. Pick a side after studying the topic and the duties of each side.
5. Have a variety and abundance of evidence; test it for character and source.
6. Understand the principles of sound reasoning.
7. Learn to recognize fallacies.
8. Prepare material for refutation and rebuttal.
9. Know how to make a strong, clear appeal.

ACTIVITIES

1. Listen to a TV debate or discussion. How did the participants' delivery hurt or harm their position?

2. Find some evidence to refute each of the following statements:

- **a.** Much of the increase in juvenile delinquency is directly attributable to the influence of television on young people.
- **b.** Under socialized medicine the individual would have no choice of doctors.
- **c.** Students who dislike high school should be encouraged to give up formal education and go to work.
- **d.** The influence of religion on the lives of young people today has declined alarmingly.

3. Study the affirmative issues of one of the two topics outlined on the Sample Charts No. 1 and No. 2 in this unit; that is, either "Capital Punishment" or "Required Public Speaking." Assemble all the proof you can find for issues stated there. Write your proof on separate evidence cards, organize the cards, and then prepare an outline of your case.

4. Refute by means of evidence and reasoning each of the four affirmative issues for which you have established a case in the preceding activity above. In presenting your refutation orally,

- **(1)** State the issue you're attacking.
- **(2)** Present your refutation, using facts, statistics, examples, testimony, etc.
- **(3)** Argue the significance and importance of your evidence.
- **(4)** Summarize your refutation and then go on to the next issue.

5. Choose a side on the topic you have selected for a practice debate (see "Getting Started," Activity 2). With a classmate for a partner, prepare a case, following the procedures described in this section.

Informal Debating

As a speech activity, debating is usually divided into general types: informal and formal. The difference between the two lies mainly in the form of organization, the manner of presentation, and the amount of preparation. Informal debating is not so tied to set rules as is formal debating. For this reason it is freer, more flexible, and fits into our normal lives better than contest debating, inasmuch as we argue informally far more than we debate formally. Yet, because the rules and requirements of formal debating are more exacting and definite, many students find it a stimulating way to learn the basic principles of persuasive speech and sound argument. There is a place for both types in most schools.

The airing of *two* sides of a question by two or more persons without set rules of organization and delivery and without the necessity of a decision as to the merits of one side over the other is what we shall call informal debating. An argument in your English class as to whether Shakespearean plays should be studied, a dispute in the gym over whether this year's basketball team is better than last year's, a discussion in a club meeting before a question comes to a vote—these are informal situations in which there may be a real give-and-take argument over certain issues. Many a discussion which is started with the purpose of viewing a problem from several sides concludes as a spirited informal debate.

A speech made in an informal debate is much like any other convincing or persuasive speech. The speaker simply presents the best arguments he has in his most convincing manner. A speaker who has learned to meet silent objections in the minds of his audience and to be clear and convincing through the use of good examples will have little trouble in an informal debate. If you follow the steps in the "General Principles of Debate" and apply what you already know about speeches which convince and persuade, you'll probably be able to hold your own in any informal debate.

Things to Remember:

1. *Be convincing* by using energetic delivery, by presenting evidence as well as opinion, and by appealing to both the mind and the emotions of your audience.

The give-and-take of informal debate can enliven a friendly conversation.

2. *Be organized* with a logical plan of what you intend to prove.

3. *Be specific* by using a variety of types of evidence—facts, examples, statistics, quotations, a variety of reasoning—generalizations, analogies, causal relationships, and a variety of human-interest material—stories, anecdotes, personal references, illustrations, and appropriate humor.

ACTIVITIES

1. Support or deny one of the following contentions in a three-minute talk. Use logical arguments and as much evidence as you can find. Be prepared to defend your stand by answering any questions or objections raised by the class.

- **a.** Poetry is greatly overrated as a form of literature.
- **b.** College admission should be based on entrance examinations only.
- **c.** Television westerns are a desirable form of entertainment.
- **d.** Our parents should give us more freedom.
- **e.** Present fashions for women are an improvement over those of the past.
- **f.** Most Americans live shallow lives.
- **g.** Our athletic program in school is well balanced.

2. Form three of these general topics into specific questions suitable for informal class debate. Then, by tryout, choose speakers to present the two sides of each question, the speeches to be followed by general discussion by the class.

Television Advertising	Soil Conservation	Student Government
Disarmament	Professional Athletics	Labor Laws

3. Listen to a television or radio debate and report to the class what you heard. What was the topic? How were the speeches presented? Who was the most effective speaker and why? How were the principles of debating applied?

4. Prepare an informal debate on any topic listed in this chapter. Be sure that another student is willing to take the other side. Present five-minute speeches followed by a short rebuttal period.

Formal Debating

Sometimes called contest, traditional, or interscholastic debating, formal debating differs from informal debating in that it requires more rules, teamwork, and preparation. More emphasis is placed on the skill of the debater in presenting one side of a debatable question than on the merits of that side or the convictions of the debater. Formal debates usually involve decisions by judges in the audience, decisions based on which team did the better debating, not on which is the "right" side. A formal debate team may debate the same or a similar topic several times on a round-robin basis or at debate tournaments with opponents from other schools. Some areas have local and statewide debate leagues. In fact, in many high schools debating is as much a school activity as is football or track.

If you have studied carefully the steps under "General Principles of Debate," you are almost ready to prepare for formal debate. But formal debate has some special procedures you must understand first. Some of what follows should sound familiar to you, as the basic principles of debate are the same; but, before you engage in a formal debate, learn to:

Choose a Formal Debate Question.
Choose a Team and Opponents.
Analyze the Question.
Plan a Case.
Gather Material.
Write a Debate Brief.
Argue Effectively Within the Rules.
Evaluate the Debate.
Understand Debate Terminology.

Choose a Formal Debate Question. Like any good debate topic, a formal debate question must be debatable, of current interest, definite, and clear. In addition, a formal debate question becomes a proposition which must be stated affirmatively in a simple declarative sentence as a resolution. For example, the proposition is not a question, "Should the government provide medical care?" but rather, "*Resolved,* That the Federal Government establish a system of free medical care for all."

Formal debating usually calls for two opposing teams of two members each.

A formal debate question should also call for a definite change from the present system or status quo. For example, "There are too many small nations in the United Nations" fails because no change is called for. "*Resolved,* That United Nations membership be limited to nations of ten million persons or more" would be better. In other words, a formal debate question calls for a stand on a policy change, not an opinion of the present or past.

The wording of a formal debate question should avoid words such as *more substantially strengthen, significantly increase,* and *greater.* Such terms only invite disputes as to their meaning.

The topic may be the National High School Debate Question formulated by the National University Extension Association's Committee on Discussion and Debate in cooperation with state and national high school debate leagues. Using this topic enables debaters from different schools, towns, and even states to prepare the same problem area so that they can debate each other on short notice. Throughout a school year, contest debaters will often debate various wordings of resolutions having to do with the same topic. Since these topics are concerned with complex social, political, and economic problems which require extensive research and analysis, it would not be practical to use an entirely different topic for perhaps twenty separate debates during the year or for four separate debates in one day at a tournament. Another advantage is that publishers and interested groups often prepare editions of material on these topics.

So, before you begin your preparation, be sure that you have the exact wording of the topic to be used in the debate. Even a one-word difference may change the entire direction of the debate.

Choose a Team and Opponents. Competitive debates usually consist of two teams of two debaters each. In some schools each debate team is expected to prepare both sides of the question, while in others each team declares for the affirmative or negative side only. Usually the assigning of debate partners will be done by the debate coach, who will be guided by his knowledge of the debaters and their abilities, temperaments, and probable balance as a team. Student preference may be considered, as it is necessary that team members work well together; but friendship is not the only requirement for a debate team. Many schools have tryouts at which students present five- or ten-minute talks on any phase of the question. The speakers are ranked by a judge, and the coach uses these rankings to match speakers of similar or complementary abilities.

For a debate within your school your opposing team may be assigned by your coach, selected by tryout, or chosen by you and your teammate. For an interscholastic debate the opponents will be selected by their coach. At a debate tournament the officials will pair the teams on a random basis usually for one or more preliminary rounds of debate. After that, eliminations take place until the naming of a winning team or teams.

The main thing to keep in mind in making up debate teams is to get the sides as evenly matched as possible. This balance will insure a lively clash of opinion, a fair chance of winning for both sides, and better teamwork. Teamwork is of as great importance in contest debating as it is in any group sport. Students must work together unselfishly for the benefit of their team; therefore, much of the success that comes to a winning debate team hinges upon the selection of the team.

Analyze the Question. The analysis of a proposition is like a doctor's examination of a patient before an operation. The doctor must know what's wrong and where it hurts before he can use a scalpel. So must you as a debater. You must study carefully the question for debate so that you know just what it means and where the strengths and weaknesses of your case lie. Here are the most important things to do:

1. *Know the Background.* A bird's-eye view of a question will help both teams to realize the significance and importance of what they are

debating. You can't argue intelligently about something you don't understand. Therefore, be sure to know

a. The origin of the question,
b. Its historical development, and
c. Its present significance.

The first affirmative speaker has the duty of presenting this material during the debate, but all members of both teams should understand the background of the problem in order to debate its causes and solutions.

2. *Define the Terms.* The first affirmative speaker is expected to define the terms of the resolution at the beginning of the debate. Without clear and accepted definitions, debaters may waste time arguing the meaning of the resolution rather than the issues. Complete prior agreement by both teams as to the meaning of the terms is helpful; but, when this is not possible, fair definitions that don't attempt to duck the issues or change the obvious intention of the resolution will usually prevent disagreement on the terms.

Several words may be combined to form one term. For example, on the topic "The Federal Government should control all public utilities" the terms which should be defined are:

"Federal Government"—Which agency or department or commission is involved?
"Should"—Will? Ought to? Must?
"Control"—Regulate? Operate? Own? Manage? Supervise? How? To what Extent?
"All"—Every company? Most of them? The major ones? Who will decide which ones will be controlled?
"Public Utilities"—What major kinds? What exceptions? Who will decide? What makes them utilities? What makes them public?

Do not use dictionary definitions *only.* Construct definitions that are specific and that fit the problem you are debating. After a precise definition of terms by the affirmative, the general position that the affirmative will defend and the direction that the debate will take should be clear. The meaning of the terms must be definite if the debate is to be definite. Vague definitions produce vague debates.

Occasionally an affirmative team will propose definitions that are not only unusual but also obviously an unfair interpretation which slants the topic away from the real issues. The negative team should call this to the attention of the audience in a brief statement explaining the situation. Then the negative team should go on meeting the affirmative arguments as well as they can, occasionally reminding the audience of the disagreement, particularly in the final summary. If the definition was "obviously unfair," it should be obvious to the judges, too.

Above all, do not argue the meaning of the terms to avoid meeting the real issues or to smoke-screen your lack of evidence. A sense of fair play and some time given to constructing good definitions is the best insurance for a worthwhile debate free of bickering over the terms.

3. *Determine the Issues.* The procedure for selecting issues was discussed previously under "Decide the Issues." Also consider these points:

a. Exclude all issues on which both sides agree or which are irrelevant.
b. Frankly admit contentions that are obviously true.
c. In many simple debates you can set up ready-made issues by answering the following questions:

(1) Is the plan necessary?
(2) Is it beneficial?
(3) Is it practical?
(4) Is it the best possible solution for the problem?

d. In more complex debates the real issues may be more difficult to determine. In that case, study the proposition from all sides and apply questions like the following:

(1) Is the present situation unsatisfactory and does it demand a change?
(2) What are the underlying causes of the situation?
(3) Is the proposed solution the best approach to the problem?
(4) What other remedies are possible?
(5) Is the suggested remedy workable in practice as well as in theory?
(6) Will the remedy improve the situation and be beneficial economically, politically, socially, intellectually, or morally?

Plan a Case. When the issues have been determined, a debate case, consisting of main points to meet the issues, should be planned. Similar points should be divided into two groups with each speaker being made responsible for one group of arguments. The distribution of arguments should be evenly balanced so that each speaker has arguments of similar length and importance. But there is a traditional arrangement of points to be proved that you must consider before deciding who will be your first and second speaker and who will be assigned which arguments.

1. *Constructive Speeches* are the prepared presentation of arguments in addition to meeting the attacks of the opposition. Each speaker is expected to perform certain duties in his constructive speech regard-

less of the particular topic. In general the affirmative must first prove that there is a need for a change from the present system, and the second affirmative speaker must show that the affirmative's plan or solution is the best practical answer. This is the affirmative burden of proof. The negative has the opposite responsibility of clashing with the affirmative arguments. Thus, the negative's case will often be the reverse of the affirmative's. Here's how a rough outline of the constructive phase of sample subject for debate would look. Note that all proof has been omitted.

a. First Affirmative Speaker

(1) Greets the audience—"Good morning, ladies and gentlemen."

(2) States the resolution—"The resolution we are debating today is '*Resolved,* That the Federal government establish a system of free medical care for all.' "

(3) Defines the terms—Federal government, establish, free, system, medical care, all.

(4) Presents the origin, historical background, and current importance of the problem.

(5) Outlines the affirmative case—"The affirmative will stand on two main lines of argument:

(*a*) The rising costs of medical care have made the present system of financing medical care inadequate.

(*b*) A federal system of free medical care will solve the cost problem and preserve the effectiveness of medical care and perhaps improve it.

I will discuss the first part and my partner will deal with the second."

(6) States any assumptions—"Before we begin, let me state that I assume the negative would agree that the cost of medical care has risen faster than the income of at least some of our citizens."

(7) States, divides, and proves the first part of the affirmative case, usually the need for a change—"We have three reasons for contending that rising costs have made our system of financing medical care inadequate:

(*a*) Rising costs force a large portion of our population to choose between no medical care or charity clinics.

(*b*) Middle-income families, even with average medical insurance protection, find it difficult to pay what the insurance doesn't cover.

(c) Medicine's most effective tool, preventive medicine, is blunted by rising costs."

(8) Summarizes the first part of the affirmative case and reminds the audience that his partner will prove the second part.

b. *First Negative Speaker*

(1) Greets the audience—"Good morning. . . ."

(2) Restates the resolution—"*Resolved,* That. . . ."

(3) Agrees with the definition of terms or raises any objections.

(4) States any negative assumptions or comments on any affirmative assumptions—"We would agree that hospital costs have risen faster than personal income, but we are not agreed that out-of-hospital medical costs have risen as much."

(5) Outlines the negative case, including the counterplan, *if used.* (The negative may, but does not have to, propose a counterplan or alternative solution to the problem. If a counterplan is proposed, the debate becomes a choice between the affirmative's and negative's plans. Generally, counterplans are less drastic solutions than the affirmative's plan.)

"The negative opposes the resolution for these reasons:

(a) Medical care is now available to all who need it.

(b) Improvements in private health insurance and government programs have been and are being made.

(c) Socialized medicine would be expensive and wasteful and would result in increasing the total cost of medical care.

(d) Government control would destroy the quality of medical care by taking medical decisions out of the hands of the individual doctor."

(6) Refutes the first affirmative's arguments by direct attack. Ideally, this can best be done by showing that the affirmative's case is contradicted by the negative's evidence for its contentions, a kind of running rebuttal.

(7) States and proves the first part of the negative case—"Medical care is available to all who need it through

(a) fee payment.

(b) local and national programs of public and private agencies for those who cannot pay.

(c) private health insurance."

(8) States and proves the second part of the negative case—"Improvements in private health insurance and government programs

(*a*) have been accomplished recently.
(*b*) are planned for the immediate future."

(9) Summarizes the negative case, showing how the affirmative case has been weakened.

c. Second Affirmative Speaker

(1) Addresses the audience—"Ladies and gentlemen. . . ."

(2) Restates the whole affirmative case, reviewing his partner's proof.

(3) Refutes the first negative's contentions and his attacks on the affirmative case.

(4) Proves the second half of the affirmative case and presents the affirmative's specific plan—"A system of Federally sponsored free medical care is the only solution to the cost problem.

(*a*) Our plan for such a system is the most practical—This is the way it would work. . . .

(*b*) Our plan is the only means of spreading the cost of medical care.

(*c*) Our plan will improve the quality of medical care by encouraging the use of preventive medicine."

(5) Summarizes the entire affirmative case, showing that it has resisted negative attacks.

d. Second Negative Speaker

(1) Addresses the audience—"Honorable Judge. . . ."

(2) Restates the whole negative case, summarizing his colleague's proof. "My partner has shown you that medical care is available to all through fee payment, private and public agencies, and health insurance. He has further shown you that improvements in these methods have been and are being made as exemplified by . . .

Now I will demonstrate that the affirmative's plan of socialized medicine would be wasteful, expensive, and would increase medical costs as a whole. I will also show that the quality of medical care would be damaged by the affirmative's plan, which would ultimately take medical decisions away from the individual doctor."

(3) Refutes the arguments of the second affirmative by attacking the weakness of the reasoning and evidence supporting them.

(4) Proves the third part of the negative case—"The affirmative plan would be:

(*a*) wasteful.
(*b*) inefficient.
(*c*) harmful to the quality of medical care."

(5) Proves the fourth part of the negative case—"The affirmative plan would ultimately take medical decisions away from the individual attending physician as to:

(*a*) choice of hospital.
(*b*) kind of treatment.
(*c*) extent of treatment."

(6) Summarizes the entire debate thus far, balancing the affirmative case against the negative case, stressing the negative's strength.

Notice that the first affirmative speaker carries a heavy burden, since he must establish the foundation for the entire debate. The other speakers, in addition to presenting their own cases, have the added responsibility of refuting points brought up by their opponents. This refutation, often called a running rebuttal, is an important part of a constructive speech. If you don't answer a major attack by your opponents as soon as possible, the audience will think you don't have an answer.

2. *Rebuttal Speeches.* Team members also divide arguments and responsibilities in the short rebuttal speeches following the last constructive speech. These rebuttals serve the double purpose of attacking weaknesses in your opponent's argument and emphasizing the strong points of your own. The order of speaking in rebuttal varies, depending on the local rules used, but often the order of rebuttals is the same as that of the constructive speeches. A speaker who is quick-thinking and analytical is often given the last or next-to-the-last position in the constructive speeches and in the rebuttal so that the most can be made of his ability. Ordinarily, this is the standard arrangement of rebuttal speeches in contest debates:

a. Rebuttal by First Negative Speaker
b. Rebuttal by First Affirmative Speaker
c. Rebuttal by Second Negative Speaker
d. Rebuttal by Second Affirmative Speaker

The affirmative has the last word because it has the burden of proof. Exactly what each speaker will say in a rebuttal is difficult to predict and depends on the cases presented. Generally, each team will divide responsibility for the arguments in rebuttal in the same way as in the constructive speeches. The first speaker for each side handles arguments concerning the present system and its problems, and the second speaker stresses the new plan for a change and its effects. In rebuttal you should:

a. attack major arguments. Don't be drawn into useless disputes on details or false issues.

b. dispute the character, source, and interpretation of evidence, not the fact itself. Introduce contradictory evidence and interpretations.

c. answer the attacks made against your case. If your opponent's attack has been scattered and disorganized, group his attacks into a few major categories and answer each category.

d. avoid introducing new lines of argument in the rebuttal. Your case should be completed in the constructive speeches. Such new points introduced in the rebuttal are not only against the rules but are also unethical, since your opponent does not have sufficient time to reply. You may, however, introduce new evidence to disprove an opponent's argument and his attacks on yours.

e. summarize the whole case often. The last speakers on each side should review the whole debate, stressing the strength of their case and the weakness of their opponents'.

3. *Cross-examination debate,* including periods of cross-questioning, has become increasingly popular in contest debates. Each speaker is questioned by an opponent after his constructive speech. The rules sometimes demand that questions concern issues the speaker has raised in his speech. However, some questions can and should be prepared in advance; if you know the issues, you know what kind of arguments your opponents will make, or at least what choices they have. Try to prepare questions for all possible lines of argument. Ask questions that help you and the audience to understand your opponents' position, the source and interpretation of their evidence, and the basic points of clash. This kind of questioning will help you make a better refutation. Usually the questioner controls the time, but complex questions often require complex answers. Time wasting, tricky questions, and evasive answers are unethical. One common way of inserting cross-examination and some common time limits are:

a. First Affirmative Constructive Speech–8 minutes
Questioning of First Affirmative by First Negative Speaker–3 minutes

b. First Negative Constructive Speech–8 minutes
Questioning of First Negative Speaker by Second Affirmative Speaker–3 minutes

c. Second Affirmative Constructive Speech—8 minutes
Questioning of Second Affirmative Speaker by Second Negative Speaker—3 minutes
d. Second Negative Constructive Speech—8 minutes
Questioning of Second Negative Speaker by First Affirmative Speaker—3 minutes
e. First Negative Speaker's Rebuttal—4 minutes
f. First Affirmative Speaker's Rebuttal—4 minutes
g. Second Negative Speaker's Rebuttal—4 minutes
h. Second Affirmative Speaker's Rebuttal—4 minutes
Total Time: 60 minutes

If necessary, all speeches can be reduced in length to fit into a class period. For example, constructive speeches: 5 minutes each; cross-examinations: 2 minutes each; rebuttals: 3 minutes each; total time: 40 minutes.

4. *Teamwork.* Whatever the time limits or kind of team debate, each debater must realize that he is an important cog in the machinery of a debate team. When the arguments have been divided, each should prepare his part of the debate to the best of his ability, without shirking responsibilities and without trying any grandstand plays which may be to the disadvantage of his team. He must be familiar with his teammate's case, must see that his own speech is closely linked to that of his colleague, and must be willing to share material with his colleague. No speaker should think that his issues are more important than those of his colleague; each one has equal responsibility for the success of his team.

Gather Material. When the question has been analyzed, the case planned, and each debater understands the responsibilities he has in the debate, gathering material to prove arguments and disprove opponents' arguments is the next step. Extensive reading on the topic is the only way to prepare a formal debate. As usual, you will have to consult libraries and more specialized sources; however, you can make a start by looking for information in general publications. Material on both sides of highly controversial questions of wide political, economic, or social interest may be found in publications such as the following:

Political Science Quarterly
Congressional Digest
Vital Speeches
Current History
Debate and Discussion Handbooks (published by the National University Extension Association on the current national debate topic)

Read all material carefully, take notes on what you read, and keep these notes on standard filing cards, as has been previously suggested. When you are ready to organize your material, you will find it easy to shuffle and arrange the cards under the headings to which they belong. Individual cards containing material for refutations and rebuttal will be very useful, too. Remember to gather far more material than you actually intend to use. You can never quite foresee what points your opponents may raise. Be ready to meet emergencies by having your filing box full of classified arguments and proof.

Write a Debate Brief. A brief is a complete outline of all the evidence and arguments, arranged in logical order. The affirmative and negative sides make separate briefs. The chief purpose of a brief is to furnish debaters a complete picture of the question, its background, the arguments, and the evidence. First drafts of a brief permit you to test the logical order of arguments and the strength of the final proof. If a team is forced to change its approach during a debate, the brief is a handy reference for checking on the overall picture of organization. Like most outlines, a brief consists of an introduction, a discussion, and a conclusion.

1. *Introduction.* This first part of the brief includes only the material that is necessary for a general understanding of the question. It contains no argument and no proof. The following headings are customary:

a. Immediate Cause of the Debate
b. Background and History of the Question
c. Definition of Terms
d. Statement of Irrelevant or Admitted Matter
e. Issues or Arguments
f. Division of the Arguments among the Speakers

2. *Discussion.* This part contains the arguments, logically arranged, and the proof which supports those arguments. Each argument must be closely related to its proof and connected by the word *because* or *for,* so that each main heading appears as a reason for the truth or falsity of the proposition, and each subheading acts as proof for the main heading under which it comes. The relationship between the headings and subheadings is indicated by indenting and alternating numbers and letters. It is customary to include the source of all proof in parentheses at the end of each statement, in the margin, or in the footnotes on each page. It is also customary to include refutation as part of the discussion. It may come after each major heading, wherever objections to the argument naturally arise, or it may be placed at the end of the entire discussion.

To understand what is required in the discussion, look again at the outlines of the debate on Free Medical Care under "Plan a Case." The main contentions for each side would be the main division of the discussion, followed by the reasons which would be the subheadings. What is missing under each subheading is the proof—the evidence and the reasoning—the longest and most detailed parts of the discussion. The exact form of outlining the proof, the way you indicate the sources, and the numbering system you use are not so important as the completeness of the proof. Your discussion should be so complete that any skilled debater could take your place after a thorough study of your brief alone.

3. *Conclusion.* This final part of the brief contains a summary of the main issues of the debate and the position of the negative or affirmative with regard to the question. There is no argument and no proof.

Argue Effectively within the Rules. Follow these simple hints for good formal debate delivery and conduct:

1. *Be dignified,* but not stuffy.
2. *Be courteous* to your opponents. Sarcasm is usually a poor substitute for a good case.
3. *Learn the specific rules,* if any, which will govern your debate. Debate leagues usually publish standardized rules.
4. *Do not give the judge directions* as to how to judge the debate. Be confident but not cocky. Let the judge do the judging.
5. *Listen while your opponents are speaking.* Whispering to your partner and other distractions are bad manners and poor debating.
6. *Do not assume that the judge is as familiar* with the details of the topic as you are after long preparation. Be clear. If you are not understood, it's your fault.
7. *Do not overuse such terminology* as *need, contention, in conclusion,* and *conclusively proved.* Debates need variety.
8. *Attack your opponent's case,* not his abilities or human errors.
9. *Avoid using evidence if you are not sure of its source.* Sources are like income-tax returns; sooner or later somebody checks one of them.
10. *Do not rely on tricks and gimmicks.* Your success as a debater will depend upon your preparation and energetic presentation of what you believe are good arguments for your side.

Evaluate the Debate

1. *Personal Evaluation*

Your debating skill won't improve from one debate to the next unless you evaluate what you have done. After each debate, ask yourself:

a. What was my most effective argument? my least effective?
b. What was the strongest argument of my opponents? Why?
c. Did my opponents and the audience appear to understand and accept my evidence?
d. Do I need more proof? Are there any areas of the problem I need to study further?
e. Did I summarize my case often enough so that it was remembered by the audience?
f. What new information or points of view did I learn?
g. Why might the judge decide that my opponents did the better debating? that my team did the better debating?

2. *Evaluation by a Judge or Audience*

The spirit of competition which is a part of all sports also exists in contest debates. High school debates may not settle any problems, but most students like to have some judgment passed as to the merits of the debating itself. In interschool league debates and in district or state tournaments, decisions are held to be necessary; and for many schools that emphasize interclass debates a decision is desirable as a reward for work or as a stimulus to greater effort.

Methods of judging vary throughout the country, the most common ones being the following:

a. Single Judge. For practice or simple interclass debates, a single competent judge, who understands debating principles and who will analyze the debate and criticize the speakers, is helpful.
b. Group of Judges. For interschool and tournament debates where the standing of the teams is at stake, a group of judges, usually three in number, is considered advisable. They should be competent, even expert, in their ability to judge what constitutes good debating.
c. Audience Decision. In debates which are directed toward convincing an audience of the merits of a question as well as the merits of the debaters, a decision given by a vote of the audience may be desirable. A small audience may vote by a show of hands; a large audience by ballot. Sometimes a vote is taken both before and after a debate, in order to measure the shift of opinion.

A sample judge's ballot of the type that is popular in many schools is the following:

Without personal bias as to the merits of the question and on the basis of my understanding of what constitutes superior debating, namely, (1) establishment of a strong constructive case, (2) effective refutation, and (3) forceful delivery,

I consider that the best debating was done by the (affirmative or negative) team.

Signed ____________________

There is no standard way of judging debates, although arguments usually carry more weight than presentation. If you judge a debate, you will find it helpful to keep a list of the arguments presented by each team and to cross-check them as they are met and disproved by the other.

Understand Debate Terminology. Like most activities, debating has its own special terminology, or jargon. Since many of these words have been used in this chapter and you are likely to hear others used in the course of a debate, study the following glossary and keep it handy. Some of the terms are common English words with a special meaning in debating. Others are more technical terms, referring to parts of a debate. Still others are words that have shifting meanings and are difficult to define definitely, but the most common meaning is given.

Glossary of Debate Terminology

Affirmative—that side in a debate which supports the resolution as stated.

Analogy—a conclusion based upon the comparison of similarities between two objects, facts, systems, or ideas.

Argument—a main point to be proved; the process of proving a point.

Argumentation—the study of reasoned proof; the process of convincing a listener.

Assumption—a statement or point of view which is accepted by both sides without proof or discussion.

Authority—a source with knowledge, reliability, and impartiality; a person expected to have sound opinion on the topic; a source whose opinion is respected by the listener.

Begging the question—assuming the truth or falsity of a statement before proving or disproving it.

Burden of proof—the affirmative's responsibility to prove the need for a change and the advantages of the change.

Brief—a complete analysis of a debate topic and a complete outline of the case of one side in a debate.

Canned speech—a memorized speech suitable only for the first affirmative speaker.

Case—the complete stand of one side on a debate question, including evidence and reasoning.

Character—the face value of evidence; the acceptability of evidence without regard to its source.

Clash—the responsibility of meeting the arguments of opponents directly; a particular responsibility of the negative to meet the affirmative burden of proof.

Common term—in a syllogism the idea which unites the major premise to the conclusion.

Contention—a stand, main point, or main argument by one side.

Counterplan—an alternative solution to the problem advanced by the negative; a debating strategy that the negative may—but need not—employ, making the debate a choice between alternatives.

Debate—any oral controversy; the advancing of arguments for or against a proposal; a formal match between two teams on a given proposition.

Deductive reasoning—arriving at a conclusion by showing how it follows logically from a more general conclusion, or law.

Definition of terms—a statement of the meaning or interpretation of the words in a debate resolution; a responsibility of the first affirmative speaker.

Evidence—that which is advanced to support a generalization; facts, examples, statistics, quotations.

Example—a particular case or instance designed to illustrate a statement.

Fallacy—an error in reasoning; a violation of the rules of logic.

Fact—an event, the actuality of which is accepted.

Forensic—having to do with speech competition; competitive debate.

Generalization—a conclusion drawn from similarities in a group of facts or other evidence; **inductive reasoning.**

Inductive reasoning—the arriving at a general conclusion based on particular evidence; scientific generalization.

Issue—a point of major conflict arising from the debate topic; a necessary clash.

Logic—the practice of correct reasoning; the rules of correct reasoning.

Major premise—the first statement in a syllogism; a general law.

Minor premise—the second statement in a syllogism; that which relates the general law to the conclusion.

Need (for a change)—part of the affirmative burden of proof; the necessity for adopting a new proposal; the evils of the present system; the unsolved problem.

Negative—that side in a debate which opposes the adoption of the resolution as stated.

Opinion—the stated judgment of any person without advancing further proof; the comment of an authority upon a problem.

Prima facie case—that which is accepted upon presentation without further proof.

Proof—that which attains acceptance from the listener; the process of using evidence and reasoning to support a conclusion; sound argument.

Proposition—the statement of that which is to be debated; a debate resolution.

Quotation—the accurate, word-for-word report of what another said or wrote; a type of evidence; the opinion of an authority.

Reasoning—the process of relating one thing to another; logic.

Rebuttal—the contradicting or answering of opponents' arguments; that period in a debate devoted to rebuttal alone; the second speech by a speaker answering objections.

Refutation—the contradicting or answering of opponents' arguments; the process of conducting a rebuttal.

Resolution—the statement of that which is to be debated, usually beginning with the word *Resolved*; a debate proposition.
Should—ought to, but not necessarily will, be done; a term often used in debate propositions.
Statistics—the numerical representation of real events or facts; any figures used as evidence.
Status quo—the present system; the state in which we now exist; the present.
Stock issue—standard points of conflict in a debate such as need for a change, practicality, beneficiality, cost, and harmful effects.
Straw man—proposal of an objection to one's stand and the answering it; a false or easily answered objection proposed against one's own argument.
Source—any reporter of events not personally witnessed by the speaker; the origin of evidence.
Syllogism—a form of reasoning in which a general law is stated, a particular statement made, and a conclusion reached from their relationship; deductive reasoning.
Term—a word or related group of words in a debate resolution.

Review of Formal Debating

CHOOSE A FORMAL DEBATE QUESTION that is

1. Debatable.
2. Clear.
3. Current.
4. A call for a change.
5. The National Debate Question (for tournament debate).

CHOOSE A TEAM based on

1. Your coach's advice.
2. Tryouts.
3. Mutual agreement.

AND OPPONENTS based on

1. Your coach's pairing.
2. Random pairing at tournaments.

ANALYZE THE QUESTION

1. Know the background.
2. Define the terms.
3. Determine the issues.

PLAN A CASE

1. Constructive speeches.
2. Rebuttals.
3. Cross-examination.
4. Teamwork.

GATHER MATERIAL by

1. Reading.
2. Taking notes.

WRITE A DEBATE BRIEF containing

1. Introduction, Discussion, and Conclusion.
2. A complete outline of your evidence and reasoning.

ARGUE EFFECTIVELY WITHIN THE RULES by

1. Knowing and following the rules.
2. Using courtesy as an effective debate technique.

EVALUATE THE DEBATE by

1. Looking for your own strengths and weaknesses.
2. Understanding the process of judging a debate.

UNDERSTAND DEBATE TERMINOLOGY

By using the "Glossary of Debate Terminology."

Topics for Debate

1. The study of poetry should be dropped from the English curriculum.
2. The reservation system for American Indians should be abandoned.
3. The President of the United States should be elected for a single term of six years.
4. The President of the United States should be permitted to serve an unlimited number of years.
5. Vivisection should be prohibited.
6. Puerto Rico should be granted immediate statehood.
7. The Federal government should control all public utilities.
8. The Federal government should revise its income-tax system.
9. A population shift from East to West in this country should be encouraged.
10. All automobile owners should be required to install seat belts.
11. A Federal Department of Urban Affairs should be created.
12. A Federal Air and Water Pollution Control Agency should be established.
13. All lumbering operations should be under Federal regulation and control.
14. The states should reassert states' rights in the areas of voting, welfare, and public works.
15. Deductions based on oil depletion allowances should be eliminated from the Federal Income-Tax Law.

16. Control of all armaments should be vested in the United Nations.
17. Newspapers should be owned by nonprofit organizations.
18. Television sponsors should not be permitted to select the programs they wish to sponsor.
19. The United States should abandon the two-party system.
20. The United States should promote a Common Market for all non-communist countries.
21. The Federal government should equalize educational opportunity by means of grants to the states for public elementary and secondary education.
22. Compulsory arbitration of labor disputes should be required in the basic industries.
23. The United States should adopt the British system of education.
24. The United States should promote the transforming of the United Nations into a World Government.
25. The United States should return the Canal Zone to Panama now.
26. The United States should recognize Red China.
27. The United States should support United Nations membership for Communist China.
28. The United States should support the policy of coexistence.
29. The United States should adopt the thirty-five-hour work week.
30. Compulsory education should end with the tenth grade.
31. The United States should adopt the policy of never being the first to use nuclear weapons in any conflict.
32. The United States should promote the entrusting of all nuclear weapons to United Nations control.
33. The United States should unilaterally abandon underground nuclear tests.
34. Automated industries should be required to provide for the retirement or reeducation of displaced workers.
35. The Federal government should directly subsidize nonprofit musical, artistic, and theatrical groups.
36. Debate in the United States Senate should be limited by simple majority vote.
37. The United States should guarantee Cuba a democratic form of government.
38. The United States should stop all aid to countries ruled by dictators.
39. No person should be photographed without his consent.
40. Wiretapping by government officials should be permitted.
41. Legalized gambling should be permitted.

42. Cigarettes should be prohibited in the same ways as narcotics.
43. Home visits by all prisoners in state and Federal prisons should be permitted.
44. All prisoners should be offered psychiatric care.

DEBATE ACTIVITIES

1. Plan a group of debates for class practice, following formal debating rules, in which a pair of teams has two speakers on a side. Choose topics of national interest for which material is available in current publications. Limit the constructive and rebuttal speeches to fit a class period. Let the audience choose the winning team at the conclusion of the debate.
2. Present a series of informal debates in which two students present the two sides of some general topic, such as those suggested on page 392. Limit talks to seven minutes; allow each speaker three minutes for informal rebuttal.
3. Choose an important issue from a current problem. Argue your side of the issue in a five-minute speech before the class. Answer questions from the audience.
4. Present a formal cross-examination debate with two-man teams. Reduce the time limits as necessary. Appoint some members of the class as judges.
5. Organize a debating activity in your school. Contact other schools to arrange for interscholastic debates or for information about debate tournaments, if any, in your area. Write for information on affiliating with the National Forensic League, a national speech honor society and debate league. Write to: Secretary, National Forensic League, Ripon, Wisconsin.

References:

An Introduction to Debate, by Thomas K. Haney. Ginn.
Argumentation and Debate, by J. R. McBurney, J. M. O'Neill, and G. E. Mills. Macmillan.
Oral Decision-making, by W. W. Braden and E. S. Brandenburg. Harper.
Competitive Debate, Rules and Techniques, by G. M. Musgrave. Wilson.
Discussion and Debate, by W. A. Behl. Ronald.
How to Debate, by H. B. Summers and others. Wilson.
Argumentation and Debating, by W. T. Foster. Houghton Mifflin.
The Debater's Guide, by J. T. Murphy and J. M. Ericson. Bobbs-Merrill.

Films:

How to Judge Authorities (Coronet). 11 min color or b&w.
How to Judge Facts (Coronet). 11 min color or b&w.
Importance of Making Notes (Coronet). 11 min color or b&w.
Learn to Argue Effectively (Coronet). 11 min color or b&w.
Fundamentals of Public Speaking. 11 min color or b&w.

Unit Twenty-one

READING ALOUD: Prose and Poetry

Reading aloud, a common kind of oral activity, is too frequently an unsatisfactory experience for listener and reader alike. Do you remember the last time you listened to someone read aloud in class—perhaps a bulletin, an announcement, a textbook selection, a magazine article, or a special report? Were you interested or stimulated? Did you enjoy it? Or was your reaction somewhere between "Who cares?" and "What was *that* all about?"

Do you remember, too, the last time *you* read aloud? Did you make any special effort to communicate with your listeners? Or were you content to say the words rather automatically without caring very much whether your listeners were getting the message?

Oral Reading Is Often Poor. Under ordinary circumstances much oral reading is poor. It seems to be such a simple, easy thing to do—just reading words—that few people think twice about their performance. They assume, because they can read silently without much conscious effort and are easily able to form words orally in ordinary talking, that all that is necessary for satisfactory *oral reading* is to put the two together and say aloud the words that are on the page.

However, in the words of a once well-known song, "It ain't necessarily so!" If you are alert, you have noticed that a student who may be able to speak interestingly when he is putting his own ideas into words, often sounds dull, monotonous, or expressionless when he begins to read aloud from material written on a page. Something happens. Good communication fails. Why?

Why? To understand what often goes wrong in reading aloud, you need to remind yourself of what happens when you speak. Your words come spontaneously, automatically reflecting your thoughts and feelings. They are *your* words, *your* thoughts, and *your* feelings, expressed freely and independently and not tied to a manuscript or a page. What hapens when you read? You forget that words are *symbols* of ideas and feelings, and you begin to treat them as if *they* (the words themselves) are what you must communicate, rather than what they stand for. The problem is complicated by the fact that the ideas and feelings behind the words are not yours but, rather, the original author's. You become preoccupied with individual words rather than with meanings, you glue your eyes to the page to get every word right, and the result is a loss of natural manner, a monotonous delivery, and often a fumbling and stumbling over words and sentences. All this obstructs communication.

Reading Is Interpretation. From the moment you begin to realize that the standard for good oral reading is not only whether the audience *heard* all the words but also whether they *received* all the ideas, you are on the way to improving your reading ability. The role you play in this kind of communication is that of an interpreter or a translator. You fill an important position in a communicative triple play—author to reader to audience. Whereas *talking* involves only two entities, you and your audience, *reading* involves three—the creator of the ideas (the author), the recipient of the ideas (the audience), and the translator of the ideas (you, the reader). You become the go-between, conveying meaning and feeling as effectively and as honestly as possible.

The Reading of Prose

Prose, by definition, is the ordinary straightforward form of written or spoken language as opposed to verse or poetry. It is not expressed metrically, and it is generally less imaginative than poetry—more matter-of-fact and closer to the patterns of everyday speech—although some forms of literary prose have many poetic qualities. Most of you have had opportunities to read some prose aloud, usually the factual, informative sort that seems to require a minimum of effort. Your interpretative skill is best challenged, however, by the reading of passages from famous writings, great books, or outstanding speeches, when your purpose is to impress, inspire, or entertain your listeners. Whatever your purpose is or the type of prose you read, you must try to establish the habit of reading *meanings* rather than words. There is no magic formula to help you do that, but if you observe the following suggestions you should be able to improve your skill.

Become Familiar with Your Selection. Begin by making yourself as familiar as possible with the prose selection you are to read. If the choice of what to read is yours, choose a selection that you know and like. Read the selection again and again. If time permits, make a copy so that you can mark it or make notes on it. Your goal at this point is to get the feel of the selection, to become familiar and comfortable with it, and to understand not only its content but also its style.

Think About Its Meaning. How carefully you answer questions like the following ones will determine whether your reading will be a shallow mouthing of words or a thoughtful presentation.

- What does the author seem to be saying on the surface?
- Is that what he really means or is there more to it?
- How does he feel about his message?
- What does he want his audience to remember?
- What emotions or attitudes does he want his reader to feel during each part of the selection and at its conclusion?

Study the Words. The uncertainty and flatness of your voice as you read a passage that contains words you do not understand will seriously weaken your audience contact. Checking the dictionary for the pronunciation and the exact meaning of all unfamiliar words is essential not only for good reading but also as a courtesy to your audience.

Mark Your Copy as an Aid to Expression. Although you may seldom have the time to prepare every detail of your reading, a good way to develop the habit of making greater use of emphasis and pause is to mark your copy of the selection (not the book) where pauses and stress might be used. A common way is to underline each word or phrase to be stressed, double underlining words to be given greater stress, and triple underlining words to be given the most stress. Pauses can be indicated by one slash (/) for a slight pause; two slashes (//), indicating a longer pause, as at commas; and three slashes (///), indicating a complete stop, as at a semicolon or period. Here is how a part of Patrick Henry's famous speech might be marked for pauses and emphasis:

"I have but one lamp / by which my feet are guided; // and that is the lamp of experience. /// I know of no way of judging the future // but by the past. /// "

Perhaps you can think of other arrangements of marking pauses and stress. Whatever arrangement you choose, your purpose should be not merely to get some marks on the paper but also to work out a way of communicating the author's ideas and feelings that you have tried to make your own. Don't let the marks become more important than the meaning; following the markings too strictly could make your reading mechanical and artificial. Once you have worked out some possible ways of reading your selection, forget about stress and pause as technical devices, and make your actual reading aloud sound as natural as possible. Your pauses and emphasis then arise out of the meaning and emotion you wish to communicate at that moment.

Watch Your Speed! The single most common fault that marks poor reading aloud is reading too fast. Fast reading is closely related to a poor understanding of your material and a lack of desire to communicate. If a reader does not clearly understand the message and mood of the author and has not practiced to find the best ways of communicating that message, making every word, phrase, and sentence play its part in the communication, there is really no other alternative for him except to mouth the words as quickly as possible. Reading too fast is not the sickness itself; it is merely the symptom of the trouble. If you are convinced of the importance of the message, understand it fully, are determined to communicate it, and use every means to get it across, your rate will be slower because you will take time to accomplish your task well.

Follow the Rules of Good Speaking. Apply as many of the rules of good speaking as you can. Adequate volume, vocal flexibility, some eye-contact, and enthusiasm are needed in oral readings, too. One temptation you must avoid is to let your voice drop at the end of each line, so that a regular and boring pattern develops—the voice starting each line high in pitch and descending to a lower pitch at the end of the sentence. Although this is a common pattern, when repeated again and again it makes the whole reading dull because every sentence sounds like every other sentence.

When we read silently to ourselves, our whole attention is focused on the words on the page; but when we listen to material being read to us, we watch the reader. Our response to what we hear depends not only upon what we hear but also what we see. If we see the reader with poor posture, face buried in the book, and a look of either discomfort or boredom, our reaction is negative. If the reader stands erect, knows his material well enough so that he can look at us occasionally to see our reaction, and is generally lively in voice and appearance, our response is lively. The moral is obvious.

What about Impromptu Reading? Aren't there occasions when you must read aloud with little or no preparation? What can you do when your teacher suddenly calls upon you to read a paragraph or someone hands you a bulletin to be read immediately? It is still possible to read aloud with reasonable effectiveness. Your previous practice with well-prepared readings will help you to understand what makes an oral reading successful. A brief reading or skimming of the material will help you grasp the main idea and mood of the selection even if you do not have time to analyze every sentence. As you read it aloud, the more emphasis, pausing, and vocal variety you use will give you more time with each sentence with the result that both you and the audience will have a chance to understand it.

Reading prose aloud can be a pleasurable experience for you and your listeners. It can be a way of sharing with others articles, stories, and good writing that you have enjoyed. It can be a way of effectively communicating, word for word, an important message. If you take time to practice reading aloud whenever you can, to concentrate on getting the ideas across, and to learn from each successful and unsuccessful oral reading you hear or deliver, you'll develop another gratifying skill in oral expression.

ACTIVITIES

1. Choose one of the following types of factual prose and prepare it for an oral reading in class:

a. A newspaper editorial.
b. An article from a news magazine such as *Time* or *Newsweek*.
c. An article from a more general publication such as *The Reader's Digest, Harper's Magazine,* or *The Saturday Evening Post.*
d. An article from a specialized publication such as *Scientific American, Seventeen, Motor Trend,* or *Sports Illustrated.*
e. A brief but interesting section from a textbook.
f. An interesting, but not too technical, passage from a nonfictional book.

2. Select a speech published in one of the following sources and prepare to read part of it to the class.

a. *Vital Speeches* (a semimonthly magazine).
b. *Representative American Speeches* (an annual series).
c. Any anthology of speeches.

3. Choose a passage from one of the following novels to read to the class. Make sure that the incident your passage will relate is interesting even if the listener does not know the rest of the story.

a. *The Pearl,* by JOHN STEINBECK.
b. *Storm,* by GEORGE STEWART.
c. *Tom Sawyer,* by MARK TWAIN.

d. *Youth,* by JOSEPH CONRAD.
e. *Animal Farm,* by GEORGE ORWELL.
f. *Cry, the Beloved Country,* by ALAN PATON.
g. *The Ox-Bow Incident,* by WALTER VAN TILBURG CLARK.
h. *David Copperfield,* by CHARLES DICKENS.
i. *The Old Man and the Sea,* by ERNEST HEMINGWAY.
j. *Wuthering Heights,* by EMILY BRONTË.

4. Choose a short story that appears in a collection of short stories or a literature anthology used in your English class. Prepare a reading of it which will convey the main plot even if you have to omit certain passages because of their length.

5. Read silently the following familiar selection from the time of the Revolutionary War. What is the point that Paine is making? Why does he choose to put it this way instead of some other way? What feelings is he trying to arouse in his reader?

These are the times that try men's souls. The summer soldier and the sunshine patriot will, in this crisis, shrink from the service of his country; but he that stands it *now,* deserves the love and thanks of man and woman. Tyranny, like hell, is not easily conquered; yet we have this consolation with us, that the harder the conflict, the more glorious the triumph. What we obtain too cheap, we esteem too lightly; it is dearness only that gives everything its value. Heaven knows how to put a proper price upon its goods, and it would be strange indeed if so celestial an article as FREEDOM should not be highly rated.

—THOMAS PAINE, *The Crisis*

6. Read the following selection, "The Battle of the Ants," from *Walden,* by Thoreau, an American individualist. Which words will most students have to look up in the dictionary? What references will the reader have to understand? Is Thoreau simply describing what he saw? Or is he using what he saw to make some comment about something else? If so, what is he really saying? Prepare the selection for a reading in class. Do not let the number of semicolons bother you. They are used in the way we would probably use periods.

The legions of these Myrmidons covered all the hills and vales in my woodyard, and the ground was already strewn with the dead and dying, both red and black. It was the only battle which I have ever witnessed, the only battlefield I ever trod while the battle was raging; internecine war; the red republicans on the one hand, and the black imperialists on the other. On every side they were engaged in deadly combat, yet without any noise that I could hear, and human soldiers never fought so resolutely. I watched a couple that were fast locked in each other's embraces, in a little sunny valley amid the chips, now at noonday prepared to fight till the sun went down, or life went out. . . . They fought with more pertinacity than bulldogs. Neither manifested the least disposition to retreat. It was evident that their battle-cry was "Conquer or die." In the meanwhile there came along a single red ant on the hill-side of this valley, evidently full of excitement, who either had dispatched his foe, or had not yet taken part in the battle . . . whose mother had charged him to return with his shield or upon it. Or perchance he was some Achilles, who had nourished his wrath apart, and had now come to avenge or rescue his Patroclus . . . he drew near with rapid pace till he stood on his guard within half an inch of the combatants, then, watching his opportunity, he sprang upon the black warrior. . . . I should not have wondered by this time to find that they had their respective musical bands stationed . . . and playing their national airs the while, to excite the slow and cheer the dying combatants. I was myself excited somewhat even as if they had been men. The more you think of it, the less the difference.

—HENRY DAVID THOREAU, *Walden*

7. Read the following selection from *Moby Dick,* by Herman Melville. Although these are the opening lines of the book, do they have anything else to say to the listener besides simply getting him interested in the book? Is there a comment made about the way men behave? Is there an attempt to show that all men are alike in some way? How? What is the mood of the paragraph? Will the length and structure of the sentences pose a special problem for reading them aloud? What should be done about it?

Call me Ishmael. Some years ago—never mind how long precisely—having little or no money in my purse, and nothing particular to interest me on shore, I thought I would sail about a little and see the watery part of the world. It is a way I have of driving off the spleen, and regulating the circulation. Whenever I find myself growing grim about the mouth; whenever it is damp, drizzly November in my soul; whenever I find myself involuntarily pausing before coffin warehouses, and bringing up the rear of every funeral I meet; and especially whenever my hypos get such an upper hand of me, that it requires a strong moral principle to prevent me from deliberately stepping into the street, and methodically knocking people's hats off—then, I account it high time to get to sea as soon as I can. This is my substitute for pistol and ball. With a philosophical flourish Cato throws himself upon his sword; I quietly take to the ship. There is nothing surprising in this. If they but knew it, almost all men in their degree, some time or other, cherish very nearly the same feelings towards the ocean with me.

—HERMAN MELVILLE, *Moby Dick*

Drawing by J. Mirachi; © 1964 The New Yorker Magazine, Inc.

"The snow had begun in the gloaming,
And busily all the night
Had been heaping field and highway
With a silence deep and white . . ."

8. Read the following excerpt from President Kennedy's most famous speech. Read the complete speech at the end of this book, to see where these ideas appeared in the speech. What special problems are there in reading aloud from another's speech? How is the style of a formal speech different from other prose? What is the point of this excerpt? Why is it placed early in the speech? What feelings should it arouse in the listener?

Let the word go forth from this time and place, to friend and foe alike, that the torch has been passed to a new generation of Americans, born in this century, tempered by war, disciplined by a hard and bitter peace, proud of our ancient heritage, and unwilling to witness or permit the slow undoing of those human rights to which this nation has always been committed, and to which we are committed today at home and around the world.

Let every nation know, whether it wishes us well or ill, that we shall pay any price, bear any burden, meet any hardship, support any friend, oppose any foe to assure the survival and the success of liberty.

—JOHN F. KENNEDY, Inaugural Address

9. Prepare a copy of one of the above selections or another prose selection approved by your teacher. Using underlining and slash marks, indicate words to be stressed and appropriate pauses. Compare your paper with others in the class. Read the selection using the emphasis and pausing you have planned.

10. Ask your teacher or a capable student to read the same selection twice. The first time it should be read monotonously and without meaning. The second time it should be read as interestingly as possible. Note what makes the difference between the two readings. Practice this exercise yourself.

11. Choose one of these poetic prose selections, practice it at home, then read it to your classmates:

Speak the speech, I pray you, as I pronounced it to you, trippingly on the tongue. But if you mouth it, as many of our players do, I had as live the town crier spoke my lines. Nor do not saw the air too much with your hand, thus, but use all gently; for in the very torrent, tempest, and (as I may say) whirlwind of your passion, you must acquire and beget a temperance that may give it smoothness. O, it offends me to the soul to hear a robustious periwig-pated fellow tear a passion to tatters, to very rags, to split the ears of the groundlings, who for the most part are capable of nothing but inexplicable dumb shows and noise. I would have such a fellow whipped for o'erdoing Termagant; it out-herods Herod. Pray you avoid it.

—William Shakespeare, *Hamlet*

Farewell at Springfield

My friends, no one, not in my situation, can appreciate my feeling of sadness at this parting. To this place and the kindness of this people I owe everything. Here I have lived a quarter of a century and have passed from a young to an old man. Here my children have been born and one is buried.

I now leave, not knowing when or whether ever I may return, with a task before me greater than that which rested upon Washington. Without the assistance of that Divine Being who ever attended him I can not succeed. With that assistance I can not fail.

Trusting in Him who can go with me and remain with you and be everywhere for good, let us confidently hope that all will yet be well. To His care commending you, as I hope in your prayers you will commend me, I bid you an affectionate farewell.

—Abraham Lincoln

Now when they were arrayed, each company with their captains, the Trojans marched with clamour and with shouting like unto birds, even as when there goeth up before heaven a clamour of cranes which flee from the coming of winter and sudden rain. . . . But on the other side marched the Achaians in silence breathing courage, eager at heart to give succour man to man.

Even as when the south wind sheddeth mist over the crests of a mountain, mist unwelcome to the shepherd, but to the robber better than night, and a man can see no further than he casteth a stone; even so thick arose the gathering dust-clouds at their tread as they went; and with all speed they advanced across the plain.

—*The Iliad of Homer,* Book III

The Reading of Poetry

When you turn your attention to the oral reading of poetry, you will plan and prepare your presentation in much the same general manner as you do for reading prose, with only a few significant differences. Those differences are related to the basic nature of poetry as a form of literature. When you are interpreting great poetic passages from the Bible, moving lines from the plays of Shakespeare or other dramatists, stirring sentences from the writings of great men, or poems of enduring charm and beauty, you are dealing with imaginative expression which rises above commonplace, workaday speech or the direct, realistic style of most prose writing.

Generally speaking, poetry expresses ideas and emotions in a more concentrated, imaginative, colorful way than does prose. Its effect is more striking to the ear and more stimulating to the imagination because of the beauty of its language, the symbolism and imagery used to give depth and richness to ideas, the arrangement of the words in verse form, and, especially, the rhythmical, musical effect of the lines. These are the qualities which require your special attention if you want to read poetry well. In preparing poetic selections for oral reading, give careful consideration to the procedures which are explained below.

Analyze the Meaning. Thorough preparation is one of the secrets of successful reading of poetry. The first step to take with any literary material you are going to read aloud is to *let your mind understand it.* The transmission of the author's thought and feeling is your chief responsibility. If you do not understand his idea and purpose, you will merely be reading a string of words meaningless to yourself and your listeners. Follow this procedure in preparing your material:

1. *Understand the general thought of the selection.* Read it silently and slowly in order to grasp the meaning as a whole. If you don't get

it the first time, read it again. Test your understanding by stating the central thought in words of your own. When you are sure of the main idea, you are ready for the next step.

2. *Break the selection into its related parts.* You've learned that a speech should be organized so that it has a beginning, a middle, and an end. Study the organization of your literary selection and observe the progression of the units of thought. What you find will help you to determine what to emphasize and what to subordinate as you read aloud.

3. *Master the individual sentences, phrases, and words within each unit of thought.* As you study the way the thoughts of your selection are grouped, be sure that you understand the meaning of each word, phrase, and sentence within each group. Decide now how you should use pause, change of pitch, emphasis, inflection, rate, and intensity in carrying meaning to your listeners.

4. *Put the pieces of the puzzle together in oral practice.* Read aloud each related part until you are satisfied that you are transmitting the author's meaning to the best of your ability; then practice the whole selection carefully for smooth phrasing between thought groups. Be particularly wary of punctuation marks, since they may lead you into awkward pauses and false phrasing. Follow the *thought* itself rather than the grammatical construction of that thought.

Analyze the Mood or Feeling. Poetry, more than prose, deals with emotion. In addition to interpreting what a good poet *means*, you must capture his *mood*, his feeling, his emotion. Therefore, to do justice to all poetry and to much poetic prose, you must learn to feel what the poet feels, when you read it aloud. This involves analyzing your selection again from a different angle. Here are the steps in the analysis:

1. *Read the selection to discover its mood.* Is it happy? Is it sad? Is it earnest? Is it fiery? Is it persuasive? Is it humorous? Does it show a combination of emotions? Is the mood conveyed chiefly through the rhythm of the lines, the music of the words, or both? When you have analyzed the mood of the whole selection and of its individual parts, you will be ready to express the feeling behind the words.

2. *Let your voice show the mood.* Use all the vocal means of good oral interpretation, which were previously explained in Unit 4.

a. Resonance	*c.* Range	*e.* Rate	*g.* Emphasis	*i.* Flexibility
b. Pitch	*d.* Volume	*f.* Inflection	*h.* Pause	*j.* Intensity

3. *Test your interpretation of mood.* As you continue practicing reading aloud, constantly ask yourself these three questions:

a. Have I identified myself with the feeling or mood of the author?

b. Is my voice carrying that mood to my listeners?

c. Am I giving my audience time and opportunity to *feel* what the author means them to feel?

Analyze the Rhythm. Poetry is essentially musical. Meaning and mood are heightened in most poetic selections by strong rhythm. Your response to the rhythm and melody of your selection is an important part of your capturing its feeling and thought. The last step, then, in the oral interpretation of poetry is to turn your attention to its sound. *Let your ear hear the music of the lines and words,* and make your audience hear it, too. Follow these steps:

Step 1. *Catch the natural swing and lilt of the lines.* All good writing, whether prose or poetry, has a rhythmic pattern. Poetry, especially, has a rhythmic flow which makes it pleasing to the ear. As you practice reading your selection, *feel* the natural rhythm of the lines and *hear* the music of the words. Is the rhythm slow? Is it galloping? Is it gentle and lulling? Is it plodding? Is it a vigorous marching rhythm? Is it gay and dancing? Whatever it is, feel it, hear it, and then carry it to your listeners. One word of warning, however, about reading selections. We have a tendency to make poetry metric rather than rhythmic when we read it aloud by stressing the mechanical regularity of the individual beats and neglecting the more subtle rhythmic structure or flow of the lines. We read as if the beats were more important than the meaning, the mood, or the melody of the poem. There is delightful variety of sound, flexibility of movement, and syncopation in most poetic rhythms. Listen for them! And above all, avoid the pitfall of singsong reading.

For example, try reading in two ways "Stopping by Woods on a Snowy Evening," by Robert Frost. First, read it stiffly, woodenly, and ploddingly, overstressing the accented beats and pausing at the end of each line, like this:

> Whose *wóods* these *áre* I *thínk* I *knów.* [pause]
>
> His *hóuse* is *ín* the *víllage thóugh;* [pause]
>
> He *wíll* not *sée* me *stópping hére* [pause]
>
> To *wátch* his *wóods* fill *úp* with *snów.* [stop]

Do you notice how artificial, singsongy and unpleasant it sounds and how the melody has been destroyed? Now read it again, this time conversationally with no overstressing of beats, no dead pauses at the ends of the first two lines, and no pause at all after the third line. Read it as if you were talking easily to someone. Notice how the poem comes to life with a natural swing of its own and how much more pleasant it sounds to the ear.

Step 2. *Notice how the sound of words can suggest mood and enhance meaning.* Words like *murmur, crash, languid, hiss, moan, hustle and bustle, bitter chill, shuffling step, gently lulling,* and *slowly and silently* can usually speak for themselves. Their sound suggests their sense. Look for key words in the selections you read aloud, and let their sounds create vivid impressions for you and your listeners.

Step 3. *Do not slight distinctness and correctness in oral reading.* As you practice reading aloud, check yourself by answering questions like these:

a. Am I pronouncing all the words correctly?

b. Is my enunciation clear?

c. Am I reading so fast that the words run together and the meaning and rhythm are lost? Or am I reading too slowly and heavily?

d. Am I using sufficient volume to be heard clearly?

e. Does the smoothness of my diction help the rhythmic flow of the lines?

Review the Essentials

You now have the essentials of learning how to improve your oral reading of poetry. Again remember how important it is to be properly and thoroughly prepared. Persistence and practice will enable you to establish a desirable relationship between what is written on a page and what your audience hears. You'll find you can bring much pleasure to others by sharing the good things of literature with them, and you can make reading aloud more fun for yourself if you will play your role properly. That role is to *interpret* poetry for your listeners, not merely to recite some lines. Help them to understand, to feel, and to respond to those qualities which make poetry a great form of literature.

1. Think of yourself as an intermediator between author and listeners.
2. Study the meaning of the selection.
3. Understand its mood.
4. Analyze the rhythm.
5. Use your voice as an instrument of interpretation to bring out the meaning, mood, and rhythm.

Interpretation of poetic passages requires especial concentration on meaning and mood and rhythm. Here Charlton Heston reads from the Bible.

6. Practice aloud patiently and often.

7. Above all, don't be mechanical, lifeless, or singsongy. Show a sensitive response to the qualities that make your selection vital.

ACTIVITIES

For understanding meaning:

1. Tell what you think the author means in each of these brief selections:

> Alas for him who never sees
> The stars shine through his cypress trees!
>
> —John Greenleaf Whittier

> To make a prairie it takes a clover and one bee,
> One clover, and a bee,
> And revery.
>
> —Emily Dickinson

At the devil's booth are all things sold,
Each ounce of dross costs its ounce of gold;
For a cap and bells our lives we pay . . .

—James Russell Lowell

Degenerate sons and daughters,
Life is too strong for you—
It takes life to love Life.

—Edgar Lee Masters

Spend all you have for loveliness,
Buy it and never count the cost;
For one white singing hour of peace
Count many a year of strife well lost . . .

—Sara Teasdale

It is a strange thing—to be an American . . .
It is strange to sleep in the bare stars and to die
On an open land where few bury before us:

—Archibald MacLeish

2. Discuss in class the meaning of each of the following poems. Select the one you like best and read it aloud, using all the vocal means you can to carry the thought of the author to your audience.

To the Virgins, to Make Much of Time

Gather ye rosebuds while ye may:
    Old time is still a-flying;
And this same flower that smiles today,
    Tomorrow will be dying.

The glorious lamp of heaven, the sun,
    The higher he's a-getting
The sooner will his race be run,
    And nearer he's to setting.

That age is best which is the first,
    When youth and blood are warmer;
But being spent, the worse, and worst
    Times still succeed the former.

Then be not coy, but use your time,
And while ye may, go marry;
For having lost but once your prime,
You may forever tarry.

—Robert Herrick

"My heart leaps up when I behold"

My heart leaps up when I behold
A rainbow in the sky:
So was it when my life began;
So is it now I am a man;
So be it when I shall grow old,
Or let me die!
The Child is father of the Man;
And I could wish my days to be
Bound each to each by natural piety.

—William Wordsworth

Loveliest of Trees

Loveliest of trees, the cherry now
Is hung with bloom along the bough,
And stands about the woodland ride
Wearing white for Eastertide.

Now, of my threescore years and ten,
Twenty will not come again,
And take from seventy springs a score,
It only leaves me fifty more.

And since to look at things in bloom
Fifty springs are little room,
About the woodlands I will go
To see the cherry hung with snow.

—A. E. Housman

An Old Story

Strange that I did not know him then,
That friend of mine!
I did not even show him then
One friendly sign;

But cursed him for the ways he had
    To make me see
My envy of the praise he had
    For praising me.

I would have rid the earth of him
    Once, in my pride! . . .
I never knew the worth of him
    Until he died.

—Edwin Arlington Robinson

Bowed by the weight of centuries he leans
Upon his hoe and gazes on the ground,
The emptiness of ages in his face,
And on his back the burden of the world.
Who made him dead to rapture and despair,
A thing that grieves not and that never hopes,
Stolid and stunned, a brother to the ox?
Who loosened and let down this brutal jaw?
Whose was the hand that slanted back this brow?
Whose breath blew out the light within this brain?

Is this the Thing the Lord God made and gave
To have dominion over sea and land;
To trace the stars and search the heavens for power;
To feel the passion of Eternity?
Is this the dream He dreamed who shaped the suns
And marked their ways upon the ancient deep?
Down all the caverns of Hell to their last gulf
There is no shape more terrible than this—
More tongued with censure of the world's blind greed—
More filled with signs and portents for the soul—
More packt with danger to the universe.

—Edwin Markham, "The Man with the Hoe"

3. Choose one of the selections listed below, analyze it by answering the following questions, and prepare it for class delivery.
   a. What is the central idea of the selection?
   b. What are the main units of thought and how are they related to each other?
   c. Do you understand the meaning of every sentence, phrase, and word in the selection? Does anything puzzle you?
   d. How can you make use of pause, emphasis, pitch, inflection, rate, and volume in interpreting this selection?

You will find many of these poems in anthologies or collections of poems in your library. Browse around a bit and see what you can find.

"Silence," by Edgar Lee Masters
"Abraham Lincoln Walks at Midnight," by Vachel Lindsay
"The Man He Killed," by Thomas Hardy
"Old Susan," by Walter de la Mare
"Grass," by Carl Sandburg
"A Ballad of Trees and the Master," by Sidney Lanier
"The Fool's Prayer," by Edward Rowland Sill
"When I Was One-and-Twenty," by A. E. Housman
"Laugh and Be Merry," by John Masefield
"Mending Wall," by Robert Frost
"Miniver Cheevy," by Edwin Arlington Robinson
"Lincoln, the Man of the People," by Edwin Markham
"Renascence," by Edna St. Vincent Millay
"The Ballad of William Sycamore," by Stephen Vincent Benét
"Miracles," by Walt Whitman

For identifying mood:

1. Identify the mood or feeling of the following lines. How do you think they should be read?

a. Strong gongs groaning as the guns boom far,
Don John of Austria is going to the war.

—G. K. Chesterton

b. Most weary seemed the sea, weary the oar,
Weary the wandering fields of barren foam.

—Alfred, Lord Tennyson

c. In the fell clutch of circumstance
I have not winced nor cried aloud.
Beneath the bludgeonings of chance
My head is bloody, but unbowed.

—W. E. Henley

d. Boot, saddle, to horse, and away!
Rescue my castle before the hot day
Brightens to blue from its silvery grey.

—Robert Browning

e. Sweet and low, sweet and low,
Wind of the western sea,

Low, low, breathe and blow,
  Wind of the western sea!

—Alfred, Lord Tennyson

f. O, there's a wind a-blowing, a-blowing from the west,
  And that of all the winds is the one I like the best . . .

—Allan Cunningham

g. Exult, O shores, and ring O bells!
  But I, with mournful tread,
Walk the deck my Captain lies,
  Fallen cold and dead.

—Walt Whitman

2. Prepare one of the following selections for reading to the class. Precede your reading with an analysis of the mood of the poem based upon these questions:

a. What is the general mood of the selection?

b. Is there any variety of mood expressed in individual parts of the poem?

c. Does the author convey his feeling through rhythmic pattern or word music or both?

There is sweet music here that softer falls
Than petals from blown roses on the grass,
Or night-dews on still waters between walls
Of shadowy granite, in a gleaming pass;
Music that gentlier on the spirit lies
Than tired eyelids upon tired eyes;
Music that brings sweet sleep down from the blissful skies.
Here are cool mosses deep,
And thro' the moss the ivies creep,
And in the stream the long-leaved flowers weep,
And from the craggy ledge the poppy hangs in sleep.

—Alfred, Lord Tennyson, "Song of the Lotus Eaters"

Last night at black midnight I woke with a cry,
The windows were shaking, there was thunder on high,
The floor was a-tremble, the door was a-jar,
White fires, crimson fires, shone from afar.
I rush to the dooryard. The city was gone.
My home was a hut without orchard or lawn.

It was mud-smear and logs near a whispering stream,
Nothing else built by man could I see in my dream . . .

Then . . .
Ghost-kings came headlong, row upon row,
Gods of the Indians, torches aglow.
They mounted the bear and the elk and the deer,
And eagles gigantic, aged and sere,
They rode long-horn cattle, they cried "A-la-la."
They lifted the knife, the bow and the spear,
They lifted ghost-torches from dead fires below,
The midnight made grand with the cry "A-la-la."
The midnight made grand with a red-god charge,
A red-god show,
A red-god show,
"A-la-la, a-la-la, a-la-la, a-la-la."

—VACHEL LINDSAY, "The Ghosts of the Buffaloes"

O world, I cannot hold thee close enough!
Thy winds, thy wide grey skies!
Thy mists that roll and rise!
Thy woods this autumn day, that ache and sag
And all but cry with colour! That gaunt crag
To crush! To lift the lean of that black bluff!
World, World, I cannot get thee close enough!

—EDNA ST. VINCENT MILLAY, "God's World"

Underneath the fallen blossom
In my bosom,
Is a letter I have hid.
It was brought to me this morning by a rider from the Duke.
"Madam, we regret to inform you that Lord Hartwell
Died in action Thursday se'n night."
As I read it in the white, morning sunlight,
The letters squirmed like snakes.
"Any answer, Madam," said my footman.
"No," I told him.
"See that the messenger takes some refreshment.
No, no answer."
And I walked into the garden,
Up and down the patterned paths,

In my stiff, correct brocade.
The blue and yellow flowers stood up proudly in the sun,
Each one.
I stood upright too.
Held rigid to the pattern
By the stiffness of my gown.
Up and down I walked,
Up and down.

—AMY LOWELL, "Patterns"

3. Bring to class some poetic selection which has a definite mood and read it aloud. Most anthologies of American and British poetry include some of these poems. Here is a list from which you might choose:

"The Bronco That Would Not Be Broken," by VACHEL LINDSAY
"A Vagabond Song," by BLISS CARMAN
"Weathers," by THOMAS HARDY
"The Glory Trail," by BADGER CLARK
"Pity Me Not," by EDNA ST. VINCENT MILLAY
"Richard Cory," by EDWARD ARLINGTON ROBINSON
"Little Boy Blue," by EUGENE FIELD
"Chicago," by CARL SANDBURG
"Columbus," by JOAQUIN MILLER
"Sneezles," by A. A. MILNE
"The Listeners," by WALTER DE LA MARE
"The Highwayman," by ALFRED NOYES
"The Death of the Hired Man," by ROBERT FROST
"Ballad of the Harp Weaver," by EDNA ST. VINCENT MILLAY
"A Farmer Remembers Lincoln," by WITTER BYNNER
"O Captain! My Captain!" by WALT WHITMAN

For practice in rhythm:

1. Read aloud the following lines for practice in rhythm and articulation:

a. The curfew tolls the knell of parting day,
The lowing herd wind slowly o'er the lea,
The plowman homeward plods his weary way,
And leaves the world to darkness and to me.

—THOMAS GRAY

b. The fair breeze blew, the white foam flew,
The furrow followed free.
We were the first that ever burst
Into that silent sea.

—S. T. COLERIDGE

c. The creeping tide came up along the sand,
And o'er and o'er the sand,
And round and round the sand,
As far as eye could see.

—CHARLES KINGSLEY

d. Serene the silver fishes glide,
Stern-lipped, and pale, and wonder-eyed!

—MAX EASTMAN

e. Come, and trip it as ye go,
On the light fantastic toe.

—JOHN MILTON

f. The cherry trees are seas of bloom and soft perfume and sweet perfume,
The cherry trees are seas of bloom (and oh, so near to London!)

—ALFRED NOYES

2. Practice reading aloud some of the following poems. They are selections which are highly rhythmical, so read them with care. Emphasize the natural swing of the lines, the music of the words, and the distinctness of your articulation. Mark the beats, if you wish, by tapping with your foot or with your hand, but do so lightly and gently. Don't let the beats become more important than the sense and feeling. Let your body respond to the flow of the lines by swaying in time with the music of the poem. Give yourself up to the pure fun of enjoying the lilt and melody in these poems.

I sprang to the stirrup, and Joris, and he;
I galloped, Dirck galloped, we galloped all three;
"Good speed!" cried the watch, as the gate bolts undrew;
"Speed!" echoed the wall to us galloping through;
Behind shut the postern, the lights sank to rest,
And into the midnight we galloped abreast.

—ROBERT BROWNING,
"How They Brought the Good News from Ghent to Aix"

Oh! young Lochinvar is come out of the west,
Through all the wide Border his steed was the best;
And save his good broadsword he weapons had none;
He rode all unarmed, and he rode all alone.
So faithful in love and so dauntless in war,
There never was knight like the young Lochinvar.

He stayed not for brake and he stopped not for stone;
He swam the Eske river where ford there was none;
But ere he alighted at Netherby gate,
The bride had consented, the gallant came late:
For a laggard in love and a dastard in war
Was to wed the fair Ellen of brave Lochinvar.

—WALTER SCOTT, "Lochinvar"

Out of the hills of Habersham,
Down the valleys of Hall,
I hurry amain to reach the plain,
Run the rapid and leap the fall,
Split at the rock and together again,
Accept my bed, or narrow or wide,
And flee from folly on every side
With a lover's pain to attain the plain
Far from the hills of Habersham,
Far from the valleys of Hall.

All down the hills of Habersham,
All through the valleys of Hall,
The rushes cried *Abide, abide,*
The willful waterweeds held me thrall,
The laving laurel turned my tide,
The ferns and the fondling grass said *Stay,*
The dewberry dipped for to work delay,
And the little reeds sighed *Abide, abide,*
Here in the hills of Habersham,
Here in the valleys of Hall.

—SIDNEY LANIER, "Song of the Chattahoochee"

Hear the loud alarum bells,
Brazen bells!
What a tale of terror, now, their turbulency tells!
In the startled ear of night
How they scream out their affright!
Too much horrified to speak,
They can only shriek, shriek,
Out of tune,
In a clamorous appealing to the mercy of the fire,

In a mad expostulation with the deaf and frantic fire,
Leaping higher, higher, higher,
With a desperate desire,
And a resolute endeavor
Now—now to sit or never,
By the side of the pale-faced moon.
Oh, the bells, bells, bells!
What a tale their terror tells
Of despair!
How they clang, and clash, and roar!
What a horror they outpour
On the bosom of the palpitating air!
Yet the ear it fully knows,
By the twanging
And the clanging,
How the danger ebbs and flows;
Yet the ear distinctly tells,
In the jangling
And the wrangling,
How the danger sinks and swells—
By the sinking or the swelling in the anger of the bells,
Of the bells,
Of the bells, bells, bells, bells,
Bells, bells, bells,
In the clamor and the clangor of the bells!

—Edgar Allan Poe, "The Bells"

Dim drums throbbing, in the hills half heard,
Where only on a nameless throne a crownless prince has stirred,
Where, risen from a doubtful seat and half-attainted stall,
The last knight of Europe takes weapons from the wall,
The last and lingering troubadour to whom the bird has sung,
That once went singing southward when all the world was young.
In that enormous silence, tiny and unafraid,
Comes up along a winding road the noise of the Crusade.
Strong gongs groaning as the guns boom far,
Don John of Austria is going to the war,
Stiff flags straining in the night-blasts cold
In the gloom black-purple, in the glint old-gold,
Torchlight crimson on the copper kettle-drums,

Then the tuckets, then the trumpets, then the cannon, and he comes.
Don John laughing in the brave beard curled,
Spurning of his stirrups like the thrones of all the world,
Holding his head up for a flag of all the free.
Love-light of Spain—hurrah!
Death-light of Africa!
Don John of Austria
Is riding to the sea.

—G. K. CHESTERTON, "Lepanto"

3. Choose for reading one of the following poems, which have been selected for their rhythmical, musical effects. Study it carefully and patiently practice it aloud at home until you capture its swing and tunefulness. Then read it to your classmates, concentrating on the music of the words and the rhythm of the lines. You'll find most of these selections in collections of modern verse such as the following:

A Little Treasury of American Poetry, edited by OSCAR WILLIAMS. Scribner.
Modern Poetry: American and British, edited by KIMON FRIAR and J. M. BRINNIN. Appleton-Century-Crofts.
New Poems by American Poets, edited by ROLFE HUMPHRIES. Ballantine Books.
Modern American Poetry, edited by LOUIS UNTERMEYER. Harcourt, Brace.
Modern British Poetry, edited by LOUIS UNTERMEYER. Harcourt, Brace.

Selections

"The Barrel Organ," by ALFRED NOYES
"Sea Fever," by JOHN MASEFIELD
"Ulalume," by EDGAR ALLAN POE
"How a Cat Was Annoyed and a Poet Was Booted," by GUY WETMORE CARRYL
"General William Booth Enters into Heaven," by VACHEL LINDSAY
"The Mountain Whippoorwill," by STEPHEN VINCENT BENÉT
"Hiawatha," by HENRY WADSWORTH LONGFELLOW
"Gunga Din," by RUDYARD KIPLING
"When the Frost Is on the Punkin," by JAMES WHITCOMB RILEY
"Eve," by RALPH HODGSON
"Time, You Old Gypsy Man," by RALPH HODGSON
"A Wanderer's Song," by JOHN MASEFIELD
"The War Song of the Saracens," by JAMES ELROY FLECKER
"The Lake Isle of Innisfree," by WILLIAM BUTLER YEATS
"Ode: We Are the Music Makers," by ARTHUR O'SHAUGHNESSY
"We'll Go No More A-Roving," by W. E. HENLEY

For general study and practice:

1. Put into practice the things you've learned so far in this unit about reading poetry aloud by preparing one of these selections for oral interpretation to the class.

Robert Frost reading to Dartmouth College students.

STOPPING BY WOODS ON A SNOWY EVENING

Whose woods these are I think I know.
His house is in the village though;
He will not see me stopping here
To watch his woods fill up with snow.

My little horse must think it queer
To stop without a farmhouse near
Between the woods and frozen lake
The darkest evening of the year.

He gives his harness bells a shake
To ask if there is some mistake.
The only other sound's the sweep
Of easy wind and downy flake.

The woods are lovely, dark and deep,
But I have promises to keep,

And miles to go before I sleep,
And miles to go before I sleep.

—Robert Frost

The Oracle

I lay upon the summer grass.
A gold-haired sunny child came by,
And looked at me, as loath to pass,
With questions in her lingering eye.

She stopped and wavered, then drew near
And bent her gay attentive head,
And o'er my shoulder stooped to peer.
"Why do you read?" she said.

"I read a poet of old time,
Who sang through all his living hours
Beauty of earth—the streams, the flowers,
And stars, more lovely than his rhyme.

"And now I read him, since men go
Forgetful of these sweetest things;
Since he and I love brooks that flow,
And dawns, and bees, and flash of wings."

She stared at me with laughing look,
Then clasped her hands upon my knees:
"How strange to read it in a book!
I could have shown you all of these!"

—Arthur Davison Ficke

When I Was One-and-Twenty

When I was one-and-twenty
  I heard a wise man say,
"Give crowns and pounds and guineas
  But not your heart away;
Give pearls away and rubies
  But keep your fancy free."
But I was one-and-twenty,
  No use to talk to me.

When I was one-and-twenty
I heard him say again,
"The heart out of the bosom
Was never given in vain;
'Tis paid with sighs a-plenty
And sold for endless rue."
And I am two-and twenty,
And oh, 'tis true, 'tis true.

—A. E. Housman

Invictus

Out of the night that covers me,
Black as the pit from pole to pole,
I thank whatever gods may be
For my unconquerable soul.

In the fell clutch of circumstance
I have not winced nor cried aloud.
Under the bludgeonings of chance
My head is bloody, but unbowed.

Beyond this place of wrath and tears
Looms but the Horror of the shade,
And yet the menace of the years
Finds and shall find me unafraid.

It matters not how strait the gate,
How charged with punishments the scroll,
I am the master of my fate:
I am the captain of my soul.

—William Ernest Henley

Thrushes

The City Financier
walks in the gardens,
stiffly, because of
his pride and his burdens.

The daisies, looking
up, observe

only a self-
respecting curve.

The thrushes only
see a flat
table-land
of shiny hat.

He looks importantly
about him,
while all the spring
goes on without him.

—HUMBERT WOLFE

THE PLAINT OF THE CAMEL

Canary-birds feed on sugar and seed,
Parrots have crackers to crunch;
And, as for the poodles, they tell me the noodles
Have chickens and cream for their lunch.
But there's never a question
About MY digestion—
ANYTHING does for me!

Cats, you're aware, can repose in a chair
Chickens can roost upon rails;
Puppies are able to sleep in a stable,
And oysters can slumber in pails.
But no one supposes
A poor Camel dozes—
ANY PLACE does for me!

Lambs are enclosed where it's never exposed,
Coops are constructed for hens;
Kittens are treated to houses well heated,
And pigs are protected by pens.
But a Camel comes handy
Wherever it's sandy—
ANYWHERE does for me!

People would laugh if you rode a giraffe,
Or mounted the back of an ox;

It's nobody's habit to ride on a rabbit,
Or try to bestraddle a fox.
But as for a Camel, he's
Ridden by families—
ANY LOAD does for me!

A snake is as round as a hole in the ground;
Weasels are wavy and sleek;
And no alligator could ever be straighter
Than lizards that live in a creek.
But a Camel's all lumpy
And bumpy and humpy—
ANY SHAPE does for me!

—CHARLES EDWARD CARRYL

HAMLET'S SOLILOQUY

To be, or not to be—that is the question:
Whether 'tis nobler in the mind to suffer
The slings and arrows of outrageous fortune
Or to take arms against a sea of troubles,
And by opposing end them. To die—to sleep—
No more; and by a sleep to say we end
The heartache, and the thousand natural shocks
That flesh is heir to. 'Tis a consummation
Devoutly to be wished. To die—to sleep.
To sleep—perchance to dream: ay, there's the rub!
For in that sleep of death what dreams may come
When we have shuffled off this mortal coil,
Must give us pause.

—WILLIAM SHAKESPEARE

PORTIA'S MERCY SPEECH

The quality of mercy is not strained;
It droppeth as the gentle rain from heaven
Upon the place beneath. It is twice blest—
It blesseth him that gives, and him that takes:
'Tis mightiest in the mightiest. It becomes
The thronèd monarch better than his crown.
His sceptre shows the force of temporal power,

There are many reasons for learning to read aloud well—as any babysitter can tell you.

The attribute to awe and majesty,
Wherein doth sit the dread and fear of kings;
But mercy is above this sceptred sway;
It is enthronèd in the hearts of kings,
It is an attribute to God himself;
And earthly power doth then show likest God's
When mercy seasons justice.

—William Shakespeare

Brutus's Explanation of Caesar's Assassination

Romans, countrymen, and lovers, hear me for my cause, and be silent, that you may hear. Believe me for mine honour, and have respect to mine honour, that you may believe. Censure me in your wisdom, and awake your senses, that you may the better judge. If there be any in this assembly, any dear friend of Caesar's, to him I say that Brutus' love to Caesar was no less than his. If then that friend demand why Brutus rose against Caesar, this is my answer: Not that I loved Caesar less, but that I loved

Rome more. Had you rather Caesar were living, and die all slaves, than that Caesar were dead, to live all freemen? As Caesar loved me, I weep for him; as he was fortunate, I rejoice at it; as he was valiant, I honour him; but—as he was ambitious, I slew him. There is tears for his love; joy for his fortune; honour for his valour; and death for his ambition. Who is here so base that would be a bondman? If any, speak; for him have I offended. Who is here so rude that would not be a Roman? If any, speak; for him have I offended. Who is here so vile that will not love his country? If any, speak; for him have I offended. I pause for a reply.

—WILLIAM SHAKESPEARE

MARK ANTONY'S REPLY AT CAESAR'S FUNERAL

Friends, Romans, countrymen, lend me your ears;
I come to bury Caesar, not to praise him.
The evil that men do lives after them;
The good is oft interrèd with their bones.
So let it be with Caesar. The noble Brutus
Hath told you Caesar was ambitious.
If it were so, it was a grievous fault,
And grievously hath Caesar answered it.
Here, under leave of Brutus and the rest
(For Brutus is an honourable man;
So are they all, all honourable men),
Come I to speak in Caesar's funeral.
He was my friend, faithful and just to me;
But Brutus says he was ambitious,
And Brutus is an honourable man.
He hath brought many captives home to Rome,
Whose ransoms did the general coffers fill.
Did this in Caesar seem ambitious?
When that the poor have cried, Caesar hath wept;
Ambition should be made of sterner stuff.
Yet Brutus says he was ambitious;
And Brutus is an honourable man.
You all did see that on the Lupercal
I thrice presented him a kingly crown,
Which he did thrice refuse. Was this ambition?

Yet Brutus says he was ambitious;
And sure he is an honourable man.
I speak not to disprove what Brutus spoke,
But here I am to speak what I do know.
You all did love him once, not without cause.
What cause withholds you then to mourn for him?
O judgment, thou art fled to brutish beasts,
And men have lost their reason! Bear with me.
My heart is in the coffin there with Caesar,
And I must pause till it come back to me.

—WILLIAM SHAKESPEARE

Reading in Groups: Choral Speaking

The first part of this unit was concerned with reading by individuals. Now we turn to *group* reading, an activity which is finding increasing popularity in schools everywhere. Verse-speaking choirs or choral-reading groups have long been popular in England. Within the past twenty years experiments with choral speaking in the United States have produced very interesting results. Group reading has proved itself to be a valuable form of artistic expression and a most helpful aid in improving speech. It is both an end in itself and a means to an end. Many people who are too self-conscious to enjoy reading aloud by themselves gain a deep emotional satisfaction from reading good literature aloud in company with others. And many students whose voices are dull and monotonous, whose enunciation is indistinct and slurred, whose expression lacks variety and vitality, find that reading in chorus offers an unusual and enjoyable means of bettering their speech and tone.

If you are given an opportunity to study choral speaking and to participate in group readings as a part of your activities in speech, accept the opportunity eagerly. This is what it can do for you.

What Choral Speaking Can Do for You

1. *Choral speaking can acquaint you with much that is great and stimulating in prose and poetry.*

2. *Choral speaking can increase your sensitive response to meaning, mood, and melody.* To be exposed to selections which seize the imagination and attract the ear, and to share the utterance of them with others is a very satisfying and broadening experience.

3. *Choral speaking can give you great freedom of expression.* Because choral speaking is a group activity, and because you can lose yourself in the crowd, you are less inhibited, less self-conscious, and less restrained than when you read aloud alone.

4. *Choral speaking can train your sense of rhythm and coordination.* This is of great importance in group reading. Learning to speak in step with other people is like learning to march in step; you acquire a sense of timing through feeling and imitation.

5. *Choral speaking can help you to make fuller use of your voice.* Resonance, flexibility, volume, range, pitch, and good use of pause, emphasis, and inflection are all necessary for group readers. Practice with others will increase your own ability in the essentials of good speech, and will help you to develop a more pleasing voice.

6. *Choral speaking can improve your enunciation.* A precise and delicate use of consonant and vowel sounds is required in group reading. Practicing with others will help you to eliminate clumsy, sluggish, and slipshod diction.

7. *Choral speaking can aid your control of breathing.* One of the first things group readers must learn to do is to regulate their intake and output of breath according to the pauses which occur in their reading. Light, quick breathing without gasping is a by-product of choral speaking.

8. *Choral speaking can give you enjoyment.* The pleasures of *singing* with a group, of letting yourself go with the swinging tune and the fine words of a good song, are the same in *reading* with a group. Once you become accustomed to the techniques of reading in chorus, you'll have many enjoyable experiences as a member of a speaking choir.

Organizing a Reading Group. Organizing a group of people and training them to read literary selections in unison is somewhat similar to organizing and training a glee club or choir. At first the main responsibility for success lies with the leader, who must have a love of poetry, a good sense of rhythm, a keen ear for tone, an ability to inspire others, and much patience. In the beginning your teacher or coach will be your leader; but later, as you acquire experience, you may have a student conductor who will direct you. He will indicate the starting signal, the changes of pace, the variety of mood, the phrasing, and the pausing, and will give any other directions necessary to keep the group together and to maintain a unity of expression while reading.

The group is usually divided by voice "color," or tone, into three sections: high, medium, and low. The high, or "light," voices, usually the girls, are used for light, happy, gay moods, for quick, dancing movements, for delicate, fairylike parts, or for emphasizing high, shrill, eerie sounds. The medium-pitched voices, often a combination of boys and girls, read lines which require no great extremes of emotion or variety of tone. The low, or "dark," voices, frequently only the boys, are given lines which reflect a masculine robustness, depth, and vigor, a slow, heavy pace, or a somber, tragic mood. The voices of all three sections, regardless of pitch, should be flexible and able to interpret many moods. The entire reading group, while striving for vocal coordination, must at the same time preserve the freshness and spontaneity of the selections it is reading.

It is customary for the readers to be grouped together on a platform or in the classroom according to their voice classifications in a manner similar to this:

Placement of Voices In a Reading Group

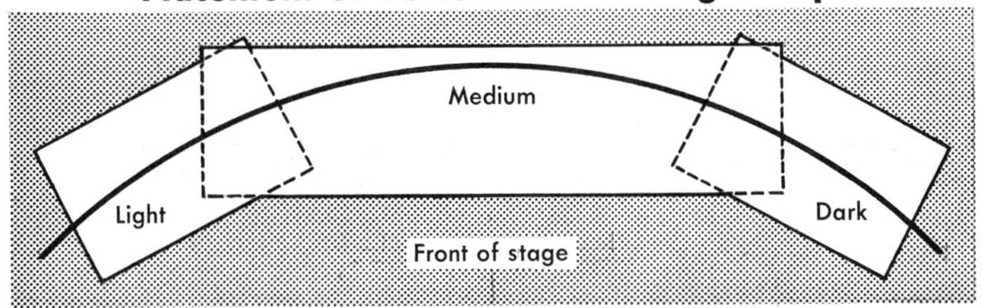

Choosing Suitable Selections. At first your leader will have the burden of selecting poems or prose passages for interpretation. But every member of a reading group should learn what is suitable for choral reading, so that he may look for selections and add them to the repertoire of his group. Here are some guides and examples:

Group 1

Begin with simple rhymes and jingles to get the feeling of chorus work. After a preliminary period of practicing such material, you should start looking for selections that seize the imagination and that have dramatic or artistic value.

Beginning Selections

Mother Goose nursery rhymes
Nonsense jingles

Marching songs
Work songs
Sea chanteys
Plain ballads with refrains or dialogue
Simple lyrics and songs
Psalms from the Bible

Advanced Selections

Odes
Elegies
Narratives of epic quality
Great lyrics
Dramatic verse
Choral drama
Antiphonal selections
Rhythmical prose; Bible passages

***Group* 2**

A poem or prose passage that has strong rhythm, good melody, and engaging ear appeal is a desirable selection for group reading.

"How They Brought the Good News from Ghent to Aix," by Robert Browning
"Boot and Saddle," by Robert Browning
"Tarantella," by Hilaire Belloc
"The Congo," by Vachel Lindsay
"The Barrel Organ," by Alfred Noyes
"I Hear America Singing," by Walt Whitman
"Christopher Robin," by A. A. Milne
"Spring," by Thomas Nash
"Battle Hymn of the Republic," by Julia Ward Howe
"The Camel's Hump," by Rudyard Kipling
"The Owl and the Pussy Cat," by Edward Lear

***Group* 3**

Narrative poems that have contrasting moods, vivid pictures, or strong climaxes are especially suitable. Poems with refrains and dialogues are always pleasant to hear. Try the following traditional ballads:

"Bonnie George Campbell"
"Barbara Allen"

"Sir Patrick Spens"
"Lord Randal"
"Edward, Edward"
"Ballad of Hynd Horn"
"Robin Hood and Allan-a-Dale"
"The Wraggle Taggle Gypsies"
"The Barring of the Door"

Also

"Lochinvar," by Sir WALTER SCOTT
"The Ballad of the Oysterman," by OLIVER WENDELL HOLMES
"Annabel Lee," by EDGAR ALLAN POE

Group 4

Lyric poetry that is simple, straightforward, and tuneful is also satisfactory. Avoid selections which are too thoughtful, subtle, personal, melancholy, or profound. Sonnets are too personal for group reading. Also avoid selections which are trite, cheap, or commonplace. Try these:

"Hunting Song," by Sir WALTER SCOTT
"Weathers," by THOMAS HARDY
"Foreboding," by DON BLANDING
"Time, You Old Gypsy Man," by RALPH HODGSON
"A Wet Sheet and a Flowing Sea," by ALLAN CUNNINGHAM
"Song of the Bow," by A. CONAN DOYLE

Preparing Selections for Group Reading. Just as it is a leader's responsibility to organize the reading group and to direct the choice of readings, so is it his obligation to see that the selections are properly prepared. But the group, too, should understand the procedure to be followed that will help to turn a mass of raw recruits into polished, smooth-spoken veterans of oral interpretation. Follow these steps:

Step 1. *Analyze the meaning and mood of each selection to be read.* After a poem or prose passage has been chosen for group reading, the leader should read it in its entirety to the choir. There follows then a complete discussion of the nature, the meaning, and the emotional feeling of the selection.

Step 2. *Study the rhythm and word music of the selection.* A reading group is unable to enter fully into the thought and feeling of a poem or prose passage until the rhythm and music have been analyzed. After your leader has read the lines of a selection to the group once or twice, emphasizing the lilt and sway of the rhythmic pattern, the group should try it, swaying, tapping, or beating in time with the beats of the lines. Be quick to discover and eliminate sluggish, dragging rhythm, unless that is the mood of the poem. Avoid awkward breaking of the rhythm or falling into a singsong tone. Remember always that it takes both *words* and *music* to make a song come to life. Discuss together any problems that arise and let your leader have the final word when decisions are to be made.

Step 3. *Watch the phrasing of the selection.* All of you must agree as to what thought should be given predominance and what ideas should be subordinated. Your breathing and pausing are dependent upon what you decide. Remember that punctuation and the ends of lines are *not* sure guides for pausing and breathing; the continuity of thought is all-important. For instance, in the following lines you must have sufficient breath at the beginning to carry the thought through to its full completion without a gasp or a pause at the end of the second line.

Boot, saddle, to horse, and away!
Rescue my castle before the hot day
Brightens to blue from its silvery grey.
Boot, saddle, to horse, and away!

—Robert Browning

Practice in thought-phrasing, especially, will help you to determine where you must pause and how you must control your breathing. It is essential that a reading group should breathe and pause as a unit without falling into mechanical sound patterns and without endangering the continuity of the lines it is reading.

Step 4. *Practice for perfection.* Having analyzed a selection for its meaning, mood, and melody, your reading choir should now be ready for the oral practice that precedes final presentation. Mastery of the fundamentals of good reading is essential. Let's review them here:

a. Voice fundamentals. One of the most important marks of a well-trained reading group is the color, life, and spirit of its voices. A group that is on familiar terms with the fundamentals of voice production can use its knowledge very effectively in making a sensitive vocal response to any selection it is reading. A bit of practice now and then will keep the choir on its toes. Refer to "Shop Talk" (Unit 4) for practice exercises in the following fundamentals of voice production:

Pause	Inflection	Resonance	Volume
Change of pitch	Tempo	Range	Flexibility

b. Accuracy of speech. Speech that is clear and precise is essential for group readers. Every group should frequently practice tongue twisters, consonant and vowel drills, and exercises for maintaining pace with accuracy. A few such setting-up exercises should be part of the group's practice every time it meets. Don't do it mechanically but rather in a gamelike spirit so that the drill is enjoyable. Practice the following exercises in unison, first slowly, then more rapidly, for the purpose of maintaining accuracy of speech at any pace.

(1) Peter Piper picked a peck of pickled peppers;
A peck of pickled peppers Peter Piper picked.
If Peter Piper picked a peck of pickled peppers,
Where's the peck of pickled peppers Peter Piper picked?

(2) Theophilus Thistle, the successful thistle sifter,
while sifting a sieveful of unsifted thistles,
thrust three thousand thistles through the thick of his thumb.
Since Theophilus Thistle, the successful thistle sifter,
while sifting a sieveful of unsifted thistles, thrust
three thousand thistles through the thick of his thumb,
see that thou, while sifting a sieveful of unsifted thistles,
thrust *not* three thousand thistles through the thick of thy thumb.

(3) There was a crooked man who walked a crooked mile;
He found a crooked sixpence against a crooked stile;
He found a crooked cat,
Who caught a crooked mouse,
And they all lived together
In a little crooked house.

(4) Sing a song of sixpence,
A pocket full of rye.
Four and twenty blackbirds
Baked in a pie.
When the pie was opened,
The birds began to sing;
Wasn't that a dainty dish
To set before the king?

c. Breath control. Your group must also be well versed in how to take enough breath before starting a selection, how to renew breath as needed, and how to regulate its output while reading, so that both short phrases and long ones are given their full value of sound. Special attention should be given to this during the preparation of each selection, and breathing exercises should be practiced as a regular procedure every time the group meets. Unit 4 includes a drill you can use.

Methods of Presenting Selections. There are many ways in which reading choirs present selections. Determining what method your group should use for a particular poem or prose passage depends upon how you analyze the construction of the selection, what its sound patterns are, how you interpret its mood and meaning, and how well trained your group may be. Here are four of the most commonly practiced methods.

Method 1. *Refrain work.* The simplest type of selection for a reading group to present is that which involves chorus or refrain work. A single speaker or a small group reads the story carried by the main stanzas, and the entire group joins in the chorus. You've sung songs in this manner, and many of you are familiar with responsive reading in Sunday school or church. It's a method of storytelling as old as literature itself; it was especially popular in the days of the wandering minstrels and troubadours from the 11th to the 13th century.

Method 2. *Two-part work.* Two-part reading, or antiphonal work, is the alternate reading of stanzas or parts of stanzas by two groups. Many poems easily lend themselves to this treatment, giving reading groups a greater opportunity for variety of dramatic expression and for improving their teamwork. Precise speech, accurate timing, vocal harmony, and sensitive interpretation of varying moods are your goals.

Usually the material for two-part work is confined to selections which have questions and answers, appeals and responses, or parallel constructions. There must be a balancing of one idea against another in antiphonal work, so that the contrasting voices may heighten the dramatic effort of the selection. "Light" voices should interpret the questions, the appeals, or the delicate, tender passages. "Dark" voices should deal with the answers, the responses, or the passionate, strenuous passages.

Method 3. *Multiple-part work.* Some selections offer a reading choir an opportunity to explore the tonal possibilities of its members by balancing one group against another. In this way the sharp differences in meaning and mood are reflected by the differences in tones, the effectiveness of the selection being thereby heightened. As your group improves in its ability, you may practice selections which offer such variety of effects. Much of the pleasure that is a part of choral reading comes from trying

The power and effectiveness of choral speaking was recognized by the ancient Greeks. The Chorus of speakers became an important part of their drama.

such multiple-part work. The choir, divided into three or more groups, analyzes the selection and then decides how the various lines or stanzas should be apportioned. Parts may be taken by single speakers, small groups of three or four, larger groups of ten or more, or by the entire choir. The important element is the effective presentation of the feeling and meaning of the poem by careful balancing of the multiple voices.

Method 4. Unison work. All your practice in studying rhythms, phrasing, refrain work, solo parts, and group work leads you to this final step in the development of a voice choir: unison reading. When the many voices of a reading group can interpret the meaning, mood, and rhythm of a poem with singleness of purpose and unity of expression as if they were one voice, they have reached a high level of achievement. It is difficult to keep together in pace and rhythm at the same time that the voice lends life and color to the words. Conscientious practice, however, will give worthwhile results. The harmony of many voices knit together in common expression lends power and beauty to many literary selections.

In planning unison work think of a symphony orchestra. The voices of your choir are grouped like the instruments of the orchestra, the deep tones in one section, the light tones in another, all balanced for the best effect. They all play together in perfect harmony, at the same time displaying subtle variations of tone and delicate shades of sound that can be delightful to hear. To achieve such a well-blended effect requires much patience, practice, and attention to detail, the most important of which is, perhaps, training the group to work in absolute unison.

Review of Group Reading

1. Group reading offers an unusual and enjoyable means of appreciating literature and improving speech.
2. Organizing a group requires a responsible leader with cooperating members classified in voice groups.
3. Suitable material for group reading should have strong ear appeal, and may include simple songs and jingles, rhythmical prose and poetic passages, narrative poems, and short lyric poems.
4. Preparing selections for reading involves careful analysis of meaning and mood, study of rhythmical pattern, careful attention to phrasing, and practice for perfection of vocal details.
5. Methods of presenting selections include refrain work, two-part work, multiple-part work, and unison reading.

ACTIVITIES

For organizing a reading group:

1. Take an inventory of the voice "color" of the members of your class. Have each student read a short selection, and let the class decide whether his normal voice is light, dark, or medium. How many voices have you in each group? If you have a tape recorder, study the playback to determine each student's vocal quality.
2. Arrange your class in three groups (light, medium, and dark) and plan a reading of the rhyme "Three Blind Mice." Have the dark voices read the first line, the medium voices read the second line, the light voices read lines 3, 4, and 5. End with the dark voices on the last line. Here is the rhyme:

dark voices	*Three blind mice, three blind mice.*
medium voices	*See how they run, see how they run.*
light voices	*They all ran after the farmer's wife;* *She cut off their tails with a carving knife;* *Did you ever see such a sight in your life,*
dark voices	*As three blind mice?*

3. Divide the class into four groups of voices, high and low for the girls and the same for the boys. Have each group select a leader, choose a short selection that suits the group's voice "color," and prepare it for unison reading. Tape-record the reading so that the class can study the vocal differences of the four groups.

4. Hold auditions for selecting two or three group leaders or conductors. The leaders should be good readers, have a good sense of rhythm, and be able to contribute imaginative suggestions as to ways of analyzing and presenting selections.

For preparing selections:

1. Have your leader read this poem to the class and then discuss it on the basis of the questions which follow it.

Experience

Deborah danced, when she was two,
As buttercups and daffodils do;
Spirited, frail, naïvely bold,
Her hair a ruffled crest of gold.
And whenever she spoke her voice went singing
Like water up from a fountain springing.

But now her step is quiet and slow;
She walks the way primroses go;
Her hair is yellow instead of gilt,
Her voice is losing its lovely lilt,
And in place of her wild, delightful ways
A quaint precision rules her days.

For Deborah now is three, and oh,
She knows so much that she did not know.

—Aline Kilmer

For meaning and mood:

a. What is the thought of the first stanza?
b. What contrasting thought is brought out in the second stanza?
c. What climax is reached in the last two lines?
d. Why is the title particularly appropriate?
e. In what way can the voices of the group reflect the contrasting moods of the poem? How do you think the climax should be read?
f. What emotional response would the group like to get from the listeners?

For rhythm:

a. How many beats or stresses are there in each line?
b. Does the rhythm of the first stanza seem gay and dancing? What is the rhythmic feeling in the second stanza? What is the difference in tempo between the two stanzas?
c. How do you think the last two lines should be read?
d. Are there any special words that give vivid impressions of mood and spirit?
e. Read the poem aloud together to get the feeling of its tunefulness.

For phrasing and pausing:

a. Why do the main pauses come at the ends of lines 2, 4, and 6 in the first stanza?
b. What is the relationship in thought between lines 5 and 6? How can you bring it out by means of pause and inflection?
c. How many ideas are brought out in the second stanza? Why are the pauses more deliberate in this stanza?
d. What is the main thought of the last two lines of the poem? How can you use pause to bring out the surprise ending?

2. Determine the meaning and the mood of each of the following brief selections.

THE WARNING

Just now,
Out of the strange
Still dusk . . . as strange, as still. . .
A white moth flew. Why am I grown
So cold?

—ADELAIDE CRAPSEY

ORNITHOLOGY FOR BEGINNERS

The bird that feeds from off my palm
Is sleek, affectionate, and calm,
But double, to me, is worth the thrush
A-flickering in the elder bush.

—DOROTHY PARKER

A late lark twitters from the quiet skies;
And from the west,
Where the sun, his day's work ended,
Lingers as in content,
There falls on the old, grey city
An influence luminous and serene,
A shining peace.

—WILLIAM ERNEST HENLEY, "Margaritae Sorori"

3. Try this rhythm practice. When you were small, your sense of rhythm was satisfied by nursery rhymes, nonsense jingles, and counting rhymes. Who hasn't said verses like this?

Bean porridge hot,
Bean porridge cold,
Bean porridge in the pot
Nine days old.

You know the rest of it. Say it, now, all together, and notice how your hands almost automatically clap out the rhythm as they once did. Say some others, as a group, beating time with the rhythm of the lines. Try "London Bridge is falling down," "Mary had a little lamb," "Yankee Doodle went to town," and "Peter, Peter, pumpkin eater." You'll find you still have a strong sense of rhythm. This rhythmical sense is very important in group reading. You must develop it, learning subtle variations and syncopations as you progress in choral reading.

4. Prepare for rhythm practice that part of Vachel Lindsay's "The Congo" which you'll find here. Let us examine some of those lines to establish the rhythm. The words that require the strong beats will be marked with a strong accent mark (/); the words or syllables requiring light stress will be marked with a breve (◡). Read the lines aloud together, pounding your desk or table with your fist only on each *strong* beat to emphasize the rhythm. Notice the poet's marginal suggestion.

Then along that riverbank
A thousand miles
Tattooed cannibals danced in files;
Then I heard the boom of the blood-lust song
And a thigh-bone beating on a tin-pan gong.
And "BLOOD" screamed the whistles and the
   fifes of the warriors,
"BLOOD" screamed the skull-faced, lean
   witch-doctors,
"Whirl ye the deadly voo-doo rattle,
Harry the uplands,
Steal all the cattle,
Rattle-rattle, rattle-rattle,
Bing!
Boomlay, boomlay, boomlay, BOOM"

A rapidly piling climax of speed and racket

—Vachel Lindsay, "The Congo"

You may find two difficulties in this first reading. First, it is hard to keep together as a group in your reading; second, you may notice a natural tendency to plod along rather heavily, in singsong fashion. The first difficulty probably will vanish as you continue practicing. The second difficulty will increase unless you modify the beats by shifting the accents slightly, as is done with ragtime music. A quick, light pause of the voice will help to accomplish that. For instance, examine the third line of the selection again. You have probably read it too stiffly and regularly, like this:

TATTooed CANNibals DANCED in FILES

If you did that, try reading it again, putting a short pause after *cannibals,* placing a light stress on the word *danced,* and running the last three words close together:

TATTooed CANNibals [quick pause] danced in FILES

You can increase the effectiveness of lines 6 and 7 by overemphasizing the heavy beat on the word *Blood,* pausing quickly, shifting all the other strong beats in the rest of those lines to light accents, and lowering the pitch of your voice.

And BLOOD [short pause] screamed the whistles and the fifes of the warriors

BLOOD [short pause] screamed the skull-faced, lean witch-doctors.

Your ear will soon tell you how syncopation of this sort can quicken the pulse of a poem, keeping it free from the dullness that comes with strict regularity of beats. Continue practicing, using a tom-tom to help you master its rhythm.

5. Ask your teacher to read aloud several times the following selections by Robert Louis Stevenson. After the first reading by the teacher, which should give you a general idea of the rhythm, keep time with a light tapping of your foot or hand. Then read aloud as a group, establishing the rhythmic feeling of the poems.

a. How do you like to go up in a swing,
Up in the air so blue?
Oh, I do think it the pleasantest thing
Ever a child can do!

b. When I was sick and lay a-bed,
I had two pillows at my head,
And all my toys beside me lay
To keep me happy all the day.

c. Dark brown is the river,
Golden is the sand.
It flows along forever,
With trees on either hand.

—Robert Louis Stevenson, *A Child's Garden of Verses*

6. For additional rhythm practice, try the selections quoted earlier in this unit under the activities for "The Reading of Poetry."

"How They Brought the Good News from Ghent to Aix"
"Lochinvar"
"Song of the Chattahoochee"
"The Bells"
"Lepanto"

7. Study the phrasing of the following selections before reading them aloud. Decide what to emphasize, where to pause, where to breathe.

a. With sloping masts and dipping prow,
As who pursued with yell and blow
Still treads the shadow of his foe,
And forward bends his head,
The ship drove fast, loud roared the blast,
And southward aye we fled.

—Samuel Taylor Coleridge

b. Orpheus with his lute made trees
And the mountaintops that freeze
Bow themselves, when he did sing.

—William Shakespeare

c. It is a beauteous evening, calm and free,
The holy time is quiet as a Nun
Breathless with adoration; the broad sun
Is sinking down in its tranquillity.

—William Wordsworth

d. I will lift up mine eyes unto the hills, from whence cometh my help.
My help cometh from the Lord, which made Heaven and earth.
He will not suffer thy foot to be moved:
He that keepeth thee will not slumber.
Behold, he that keepeth Israel shall neither slumber nor sleep.
The Lord is thy keeper:
The Lord is thy shade upon thy right hand.
The sun shall not smite thee by day, nor the moon by night.
The Lord shall preserve thee from all evil:
He shall preserve thy soul.
The Lord shall preserve thy going out and thy coming in
From this time forth, and even for evermore.

—Psalm 121

e. The night has a thousand eyes,
And the day but one;
Yet the light of the bright world dies
With the dying sun.

The mind has a thousand eyes,
And the heart but one;
Yet the light of a whole life dies
When love is done.

—F. W. Bourdillon

For methods of presenting selections:

1. Practice the following poem for refrain work. Notice that the last three lines of each stanza are the chorus. Let a solo speaker read the first four lines in each stanza and let the entire group read the last three lines. The solo speaker may be changed for each stanza to give more students an opportunity to read. He must always keep the rhythm free and moving so that the chorus may answer in perfect time without destroying the pace of the poem. Be sure that the chorus speaks with distinctness and that it keeps up the spirit of the selection.

The Fox

Fox went out on a chilly night,
Prayed to the moon for to give him light,
For he'd many a mile to go that night
Afore he reached the town-o,
The town-o, the town-o,
He'd many a mile to go that night
Afore he reached the town-o.

He ran till he came to a great big pen,
Where the ducks and the geese were put therein,—
"A couple of you will grease my chin
Afore I leave this town-o,
Town-o, town-o,
A couple of you will grease my chin
Afore I leave this town-o."

He grabbed the grey goose by the neck,
Throwed a duck across his back,
He didn't mind their "Quack-quack-quack,"
And the legs all dangling down-o,
Down-o, down-o,
He didn't mind their "Quack-quack-quack,"
And the legs all dangling down-o.

Then old mother Flipper-Flopper jumped out of bed,
Out of the window she cocked her head,–
Crying, "John! John! The grey goose is gone
And the fox is on the town-o,
Town-o, town-o!"
Crying, "John! John! The grey goose is gone,
And the fox is on the town-o!"

Then John, he went to the top of the hill,
Blowed his horn both loud and shrill;
The fox, he said, "I better flee with my kill
Or they soon be on my trail-o,
Trail-o, trail-o."
Fox, he said, "I better flee with my kill,
Or they soon be on my trail-o."

He ran till he came to his cozy den,
There were his little ones eight, nine, ten,–
They said, "Daddy, you better go back again,
'Cause it must be a mighty fine town-o,
Town-o, town-o."
They said, "Daddy, you better go back again,
'Cause it must be a mighty fine town-o."

Then the fox and his wife without any strife,
Cut up the goose with a fork and knife;
They never had sich a supper in their life
And the little ones chewed on the bones-o,
Bones-o, bones-o,
They never had sich a supper in their life
And the little ones chewed on the bones-o.

2. Select one of the following poems for group reading. Hold tryouts to choose solo speakers for the narrative parts. Refrains should be read by the whole group.

"Boot, saddle," by Robert Browning
"Barbara Allen," Traditional
"Duncan Gray," by Robert Burns
"The Stolen Child," by W. B. Yeats
"The Night of Trafalgar," by Thomas Hardy
"A Tragic Story," by W. M. Thackeray
"Spring," by Thomas Nash
"When Icicles Hang by the Wall," by William Shakespeare
"Blow, Blow, Thou Winter Wind," by William Shakespeare
"Ballad of Hynd Horn," Traditional

"Shoes and Stockings," by A. A. MILNE
"The Smuggler's Song," by RUDYARD KIPLING

3. One of the simplest yet most moving selections for your reading group to try is the Beatitudes, Matthew 5:3-11. Have the girls read the parts beginning with the word *Blessed* and ending with the colon (:) mark; have the boys read the responses, beginning with the word *for* in each verse and ending at the period. The last verse can be read by the entire group.

THE BEATITUDES

Blessed are the poor in spirit: for theirs is the kingdom of heaven.

Blessed are they that mourn: for they shall be comforted.

Blessed are the meek: for they shall inherit the earth.

Blessed are they which do hunger and thirst after righteousness: for they shall be filled.

Blessed are the merciful: for they shall obtain mercy.

Blessed are the pure in heart: for they shall see God.

Blessed are the peacemakers: for they shall be called the children of God.

Blessed are they which are persecuted for righteousness' sake: for theirs is the kingdom of heaven.

Blessed are ye, when men shall revile you, and persecute you, and shall say all manner of evil against you falsely, for my sake.

4. Try A. A. Milne's "Journey's End," given below, for further practice in two-part work. Watch your phrasing, keep together, and give the poem a light, whimsical touch. Let the girls read the questioning lines and the boys the responses.

JOURNEY'S END

Christopher, Christopher, where are you going,
Christopher Robin?
"Just up to the top of the hill,
Upping and upping until
I am right on the top of the hill,"
Said Christopher Robin.
Christopher, Christopher, why are you going,
Christopher Robin?
There's nothing to see, so when
You've got to the top, what then?
"Just down to the bottom again,"
Said Christopher Robin.

—A. A. MILNE

5. Select one of the following for additional two-part work:

"Lord Randal," TRADITIONAL
"Edward, Edward," TRADITIONAL
"Bessie Bell and Mary Gray," TRADITIONAL
"Joy of the Open Road," by BLISS CARMAN
"The Camel's Hump," by RUDYARD KIPLING
"Big Steamers," by RUDYARD KIPLING
"Under the Sea," by ALFRED, LORD TENNYSON

6. Divide the choir into three groups, light voices, dark voices, and medium voices. Now practice reading "Cargoes," by John Masefield. The light voices will read the first stanza; the dark, the second; and the medium, the third. Each group should carefully study its stanza for meaning, rhythm, phrasing, and tone color, and practice it for perfection before joining with the other groups for the finished presentation. Here is the poem with some suggestions for interpretation.

CARGOES

Quinquireme of Nineveh from distant Ophir
Rowing home to haven in sunny Palestine,
With a cargo of ivory,
And apes and peacocks,
Sandalwood, cedarwood, and sweet white wine.

Stately Spanish galleon coming from the Isthmus,
Dipping through the Tropics by the palm-green shores,
With a cargo of diamonds,
Emeralds, amethysts,
Topazes, and cinnamon, and gold moidores.

Dirty British coaster with a salt-caked smoke stack
Butting through the Channel in the mad March days,
With a cargo of Tyne coal,
Road-rail, pig-lead,
Firewood, iron-ware, and cheap tin trays.

First stanza. *Gentle and flowing.* Voices delicate and dreamy, reflecting the Oriental splendor of the kind of cargo carried by early five-tiered slave galleys.

Second stanza. *Robust and rolling.* Voices warm and lusty, reflecting the adventurous, buccaneering spirit of Elizabethan times and the richness of the cargo.

Third stanza. *Uneven and jerky.* Voices staccato, nasal, and metallic, reflecting the unromantic nature of present-day ships and their cargoes.

7. Practice the following poem for multiple-part work. Divide it among groups as suggested in the margin. After you have practiced it this way, you may plan an arrangement of your own, using more than three groups and perhaps some solo parts.

Falmouth

Medium voices

O, Falmouth is a fine town with ships in the bay,
And I wish from my heart it's there I was today;
I wish from my heart I was far away from here,
Sitting in my parlor and talking to my dear.

All voices

For it's home, dearie, home—it's home I want to be.
Our topsails are hoisted, and we'll away to sea.
O, the oak and the ash and the bonnie birken tree
They're all growing green in the old countrie.

Light voices

In Baltimore a-walking a lady I did meet
With her babe on her arm, as she came down the street,

Dark voices

And I thought how I sailed, and the cradle standing ready
For the pretty little babe that has never seen its daddie.

All voices

And it's home, dearie, home—it's home I want to be.
Our topsails are hoisted, and we'll away to sea.
O, the oak and the ash and the bonnie birken tree
They're all growing green in the old countrie.

Light voice

O, if it be a lass, she shall wear a golden ring;

Dark voice

And if it be a lad, he shall fight for his king:

Dark and medium

With his dirk and his hat and his little jacket blue
He shall walk the quarter-deck as his daddie used to do.

All voices

And it's home, dearie, home—it's home I want to be.
Our topsails are hoisted, and we'll away to sea.
O, the oak the ash and the bonnie birken tree
They're all growing green in the old countrie.

Medium

O, there's a wind a-blowing, a-blowing from the west,
And that of all the winds is the one I like the best,
For it blows at our backs, and it shakes our pennon free,
And it soon will blow us home to the old countrie.

All

For it's home, dearie, home—it's home I want to be.
Our topsails are hoisted, and we'll away to sea.
O, the oak and the ash and the bonnie birken tree
They're all growing green in the old countrie.

—W. E. HENLEY

8. Prepare one of the following poems for multiple-group reading:

"Gifts," by JAMES THOMSON
"Laugh and Be Merry," by JOHN MASEFIELD
"Pioneers! O Pioneers!" by WALT WHITMAN
"Beat! Beat! Drums!" by WALT WHITMAN
"The Bells," by EDGAR ALLAN POE
"Recessional," by RUDYARD KIPLING
"Danny Deever," by RUDYARD KIPLING
"Song of the Bow," by A. CONAN DOYLE
"Drake's Drum," by HENRY NEWBOLT
"All That's Past," by WALTER DE LA MARE
"Barrel Organ," by ALFRED NOYES
"Cradle Song," by A. A. MILNE

9. Try this poem for unison work. It is gentle in mood, slow in rhythm, subtle in word music. Study the metric pattern, decide upon phrasing and breathing, notice the lovely sounds, and practice for unity of expression and delicacy of touch.

CRADLE SONG

Sweet and low, sweet and low,
Wind of the western sea,
Low, low, breathe and blow,
Wind of the western sea!
Over the rolling waters go,
Come from the dying moon, and blow,
Blow him again to me;
While my little one, while my pretty one, sleeps.

Sleep and rest, sleep and rest,
Father will come to thee soon;
Rest, rest, on mother's breast,
Father will come to thee soon;
Father will come to his babe in the nest,
Silver sails all out of the west
Under the silver moon:
Sleep, my little one, sleep, my pretty one, sleep.

—ALFRED, LORD TENNYSON

10. Read in unison "Why So Pale and Wan?" It is light and flippant in mood, quick, yet subtle, in rhythm, and requires great precision and accuracy of speech.

WHY SO PALE AND WAN?

Why so pale and wan, fond lover?
  Prithee, why so pale?
Will, when looking well can't move her,
  Looking ill prevail?
  Prithee, why so pale?

Why so dull and mute, young sinner?
  Prithee, why so mute?
Will, when speaking well can't win her,
  Saying nothing do 't?
  Prithee, why so mute?

Quit, quit for shame! This will not move;
  This cannot take her
If of herself she will not love,
  Nothing can make her:
  The devil take her!

—SIR JOHN SUCKLING

11. Try one of the following poems for additional practice in unison work:

"Vagabond Song," by BLISS CARMAN
"Tarantella," by HILAIRE BELLOC
"Weathers," by THOMAS HARDY
"Sands of Dee," by THOMAS KINGSLEY
"The Shepherdess," by ALICE MEYNELL
"A Cradle Song," by PADRAIC COLUM
"Crossing the Bar," by ALFRED, LORD TENNYSON
"Boots," by RUDYARD KIPLING
"Sea-Fever," by JOHN MASEFIELD
"A Musical Instrument," by ELIZABETH BARRETT BROWNING

12. Plan a program of group reading to be presented before some of the English classes in your school. Select a classmate to be your leader, and choose a variety of selections which in your judgment will interest and entertain your audience. Here is a sample program based on selections included in this unit:

a. Brief explanation by your leader of the purpose and value of group reading.
b. "The Fox," traditional
c. "Journey's End," by A. A. MILNE
d. A section of "The Congo," by VACHEL LINDSAY
e. The Beatitudes

f. "Cradle Song," by ALFRED, LORD TENNYSON
g. "Why So Pale and Wan?" by SIR JOHN SUCKLING

13. Divide your class in halves, and plan a verse-reading contest between each half. Each side should have an equal number of boys and girls, with an equal balancing of voices. Let each group select a varied program, practice independently, and come together in final competition, with the teacher acting as judge.

References:

Oral interpretation:

The Art of Interpretative Speech, by C. H. Woolbert and S. E. Nelson. Appleton-Century-Crofts.
Interpretative Reading, by Sara Lowrey and Gertrude E. Johnson. Appleton-Century-Crofts.
Oral Interpretation, by Charlotte I. Lee. Houghton Mifflin.
Reading Aloud, by W. M. Parrish. Ronald.
Reading Aloud Effectively, by Ben G. Henneke. Rinehart.

Choral speaking:

Choral Speaking, by Marjorie Gullan. Expression Company.
Choral Speaking, by Letitia Raubicheck. Noble.
Choral Verse Speaking, by Elizabeth Keppie. Expression Company.
Holiday Book for Verse Choirs, by Gertrude Enfield. Expression Company.
Poetry Arranged for the Speaking Choir, by Marion P. Robinson and R. L. Thurston. Expression Company.
The Reading Chorus, by Helen Hicks. Noble.

Films:

Let's Try Choral Reading (MH). 11 min b&w.
Better Reading (MH). 13 min color or b&w.
Let's Read Poetry (Bailey). 10 min b&w.

Records:

Great American Poetry (Caedmon). Two 12″ records 33⅓ rpm.
Famous American Story Poems (EAV). Two 12″ records 33⅓ rpm.
Great Stories in Poetry (Educational). One 12″ record 33⅓ rpm.
American Short Stories (Educational). One 12″ record 33⅓ rpm.
Ogden Nash Reads Ogden Nash (Caedmon). One 12″ record 33⅓ rpm.
Conversation Piece (Folkways). One 12″ record 33⅓ rpm.

Unit Twenty-two

ON STAGE: Dramatics and Play Production

The houselights don't have to dim, the audience become hushed, and the curtains rise for us to be in the realm of drama. We are, in fact, seldom out of it. Just as soon as two or more people assemble, the play begins, because everyone is trying to play a role in order to satisfy an inner need, whether it be to create an impression or image of self upon someone else, or to gain some predetermined goal. The way we walk, talk, dress, gesture, and give way to or control emotion is a result of our own character in action. This is our way of seeking adjustment to the social situation, our way of playing out the drama of living with others. In fact, we act much of the time on the stage of life as we attempt to influence, control, persuade, and win approval from family, friends, and strangers.

In addition to this unconscious acting, we deliberately use pretending for recreation. All of us as children played a part in the world of make-believe, which is the world of the theater, in our little backyard dramas of "house" or "store" or "cowboys" or "cops and robbers." As we grew older, we often entered into the portrayal of people and situations that became real to us because an author's creation has made them so.

Through the medium of the play we can escape into other ages, other lives, or other events. With the simple raising of a curtain we can explore *Lower Depths* or thrill to *High Tor*. We can take Shakespeare's hand and slip away for a visit to the court of Henry V. We can lose ourselves in the character of Juliet, famous daughter of the house of Capulet. We can take a moment for sober reflection upon the evils of Fascism through the presentation of *It Can't Happen Here*. We can enter the minds of Yank in *The Hairy Ape* and MacGregor in *My Heart's in the Highlands*. All these things we can do, whether we are part of the cast or part of the audience.

But there are values to be gained beyond the mere fun of casting off your personality to become someone else. As a member of a group you learn to work with other people and to appreciate how important each person's effort is to the achievement of a unified result. Everyone, from the lead to the carpenter who drives a nail into the corner block of the flat used in the second act, is an integral part of the production team. As an individual you will gain skill in the communication of ideas and situations, around which plays are built. Communication consists not only of understanding these ideas and the motives that underlie action but also of interpreting them in such a manner that the audience can understand them, too, and have the desired emotional responses. With the development of your understanding and interpretation will come a knowledge of why people behave as they do, for the drama is a medium for reflecting life.

In acting before an audience you will also gain poise and confidence. High school students who come to a course in public speaking with a background of experience in dramatics find that they can speak before a group for the first time with much more assurance than other beginners. Your playing roles will teach you effective use of your voice, command of your body, and the language of the people you are portraying. And from the whole process of reading plays for enjoyment, as well as studying them for production, you will assume a critical judgment that will enable you to distinguish between the good and the bad in both plays and movies.

All these values, then—an understanding of life and of the behavior of people, learning to communicate ideas and situations to others, learning how to work with a group toward an artistic unity, and gaining a critical sense of dramatic worth—can come from the study and interpretation of plays to help you to become a poised, confident, interesting, and vital person. Do you think this sounds worthwhile? Then let's learn how to put on a play.

First Things First

Before you put on your greasepaint and step dramatically onto the stage, you have a little spadework to do. Consideration of acting, lighting, and staging will have to be delayed until some preliminary action has been taken. All you know right now is that you are full of vim and eager to produce a play, but good generals don't go into battle without plans, or without an *evaluation of the situation.* For you, this means taking stock of what you have in terms of the play you are going to select. Your selection will be guided by the answers to a number of questions. How many people are interested in putting on a play? How many of these are boys and how many girls? Before what kind of audience will the play be given? What are the limitations in costumes, scenery, lighting, and building facilities? What previous dramatic experience have the members of the cast had? How much talent have they? How much time is there to prepare a production? How much money? What is the *purpose* of this play? Regardless of the answers to these questions, the guiding consideration should be to choose a play that will provide a rich, satisfying, educational experience—a play that embodies the values already mentioned as possible in a study of drama and dramatics.

No attempt is made here to provide exhaustive lists and anthologies of plays. The plays listed below are representative and worth both your reading and your producing. Play catalogs, which are easily obtained, will give you the additional information and suggestions that you desire.

One-Act Plays

Back of the Yards, by Kenneth S. Goodman. Social drama.
Ile, by Eugene O'Neill. Drama of idea and mood.
Riders to the Sea, by John Millington Synge. Poetic tragedy.
Where the Cross Is Made, by Eugene O'Neill. Psychological.
A Night at an Inn, by Lord Dunsany. Drama—a play of mood.
The Finger of God, by Percival Wilde. Serious drama.
Dust of the Road, by Kenneth S. Goodman. Christmas drama.
The Birthday of the Infanta, by Oscar Wilde. Tragedy.
Trifles, by Susan Glaspell. Mystery melodrama.
Half an Hour, by J. M. Barrie. Comedy drama.
The Will, by J. M. Barrie. Comedy drama.
Seven Women, by J. M. Barrie. Modern comedy.
The Marriage Proposal, by Anton Chekhov. Farce.

Collections of One-Act Plays

Christmas Plays for Young Actors, edited by A. S. Burack. Plays, Inc.
Thirty Famous One-Act Plays, edited by Bennett Cerf and Van H. Cartmell. Modern Library.
24 Favorite One-Act Plays, edited by Bennett Cerf and Van H. Cartmell. Doubleday.

One-Act Plays by Modern Authors, edited by HELEN COHEN. Harcourt, Brace.
Plays for Great Occasions, by GRAHAM DUBOIS. Plays, Inc.
Health and Safety Plays and Programs, by AILEEN FISHER. Plays, Inc.
Radio Plays for Young People, by WALTER HACKETT. Plays, Inc.
Twenty-Five Plays for Holidays, by MILDRED HARK and NOEL MCQUEEN. Plays, Inc.
Modern Comedies for Young Players, by MILDRED HARK and NOEL MCQUEEN. Plays, Inc.
Special Plays for Special Days, by MILDRED HARK and NOEL MCQUEEN. Plays, Inc.
The Bag of Fire, by FAN KISSEN. Houghton Mifflin.
The Straw Ox, by FAN KISSEN. Houghton Mifflin.
Twenty Short Plays on a Royalty Holiday (3 volumes), edited by MARGARET MAYORGA. French.
Holiday Plays for Teen-Agers, On Stage for Teen-Agers, by HELEN L. MILLER. Plays, Inc.
One-Act Plays for All-Girl Casts, by MARJORIE B. PARADIS. Plays, Inc.
Book and Library Plays (2 volumes), by EDITH M. PHELPS. Wilson.
Plays, published monthly by Plays, Inc.
Plays for Players and a Guide to Play Production, by VERNE E. POWERS. Row Peterson.
Plays of Far Places, by OLIVE PRICE. Walter H. Baker.
Career Plays for Young People, by SAMUEL S. RICHMOND. Plays, Inc.
Plays for Our American Holidays, edited by R. H. SCHAUFFLER and A. P. SANFORD. Dodd, Mead.
Fifty More Contemporary One-Act Plays, by FRANK SHAY. D. Appleton and Co.
A Treasury of Non-Royalty One-Act Plays, by BETTY SMITH and others. Doubleday.
Modern Short Plays, edited by FELIX SPER. Globe.
Modern One-Act Plays, edited by FRANCES GRIFFITH and JOSEPH MERSAND. Harcourt, Brace.

Longer Plays

Older Comedies

The Rivals, by RICHARD BRINSLEY SHERIDAN.
She Stoops to Conquer, by OLIVER GOLDSMITH.

Comedies of Fantasy

Dear Brutus, by J. M. BARRIE.
The Poor Little Rich Girl, by ELEANOR GATES.
A Kiss for Cinderella, by J. M. BARRIE.

Modern Comedies and Comedy Dramas

The Admirable Crichton, by J. M. BARRIE.
The Poor Nut, by ELLIOT NUGENT.
The Show Off, by GEORGE KELLY.
You Never Can Tell, by GEORGE BERNARD SHAW.
The Charm School, by ALICE DUER MILLER and ROBERT MILTON
Come Out of the Kitchen, by ALICE DUER MILLER.
The Patsy, by BARRY CONNERS.
The Passing of the Third Floor Back, by PETER JEROME.
Merton of the Movies, by GEORGE S. KAUFMAN and MARC CONNELLY.
The Goose Hangs High, by LEWIS BEACH.
Seventeen, by BOOTH TARKINGTON.
Little Women: novel by LOUISA MAY ALCOTT; play by ROGER WHEELER.
The Young Idea, by NOEL COWARD.
Stage Door: novel by EDNA FERBER; play by GEORGE S. KAUFMAN.
Holiday, by PHILIP BARRY.
The Peace Corps Girls, by DAVID ROGERS.
Take Me to Your President, by LEONARD WIBBERLEY.
Star Dust, by WALTER KERR.

Dramas of Fantasy

The Yellow Jacket, by GEORGE C. HAZELTON and J. H. BENRIMO.
The Blue Bird, by MAURICE MAETERLINCK.
The Gods of the Mountain, by LORD DUNSANY.
Peter Pan, by J. M. BARRIE.
Bethlehem, by LAURENCE HOUSMAN.
Death Takes a Holiday: novel by ALBERTO CASSELLA; play by WALTER FERRIS.
The Scarecrow, by PERCY MACKAYE.
Captain Applejack, by WALTER HACKETT.
The Ivory Door, by A. A. MILNE.

Others

Abraham Lincoln, by JOHN DRINKWATER. Historical drama.
Nathan Hale, by CLYDE FITCH. Historical drama.
Seven Keys to Baldpate, by GEORGE M. COHAN. Melodrama.

The Arrow-Maker, by Mary Austin. Historical drama.

The Thirteenth Chair, by Bayard Veiller. Melodrama.

Sherwood, by Alfred Noyes. Poetic drama.

Treasure Island: novel by Robert Louis Stevenson; play by Kenneth S. Goodman. Melodrama.

Cradle Song, by G. Martinez Sierra. Spanish drama.

The Melting Pot, by Israel Zangwill. Social drama.

The Winslow Boy, by Terence Rattigan. Drama based on real court case.

Our Town, by Thornton Wilder. Unique drama with imaginative techniques.

The Glass Menagerie, by Tennessee Williams. Retrospective drama.

Murder in the Cathedral, by T. S. Eliot. Poetic drama of Thomas à Becket.

The Heiress, by Ruth and Augustus Goetz. Based on Henry James's *Washington Square.*

Daughters of Atreus, by Robert Turney. Modern treatment of the Helen of Troy theme.

For an additional list of longer plays see:

Directing for the Theatre, by W. David Sievers. (*Appendix B. Lists of Recommended Plays for High Schools,* pp. 256-261. Wm. C. Brown Publishers, 135 South Locust Street, Dubuque, Iowa.)

Where to Get Plays

Whether or not you have selected your play, it is well for you to have on hand some catalogs of plays. If you have not chosen the play, the information in the catalogs will probably help you, because there you can find a short description of each play, the number of male and female characters in each, and a notation on the royalty. If you *have* determined which play you want to produce, you may need the catalogs to find out which company publishes that play in acting form. The publishers will be glad to furnish you catalogs upon request. If you are lucky enough to live in the vicinity of a publishing house, it will be possible for you to look at both the catalogs and the plays themselves and thus be sure you're getting the right play before you order a number of copies for the cast.

Ordinarily, you will want a copy for each member of the cast, a prompt book, and a copy or two for the technicians. If you're on a limited budget, however, you will have to do some doubling up, perhaps circulating copies among the minor characters until they have memorized their lines. Don't forget that the copyright laws make copying material from plays illegal.

The catalogs will be especially helpful to you if your choice of play is dependent upon your budget. The majority of plays have royalties ranging from a few dollars to fifty dollars, some have no royalty, and others are almost prohibitively high for the average high school. Knowing beforehand what your financial obligation will be for both playbooks and royalty, you can decide which plays you will be able to produce. Make your royalty arrangements with the publishing house, giving details as to the number of performances you plan, whether or not you have a paying audience, and whether you are giving a benefit performance. Circumstances generally alter the royalty restrictions.

But remember this: the primary consideration is the worth of the play and the anticipated values coming from it. You should not produce trashy plays just because they are cheap, nor should you judge the merit of a play by the size of its royalty. Be sure you have the play you want, and make any reasonable sacrifices to put it on.

Here is a list, with addresses, of some of the major houses that publish plays.

Atheneum Publishers, 162 East 38th St., New York, N.Y. 10016.
Baker's Plays, 100 Summer St., Boston, Mass. 02110.
Chandler Publishing Co., 604 Mission St., San Francisco, Calif. 94105.
T. S. Denison and Co., 321 Fifth Ave., Minneapolis, Minn. 55415.
The Dramatic Publishing Co., 179 North Michigan Ave., Chicago, Ill. 60601.
Dramatists Play Service, Inc., 14 East 38th St., New York, N.Y. 10016. (This company has rights to most recent Broadway successes.)
Samuel French, Inc., 25 West 45th St., New York, N.Y. 10036.
Harper & Row, Publishers, 49 East 33rd St., New York, N.Y. 10016, and 2500 Crawford Ave., Evanston, Ill. 60201.
Hill & Wang, Inc., 141 Fifth Ave., New York, N.Y. 10010.
Little, Brown and Company, 34 Beacon St., Boston, Mass. 02106.
David McKay Co., Inc., 750 Third Ave., New York, N.Y. 10017.
Plays, Inc., 8 Arlington St., Boston, Mass. 02116. (Publishers of royalty-free plays for young people.)
Random House, Inc., 457 Madison Ave., New York, N.Y. 10022.
Stein & Day Publishers, 7 East 48th St., New York, N.Y. 10017.
Theatre Arts Books, 333 Ave. of the Americas, New York, N.Y. 10014.

Participating in a play, from tryouts to final curtain, is a demanding, rewarding experience.

Casting the Play

"I won't play unless I can be captain!"—ANONYMOUS

Now that your play has been selected, you have to find the people best adapted to the roles. Let's suppose that your director has chosen a casting committee to help him with this very important step in production, or that are just looking through his eyes at the problem. What is the first thing to do?

Decide upon the Overall Approach. Study the play to determine the interpretation and overall effect desired. For example. if the play selected was the melodrama *East Lynne,* it could played in the manner of the original presentations as a sort of historical study in the development of drama and acting, or it could be played as a farce, depending upon the talent you have in your group. At the same time ask yourself which type of interpretation your audience will be likely to prefer. It may be that you will have to change your approach after casting is under way and you realize that such an approach can't be successfully undertaken. This initial study will also give you a good chance to reevaluate the play in terms of the values that determine choice.

Open Tryout. Call for an open tryout. This is probably the best means of casting, since it ensures everyone a fair chance at a part, and fairness rather than favoritism must be your guide. The effectiveness of the tryouts will be increased greatly if your committee and your director make copies of the play available at an early date to those wishing to try out. Further, you should post notices indicating which scenes will be used and suggest what interpretation you expect. Before the tryouts begin, summarize the play and discuss the character briefly so that the contestants can make some effort at characterization. If for any reason you are unable to fill all the roles at first, or if there are decisions you want to delay, at least eliminate those contestants who show no great promise. Call for a second tryout, posting the names of those who should appear. When final choices have been made, consider the nail-biting suspense that is gripping all the contestants and let it be known immediately who has won the various parts.

The Players and Their Roles. Try to picture each person who tries out as he will be after five or six weeks of training. Your director, since he has the chief responsibility, will try to help his committee to see each contestant as he will appear eventually, how he will develop in interpretation, how he will fit in with the rest of the players and the production as a whole. For instance, the hero should be as tall, or taller than, the heroine unless you are striving for a comic effect. A henpecked husband should not be a magnificent physical specimen. A dignified judge should not be roly-poly and boyishly open-faced. Nor would you want a hero whose voice was either higher or weaker than the heroine's. In attempting to look ahead you have other considerations, too. Does the contestant have a voice that will carry to all parts of the auditorium? Is he able to use the range and color of his voice to capture the sound of the character's voice? Is he able to suggest character vocally? Does he have the ability to assume mannerisms that will allow him to create the illusion of a real person? Are his facial features such that with a reasonable amount of makeup he will suggest the character? Is he capable of understanding the role and its relation to the play? Does he have the imagination to grow in his part? Will he be able to take direction? If the answer to many of these questions is "No," you had better consider someone else for the part.

Choose Dependable Players. Choose dependable people who are willing to work. Executing a play calls for seemingly endless labor for everyone, and a person who isn't willing to spend long hours studying his part, who resents the trying sessions during rehearsal, who is late for, or absent from, rehearsals, who constantly makes excuses for failures, and who wastes valuable time showing off should never be allowed in the cast.

Select Two Casts. Select two casts or, if this is impracticable, have understudies for the main characters. Not only will this spur the main cast to best effort, but also it will insure against minor catastrophe in the case of accident or illness. In this connection, if you are *in* the play and there is necessarily only one cast, don't let your head swell until your eyes are closed to the simple truth that you are on a *team*. And, if by any chance you didn't get the part you wanted, try for another. Don't *pout*! Try to play in the game, even if you aren't captain.

Director's Book

Before rehearsals begin, there's some homework to do. Your director will carefully prepare a detailed analysis of the play, an analysis you should understand. This *director's book* contains his interpretation of the play's meaning, his conception of the form it will take on the stage, a detailed chart of stage movements, entrances, exits, groupings and stage business, and his prediction of the audience reaction.

Assuming that a sample director's book might contain the following considerations, study the play and then test your understanding of it by answering the questions in each of the sections in Part I. Check your answers with your director.

Part I—Statement of the Director's Intention

A. THE NATURE OF THE PLAY ON THE PAGE

1. The Dramatic Idea: The director's description of the playwright's intention.

a. What is the play about? What is its basic idea? What is the playwright's intention? What did he want to say in his play?
b. What does the idea of the play mean to you? How do you feel about it? Illustrate by quoting the key speech from the play that proves your concept of the idea.
c. What is the playwright trying to show in his play? What is his personal vision? Illustrate by quoting from the text.

2. **The Director's Function:** To create on the stage the meaning, mood, and spirit of the playwright's intention through use of actors, setting, costumes, etc.

B. THE FORM OF THE PERSONAL IMAGE ON THE PAGE

1. **The Production Idea:** The director's theatrical key to the dramatic idea. His analysis of the form of the production. His plan to make the play an artistic realty.

   a. How do you plan to fulfill the dramatic idea in theatrical terms? What is your major production idea?
   b. What is the inner movement, or action of the play? What deep struggle gives it purpose and character?
   c. Main actions of play and characters.
      (1) What is the function of each scene and act in the fulfillment of the main action of the play? (The playwright's intention.)
      (2) What does each character want to do (his drive, goal, motive) in order to achieve the playwright's intention? This is called his "action."
      (3) Why does each character want what he wants?
      (4) Why does he say what he says?
      (5) Why does he do what he does?

   d. Express your theatrical plan as it illuminates, interprets, and contributes to your personal image of the dramatic idea.

2. **The Director's Function:** To coordinate the various elements of the production through his interpretation of the play, and to conceive its unifying image.

3. **His Personal Image:** The form of the play grows out of the scene-by-scene fulfillment of the main intention, or action of each character in relation to the dramatic idea.

C. THE FORM OF THE PLAY ON THE STAGE

1. **The Production Plan:** The director's theatrical realization of the dramatic idea. His use of the production elements to achieve the form of the play on the stage. The stage elements added to heighten and clarify the idea, or sense of the play.

   a. What instructions will you give your artistic collaborators in order to help them fulfill your production idea, image, and plan? (actors, scene and light designers, costumer, composer, choreographer, etc.)
   b. Describe their functions in helping you to achieve your intentions as a director.

2. **The Director's Function:** To translate the text of the play into stage terms; to make the idea of the play (as written) clear, interesting, and enjoyable by using actors, sounds, movements, colors; to find the unifying theatrical image of the entire production through a personal interpretation, and to seek in this scenic world the required style of treatment of the play in order to express its inherent nature and form.

D. THE PLAY IN PERFORMANCE

1. **The Audience Reaction:** The director's projection of the effect he intends his theatrical and personal interpretation to have on the audience. The result of the director's fulfillment of the dramatic idea in performance.

   a. What do you want the audience to *know*?
   b. What do you want the audience to *feel*?
   c. What do you want the audience to *enjoy*?

2. **The Director's Function:** To achieve a desired satisfactory audience reaction, and to be able to say: *this* is what the playwright wanted to say to the audience; *this* is the theatrical result the stage collaborators wished to achieve in order to realize their intention with *this* production, in *this* style, in *this* mood, on *this* stage.

Part II—The Director's Promptbook

A. Research
   1. History
      a. Play
      b. Period
      c. Playwright
   2. Comparison with previous productions
   3. Bibliography

B. Ground plan of the set (to scale)

C. The play script

D. Blocking of the scenes
   1. Stage movements
   2. Stage business
   3. Entrances
   4. Exits
   5. Groupings
   6. Etc.

E. Production plots
   1. Lighting
   2. Properties
   3. Costumes
   4. Makeup
   5. Music
   6. Sound
   7. Dance

F. Improvisations, acting exercises, and other creative notes relating to the director's interpretation.

First Rehearsals

Now you are ready for the first rehearsal. You are on time, you're in your seat, and the director has just given you a copy of the play—or maybe you're sharing a copy. There may be a few cuts and changes to be made, and you listen carefully to the director as he points these out, doing exactly as he says.

Look and Listen. When the revisions are complete, you will read the play together, each taking his part. In this first reading, the most important task for you, the actor, is to listen with your ears, and mind, and entire being. Look at the actor speaking to you. This means that you must take your eyes off your script, holding your finger on your next speech while you listen to him speak. Concentrate your complete attention on what he is saying: What does it mean? He is looking at you, speaking to you; you are listening. What are you thinking while he is talking? Do you have an impulse to answer? You will if you are listening and he is really talking to you. Then, when he has finished, look at your speech where your finger points to the place; and, with your impulse to answer, say your lines to him, using the meaning and sense of the line in your response.

There, do you see? He speaks to you, and you answer him, simply, honestly. Already a small part of the meaning of the line and your character is present in the response. Otherwise, if you read his speech while he is reading and neither of you is looking at the other, when it is time for you to speak, you merely read the lines of your script and no communication has passed between you. You both are reading aloud, alone. Any parrot can do this!

Sit in a Circle. At this first reading it is essential that you and your fellow actors find out what the play is about, what kind of people you are supposed to be, and what you are supposed to say, think, feel. Talking and listening to each other is the only way this most important task can be accomplished. A very helpful way to accomplish this kind of talking-listening communication at this first reading rehearsal is to sit in a circle, with you and your fellow actors sitting next to each other in terms of the relationships in the play and the scenes you have together. If it is necessary to change seats occasionally in a musical-chairs manner, do it before the scene begins. This not only forces you and the other actors to talk and listen to each other but also helps everyone to find out about the play: the story, your character, the other characters and your relationships with them, the theme, dramatic ideas, major conflict, and the scope of the acting problems.

Gain Understanding. This kind of internal exploration of the human values and ideas of the play, combined with group discussion, should be continued for at least the first week of rehearsals and before the staging begins. Without such careful initial exploration of the inner life of the play by the entire cast, led by the director, traffic patterns will be meaningless. It is important that no one be excused from these sessions for any reason, except perhaps illness, despite the smallness of the role. This will ensure a mutuality of understanding and feeling about the play that cannot otherwise be achieved.

Make Suggestions. In this first rehearsal the director is going to try to give you the feeling of the play as a whole and of your role in particular. If you have suggestions, don't be afraid to tell him what they are; give him a chance to show you why his idea is better, or to see the merit of yours and make revisions accordingly.

Hold a General Discussion. After you have read through the play, hold a general discussion and let the director find out how you feel about your role, how well you understand the motives and aspects of the character you are to play, and whether or not you see the relationship between your part and the plot and theme of the play. And then, before you leave for home, discuss briefly the best times to meet for rehearsal. Reach a working agreement so that your director can make and post a rehearsal schedule for the first week.

Gain New Insights. During the rest of the first week, continue to read and discuss the play scene by scene, act by act, until you have read it through several times. You will find new insights, new ideas, new meanings, new character revelations during this reading and study period. Go into such matters as the history, customs, social attitudes and beliefs of the period; the author's life and other works; the history of the play's original and subsequent productions; reviews and stories about the play; and, in fact, any information that will help you and the director create the climate and environment of the play before you arrive at the actual staging process. Your study of the play will lead to a deeper understanding and appreciation of the inner meanings of your lines, your character, and your other acting needs.

Second Week

"Block" Your Actions. Now you're ready to "block" the first act, if you are working on a longer play. If the act is divided into scenes, you will work on one at a time; if there are no scenes, convenient units of the act can be blocked, for blocking is a slow process, and the smaller the unit the fewer the people who will have to wait around. The director blocks action by telling you where and when to move, how crosses should be made, what positions you will take, and how and where groups will be formed.

Why Do You Move? It is most important that the director tells you *why* you move each time he gives you a cross, a position, or some other stage "business." If he doesn't tell you, ask him, or else figure it out for yourself. Whether you realize it or not, you never move in life without a reason, so why move on the stage just for the sake of movement or because the director tells you to move? Ask yourself: Why would I move, sit, stand, cross, etc., if I were the character in this situation? What do I want in the scene, in the act, in the play? And why do I want it? This analysis is your actor's homework. It is a never-ending process.

Your Actor's Book. Write your reasons in your script. Keep a notebook, and record all your thinking, all your work on the role; it will become a log, a creative diary of your director's comments and instructions and of your own comments and instructions. This actor's book will be a constant source of nourishment for you when you have reached the final rehearsals and performances. You will find it helpful and stimulating to look over your notes while you are preparing for each performance. It is as important that you prepare yourself internally to act as it is to put on makeup and costume.

A Week's Work. During the blocking process you will be memorizing, or "canning," your lines and working privately on your characterization. By the end of the week you will have established movement, learned your lines, and run through the act a number of times to bring about continuity of action.

Third and Fourth Weeks

Weeks 3 and 4 are spent on Acts II and III in the same way the second week was devoted to Act I. A review of Act I during the third week and of Act II during the fourth week is advisable, for the process of forgetting sets in quickly.

Fifth Week

It's time now to run through all three acts so that you will feel that the production is unified. Add your final bits of stage business, pick up your cues quickly, and polish your characterization. Spend extra time on the rough spots, ignoring, if necessary, the portions of the play that you are doing well.

Sixth Week

If the production has developed faster than you expected or if you are pressed for time, you may have to combine the work of the fourth and fifth weeks. Many directors feel that a minimum of six weeks is necessary to prepare for a satisfactory production. Whatever the case, you still have much work to do. The stage crew has finished the set (or sets) and is ready to put it up. Costumes must be tried on and the necessary alterations made. All properties are gathered. Makeup is applied and tested under the lights you are going to use. The jigsaw puzzle has been assembled, and you are viewing the complete, live picture. During the rehearsals of this important period, you add the final polishing touches, and your play is ready.

It is always a good idea to invite a few people in to see the last two rehearsals. If your play is a comedy, you can find out where the best laughs come, how long to wait for them, and what general reaction to expect from an audience. If you are producing a serious drama, you have a chance to detect in "heavy" scenes weakness that may either lessen the emotional quality of those scenes or produce unexpected laughter, a disastrous reaction that sometimes occurs in amateur productions. It is better to sample audience reaction ahead of time than to gamble on your judgment alone.

Characterization

Creating a character in a play requires putting yourself in his place and doing all the little things as well as the big ones that he would do if he were a real person, for your character must be convincing. Try to find someone who is like the character you are going to portray and then observe him in a number of situations. How does he walk? stand? sit? Is he generally slouchy, or is he firm in his movements? Do his clothes show taste? Are they neat and well fitting? Is his hair well groomed or unkempt? How does he use his hands? Does he look you straight in the eye when he talks to you, or does he avoid your gaze? And what about mannerisms? Does he bite his nails? scratch his nose or hair when nervous? play with coins? point his index finger when speaking? Or what *does* he do?

You Must Know the *Why*. Now, in order to understand what he *does,* you, the actor, must first find out WHY he does what he does! We know that, in life, cause leads to effect. If we want to turn on the light, we flip the switch. The movement of the switch to the "on" position causes the electricity to flow into the bulb, thus activating the light. CAUSE—EFFECT! Somebody says something funny—you laugh. You look at the exam paper—(you flunked! !)—you frown, you cry. CAUSE—EFFECT! First, the event, then your reaction to it. This occurs all the time in life.

What happens, then, in the theater, where a play mirrors life? Here the playwright reverses the process. He gives you, ready-made, the situation, circumstances, character, relationships, thoughts, words, actions, even your emotional responses: "you cry, you laugh, you are angry, you frown, you are happy, etc." It's the EFFECT he wants, the result. He tells you what you say, and do, and feel, at this moment, now, on this line. Then, it's up to you to figure out: WHY? CAUSE! So, you see, the order is reversed on the stage. Before you can truthfully achieve the effects called for by the playwright, you must find the causes, either in the play or within yourself.

The best way to start the process of looking for the cause is to ask yourself some simple questions:

1. Who am I? (character)
2. What do I want? (goal)
3. Why? (cause)
4. Under what circumstances? (story)
5. Where? (place)
6. When? (immediacy)
7. With whom? (relationships)
8. What and who gets in my way? (obstacles)
9. What do I have to do in order to achieve my goal? (actions)

When we ask, "What do I want?" we imply that there is an important need, desire, drive, or motive underlying each human action whether or not we are aware of its presence. Accompanying each need is an urgent reason, a motivation based on human character and situation. Therefore, all human action and utterance are results of these inner drives and are external expressions of their immediate and urgent power. You, the actor, must discover these character needs and desires in your stage life in order to transform yourself into the exciting expression of the playwright's intention. You must find this inner life before you can articulate it in movement, vocal expression, and characterization so that everything you do and say in the play is the direct result of this particularization. For example:

"Does he scratch his nose?"

WHY? What inner tension, anxiety, fear does this express? What is he hiding? Does he have trouble breathing? Is he crafty, is he trying to divert attention, or is he trying to figure out what to say or do? *WHY does he scratch his nose?*

"Is he slouchy?"

WHY? What caused this slouch? When did it begin? Was it because he was too tall as a youngster, and he tried to hide his size? Was his a life of hard physical labor? Is it an emotional reaction? *WHY is he slouchy?*

"Does he bite his nails, play with coins, point his index finger when talking?"

WHY? What does each physical action reveal about the inner needs and peculiarities of the character?

Write a Character Sketch. It helps the beginning actor when he starts to explore the inner and outer aspects of his role to write a detailed biography, or character sketch. This should include:

1. *Physical appearance.* What does he look like? How does the playwright describe him? How do other characters in the play describe his appearance? What does he say about the way he looks?
2. *Psychological makeup.* What does he like, dislike? What makes him cry, laugh, be happy, sad, angry, despondent, disappointed, etc.
3. *Environmental history.* What is his background? (family, school, friends, religion, neighborhoods, sports, games, travel, etc.)

Study Speech Habits of Character. Besides considering appearance, psychology and environment, you must study the general speech habits of people like your character. From what part of the country or the world does the character come? What is his occupation? What education has he had? Could he have picked up different pronunciations and inflections from parents who are foreign-born? How old is he? Does he have an impediment in his speech? Does his personality demand a vigorous manner of speaking, or is he reserved?

What kind of character sketch would you write if you were assigned the role of Macbeth? of his friend Banquo? of one of the Three Witches?

Characters Are Complex. Remember that most characters are many-sided creatures, and your portrayal must show these sides if it is to do justice to the characterization. True, in the days of the old melodrama you were either a hero or a villain, and you had only to give the audience a white picture or a black one. But such is not the standard of our modern productions. Take, for example, the character of Hamlet. He is violent in his wrath, logical and forceful in his reasoning, strange in his love for Ophelia, scathing in his accusations against his mother because she married his father's brother when his father was not long dead, distraught and sorrowful when he kills Polonius by mistake, steadfast in his devotion to his loyal friend, Horatio, and unforgiving in his desire for revenge upon those who killed his father. Strong motives drive him to all his actions, with the result that he comes to us across the footlights as an understandable and tremendous character, neither all good nor all bad.

A Review of Characterization

As a review of the considerations that will aid you in creating a character, let's imagine that you have been assigned the role of Grandpa in Kaufman and Hart's *You Can't Take It with You* and follow you through your preparation for it.

1. First, you'll study the whole play to find out just what the author wants in your portrayal. In his description preceding the entrance of each character there are valuable hints.

2. Next, study the play to find out what the other characters in the play say about you so that you will know how you appear to others.

3. Study your own speeches, for what you say will reveal how you feel about other people, how you accept life, what things you believe, and how you react emotionally.

4. What are your *actions* in the play? Where have you been and what have you done in the past?

5. Review your actor's questions concerning goals and motivation: What do I want, why, and what must I do to achieve it?

(Grandpa: "I want to enjoy life by doing what I enjoy most. Because wealth cannot compare with the joy of human affection and the pleasure of doing what really interests me, I will achieve it by teaching this philosophy by example, by living it.")

6. So far as age is concerned, you can picture a man with a voice that has lost some of its force and resonance, with a walk that has lost some of its briskness, and with hair that has turned gray. Grandpa probably is bent a little and has become careless in his dress and habits. Motivate the physical mannerisms.

7. The rest of your characterization of Grandpa must come through your observation of old people and your establishing and practicing the mannerisms, gestures, and kind of speech delivery peculiar to them. How far you go beyond this point will depend upon your own imagination and creative ability.

8. Be sure you find a strong motivation for everything you do, say, feel. Find important, urgent, immediate reasons, reasons that you can believe, reasons that will make you act in character as if you were that old man, Grandpa, in those circumstances and environment, with that family, and driven by those urgent motives.

Achieving a high degree of naturalness in characterization is your goal. You will reach it by painstaking study and endless rehearsal, at first practicing each aspect alone, and then trying all together until you have a convincing creation in harmony with the rest of the production.

ACTIVITIES

1. Try the following exercise: Come into the room to look for something you need NOW. WHY? Decide what the circumstances are, where this place is, who you are, and why you want it. Be sure your reasons are urgent and immediate. Prepare before you enter by picturing what you want, where it might be, why you need it right now. Then decide what you would do if these were really the circumstances—and do it! (Use real props.)

Come into the room:

a. to get your wallet.
b. to select a book.
c. to check the time.
d. to look up a phone number.
e. to get a chair.
f. to find a key.
g. to look for a pencil.
h. to find your assignment.
i. to find a letter.
j. to look for a contact lens.
k. to look for a handkerchief.
l. to look for an earring.
m. to look for a band-aid.
n. to look for a stamp.
o. to inventory furniture
p. to look for a lost coin.
q. to look for your glasses.
r. to find a needle.
s. to get a piece of chalk.
t. to look for a glove.

It might help you to have someone put the object you are seeking somewhere in the room while you are preparing to enter. This will lend a spontaneous reality to the exercise. The important thing is to look for it for an urgent, immediate reason. You may find it, or you may decide you can't find it. In either event, do only what you need to do in order to accomplish your task. Don't be concerned with showing anybody your reasons. Know what they are, and do only what you have to do in order to accomplish your action, your goal.

Ask yourself: When did I begin to believe what I was doing? When did it become true? You will discover that you have been focused and concentrated when you thought only of the object you were looking for and the urgent, immediate reason you needed it. Your awareness of yourself, how you looked, and your preoccupation with showing your audience what it was that you were supposed to be doing disappeared in the process.

2. Try another exercise: **Come into the room to read a newspaper, in order:**

a. to look for information about an apartment.
(Why? To find the $45 apartment before anybody else sees it.)
b. to confirm the report that there was a review of the play you opened last night.
(Why? To find your name in the review—it's a good notice!)
c. to get information—seats for a show.
(Why? To look for dollar seats for a show to take your class to—only twenty dollars available.)

Supply your own why:

d. to look for a job.
e. to look for a roommate.
f. to look for a casting notice.
g. to look for a death notice.
h. to look for football scores.

i. to find the time of a movie.
j. to find a used automobile to buy.
k. to find arrival time of train.
l. to find an engagement picture.
m. to look for a sale.
n. to look for a TV program.
o. to confirm information on a sale of phonograph records.

In this exercise it is necessary to use a real newspaper. When you look in the paper, actually use what you can see. Don't pretend to see it. Really find something on the specific page: a picture, real numbers, names. Don't show anyone that you are looking. Really look—and see something on the page. As closely as you can, relate what you see to what you are looking for, to what you need to find. Don't give up after looking thoroughly because the fact is not there. Find it by relating to something that you can find, something that reminds you of the fact. It is AS IF it were there when you are able to find a number, or a picture, or some fact that is similar to the one you are seeking. Relate to it when you find it. That new fact becomes stage fact, and that is what the actor needs. At that moment it is AS IF it were true because there's enough truth in the pretense to help the actor convince himself that it IS true. That is what you would really do under those circumstances if you were looking for a job, an apartment, a sale for *that* reason at *that* time.

Emotions

> O, it offends me to the soul to hear
> a robustious periwig-pated fellow
> tear a passion to tatters, to very rags. . . .
>
> —SHAKESPEARE

Emotion *Follows* Understanding. Successfully achieving the emotions of the character as called for by the playwright is the mark of a good actor. Practically anyone can puff, snort, rage, or fling his hands and body around in exaggerated emotional reaction; actors in the old melodrama and in the first motion pictures did just that. You know the results and laugh at them. But don't laugh too hard until you've seen what *you* can do. Amateurs always discover that they are trying to force the emotional results of the scene before they really know what they are doing. The emotion is a result, and the danger in trying to play preconceived results is that you look into the mirror and try to assume the mask you see in the reflection. It is much better to work for a deep understanding of your character in the circumstances of the play, trying to find urgent reasons for accomplishing your goals, and then letting your performance develop. If your creative work has been deep and honest, the emotional results will take place spontaneously, naturally, simply. And, if your preparation and rehearsals have been thorough, your emotional responses to the stage situations will instinctively be correct.

Words like *underplaying* and *overplaying* when referring to emotion on the stage are as meaningless as *light* or *heavy, soft* or *loud,* and *fast* or *slow.* They are generalities that describe effects without relating to their causes. Any concern with trying to play under or over the role's emotional requirements leads the actor to a constant preoccupation with showing results. His entire concentration then is on holding, "as 'twere, the mirror up to" his own nature, and trying to assume the postures, attitudes, facial expressions, and sounds of emotions without regard to their causes.

Mimicry Is Not Enough. Observations of how we respond emotionally may be successfully recorded by a careful watching and analysis of how people appear when yielding to emotion, but mimicry will not produce satisfactory results for the actor who must respond with the correct emotional reaction at the same moment, night after night. He may produce mechanically the required emotional result the first few times; but when the inspiration wears off or his memorized reaction hardens into a false, mechanical sound, pose, and gesture, he is lost because he cannot honestly remember or reproduce the original cause.

Leave Your Emotions Alone. How you look, how you sound, and what you do in the expression of strong emotions, such as anger, grief, terror, revulsion and hate, can be generally described. But we must always remember that it is false and dishonest to show emotional results. The actor must prepare himself to respond emotionally by developing his belief in the situation of the play, his goals, motivations, and character. Leave your emotions alone! They are there for you to use when the proper moment comes. But when you try to force them, they result either in general hysteria or in hardened facial masks, posed gestures, and memorized hollow sounds. You must concern yourself with the situation and your needs within it. Think of your goal: What do I want, and why? Then play it fully, with urgency and immediacy. Then, if you know your character and can believe in the stage truth as if it were really fact and happening to you, you will have the correct emotional impulses. You will respond as you would if the event were really happening to you, as, indeed, it is!

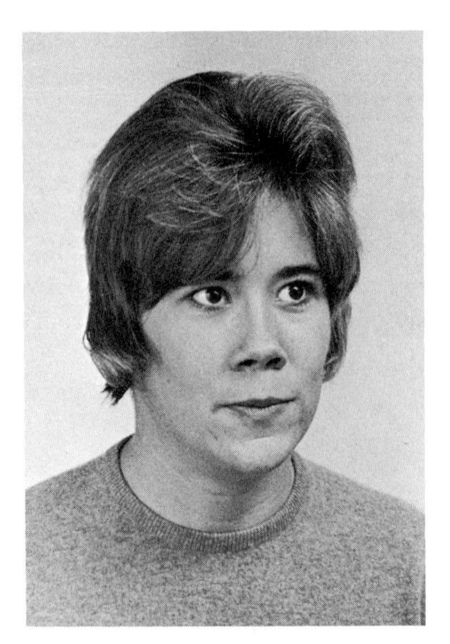
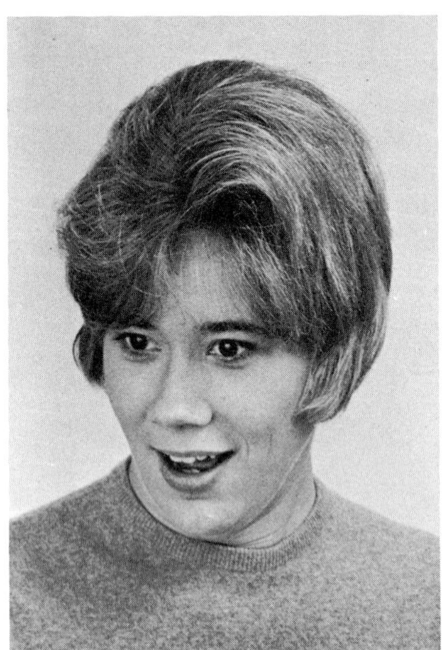

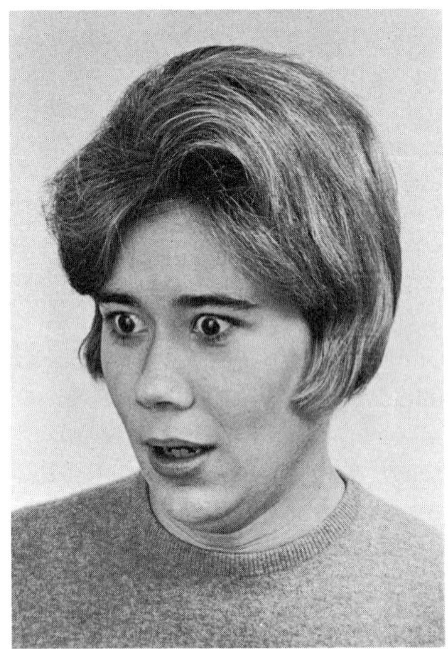

React as a person, not as an actor. When you feel the emotion honestly yourself, your face and posture and gestures will spontaneously assume the natural attitudes. What is a situation that might make you feel controlled anger? pleasant surprise? uninhibited, wholehearted enjoyment? horror?

ACTIVITIES

1. Listed below are some general emotions.

controlled anger	terror	fear	discouragement
explosive anger	horror	dislike	contempt
intense hatred	triumph	sorrow	bitterness
radiant happiness	boredom	worry	friendliness

Use your imagination. Think of a situation in which you want something very much and a very powerful obstacle prevents you from achieving it. Invent immediate, urgent reasons. Use yourself. What would you do under similar circumstances? Give yourself important reasons for wanting to do something; then try to do it. Overcome the obstacles if you can. See what happens. You will find that if you concentrate on what you must do in order to get what you want, in the process something will happen to you; the emotion will come as you attempt to fulfill your need. You will not have to be concerned with *how* to respond; you will respond fully if you really believe in the situation.

For example: controlled anger

Circumstances: You are a student doing your homework in your room. You are being punished by your mother because your report card indicated that your low grade in English was a result of sloppy, carelessly written themes. She has made you recopy your latest theme three times because she found spelling errors and poor punctuation. You are writing it again for the fourth time. You have made a date to go to the movies, and your friends are waiting for you outside in a car. You have ten minutes to copy the theme to your mother's satisfaction. Otherwise, she will not let you go. It is a movie you have wanted to see, and tonight is the last performance. They keep blowing the car's horn. (Use a real essay that you have written and copy it carefully but quickly. Have someone simulate the sound of the horn.)

Actor's questions:

a. What do I want?
b. Why?
c. What obstacle do I have to overcome?
d. When? How soon?

Now do what you would do if you found yourself in those circumstances. Concentrate on the writing. See what happens to you after a few minutes. See if you don't begin to feel controlled anger. If you begin to believe in the situation, and it becomes true, you will experience the correct emotional response to the situation.

explosive anger:

I had to copy it again for the fifth time! My friends left! I am stuck! (What would you do? DO IT!)

intense hatred:

Look at the theme again. Look at all the discarded copies, all four of them. There they are, the cause of your troubles. Express yourself. Take out your frustration on them. Tear them, beat them with your fists, stamp on them with your feet, scatter them around the room!

See what happens? Your emotion comes as a result of your involvement with the situation and your strong needs. **Cause—Effect!**

2. Now, let's try to extend the first exercise. Let's add two nouns (objects) to the emotion. Pair with a classmate, or two if you wish, and invent a story which involves these words. Decide on your characters, keeping them within your own age range, and work out your goals, motives, and obstacles.

   Act them out, improvising the dialogue. Use real props. Don't work out the story outline beyond the circumstances, character, place, time, and obstacles. Let the improvisation take you where it develops, and notice how the emotions which are part of the scene happen naturally as a result of overcoming the obstacles in the way of getting what you want. They will result from your playing the causes and allowing yourself to react to the situation as you would do in life. Concentrate on what you want to do, and why. The reason must be urgent, and your need must have immediacy. Don't think about the emotion. You will find that the correct result will occur if you believe in the circumstances and do what you would do if this were really true.

Exercises in Playing Word Improvisations

afraid rain paint	proud newspaper milk	ashamed glove clock	grateful handbag lamp
jealous orange book	admire window table	suspicious actor door	revenge curtain horse
hate ring hat	grateful money letter	grief dress haircut	laughter fur coat beard
envious coat car	pity photograph house	tender stocking tree	love belt flower
angry key pencil	disgust candle tea	anxious umbrella jug	excited car dinner plate
afraid picture shoe	timid fan stick	delight glass pipe	sorrow spoon cow
vain phonograph elephant	ambitious mouse violin	jealous key trolley	greedy briefcase stone
admire stage bus	joy chair floor	flirt jewelry shirt	remorse raincoat looking glass

pleased	rage	flattered	apologetic
pot	knife	radio	snow
cork	sea gull	pickle	ping-pong

3. Invent dialogue for these situations, and act them out. Put your emphasis upon characterization. Supply circumstances, goals, and motivations. Add obstacles to increase the conflict.

   a. A high school boy is asking his father for the family car to take his date to a movie. Afraid of his father's reaction, he is reluctant to come right to the point.
   b. A patrolman has stopped a speedster and his loving wife. The officer is bored with alibis he has heard a million times, the speed demon is sure he can talk his way out of the trouble, and the wife thinks her husband can do no wrong.
   c. A minister is talking to two young men who have stolen a car and are now in jail. One of the boys is ashamed, repentant, and worried. The other is sullen and defiant.
   d. A man is summoned home from a business trip by a telegram informing him of his wife's sudden illness. He is met in his living room by the doctor, an old friend, who tells him his wife is dead.
   e. A housewife has telephoned for a plumber. By mistake he goes to the house next door and is met by a courteous old lady who invites him in, thinking he is an expected friend of the family's. It is some time before their conversation leads to a realization of the truth.
   f. An excited group of young people are planning a surprise party. Everyone is full of ideas and wants to talk. Develop your dialogue so that characters break in on each other, speak in single words and phrases, laugh a good deal, and enjoy themselves thoroughly.

4. Have your teacher select some short scenes from good plays for you to act out before your class. Now is your chance to incorporate what you have gained from the previous exercises into a real acting situation.

Stage Action

Stage action is a term that refers generally to all stage movement. It includes exits, entrances, and crossings; special bits of action that reveal character, develop plot, or provide comic relief; and any other unclassified stage movement. Since amateur actors usually feel ill at ease on the stage, they tend to do nothing for fear they will appear ludicrous, with the result that the play seems stiff and lifeless. You must remember that in a play, too, "actions speak louder than words."

Stage Business. *Business*, the special bits of action mentioned above, is useful in creating character. For example, the crook in *Winterset* might have a nervous habit of biting his nails, or he might display a facial twitch. An old woman might have false teeth that she must unconsciously work at keeping in place. A flighty woman could have a characteristic habit of patting her hair or hauling out her compact every few moments to add a dab of lipstick or powder. A blustering "big shot" might pointedly flick cigar ashes on the floor. A weak little male character might jump when anyone speaks to him. If the business is to advance plot, it must stand out so that everyone in the audience is aware of the action and its significance. When the business is to give comic relief or heighten comedy, it must, whatever its form, be allotted time and must *not* interfere with speeches. Remember always to ask why of every piece of business and character detail. Motivation works for you and deepens your character.

ACTIVITY

Try these physical activities in pantomime. Do not use real objects. Picture the activity before you do it. When you have a clear image of the object and the activity, perform it as if it were true. Justify each activity in terms of character. What kind of person are you? Why are you doing it? Where are you? Etc.

Do what you would do if you were:

a. waxing the floor.
b. shaking out small throw rugs.
c. mowing the lawn.
d. throwing a baseball.
e. serving a tennis ball.
f. kicking a football.
g. shooting a rifle.
h. catching a pitched baseball.
i. shooting a basket.
j. driving a golf ball.
k. lighting a kerosene lamp.
l. sewing a patch on trousers.
m. chopping wood.
n. catching a fish.
o. dressing yourself.
p. shaving.
q. washing your inky hands.
r. eating hot soup.
s. slicing an onion.
t. picking up beads from a broken necklace.
u. painting:
 a wall.
 a chair.
 a picture frame.
v. washing:
 a window.
 a car.
 a pot.
 the floor.
w. touching:
 a hot radiator.
 ice.
 a silk stocking.

Entrances. In dramatic work an entrance is more than just arriving on stage. It is a significant gesture involving a revelation of character, a development of plot, a securing of attention and interest, and an establishment of new relationships and circumstances. The author has built his entrances thoughtfully; read his directions with care, and don't let him down. These tips on entrances should help you:

1. *Be sure you are in character before you enter.*

Stage Areas and Directions

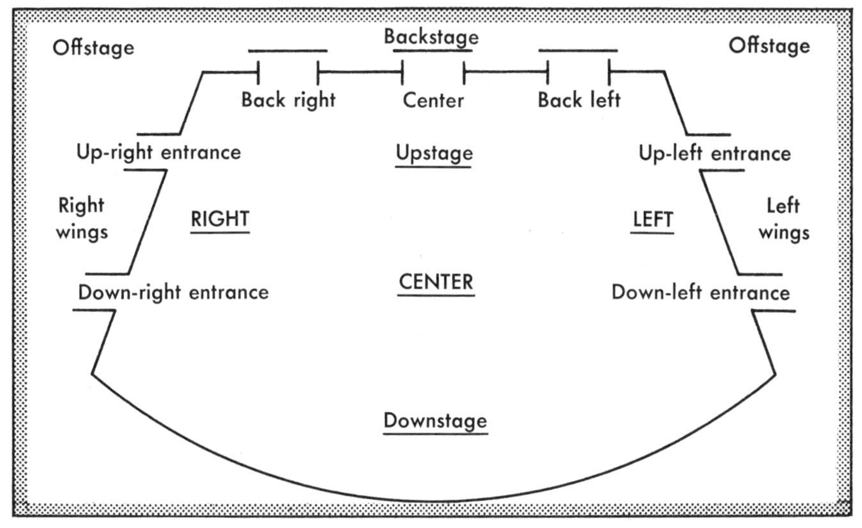

2. If you are supposed to be engaged in conversation with another person as you both enter, start the conversation offstage.

3. If you are supposed to have been running before you enter, come in hurriedly and with rapid breathing.

4. Don't start your entry at the stage door; begin your steps several feet away.

5. Watch the *timing* of your entrance.

6. If you have to shut a stage door behind you, close it as you would any door with whichever hand is closer to the doorknob and without turning to look at the door.

Exits. Just as there is a good reason for every entrance, there is a reason for every exit; you don't leave the stage merely because the next scene doesn't include you. If you know exactly why you are leaving and show that purpose in your manner, your exit will be successful. You will add to the effectiveness of your exit by following these general rules:

1. *Be sure you are in character when you leave.*

2. Time your exit carefully.

3. Be reasonably close to the exit before finishing your last line unless a long walk has dramatic value in a particular scene.

4. Although it is not a "must," leaving on the upstage foot is considered desirable in side exits.

Crossings. A crossing is a movement across the stage. It may follow an entrance, precede an exit, or simply involve change of position on the stage. These suggestions apply:

1. Crossings must be *motivated.* There must be a reason for the movement, and the director will supply it if the author has not done so.
2. Don't cross when someone else is speaking, for attention will be drawn away from his speech.
3. Unless there is a specific reason for your talking as you make your crossing, wait until you have crossed before delivering your line.
4. Tradition says that crossings should be made in straight lines, that you should go directly to the door, to a piece of furniture, or to another person. This is certainly true of short crossings or of longer crossings that are motivated by haste or strong emotion, but such technique may not apply to all long crossings. It is quite often desirable to eliminate the rigidity of the long, straight-line crossing by breaking it into a graceful curve or two.
5. You will nearly always cross *in front* of other persons on the stage. Your downstage position helps to keep interest on you. If the script requires you to cross *behind* someone as you speak a line, it's better to break the speech slightly as you pass him.
6. If you have been crossed, you have two responsibilities: one is to show by some bodily movement that you know you have been crossed; the other is to help to preserve stage balance by moving in the opposite direction when you have been "covered" by a crossing that has stopped too short. Although rehearsals will generally eliminate the possibility of someone's stopping in front of you, or nearly so, such an accident *may* happen and *it's your move.* Movements to maintain balance are called countering or "dressing" the stage.

Other Stage Movements. Stage dictum has for a long time insisted that characters make their turns *toward* the audience. Present practice isn't so severe. If the focus of attention is upon the action and it should be completed speedily, the turn should be made in the direction that is easiest and fastest. In some instances a back-to-the-audience position may be desirable; and, even though there is no hurry, a three-quarter turn toward the audience from a position facing left or right would be poor form. When no special considerations apply, turn in the direction of the audience.

Movement *of* a group and *within* a group should not be left to chance but should be worked out carefully. The group has formed for a definite reason, perhaps to listen to a character, perhaps to show dramatic conflict, or perhaps to take strong action (as the scene in *Julius Caesar* where the mob has come to kill Caesar). There are two things to watch in group business: all members of the group must have some little business planned to suggest that the group is not merely a collection of bodies but is made up of real people who have different reactions; and the group must not indulge in unrestrained movement that will destroy its unity and the stage balance.

Stage Balance. Stage balance, as discussed here, is a relationship between groups of people, or between persons and objects, expressed in satisfying arrangements. The term *balance* implies that equal units or values are poised against each other, and so any kind of symmetrical arrangement is in that sense balanced. But symmetry in the positions of persons or in the arrangement of furniture is not the kind of balance that ordinarily is sought on the stage. There the author and the director try to bring balance between forces, elements of interest, or important and less important characters. No matter what the situation may be, there is a reasonable degree of balance if approximate halves of the stage have equal centers of interest or equal opposing forces. As a character approaches center stage, his force and importance increase, and he can oppose a larger group or a stronger center of interest. Characters whose importance must be built up in the minds of the audience should be given center stage a generous portion of the time.

A few examples of stage balance between groups of unequal size will illustrate for you the theory expressed above. The heroine, who is angry and leaving home, can balance her whole family—and even some of the neighbors—as she "tells them all off." A character, aided by some property in which there is a lot of interest, can balance a group of people. One person can command attention and balance a group simply by elevating his position—jumping upon a hassock, a chair, or a table, or sitting on a raised platform, as in the case of a judge. An important property, such as a knife sticking in the wall or a jewel gleaming on a table, can balance any number of persons across stage who are directing their attention toward it. Variations in the actual placing of the balancing forces depend upon the imagination and ability of the director, not upon the limitations of the scene.

ACTIVITIES

1. Use the situations that follow for practice in making entrances and exits and in maintaining stage balance. Supply your own circumstances and motivate everything you do.

a. You enter quietly downstage right, pause with your hand still on the doorknob, face your father, who is directly across stage from you, and then start slowly toward him.
b. You have been running. Enter quickly from upstage center, leave the door open, glance hurriedly about the room, find the person you want to see downstage left, and move in that direction.
c. Enter gaily with several of your classmates from up left upon a room full of people who are having a party. Disperse quickly and become part of the larger group.
d. You are still at the party. Suddenly you remember something in your car that you wanted to show to everyone. Exit up left, telling everyone you have a surprise and will be gone only a minute.
e. You are at center stage facing two hostile men. Slowly back toward an exit down right. Open the door without looking around, and slam it shut once you're out.
f. You are down front arguing with a friend. Suddenly look at your watch, say you have to go, and start for the exit up center. Make several stops on the way to the door, each time turning around and arguing a little more. Exit half-facing the audience while you're still talking.

2. Practice these crossings:
   a. From entrance up center to fireplace down right. You have entered quietly and want to surprise someone who is sitting with his back toward you by the fire.
   b. From center right to center left. The stage is dimly lit and empty. You come in one door and go out the other. Your manner is hesitant and suspicious. Don't make a straight-line crossing.
   c. From down right to down left, and then around the room until you reach down right again. You are the charming hostess who is greeting clusters of guests located roughly in a half-circle. The most important guests are those that you crossed to immediately down left. There is no stage furniture in the way of that first direct crossing.
   d. From up right to down left. Your sister is down right, your boyfriend at center, and your mother down right. Talk to your mother during the entire cross, taking time only to say "Hi!" to your sister as you enter and giving your friend a big smile as you cross behind him.
   e. From up left to center right. It is important for stage balance that you cross when two other characters take down left. Move casually and don't draw attention to yourself.

The Actor's "Will" Guide

The tips in the "Will" guide are both new and review material and provide for you a compact guide to better acting.

I will try out for any part in which I have an interest and for which I am suited, and I will always remember the saying "There are no small parts, only small actors."

I will be on time for all rehearsals for which I am scheduled and show that I'm there to do the job.

I will listen carefully to the director's instructions, write them into my copy of the play at the first plotting rehearsal, and learn them just as I do my lines.

I will strengthen my interpretation of my role by studying people who resemble the character and by finding reasons for their behavior.

I will react to what is being said to me, and know why.

I will act with my mind and my body and my voice.

I will learn my lines so well that I can concentrate on stage business and on my cues in order that I may contribute to timing and pace.

I will not "hog" the stage by upstaging other actors or by moving when others are speaking, unless so directed.

I will at all times *maintain* character on stage, *keep* in character until I am well offstage, and *assume character before* I make an entrance.

I will be quiet when offstage so that no sound will disturb either the audience or the actors on stage.

I will not stop in front of another actor nor allow myself to remain behind one who has accidentally "covered" me.

I will maintain poise and stay in character when something goes wrong on the stage, doing whatever I can to pass the error off unnoticed.

I will not lend amateurishness to the production by peeking through the curtain to spot my friends or to determine the size of the audience.

I will remember always that the director is in command and that his orders are to be followed.

I will try to serve the play, and I will subordinate my own ego in order to accomplish the needs of the character as honestly as I can.

Stage Chores

Your director is responsible for the final production of the play, but he can't do the job alone; he *must* have help. Training the cast is only a part of the whole task, for sets have to be built and assembled, lighting must be provided, properties must be located, costumes have to be made, rented, or borrowed, makeup must be tested and applied, and the business end of the play has to be handled. All this means a reasonable amount of work for an adequate staff or a great deal of work for a few people. The audience never realizes how much effort goes into the technical phase of production, but this doesn't lessen its importance.

Stage Crew. Since most high schools never produce plays under ideal conditions, setting up an ideal staff or stage crew is a rather meaningless gesture. In all probability one person will have to do several jobs, and that's all right if he has time. The important thing to avoid is having several divisions of the stage crew responsible for the same work. Responsibility should be definitely and clearly established early if successful production is to result. The chief areas of work for which someone must take charge are:

1. Managing the entire stage crew. Stage workers take orders from the stage manager, who in turn gets his instructions from the director.
2. Carpentry work. Building of flats, window or door frames, fireplaces, steps, or whatever else has to be built.
3. Gathering of properties, seeing that they are ready for use, and returning them.
4. Electrical work, which includes all stage lighting and switchboard operation.
5. Providing costumes, making alterations, and returning borrowed or rented costumes.
6. Changing sets and operating the equipment in the fly gallery, if there is one. On a modern stage with good equipment the work falls into two areas and demands separate responsibilities.
7. Making business arrangements such as advertising, selling tickets, running the box office, ordering and paying for copies of the plays, paying royalties, providing ushers and ticket-takers, and paying local bills.
8. Prompting and curtain pulling.

How to Build Flats. If you don't use a cyclorama (a curtain of heavy material for the walls of your stage room), you will use a set made of flats. A flat is a painted, canvas-covered framework approximately four to six feet in width and as long as the height of your stage necessitates. It is made with or without openings, depending upon whether or not it includes a window or a door. If you have no flats, or if you must build some new ones, examine Figure 1 for details of construction. The frame is made of soft white-pine strips held together by corrugated fasteners and strengthened by plywood triangles. The strips are one inch thick and usually three inches wide, and the plywood is at least one-fourth of an inch thick. To ensure strength, the plywood blocks are always nailed down with nails that are long enough to be clinched.

An easy way to be sure the frames are nailed together into a true rectangle is to make a corner form. This is done by nailing two three-

Figure 1. Frame for flat

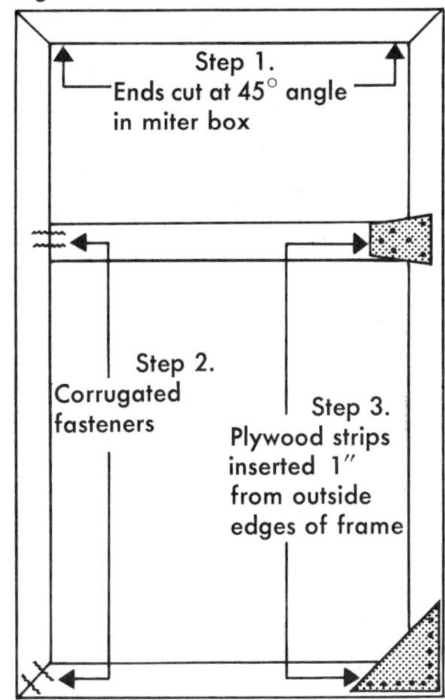

Figure 2. Constructing corners

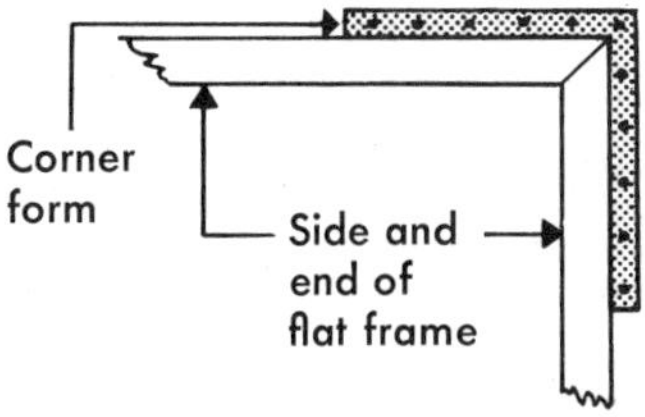

Corner
form
Side and
end of
flat frame

Figure 3. Design of doors and windows

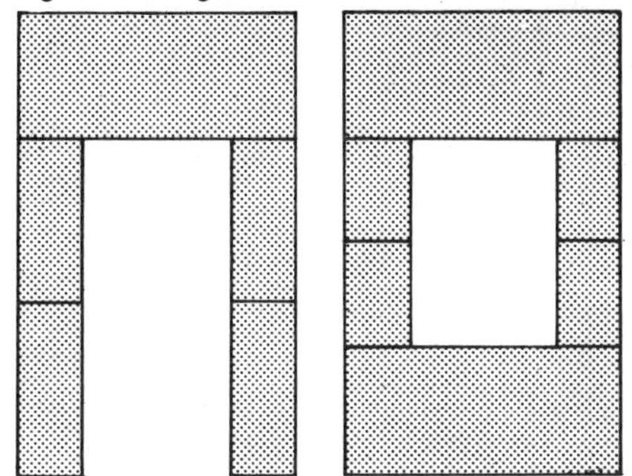

foot strips of lumber to the floor in an **L** shape, which can be made true with an ordinary carpenter's square. A side strip and an end strip can be pushed snugly into the form and secured with the corrugated fasteners, as illustrated in Figure 2.

If a door or a window must be put into the flat, the construction of the flat is the same as that of any other simple flat. The drawings in Figure 3 show the placement of the pine strips in flats that are designed for doors and windows. Simple window and door frames can be built and slipped into the flats to add a realistic touch.

The next step in making a flat is covering the frame with muslin or theater canvas. This is done by tacking the material lightly to the inner edge of the pine strips, as shown in Figure 4. Don't stretch the material too tight because it will shrink somewhat and take up any slack after sizing and paint have been applied.

Pull the edges of the material back and spread some glue on as illustrated in Figure 5. Now press the muslin or canvas down smoothly and firmly on the glued surface and allow it to dry thoroughly. After the glue has dried, pull out the tacks and trim the overhanging material around the edge of the flat with a sharp knife or razor blade.

A satisfactory kind of glue for fixing the material to the frame is a ground glue that is melted in a glue pot or any kind of double-boiler ar-

Figure 4. Tacking on canvas

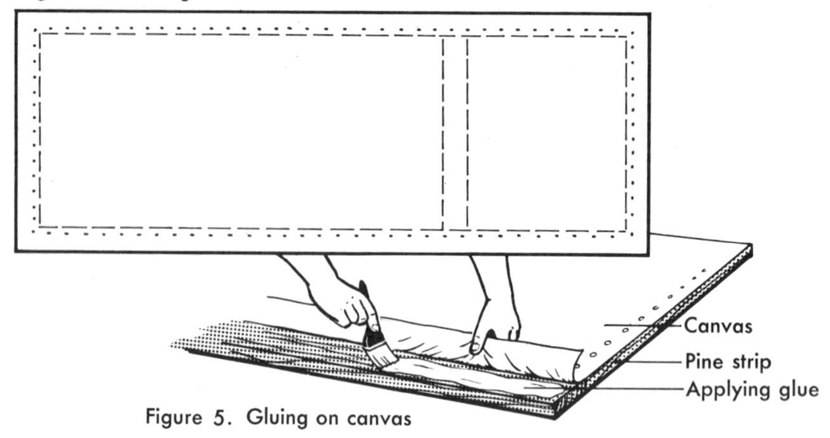

Figure 5. Gluing on canvas

rangement. Ground glue can be purchased in any hardware store; both directions and a little experimenting will enable you to get the right proportion of glue and water.

Scenery paint of the powdered variety is the most inexpensive and the most efficient. This is mixed with "size water," a mixture of one part glue (white flake glue which is melted) and ten parts water. If the water is not hot when added, the glue will coagulate. Place the dry scenery paint in a container large enough to hold all the mixture you'll need, and add size water until the mixture has the consistency of thick milk, stirring long enough to be sure all the glue has dissolved. Your product is properly mixed if it seems tacky when pinched between your fingers.

No generalization can be made in regard to the colors you'll paint your sets for different period plays, but it is usually true that comedies should have light or gay colors; tragedies should have somber or deep, glowing colors.

After you have brushed, sponged, or rolled the paint onto the flats and they have dried, you have only to fasten cleats to the back of the frame in order to lash or hinge it to the flat next to it and to brace it to the floor.

Assembly of Set. Assemble the set as soon as possible. Your set should be completed and ready for use by at least the time the first dress rehearsal is scheduled. It is quite disconcerting to the cast to rehearse on an empty stage until the night of the performance and then find that the entrances are not where rehearsals placed them and that the depth of the stage has changed. Getting your set up early will give you a chance to detect flaws and make corrections. You might, for example, discover that a portion of the set sways because it has not been well braced. If your play calls for a change of sets, early assembly of the set will allow the stage floor crew to mark the locations of each piece of scenery so that changes can be made swiftly on the night of final production.

How Important Is a Set? In the final analysis you must not forget that the set is not the whole show; and, even if you have unlimited resources, you don't want your set so elaborate that it detracts from the idea of the play and the excellence of the acting. A Broadway producer, whose eagerness for realism in his sets led him to reproduce a famous New York restaurant on the stage, was dismayed to observe that the audience *oohed* and *ahed* at the realistic set as their interest wandered from the play itself. On the other hand, a recent production of O'Neill's *The Great God Brown* in an old church with a most inadequate stage and only the barest suggestion of scenery was a thrilling experience. Brown's office, for instance, had only a screen with a few plans tacked on it to suggest an architect's place of business, but the suggestion was clear, the lighting good, and the acting superb. So, if you have no sets and can't afford to build one, don't be discouraged. Get some large pieces of the kind of material that will hang well and make draped doorways or arches or whatever you need. With a little imagination you can suggest hidden windows if necessary. Then get down to serious work and put on a good show, for "the play's the thing."

Lighting. Successful stage lighting will depend upon more technical and more extensive information than can be given here. Your director has that knowledge and will be able to help the electrician work out the details of lighting. These general principles will give you some notion of what equipment is used and what problems will arise:

1. The chief devices for lighting the stage are striplights, spotlights, and floodlights.

A *striplight* is a group of lights arranged in a row in a reflector and wired in parallel circuit so that if a bulb burns out, the other lights will not be affected. The footlights built into your stage are nothing more than a stationary striplight. This type of light is also used for overhead illumination.

A *spotlight,* as its name indicates, is used to throw a controlled beam of light on a particular area. Its intensity comes from a high-powered bulb, a good reflector, and a lens. There is almost no limit to the number of places a spotlight may be placed to aid general illumination or to produce a special effect.

A *floodlight* is roughly like a spotlight without a lens, differing mostly in its larger size and more diffuse light.

2. Color effects can be achieved by placing gelatin slides over the floods and the spots and by inserting colored bulbs in the strips.

Warm color effects are produced by amber, red, "surprise pink," and variations of these shades.

Cold scenes result from the use of a great deal of blue. Moonlight, for example, is predominantly blue light.

Eerie, ghostly, or weird effects are caused by a strong use of green.

3. One principle of lighting is that light should seem to be coming from a definite and legitimate source. If you have a daytime scene, the light should apparently be coming from the sun; if your scene is laid at night, the obvious sources of light should seem to be furnishing the stage light.

4. Don't arrange your lighting so that actors and properties throw grotesque shadows, unless you want that effect. By the same token, don't eliminate every shadow onstage, for that will bring about an undesirable artificiality. Try mainly to *soften* natural shadows.

5. The *amount* of light used is quite important. Overlighting, particularly with white light, makes everything look raw and unrealistic. Conversely, a dark scene that is underlighted causes the audience to strain excessively to see what is going on.

6. Whenever it is possible, heighten natural colors by using colored lights of the same hue. Experimentation will show you where you have been successful and where you have created dull or sickly effects.

7. Test all lighting effects *after* costumes are on and makeup has been applied. Under a blue light, red appears black, and you may have to change the shade of lipstick in a moonlight scene to keep the ladies from looking gruesome.

8. *Be careful with your wiring! Don't create fire hazards by putting too many lights on one circuit, permitting the cast to walk on lamp cords, or running wires across each other. Don't leave any wires exposed; electrical power can be dangerous!*

Stage Properties. The property manager and his assistants have the task of finding all properties, having them ready for use at rehearsals, and returning them after the show is over. Included under properties are the stage furnishings, the props to be used by the actors, and special properties such as trick devices. Many times properties can't be borrowed or rented; then the prop manager will have to make or have made what he needs. In one student production of *The Green Dragon Emerald* several large statues of Buddha and a special box to hold the emerald were on the property list. The students assisting the property manager had no trouble constructing the box and giving it a phosphorescent glow, but making the statues was another thing. The ingenuity of the director and the modeling talent of one of the students solved the problem. An original Buddha was made from clay found near the school. Then alternate layers of wet burlap strips and plaster of Paris were formed around the clay statue. When this shell was dry, it was sliced along one side, lifted from the clay form, taped back together, and painted. Three such shells were completed for the play, to the extreme satisfaction of the property crew and the delight of all who viewed the scene.

Many times the search for certain properties becomes almost a scavenger hunt as the responsible students scour the community. The following suggestions may be of help to the property manager:

1. If there is an antique shop in your community, make friends with the owner; he may lend you properties you need. Be careful of what you have borrowed and return it promptly.
2. Start a property collection and keep it in a cabinet used only for that purpose. It's surprising how something you almost discarded will turn out to be just what you need.
3. Have properties, or reasonable substitutes, ready for use early in rehearsals. Real properties should be employed at least during dress rehearsals.
4. Deliver personal properties, such as letters, papers, or trinkets to be used in business, to the actor just before he goes on the stage.
5. *Be sure that onstage properties are placed exactly where they have been placed during rehearsals.*
6. Take care in achieving as much realism as possible in your properties. A young lady who was property manager in a college production lost an important prop letter. Since the letter was necessary to the stage business that followed the actress's entrance, the manager grabbed a piece of Kleenex and stuffed it into the envelope. When the actress came to the business of reading the letter, out came the flimsy piece of paper tissue. She couldn't hide her shock, and the audience couldn't conceal its amusement.
7. Arrange your personal properties on a convenient table so that you

can find each quickly when it is needed. Allow no one to handle any of these properties for which *you* are responsible.

8. Don't furnish sweet liquid refreshments to the actors in scenes calling for sodas or cokes or whatever the drink may be. Sugar makes the throat "sticky" and speech difficult. Milk has the same temporary effect. Plain water and artifical coloring will take care of most demands.

9. Rarely will you need to serve real food in an eating scene. For inexperienced actors it is better if you don't, since it is not only hard to prepare but encourages actual eating, a practice that stage "eaters" should avoid. Seeming to eat is all that is necessary, and artificial food will appear realistic enough if made with cotton, absorbent paper, pieces of sponge, or slices of old bread splashed with boiling water so as to give off steam.

Costuming. Your work as costume manager will range from slight expenditure of effort if the play is one concerning modern teen-agers to a great deal of effort if it deals with adults in colonial times. If you do a good job, no matter what the play you will always have plenty to do.

After you have established the period of the play and planned the kinds of costumes you will use, you have to consider individual costumes in terms of each character to be portrayed. How old is he, for instance? How wealthy? What is his physical build? What is his personality? How can he have individuality and yet not dress out of harmony with others of his social class? A few principles of design, in terms of line, color, pattern, and material, should aid you in costuming.

Lines. The appearance of slimness is achieved by lines running the length of the costume, just as real slimness is accentuated by them. Conversely, stoutness is suggested by lines running around the costume. Tallness, severity, and dignity are associated with long vertical lines, while cross lines, broken-line combinations, circles, and curves are related to shortness, gaiety, flamboyance and comedy. A lack of any noticeable line may produce the effect of drabness, and a poor combination of lines can lend frowziness to dress. Effective combinations of lines, such as horizontal lines through the shoulders of a gown to give breadth and long vertical lines from the waist down to create slimness and height, are desirable for special effect.

Colors. For centuries certain traditions have been observed in representing things by particular colors. Royalty has been purple; virtue, white; death, black; passion, red; and jealousy, green. The "good" elements have been light in color and the "bad" ones dark. What girl ever dreamed of her Prince Charming as other than Superman riding in *shining* armor and on a *white* horse? What little boy, struggling with darkness, ever pictured a bogeyman dressed in a gay blue suit? Light, gay colors have also been connected with youth, festive occasions, and hope, just as dark or somber colors have characterized old age, solemn occasions, and despair. The warm colors—red, yellow, and orange—are for youth, strength, passion, and intensity. The cool colors—violet, blue, and green—are appropriate for serenity, advanced age, and a retiring nature. Pastel shades suggest femininity, daintiness, innocence, and spring. Don't lose sight of the fact that these color-character associations are generalizations and may not apply at all to a particular role.

Patterns. As it is used here, the word *pattern* refers to the figure, check, or stripe of material. Since pattern and color are often so closely related in an overall effect, it is difficult to tell when pattern alone is responsible for that effect. It seems, however, that men who never abandon youth and who like noise and crowds and admiration dress in showy clothes. Loud checks and prominent stripes in suits and blazing figures in sportswear help to characterize that type of man. Likewise, women who habitually wear splashy patterns show lack of restraint. Stout women who dress with care and taste don't wear dresses with large floral patterns. Quietness, dignity, old age, and conservatism are associated with inconspicuous patterns or none at all. Youth and exuberance claim the patterns that almost literally knock people's eyes out, and these two characteristics, plus a desire for admiration, demand the extremes in fashion.

Materials. Your own knowledge of the kinds of materials people wear is likely to be superior to any general advice that might be offered. Whereas at one time there was a great difference between the clothes worn by the wealthy and those worn by the poor, there is now less difference in the quality and practically no difference in the appearance, for clothing manufacturers are now making stylish cheap clothes of new materials that look expensive. If you are faced with the problem of making period costumes that are rich-looking, there are certain substitutes for costly material which you can use on the stage. A cloth that is widely used for period costumes is a good grade of unbleached muslin. It can be inexpensively dyed and decorated to suggest clothes of both the poor and the rich. Duvetyn or cotton flannel can be dyed to look like heavy wool. Velveteen is a cheap but excellent substitute for velvet. Lightweight corduroy is also a good material for clothes that should have a velvetlike appearance. Rayon satins can suggest great wealth and are beautiful on the stage because they reflect light well. Gingham, calico, and cheesecloth make very suitable classical costumes. Such accessories as sashes, handkerchiefs, veils, and scarfs may be of real silk or satin, for usually these can be borrowed without any expense.

Warning. Don't ruin the appearance of costumes made from cheap material by allowing any of the cast to wear costumes made from real silk, satin, or other expensive materials that make the substitutes look shoddy by comparison.

This warning applies to costume jewelry, too. If it is possible for each actor needing jewelry to provide his own and he can find real jewelry, for which he is willing to assume risk, you have no responsibility; but if the play calls for much jewelry that you must provide, get it from a ten-cent store and see that no one wears genuine ornaments that show up the cheap ones.

Other Considerations. In the costume manager's checklist that follows, the items concerning availability of costumes by the time dress rehearsals begin should receive especial attention. The quality of acting will suffer if the actors are not used to their costumes. Girls who must wear dresses with trains need a great deal of practice in managing these unwieldy costumes if they are to appear graceful and at ease. Male characters clad in tights will seem more natural if the actors have had sufficient time to get over the feeling of looking foolish. Girls who are to wear high heels during the performance must be sure to practice in them when dress rehearsals begin, for besides learning to walk gracefully, the high-heeled actress has a new number of steps to learn for stage movement since low shoes permit longer strides. Men who have to wear high, tight collars will at first feel that they can neither breathe nor speak, and they will look as if the head-neck-back portion of the body were held together by a stiff iron rod.

Costume Manager's Checklist

1. Determine the period of the play and what costumes will be appropriate.
2. Talk over with the director plans for achieving color harmony and any special dress effects.
3. Consider the budget and decide with the director which costumes can be borrowed, which can be made, and which must be rented.
4. Make a list of the names and addresses of people from whom costumes have been borrowed.
5. Order material for costumes that are to be made.
6. Order rental costumes in time for their arrival at the time dress rehearsals are to begin.

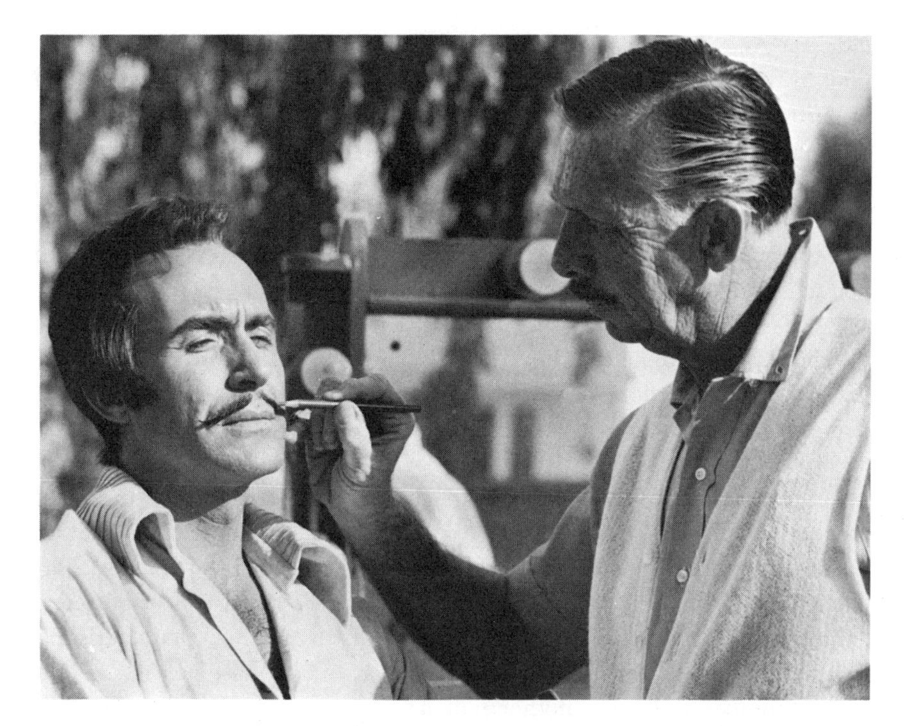

Makeup adds a villainous touch to Ricardo Montalban as the pirate Jean Lafitte.

7. Complete costumes that are being made.
8. Procure all costume jewelry.
9. Point out to each actor that he is responsible for his costume during the time it is in his possession.
10. Sit out front with the director during dress rehearsals and study the individual costumes for fit and the collective costumes for harmony and effectiveness.
11. Make necessary alterations.
12. Collect, clean, and return borrowed costumes, and collect and return rented costumes when the play is over.

Makeup

There are a number of reasons for using makeup in stage productions. In the first place, most theaters are large, and the actors need the added emphasis of features that makeup will give. Also, the intense stage lights tend to "kill" features and natural coloring, thus detracting from the power of a character's face. If you must grow older during the course of the play, makeup will make the change believable by allowing graying hair, sagging face muscles, and wrinkling skin. Further, if you are in a play in which close resemblances or strong differences in appearance are important to the action, makeup will permit these illusions, just as it will make possible the illusions of racial characteristics and changes in body structure. Finally, when you are in makeup and costume, you feel more like the character; you can more easily cast off your own personality and assume another. It is also easier for your fellow actors to play with you when you look like the character you are portraying.

Who Applies Makeup? For your production you will probably have, under the supervision of your director, a crew that is responsible for makeup. Some of your cast will be able to put on their own makeup, as professional actors nearly always do; in some cases the director will have to apply makeup for a difficult characterization; in most instances the crew will have the job. One kind of crew organization is that in which directors give each crew member a description sheet for the character he is to make up. Included will be specifications concerning age, complexion, type, hair, and any special distinguishing characteristics. In another kind of organization one member will do base colors, another lining, another rouging, another hair arrangements, and so on. For educational purposes, the first kind of organization is better; for saving time with an extremely large cast, the second is preferable.

Equipment. The following tips on makeup equipment may help:

1. ***Base paint.*** Foundation greasepaint usually comes in two forms: stick and cream. The stick type is manufactured by Stein and requires a thin film of cold cream before application. The cream type, in tubes, is a product of Max Factor and needs no cold-cream base. Base paint comes in shades ranging from light pink to dark brown and black.
2. ***Cold cream.*** Buy theatrical cold cream; it is cheaper than commercial cream and serves its purpose just as well.
3. ***Eyebrow pencils.*** Another name for these liners is dermatograph pencils. They are used for making age lines, for lining the eyes, darkening the eyebrows, creating shadows, and minimizing features.
4. ***Liners.*** Liners are small sticks of greasepaint that come in the colors white, gray, blue, brown, and black. In the dark colors they are used to accentuate age lines and shadows or to produce subtle age effects.
5. ***Eye shadow.*** Eye shadow is a greasepaint that is used on the eyelids to give the eyes a deeper, larger look. Since liners can be used for this purpose, special eye shadow is not a necessary part of equipment.

6. Rouge. Coloring for the cheeks that comes in cake form or as a greasepaint.

7. Lipstick. Is there anyone who doesn't know what lipstick does?

8. Crepe hair. This synthetic hair material, made from wool, comes in a wide range of colors and may be bought by the inch or the foot. It is used for any type of facial-hair adornment.

9. Spirit gum. Spirit gum is a sticky liquid that holds crepe hair securely to the face. Don't apply it over cold cream or greasepaint without first powdering the area heavily.

10. Collodion. This is a liquid that has the effect of puckering up the skin when it dries. It is particularly useful in making stage scars.

11. Putty. Putty is a flesh-colored, pliable material that is used to build up such facial features as noses, brows, and cheekbones. It will adhere to the skin before cold cream or greasepaint has been applied, and can be painted just as the skin can be painted.

12. Powder. Powder, like cold cream, is produced for theatrical use and come in shades that correspond to greasepaints. It is brushed or patted lightly over the finished makeup and has the effect of softening harsh colors and preventing shininess.

Straight Makeup. When an actor needs only to enhance his appearance and to overcome the effects of lights and distance from the audience, his makeup is called straight. Unless there is reason to change the features, all young characters take straight makeup. Here are the steps in application:

1. Put cold cream on all areas that will later take greasepaint or powder and then *carefully wipe it off.*
2. Apply a thin coat of base paint on all areas that will be exposed—face, neck, arms, and legs—*and spread the paint evenly.* Blonds and people who spend much time indoors will take a pink shade of paint; the outdoor and Latin types will need a brown shade. Liquid makeup of the same shade can be used for large areas.
3. Place a small spot of rouge on the cheek and work it out toward the edges of the rouged area. This blending process is important in avoiding unnatural color spots. Rouge is generally spread high on the cheek—higher on women than on men—although facial contour will be a determining factor. A round-faced, rosy-cheeked person, for example, should have a larger rouged area and should wear it a little lower than a person who has high cheekbones.

4. Apply eye shadow to the eyelids and line the eyes to accentuate them, drawing the lines a little past the corners of the eyes. Emphasize the eyebrows with pencil or liner but don't make them too thick or the character will appear villainous.

5. So far as color is involved, put on lipstick in shades that harmonize with complexion and color of hair. Most high school girls have good judgment in this respect. Stage women apply lipstick rather heavily, and stage men use just enough to suggest lip coloring. Remember that makeup to be used under blue light must be tested for effect.

6. Cover the entire makeup generously with power and remove the excess with a soft brush or cotton. Now you're ready to go on the stage!

Character Makeup. Character makeup includes makeup for middle age, old age, another race, deformities, or anything different from straight makeup. Here you are concerned with sagging flesh for old age, mustaches, beards, wigs, livid scars, bulbous noses, protruding brows, slanting eyes, and as many other characteristics as you have seen or can imagine. Because amateur productions usually have only the problem of showing *age* in characters, that technique alone will be treated.

Age is achieved by the use of highlights and shadows. A highlight is a light spot placed on a particular feature in order to emphasize it, and a shadow is a dark spot on a feature to minimize it. Both are imposed upon a sallow complexion ordinarily, although some old people have florid complexions. In addition, there is a graying or loss of hair. Figure 6 shows the wrinkled and sagging areas that must be highlighted and shadowed with liners. The steps in the application of makeup are as follows:

1. Apply cold cream and *wipe it off*.

2. Spread the foundation paint—usually a sallow, grayish color, or a liverish yellow—*evenly* on all skin areas visible to the audience.

3. In order to have the area below the cheekbones appear sunken, darken it with gray liner and highlight the cheekbones with white liner. The contrast has a heightening effect.

4. Add dark lines as shown in Figure 6 and highlight the deep wrinkles with light liner to make them appear deeper. Remember that deep wrinkles are characteristic of great age, not of younger "old age."

5. Blue liner used as lipstick will hide healthy, red young lips and add to the grayness of age. Older people who have flushed, full faces will need a touch of red lipstick, just as will stylish modern women who refuse to recognize the advances of age.

Old-Age Wrinkles

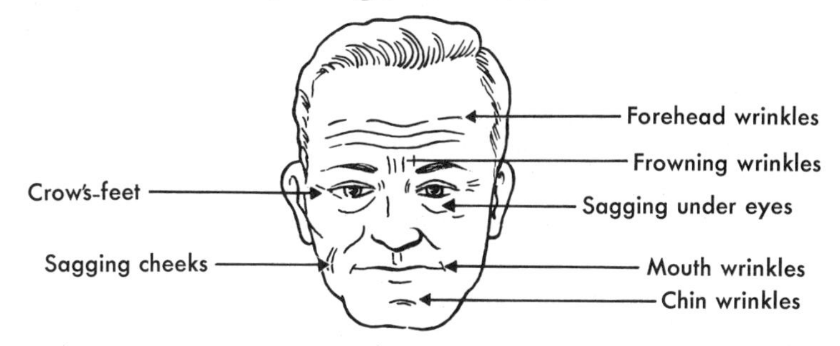

6. Gray the hair and eyebrows with a light powder, cornstarch, or white mascara. Although many old people do not have gray hair, it is still a good idea for young actors to add gray hair to their makeup in the attempt to age themselves.

7. Apply powder over the whole makeup and brush off the excess.

Don't Forget:

To exaggerate makeup beyond what is pleasing at close range.
To blend base paint into the hair line.
To test all makeup under stage lights.
To check makeup after each act to see if it needs freshening.
To blend rouge, highlights, and shadows into the base paint.
AND—That bright makeup colors will ruin the effect of old age.
That young male leads must not be made too pretty.
That stage kisses won't smear if the lipstick is powdered.
That a person with good face coloring may not need base paint.
That spirit gum is easily removed with ether or alcohol.
That you need an abundance of soft cloth, cheesecloth, or face tissues.

Now Put on Your Play! With the last dab of greasepaint, the last brush of powder, and the last admiring glance into the mirror you have completed your long trail to the footlights. True, you still have a few last-minute jobs to take care of, a few last butterflies in your stomach to quiet, but the long haul is over. Everyone is at his station, and the team is ready to perform in two hours what has taken six weeks to prepare. If you have chosen a good play, if your director has carefully worked out his plans and you have cooperated in helping him execute them, if your set is effective, if your lights are properly handled, if your makeup has been applied with skill, *and* if you are no longer yourself, but a character who knows exactly what his role is in this exciting game, *then* you are ready to put on your play!

References:

Drama in the Junior High School

Creative Dramatics in the Upper Grades and Junior High School, by Winifred Ward. Appleton-Century-Crofts.

Drama in the High School

Dramatics in the Secondary School, by Winifred Ward. Special issue of *The Bulletin of the National Association of Secondary Principals,* 1949. Available through American Educational Theatre Association.

Educational Theatre

"Educational Theatre," by Gilbert V. Hartke, *Educational Theatre Journal,* Vol. 8, No. 1 (March, 1956), pp. 39–45.

"A Symposium on Aims and Objectives in Educational Theatre," by Francis Hodge, *Educational Theatre Journal,* Vol. 6, No. 2 (May, 1954), pp. 106–119.

"A Method of Integrating the High School Drama Program," by Charlotte Kay Motter, *Educational Theatre Journal,* Vol. 12, No. 2 (May, 1960), pp. 94–97.

Acting

Acting: The First Six Lessons, by Richard Boleslavsky. Theatre Arts.

Acting: A Handbook of the Stanislavski Method, edited by Toby Cole. Crown.

Actors on Acting, edited by Toby Cole and Helen Krich Chinoy. Crown.

Method or Madness? by Robert Lewis. French.

Modern Acting: A Manual, by Sophie Rosenstein, Larrae A. Haydon, and Wilbur Sparrow. French.

First Steps in Acting, by Samuel Selden. Appleton-Century-Crofts.

An Actor Prepares, by Constantin Stanislavski. Theatre Arts.

Play Production

Producing the Play, by John Gassner. Dryden Press.

Modern Theatre Practice, by Hubert C. Heffner, Samuel Selden, and Hunton D. Sellman. Appleton-Century-Crofts.

Direction and Production

General Principles of Play Direction, by Gilmor Brown and Alice Garwood. French.

Fundamentals of Play Directing, by Alexander Dean. Farrar & Rinehart.

Play Production: Theory and Practice, by Bernard Hewitt, J. F. Foster, and Muriel Sibell Wolle. Lippincott.

The Stage in Action, by Samuel Selden. Crofts.

Directing for the Theatre, by W. David Sievers. Wm. C. Brown.

My Life in Art, by Constantin Stanislavski. Theatre Arts.

Stage Management

The Stage Manager's Handbook, by Bert Gruver. Harper.

Stage Management for the Amateur Theatre, by William P. Halstead. Crofts.

Costume

Historic Costume for the Stage, by Lucy Barton. Walter H. Baker.

What People Wore: A Visual History of Dress from Ancient Times to 20th Century America, by Douglas Gorsline. Viking.

Lighting

Method of Lighting the Stage, by Stanley R. McCandless. Theatre Arts.

Stage Scenery and Lighting: A Handbook for Nonprofessionals, by Samuel Selden and Hunton D. Sellman. Appleton-Century-Crofts.

Scenery

Scenery for the Theatre, by Harold Burris-Meyer and Edward C. Cole. Little, Brown.

Stage Scenery and Lighting: A Handbook for Nonprofessionals, by Samuel Selden and Hunton D. Sellman. Appleton-Century-Crofts.

Films:

Julius Caesar (MH). 33 min b&w.
The Man without a Country (MH). 25 min b&w.
Acting Problems (IFB). 11 min b&w.
Building a Set (IFB). 11 min b&w.
Designing a Set (IFB). 11 min color.
Directing a Play (IFB). 11 min b&w.
Make-up for Boys (IFB). 11 min color.
Make-up for Girls (IFB). 11 min color.
Managing a Play (IFB). 11 min b&w.
The Canterville Ghost by Oscar Wilde (Dynamic). 15 min b&w.

Records:

The Barretts of Wimpole Street (Caedmon). One 12″ record 33⅓ rpm.
Anta Album of Stars—1 (Decca). One 12″ record 33⅓ rpm.
Dear Audience (Folkways). One 12″ record 33⅓ rpm.
Listen to Literature (Ginn). This series includes the following albums, each consisting of two 12″ records 33⅓ rpm, which contain drama selections: **Introduction to Literature; The Study of Literature; Understanding Literature; Types of Literature; English Literature.**

VOICE OF AMERICA

Unit Twenty-three

RADIO BROADCASTING: A Miracle of Communication

Radio is truly one of the marvels of the marvelous 20th century. Music and voices travel through the air, over cities, and across continents, permitting listeners to be entertained and to keep in touch with the world merely by their turning a little dial!

Wherever You Go . . . Radio! Fifty years ago a high school student would take turns with his family listening to a radio instrument via headphones until a loudspeaker eventually made it possible to project the sound into the room. Today it is possible to enjoy the radio not only at home but also in automobiles and virtually anywhere a person wishes to travel with a pocket transistor radio. Because of this convenience, broadcasters like to think of radio as a personal companion for all of us. This idea stresses the very direct and close communication which radio makes possible.

The major entertainment function provided by radio during its first thirty years was later assumed by television, requiring radio to reevaluate its unique strength. Many stations began concentrating on playing popular records while other stations emphasized conversation. Both types of stations have proved very successful; "Top 40" music stations appeal to listeners who enjoy the most popular recordings, while "talk" programs make it possible for people in all walks of life to hear programs directed to their special interests, and they in turn occasionally use radio to express themselves. Sports enthusiasts, for instance, enjoy listening not only to athletic events but also to interviews and discussions among sports figures.

The same is true for listeners interested in religion, science, literature, fashion, movies, business, health, current events, hobbies, and so on. Several stations include regular discussions among young people, and the young person's views of controversial subjects are sought by radio stations for broadcast to a large audience.

Today, more than ever before in the half-century history of broadcasting, exciting possibilities lie ahead for people who would like to use radio for communication that is dynamic as well as far-reaching.

Perhaps you are such a person. Familiarity with radio broadcasting may make it possible for you to use this very flexible medium in a wide variety of ways. Individual or group achievement can be announced to a large audience; important activities can be widely publicized; significant problems can be documented and dramatized in a persuasive manner. Broadcasting can be a great deal of fun, an unusually rewarding experience for the creative person, and an exciting means of communicating to a very wide audience, not just in one community or nation but throughout the entire world!

Studio Talk

The equipment used in broadcasting, together with unique production practices, has given rise to a number of strange terms. Some of these have been borrowed from other creative activities and have assumed a special meaning for the broadcaster. How many do you already know?

Ad-lib: To improvise comment rather than to follow a script in a literal manner; to depart temporarily from a script or to speak extemporaneously without any script whatsoever.

Audition: A talent tryout performed for producers who are looking for a certain kind of voice or standard of performance.

Background: Sounds that are heard in the distance rather than in the foreground; sound effects, music, speech, etc.

Beam: The sensitive area of the microphone, as contrasted with "dead" areas in which sound is not picked up as well.

Blast: Speaking too loudly or too close to the microphone, resulting in a distortion of sound.

Board fade: The technique by which all existing sound is faded out by the engineer turning down a volume control.

Cold: (1) Beginning a program with no preliminary music or normal introduction; (2) reading a script without any prior familiarity.

Cross fade: Slowly fading out one sound or voice while simultaneously fading in another; at midpoint the two sounds will be heard before the original is lost altogether and the second is heard exclusively.

Cue: A signal to begin or to take a prearranged action in the program.

Cushion: Speech, music, sound effects, applause, or other material placed near the end of the program to assist the producer in controlling the exact length of time occupied by the program.

Cut: (1) A signal given to stop; (2) the deletion of specified program material.

Fade: The lessening of volume, quickly or slowly, either vocally by the speaker or electronically by the engineer.

Fill: Low-priority material that can be added to a show to extend its time to the desired length.

FCC: Federal Communications Commission, the government agency which authorizes radio-station operation in addition to overseeing many of the communications operations throughout the United States.

Montage: (mŏn täzh′) A production technique whereby a series of program ingredients such as speech or music or sound can be arranged in a fairly rapid sequence in order to suggest a great deal of activity over a longer period of time, or to enhance a particular mood.

Segue: (sā′gwā) Proceeding from one program element to another without any interruption between.

Tight: So much material to be accommodated with a fixed time period that little or no flexibility exists.

Transition: Proceeding from one part of a program to the next by means of some such production device as music, sound effects, narrator, fading, or silence.

Tools of the Trade

Your high school may be one which enjoys its own campus-wide radio station operated by students. The opportunity to broadcast news, school events, talks, discussions, sports, drama, and music will prove to be a useful and rewarding experience for everyone concerned.

Your Classroom Is Your Studio. Any classroom can be equipped very easily to duplicate radio-station facilities. It is a mistake to assume that

Performers use a tape recorder to play back their practice sessions and to preserve their best effort for radio broadcasts or other programs.

radio stations are all very spacious and glamorous, decorated with chromium, glass, carpets, and acoustical ceilings. The fact is that most radio stations are very modest in appearance with sparsely furnished studios much smaller than your classroom. You can create a professional atmosphere in your room with a single microphone and a tape recorder.

Tape recording makes it possible to record your class projects for study and review, for broadcast over your high school station if you have one, or possibly for presentation in a school assembly. If no tape recorder or microphone is available, similar experience can be gained by making a dummy microphone and following the same techniques that will be described in this chapter. The important thing is to learn how to use radio, to use it intelligently, effectively, and in a responsible manner. It is an enormously powerful medium of communication.

Now, let's take a look at some of the hardware:

Meet Mike. While every piece of equipment used in broadcasting has its own important function, the microphone is one of the most essential tools in the process of radio communication. It converts the human voice into an electronic equivalent, destined to be amplified many times, pushed through the air, received by equipment in distant areas, relayed to a loudspeaker and, through a process of vibration, reconverted into audible sound which closely resembles the original voice.

There are several kinds of microphones, each of which has been developed to serve some particular kind of function. One microphone will be best for music, another best for an individual speaker, another best for drama involving a number of people, and another best for group discussion. The basic difference, in terms of use, is in regard to the directional pattern of microphone sensitivity.

A microphone which is said to be *unidirectional* is one that is "live" on one side and "dead" on the other. The "dead," or nonsensitive, area minimizes the amount of reverberation or echo within a given room and generally produces a better quality of sound when only one person is speaking.

On the other hand, where two people are involved as in an interview or dramatic scene, it is better to have a microphone with a *bidirectional pattern,* one which roughly resembles a figure 8 and is "live" on both sides of the microphone. Such a microphone is still "dead" on the other two sides.

A *nondirectional* microphone has no particular directional characteristic but is equally "live" on all sides, making it particularly useful for group discussion. There are great differences in the quality and construction of different microphones, differences which are chiefly the concern of technicians. If you are planning a broadcast, your principal concern will be the best uses of these important tools.

Microphones may be installed in small desk stands or wall mountings, hung from portable booms, or mounted on floor stands which can be moved about the studio. Unless unusual portability is required, as in the instance of your moving about a room or on a street, it is not a good idea to hold the microphone by hand. Such handling increases the amount of unwanted noise that is broadcast while risking a good balance of voices.

Mike Is Sensitive. Great care must be taken in handling such sensitive equipment. In a network station no one but an engineer is permitted to handle the microphone, including even the simple operation of raising or lowering the stand. The same care should be exercised in your

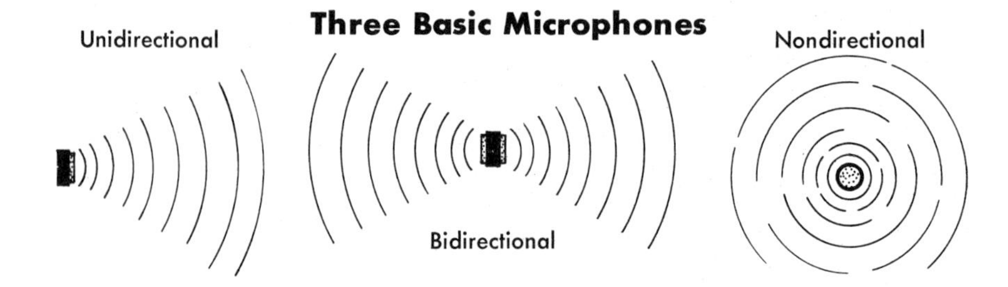

classroom. One should never blow into a microphone to see if it is on, for instance; although this treatment can be absorbed by certain very rugged outdoor microphones, excessive pressure caused by blowing or shouting could be very damaging to a studio microphone. When in doubt, be cautious.

Here are a few more tips:

- Be aware that the microphone is sensitive to *all* sound, including any noise you might not wish to have broadcast. This includes any whispers, heavy breathing, rattling pages, etc. The microphone cannot discriminate between a cough and a word; it will transmit both of them very faithfully.
- Handle the pages of the script very quietly. One suggestion is to remove any staples or paper clips so that each page can be placed silently beneath the pile as it is completed.
- Your distance from the microphone makes a big difference. If you are too far away, you will sound faint; turning up the volume control only makes the microphone more sensitive to all other noises in the room. On the other hand, if you are too close, certain plosive sounds (*p, b, d, c, t,* and *k*) will "blast" the microphone by pushing too much air and will produce considerable distortion. A comfortable and effective position will be approximately the length of your script page away from the microphone.
- Don't be a "creeper." Having established a comfortable relationship with the microphone, stay in place rather than creeping forward every time it's your turn to speak. Be sure there is ample room for others who must use the microphone.

ACTIVITIES

1. Experiment with the directional characteristics of your microphone. See what happens to your voice when you stray out of the "beam," when you are too close or too far away.
2. Select a news item from a current newspaper and rewrite the information for presentation as a radio news bulletin. Assume that exactly two minutes have been allotted for your announcement and see how close you can come to hitting the time target "right on the nose."

A correct position for the script and for distance.

3. Read your newscast "on mike," establishing and maintaining the correct distance. Hold your script to one side where it will be easy to read without blocking your voice from the microphone.

Handle with Care. *Remember:* Extreme care in handling the microphone should be practiced from the very first activity.

The Importance of the Tape Recorder. Microphones capture sound, but it is the tape recorder which makes the best use of such captivity. Voices and sounds stored on tape may be retained, employed, or disposed of at your pleasure.

Miniature tape recorders have revolutionized modern broadcasting because they can be carried around with reporters who are covering a variety of stories in the field rather than relying upon interviews within the radio studio.

Tape recording serves as more than a memory for radio; it becomes the raw material of broadcasting for many news and documentary programs, material that is collected on the spot and later reviewed, edited, broadcast, and stored for other uses later on. It is a remarkable means of preserving the sound of the people, places, and events in our lives; history will be told tomorrow in large part through the sounds that are thus collected and which will vividly supplement the resources of history books. You will find this kind of recording to be a very interesting experience, and it is well worth the time spent in practice right now.

There are many additional tools which the broadcaster finds useful; but with the microphone and the tape recorder—an effective combination—a single person, a small group, or a large production team can organize, edit, and produce a complete radio program ready for use in the classroom or on the air.

ACTIVITIES

1. Learn to use the tape recorder in your classroom. Practice with the microphone and controls until you are sure that you can handle the following techniques yourself: **(a)** threading a tape for recording, **(b)** starting the recorder and making a recording at the correct volume, **(c)** stopping and rewinding the tape, **(d)** playing the tape through, **(e)** locating a specific place on the tape for an instant start when needed.
2. Record one of your classmates commenting upon a current news item. Prepare a short news bulletin which will include the recorded statement as well as your own narration. Read your bulletin into the microphone, introducing the recording in an appropriate manner and playing the recording at just the right moment for it to become part of your newscast.

The Radio Voice

Radio is exclusively sound. When you speak over the radio, there is no one in your audience who can see you. The listener has no clue whatsoever to your appearance because there is rarely any direct connection between the sound of your voice and your actual appearance. Consequently, the listener attaches a great deal more importance to your voice that he would if he were seeing you on television or meeting you in person. Your voice alone carries the full burden of communicating your personality, your conviction, your mood. Everything that you might communicate to others by means of facial expression or gesture must be communicated through the single medium of your voice.

What Does Your Voice Say about You? How interesting a person are you? As far as your radio audience is concerned, your voice provides the only clues. Does it have vitality? Does it have variety in pitch and rhythm, or is it flat and monotonous? You may be a very personable individual, but, unless your voice conveys this quality, there is no way the listener can get a correct impression. If your voice is dull, as far as your audience is concerned, *you* are dull. You can see now why radio speech provides such excellent training for your voice.

Even though your audience cannot see you, you will find that it is a good idea to use gestures and facial expressions which seem appropriate to you and which you would certainly include if you were facing your audience. Effective speaking involves more than your vocal cords; your whole body is involved; and, even though no one will see these physical reactions, they will be evident in the tone of your voice.

The Radio Voice Should Be Believable. Some people have beautiful, resonant voices, free from defects. More important than a cultured voice, however, is a voice that is *believable.* Radio stations do not look for the kinds of announcers who might be admired, but for those who will inspire confidence in their listeners. The quality that you want in your voice is one of conversation; radio is a person-to-person form of communication despite the fact that you may have an audience of millions. You will be making a great mistake to think in terms of a "vast radio audience" because the formal lecture style that might creep into your voice will separate you from your nearest audience, the individual listener. Talk to *one* person, real or imaginary.

Listen Carefully to Your Voice. Radio magnifies a voice so that it literally can reach around the world, but in so doing it also magnifies any defects in voice or delivery. Artificial effects or an exaggerated style sound all the more phony in a radio voice. Practice in straightforward and interesting speech is well worth a little effort.

You can hear what your radio voice sounds like to others simply by recording a short speech and listening to the result.

Caution: Brief Disappointment Directly Ahead. Be prepared for a disappointing surprise when you play the recording back. The tape recorder will seem to work very well for everyone in the class except yourself! The recordings of their voices will sound just as they should, but the recording of your voice will seem strangely lifeless. It may sound nasal or much more breathy than you thought it would be. Actually, if all the other voices sound about right, you will have to accept the fact that your voice sounds just as natural to your classmates. It sounds different to you because you hear your own voice with certain built-in advantages, particularly in regard to resonance. If you are disappointed in the recorded sound, rather than vowing never to try again, record your voice many, many times. Practice can help make your voice sound more the way you would like it to be, and frequent recording is a good way to check progress.

Reading Script

Don't Be Trapped by Your Script. If you are reading from a script, you must be certain to become very familiar with its contents before reading it over the air. Reading from a script is in some respects the most difficult kind of radio speech to make effective because it represents such a dangerous trap to the uninitiated broadcaster. The inexperienced speaker will read words from a paper in such a way that everyone *knows* he is reading. How? By reading aloud without permitting the written words to pass first through the mind and heart in such a way as to color them with meaning and feeling before they are spoken. When you speak without a script, you generally are very conscious of what you are saying and are likely to sound as if what you are saying means something to you. In reading words from a page you must be careful to think about what you are saying so that the audience will get the most important part of your message: *believability.*

More Tips on Reading from a Script. Because of the nature and the strangeness of the broadcasting experience, you're likely to find yourself speaking more rapidly than usual. This increased rate of speech makes you more aware of the fact that something strange is going on, and this in turn makes you want to speed up even more. The vicious cycle can lead to stumbling at worst and monotony at best. By intentionally speaking a bit more slowly than you want to at first, you will probably end up operating at your natural rate, speaking with greater expression and feeling much more comfortable as a result.

Reading from a script also offers you the temptation to read sentences at a very routine and even rate, giving each word and each idea the same value, squeezing out the variety that would otherwise make your voice sound genuine, conversational, and interesting. It is not necessary to work out artificial pauses and changes of pace with elaborate marks on your paper, but it is a good idea to underline certain words you want to be sure to emphasize or to make other marks that might help you with pronunciation.

Watch Out for Words That Can Play Tricks on You. Reading aloud differs from reading to yourself in that you may occasionally encounter a word combination which presents no problem whatsoever as you silently read the sequence to yourself but which, when read aloud, twists the tongue or runs together to produce some strange results to the ear.

Presenting a play through sound. (Members of the Tyrone Guthrie Theatre Company.)

Words! Words! Words! Words are the raw material of radio communication; an announcer works with words all day long. He must have some familiarity with current events, geography, and musical terms to avoid embarrassing mispronunciations. It is difficult for anyone to keep up with all the foreign names which arise in the news, but basic familiarity with various languages and their rules of pronunciation proves extremely valuable to radio announcers. Even our own language contains many simple words which the careless person tends to mispronounce.

ACTIVITIES

1. Study these twenty words which are familiar to you but which you should check for pronunciation. Read them aloud and have someone verify your pronunciation:

adult	equitable	integral	preferable
advertisement	etude	laboratory	prelude
athletics	exquisite	library	revocable
deluge	formidable	mischievous	Soviet
envoy	gala	pianist	temperature

2. Prepare a two- or three-minute speech for recording. Listen to the result and judge for yourself whether your voice is communicating the meaning of what you have to say in an effective and interesting manner. Consider such matters as your rate of speech and the variety in your voice with regard to changes of tempo

and intensity. Do you think you are speaking too rapidly? Does your voice sound natural? What can you do that will make your speech sound more conversational and more interesting to listen to?

Having thought through some of these questions, record the same speech once again and compare the results. This kind of practice not only improves a given exercise but also enables you to become much more at ease with broadcasting equipment. The less you are distracted by the hardware of the studio, the more you can concentrate upon the really important task of communicating with your listeners.

3. Listen to a variety of radio speakers whose voices differ from one another. What is it about their speech which you admire or dislike? Do their voices seem natural or artificial? Are there any techniques being used by announcers which you could apply to your own radio speech?
4. Select a news item of current interest in a magazine and read it as news, recording your speech for later review. You may prefer to write a brief sportscast or similar feature of your own, summarizing items from the daily newspaper. Think about what you are saying. What does it mean? How do you feel about it? *If what you're saying doesn't interest you, the chances are that it will not interest your audience.*
5. Turn on the tape recorder, select a page at random near the end of this book, and read it aloud without any prior rehearsal. Turn off the recorder and spend a few minutes rereading the same material, rewriting where you find it helpful to make it sound more conversational. Mark any awkward word groupings or other difficult spots. Record another reading of the same page and then listen to both readings in sequence to note the difference between a "cold" reading and a statement of familiar material.
6. Just for fun, try recording your voice while disguising it in as many ways as you can. Invent characters by changing your voice with a regional accent or some other distinct characteristic of speech. Try to sound younger or, to use the radio actor's term, "put whiskers on it" by making your voice sound aged. Listen to the recordings of these different voices to see how successful you have been in presenting different images to the listener.
7. Write a short radio commercial for a real product and deliver the sales message in as persuasive a manner as you can. It's fun to parody radio commercials, but see how effective your radio voice can be in a realistic situation.

Producing a Radio Program

Every kind of program requires the direction of a person generally referred to as the producer. This is true of a radio speech, a newscast, or a very complicated dramatic or documentary show. Someone must be responsible for the preparation and presentation of this material on the air. There are many details that need looking after, details involving writing, talent, rehearsal, engineering, music, and so forth. Very often there is a good deal of executive or administrative work in handling contracts, in making arrangements with people to appear, or in securing permission for something to be included in a broadcast. The radio producer, therefore, must have managerial skills, and he must also be a creative person who can inspire the confidence of others upon whom he will depend for the success of his radio program.

Production does not begin with the assembling of a cast or the assigning of reporters to cover a story or the planning of sound effects and music with technicians. Production always begins in the mind of someone who has a sense of what is important, interesting, or entertaining to a large number of listeners. In short, production begins with an idea or a purpose.

Whatever radio projects are undertaken by your class, they should be preceded by careful thought regarding objectives, balance of ideas, and point of view. The best use of time is not to hurry but to plan so that each step is taken in proper sequence, avoiding wasted effort. In radio, where time is so very important, producers learn that advance planning proves to be the single most important investment of time and energy.

Let's consider one aspect of production—sign language—and then turn to three kinds of production: the interview, the panel, and the documentary.

Radio Sign Language. For all its great sensibilities the microphone has one great weakness: it cannot decide which sounds you want to broadcast and which sounds you would rather keep in the studio. Its solution is to pass each and every sound along, all whispers included. This means that any communication between people in the studio or between the studio and a soundproof control room must be silent. To assist broadcasters a sign language has been developed, one which is now used by

Ten Basic Radio Hand Signals

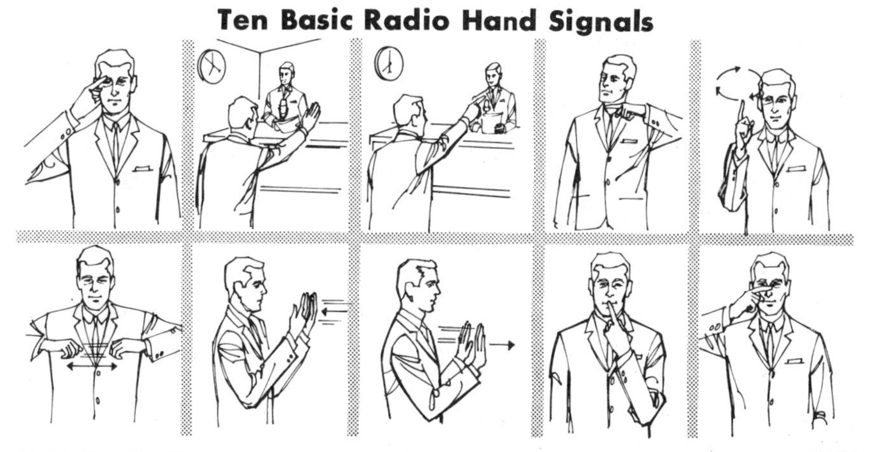

all stations. Like verbal vocabularies, language used with the hands will be fairly complicated in some areas and simplified in others; there is even a certain amount of slang. The basic signals are as follows:

Watch me for a cue or signal.	Tap finger near eye.
Stand by; cue is imminent.	Hold hand up, palm outward.
Cue! Begin!	Extend arm and point index finger at a person.
Cut! Stop where you are.	Draw finger across throat.
Speed up a little, or, if index finger is moving rapidly in large circle, hurry up!	Revolve index finger in small circle.
Slow down (a little or a lot, depending upon vigor of the sign); we're getting ahead of ourselves.	Stretch two hands out as if pulling taffy.
Come closer to the mike; you're far off.	Move one or both hands close to mouth, beckoning inward.
Get back a bit, you're crowding the microphone.	Push two hands away from chest, palms outward.
Not so loud.	Raise one finger to lips.
We're right on time.	Tap nose with index finger.

Now You're Ready to Produce a Show: The Interview

Let's start with a simple kind of program, the radio interview. Because people are interested in people, the interview will remain one of radio's most permanent features.

Careful Planning. Sometimes it is possible for the interviewer to meet his guest ahead of time to become acquainted with him as a person and to gain some familiarity with the subject to be discussed. This preplanning provides an advantage in exploring possible questions and helps the guest to become more familiar with the experience that lies ahead. It also helps to eliminate rambling or spending too much time on any one subject at the expense of others, as well as to allow the interviewer the opportunity to size up his guest, sensing whether or not the person will speak freely or will require encouragement.

Spontaneity. Just as frequently, however, the interviewer and guest are not able to meet ahead of time. The guest may arrive while the radio interviewer is already engaged in a program, and there is no opportunity to compare notes or to discuss the interview that is about to take place. This situation has advantages, also, in that it ensures a spontaneity which might well be lost if questions are planned too thoroughly in advance. Free from the restriction of prepared questions and anticipated answers, the resulting interview will sound more natural than polished. If the interviewer is genuinely interested and the guest is familiar with his material, neither is likely to be at a loss for words. An experienced interviewer can keep one eye on the clock and not permit himself either to skip around or to dwell too long on any one subject.

Simplicity. The simplicity of the radio interview is perhaps its greatest danger. It seems so very simple; two people sit down and talk to each other, one asking questions and the other answering them. What could be easier? A skilled interviewer knows that few programs are more *difficult.* The "easy" interview often consists of a scattered sequence of unrelated questions and answers which wander about aimlessly and end abruptly when time runs out. A successful interview is one which proves to be concise, entertaining, and thoughtful as it progresses from one idea to the next and concludes in an appropriate manner. A radio interview requires a great deal of thought, planning, and experience if the pitfall of "simplicity" is to be avoided.

Tips for the Interviewer

Be a Good Host. Remember that you are the host. It is your job to introduce your guest to the listeners, and such an introduction includes making the audience as interested as possible in the person being interviewed without overdoing it. Remember also that the audience cannot see your guest and that frequent references to this person by name and occasional mention of his background will be of assistance to those who tune in late. Certainly this information, even in summary form, should be repeated at the close of the interview.

Be Relaxed. As host, you will also set the tone of the entire program. If you are relaxed and friendly, your guest can more easily assume the same attitude. Your manner is doubly important if the guest is unfamiliar with broadcasting and is apprehensive about the experience. By keeping the emphasis away from the strangeness of broadcasting and by stressing the familiarity which all of us have with genuine conversation, you are much more likely to enjoy an interview that sounds friendly and relaxed, inviting the listener's attention.

Be a Good Listener. One of the most important things an interviewer can do, and yet one of the things which many beginning interviewers fail to do—with disastrous results—is to *listen* to the answers to his questions. An inexperienced interviewer will come to his assignment armed with a list of questions which he doggedly pursues rather than using such questions as a point of departure, putting his list aside or modifying it to fit the resulting conversation. The worst thing you can do is to ask a question, wait out the answer, and then arbitrarily ask the next question on your list. Rather, you must learn to ask a question and then to listen carefully to the answer, which will very likely suggest the next question. The answer to that next question, if you listen to it carefully, should provide the basis for the question to follow. Any one of these answers may lead you back to a question on your original list, though not necessarily in the order in which you had anticipated. The most interesting interviews do not spring from a predetermined list of questions and answers but from a conversation which develops very naturally from one subject to the next.

Keep the Listener in Mind. The questions you ask should be questions the listener would want to ask if he had the opportunity to be in your place, which suggests that you are not expected to be an authority on the subject being discussed. Your guest quite possibly *is* an authority; that is why he is being interviewed. For your part, you represent the average listener who is interested in the subject. It is foolish to pretend expert knowledge; it is more proper to represent the listener by asking whatever questions you think would occur to him if he were in your place.

Here is a special tip. If you find yourself at a loss for questions, consider the 5 *W's* and an *H* that the journalist carries to every story: Who, What, Why, When, Where, and How.

Wrap It Up! Be sure to conclude the interview in a manner which suggests that the conversation has come to an interesting ending rather than an impolite interruption because "our time has run out," leaving everyone with a sense of unfulfillment. The conclusion to the interview can be very brief, with a few words of summary or general comment, a reminder to the late listener about the person and subject of the interview, and a genuine expression of gratitude to your guest for his appearance.

Tips for the Person Being Interviewed

The Listener Is Interested in You. You have been asked to appear because you are well known, because you are an expert in some given field, because you represent an organization, or simply because you have opinions to share or a story to tell that the radio programers feel will be interesting to others. In other words, your preparation for the interview is already complete. There will, of course, be circumstances when it is advisable to secure additional information or up-to-date facts.

Stick to Conversation. In most instances a relaxed and informal manner will be appropriate for the interview. If statistics or quotations are important and accuracy is essential, have this kind of information written down and readily accessible. Other than this, an absolute minimum of notes will prove to be better than more formal preparation. The audience expects to hear conversation, not a recitation.

Don't Leave Important Points to Chance. If you have an opportunity to meet the interviewer ahead of time, it will be possible for you to discuss the area that will be covered during the program. If such a meeting is not possible, you may want to guard against the possibility of omitting a significant topic by leading the conversation yourself in that direction through one of your answers or, if need be, by initiating the new subject at some point within the program.

Remember that most interviews have a definite cutoff point beyond which there can be no further discussion. Make sure you know the length of the interview before it begins, so that you can plan to include the most important things you wish to say.

Producing a Panel Discussion

Many of the same suggestions for the interview apply to the panel discussion, which is, in a sense, a group of simultaneous interviews. Discussion programs usually begin with direct statements of some predetermined length with an exchange of questions and answers later on. Again the job of the moderator or master of ceremonies is that of a program host who introduces his guests and directs their conversation for a specified period of time. Such direction involves the preparation of questions in advance, either with the assistance of individual participants or without benefit of their guidance. Thoughtful questions are very useful in keeping the discussion going in an orderly manner but should not force comments to revolve around a rigid outline.

Tips for the Moderator

Be Sure Your Procedure Is Fair and Understood. Introduce your guests either all at one time or individually if each one is going to make

A radio panel is often planned around a community problem, for which panel members suggest possible solutions.

a separate presentation. Be sure you have established ground rules for the discussion so that each person knows the approximate amount of time for his individual presentation. If the subject is very controversial, it is particularly important to establish agreement whereby each participant is assured of a fair share of the time to make his position clear. The form of the program should be determined by such considerations as subject matter, number of guests, available time, and the presence or absence of a studio's audience which might be drawn into the discussion.

Keep Good Control. Once the discussion begins, your job is to keep it on the main topic or to bring it back if it becomes sidetracked. If one or two of the panelists dominate the discussion, it is your job to direct questions to other members of the panel who have not had as much opportunity to speak. Panelists should be given an opportunity to question one another, relieving the moderator of some of this activity but not of his responsibility to see that the discussion remains balanced and comprehensive. Remember that you are representing the audience; you must be sensitive to what they would like to hear and must direct the program accordingly.

Watch Your Time. Allow sufficient time to permit a strong conclusion to your broadcast. The termination of a radio discussion, unfortunately, often has less to do with the completion of the program itself than with the passage of an allotted period of time. "Running out of time" is a common occurrence which leaves the audience with a sense of disappointment and frustration. You can guard against this problem by keeping a close watch on your time throughout the discussion and by reserving enough time at the end to conclude the program in an appropriate manner.

You may want to ask each of the members for a brief final statement, or you may attempt to summarize the discussion yourself. In any event be sure that some sort of obvious and lasting conclusion is made to the broadcast.

Courtesy! Your final responsibility to your guests, as in the interview, is to thank them publicly and privately for their participation and contribution.

Tips for Panelists

Each Member of the Group Is Important. Remember that you are one of a group and that each member is there for a reason. You have been invited because of your familiarity with the subject or your personal interest in it. As with the interview, do not prepare elaborate notes; but, if accuracy is important, do come prepared with quotations or statistics. It is important that you neither dominate the discussion nor remain apart from it. Be very attentive to the questions that are directed to others so that you may comment appropriately or ask questions yourself. It is a temptation sometimes to sit back for a while after having participated and to tune out of the discussion, sometimes with embarrassing results when the next question comes to you. Do not allow yourself to think too far ahead toward your next question when, in so doing, you may miss points being made which might very well affect the question you are thinking about asking.

The Goal Is Communication. Keep in mind that even the most controversial discussion is not designed as a contest to see who can score the most points. Discussion, if it is to serve any purpose at all, must be a cooperative effort among participants who have been asked to *discuss* a given subject with one another. This is conversation of a very high order, involving respect for one another's views and a willingness to put forth one's own position. It gives you a good opportunity to exchange ideas with people whose backgrounds, experiences, and points of view are different from your own. It can be a profitable experience for listeners only when the participants keep these values before them and do their very best to make the discussion meaningful and interesting.

Producing a Documentary Broadcast

One of the most interesting and dynamic kinds of radio production is the documentary, a form of broadcasting that may be quite simple and direct or extremely ambitious in scope and production effort.

The term *documentary* can be applied to a variety of program forms and techniques which have one purpose in common: to explore a realistic subject in a dramatic manner. The specific approach to any given subject will depend not only upon the subject itself but also upon the amount of time available for production, the limitations of budget, the availability of resource material, and the imagination of the production crew.

The flexibility of radio recording equipment today makes it possible for a small group to cover a wide variety of subject matter which later can be edited in such a way as to provide comprehensive coverage of a given subject with many changes of voice and location. The documentary occasionally exists in a radio studio but more often includes sequences extracted from the real world. This kind of radio production provides the greatest challenge to broadcasters who are conscious of their opportunity to draw attention to special people, places, and events.

Your own speech class might serve as an example of a subject for a documentary radio program. In its simplest form such a broadcast might consist of descriptive narration supplemented with one or two interviews in the studio or a brief period of group discussion. The same subject can be made more interesting and effective by recording several interviews at different locations around the school in order to determine the attitude of faculty members and students toward the importance of improving speech skills. Some of the resulting interviews may be used only to provide information for the narrator; some of the tapes may be shortened for use on the air, while others may be used in their entirety.

Dramatization, music, and sound effects may be added to attract greater interest or to heighten a particular mood where such additional effects prove useful. Here is an example of how such a program might begin, prepared in proper script form using capital letters to separate production directions from words that are intended to be spoken over the air:

Unaccustomed as We Were to Public Speaking . . .

VOICES: (ANGRY, LOUDLY ARGUING ABOUT SOMETHING)

SOUND: (GAVEL RAPS ON TABLE)

CHAIRMAN: (RAISING VOICE OVER CROWD) Order, please! Order! Quiet down!

VOICES: (QUICKLY SUBSIDE)

CHAIRMAN: Shouting isn't going to settle anything. We might as well adjourn the meeting and forget the whole thing.

ARTHUR: Wait, Mr. Chairman!

CHAIRMAN: What is it, Arthur?

ARTHUR: It's easy to understand the reason for this argument. There are two sides to the issue and . . . well, each of us is acting on convictions that mean a great deal to us. There's one thing that all of us agree on, however: This is a problem that *has* to be solved, and our only chance lies in working together toward a solution. (START FADING OFF MIKE, CONTINUING TO SPEAK IN BACKGROUND) Let's start with what we have in common, and then proceed to work toward the point at which the first conflict begins to appear. If we can resist jumping feet-first into an argument at every checkpoint, we can work out our differences one by one until the last of them has been resolved. I'm not suggesting that both sides compromise on each and every point, but rather that we explore this problem with an open mind, holding on to those principles which should never be compromised but extending the same respect to the other fellow when it's deserved. (FADE BACK ON MIKE) Now what do you say? Are we going to lick this problem?

NARRATOR: The person who is speaking is about to become the most important member of his group. (PAUSE)

He's important because he is able to lead. (PAUSE)

He can lead because he has learned to respond to the world around him, to think clearly, and to get on his feet to express his convictions to others who listen.

VOICES: (AD-LIB ENTHUSIASTIC AFFIRMATIVE RESPONSE, INCLUDING APPLAUSE)

MUSIC: FAMILIAR SCHOOL SONG PLAYED OR SUNG FOR ABOUT TEN SECONDS; FADE TO BACKGROUND AND CONTINUE UNDER ANNOUNCER.

ANNOUNCER: "Unaccustomed as We Were to Public Speaking," a spe-

cial documentary broadcast written and produced by the ____________________ of ____________________ High School.
(name of class) (name)

MUSIC: FADE UP FOR APPROXIMATELY FIVE SECONDS AND THEN FADE OUT UNDER NARRATOR.

NARRATOR: It wasn't always this way for Arthur or the many others like him who, just a short time ago, would do anything to avoid having to stand up and give any kind of "speech" before an audience. It was Arthur's counselor, ________________, (name) who made this suggestion one day when they were discussing his program.

COUNSELOR: LIVE OR TAPE-RECORDED COMMENT

NARRATOR: (REPEAT LAST LINE OF COUNSELOR'S COMMENT, IF APPROPRIATE)
That made good sense to Art, but he also wanted to talk to a few classmates who had been through the course to get their personal reactions. He talked to as many different people as he could find, and their experiences proved very interesting.

STUDENT #1: (LIVE OR TAPE) BRIEF COMMENT

STUDENT #2: (LIVE OR TAPE) BRIEF COMMENT

STUDENT #3: (LIVE OR TAPE) BRIEF COMMENT

MUSIC: ANOTHER PHRASE OF SCHOOL SONG; FADE UNDER NARRATOR

NARRATOR: Arthur elected to take the course in speech, and the very first meeting of the class convinced him that he had made a decision which represented a very good investment in his personal future.

TEACHER: COMMENT ON OBJECTIVES OF SPEECH COURSE; LEAD CLASS IN BRIEF DISCUSSION OF OBJECTIVES AND VALUES. CONCLUDE WITH FIRST ASSIGNMENT.

SOUND: CLASS BELL RINGS, NOISE OF CLASS LEAVING ROOM.

NARRATOR: That first assignment was helpful to Arthur in more ways than one. He didn't think he did well at all, but he learned *specific* ways to improve. He was impressed by the way some of his fellow students handled the same assignment in an original and effective manner. __________________, (name) for instance, began with an introduction that immediately caught his attention.

STUDENT #4: INTRODUCTION TO SPEECH

NARRATOR: Another good example was provided by ______________ (name) who seemed to have an effective way of putting points across, instead of just standing up there and reciting as Arthur had done.

STUDENT #5: EXAMPLE OF GOOD DELIVERY
SOUND: SCHOOL BELL
NARRATOR: Each time that Arthur came to class he found that he and his classmates continued to move along with greater assurance and effectiveness. Some of the assignments they tackled were as entertaining as they were useful. For instance . . . . . .

ACTIVITY

Complete the documentary broadcast that is suggested in the script example above. In order for your class to do this, it will be necessary to organize a production team, as follows:

1. A *producer* to coordinate the entire project.

2. An *assistant producer* to carry out such details as the scheduling of interviews, distribution of tapes and scripts, planning a rehearsal schedule and other requirements of production.

3. One or more *engineers* to handle the recording and editing functions.

4. *Sound effects* and *music* can be handled by another member of the production team.

5. One or more *writers* will be needed to prepare narration throughout the program, linking the various elements together in a logical and interesting sequence, and leading to a strong conclusion.

6. *Talent* for the show will include a narrator, an announcer, and several student participants.

Do not hesitate to modify the suggested script or to set it aside completely if another approach will be more adaptable to your class. Make this exercise an interesting experience as well as a learning situation, but, above all, make a point that will stick with your listeners.

The Professional Attitude

Whatever the radio activities you and your class choose to practice, the important thing is to begin immediately with a professional attitude about what you are doing. Broadcasting is fun, but it is much more than that. The fact that you are addressing yourself to a very large number of listeners involves a great deal of responsibility on your part. There is no room for horseplay where valuable equipment is involved and no room for irresponsibility when the use of the public airways is extended to you. Take all assignments seriously, even though your particular contribution may appear to be very small. There can be nothing small about a medium which covers our entire nation and planet. Within these brief class projects you must begin to develop an attitude toward broadcasting which should take this larger responsibility into account.

As in any other act of speech, you should not use radio until you have something to say. When you do have something to say and you have learned to say it on radio, you must keep in mind the additional fact that your audience may be greater at any one moment than is possible through any other means of communication. Certainly this consideration suggests careful preparation on your part.

References:

General

Television and Radio, by Giraud Chester and others. Appleton-Century-Crofts.
Broadcasting in America, by Sidney Head. Houghton Mifflin.

Announcing

Radio and Television Announcing, by Lyle D. Barnhart. Prentice-Hall.
NBC Handbook of Pronunciation, by James Bender. Crowell.
The Announcer's Handbook, by Ben Henneke and Edward S. Dumit. Holt.
Television and Radio Announcing, by Stuart Hyde. Houghton Mifflin.

Radio Drama

Radio and Television Acting, by Edwin Duerr. Holt.
Radio Drama Acting and Production, by Walter Kingston and Rome Cowgill. Holt.
Drama On the Air, by D. R. Mackey. Prentice-Hall.
Creative Broadcasting, by H. J. Skornia and others. Prentice-Hall.

Production

Handbook of Radio Production, by Erik Barnouw. Little, Brown.
Radio Production Directing, by Albert Crews. Houghton Mifflin.

Tapes and Transcriptions

Educators Guide to Free Tapes, Scripts, Transcriptions, Educators Progress Service, Randolph, Wisconsin.
National Tape Recording Catalogue, Department of Audiovisual Instruction, NEA, University of Colorado, Boulder, Colorado.

Films:

Using Your Voice (MH). 10 min b&w.
Getting Yourself Across (MH). 21 min b&w.
Say What You Mean (MH). 20 min b&w.

Filmstrip:

Radio (MH). 47 fr b&w.

Records:

History of Broadcasting: A Word in Your Ear (Folkways). One 12″ record 33⅓ rpm.

History of Broadcasting: I Know What I Like (Folkways). One 12″ record 33⅓ rpm.

2

Unit Twenty-four

TELEVISION: A New Dimension for Speech

Effective speech—no matter what the subject or who the audience—produces effective response. You know this already from your experience and your study of this book. Such is the case for any speaking situation from a conversation in your cafeteria to a political speech in the Los Angeles Coliseum. There is a difference, of course: the size of the audience.

Now consider the size of the television audience! This most modern means of mass communication has put millions upon millions of people within sight of their President and other leaders at all levels of government; it permits an audience of millions to witness a ball game or a musical program or a national tragedy, as was the case when television made it possible for the entire world to witness the funeral of President Kennedy.

Day by day, in less dramatic communication, television permits a community or a network of communities to enjoy close contact with those who have something to say. Formal or informal speeches, interviews, conversations, panel discussions, and other program forms concerned with public address place speakers in close contact with those who choose to listen.

Because its reach is so great and its impact so strong, television is an unusually exciting medium in which to work. Anyone studying speech today should become familiar with this marvelous instrument of communication.

How TV Works

The real miracle of TV lies in the electronic field. Television consists of two complicated operations—the simultaneous transmission of sound (audio) and sight (video)—which amount to two broadcasts being received at the same time by your TV set. Audio transmission works the same as in radio. Video transmission is more complicated.

When a performer faces the TV camera, this is what happens:

The camera takes a continuous picture of the performer and passes the image to a sensitive plate, or *mosaic,* within the pick-up tube. As the front of this mosaic receives the black-and-white image, the back of it is being swept, or *scanned,* by an electronic beam. This beam sweeps back and forth across the mosaic 525 times every one-thirtieth of a second and changes the black-and-white light patterns into patterns of electrical charges.

Color television is even more complicated; the single pick-up tube must be replaced by three separate tubes, one for each primary color: red, green, and blue. (These are the primary colors for *lights* as differentiated from the primary colors for *pigments:* red, yellow, and blue.) The picture that is captured by the camera lens becomes separated into these three colors, each of which is directed to the appropriate color-sensitive tube where the scanning process takes place.

Whether black-and-white or color, the signals are converted to electrical charges as described above. These charges are carried by cables to the control room and the transmitter. After being strengthened there, they are sent out into space from the TV station's tower. At the same time and from the same tower (but over separate antennae) the sound, or audio, portion of the program is being broadcast.

As the sound and picture impulses are flying through space, your TV antenna at home picks them up. The audio portion is changed back into sound by the tubes in your set and by the loudspeaker.

The video impulses are drawn into the picture tube and are changed into black-and-white or color patterns by an electronic beam which scans the inner surface of your picture tube in the same way and at the same rate as was done in the pick-up tube in the studio camera. This carefully synchronized effort enables you to see and hear what is being produced on the studio stage within a split second after it occurs.

Television in America

Television in the United States now operates through local stations, a majority of which are organized into three separate commercial net-

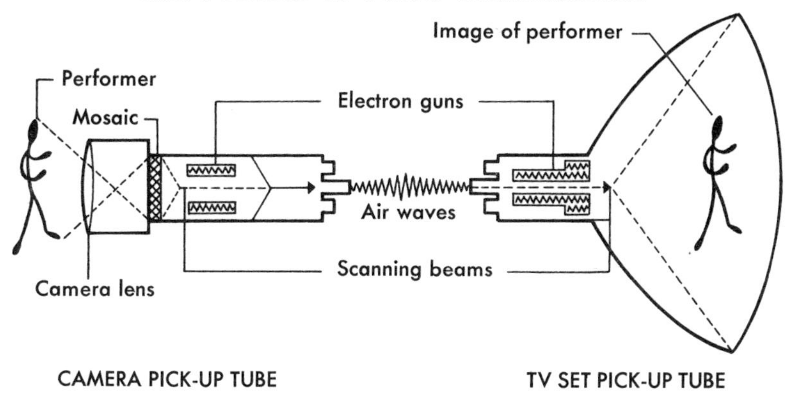

works and one educational network. The Columbia Broadcasting System (CBS), The National Broadcasting Company (NBC), and The American Broadcasting Company (ABC) comprise the commercial companies. National Educational Television (N.E.T.) is the educational television tape network.

The commercial networks and their affiliated stations must depend for support upon advertisers and advertising. Commercial network and station programs are many and varied. Most are pure entertainment; some (news and news commentary, for instance) are informational; and a very few are strictly educational. All are interspersed with commercials.

There are no commercials on educational television stations. The rules of the Federal Communications Commission forbid this. National Educational Television and its affiliated educational stations depend mainly upon gifts, grants, and appropriations from federal, state, and private sources. Educational television stations now number above 105 stations and are increasing rapidly. Programs are mainly educational, informational, and cultural. Few are pure entertainment.

No matter what the program, however, the audience is always mammoth in terms of a single coliseum or stadium. It is not uncommon for seventeen to eighteen million homes to be tuned in on a top-rated commercial network program or ten million on a low-rated one. Even on a local educational or commercial station a popular program may command an audience of many thousands.

For the majority of the programs reaching these vast audiences, speech is the crucial ingredient. Imagine yourself as a speaker, an actor, a participant in an interview or panel, a newscaster, or a news analyst speaking to forty thousand or even forty million people. With television this takes place every day. Is what you have to say and how you say it important under these circumstances? When millions of families are watching a single program, is the content of that program important? Is what it teaches or implies significant? We think it is!

The Audience, the Program, and You

The TV Audience. The potential television audience is a big one, 90 percent (and growing) of all the homes in the United States. This fact means that any television audience is composed mainly of thousands, or often millions, of family audiences in their homes. For special programs there is often viewing in classrooms, public establishments, and theaters, but the great bulk of any television audience consists of members of a family watching at home.

TV Communication Is Intimate. What does this fact reveal about the television audience? It suggests that you are speaking to an intimate audience and that your speaking approach, therefore, must be intimate. There is no need to shout in a family room or a den; a quiet, conversational quality is much more fitting, emotionally intense where necessary, but seldom loud. Every member of your audience is close to you, close enough to see every small expression, each important movement or object in detail. You are obligated to show yourself and any objects vital to your subject in close-up. Your viewers demand this for a very natural reason: they wish to see as closely on television as they would in the room in which they are viewing television.

TV Ratings. For information concerning the type of programs preferred by the television audience you must turn to other sources. The 1965 *Broadcasting Yearbook* listed fifty-six audience measurement services. Of these, A. C. Nielsen Company, The Pulse Incorporated, C. E. Hooper Incorporated, and Trendex Incorporated may be familiar names to you. Such companies are engaged for profit in studies of audience, marketing, programing, and other areas of communication research. Network and local stations depend upon them to determine their audience size and program ratings.

How Do We Evaluate TV Programs? What criteria are involved in the selection of programs by an audience? Choices are made through good taste and sound judgment based upon wide knowledge, experience, and understanding. What makes a good children's program or a good western drama, for instance? In the case of a program for children, a sound knowledge of child psychology and development is essential. Does the program challenge the child's imagination and help him grow, or is it simply a program that sops up his attention for the moment? Does the western drama have something to say about human behavior or is it once more the trite restatement of the conquest of good over evil? Does it deal with real people in real situations? Does it baby-sit your mind or challenge you to feel and think? These are the kinds of questions you must ask in making decisions about programs. When you are equipped to make such judgments, you can sift and view selectively. You should, you must, equip yourself to do so.

How Can We Help to Improve TV Programs? But what if you feel that present programing is inadequate, that there is too much escapism and not enough challenge for the more than fifty million families with television sets? What can you do? You can write your local stations, the networks, program sponsors, the Federal Communications Commission, and the critics to express your views. This is not only your privilege but also in a real sense your obligation, for the TV channels are public property.

By the same token, you should utilize these same methods to communicate your appreciation for programs which prove valuable to you. Correspondence provides the broadcasters with information that is much more explicit than a mere statistic in a rating booklet, and the response that you receive will in turn help you more fully to appreciate the nature of this gigantic communications system.

ACTIVITIES

1. Visit a nearby educational or commercial television station so that you may observe the equipment and space that are needed. Be prepared to ask questions.
2. From the following list select a topic for investigation in preparation for a panel discussion on the subiect of television:

   a. Historical Development
   b. Federal Communications Commission
   c. Educational Television
   d. Closed-circuit Television
   e. TV Commercials
   f. Censorship
   g. Future of Television

The Studio and You, the Speaker

The emphasis on your performance in a TV show will be directed in this unit toward "talk" programs—speeches, demonstrations, interviews, newscasts, and panel discussions. Though what is said may also sometimes apply to dramatic productions, the chief intent of the instruction that follows is to help you to understand the equipment, materials, and personnel of a TV studio as they affect you in your television talk programs. You will also learn how best to appear on TV, how to take cues, and how to work with others in such programs. If you are attending a school that is able to present full-scale television productions, your teacher can provide additional instructional material. The book list at the end of the unit will also be of interest and help.

The television studio is the place in which most "live" and "taped" programs are produced. "Live" means being broadcast at the time of performance; "taped" refers to a program recorded on video tape for later broadcast. Today most network dramas and many variety programs are filmed in segments over a period of time prior to the broadcast; also, there are a great many remote programs (sports, for instance) which are carried live or recorded for delayed broadcast outside the studio. Virtually all discussion programs, however, are produced in television studios.

The Camera. Figure 1 is a photograph of a talk program taking place in one area of a large studio. All the basic studio equipment and personnel are shown and identified by letter. You should know how each applies to you, the speaker (A). (B) is the television camera. It can move toward, away, across, and with you. These movements are called *dolly in* (toward you), *dolly out* (away from you), *pan right* or *pan left* (across you), *truck right* or *truck left* (with you horizontally), and *boom up* or *boom down* (across or with you vertically). On the front and top of each camera are red lights, called tally lights (C). These tell you which of two or more cameras is taking your picture.

The Lenses. Also on the front of the camera are four lenses which protrude at various lengths from its face. The longer the lens, the closer the picture of you. On the camera illustrated are a 50 mm lens (D) for wide-angle shots; a 90 mm lens (E), the most natural picture-taking lens; a 135 mm lens (F) for medium close and close shots; and an 8½ inch lens (G) for extreme close-ups. Some of the most modern cameras employ a single lens capable of "zooming" to various degrees of distance within the picture which is produced.

Figure 1. For an explanation of what the letters represent, see pages 576–580.

The Microphone. Figure 1 shows a neck (lavalier) microphone (H), the type usually used for a talk program. When it is suspended correctly from your neck and rests on your chest, you need not worry about its use. You must learn to handle with ease the cable that is attached to the microphone as you move from place to place on the set.

Lights. In order to be seen on television, you must be lighted. Notice the scoop (I), which is used for general, overall lighting; and a spotlight (J), which is used for narrower, more specialized purposes. There are several uses for spotlights, including modeling (to give natural shadow contours to your face and figure) and backlighting (to give the illusion of depth in a two-dimensional medium). As a performer, all you must know about lighting is how to feel the presence or absence of a spotlight without looking at it. If you are out of position, you may be in a shadow when you should be in a pool of light.

Other Considerations. You will be backed by a setting which should be appropriate to the program content and mood. Such a setting, with proper lighting added, serves to make your program more interesting to the eye. "Home base" for your talk will be the podium (K). It is from here that you will move to other parts of the set in order to make use of set and hand properties which are placed away from the podium table (L). Movement is important for variety, but it should always be motivated and natural.

Help Your Audience to "See" Your Talk

The subject matter of any speech should always be clear, but this requirement is particularly true of a talk which is being televised to a large audience that cannot respond with questions.

Visual aids not only serve to clarify a subject but also lend themselves nicely to the television camera. Some will be large set devices; some illustrations will be small and light enough to hold when necessary. These will be placed variously within and as a part of the set, some nearby, others away.

Visual Aids. Visual aids may be hand-held or placed on a title stand (M). If they are hand-held (often called hold-and-show illustrations) near the podium table or elsewhere, be certain you know which camera is taking the picture (tally lights on). Your illustration will be in close-up, so hold it straight and steady until the tally lights have gone off. Be at ease in picking up the illustration, moving it into a predetermined position for the camera and returning it and yourself to former positions after the shot is completed. Books should be held so that the page with the illustration is perpendicular to the camera lens. All flat illustrations must be prepared in a 3 by 4 relationship, 9 inches by 12 inches, for instance, for easy framing by the television camera, which has a picture size of four parts wide to three parts high. In a talk on world geography a model of the earth would be essential. If your subject has to do with the history of the telephone, several *real* telephones could be used to illustrate changes in design which have taken place over the years.

Greenboard. Greenboards (green blackboards) may be portable (on casters) or a part of the set (N). They are useful for outlines, line drawings, and simple illustrations placed there prior to your talk or while you are talking. Regular chalk is too narrow to be clear on television; oversize chalk should be used. Illustrations should be drawn in a 3 by 4 relationship for easy framing. Written material should not exceed the horizontal limits of the camera, but may be longer vertically since the camera can tilt down as the material is being read.

Feltboard. Another useful item is a solid frame covered with felt. Illustrations backed with felt will stick to the feltboard when contact is made between the two. The feltboard is particularly useful when quick rearrangement of illustrative elements is important. It, too, may be portable or a part of the set.

Rear Projection. Whenever pictorial illustration is called for, you may make use of slides. (In a talk on Degas, for example, slides of his famous paintings would be essential.) From the rear of the set the slide is projected in reverse on the back of a translucent projection screen (O). From the front the image will appear as it should be seen. Pointer in hand, you stand near the projected image and point out its salient aspects. Camera shots may be of you and the slide or of the slide alone.

Slides. 2 by 2 color slides can also be shown by separate projectors which fill the entire TV screen. Such technique has the advantage of maximum enlargement and frees the studio cameras to prepare their next pictures. In contrast to the rear-projection technique, however, the full-screen use of slides does not permit interesting camera movement or references to the picture that the speaker might wish to make with a pointer.

Film Clips. Short motion-picture scenes are frequently useful for clarification. In a talk on highway safety, for instance, a film clip could dramatically demonstrate the dangers of passing on a curve. Clips will be cued in from the control room and carried on the set monitor (P), where you may see what is going on as you continue your talk.

Dress to Look Your Best. As a performer you must be dressed for the mood and character of the program. The speaker in Figure 1 wears a dark suit, a tie in keeping with the suit, and an off-white shirt. The rules are these: wear clothes that are not too black, too white, or too "busy." White garments—a white shirt, for instance—are less preferable than light blue or beige. Always avoid startling contrasts in clothing, and never wear bright jewelry which will reflect light.

Makeup. Except for dramatic programs, makeup is optional. Men with extremely dark beards should shave just before showtime and apply flesh-toned powder. For women, careful street makeup without extreme shadows and contrasts is satisfactory.

Television Production

The Crews. In rehearsing and performing a talk program you will work with a production crew consisting of *floor manager* and *cameramen* on the studio floor and *director*, *technical director*, and *audio engineer* in the control room. An intercom system (Q) provides the means for members of the crew to talk with each other.

Production Crew. The floor manager (R) takes orders from the director. He sees that titles and stand-held illustrations are in position for the camera, on time, and changed according to plan. He cues performers to take the air, gives signals for unplanned changes in performer position, cues the speaker's look from camera to camera, and gives time and closing signals. You must know these cues and signals and learn to obey them quickly and unobtrusively.

Cues and Signals. When the time comes to begin your program, the floor manager will cue you, having given you a sixty-, thirty-, and fifteen-second countdown. On cue he points directly at you. When a change in camera is about to take place, the floor manager, standing between the two cameras, will place his index finger close to the lenses of the camera on the air. A split second before the shift is called, his finger will move swiftly to point to the other camera. At this time your look should shift smoothly and naturally.

Occasionally a speaker or performer will get out of his planned position. Below are standard hand signals the floor manager will use to move you back into position. Be sure you understand and obey them quickly.

Come close to this camera	Stand near camera in question and beckon toward it.
Move away from this camera	Stand near camera in question and thrust hands away.
Get closer together	Move palms of hands together accordion-style.
Get further apart	With hands back-to-back move them abruptly apart.

Four Basic Television Hand Signals

When you approach the close of your talk, the *floor manager* will give you time signals in minutes left for you. Normally these are five-, four-, three-, two-, and one-minute, thirty seconds, and fifteen seconds, which means "wrap it up" or close promptly. These may be given on cards or by hand. In either case they are shown close to the camera on the air so that you can see them easily. Hand time signals are communicated by spread fingers: five minutes, five fingers; four minutes, four fingers; and so on through one minute. Thirty seconds is represented by a raised but closed index finger, and cut (stop now) by drawing the index finger rapidly across the throat.

Never acknowledge any signal with eye movement or a nod of the head. Such movements are communicated to your television audience as well as to the floor manager.

Control-room Crew. Figure 2 (p. 582) is a photograph of *control-room* personnel and equipment for the talk program pictured in Figure 1. The director (A) is in charge of all aspects of the program, including program planning and rehearsals. He will help you select illustrative materials and explain where they should be placed on the set. Usually, talk programs are not fully rehearsed because of the danger of losing spontaneity. The opening and closing and movements around the set will be rehearsed or carefully planned. During rehearsal and performance the director gives all commands through the intercom system.

Each camera on the floor of the studio is connected with a monitor in the control room, camera 1 to monitor 1 (B), camera 2 to monitor 2 (C), and so on. The director decides which of these will be on the air

Figure 2. For an explanation of what the letters represent, see pages 581–582.

and gives commands to the technical director (D) to select the camera picture desired by punching the appropriate button on the switcher (E). The director also gives commands for the types of camera shots and movements to the cameramen on the studio floor and relays messages to the performer through the floor manager.

The *audio engineer* (F) is responsible for microphone adjustment and placement in the studio, for microphone volume control through the audio console (G), and for the cuing and control of recorded sound effects and music from either the tape recorder (H) or the transcription tables (I).

The Crews and the Performer. To understand how the production crew in Figure 2 would work closely with the studio crew and performer in Figure 1, eavesdrop for a minute on the "party line" communication link which the audience never hears:

INTERCOM	*BROADCAST*
DIRECTOR: Cue him to Camera One. Camera Two, your	SPEAKER: You are seeing and hearing me at this very mo-

next shot will be tight on that big gadget on the table, right next to the diagram. Then you'll pan left.

FLOOR MANAGER: Should we change the slide?

DIRECTOR: Hold on; Audio, watch your level. He's going to be talking down right into his mike. Camera One, dolly in slowly on that mike.

TECH DIRECTOR: Camera Two, sharpen focus.

DIRECTOR: Ready Two . . . Take Two! Camera One, back to medium shot. Stand by to pan left, Two . . . Pan left. Frame up on that telegraph key. Stand by One . . . Take One. Camera Two, pan right to that diagram. We'll start on the left side of it and pan slowly right while he talks.

CAMERA ONE: Do you want me to pan down the cord when he handles it?

DIRECTOR: No. Stand by to dissolve to Two. Give him a speed-up signal, we're dropping behind . . .

ment as a consequence of a modern miracle of communication, and any explanation of how it actually happens does little to reduce the miraculous nature of the whole thing. The sound of my voice is the simplest part of the process, starting here with this little microphone.

The microphone is so sensitive to the vibration produced by sounds that a little mechanism inside picks up these vibrations every time a sound is heard. It vibrates one way if a steady tone is generated . . . and another way if an intermittent click is produced . . . and still another way if I were to sing a song, which I hasten to assure you I'm not about to do. This very sophisticated vibration is simultaneously translated into an electromagnetic equivalent, a series of faint electronic impulses which travel along this cord and out to an amplifier where they can be reinforced and given strength before being pushed out into the blue yonder.

Television is a frantic, fascinating business, with plenty of opportunities for people who have something to say to a large audience and who learn how to use the techniques of electronic communication.

Speech Is Important on TV

There are few programs on television in which speech is not a crucial ingredient. Symphonies, ballets, and pantomimic comedy are examples of non-speech program material, but even here speech is necessary for introduction and, perhaps, explanation. In the interview, the panel, the newscast, the drama, and the talk, speech is an essential element. We have considered the talk. In brief, let us look at the other programs.

The Interview. Interviews are limited to two or three participants: the interviewer and one or two guests. The interviewer is normally a member of the station staff. The guest is well known in his own right or has something to say that will be of interest to the television audience. He might be, for example, a popular recording star, an eminent nuclear physicist, or a community leader. The program consists mainly of questions and answers built around a central theme relating to the work or activity of the guest. The interviewer prepares these questions, usually in conference with the guest. For safety it is well to prepare more questions than seem to be necessary to fill the time of the program.

The interview is staged in a small set with the participants seated in easy conversation-angles at a table or, more comfortably, in armchairs by a coffee table. On cue the interviewer opens the program by welcoming his audience, identifying the subject, and introducing his guest. The body of the interview should seem more like a conversation than a series of questions and long answers. It can be helped by the interviewer's breaking in to add an occasional comment and supplementary questions. The conclusion is simply a brief summation with a word of sincere appreciation to the guest.

Production is similar to the talk program, utilizing the same crew complement, the same signals, and the same cues. The interviewer, however, must accept and respond to all signals and cues. He is completely responsible for the smoothness of the performance.

Panel Discussion. Although the size of the group may vary to suit the occasion, a panel discussion generally involves from three to five participants in addition to a host or moderator. The moderator is in charge, opens the program, introduces the panel members, keeps the program moving, and closes on time. In the strict sense of the word panels are discussion-opinion programs. Panelists are selected because of their depth of knowledge and point of view. The moderator is also an expert, but often in a broader sense. The subject is usually controversial, each side of the issue being represented by one or more panel members. After short formal statements by each participant, the program is opened for discussion (often heated), with the moderator in command.

Mrs. Evelyn Lincoln, President Kennedy's secretary, is interviewed on TV.

Usually the panel members are seated, with comfortable separation, along one side of an oversize table or desk. The moderator is seated at one end or at a separate desk close by. Production techniques are very similar to those that are employed in televising the talk or interview.

There are numerous variations on this pure or formal style of the panel, including the popular quiz program, but all have the common similarity of questions and answers.

News. The newscast is a talk program in which the material is delivered in a precise manner rather than extemporized. Many news programs are performed by one man. Some are shared by two or more, each assuming responsibility for a part or parts of the program. Well-produced newscasts use varied illustrative devices, including maps, charts, film clips, and photographs.

The newscaster may secure some of his material from local sources and reporters. Most of what he reads, however, will be selected from one of the wire services, syndicated news services which furnish clients with continuous news printed by teletype machines at the stations. All of the newscaster's material should be carefully edited and read aloud prior to air time, ensuring a smooth performance without mispronunciations of difficult names and places.

During the air show the newscaster may sit or stand. In either case he should have in front of him a lectern upon which to rest his copy. In the camera picture the lectern must not be obtrusive and may at times not be seen at all. In delivery the newscaster should maintain as much audience eye-contact as possible; he should never remain glued to his material.

Drama. With few exceptions drama is filmed for television. Live or taped television drama—a play performed in a television studio—does not take place today except occasionally in educational stations or in commercial stations where there remains an interest in experimentation.

Whether a play is performed live, on tape, or filmed in segments for later editing and assembling as a completed story, you can learn a great deal about acting by applying critical standards to the performances.

- Was the acting convincing? Did the actors establish definite characters and maintain these throughout the play? Were the gestures too broad for television, or were they easy and comfortable?
- Were the voices in character? Did they seem to be overprojected, or were they conversational, although emotionally intense when necessary?
- Did the actors move, sit, rise, and turn as though they had lived in the place where they were acting? Or were these movements exaggerated at times?
- Were the performers costumed in character? Did they wear and move in their clothes as though they belonged in them?
- Did you ever notice an actor out of position for the camera or for the lighting?
- Were small properties handled with ease?
- Was the makeup noticeable or natural?

Tips for TV Speech

Be Direct. Your audience may number in the thousands but is composed of very small groups. Use a simple, direct, and personal approach in constructing and delivering your talk.

Keep It Visual. Use as many illustrations and illustrative devices as you think necessary to make your subject matter clear. Never use an illustration or an illustrative device, however, unless it will help you clarify your subject matter.

Keep It Lively. Your speech must sound spontaneous. Don't write it out word for word, therefore, or memorize it. Use an outline written on 5″ × 8″ cards, if you must, to remind you of next points.

Plan Your Movements. Give some thought to planning the physical movement of your speech. Using notes from your visit to the local television station or from this text, draw a floor plan to scale of that portion of the studio you will use for your talk. Place in it the podium, podium table, title stand, and any other illustrative device you plan to use. Diagram your proposed movements. Remember, you are talking to a few people in a small room. Plan your movements with this in mind.

ACTIVITIES

1. Prepare for a TV talk. Select a subject you would like to present on a topic that can be covered in five minutes while lending itself to one or more means of visual illustration. You might wish to present a newscast, a sports review, or a carefully planned interview which involves the handling of objects or visual aids.
2. For practice, use your classroom as a studio and your classmates as production personnel. Move the seats to the walls. In one corner of the classroom place your set pieces according to your floor plan, using classroom furniture to simulate the studio. Cameras may be chairs with gliders or, preferably, rollers; your podium and podium table may be the teacher's desk and lectern; and other illustrative devices may be represented by stools and benches. Assign your director and floor crew from members of the class: camera one, camera two, and floor manager.
3. Rehearse your talk as though you were in an actual studio. The floor manager should give you a countdown and cue to begin, wave-overs from camera to camera, time and closing cues, and whatever other signals seem to be necessary. Cameramen should move their chairs as if they were actually operating cameras. As speaker, follow the suggestions which have been made concerning eye-contact with your audience, shifting your look with ease from camera to camera, and using illustrative devices. Later, your teacher will give you criticisms.
4. Repeat this procedure, changing the floor crew for each talk so that everyone has the opportunity to serve as director, cameraman, and floor manager at least once.

References:

The Television Program: Its Direction and Production, rev. ed., by Rudy Bretz and Edward Stasheff. Hill & Wang.

The Television Actor's Manual, by William Hodapp. Appleton-Century-Crofts.

Television and Radio Announcing, by Stuart Hyde. Houghton Mifflin.

Television Writing and Selling, 3d ed., by Edward B. Roberts. Writer, Inc.

Television and Radio News, by Bob Siller, Ted White, and Hal Terkel. Macmillan.

Films:

Television: How It Works (Coronet). 11 min color or b&w.

Television Serves Its Community (FAC). 14 min color or b&w.

Filmstrip:

Television (MH). 47 fr b&w.

Appendix A

Audio-Visual Materials

As an Aid to the Speaker. The list of visual and audio devices that speakers may use for demonstrations or as aids to communication is lengthy. It includes exhibits, models, maps, globes, displays, pictures, slides, drawings, diagrams, charts, samples, and objects—anything that can be easily seen and handled. It also covers blackboards, bulletin boards, flannel boards, dioramas, projectors, films, records, tapes, and transcriptions, as well as radio and television. Such aids help the speaker to communicate facts, illustrate points, clarify ideas, and add to knowledge. They help listeners to understand, to believe, and to remember what the speaker has to say. When well handled, they contribute interest and impressiveness as well as clarity to a talk, serving as an additional means of communication and offering a dramatic reinforcement to language. The saying "One picture is worth a thousand words" generally exemplifies the value of skillfully used visual materials.

Tips to the Speaker

- Use only those visual materials that are related closely to your subject or essential to its development.
- Be sure that your materials are large enough to be seen easily by everyone.
- Avoid long explanations and intricate displays.
- Direct your voice and your eyes toward your audience as you exhibit your material, making exception to this rule only when it is imperative that you look at your exhibit for instructional purposes.
- If your displays are not mounted in stationary frames or hung on a wall, hold them at a convenient visual angle and turn them *slowly* in a flat arc so that everyone has comfortable vision.
- Don't pass to your audience pictures, relics, or other small objects of display for examination during your talk. You will lose a good part of your listeners. Instead, invite the members of the audience to look at your displays after you have concluded what you have to say.
- Prepare blackboard or bulletin board displays ahead of time if possible. If not, establish the visual aids efficiently and quickly as you talk. Stand to one side as you pin, tack, draw, or talk.
- When you are handling objects or models, touch them only as they are important to your demonstration. Don't use them as objects to twirl, finger, or clutch to relieve your nervous tensions.
- Exercise caution in the *number* of materials you use for demonstration. Too many exhibits may serve only to confuse, and you will lose the impact of your

observations because there seems to be no continuity in your speech. Always keep in mind that you are trying to make a point or sell an idea and that the visual materials are *aids,* not ends in themselves.

- Follow the showing of your visual aids with interest-arousing statements or a summary that will bring attention back to you and your talk.
- Prepare all details carefully ahead of time so that your handling of materials is skillful and effective.

As an Aid to Classroom Learning. The same audio-visual materials that speakers use to enliven and clarify their subjects are also useful for educational purposes in the classroom. In particular, projectors and tape recorders, plus films, filmstrips, records, tapes, and transcriptions can be valuable supplements to conventional methods of teaching, helping you to see as well as to hear as you learn in your speech class.

Hearing yourself as others hear is an important first step toward self-improvement in speaking. If you have a tape recorder, you can record your voice, analyze its quality, study your speech habits, practice your talks, rehearse programs, and play the tape for critical evaluation. You can also record speeches, discussions, interviews, readings, debates, or plays for classroom study.

Tips on Voice Recording

- Treat the recording equipment with care and respect.
- Early in your speech course, record your voice for diagnosis and analysis by reading or speaking for two or three minutes into the microphone.
- Don't be shocked the first time you record. Even though it may sound strange, the voice you hear will be your own—as others hear you.
- With the help of classmates and teacher, make a chart or evaluation sheet of your voice. Analyze fundamentals, such as breath control, vocal quality, volume, pitch, rate, articulation, pronunciation and general speaking pattern.
- If possible, arrange additional recordings to check how you sound in informal conversation, when relating a story or incident, while giving a speech, when reading or interpreting prose or poetry.
- Understand your personal speaking habits thoroughly and take definite steps to improve yourself.

The use of films, tapes, and records for supplemental learning and enrichment of experience is highly recommended. Such audio-visual material is in great supply. Catalogs are easily available, and sources are many, far more than can be listed in this appendix. If there is no audio-visual center near your school or no teacher in charge of audio-visual activities, you can write for information to the Department of Audio-Visual Instruction, National Education Association, 1201 Sixteenth Street, N.W., Washington, D. C., or to Kent State University, Kent, Ohio, a national repository of material.

Tips on Using Films, Records, and Tapes

- Select material that is interesting, worthwhile, and suitable for your purpose.
- Precheck, preview, or preaudit the material, if possible, and build up group interest ahead of time.
- Anticipate and prepare for special terminology, acoustical problems, or mechanical deficiencies that interfere with communication. Check seating, placement of equipment, sound volume, amount of light, timing, ventilation, etc.
- Afterwards, evaluate the experience in its relationship to class work. If possible, plan appropriate follow-up activities that complement the learning experience.

Key to Producers and Distributors of Audio-Visual Aids

Records:

CAEDMON	Caedmon Records, Inc., 461 Eighth Ave., New York 1, N. Y.
DECCA	Decca Distributing Corporation, Educational Division, 445 Park Ave., New York 22, N. Y.
EAV	Educational Record Club, Popular Science Publishing ville, N. Y.
ERC	Educational Record Club, Popular Science Publishing Company, Audio Visual Division, 355 Lexington Ave., New York, N. Y. 10017.
EDUCATIONAL	Educational Record Sales, 157 Chambers St., New York 7, N. Y.
ENRICHMENT	Enrichment Records, 246 Fifth Ave., New York 1, N. Y.
FOLKWAYS	Folkways Records & Service Corp., 117 W. 46th St., New York, N. Y.
GINN	Ginn and Company, Statler Bldg., Boston, Mass. 02117

Films:

BAILEY	Bailey Films, Inc., 6509 De Longpre Ave. Hollywood 28, Calif.
BASIC	Basic Skill Films, 1355 Inverness Dr., Pasadena 3, Calif.
CORONET	Coronet Instructional Films, Coronet Bldg., 65 East So. Water St., Chicago 1, Ill.
DYNAMIC	Dynamic Films, Inc., 405 Park Ave., New York 22, N. Y.
EBF	Encyclopaedia Britannica Films, Inc., 38 W. 32d St., New York 1, N. Y.
FAC	Film Associates of California, 11014 Santa Monica Blvd., Los Angeles 25, Calif.
IFB	International Film Bureau, Inc., 332 South Michigan Ave., Chicago 4, Ill.
MH	McGraw-Hill Book Company, Text-Film Div., 330 W. 42d St., New York 36, N. Y.

SVE	Society for Visual Education, Inc., 1345 Diversey Pkwy., Chicago 14, Ill.
TFC	Teaching Film Custodians, 25 W. 43d St., New York, N. Y.

Appendix B

Selected Speeches

Inaugural Address

President John F. Kennedy

President Kennedy's Inaugural Address was delivered January 20, 1961. The speech outlined his idea of the nation of the future. It revealed an attention to history, a unity of thought, and a ringing rhetoric not often found in modern political statements.

We observe today not a victory of party but a celebration of freedom, symbolizing an end as well as a beginning, signifying renewal as well as change. For I have sworn before you and Almighty God the same solemn oath our forebears prescribed nearly a century and three-quarters ago.

The world is very different now. For man holds in his mortal hands the power to abolish all forms of human poverty and all forms of human life. And yet the same revolutionary belief for which our forebears fought is still at issue around the globe, the belief that the rights of man come not from the generosity of the state but from the hand of God.

We dare not forget today that we are the heirs of that first revolution. Let the word go forth from this time and place, to friend and foe alike, that the torch has been passed to a new generation of Americans, born in this century, tempered by war, disciplined by a hard and bitter peace, proud of our ancient heritage, and unwilling to witness or permit the slow undoing of those human rights to which this nation has always been committed, and to which we are committed today at home and around the world.

Let every nation know, whether it wishes us well or ill, that we shall pay any price, bear any burden, meet any hardship, support any friend, oppose any foe to assure the survival and the success of liberty.

This much we pledge—and more.

To those old allies whose cultural and spiritual origins we share, we pledge the loyalty of faithful friends. United, there is little we cannot do in a host of cooperative ventures. Divided, there is little we can do, for we dare not meet a powerful challenge at odds and split asunder.

To those new states whom we welcome to the ranks of the free, we pledge our word that one form of colonial control shall not have passed away merely to be replaced by a far more iron tyranny. We shall not always expect to find them supporting our view. But we shall always hope to find them strongly supporting their own freedom, and to remember that, in the past, those who foolishly sought power by riding the back of the tiger ended up inside.

To those peoples in the huts and villages of half the globe struggling to break the bonds of mass misery, we pledge our best efforts to help them help themselves, for whatever period is required, not because the Communists may be doing it, not because we seek their votes, but because it is right. If a free society cannot help the many who are poor, it cannot save the few who are rich.

To our sister republics south of our border, we offer a special pledge: to convert our good words into good deeds, in a new alliance for progress, to assist free men and free governments in casting off the chains of poverty. But this peaceful revolution of hope cannot become the prey of hostile power. Let all our neighbors know that we shall join with them to oppose aggression or subversion anywhere in the Americas. And let every other power know that this hemisphere intends to remain the master of its own house.

To that world assembly of sovereign states, the United Nations, our last best hope in an age where the instruments of war have far outpaced the instruments of peace, we renew our pledge of support: to prevent it from becoming merely a forum for invective, to strengthen its shield of the new and the weak, and to enlarge the area in which its writ may run.

Finally, to those nations who would make themselves our adversary, we offer not a pledge but a request: that both sides begin anew the quest for peace, before the dark powers of destruction unleashed by science engulf all humanity in planned or accidental self-destruction.

We dare not tempt them with weakness. For only when our arms are sufficient beyond doubt can we be certain beyond doubt that they will never be employed.

But neither can two great and powerful groups of nations take comfort from our present course—both sides overburdened by the cost of modern weapons, both rightly alarmed by the steady spread of the deadly atom, yet both racing to alter that uncertain balance of terror that stays the hand of mankind's final war.

So let us begin anew, remembering on both sides that civility is not a sign of weakness, and sincerity is always subject to proof. Let us never negotiate out of fear. But let us never fear to negotiate.

Let both sides explore what problems unite us instead of belaboring those problems which divide us.

Let both sides, for the first time, formulate serious and precise proposals for the inspection and control of arms, and bring the absolute power to destroy other nations under the absolute control of all nations.

Let both sides seek to invoke the wonders of science instead of its terrors. Together let us explore the stars, conquer the deserts, eradicate disease, tap the ocean depths and encourage the arts and commerce.

Let both sides unite to heed in all corners of the earth the command of Isaiah to "undo the heavy burdens . . . [and] let the oppressed go free."

And if a beachhead of cooperation may push back the jungle of suspicion, let both sides join in creating a new endeavor, not a new balance of power, but a new world of law, where the strong are just and the weak secure and the peace preserved.

All this will not be finished in the first one hundred days. Nor will it be finished in the first one thousand days, nor in the life of this Administration, nor even perhaps in our lifetime on this planet. But let us begin.

In your hands, my fellow citizens, more than mine, will rest the final success or failure of our course. Since this country was founded, each generation of Americans has been summoned to give testimony to its national loyalty. The graves of young Americans who answered the call to service surround the globe.

Now the trumpet summons us again—not as a call to bear arms, though arms we need; not as a call to battle, though embattled we are; but a call to bear the burden of a long twilight struggle, year in and year out, "rejoicing in hope, patient in tribulation," a struggle against the common enemies of man: tyranny, poverty, disease, and war itself.

Can we forge against these enemies a grand and global alliance, North and South, East and West, that can assure a more fruitful life for all mankind? Will you join in that historic effort?

In the long history of the world, only a few generations have been granted the role of defending freedom in its hour of maximum danger. I do not shrink from this responsibility; I welcome it. I do not believe that any of us would exchange places with any other people or any other generation. The energy, the faith, the devotion which we bring to this endeavor will light our country and all who serve it, and the glow from that fire can truly light the world.

And so, my fellow Americans, ask not what your country can do for you; ask what you can do for your country.

My fellow citizens of the world, ask not what America will do for you, but what together we can do for the freedom of man.

Finally, whether you are citizens of America or citizens of the world, ask of us here the same high standards of strength and sacrifice which we ask of you. With a good conscience our only sure reward, with history the final judge of our deeds, let us go forth to lead the land we love, asking His blessing and His help, but knowing that here on earth God's work must truly be our own.

In Memoriam

Senator Frank Church

This tribute to the late President John F. Kennedy was given at memorial services held at the River Road Unitarian Church in Bethesda, Maryland, on Sunday, November 24, 1963.

It is not my purpose or place to deliver the sermon this morning. That is properly a service for your own pastor to perform. It is, rather, my purpose to say a few words in tribute to our fallen President.

I hope you will understand if I speak of him in somewhat personal terms, for this is the way I shall remember him.

He was my friend. I loved and honored him. I was proud for my country that he was our President.

John Fitzgerald Kennedy was one of those rare human beings about whom it could be truly said . . . "the elements so mixed in him that Nature might stand up and say to all the world 'This was a man!' "

He was as handsome as a storied prince; his wife, Jacqueline, as fair as any princess of song or legend. With his encouragement, she made the White House a place of impeccable beauty, where occasions of state were conducted in the style, and with a graciousness and gaiety that befits a great nation. Whenever I was present on these occasions, I never failed to marvel at the President's composure. His dignity was natural to him, and his friendliness always set his guests at ease. How unprepared they were to discover in him that endearing quality of self-effacement, which he often revealed through some light-hearted witticism, but which invariably disclosed his underlying humility. Once, in a toast to the King of Afghanistan, I recall how he explained why the Constitution limited the President to eight years in office. The amendment had been adopted, he said, partly out of consideration for the well-being of the President, but mainly, he added with a smile, out of consideration for the well-being of the country.

Many of you will remember the celebrated comment he made to that illustrious company of Nobel Prize winners who came to dine with him at the White House. Never, he remarked, has so much talent been gathered at one time under this roof, since Thomas Jefferson used to dine here alone!

Such was the brilliance of the social life which John and Jacqueline Kennedy brought to the Presidential Mansion. But more important was the kind of family life they implanted there. Somehow they managed to make that big house a home. Along with other playmates, their daughter, Caroline, and their little son, whom the President liked to call "John-John," used to gather in the play yard, within easy view of their daddy's office. He was seldom too busy to be interrupted by them; he refused to permit the heavy burdens of his office to usurp his family function as a loving father. The personal attention he gave to his children, and to the needs of his grief-stricken wife, when their infant son, Patrick, died soon after birth a few months ago; the tender pictures of John-John on the south lawn awaiting his father's arrival by helicopter, or crawling through the trapdoor in his father's desk, while the President was sitting there absorbed with his evening's work; the familiar sight of Caroline clutching her father's hand as he led the family into church on a Sunday morning—all combined to present to the country the finest example of a devout and affectionate family, setting a moral standard of the highest order.

The many attributes that made John F. Kennedy such an exceptional person cannot be compressed into the short tribute I pay him this morning. Well known was his bravery in battle; his literary talents which won for him the Pulitzer Prize; the fortitude with which he bore the pain in his injured back; the ceaseless energy with which he pursued his quest for self-fulfillment through seventeen years of honorable service in the House of Representatives, the Senate, and finally, the White House itself.

History will judge his greatness as a President, but already it is clear that he will be remembered for the strength of his statesmanship which saw us through the dread missile crisis in Cuba a year ago, when the world trembled on the brink of thermonuclear war. And he will be remembered too for the initiative he brought to the search for peace—for the first step along that road he made possible through the nuclear test ban treaty. Not since Lincoln has any President been so deeply committed to the cause of equal treatment for all Americans.

The tragedy of his death is heightened because it came so cruelly at the prime of his extraordinary life. It came as he was grappling with the gigantic problems of our times with the skill and courage of a young David—only to be struck down by an assassin in his own country, in a foul and cowardly murder which crosses us all with shame.

Once, when he faced a crucial primary test, in that long, arduous trek he made toward the Presidency, I asked him whether he believed in prayer. He said he did, and he seemed genuinely moved when I told him I would pray for him. Now, I think, he would want us all to pray for our new President, in faith that a national revulsion against every kind of fanaticism will wash the land clean, so that the hand of Lyndon B. Johnson may be upheld by the councils of reason and decency against the councils of ignorance, bigotry, and hate.

May God preserve this Republic and keep her sensible, strong, and free. Amen.

INDEX

PHOTO CREDITS:

Acme Photo: p. 350; Ampex Corporation: p. 548; *Better Living:* p. 322; Black Star: p. 151 (Lanks), p. 236 (Smith); Bob Blanch Advertising Photography, Inc.: p. 555; Communication Center Photo Lab, Univ. of North Carolina: pp. 577, 582; Community Relations Service: p. 330; A. Devaney: pp. 4, 131, 134, 551; Dr. Harold E. Edgerton: p. 192; Egyptian State Tourist Administration: p. 166; FPG: p. 257 (Gilman); Ewing Galloway: p. 335; Harvard University: p. 158; Weston Kemp: pp. 11, 50, 186, 228, 249, 367, 378, 382, 386, 417, 419, 502, 518; Keystone: p. 395; Minnesota Mining and Manufacturing Company: p. 570; Monkmeyer: p. 20 (Shelton), p. 26 (Morin), p. 294 (Hays), pp. 306, 341, 344 (all Shelton), p. 362, p. 469 (Bloom); National Tourist Organization of Greece: p. 479; *The New York Times:* p. 98 (Tames); Peace Corps: p. 71; PIX: p. 37 (Purcell), p. 154 (Bognar-Kegl); H. Armstrong Roberts: pp. 32, 86, 146, 239, 314; The Scottish Tourist Board: p. 513; Edwin Snyder Photo: p. 494; Society for the Preservation of New England Antiquities: p. 390; Standard Oil Co. (N.J.): p. 464; Sun Valley News Bureau: pp. 171, 175; Mart Toggweiler: p. 198; Twentieth Century-Fox Film Corp.: p. 42; United Air Lines: p. 327; United Nations: pp. 10, 214; United Press International: pp. 15, 212, 261; Vanguard Records: p. 452; Voice of America: p. 544; Wide World: pp. 106, 138, 173, 217, 224, 264, 288 (both), 310, 338, 438, 537; WGBH-FM: p. 562; WNAC-TV: p. 585

CDEFGHIJ 0698
PRINTED IN UNITED STATES OF AMERICA
083–B–F